01-132

D1599555

GLENCOE

Writer's Choice

Grammar and Composition
Grade 11

 **Glencoe McGraw-Hill**

New York, New York   Columbus, Ohio   Woodland Hills, California   Peoria, Illinois

ACKNOWLEDGMENTS

Grateful acknowledgment is given authors, publishers, photographers, museums, and agents for permission to reprint the following copyrighted material. Every effort has been made to determine copyright owners. In case of any omissions, the Publisher will be pleased to make suitable acknowledgments in future editions.

Acknowledgments continued on page 929.

The Standardized Test Practice pages in this book were written by The Princeton Review, the nation's leader in test preparation. Through its association with McGraw-Hill, The Princeton Review offers the best way to help students excel on standardized assessments.

The Princeton Review is not affiliated with Princeton University or Educational Testing Service.

The **Facing the Blank Page** feature in this book was prepared in collaboration with the writers and editors of *TIME* magazine.

Glencoe/McGraw-Hill

A Division of the **McGraw-Hill** *Companies*

Send all inquiries to:
GLENCOE/MCGRAW-HILL
8787 Orion Place
Columbus, OH 43240-4027

ISBN 0-07-822660-0
(Student Edition)
ISBN 0-07-822661-9
(Teacher's Wraparound Edition)

4 5 6 7 8 9 10 027/043 05 04 03 02 01

PROGRAM CONSULTANTS

Mark Lester is Professor of English at Eastern Washington University. He formerly served as Chair of the Department of English as a Second Language, University of Hawaii. He is the author of *Grammar in the Classroom* (Macmillan, 1990) and of numerous other professional books and articles.

Sharon O'Neal is Assistant Professor at the College of Education, Southwest Texas State University, where she teaches courses in reading instruction. She formerly served as Director of Reading and Language Arts of the Texas Education Agency and has authored, and contributed to, numerous articles and books on reading instruction and teacher education.

Jacqueline Jones Royster is Associate Professor of English at The Ohio State University. She is also on the faculty at the Bread Loaf School of English at Middlebury College in Middlebury, Vermont. In addition to the teaching of writing, Dr. Royster's professional interests include the rhetorical history of African American women and the social and cultural implications of literate practices.

William Strong is Professor of Secondary Education at Utah State University, Director of the Utah Writing Project, and a member of the National Writing Project Advisory Board. A nationally known authority on the teaching of composition, he is the author of many volumes, including *Writing Incisively: Do-It-Yourself Prose Surgery* (McGraw-Hill, 1991).

Jeffrey Wilhelm, a former English and reading teacher, is currently an assistant professor at the University of Maine, where he teaches courses in middle and secondary level literacy. Author of several books and articles on the teaching of reading and the use of technology, he also works with local schools as part of the Adolescent Literacy Project.

Denny Wolfe, a former high school English teacher and department chair, is Professor of English Education, Director of the Tidewater Virginia Writing Project, and Director of the Center for Urban Education at Old Dominion University in Norfolk, Virginia. Author of more than seventy-five articles and books on teaching English, Dr. Wolfe is a frequent consultant to schools and colleges on the teaching of English language arts.

Advisors

Educational Reviewers

Student Advisory Board

BOOK OVERVIEW

v

CONTENTS

Part 1 Composition

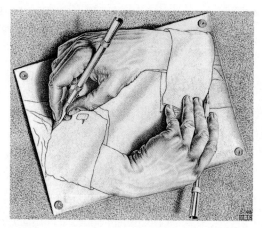

 # Business and Technical Writing 408

Instruction and Practice

Part 2 Grammar, Usage, and Mechanics

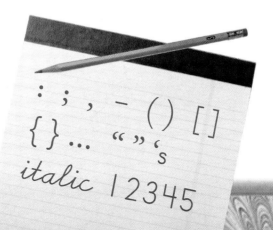

Part 3 Resources and Skills

LITERATURE MODELS

Composition Models

Each literature selection is an extended example of the mode of writing taught in the unit.

Skill Models

Excerpts from outstanding works of fiction and nonfiction exemplify specific writing skills.

LITERATURE MODELS

Language Models

Each Grammar Review uses excerpts to link grammar, usage, or mechanics to literature.

LITERATURE MODELS

FINE ART

Fine art—paintings, drawings, photos, and sculpture—is used to teach as well as to stimulate writing ideas.

"Not I, not any one else can travel that road for you.
You must travel it for yourself."

—Walt Whitman, "Song of Myself"

Conrad Buff, *Ocean Vista*, 1925

PART 1

Composition

"*Seized with a determination to learn to read, at any cost, I hit upon many expedients to accomplish the desired end.*"

—Frederick Douglass, *My Bondage and My Freedom*

Writing in the Real World

Rich storytelling flows naturally from Cléo Boudreau (boo-DROH), who has chronicled his personal adventures for over a decade. In 1984 Boudreau exchanged his life as a professor for the "complete freedom" of a life spent sailing between Jamaica and Venezuela. His long, lively letters to his son Will about his nautical adventures eventually grew into a twice-yearly newsletter, the *Melibea News*. The following is an excerpt from the online version of the newsletter, *Cruising the Caribees.*

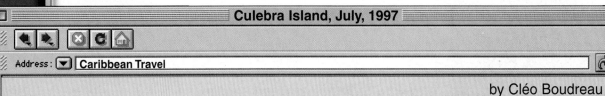

Culebra Island, July, 1997

Address: Caribbean Travel | Go

by Cléo Boudreau

Rain was coming down hard at Chaguaramas on this date two years ago. Big rain, pelting down in bursts. Susan was soaked, I was drenched, and Terry was prowling the edge of the forest looking for butterflies. We thought the bus wasn't coming, maybe it skidded off into a ditch, maybe the road got washed out, maybe the windshield wipers weren't working, maybe the driver had a coronary. . . .

Susan and I decided to walk back. It was only a couple of miles anyway, and we were soaked already, so what difference could it make. Terry was doing okay on the butterflies—he's a collector—and he figured he'd hang in for a while longer. Wet butterflies. Who ever heard of collecting wet butterflies?

"He's not collecting," Susan said. "He's just looking."

"Fine. Let's go." And we headed off at a fast pace in what looked like a lull between cloudbursts. That was all relative, because even in the lull it was still pouring hard. We didn't get beyond the nearest bend in the road when it really began to come down, though. I mean, you have no idea at all

about rain until you've seen how it comes down on Trinidad. Stupendous torrents of raindrops big as kumquats. And they hurt. . . .

Up ahead was a small wooden building. . . . "Come on, Susan, let's run!" I grabbed her hand and yanked. . . . We actually worried about drowning before we got there, it was so hard to breathe under all that falling water. . . .

We huddled [in the building] the best we could, wet, cold and miserable. Every once in a while loud crashing noises came out of the rain forest, as of branches breaking and falling. . . .

"Hello."

I jumped at the man's voice. He came right out of the rain forest and stepped into the pump-house. Susan saw him before I did and she yelped in fear. . . . [T]his guy . . . had a machete in his right hand, and there was a wide rectangular basket hanging from a cord around his neck. His long hair was streaming down around his shoulders, and I saw long scars on his face. . . . On appearances alone, this was the kind of man you wouldn't want to meet in a dark alley. He turned out to be one of the most fascinating individuals I've met in a lifetime.

I stepped forward to place myself between him and Susan. . . . The man smiled at my move and put down his machete. . . . "No need for worry," he said. "No harm here."

We stood without speaking for a while, all three of us. I got curious about his basket, though, and wondered what he had in it. . . . There were short chunks of tree branches, . . . and small bundles of leaves held together with strings, and roots of different colors and shapes. . . .

"What've you got there?" I asked.

"These are medicines," he said. "Old people buy them."

"Old people?"

"Yes. People who don't have money for regular doctors, old people. I sell to the duendes, the herb doctors. Sometimes I go into Port of Spain, into the poor sections, and the old people come out of their houses to meet me." . . .

"Here, let me show." He rummaged through his basket and pulled out an orange colored root, washed it clean under a stream of water pouring down from a broken drain pipe, and then began to slice it with his machete. Whack! Whack! That machete was two feet long and he was holding the piece of root in his left hand, whacking off slices thin as razor blades. Susan winced every time the machete came down. She told me later I was wincing too. . . .

We stayed about half an hour watching this man wash, peel, slice, trim and otherwise prepare his forest medicines for the old people. . . .

Internet zone

A Writer's Process

Prewriting
Reeling in Ideas

Before retiring, Boudreau had never attempted any personal writing. Now he says, "To sit down and try to match up a style with an actual event that you have had a part in—I never realized it was such a challenge. To use words as one would use paints—to let them shed their color on each other in a way that highlights an adventure—is rewarding."

His ship's log is "perhaps the chief sourcebook for the newsletters," the captain says. He tries to "make little vignettes or anecdotes out of the entries." "Culebra Island, July, 1997" is an example of a vignette that grew out of a log entry.

The newsletter sometimes features life-and-death adventures, such as one in which Boudreau described a terrifying hurricane. Other issues are more lighthearted. One issue described the process of baking bread. In the middle of the churning ocean, even baking bread can be an adventure.

Boudreau's life aboard the Melibea *provides material for his writing journal.*

Ashore at St. Thomas, the captain finds a quiet place to think and write.

Writing in the Real World

Drafting/Revising
Describing the Events

Boudreau does most of his writing before 10:30 A.M. in an idyllic setting: "From when the sun comes up until the trade winds fill in, it's delightfully cool. I have a cockpit in the sailboat with a canvas top on it. I can just sit there at my writing table . . . looking out over the harbor, the palm trees, and the mountains."

Usually Boudreau has a definite idea in mind before he begins writing. He first composes his newsletter in pencil, even before he has a particular reader in mind. After writing a couple of drafts, he chooses the best one and revises it again as he types it on his computer. "I let it sit for a couple of weeks or so. Then I go back and do a final draft," he explains. "About four or five run-throughs is my average."

Boudreau strengthens his writing with vivid description, interesting facts, personal and sensory observations, and a strong sense of narrative. All of those elements came together in his account of an encounter with a West Indian herb gatherer.

Revising/Editing
Continuing "Until It's Right"

The *Melibea* was designed to be sailed by a lone sailor. For Boudreau, writing is a solitary endeavor as well.

Boudreau's recipe for flying fish as well as letters to his son and newsletters reprinted in a St. Thomas newspaper

"If there's anybody I write for, it must be myself," says the captain.

He is also his own editor, so he must rely on his own instincts to decide when his work is complete. "Because of my lifestyle," he notes, "I can take time to make sure that I find the pleasure that I'm looking for in it, simply by revising until it's right."

Publishing/Presenting
The Newsletter Is Printed

Once Boudreau has completed his newsletter, he gives a copy of it to his son Will, who takes it back to the United States for duplication and mailing. The original handful of readers has grown to a circulation of more than 150 friends and relatives. Boudreau's "hurricane edition" garnered an even wider audience when it was reprinted as a three-part newspaper series in the *St. Thomas Courier.*

Readers of the newsletter frequently urge Boudreau to reprint some of his other issues, but he laughs. "I don't know why everyone wants to put me to work. I'm having so much fun!"

Analyzing the Media Connection

Discuss these questions about the article on pages 4 and 5.

1. What mood does Boudreau evoke in "Culebra Island, July, 1997"? How does he evoke this mood?

2. What literary devices does Boudreau use to enliven his writing?

3. In what ways does Boudreau's use of dialogue add to the power of his piece? Explain.

4. In what ways are Boudreau's real-life account and a short story similar? Is there rising action, a conflict, a climax, a denouement, and/or falling action?

5. How does Boudreau create suspense in his narrative?

Analyzing a Writer's Process

Discuss these questions about Cléo Boudreau's writing process.

1. Why does Boudreau find the writing he does difficult?

2. Where does Boudreau get ideas for his writing?

3. For whom does Boudreau write? Why?

4. What techniques does Boudreau use when revising his writing?

5. What are the advantages and disadvantages of Boudreau's serving as his own editor?

Use commas with coordinating conjunctions.

One kind of run-on sentence occurs when the writer omits a comma before the coordinating conjunction in a compound sentence.

Notice how Boudreau uses a comma:

She was a little scared too, and I wasn't feeling very good about things either.

Fix each run-on below.

1. Jane wrote a postcard to Elizabeth but her mother forgot to mail it.

2. Andy called his sister in Florida and we both told her the good news.

3. The weather is getting warmer every day and now the tulips are starting to bloom.

4. We ordered three fish platters but the Jacksons wanted the shrimp special.

See Lesson 13.10, pages 553–555.

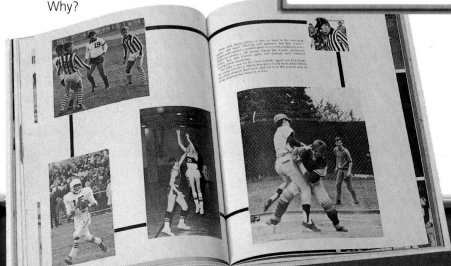

Writing to Discover

*W*riting about your own thoughts, feelings, and experiences is called personal writing. Often based on exploration of your past, personal writing can either be kept confidential or be shared, as Annie Dillard does with this meditation on the value of writing.

Malvin Gray Johnson,
Self-Portrait (detail), 1934

Literature Model

*W*hen you write, you lay out a line of words. The line of words is a miner's pick, a woodcarver's gouge, a surgeon's probe. You wield it, and it digs a path you follow. Soon you find yourself deep in new territory. Is it a dead end, or have you located the real subject? You will know tomorrow, or this time next year.

You make the path boldly and follow it fearfully. You go where the path leads. . . . The writing has changed, in your hands, and in a twinkling. . . . The new place interests you because it is not clear. You attend. In your humility, you lay down the words carefully, watching all the angles.

Annie Dillard, *The Writing Life*

What does Dillard mean when she says, "You make the path boldly and follow it fearfully"?

Dillard uses words as tools for digging out ideas that are new, unknown, and interesting. Malvin Gray Johnson used paint to explore images of himself in his self-portrait. Taking a paintbrush or a pen in hand reveals thoughts you never knew you had.

Create a Life Map

Just as a road map helps a traveler plan a trip, a life map helps you identify events in your life that offer intriguing possibilities to explore in your writing.

Charting the significant people, places, and events in your life can give you an overview of your life's high points, low points, and turning points. If you make a map of challenges you have met and disappointments you've overcome, you'll notice patterns that will help you answer questions such as When do I feel happy? What are my interests? What type of work do I like? Who are my friends? The life map below shows the kinds of events one student might note.

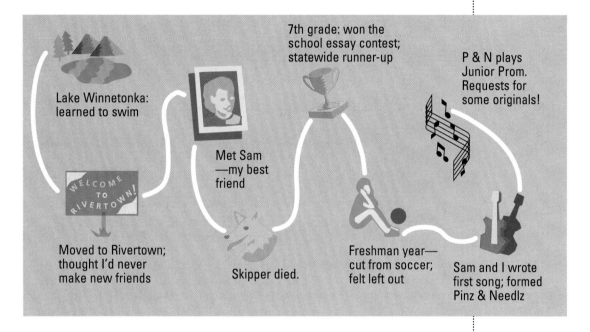

Lake Winnetonka: learned to swim

Moved to Rivertown; thought I'd never make new friends

Met Sam —my best friend

Skipper died.

7th grade: won the school essay contest; statewide runner-up

Freshman year— cut from soccer; felt left out

P & N plays Junior Prom. Requests for some originals!

Sam and I wrote first song; formed Pinz & Needlz

Once you sketch a life map, look for patterns that connect the events. The student who drew the map above might notice that the low points in his life have inspired him to do things that led to success. In your own writing, you might want to focus on the connection between two or more events.

Journal Writing

Sketch your life map. Find and describe a pattern among the highs, lows, and turning points. List the specific events that are part of that pattern.

Share Discoveries

As you write about events from your life map, you might want to ask a small group to read and respond to your writing. A group's purpose is not to evaluate your experiences, but rather to let you know whether your writing expresses what you want to say. The script below shows the kind of conversation you and your readers might have.

WANDA, THE WRITER: Do you think I gave too much information about the first driving lesson? Is it boring?

ANDY: Some of these details about what the teacher told you to do and how confused he made you are funny. They make the story come alive.

BARBARA: One thing I liked was that this reminded me of the time when I was learning to drive. But I don't like the ending. I don't know why.

ANDY: I disagree. I think the ending is really good, but it takes too long to get into the story.

WANDA: Do you think I should cut the first couple of paragraphs? I wondered whether people needed that information to understand what comes later.

Exchanging ideas can improve anyone's writing. Listen to feedback carefully. Write down all responses; even if you disagree now with some ideas, you might reconsider them as you revise your writing. You will also learn by giving feedback to others. Use the following guidelines.

Guidelines for Groups

LISTEN	RESPOND	CLARIFY	COOPERATE
Make eye contact, nod, and tune in to each person as he or she speaks. Take notes and ask questions.	Stay on the subject. Be brief. Make it clear that you disagree with ideas rather than people.	If you don't understand what someone else has said, ask for clarification.	Offer compliments to each member. Give encouraging feedback such as, "I like Joe's suggestion because . . ."

Write About a Personal Episode

Write a few paragraphs about a significant event or person in your life. You might write about how one person influenced a decision you made, about how it felt to move to a new town, or about another occurrence of your own choosing. Use a life map and brainstorm a list of relevant words and phrases to organize your ideas.

PURPOSE To describe an important event or person in your life

AUDIENCE Yourself and your peers

LENGTH 2–3 paragraphs

WRITING RUBRICS To write a vivid personal narrative, you should

- provide details that will make your writing come alive

- consider using dialogue if it's appropriate to your narrative

- review your essay to find incorrect pronoun shifts

Listening and Speaking

COOPERATIVE LEARNING Read your narrative to a small group. The objective of presenting your work is to discover if you have conveyed your experiences effectively. Can the others clearly see your descriptions or hear your dialogue? What are some of the group's suggestions for revision? When listening to other students' work, remember that your job is to give them constructive feedback so that they can find the clearest way to express themselves in their writing.

Avoid incorrect pronoun shifts.

Notice how Annie Dillard uses the pronoun *you* consistently:

> When you write, **you** lay out a line of words.

Revise the sentences below by making sure the pronouns are consistent.

1. I love going to the beach at times when you can avoid the crowds.
2. One needs to consider carefully each college and university; you shouldn't choose a school blindly.
3. You should always travel without an itinerary so that one's vacation turns into an adventure.
4. If people don't follow their dreams, you lose your zest for life.
5. He takes a shortcut where you rarely encounter traffic.

See Lesson 17.6, pages 632–636.

Cross-Curricular Activity

ART Review the life map you created. Illustrate four or five events on the map. Then, in a small group, share your life map. Explain each event you have illustrated and what the illustration tells about that event.

Writing in a Journal

A writer's journal is a place to record thoughts for future reference. In the following models, Joan Frances Bennett and Loren Eiseley use journals to jot down impressions.

Literature Model

Sometimes when I come across an old photograph of myself, particularly one of those taken when I was ten or twelve or thereabouts, I stare at it for a while trying to locate the person I was then, among all the persons I've been, trying to see stretched out down the years the magnetic chain linking the onlooker and the looked at, the gay expectant child and the sober near-adult. If I am successful, and very often I am, the two merge and I recall little snatches of life. Running through the wet grass in the dusk of early evening. My father's vulnerable smile as I walked down the aisle on graduating from kindergarten. . . .

Joan Frances Bennett
Members of the Class Will Keep Daily Journals

What triggers Bennett's memory of her kindergarten graduation?

Literature Model

Last evening the largest house centipede I have ever seen died peacefully on our bathroom rug. . . . Like two aging animals who have come into a belated understanding with each other, we achieved a mutual tolerance if not respect. He had ceased to run with that flowing, lightninglike menace that is part of the horror of centipedes to man; and I, in my turn, ceased to drive him away from the woolly bathroom rug on which his final desires had centered.

Loren Eiseley
The Lost Notebooks of Loren Eiseley

What features of this journal entry are clues that these are the personal reflections of a scientist?

Write Now for Later

Many writers store impressions and bits of information in journals to refer to as they write. When novelist F. Scott Fitzgerald overheard the intriguing comment "He wants to make a goddess out of me and I want to be Mickey Mouse," he wrote it in a notebook. The same words later came out of the mouth of a character in his story "On Your Own."

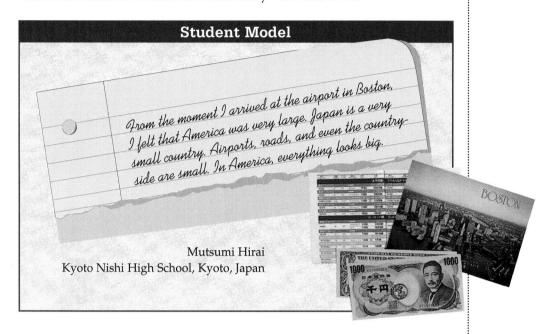

Student Model

From the moment I arrived at the airport in Boston, I felt that America was very large. Japan is a very small country. Airports, roads, and even the country-side are small. In America, everything looks big.

Mutsumi Hirai
Kyoto Nishi High School, Kyoto, Japan

Other writers return to journal entries written years earlier and comment on the views they held then. When Louisa May Alcott's publisher asked her to write a book for girls, she wrote in her journal, "I don't enjoy this sort of thing. Never liked girls or knew many, except my sisters; but our queer plays and experiences may prove interesting, though I doubt it." Years later, following the tremendous success of her novel *Little Women*, Alcott wrote "Good joke" beside this passage. The impressions you record in your journal now might seem insignificant, but in the future these impressions may hold more importance.

The journal excerpt on this page, by Japanese exchange student Mutsumi Hirai, will preserve Mutsumi's initial impressions of the United States long after she ceases to find American ways remarkable.

Journal Writing

Look around your classroom and make rapid notes for twenty minutes. Use your immediate environment as a stimulus, but write about anything that comes to mind. Don't stop until the twenty minutes are up. Then read your notes. Which do you find most surprising?

Make It Your Own

What you write in your journal is up to you. You might report observations, record impressions in poetry, or invent characters and situations for a short story. Several possible journal responses to seeing a street musician are illustrated below.

Street Musician

Nonfiction

More and more people seem to be performing on the streets these days.

Poetry

Strong, sweet,
Singing, drumming,
Lyrical, rhythmical,
Ringing, strumming,
Street song.

Fiction

Playing music always took Edward's mind off the stress and turmoil of his life.

Whatever you call it—a journal, a diary, a daybook, or a log—a journal will express your own sensibilities. It can be a bound book with a lovely cover, a spiral notebook, a looseleaf binder, a computer file, or a stack of index cards. The important thing is to try to record something in it every day.

Your journal can include your thoughts and ideas, lists, titles, outlines, first sentences, sketches and photographs, ticket stubs, diagrams, quotations, newspaper clippings, letters, interesting dialogue, or notes. As novelist and essayist Virginia Woolf explains below, a journal can be that desk drawer of your mind into which you put everything you want to keep.

How would you describe the kind of diary Woolf wants to have? What other kinds of diaries or journals might one keep?

Literature Model

What sort of diary should I like mine to be?
Something loose knit and yet not slovenly, so elastic that it will embrace anything, solemn, slight or beautiful that comes into my mind. I should like it to resemble some deep old desk, or capacious hold-all, in which one flings a mass of odds and ends without looking them through.

Virginia Woolf
A Writer's Diary

Write a Journal Entry

Choose a topic from the list below or a topic of your choice and use it as the basis for a journal entry.

- an old photograph of yourself
- an animal or insect you have encountered
- an article in a newspaper or a magazine
- a person you don't know very well but find intriguing

PURPOSE To record your impressions in a journal
AUDIENCE Yourself
LENGTH 1 page

WRITING RUBRICS To write an effective journal entry, you should

- open your mind and record as many thoughts, impressions, and details as you can
- use language that is as specific and vivid as possible
- review your journal entry for verb tense consistency; for example, if you describe an event from the past, use past tense verbs

Specific adjectives can make a piece of writing come alive.

Notice how Virginia Woolf uses adjectives—*slovenly, elastic, solemn,* and others—to describe the variety of her diary.

Add specific adjectives to the following sentences to create strong word pictures.

1. The girls took the path home.
2. The elms shook as the wind grew stronger.
3. The noise woke the sleeper from a dream.
4. The dog howls every day when its owner leaves for work.
5. In childhood I always pulled the blanket over my head at bedtime.

See Lesson 10.4, pages 456–461.

Cross-Curricular Activity

HISTORY Locate a painting that shows a group of people who lived at another time in history. Reflect on what life may have been like for these people and how life has changed since that time. Freewrite for ten minutes about any related ideas the painting suggests to you. Then, write a paragraph describing the characters in the painting. Explain the circumstances in the people's lives.

Listening and Speaking

COOPERATIVE LEARNING As an extension of the Cross-Curricular Activity, join several other students and present a dialogue that in your view reflects what the people in a particular painting might be talking about. Before presenting your dialogue, brainstorm to decide on possible directions the dialogue might take. Then present your dialogue to the class, either from written scripts or as an improvisation. Afterwards, have a class discussion about your dialogue to determine how well it reflects the sense of the painting.

Writing to Learn

A learning log is a kind of journal in which you record observations about how and what you are learning. In the learning log entry below, Peter Ivaska notes his progress and considers his strengths and weaknesses in a trigonometry class.

Personal Writing

Student Model

I have just spent another 45 minutes in trigonometry. We had a quiz on probability today. I went into class uncertain whether I understood combinations and permutations because I have been absent for most of the unit, but everything worked out and I did very well. . . . Doing well on the tests should be a good indication of how well I understand the material. Sometimes, though, I fall into the trap of thinking that I can get by without doing my homework. I wish that I could get rid of this recurring laziness. The assigned homework is usually not very long or difficult, but it is hard to do when it just seems like busy work.

Peter Ivaska
Evanston Township High School, Evanston, Illinois

What insights might Peter gain from this passage in his learning log?

The values of keeping a learning log are many. A learning log lets you step back from your schoolwork to analyze what you know, as well as your strengths, weaknesses, and progress. It also allows you to examine from several different angles material you find unclear. By assessing where you are in your learning, you can get more out of the time you spend studying.

Raise Your Learning Level

If you keep a learning log, you'll have several strategies for increasing the amount of information you retain. In a learning log, you can grapple with the facts and concepts introduced in your classes. When you become actively involved with facts and concepts by testing and using them, real learning takes place.

A log also can help sort out what you know and don't know so you can decide how to focus your study time. A list like the one to the right showing general headings can help you prepare for a chemistry lab, or research a history paper, or study for a literature exam.

Another learning log technique is to imagine yourself in a situation and then think about how you might be affected by it. For instance, you might rephrase the review question "What were the ramifications of the cotton gin on the southern economy?" by asking yourself, "If I had been a southern farmer in the early nineteenth century, how would buying a cotton gin have affected my operations?"

You can keep your learning log in a separate binder or notebook. You can also incorporate your log into your regular notebook. Use the left-hand page for comments on notes that are on the facing right-hand page. You can also divide each page of your notebook in half. Use one half of the page for notes, the other half as a learning log.

What I understand
Matter = anything that occupies space
Atom = fundamental unit of matter

What I'm uncertain of
What's the difference/relationship between protons, neutrons, and electrons?

What I need to find out
What is an isotope?

Matter i
occupies
unit of n
relation
neutrons
in conju
fundame
isotopes
electrons
differenc
protons

Journal Writing

Experiment with a variety of learning log techniques: evaluate your progress in class; write a dialogue debating an idea you find unclear; explain to a child what you have been studying; or make up your own essay test and answer one of the questions.

Know Your Style

Once you know what you need to learn, it's helpful to understand how you learn best. Experiment with a variety of learning log techniques, including the ones below. You'll find out which help you most.

- Evaluate progress in a class. Assess strengths and weaknesses.
- Write a dialogue in which you take turns arguing for and against an idea you find confusing or intriguing.
- Try explaining to a child what you have been studying.
- Make up your own essay test for a class. Answer one of the questions yourself.

Another way to improve your learning is by understanding how you process information. You probably use one of three basic learning styles: visual, auditory, or tactile. Visual learners do best when they can read or see things in front of them. Auditory learners prefer to hear an explanation of what they are trying to learn. Tactile learners benefit from actually handling and manipulating material. Many people use a combination of learning styles, but most people find that one style dominates.

Experiment with the three learning styles, and record the results in your learning log to better understand your learning strengths and weaknesses. One way to get started is to reserve a section in a notebook for each of your subjects and to write in the log on a regular basis. At first you might simply keep track of your progress in each class, dating each entry. Next you might try recording the results of experimenting with the three learning styles. Which style resulted in improvement, confusion, or mastery of a topic? You may achieve insights like those illustrated below.

Tactile Learner
The best way for me to learn is to get my fingers on the keys and play the piece over and over.

Auditory Learner
The best way for me to learn a song is to listen to recordings and hear the way other musicians play the piece.

Visual Learner
The best way for me to learn a song is to study the sheet music.

Write an Entry in Your Learning Log

Look through a textbook from one of your classes and choose a chapter you have already studied. Determine which sections give you difficulties and which you understand. In your learning log, write one or two paragraphs focusing on problem areas and one or two paragraphs evaluating strengths.

PURPOSE To use a learning log to evaluate your strengths and weaknesses in a subject

AUDIENCE Yourself

LENGTH 2–4 paragraphs

WRITING RUBRICS To write an effective entry in your learning log, you should

- list what you understand and what you need to find out
- ask yourself questions about the subject that you find troublesome
- analyze your learning style
- record some learning strategies that might help you learn the material
- proofread your entry and correct mistakes in spelling and punctuation

Using Computers

Collaborate with another student to develop a format for a learning log that each of you finds effective and convenient to use. With your partner, use a computer to design a template that can be used in a variety of subjects. If your school has a Web page, share your findings by publishing your template.

Grammar Link

Keep verb tense consistent if events occur at the same time.

Don't change verb tense when writing about things that happened at the same time:

*We **had** a quiz on probability today. I **went** into class uncertain. . . .*

Revise the sentences below. Make sure that the verb tenses are consistent.

1. It is a beautiful day and we were happy to bicycle to the picnic.
2. Because we swam a long distance to the dock, we stop to sunbathe before turning back.
3. As Laura sang in chorus, she focuses on the music in front of her.
4. Just as the sitter rings the doorbell, the baby awoke crying.
5. Whenever Pete eats spicy food, his stomach ached all night.
6. When Jill got to work, her boss leaves.
7. When the students finished researching, they all write an essay on weaving.
8. Susan inherited money from her grandmother and buys a train ticket.
9. Joe caught the ball and tosses it to Zoe.
10. After Tony's dog had been trained, his mother buys another puppy.

See Lesson 15.3, pages 579–582.

Listening and Speaking

COOPERATIVE LEARNING In a group, brainstorm a list of time-management techniques that might help you study for tests. Share the best strategies with other groups.

LESSON
1.4

Writing a Letter

*L*etter writing is a form of personal writing that may provide insight and understanding to both writer and recipient. Notice in the following model how Michelle Eddy uses shared memories to get a response from her friend Sarah.

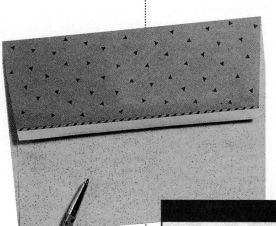

Student Model

Dear Sarah,
It's so sad how we used to write to one another every other week, and now only once every four or five months. I guess as we got older we also got much busier. . . . Still, I miss not having my best friend, Short Legs, here to share everything with me.

I played tennis again this year, and my partner in one doubles was Mary Trujillo. I know you remember Mary. She is still a clown and a good friend. . . . We did really well this season, and went to the state tournament that was held here in Pueblo. We made it to the second round and lost to a team we should have beaten. Isn't that always the story? Oh well! This summer, I am going to take private lessons from the coach at Cheyenne Mountain High School. . . .

What about you? What are you going to do this summer? I know you have been in some successful plays this year that you need to tell me about. . . . I know you're busy too, but try to respond soon. I'll be thinking about you!

Love always,
"Mish"

Michelle Eddy
Centennial High School, Pueblo, Colorado

> How does Michelle express her feelings about Sarah in the first paragraph?

> What is the purpose of Michelle's last paragraph?

Consider Your Audience and Purpose

Once you move beyond purely private journal writing into letter writing, you need to think about your audience. Are you writing to a friend as Michelle was? Or are you writing to people you have never met? In each case, you should try to anticipate your audience's interests and depth of knowledge about your topic. For example, if Michelle had been writing to someone she didn't know, she would have provided more background details about each person mentioned in her letter.

In addition to content, the language and tone of your letters will also depend on your audience. For example, even though you might write letters to your friend and your aunt on the same day about some of the same topics, you can't quickly revise a letter to a friend to make it a suitable thank-you note for your aunt. Though there may be some topics that interest both your aunt and a friend, much of what you write about and how you write it will depend on your audience. This diagram illustrates the way Michelle's choice of topics may change for a letter to a friend and a letter to her coach.

Your purpose in writing should be clear to both you and your audience. For example, you may decide that your purpose in writing is to inform, persuade, entertain, narrate, or describe. Michelle probably had several purposes in writing to Sarah: to rekindle that old spark of friendship and to get Sarah to fill her in on what has been happening in her life.

Letter to a friend
- Friendship
- Tennis partner
- Feelings about tournament loss

Elements in common
- The state tournament
- Plans to take private lessons

Letter to tennis coach
- Schedule for lessons
- Tennis skills to be improved

Journal Writing

Make notes about two letters you want to write to two different people. List the topics you would cover in each letter. Put a check by the topics you would mention in both letters.

Maintain Relationships

No matter what it says, a good letter begs for an answer. Many relationships have been preserved through the regular exchange of letters. These letters between American writers Zora Neale Hurston and Fannie Hurst, written in the 1940s, are an example of written communication between friends.

Literature Model

Dear, dear, Friend,
    I cannot tell you how shocked I am to hear that you have been ill at all, let alone being in a hospital! I have never conceived of you as either ill nor ailing. I see you always swirling the waving veils of space like a spear of flame.
    Now what can I do about it? Do you need me in any way? I am at your feet and at your service. There is nothing I would not do for my benefactor and friend. You know that I can type now. I can cook as always, [and] I can do many more things than I could when you scraped me up out of the street. If there is anything that you feel I could do to please you, you must let me know. I should pay back for all that I have received somehow. . . .

Most devotedly,
Zora

> What does Hurston say to convince Hurst that her offers to help are sincere?

Literature Model

Dear Zora:
    Thank you for your warm and understanding letter. In this torn and harassed world, the stability of friendship is about the only staff of life we have left.
    I am just about emerging from my fantastic convalescence and hope that you will soon be in New York so that I can prove to you that I am back in my seven league stride.
    Are you doing a book? I hope so.
    I am on a second draft of a fat novel. The illness interfered horribly, but I am about to resume work. . . .

Thine,
Fannie Hurst

> How does Hurst respond to Hurston's concern?

Write a Letter

Write a short letter to a relative or friend telling about a recent experience and your feelings about it.

PURPOSE To describe an experience in your life
AUDIENCE A friend or relative
LENGTH 2–3 paragraphs

WRITING RUBICS To write an effective letter, you should

- decide on a purpose and stick to it
- keep your audience in mind
- invite a response
- ensure that your letter is legibly written

Cross-Curricular Activity

GEOGRAPHY Locate a photograph of a scene from another country or another region of the United States. What questions does the photograph raise? Jot down your impressions and questions. Then write a letter to someone who might be interested in the country or region. Include in your letter your feelings and observations, as well as some of your questions and possible answers.

Listening and Speaking

COOPERATIVE LEARNING Compose a letter to a person of your choice—perhaps a relative or a classmate who has moved to another neighborhood. In the letter, describe how the current

Capitalize proper nouns.

Names of specific people and places should be capitalized.

Sarah, Cheyenne Mountain High School

Revise the following sentences, using correct capitalization.

1. The drive from Trenton, new Jersey, to augusta, Maine, feels endless.
2. I wrote to aunt Alice, but I haven't heard from her yet.
3. Ms. Smith's class is studying the earth's rotations.
4. Mercury and venus are the closest planets to the sun.
5. If you see the grand canyon at sunrise, it will take your breath away!

See Lesson 20.2, pages 696–701.

school term is going. Then, in a small group, read your letter aloud. Discuss each group member's letter. Consider questions such as the following: Are the language and tone appropriate for the audience? Is the letter writer's purpose clear? What has the writer done to engage the reader? How can the letter be improved? Revise your letter based on feedback from the group.

1.5

Writing a College Application Essay

A college application essay, although for an audience you don't know, must be personal to succeed. In the essay below, the writer uses one extracurricular activity to reveal personal strengths that are valuable in other areas.

Personal Writing

Student Model

"Swimmers up, take your mark, BANG (the Gun Shot)." Splash! I am in the water now and my heart is racing. One lap completed; nineteen more to go. Boy, nineteen laps. Four hundred fifty yards. I have to think about something. Sometimes I sing fifties' songs; or if I am especially hungry I'll think about a yummy hamburger with everything on it. No, wait, I need to concentrate on my stroke and breathing. Is the girl in the lane next to me gaining? Faster, faster! Good, lap nine. I can hear people screaming; they're counting on me. I have to do well.

I've spoken in front of hundreds of my peers in school assemblies, talked to the entire teaching staff, and led cheers before an audience of thousands. I shouldn't be nervous having a friendly swim competition with five other girls with fewer than 200 people watching, but I am. This type of stress to win goes way beyond the amount of practice time one puts in . . . it has to do with a toughness—not physical, but mental.

I am one of the few people the coaches do not have to beg to swim the 500. This is not because I am an exceptional swimmer (my times are just above average in our league). It is because I have the mental toughness to take things to the very end. . . .

Anna Strasburg
Quartz Hill High School, Quartz Hill, California

The essay focuses on a single talent: swimming.

What does Anna say to convince college officials that she has the mental toughness needed to complete college?

Emphasize Your Individuality

Deans of college admissions say the essay is the part of the entrance application they most enjoy reading. A well-written essay can help you stand out from all the other applicants with similar grades, test scores, and extracurricular activities.

Some colleges will allow you to answer at length one question from a list of specific questions. Others will simply ask you to "tell us a little about yourself." Either way, the point is to get you to express something about your individuality.

Take a look at your topic—yourself—from different angles. How would a friend describe you? How has your family influenced you? Probe your feelings about events or accomplishments in your life. Use the checklist above to guide your exploration.

A laundry list of accomplishments won't create an interesting essay. Focus your writing; select one activity or image to illustrate your unique personality. Anna used a swimming competition to show her mental toughness, the character trait she decided to highlight. Anna might have used notes like these to plan her essay.

Self-Assessment Checklist

- What feat am I proudest of? Why?
- How would my best friend describe me?
- What roles have my family and community played in my development?
- In what ways is this picture of me incomplete?

Personal Writing

Qualities to emphasize
- *perseverance; mental toughness*
- *ability to perform under stress*
- *ability to perform before a crowd*
- *ability to set and achieve goals*

Activity that portrays qualities
- *swimming, not only competitive, but distance*

How to portray
- *stream of consciousness; thoughts that keep me going*

Journal Writing

List four accomplishments of which you are proud. Next to each one, list any traits, such as initiative, perseverance, or creativity, that you used to achieve it. Then write a paragraph describing one of the achievements and why you are proud of it. What activities or images can you think of that could help you illustrate these traits and achievements?

Calvin and Hobbes by Bill Watterson

Put the Pieces Together

Even if you're much older than Calvin, don't let your application essay run on and on. Once you've written your essay, reread it to be certain each detail makes an important point. Aim for clear, natural language that draws attention to what you say, not how you say it.

Literature Model

My father has always said that I have "brain surgeon hands," probably because they're rather large with fingers so long and thin that my school ring has to be held on with masking tape. . . .

When I was a child, these hands curled themselves around a crayon to scrawl my first letters; they clutched at the handles of a bicycle, refusing to trust my training wheels; they arched delicately over my head in pirouettes and slid, wriggling, into softball gloves. . . . These hands once plunged deep into the pinafore pockets of my candy-striped uniform, emerging to write messages and lab orders, punch telephone numbers, steady syringes. . . .

Someday, these hands will grip forceps and retractors, tense and slick; they will rake through my hair with fatigue as I sit in library carrels studying graphs and figures. Someday soon, they will hold a daisy-adorned diploma from Lincoln School, and they will hold again, as they have in the past, trophies and book awards and certificates. I have confidence that they will become the hands of an M.D., with the power to heal and comfort. . . .

Joanne B. Wilkinson
from *100 Successful College Application Essays*

> What does Joanne tell the admissions committee that might convince them of her commitment to a career in medicine?

> Does Joanne expect the road to career success to be easy? How can you tell?

Write a Short Essay

Write a short college application essay that reveals something about yourself. Focus on one event or experience that was particularly meaningful. You might describe how a part-time job changed you, how you overcame a handicap or obstacle to achieve something, or how a family member influenced you.

PURPOSE To present yourself as a strong candidate to a college admissions committee

AUDIENCE College admissions personnel

LENGTH 3–4 paragraphs

WRITING RUBRICS To write an effective college application essay, you should

- examine your feelings and viewpoints about the experience
- include details that emphasize the point you want to make
- use direct language that is simple and clear
- proofread your essay carefully
- exchange drafts with a partner and comment on each other's essays

Using Computers

If you use a computer to write your essay, store each draft in a separate file. This will free you to be ever more creative in your writing, knowing that if you go too far in any one draft, the earlier version has not been destroyed.

Use commas and semicolons to separate words in a series.

Revise the following sentences by putting commas or semicolons in the appropriate places.

1. Three remarkable women in history are Virginia Woolf a writer Marie Curie the first female Nobel Prize winner and Eleanor Roosevelt author of the human rights credo for the United Nations.

2. The paintings that impressed me the most were Avery's *Mother and Child* Hopper's *Early Sunday Morning* and Picasso's *Guernica.*

3. The video store had a number of movies we were interested in: The Marx Brothers' *Duck Soup* a comedy *Young Sherlock Holmes* a mystery-thriller *Planet of the Apes* science fiction and *Sounder* a coming-of-age story.

4. If you observe the marsh area carefully, you will see several species of ducks— mergansers mallards and wood ducks a green heron and two species of geese— Canada and brant.

See Lesson 21.5, pages 720–721 and Lesson 21.6, pages 722–730.

Viewing and Representing

CREATING A LIFE MAP To help get started on your college application essay, use the technique of creating a life map, discussed in Lesson 1.1, page 9. You might use the map you created then or create a new one to spark an idea for the essay. Share your life map with a partner and discuss what parts of your life maps might suggest topics for a college application essay.

WRITING ABOUT LITERATURE
Writing About Nonfiction

*W*riting about nonfiction *is a way of recording personal responses and reactions. After you read the article below, read the response that one reader had to it.*

Literature Model

Patricia Szymczak was 36 years old when she decided to pursue a quest she had contemplated since childhood: finding her mother. . . . She knew the woman's name and hometown from a 1953 Illinois adoption decree, obtained when she turned 18 from her adoptive mother. Szymczak called the local post office, found a retired mailman, and got him talking about the family—*her* family. She contacted old neighbors, who led her to friends. Some had seen the woman, who now lived out of state, at a recent high school reunion.

. . . The long search ended with a three-hour call from a pay phone. By the end of the conversation, it was after midnight on the second Sunday in May. Patricia Szymczak smiled and wished her newfound relation a happy Mother's Day.

Elizabeth Taylor, "Are You My Mother?" *Time*

Model

I really enjoyed this article. It started me thinking: Is it a good idea for an adoptee to search for his or her birth parents? It seems that you never know what you might turn up, so why not leave well enough alone? On the other hand, you may be able to answer questions about yourself that would otherwise be forever unresolved. The article basically says that each case is unique. Many people are happy that they went to the trouble to locate their birth parents. Searches don't always end happily, however.

The writer begins this response by asking and then answering a question. What other question could be asked to begin a response to this article?

Respond as a Reader

The more involved you are in what you read, the more you benefit from it. By recording your responses on paper, you can clarify your thoughts as well as create a record to refer to in the future.

A reader-response journal, a notebook in which you record your reactions to books and articles, can be a tool for staying involved in your reading. It can also be a place to record your changing ideas as you increase your knowledge and understanding of various topics.

Ideas in a reader-response journal need not be organized or developed like those in the model on page 28; they are simply kernels you can later decide to explore and develop. This sample from a reader-response journal illustrates one reader's reactions to Taylor's article.

Quotation or paraphrase from text	What text makes me think of
When she turned 18, she obtained her adoption decree from her adoption mother.	This made me wonder how adoptive parents feel about their children searching for their birth parents.
The author used Mother's Day to represent the happy reunion.	Mother's Day might mean different things to different people. But for those who can't be with their mothers and for those who don't even know them, it may bring sadness.
Szymczak obviously spent a lot of time and money trying to track down her birth mother.	Szymczak's drive to make a connection with her birth parents must have been powerful. I wonder why the connection was so important to her.

Journal Writing

Examine a work of nonfiction that affected you strongly in either a positive or a negative way. Quote or paraphrase information from the work. Respond to it by asking one question about the topic and answering it.

Expand the Response

Sometimes you will want to write more than brief notes to respond to a nonfiction article. The article that follows, for instance, might inspire a variety of more fully developed responses.

Student Model

Anyone whose parents have divorced and remarried will know what I'm talking about. . . . You need maps, calendars, and a collection of used airline tickets to make any sense out of [my family]. Heather and I lived in Tennessee with my mother and stepfather. We were from California—which is where my father and stepmother lived. My stepfather's first wife also lived in California with their four children, Mike, Tina, Angie, and Bill, my step-siblings.

Confused? So was I.

. . . How do you separate out all of your feelings about divorce, remarriage, and these strangers who are supposed to be your family? You can't. But you can try to see your stepbrothers and sisters as people. . . . Figure out who they are, not just the role they play in your circumstances, [and] chances are you'll have an easier time understanding them. They've seen the same kinds of hard times that you have and will probably share similar feelings. . . .

Ann Patchet
"Step-Siblings," *Seventeen* magazine

The chart below suggests some ways you might respond to this or another nonfiction article that you found particularly interesting.

Read an Interesting Article, and . . .			
Write a research paper on the same topic:	**Write a poem or notes for a poem:**	**Write a second article with a different emphasis:**	**Write a play or script:**
"What is the contemporary family really like? How many children live with stepparents and siblings from a previous marriage?"	"My stepsister called. Jealousy, again. Somehow when the phone rings I can tell who it is."	"Money is an issue in any family. But when stepchildren are involved, the issue becomes even more complicated."	"**Ursula:** I hate you! I always will. [turns back to John] **John:** Is it me you hate? Or the fact that your parents are divorced?"

30 Unit 1 Personal Writing

Make a Dialogue

Write a one-act play that will provide entertainment and information on an issue you care about. Read two or three nonfiction magazine articles about the topic. Create two characters who represent different views on the topic, and then write a dialogue in response to the articles. One of the characters should express views that are essentially your views; the other character should present an opposing opinion. Be as fair as possible in presenting both points of view, but make it clear which opinion you find most valid.

PURPOSE To respond to an issue creatively
AUDIENCE Your classmates
LENGTH 1–2 pages

WRITING RUBRICS To write realistic dialogue, you should

- make your dialogue informative and entertaining
- be sure both viewpoints are reasonable
- use views that provoke response
- be sure that pronouns agree with their antecedents

Using Computers

If you have access to a computer or a word processor, you may find it useful in writing and printing a script. The word-processing program probably allows you to create lines with a hanging indentation. This feature lets you put the speaker's name on the left, while all the dialogue that the character speaks is indented to the right of the name. Printing dialogue using hanging indentations makes it easier for actors to identify and memorize their lines.

Personal Writing

Grammar Link

Make sure that pronouns agree with their antecedents in number and gender.

*Many people are happy that **they** went to the trouble to locate **their** birth parents.*

Complete the following sentences by supplying pronouns that agree with their antecedents in number and gender.

1. Mr. Sims, the driver, took Helen to the wrong restaurant because _____ wouldn't listen to _____ directions.
2. Oswald had already ordered _____ first course, and _____ had been served.
3. Since Helen and Oswald were old friends, _____ late arrival did not cause _____ to argue.
4. When Helen saw that he had ordered snails, _____ wondered if _____ could watch _____ eat _____.
5. When the waiter brought Helen _____ frogs' legs, Oswald could not look at _____.

See Lesson 17.6, pages 632–636.

Listening and Speaking

COOPERATIVE LEARNING With the help of a partner, perform your dialogue for the class. Be sure each speaker in the dialogue presents clear ideas and logical support. The effective use of pitch and tone of voice as well as eye contact can help the speakers emphasize their main points. After performing the dialogue, discuss your presentation with the class and accept suggestions for improvement.

WRITING ABOUT LITERATURE
Writing About Poetry

A response to a poem is a personal matter; different people will respond in different ways. Listen as a classmate reads the following poem, which Irish writer Christy Nolan created at age eleven. What is your response to the poem?

Literature Model

"On Remembering the Beara Landscape"

Lakes and rivers, lovely scenery,
Parks and skies, mountain greenery,
A lovely day awaiting.
Away we drive through lonely roads,
Late Fall played a tune on our motor car,
We laughed and sang as we sped along,
Pores open wide along polar jaws.
A possie occurred riding,
Along lonely laneways speeding,
A herd of cattle steaming,
Which brought us to a halt.
A paper passed on an ethereal, rapier-
    like wind,
A song bird flew on fiery wing,
Over hill and dale clouds billowed,
Dancing the dance of golden dreams.

Christy Nolan

Tune In to Impressions

There is no "right" way to respond to a poem. The important thing is to tune in to the personal feelings the poem awakens in you. Following are two responses to Nolan's poem.

The first student liked the poem and was inspired to write a few lines of poetry that used one of Nolan's images.

Model

I really like the way Christy Nolan puts certain words together.
A song bird flew on fiery wing—Nolan

My cat flew at the fiery jay,
The jay laughed raucously from its high perch—Me

Even though the second student was less enthusiastic, she provides reasons for her response.

Model

Today we read Christy Nolan's poem, "On Remembering the Beara Landscape." I enjoyed it, but I was not as swayed by it as some people seemed to be. I know that Nolan was only eleven when he wrote it, but I still think it's a little too childlike. For instance, the opening lines about "lovely scenery" and "mountain greenery" are pretty predictable.

I do like some of the lines, though. I especially enjoy this line even though I don't have any idea what it means:
Pores open wide along polar jaws
Goose bumps maybe?

What does this writer dislike about Nolan's poem? What does this writer like about the poem?

Each person who reads a poem will respond to it in a different way because every reader brings his or her own expectations and experiences to the poem.

Journal Writing

Write your own response to "On Remembering the Beara Landscape." Allow your response to reflect feelings the poem awakens in you. You may either write a creative piece of your own, using the poem as inspiration, or find examples in the poem to explain your reaction.

Spin Off from the Poem

You can move past your immediate, emotional reactions to a poem and enrich your responses even more. Here are a few ways to do this.

Read a Poem about a Trip to the Countryside, and . . .			
Write an essay:	**Write a journal entry:**	**Research the poet:**	**Write a poem:**
"This poem is full of words connoting graceful movement. . . ."	"This poem reminded me of a country drive my family made years ago."	"Christy Nolan succeeded in expressing himself despite his disorder. . . ."	"Sand and grass, pale pink shells and gray-green tendrils . . . "

Below are Curran Walker's responses to "On Remembering the Beara Landscape." In the first model he uses personal reactions to create an original poem. The second model expands that poem into fiction.

Student Model

The crisp cool air stirs before a storm.
From atop the mountain meadow, I saw clouds forming.
A horse and rider trotted through the cool, fall air
    before a mountain storm.
The wind soared across meadow and wood,
    whistling along its way.
Leaves fluttered and fell to earth as the wind
    danced among the trees.

Curran Walker
Austin High School, Austin, Texas

Student Model

Leaves fluttered to earth. Nathaniel buttoned his coat while he watched the dark towering clouds coming in over the mountain. He shivered. As he guided his horse, Blue, down the mountain, the sky grew black. Wind soared across meadow and wood, whistling along its way. Then lightning flashed and thunder boomed like a thousand cannons. His horse broke into a dead run down the side of the mountain. After what seemed like an eternity to Nathaniel, he regained control of Blue—only to find that he was in unfamiliar surroundings.

Curran Walker
Austin High School, Austin, Texas

Write a Response to a Poem

Respond to a poem of your choice by describing its content, explaining how it touched you in unexpected ways, or writing a new poem that expresses your feelings about it.

PURPOSE To respond personally to a poem
AUDIENCE Yourself
LENGTH 3–4 paragraphs

WRITING RUBRICS To effectively respond to a poem, you should

- record your impressions as you read
- examine the reasons for your reactions
- select the details and language that seem to elicit the deepest response

Cross-Curricular Activity

HISTORY The painting on this page inspired W. H. Auden to write the poem "Musée des Beaux Arts." Find the poem. Read and discuss it in a small group. Have one person research the myth of Icarus; another the painter Pieter Brueghel; and another the poet Auden. Ask each person to share his or her findings with the group.

Viewing and Representing

In your group, write an interpretation of the relationship between the painting and Auden's poem, "Musée des Beaux Arts." Afterwards, discuss ideas on the difference between feelings expressed in words and those expressed in visual images.

Grammar Link

Use precise verbs.

Curran Walker used *fluttered, soared,* and *boomed* to make his writing vivid.

Revise this descriptive paragraph by using stronger verbs.

The children [1]**walked** together on the beach in the early morning. My friend and I [2]**watched** a little girl run through the puddles [3]**left** by the tide. The children [4]**looked** at the silvery shells [5]**lying** along the shoreline.

See Lesson 10.3, pages 449–455.

Pieter Brueghel, *The Fall of Icarus,* 1564

Writing Process in Action

Personal Writing

In previous lessons you have learned that there are different kinds of personal writing. You've also had a chance to write your responses to the personal experiences of others. Now it's time to invite your readers to step into an episode from your life. In this lesson you'll write a personal narrative in which you balance narration, description, and reflection to give others an idea of who you are.

Assignment

Context	In a college board review course, you are asked to write about a particularly meaningful personal experience—something you had a strong reaction to or that affected your values. The topic is loosely defined. Focus on your personal impressions and feelings.
Purpose	To write a personal narrative essay that connects with the reader and conveys the real you
Audience	A college admissions panel or a job application review board
Length	1 to 2 pages

The following pages can help you plan and write your personal narrative. Read through them and refer to them as you need to. But don't let them limit you. This is your story.

WRITING Online

Visit the Writer's Choice Web site at **writerschoice. glencoe.com**, for additional writing prompts.

Prewriting

What experience from your past strikes you as particularly meaningful? You will probably find several good topics in your personal writing journal. Remember that simple and ordinary experiences can reveal just as much about the real you as dramatic events.

Once you've chosen an experience, close your eyes and imagine yourself back in time, going through what happened. Make notes about the Prewriting Questions at the right to help yourself remember. Keep going until the situation is so vivid in your mind that you can re-create both the incident and your feelings in words that a reader can relate to.

Prewriting Questions

- How did my surroundings look, smell, and feel?
- What were my emotions at the time?
- How do I feel about the experience now?
- How did the experience change me?
- What did I learn about myself?
- What did I learn about others?

Drafting

To begin drafting, think about how to open your personal writing. There are several possibilities:

- Plunge immediately into the action.
- Provide background information the reader will need to know to understand your experience or viewpoint.
- Raise a question that your response will answer.
- Offer a provocative statement about the subject.

The natural order of events in a narrative is chronological: what happened first, second, third, and so on. But for dramatic effect, you could start at the culminating event and then flash back to the beginning.

During drafting think about the tone or voice. Do you want to sound casual and friendly or distant and formal? Is your approach humorous or serious? Your tone conveys your attitude toward your audience and the topic.

Your tone will help you decide what to say and how to say it. In the model on the following page, the description of a basketball game is clipped and direct in order to show that the narrator is serious, abrupt, and shy.

Literature Model

Suddenly I saw her mirror image compose itself into a frightening look. Her eyes widened and gazed into some sorrowful romantic distance; her nostrils dilated; her full lips spread into a weird close-mouthed smile. I knew that, to her, this was her favorite image of herself; I could tell by a kind of relaxed triumph that came over her. "Stop that!" I cried. "Stop looking like that," for as long as she did, my mother was lost to me.

Gail Godwin, from "My Face"

Although drafting is not the time to agonize over word choice and sentence structure, do consider the voice and tone you will adopt. A comic tone will lead you to make choices that are different from those you would make to convey a serious attitude toward your subject.

Conclude your draft by reinforcing your main idea. You might come full circle, or you could forecast how the future will affect your features. Be sure to include what this close look at yourself has taught you. You might also ponder large questions, as Gail Godwin does in this excerpt from "My Face." Here she focuses on the link between looks and identity and goes on to make us think about the differences between how we see ourselves and how others see us.

Literature Model

After all, the mirror shows us the reverse of the self others see. Stand in front of the mirror with someone whose face you know well. His face in the mirror will not look quite the same. It may even look strange to you. Yet this is the face he sees every day. What would be strange for him would be to see his face as you see it at at its most familiar.

Gail Godwin, from "My Face"

Revising Checklist

- Have I focused on my topic?
- Have I selected details that best convey my attitude toward my picture?
- Are there any words or images that interfere with a consistent tone?
- Do my introductory and concluding paragraphs successfully perform their functions?
- Are there any places where transitions are needed?

Revising

To begin revising, read over your draft to make sure that what you've written fits your purpose and your audience. Then have a **writing conference.** Read your draft to a partner or small group. Use your audience's reactions to help you evaluate your work so far. The Revising Checklist can help you and your readers.

Editing/Proofreading

Once you are satisfied with the basic content and setup of your personal essay, **proofread** it carefully for errors in grammar, usage, mechanics, and spelling. Use the questions at the right as a guide.

In addition to proofreading, use the self-evaluation list below to make sure your personal narrative does all the things you want it to do. When you are happy with it, make a clean copy of the essay and proofread it one more time.

Self-Evaluation

Make sure your personal narrative

✔ focuses on a significant personal experience or viewpoint

✔ explores your thoughts and feelings

✔ describes events, people, and places in specific sensory detail

✔ reflects your unique personality

✔ follows correct grammar, usage, mechanics, and spelling

Publishing/Presenting

Keep your personal narrative in a safe place until you begin applying to colleges. It can serve as the basis for any number of application essays. You can also share your essay by submitting it to your school literary magazine or to a magazine for high school readers.

Editing Checklist

- Is my use of pronouns consistent and correct?
- Are all my verb forms and tenses correct?
- Have I capitalized all names and places correctly?
- Have I used commas and semicolons in a series?
- Have I checked the spelling of any words I'm unsure of?

Personal Writing

Proofreading Tip

What kind of mistakes do you make most often in writing? Keep them in mind as you proofread your personal narrative. For proofreading symbols, see page 92.

Journal Writing

Reflect on your writing process experience. Answer these questions in your journal: What do you like best about your essay? What was the hardest part of writing it? What did you learn from readers' responses? What new thing have you learned as a writer?

Literature Model

Black Ice is the story of a bright, young African American girl who entered a well-known formerly all-male boarding school. As you read this autobiographical selection, notice how Lorene Cary's personal reactions to unfamiliar experiences make connections with the reader. Then try the activities in Linking Writing and Literature on page 44.

BLACK ICE

by Lorene Cary

Fumiko met me on the way to soccer. "Do you play basketball?" she wanted to know.

"Nah." I felt rough in her presence, square-fingered, and loud.

"I like basketball. In Japan, I played a *lot* of basketball. Don't you play at all?"

"A little bit. I don't shoot so well."

"I can teach you! It's easy. I'll teach you." She looked at her watch. "Come on. We have time."

In the gymnasium we heard the commotion below in the locker rooms. Fumiko ran to the wall behind the basket where a few balls lay beside each other. She picked one, dribbled it, and then passed it to me. She ran onto the court, and I passed it back to her. She shot the ball. It headed toward the basket in a low arc and dropped through. She ran hard to retrieve her own rebound. There could have been four girls after her, as hard as she ran. She snatched the ball out of the air and then leapt to make a lay-up. It hit the backboard softly and fell through the hoop. Then she passed me the ball.

I hesitated and passed it back. She thrust it at me. I caught the pass, chest-high. She threw it as perfectly as a diagram, harder than my old gym teacher, and with no effort I could see.

I did not want to play. I wanted to watch. But she seemed intent on teaching me. Her intelligence and force were as obvious as her athleticism. I had seen none of it before, because I'd been so eager to assume her need for me.

"Hold like this," Fumiko said. She stood behind me in order to position not just my fingers but my arms as well. She pushed me with her body. I was confused. Her language had been so delicate that I hadn't expected the shove.

I shot. The ball bounced off the rim.

"Hah!" Fumiko zoomed down the key for the rebound and rocketed another pass to me.

I caught it. My palms tingled. This time she told me to dribble to the basket. She followed me close. Her body was so close and new that I dropped the ball. She laughed.

Out of the corner of my eye I watched her as we walked to soccer practice. "You are really good." I felt ashamed for having thought of her as a geisha girl. I had done to her what I suspected white people did to me. She did not answer me. I did not repeat myself. It would've been too much like amazement; after all, the girl had told me that she could play.

Green fields stretched out before us. Two soccer fields lay end to end. A line of white paint on the grass divided them, and the four goals

John N. Robinson, *Reclining Woman*, 1976

lined up like giant white wickets. Beyond them were clay tennis courts and a gravel track. Football fields hid behind a stand of trees at the end of the track. Big and small boys ran past us toward the far fields. Fumiko broke into a run, too, and I trotted along. By the time we got there, I was out of breath.

We flung ourselves onto the damp grass to lounge in the sun with the other girls.

"Have you people finished your laps already?" The voice behind us was blunt, the pronunciation lippy and controlled. Miss Breiner, the modern-languages teacher, appeared in pastel-colored shorts and knee socks. She was one of the few women at the school who wore makeup. "Four laps. Four laps, please, so we can get started."

I could not help but stare at the field. It was as big around as a Philadelphia city block. I knew people who would get in their cars and *drive* that far. The other girls groaned dramatically and started running. I couldn't do it. I'd die.

"Excuse me, Miss Breiner," I said. This would look like shirking, I knew. Her powder-blue eyes studied a clipboard.

"Yes," she said without looking up.

"My parents wrote to the school this summer to tell them that I have asthma."

"I see," she said looking at me. "I know a couple other girls here who have asthma. Do you take medication? Do you have pills?"

Behind me I heard the thunder of distant cleats. "No." I didn't know there *were* pills for asthma. "But I use an inhaler when I need to."

Miss Breiner was finished regarding me. I could see myself in those blue eyes: a robust black girl talking about asthma and didn't even have pills. "Do what you can," she said. "You may find that the exercise will actually help your asthma."

I fell in. What had started as a pack stretched into a column nearly a quarter lap long. Ahead of me girls talked to each other as they ran. One sprinted to sneak up behind another and give her ponytail a yank. Ponytails flashed in the sun. Striding legs stretched out before me like a movie. My breath came so fast now that I had to concentrate as if to break through some partition stretched across my lungs. It had to be some failing of mine. I was breathing too fast, that was it. I'd slow it down and let the air go deeper. But then I began to wheeze, and the long, lithe girls in front of me were coming up behind me now, passing me. How had I dropped so far behind? I pumped my legs as hard as I could.

"Do not cut corners. Do not cut corners." Miss Breiner's voice caught me out. She'd be watching me now, for sure.

My arms flailed. I'd never run so far in my life. What were those pills? The top of my body swung from side to side, and none of it, the pumping or flailing or desperate prayer, pushed me forward.

When everyone else finished, I slunk into the huffing group. I was gulping at the air. It came into my lungs in teaspoonsful. One girl asked me if I was all right. I nodded. It cost too much air to talk.

Then practice began. We passed and kicked and chased the ball. It changed direction in an instant. It was tyrannical, capricious. At the end of practice we did little sprints. Fumiko won most of them. After practice she grinned at me. Her face was flushed and happy.

"I can't do this every day, Fumiko," I said as we walked to Simpson.

In my room I sat on the bed and sucked at my inhaler. The medicine spread through my chest like warmth blown in through tiny cop-

R. Delaunay, *The Runners*, 1925

per wires. I thought hard about how to handle this soccer business, and decided to get to practice early in order to do laps before Miss Breiner appeared. After two slow ones, I could quit without being suspected—and still have time to get my wind back before practice. . . .

About forty minutes was allotted in the community schedule for bathing and dressing before class at 5:15. At first, eighth-period class seemed cruel and redundant. We carried with us the fatigue of the day but also, much as I hated to admit it, the weary refreshment of exercise. Our teachers, tired from their own classes and sports, seemed less critical and demanding. I felt less competitive. I had made it through another day, and dinner was imminent. Night was coming, and the dark pushed us closer together.

Linking Writing and Literature

Readers Respond to the Model

How does Lorene Cary's writing make personal connections with the reader?

Explore Lorene Cary's autobiographical writing by answering these questions. Then read what other students liked about Cary's writing.

1. Lorene Cary's experiences are told from the first-person point of view. How does that perspective affect the story's purpose and audience?
2. Have you ever realized that your first impression of someone was wrong? Were you ashamed, like Cary? How did your relationship change?
3. Think about a situation when you had to learn something new. How did you feel? How does your reaction compare with Cary's?

What Students Say

❝The selection from *Black Ice* is about a girl who realizes that it is necessary to search beyond first impressions. Because Fumiko was Japanese, the narrator assumed that Fumiko was a geisha girl. Later she realized that Fumiko was intelligent and athletic. The narrator discovered that people not only depend on her, but that she also depends on them.

This selection was easy reading. From the excerpt, it seems to be an enjoyable story in which many people would be able to see themselves. ❞

Marsha Novak

❝I liked the use of a first-person speaker. The passage became much more interesting because the reader was able to get inside the speaker's head and learn her true feelings and emotions. The passage is extremely readable. ❞

Mathew Isaac

UNIT 1 Review

Reflecting on the Unit

Summarize what you have learned in this unit by answering the following questions.

1 How does a life map help you select or develop a topic for personal writing?

2 How can you get constructive criticism from other students?

3 In what ways can a journal help you discover problem areas in your schoolwork or study habits?

4 How does a personal letter express your personality?

5 What are the purposes of a college application essay?

6 How can a journal help you make discoveries about yourself? List the kinds of entries you can make in a journal.

7 What process do you use for writing a college application essay?

8 What did you learn about the effectiveness of first-person narration from the excerpt from Lorene Cary's *Black Ice*?

Adding to Your Portfolio

CHOOSE A SELECTION FOR YOUR PORTFOLIO Look over the personal writing you have done during this unit. Select a completed piece of writing to put into your portfolio. The piece you choose should have some or all of the following:

- a clear sense of purpose
- reliable evidence
- a logical order
- strong details along with your personal feelings, observations, and impressions
- language and tone that anticipates your audience

REFLECT ON YOUR CHOICE Attach a note to the piece you choose, explaining briefly why you chose it and what you learned from writing it. What criteria led you to believe that this was your best piece of writing?

SET GOALS FOR YOUR WRITING How can you improve your writing? What skill will you focus on the next time you write? How can you use activities in this unit to strengthen your writing in other classes or to frame questions for future writing?

Writing Across the Curriculum

MAKE A HISTORY CONNECTION Think of an event that you have studied recently in history that moved you in some way, such as the Black Plague killing thousands in the Middle Ages or the signing of the Declaration of Independence. Write a brief personal response to the event. First tell about the circumstances surrounding the event, and then explain why it moved you.

> "And all the while the dog sat and watched him, a certain yearning wistfulness in its eyes."
>
> —Jack London, "To Build a Fire"

Writing in the Real World

Like other kinds of writing, cartooning involves gathering ideas, producing drafts, and revising for clarity and effectiveness. The following cartoons were created by Barbara Brandon, the first African American woman to have a nationally syndicated comic strip. Her cartoons originally appeared in the *Detroit Free Press*.

Where Brandon's Characters Come From

*Cartoonist
Barbara Brandon*

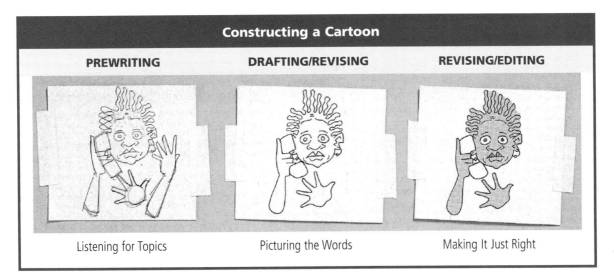

Constructing a Cartoon

PREWRITING	DRAFTING/REVISING	REVISING/EDITING
Listening for Topics	Picturing the Words	Making It Just Right

A Writer's Process

Prewriting
Listening for Topics

Brandon keeps a pad of paper near her bed, and she also carries a notebook around so she can jot down possible topics and pieces of dialogue for her strip.

Brandon gets most of her ideas for dialogue from the things people say, so she has to listen carefully when her friends talk. "I have friends who are open and honest with me, and that's great for my humor," she said. "I egg them on, and what they say ends up in my strip."

The cartoonist also admits to being an incurable eavesdropper. "My ears perk up when I hear people, especially men, talking about relationships."

Occasionally, getting ideas involves more than just listening. Brandon often goes out of her way to join a conversation even if she must talk to complete strangers. By listening, observing, and reflecting, Brandon discovers the many points of view that appear in her comic strip.

Writing in the Real World

Drafting/Revising
Picturing the Words

In many cartoons, words are subordinate to the visual gags. But with Brandon, the words always come first. Before she writes, Brandon thinks carefully about her audience: Will her readers understand the strip? Will they relate to it? As she writes, she tries to focus on one main idea and to create a certain mood—sometimes humorous, sometimes serious or ironic.

"First, I put down an idea and try to come up with dialogue to make that point," she explained. "Then I ask myself which of my characters would say these things. How one character might react is not the same as how another might."

After choosing her characters and writing a rough draft of the dialogue, Brandon begins sketching. "I come up with the [facial] expressions to go with the words," she says. Brandon keeps a file on her recurring characters, including flighty Nicole and solid, dependable Judy, the lovesick Cheryl, and the socially conscious Lekesia.

"If I do a particular facial expression, I might want to use it again," the artist explained. "If I have it on file, I can . . . just alter a few lines."

Revising/Editing
Tightening the Focus

Brandon began with twelve characters but has eliminated three of them—just as a writer might edit out characters in a novel or a play. "I used to create a new character every time I did a strip." she recalls, "but my editors in Detroit said it's better to use the same characters so the reader can get used to them. . . . I have about nine characters now."

Revising/Proofreading
Making It Just Right

Brandon draws four to eight cartoons, then begins revising. "I never have liked anyone to look over my shoulder, so I don't really use people as sounding boards," she said. But Brandon does ask her roommate to check for spelling errors before she sends her strips to the syndication company.

Publishing/Presenting
Listening to Criticism

Before her work was accepted for national syndication, Brandon spent one year on a trial contract. She would send as many as eight strips in pencil each month to the syndication company. "They would tell me which ones they liked and which ones they didn't," she said. "If I thought their criticism was something I could learn from, I'd listen. If I thought they were wrong, I'd try to make my point more clearly. By the time I put ink on the cartoon, it had changed."

Examining Writing in the Real World

Analyzing the Media Connection

Deconstruct or analyze Brandon's cartoons on page 48 by discussing the following questions.

1. What topic do the two cartoons reproduced on page 48 share?
2. What word would you use to describe the tone of the dialogue in the cartoons?
3. In your opinion, could the words in the cartoons stand alone, without the pictures? Why or why not?
4. What point do you think Brandon is making about relationships in the two cartoons?
5. What techniques does Brandon use to make the dialogue in these cartoons realistic?

Analyzing a Writer's Process

1. Many of the strategies Brandon uses in creating a cartoon strip are also used by other kinds of writers. What are some of these strategies?
2. How does Brandon gather ideas for her comic strips? Why is being a good listener important to any writer?
3. What questions does Brandon ask about her audience before she begins writing?
4. What role does the "real world" play in Brandon's cartoons?
5. How does Brandon respond to criticism from the cartoon syndication company? What use does she make of it?

Use commas to make your writing clearer.

Use commas with words used in direct address, tag questions, parenthetical expressions, and interrupting words such as *yes, on the other hand,* or *by the way.*

Write the sentences below, placing commas where they belong.

1. I asked for rice pudding didn't I?
2. Gene told me by the way where you got your haircut.
3. Yes I should lock the back screen door shouldn't I?
4. Rachel those children should have been in bed an hour ago!
5. The auction if you're really interested is Friday evening Marcus.

See Lesson 21.6, page 722.

LESSON 2.1

Writing: A Five-Stage Process

The writing process involves five stages—prewriting, drafting, revising, editing/proofreading, and publishing/presenting. In an interview on National Public Radio, John McPhee describes how the process of writing unfolds for him.

TIME

For more about the writing process, see **TIME Facing the Blank Page,** pp. 111–121.

Literature Model

You do not write well right away, and if you're going to get anything done at all you have to blurt out something. And it's going to be bad. And to sit there and do something that's bad all day long is unpleasant—but when you've done this enough, you have the so-called rough draft. And at that point, when I do have a draft—something's on paper, and it's really miserable . . . I can work on it and make it better, and I relax a little, and I get a little more confident when I'm in that second, third phase, or however many times it takes.

Author John McPhee, interviewed by Terry Gross at WHYY-FM for National Public Radio's "Fresh Air"

Two-way traffic ahead

Fog Area

Understand the Process

When you write, your own mind, methods, temperament, and interests will make your writing unique. Like all writers, however, you will move through a series of stages to create a finished product. Understanding the writing process, from prewriting through publishing/presenting, will help you know how to proceed, whether that means taking two steps forward or one step back.

The diagram below shows that you cannot find a shortcut from start to finish, but you can follow many different paths. You may choose one that leads to a dead end. You may make a discovery that opens up new directions. At any point, you may decide to return to the prewriting stage. Even as they are revising or editing, successful writers often return to earlier stages to clarify or expand their thinking.

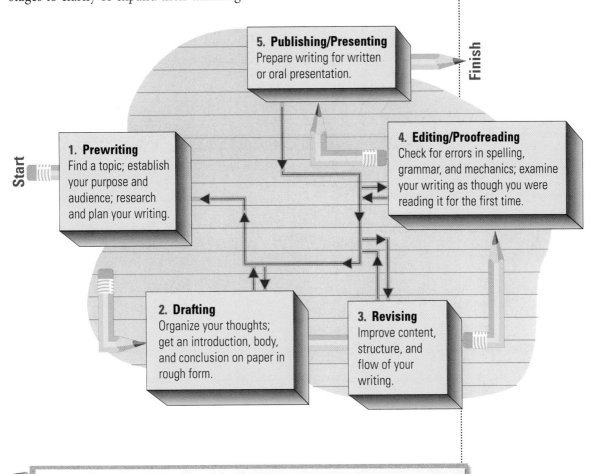

Start

Finish

5. Publishing/Presenting
Prepare writing for written or oral presentation.

1. Prewriting
Find a topic; establish your purpose and audience; research and plan your writing.

4. Editing/Proofreading
Check for errors in spelling, grammar, and mechanics; examine your writing as though you were reading it for the first time.

2. Drafting
Organize your thoughts; get an introduction, body, and conclusion on paper in rough form.

3. Revising
Improve content, structure, and flow of your writing.

Journal Writing

You have to write an essay for class. How will you go about it? Recall how you have worked on writing assignments in the past. Write a description of the stages you will go through. Which stage do you think that you will enjoy the most?

Write It Your Way

There are as many ways to write as there are books in a library. Some writers like quiet; some like noise. One writes a dozen drafts; another writes two. Each applies a unique mix of discipline and creativity to writing. As you write, you'll discover the way that works best for you.

Finding out what others say about their writing can also help you understand your own. Look at what the following writers said about how they write, and compare their writing processes with your own. Pay special attention to strategies that you might like to use. Think about what works best for you, and then *try* it.

How Professionals Write

VLADIMIR NABOKOV
I have rewritten—often several times—every word I have ever published. My pencils outlast their erasers.

KATHERINE ANNE PORTER
If I didn't know the ending of a story, I wouldn't begin. I always write my last line, my last paragraphs, my last page first.

ANTHONY BURGESS
I don't write drafts. I do page one many, many times and move on to page two. I pile up sheet after sheet, each in its final state, and at length I have a novel that doesn't—in my view—need any revision. . . . Revising is done with each page, not with each chapter or the whole book.

How Students Write

NINA E. MOLUMBY *Evanston, Illinois*
I usually write a first draft in a spiral notebook and make changes on paper. Later I move to my computer. I try to find a quiet room where I can spread out. The time of day doesn't matter as long as I have the inspiration to compose on paper.

MICHELLE EDDY *Pueblo, Colorado*
I write from my heart. I write what I feel and then go back and revise.

NEELESH CHOPDEKAR *Edison, New Jersey*
Once a good introduction is complete, the rest just flows naturally.

MELISSA FROHREICH *Bay Shore, New York*
I write about 1,000 rough drafts about completely different things; then, at about three in the morning, inspiration hits me.

ERIK NAGLER *Aurora, Colorado*
I wait until eleven o'clock the night before it is due before I start writing. Panic usually takes over for inspiration.

Write About Yourself as a Writer

Think over your writing experiences. Then, in your journal, write a brief piece about who you are as a writer.

PURPOSE To analyze your own writing process
AUDIENCE Yourself
LENGTH 1–2 paragraphs

WRITING RUBRICS To evaluate yourself as a writer, you should

- reflect on your approach to writing
- determine in what setting you prefer to write
- evaluate your writing habits

Cross-Curricular Activity

ART Write a paragraph about the drawing below. What ideas about writing does the work suggest? How does the artist use color? What might the position of the images mean?

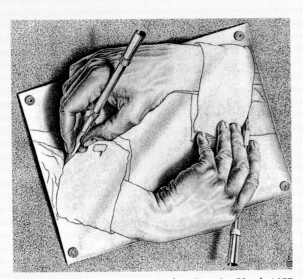

M.C. Escher, *Drawing Hands,* 1977

Grammar Link

Use *good, well, bad,* and *badly* correctly.

Good and *bad* are adjectives. They precede nouns and follow linking verbs.

Use *well* as an adjective only to mean "in good health." Otherwise, *well* and *badly* are adverbs and modify action verbs.

Complete each sentence with the correct word in parentheses.

1. Those turkey burgers tasted particularly (bad, badly).
2. I don't think Caroline seasoned them very (good, well).
3. It's true that no other dish was prepared (bad, badly).
4. But my stomach is churning, and I don't feel (good, well) at all.

See Lesson 18.5, page 657

Listening and Speaking

EVALUATING Select a recent piece of writing from your portfolio. Draw a graphic like the one on page 53 to show the writing process you followed to create it. Use arrows to indicate the steps you took and perhaps retook, and note what problems you solved at each stage. Compare your graphic with that of a classmate and discuss your writing processes.

LESSON 2.2

Prewriting: Finding Ideas

In the model below, Eliza Miller used freewriting to look for writing ideas. Freewriting and creative tree charts are two ways to begin finding your unique perspective on a writing topic.

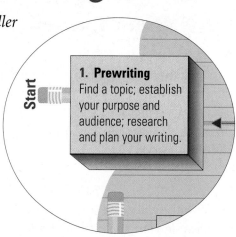

Start

1. Prewriting Find a topic; establish your purpose and audience; research and plan your writing.

Student Model

With what kind of observations does the writer begin her freewriting? Why?

What associations does the writer make to get from the subject of her alarm clock to Newton and Einstein?

My alarm clock is small and black. It beeps eight times in a row, tiny shrill beeps, then pauses for a second or two and does it again. I put it across the room on my bookcase so I have to get out of bed to shut it off. Even so, I still oversleep. Somehow my sleep-mind rationalizes getting back in bed every single morning, even though I know I will fall back asleep: It's okay, I'll just lie here for ten minutes and not fall asleep. . . . It's too cold to go to school. . . . I have to finish my dream. . . . It's probably Saturday anyway. It's strange the things your mind will think up when it's still asleep. The other day I woke up thinking about math; I don't know why. It seemed to me that I had invented a whole new theory of mathematics. I suddenly understood everything. I was like Einstein or Newton or Pythagoras or any of those amazing mathematicians, and my theory would change everything and make it possible for people to do something impossible, like fly or read minds. I finally woke up all the way and realized I was wrong. There is nothing so disappointing as waking up after a wonderful dream and finding yourself back in your cold room and reality, and it's 7:15 and you have only ten minutes before you have to be out the door.

Eliza Miller, Concord Academy, Concord, Massachusetts

Find New Ideas

Freewriting can help you find ideas and write about them more fluently. Writing starters, such as those on the right, can get you going. Try creating your own list of starters.

Writing topics can also come from observing the world. Study the way a person walks against the wind or fights with an umbrella. Think about why you didn't like a TV show. Then compose a list of writing ideas from your observations. When you settle on a topic, explore it. Make a tree chart to give you different ways to think about your topic.

Writing Starters

My inner voice tells me . . .

I wouldn't hesitate to . . .

I know a kid who is so . . .

If people could be more . . .

If I were an insect . . .

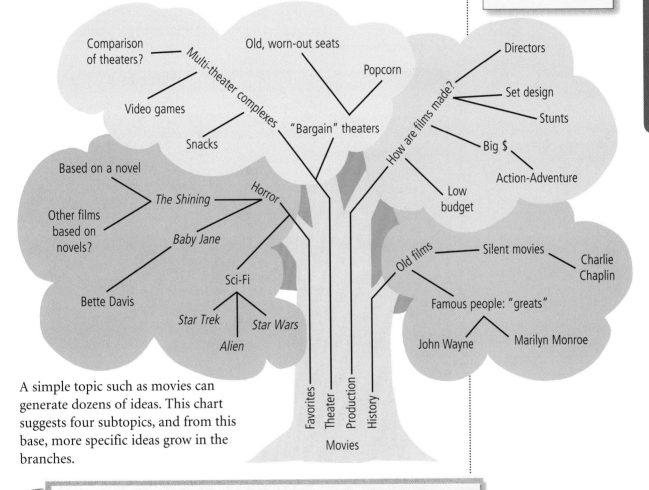

A simple topic such as movies can generate dozens of ideas. This chart suggests four subtopics, and from this base, more specific ideas grow in the branches.

Journal Writing

In your journal, try freewriting about an unusual idea. Start on your own, or fill in the blanks of this question: "What if _____ were _____?" Let your imagination run wild.

Turn Ordinary Life into Great Writing

Writing topics don't have to be unusual. Everyday occurrences in the lives of average people have inspired great literature. Your vision and experience can take familiar scenes or events and transform them into unique impressions. Below is one such personal vision.

Giovanni starts with ordinary events and objects. These lead to memories that are both disturbing and poignant. As you think about the feelings this poem evokes in you, remember that when you write, the way you describe events and objects can transform the most familiar subject into your personal vision.

Look over the details of the topic that you explored through freewriting and drawing tree charts. Choose details that will lead your readers to experience your unique perspective.

Literature Model

> The poet begins by describing items and events of everyday life.

I always like summer
best
you can eat fresh corn
from daddy's garden
and okra
and greens
and cabbage
and lots of
barbecue
and buttermilk
and homemade ice-cream
at the church picnic
and listen to
gospel music
outside
at the church
homecoming
and go to the mountains with
your grandmother
and go barefooted
and be warm
all the time
not only when you go to bed
and sleep

> What does this poem tell you about the other seasons of the year in the speaker's life?

Nikki Giovanni, "Knoxville, Tennessee"

Determine a Topic

Take some time to select a topic that will lead to a five- or six-paragraph essay. You will be working with this topic through a series of lessons while you move through the stages of the writing process, so you will need to be sure that the topic interests you. Create some prewriting notes.

PURPOSE To select a writing topic
AUDIENCE Yourself
LENGTH 1/2–1 page

WRITING RUBRICS To select a writing topic, you should

- use freewriting, observation, and other techniques to generate topic ideas
- select an essay topic and explore it through a tree diagram
- record details that could give your topic a unique slant

Using Computers

If you are a fast typist, a computer may help you freewrite. By typing, you can keep up with your thoughts faster than if you were writing by hand. Don't stop to check your spelling, and don't worry about margins. Just keep thinking and typing. When you are finished, you may want to save and work on some sections. Copy them into a new file, and start your tree chart or first draft here. Be sure to save your file so you can use it later.

Grammar Link

Form possessive pronouns correctly.

Do not use apostrophes with possessive pronouns: *his, hers, yours, theirs, ours, its.* Do not confuse the possessive pronouns *its* with the contraction *it's:*

It's [it is] too cold to go to school.

Rewrite the sentences below, using apostrophes correctly.

1. Its getting late; their bus will probably arrive before our's.
2. The T-shirt on the dresser was her's before it was mine.
3. Jay, is that my CD or your's?
4. Gramps sat down next to his cat and stroked it's neck.
5. Our computer isn't heavy; that bulky 1928 Royal typewriter is her's.

See Lesson 17.1, pages 623–625

Listening and Speaking

COOPERATIVE LEARNING In a small group, brainstorm to create a list of broad topic areas that might serve as starting points for a one-page essay. Go around the group several times, with each person offering favorite experiences in sports, music, art, and so on. Don't worry now about focusing the topic. Concentrate on finding subject matter that interests you.

Prewriting: Questioning to Explore a Topic

Writing ideas often begin as questions in the writer's mind. But the writer must ask the right questions.

Literature Model

Bud: You know, strange as it may seem, they give baseball players peculiar names nowadays. On the St. Louis team Who's on first, What's on second, I Don't Know is on third.

Lou: That's what I want to find out. I want you to tell me the names of the fellows on the St. Louis team.

Bud: I'm telling you. Who's on first, What's on second, I Don't Know is on third.

Lou: You know the fellows' names?

Bud: Yes.

Lou: Well, then, who's playin' first?

Bud: Yes.

Lou: I mean the fellow's name on first base.

Bud: Who.

Lou: The fellow's name on first base for St. Louis.

Bud: Who.

Lou: The guy on first base.

Bud: Who is on first base.

Lou: Well, what are you askin' me for?

Bud: I'm not asking you. I'm telling you. Who is on first. . . .

Lou: [Trying to be calm.] Have you got a first baseman on first?

Bud: Certainly.

Lou: Well, all I'm tryin' to find out is what's the guy's name on first base.

Bud: Oh, no, no. What is on second base. . . .

> Bud Abbott and Lou Costello, "Who's on First?"

Ask Questions

Different questions serve different purposes, and knowing what kind of question to ask can be as important as knowing how to ask it clearly. Personal questions ask about your responses to a topic. They help you explore your experiences and tastes. Creative questions ask you to compare your subject to something that seems different from it, or to imagine observing your subject as someone else might. Such questions can expand your perspective on a subject. Analytical questions ask about structure and function: How is this topic constructed? What is its purpose? Analytical questions help you evaluate and draw conclusions. Informational questions ask for facts, statistics, or details.

The examples below show how questions can help you take a subject that intrigues you and turn it into a topic that you can write about.

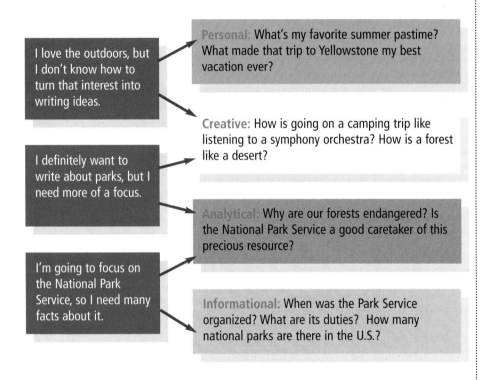

I love the outdoors, but I don't know how to turn that interest into writing ideas.

Personal: What's my favorite summer pastime? What made that trip to Yellowstone my best vacation ever?

Creative: How is going on a camping trip like listening to a symphony orchestra? How is a forest like a desert?

I definitely want to write about parks, but I need more of a focus.

Analytical: Why are our forests endangered? Is the National Park Service a good caretaker of this precious resource?

I'm going to focus on the National Park Service, so I need many facts about it.

Informational: When was the Park Service organized? What are its duties? How many national parks are there in the U.S.?

Journal Writing

Choose a simple object or idea that you know something about—a sneaker, your locker, your favorite car, swim meets—and write at least ten good questions that could help you explore it as a writing topic. Include questions that are personal, creative, analytical, and informational.

Ask More Questions As You Write

Just as you use questions to get started, you can also question your writing as it develops. For example, if you were to write, "The woman rose from the table and walked to the window," you might ask yourself: "What does the table look like? What does the woman see out of the window? Does she walk quickly or slowly?" With the right questions, you can create infinite depth and detail.

The excerpt below by Estela Trambley is from a short story about an old Mexican peasant woman, Lela. As you read, keep in mind that to develop this scene, the writer had to ask many questions: "What did Lela see next? How does it feel to pick up sand? To sleep with a fever?"

Literature Model

What happens to someone in free fall? The writer envisioned Lela's lungs filling with air.

What questions might the writer have asked herself in order to describe the sand in this part of the story?

How would Lela react to this crisis? The writer had to ask questions like this to develop the details in this passage.

She lost her footing and fell down, down over a crevice between two huge boulders. As she fell, her lungs filled with air. Her body hit soft sand, but the edge of her foot felt the sharpness of a stone. She lay there stunned for a few minutes until she felt a sharp pain at the side of her foot. Somewhat dizzy, she sat up and noticed that the side of her foot was bleeding profusely. . . . She looked up at the boulders that silently rebuked her helplessness; then she began to cry softly. She had to stanch the blood. She wiped away her tears with the side of her sleeve and tore off a piece of skirt to use as a bandage. As she looked down at the wound again, she noticed that the sand where she had fallen was extremely crystalline and loose. It shone against a rising moon. She scooped up a handful and looked at it with fascination. "The sand of the gods," she whispered to herself. She took some sand and rubbed it on the wound before she applied the bandage. By now, she felt a burning fever. She wrapped the strip of skirt around the wound now covered with the fine, shining sand. Then she slept. But it was a fitful sleep, for her body burned with fever. Half awake and half in a dream, she saw the sands take the shapes of happy, little gods. Then, at other times, the pain told her she was going to die. After a long time, her exhausted body slept until the dawn passed over her head.

Estela Portillo Trambley, "The Burning"

Can you imagine what this passage would be like if the writer had settled for a limited description of a woman falling and injuring herself?

Explore Your Topic

As you focus on your topic, ask questions to discover how you will approach it. In your prewriting notes, write two or three questions for each category below.

PURPOSE To ask questions and explore your topic
AUDIENCE Yourself
LENGTH 1 page

WRITING RUBRICS To explore your topic, you should

- write personal questions to explore your own responses to the topic
- write creative questions to make comparisons or see the topic from other viewpoints
- write analytical questions to explore your purpose and draw conclusions
- write informational questions to see what facts or statistics you need

Viewing and Representing

EXAMINING MEDIA With a partner, examine several forms of mass media, such as print and TV advertisements, news broadcasts, and newspaper articles and editorials. What kinds of questions does each type of media seem best at answering? Are the questions personal, creative, analytical, or informational? How effective is the media itself in involving viewers or readers in the issues it presents? Write a report based on your research and share it with the class.

Cross-Curricular Activity

ART In a group of four students, brainstorm about the content, colors, subjects, and setting of a painting in this book. Assign one type of question to each person: personal, creative, analytical, and informational. As a group, use these questions to write a three- or four-paragraph description or story about the painting.

Grammar Link

Use the principal parts of verbs correctly.

The base form or past form of a verb *does not* need to be preceded by an auxiliary verb if it is the predicate of the sentence. A participle, either past or present, *does* need to be preceded by an auxiliary verb if it is to function as the predicate of the sentence. Be particularly careful with forms of irregular verbs.

She **lost** her footing and **fell** down . . .

In the sentences below, use the principal parts of the verbs correctly.

1. The people at McGuire's Cafe (has + *see*) all of Mel Gibson's movies.
2. Classes in sketching and acrylics (past tense of *begin*) at 9:30 A.M.
3. We (were + *scrub*) apples, oranges, and kiwi before cutting them into bite-sized pieces.
4. I (had + *run*) to catch the first bus for three days in a row.

See Lessons 15.1 and 15.2, pages 575–578.

The Writing Process

Prewriting: Audience and Purpose

*P*art of your job as a writer is to know your audience and your reason for writing. In the cartoon below, the writer, Zeek, shapes his words to tantalize his fellow canines. How would the writing change if the mail carrier were composing the story to amuse his fellow workers?

THE FAR SIDE   By GARY LARSON

Creative dog writing

Determine Your Audience and Purpose

Before you begin any writing task, you must know who your audience is. Are you writing for your classmates, your best friend in another city, the members of your local school board, your parents? Each audience may require a slightly different way of presenting a topic.

You must also pin down your purpose for writing. You will usually select one central purpose: to describe, to explain, to persuade, or to narrate. Knowing this purpose helps you reach out specifically to your audience. If, for example, you want to persuade your classmates to elect Carla to the student council, make every sentence grab a vote.

Throughout the writing process, take care to use ideas and language that are appropriate for your audience and your purpose. If you write a speech for your history class, you might include lively anecdotes and use informal language. But if you're presenting it to the local historical society, you might use more formal language and make absolutely certain that you have all the facts straight.

Create a chart like this one to help you explore different audiences and purposes. Notice how your purposes might vary if you were writing for the first audience as opposed to the second one.

If your audience were parents and your purpose to convince them of the value of video games, you might write a piece like the following example.

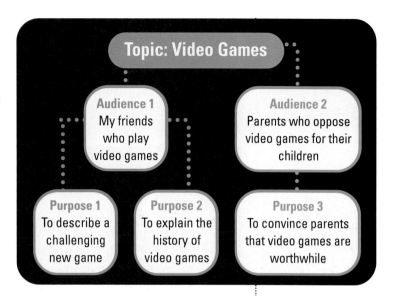

Topic: Video Games

Audience 1
My friends who play video games

Audience 2
Parents who oppose video games for their children

Purpose 1
To describe a challenging new game

Purpose 2
To explain the history of video games

Purpose 3
To convince parents that video games are worthwhile

Model

Parents, before despairing that your son or daughter plays video games, consider these arguments on behalf of the sport.

Video games have redeeming qualities that you may have overlooked. They are not only fun, but they also require quick thinking, good reflexes, and keen hand-eye coordination. With practice, virtually anyone can excel at video games. They thus offer an opportunity for friendly, healthy competition. Playing these games can strengthen self-esteem and confidence. Most important, video games force the player to concentrate and to perform well under pressure.

Take some time out to visit a video arcade and to savor the experience of video games. Perhaps you'll gain a new skill; you can certainly count on having a great time.

Find examples of how the writer tailored the language to suit his audience.

Journal Writing

Choose a topic you could write about, such as a favorite hobby or pastime. In your journal, list possible audiences and possible purposes for the topic you've chosen. A chart like the one above may help you.

Know Your Purpose

Below, different authors write about the same topic, breakfast cereals. The purpose of the first selection is to teach; therefore, the writers address their audience as instructors would. The purpose of the second selection is to entertain a family audience. Notice the difference in the tone of these two passages.

From reading the first sentence, who do you think is the writers' intended audience and what is the writers' purpose?

What is the tone of this paragraph? How would you describe the choice of words?

What is Erma Bombeck's purpose in writing this piece? What clues can you find in the first sentence to support this purpose?

Literature Model

Cooked cereals are excellent, because the B vitamins stay right there in the water, and the lysine is not destroyed. Besides, could anything be more satisfying than hot, whole-grain porridge? With sliced bananas, raisins or dates, dried apricots or nuts, hot cereal can be mouthwatering to even the pickiest little one. I always thought it had to be sweetened, but try it with Better-Butter. Milk is traditional, but buttermilk and cottage cheese both go well with hot cereal.

Laurel Robertson, Carol Flinders, and Bronwen Godfrey,
Laurel's Kitchen: A Handbook for Vegetarian Cookery and Nutrition

---

I told the kids I had had it and there would be no more new cereal brought into the house until we cleaned up what we already had. . . . Eventually we polished off every box, only to be confronted with the most important decision we had ever made as a family: the selection of a new box of cereal.

I personally favored Bran Brittles because they made you regular and offered an African violet as a premium.

One child wanted Chock Full of Soggies because they turned your teeth purple.

Another wanted Jungle Jollies because they had no nutritional value whatsoever.

We must have spent twenty minutes in the cereal aisle before we decided on Mangled Wheat Bits because "when eaten as an after-school snack, will give you X-ray vision."

Erma Bombeck, *Aunt Erma's Cope Book*

Identify Audience and Purpose

Shape your approach to your topic by determining whom you are writing for and what your purpose is.

PURPOSE To focus your topic by determining your audience and purpose
AUDIENCE Yourself
LENGTH 1 page

WRITING RUBRICS To focus your topic by identifying your audience and purpose, you should

- create a chart to explore various audiences and purposes
- determine which approach to your topic would most appeal to the audience you've chosen
- note the tone and kind of language you will use

Pablo Picasso, *Carafe, Jug and Fruit Bowl*, Summer 1909

Use commas to separate items in a series.

In the sentences below, add commas where they are needed in a series.

1. "I need you three," Mrs. Gabriel said, pointing to Randy Grace and Jose.
2. Don't handle insecticide poison-ivy killer or corrosive chemicals without your gloves.
3. The choice was bleak: chicken potpie macaroni and cheese or pork.
4. Well, Phyllis, you have done well at following directions managing bank deposits encoding data and greeting customers.

See Lesson 21.6, pages 722–730.

Cross-Curricular Activity

ART Write two explanations of the meaning of the painting on this page—one for elementary school children and the other for adults. Write 200–250 words for each, tailoring your remarks and vocabulary to fit your audience.

Listening and Speaking

SPELLING Keep a list of the words that you frequently misspell. Practice spelling these words with a partner. To help with memorizing the spelling of a troublesome word, say the word first. Then spell it, syllable by syllable. Visualize the word as you spell it.

Prewriting: Observing

A good writer, like an impressionist painter, selects and combines a multitude of carefully observed details to convey a single vivid impression.

Claude Monet,
Bridge at Argenteuil,
1874

Observe Details

Certain observation techniques that painters use can also be employed effectively by writers. One is to take the time to note small details, instead of settling for a passing glance. Another is to study a subject from many views, such as looking at an object from the front, back, sides, and top.

Sometimes when you write, you will find one of these techniques appropriate to your purpose. In the following excerpt, notice the way Alice Munro uses details to create an overall impression not unlike a verbal painting.

Literature Model

Flo at this time must have been in her early thirties. A young woman. She wore exactly the same clothes that a woman of fifty, or sixty, or seventy, might wear: print housedresses loose at the neck and sleeves as well as the waist; bib aprons, also of print, which she took off when she came from the kitchen into the store. This was a common costume at the time, for a poor though not absolutely poverty-stricken woman; it was also, in a way, a scornful deliberate choice. Flo scorned slacks, she scorned the outfits of people trying to be in style, she scorned lipstick and permanents. She wore her own black hair cut straight across, just long enough to push behind her ears. . . .

Alice Munro, "Royal Beatings"

Is Flo a conformist or a nonconformist? What details in the text support your answer?

The writer observes not only what Flo wears, but what she doesn't wear, which is just as significant.

When you study a person or scene, try to develop your powers of observation. Use your sense of sight, as Munro does; use your other senses as well. Below are some basic observations of the sensory details observed during a traffic jam.

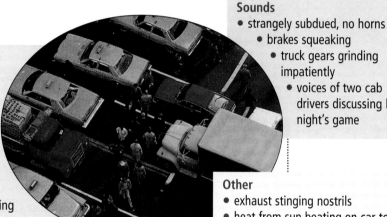

Sounds
- strangely subdued, no horns
- brakes squeaking
- truck gears grinding impatiently
- voices of two cab drivers discussing last night's game

Sights, colors
- cobalt blue hatchback, driver on a car phone
- hot red pickup piled precariously with granite blocks
- huge turquoise truck in middle of intersection
- bright clear blue sky
- pedestrians heedlessly weaving through cars to cross street

Other
- exhaust stinging nostrils
- heat from sun beating on car tops
- aroma from nearby bread factory

Journal Writing

In your journal, write as many sensory details as possible of a scene that you've observed. Create a list of those observations that support one clear idea.

Choose the Best Details

The longer and more carefully you look at something, the more you're bound to see. Go beyond simple sensory details to detect more about a person or a situation. Suppose you spent a long time observing and analyzing the traffic jam described on the previous page. The details might lead you to make the following connections.

Associations

- Where we used to live, drivers were rude.
- What if you were about to have a baby and had to get to the hospital?
- Like that 2-hour jam coming back from Sox game. Dad says driving through Lincoln Tunnel is like smoking a pack of cigarettes—wonder how healthy the air is out here?

Other Perspectives

- Wish I could hop from car top to car top.
- From sky, looks like a checkerboard of cars.
- Should have taken the bypass.

Figurative Language

- Woman's drooping hair looks like a wilted salad.
- Like a stadium crowd trying to move through a turnstile.

Emotions, Impressions

- Sense of camaraderie, good-natured resignation.
- Driver of hatchback looks cool, oblivious to it all.
- I hate being stuck behind a truck; can't see what's causing the jam.
- Bread smell makes me even more impatient to get home and eat.
- Irony: cars speed us up; traffic slows us down.

If you've done your job as an observer, you may have pages and pages of notes. Before you start writing, however, there's more to do. Take time to read your notes. Digest them and continue thinking about them. Jot down other memories, emotions, or thoughts that come to mind. When you know your material well, you may decide that some details are more important than others. Try putting asterisks next to observations that seem particularly useful, striking, or unusual.

You might also go back to your subject on another day or at another hour to see how the atmosphere can change. Think of details as raw material that you can use to paint a sharp and vivid word picture for your reader.

The Writing Process

Select Appropriate Details

Begin planning ways to bring your topic to life with well-chosen, specific details. Keep your purpose and audience in mind as you select appropriate details.

PURPOSE To select appropriate details to develop your topic

AUDIENCE Yourself

LENGTH 1 page

WRITING RUBRICS To develop your topic, you should

- record details that appeal to the senses
- record details based on impressions, associations, and other perspectives
- mark those details that seem particularly useful or effective

Listening and Speaking

COOPERATIVE LEARNING With four other students, plan and write an essay describing the lunchtime scene in your cafeteria. Assign each

Using Computers

Arranging the details you've gathered in a table will help you plan how to present the ones you select in your writing. Create a table following the guidance of your word processing program.

member of your group one of the senses. During one lunch period, go to the cafeteria and take notes on your assigned sense. Meet again and read your notes out loud. Ask each other a variety of questions to help develop your notes with details. If necessary, go back to the cafeteria for more observation. Now, each member will write a one-page description of the cafeteria from the perspective of his or her assigned sense. Combine the best parts of each description in a group essay.

Choose carefully between words that sound alike.

Choosing the right word often requires a knowledge of words that sound similar but have different meanings, such as *lose/loose* or *then/than*.

> She wore exactly the same clothes that a woman of fifty, or sixty, or seventy, might wear: print housedresses *loose* at the neck . . .

Determine the correct choice in each.

1. Talking about the (passed/past) brought tears to her eyes.
2. Did you (lose/loose) your wallet?
3. Their house was not (effected/affected) by the storm.
4. Do you know (weather/whether) they plan to be there?
5. She was proud to (accept/except) the award.
6. (Accept/Except) for Jane, the group had a good time in-line skating.

See Unit 19, pages 673–687.

Drafting: Achieving Unity

For a piece of writing to achieve unity, each sentence must support the main idea of each paragraph, and each paragraph must support the main idea of the essay. In the model below, each sentence supports the idea that plastic is an "uncontrolled killer."

Student Model

There is an uncontrolled killer in the oceans of the world. Each year it destroys thousands of innocent and unknowing mammals. In fact it can annihilate any marine animal that comes in contact with it. The name given to this murderer is *plastic*. It is a manmade substance which has been carelessly thrown into the oceans for many years. Each year ships haphazardly discard fourteen billion pounds of waste into the waters of the world. The National Academy of Sciences estimates this rate to be more than 1.5 million pounds of refuse each hour of the day. Thankfully the paper is able to decay and the glass and metal usually sink, but plastic does not decay or sink. By accumulating and floating on the water, plastic turns into a killer.

Heather Ann Sweeney,
William V. Fisher Catholic High School, Lancaster, Ohio

What is the main point of this paragraph? Why do you think the student waits until the end of the paragraph to express it?

Find a Focus

The main idea, or focus, of your paragraph or essay determines which details, facts, and examples you include in that piece of writing. You should be able to express your main idea in a topic sentence when you write a paragraph, or in a thesis statement when you write an essay.

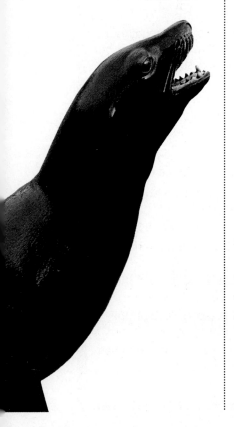

The Writing Process

If you are having trouble expressing your main idea, one strategy is to look at your prewriting notes and allow the idea to emerge from the specific details. Notice the details Heather might have come up with in preparing to write about the problems of plastics in our environment. In drafting possible thesis statements, she would have thought about what these details suggested and what would interest her readers.

Plastics			
SENSORY AND CONCRETE DETAILS	**REASONS**	**FACTS OR STATISTICS**	**EXAMPLES OR INCIDENTS**
• dirty plastic bottles washed ashore on a clean beach • plastic cup left in a beautiful park • cries of baby porpoise struggling to break free of plastic containers	• Plastic is more of a hazard than paper because plastic does not readily decay. • Mammals are more likely to encounter plastic than metal because plastic floats.	• Plastic takes hundreds of years to decay. • Americans throw out billions of tons of plastic every year. • Ships discard 14 billion pounds of waste annually.	• landfill overflowing with plastic • a dolphin head trapped in a round piece of plastic, dies of starvation • plastic rings from soda cans strangle seagulls

THESIS STATEMENTS

1. **The use of plastics in industry is a modern phenomenon.**

2. **Irresponsible disposal of plastic destroys natural beauty.**

3. **Discarded plastic kills sea mammals.**

After examining these details, Heather would have rejected the first thesis because it did not fit her data. The second thesis could be supported by the data, but the general reader would already know a great deal about the topic. Moreover, since Heather's intention was to strongly affect her readers' feelings, the third thesis was a better choice. Much of the data supported this thesis, the subject was less widely known, and the details about sea mammals would have a great emotional impact.

Once you've pinned down a thesis statement, some of your details will become irrelevant, as in the example above. Other data may be missing, so you will have to return to prewriting and do more research on your topic.

Journal Writing

Make a diagram like the one above for a topic such as a compelling school or community issue. List at least three possible controlling ideas, and circle the one that seems best suited to the information.

Let Go of Irrelevant Details

One of the most difficult aspects of writing is deciding what to leave out. If you include information that does not support your main idea, your essay will be less effective. The following writer returned from vacation eager to write about the startling moment of his encounter with a moose. As he read his notes, he crossed out items that didn't support his main idea and jotted down questions about others.

Rowboats on Lake Azisgahos
Will the image of the rowboats set up the encounter well?
~~A moose can weigh up to 1800 lbs.~~
Sunrise on the lake *Will it help my story to start by establishing time of day?*
Thick brown fur, matted, coarse
Antlers that stretched nearly six feet across
Brown fuzz on the antlers
~~Even in August, cold nights~~
Until now Bullwinkle was my only idea of a moose
Funny, but will this distract the reader from the mood?
Big brown eyes *Too sweet—huge brown eyes?*
~~Also saw two deer the day before~~

Such choices can be painful. The Bullwinkle comment was one of the writer's favorites, but he had to admit that it didn't fit in. As he continued to work, other ideas began to surface. He continued the process of deleting and adding details until the writing felt right.

Model

It was just after sunrise, and the mist was rising on the lake. Several early-risers in rowboats were gently bobbing on the quiet lake, fishing for their breakfasts. Suddenly, I heard hoof-beats like muffled thunder in the meadow. The moose's massive frame burst from the forest, and he stopped, as surprised to see me as I was to see him. His thick brown fur was matted and coarse. His antlers stretched six feet across, like a giant crown lit by the glow of the early sun. I was close enough to see that they were covered in soft fuzz. His huge brown eyes darted right and left, looking for escape. I felt afraid, but also—strangely—glad; I was standing face to face with the grandeur of nature. Steam blew from the moose's nostrils. He gave a great bellow and turned suddenly, heading back into the forest.

Begin Your Draft

Begin to tentatively put your writing together by making sure all the parts will connect to make a unified whole.

PURPOSE To begin building your essay around a thesis statement

AUDIENCE Yourself

LENGTH 1 page

WRITING RUBRICS To begin writing a first draft, you should

- organize and examine your prewriting notes
- cast your main idea into a thesis statement that reflects your notes
- eliminate irrelevant details and add new ones as needed

Listening and Speaking

THESIS STATEMENT Pair up with another student and share your thesis statements. Evaluate whether each thesis statement is focused. Will it appeal to the audience that the writer wants to reach? Discuss which prewriting notes support the thesis and what additional information is needed.

Using Computers

Using a word processor, you can store deleted text as you draft. This can help you if you want to restore that text later or if you want to use it for another assignment. Create a new document called Leftovers, Extras, or Trims. Whenever you delete a block of text or list of details, copy it into this document. Make sure to save the document immediately.

Grammar Link

Make pronouns agree with their antecedents.

Be sure that a pronoun agrees with its antecedent in person, number, and gender.

The name given to this murderer is **plastic**. *It is a manmade substance. . . .*

Compare pronouns and antecedents in the following sentences. Replace pronouns that do not agree with the terms they refer to.

1. The salesman parked its car at the base of the mountain.
2. You should look at that magazine for their story on teenage actors.
3. The filmmaker Jean Renoir noted that the only tragedy is that each man has their reasons.
4. Serena and Jared like playing tennis because it gives you good exercise.
5. Both students left his homework in the library.
6. Each of the girls was wearing their soccer uniform.
7. I don't like roller coasters because they give you a stomach ache.
8. Any boy chewing gum will lose their place in line.
9. The bird lost his balance and plummeted out of its nest.
10. All students should bring their music sheets to chorus on Wednesday.

See Lesson 17.6, pages 637–641.

Drafting: Organizing an Essay

Like the parts of a collage that are assembled to express one central idea, the supporting details, reasons, facts, and examples of an essay need to be organized to make a coherent piece with a beginning, a middle, and an end.

Choose the Right Organization

When it is time to write your essay, you may find that you do not know how to organize the array of details, reasons, facts, and examples you have collected. Here are five possible organizing techniques you can use to pull together your mass of material.

Common Organizing Techniques	
COMPARE AND CONTRAST	Shows similarities and differences between two objects, persons, or incidents.
ORDER OF IMPORTANCE	Presents details in order of increasing (or decreasing) significance or scope.
PRO AND CON	Presents first positive, then negative, aspects of a product or course of action.
SPATIAL ORDER	Shows the details of a scene, object, or person according to their relative positions.
CHRONOLOGICAL ORDER	Describes an event or a process in sequence as it occurs over time.

Kurt Schwitters, *Opened by Customs*, 1937–38

But how do you choose the right organizing technique? A good strategy is to let your purpose determine the way you order your material. Suppose your general topic were "garbage." The chart on page 77 demonstrates different purposes with the corresponding organizing techniques.

Selecting an Appropriate Organizing Technique

Purpose: To explain that Americans generate much more garbage than people in other countries do.

Data: Statistics on landfills, including kinds and amounts of garbage generated in the United States and in other countries.

Organizing Technique: Compare and Contrast

Purpose: To make a compelling argument that disposal of garbage is extremely expensive.

Data: The cost of disposal of a variety of products including glass (expensive), paper (very expensive), waste water (exorbitant).

Organizing Technique: Order of Importance

Purpose: To give a balanced view of the difficulties and rewards of being a garbage collector.

Data: Details and examples of the problems of the job; details and examples of the benefits of the job.

Organizing Technique: Pro and Con

Purpose: To write a description of a landfill that emphasizes its size and diverse content.

Data: Details of visit to local dump: description of the layers of landfill, from underground to the highest "hills"; description of landfill observed from left to right and from foreground to horizon.

Organizing Technique: Spatial Order

Purpose: To provide clear instructions on making toys from trash.

Data: Suggestions for appropriate material such as empty containers and paper; examples of toys that can be made; descriptions of each step in constructing several such toys.

Organizing Technique: Chronological Order

Sometimes you need to use a combination of methods. If you wanted to show that Americans produce more garbage than people in other countries and that the amount has been increasing every year, you would use compare and contrast *and* chronological order.

Journal Writing

Create a chart on the topic "high school." Brainstorm three different purposes for writing about this topic. Include the kinds of data to be used and the best organizing technique for each.

Write Your Essay

Each of the three parts of your essay—the introduction, the body, and the conclusion—has its own unique function and contributes to the overall picture you create. Normally, you start with the big picture, the essay's main idea. Next, you present your material piece by piece. Then you end by stepping back for a final overview.

INTRODUCTION	BODY	CONCLUSION
• How can I get my reader's attention? • How can I introduce my main idea? • What tone do I want to set?	• How can I develop and support my idea? • How can I organize my writing? • How can I tie my ideas together?	• How can I create a strong last impression? • What is the best way to bring this writing to a close?

Get Off to a Good Start   In the opening scenes of *Raiders of the Lost Ark,* intrepid archaeologist Indiana Jones narrowly escapes a giant rolling boulder, poisoned darts, and flying spears in a hair-raising flight. Director Steven Spielberg knew how to bring you to the edge of your seat even before the title appeared. He seized your attention and set the stage for the next ninety minutes of danger and suspense.

Like the opening scene of a well-directed movie, the introduction to a written work should capture your audience's attention and show where the writing is going. As author John McPhee put it, an introduction "ought to shine like a flashlight down into the whole piece." An effective introduction will engage the audience, present the main idea, or thesis, and establish the tone and organizing strategy for the rest of the piece.

Organize the Body Logically   The body of your essay presents your supporting material in an order appropriate to your thesis and purpose. Once you have selected an organizing technique, divide your argument into logical sections. As a rule, you will present each section in one or more paragraphs.

The first paragraph of each section should contain a topic sentence. Use supporting details—examples, statistics, quotations from one or more authorities—to amplify or reinforce the topic sentence, and be careful to include only the details that are essential to your thesis.

As you move from one topic to the next, remember to take your reader with you. Transitional words, such as *first, second, therefore,* and *as a result,* can help your reader follow your argument. Longer essays may require transitional paragraphs to sum up the points made so far and introduce the next topic. Keep in mind that your paragraphs should follow an orderly sequence.

Conclude Effectively   The strongest and most effective conclusions are those that leave the reader with a new way of seeing the main point. If the body of your essay is long and complicated, you may need to summarize or restate your main ideas in your concluding section. Shorter essays may not require a repetition of all of the key points, but instead may conclude with an anecdote, an analysis, a quotation, or a striking fact that you've saved for the end to have a dramatic effect.

The following is a concluding paragraph from an essay asserting that television is harmful to society. In the essay, the writer makes three main points about TV: It shows too much sex and violence, it stifles creativity, and it gives viewers a false sense of reality.

Student Model

In short, television is hurting our society more than it is helping it. The general consensus of authorities suggests that although television can be a valuable tool, it is not being used as such. Dr. Neil Postman said, "Words, not visual images, are still the coin of the realm for serious culture." There is much to be learned from television, but one must remember not to become completely absorbed. One should watch television with an inquisitive mind and never become complacent.

> Matthew Asbury, Claremont Northeastern High School,
> Batavia, Ohio

> How does this conclusion go beyond mere summarizing?

Journal Writing

Consider the last essay you wrote for another class or one you are working on currently. How is your information organized? Consider the techniques explored in this lesson, and jot down in your journal ways your organization could improve. Think how your essay builds to a conclusion, and write how you could strengthen your conclusion, as well.

Put It All Together

When the tape deck was stolen from her car, Ellen Goodman, a newspaper columnist, wrote a humorous essay about the incident.

What indications does Goodman give you in the first paragraph that this will be a humorous piece?

> ### Literature Model
>
> Let me begin this tale of urban crime with a small piece of family lore. My father was a man so intent on believing in an honest world that he wouldn't, on principle, lock the car. I don't mean the doors to the car. I mean the ignition.
>
> For this particular principle he was well rewarded, or should I say targeted. During one brief period in the early sixties, our car was driven off no less than three times.
>
> I, however, have always considered myself relatively (to him) street-smart, somewhere between savvy and paranoid. Nevertheless, last week I got ripped off and it was, everyone seems to agree, my own fault.
>
> Where did I go wrong? you ask. I blush to confess this, but I was foolish enough to actually be the owner of an automobile radio with a tape deck.
>
> Ellen Goodman, "Confessions of a Tape-Deck Owner"

The body of the essay details the matter-of-fact reactions of friends to Goodman's tale of woe: "Indeed, one colleague suggested that having a tape deck in a car was in and of itself a form of entrapment." She ends her essay with a wry, decisive conclusion.

The essay feels finished. Why?

> ### Literature Model
>
> With all this advice, I now face two alternatives. I can chuck the music and the illusion that someday I will spend my commuting hours learning French. Or I can spend $550 for the protection of my right to hear a $5.95 tape.
>
> Of course, I have another thought, that I don't even say out loud: Maybe the thief will be caught and the audio system returned. I guess that's the sort of fantasy you'd expect from someone who'd put a tape deck in a city car.

Write Your First Draft

Gather all the notes and plans you've worked on so far. Now you will draft your essay.

PURPOSE To write the first draft of your essay
AUDIENCE Yourself and your teacher
LENGTH 5–6 paragraphs

WRITING RUBRICS To write an effective first draft, you should

- choose an appropriate organizing technique
- incorporate your thesis statement into an attention-getting opening paragraph
- organize relevant supporting details in the body paragraphs
- write an effective conclusion

Listening and Speaking

COOPERATIVE LEARNING In a small group discuss style and content of the painting on this page. How would you feel if the painting were displayed in your school lobby? Have one person take notes. Together, draft a two-paragraph essay for or against putting the painting on display. Use the chart on page 78 to help you organize your paper. Present your essay to the class.

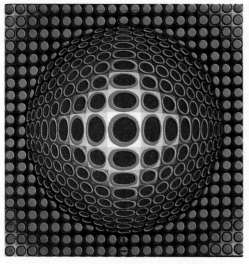

Victor Vasarely, *Vega-Tek*, 1969

Subjects and verbs must agree regardless of intervening elements.

The verb agrees with the subject, not with the object of the preposition.

The . . . **consensus** *of authorities* **suggests** *. . .*

Rewrite the sentences below, making subjects agree with verbs.

1. Mr. Coleman, as well as his daughters, are attending the conference.
2. The composer of those folk songs take no credit for their success.
3. The TV dinner, along with many of Ada's frozen items, are thawing.
4. Mr. Magico, accompanied by an assistant, perform every weekend.
5. Mattie remarked, "Joe, not the other cousins, were cooking breakfast."

See Lessons 16.1, pages 601–602, and 16.6, pages 609–610.

Using Computers

A word processing program can help you organize your essay. Use a numbered list to plan the order in which you will reveal details or ideas. For a pro- and con- or a compare-and-contrast organization, record your ideas in a two-column chart.

The Writing Process

Drafting: Writing with Coherence

*T*he following dialogue is hard to follow because it is linked by puns, or plays on words' sounds. Although the effect here is humorous, your sentences and paragraphs must be connected in a more logical manner.

Literature Model

FINANCE MINISTER: How about taking up the tax?

FIREFLY: How about taking up the carpet?

FINANCE MINISTER: I still insist we must take up the tax!

FIREFLY: He's right. You've got to take up the tacks before you can take up the carpet.

FINANCE MINISTER: I give all my time and energy to my duties and what do I get?

FIREFLY: You get awfully tiresome after a while.

FINANCE MINISTER: Sir, you try my patience!

FIREFLY: I don't mind if I do—you must come over and try mine sometime.

From the movie *Duck Soup*

Make Connections

Coherent writing develops connections between one sentence or paragraph and the next. Sentences and paragraphs must be arranged in a clear, logical order so that thoughts flow smoothly. You observe many of the rules of coherence automatically when you speak or write:

"*Mary* said it was nice out. *She* told me not to bring a sweater." (pronoun reference)

"*First,* make sure you have all your ingredients. *Then* you can begin to cook." (transition)

"*I asked you* to take out the garbage. *I asked you* to clean up your room. *I asked you* to look after your sister. What did you do? You watched television!" (repetition, parallelism)

Student Model

My dad rushed downstairs for ammunition. Meanwhile, my aunt staggered from her room to investigate the commotion. When she saw the bat, she sprinted wildly to her room to get a flowered shower cap so that the bat could not get caught in her hair. My father was doing his own mad sprint back up the stairs, now armed with my brother's fencing helmet and two tennis racquets. One of the racquets was mine. My brother stood and refereed Dad's "bat-minton" game.

The bat's sonar enabled him to dodge my dad's swings with the tennis racquet. Dad cursed in frustration. I wanted to curse when I saw what he was doing to my tennis racquet. We heard Dad's feet smooshing into cushions as he galloped from chair to bed to chair. We heard the thuds and smacks of the racquet as it crashed into door frames and lamps. And we heard my aunt's yelps of encouragement and advice to my dad. Finally there was a triumphant yell. My fearless father had vanquished the "winged invader."

Merry Margaret Carlton, Princeton High School,
Cincinnati, Ohio

Coherence Devices	
TRANSITIONAL WORDS	"Meanwhile" . . . "When she saw". . . "Finally"
LOGICAL ORGANIZATION	Sequential reactions of dad, aunt, brother, and narrator
SPORTS LANGUAGE AND IMAGERY	"mad sprint," "fencing helmets," "tennis racquets," "refereeing," "'bat-minton'"
PRONOUN REFERENCE	"my aunt . . . she," "my father . . . he," "the racquet . . . it"
REPETITION AND PARALLELISM	"sprinted . . . sprint," "Dad cursed . . . I wanted to curse," "We heard . . . We heard. . . And we heard . . . "

Journal Writing

Look at a piece of your own writing. Note all of the coherence devices you used in the passage, referring to the chart above. Then write an evaluation of the coherence of the piece.

Find the Invisible Threads

Readers don't usually stop to think about why the passage they're reading is coherent. But they'll certainly notice if it's *not* coherent.

> Our high school was named Hoover after Herbert Hoover. Every fall the parking lot became a lake. I caught an eight-pound carp and kids would go fishing. Someone called the newspaper in Portland. A photographer showed up and wrote about it.

A few connections are suggested here, but none are clear. Is the parking lot at the school? Why did someone call the newspaper? What is the "it" that someone wrote about? Now, compare the paragraph with the following passage from a novel by David James Duncan.

Literature Model

One of the images that ties this paragraph together is the juxtaposition of unlike objects, such as a parking lot and a lake. What other incongruities do you observe?

What examples of repetition and transitional phrases can you find in this paragraph? See page 216 for a list of transitional words.

Our high school was named Hoover, after Herbert, but we called it "J. Edgar" to capture the spirit of the place. Whoever designed the J. Edgar parking lot didn't know much about Oregon; every fall the lot became a lake. One spring I stocked the lake with an eight-pound carp that lived in there for three weeks before someone spotted it feeding by a stalled-out Studebaker. Word got around; kids chased it and fished for it, but it was a strong, smart old fish; somebody called the Portland newspaper—they ran an AP photo of the lot and a write-up in the sports section by one of the senile but tenured editors that the paper was renowned for. This editor calls his column "The Fishing Dutchman." In the column he accounted for the carp's presence by noting the existence of a three-season sewer ditch a quarter mile away; he theorized that the fish, one flooded night, half swam, half crawled its way overland to the J. Edgar parking lot. He then, for the tenth time in the history of his column, went on to say that to cook a carp you broil it on a cedar shingle till it turns golden brown, then throw away the carp and eat the shingle.

David James Duncan, *The River Why*

Although Duncan's writing appears to be rambling and impressionistic, each sentence follows from the one before, and every transition and reference is immediately clear.

Check Your Draft for Coherence

Evaluate the first draft of your essay to make sure connections between sentences, paragraphs, and ideas are clear.

PURPOSE To make sure your first draft is coherent
AUDIENCE Yourself and your teacher
LENGTH 5–6 paragraphs

WRITING RUBRICS To write a coherent draft, you should

- incorporate transitional words and phrases
- check for correct pronoun reference
- repeat key phrases and wording patterns

Viewing and Representing

COMMUNICATING MEANING Write two or three paragraphs describing the painting *Little Blue Horse*. What reactions do you have to the painting? How would you describe its style, content, and colors? What ideas might the horse represent? Use the techniques you have learned in this unit to make your writing unified and coherent.

Using Computers

Use the Find command (check under Edit in the menu bar) to locate repeated words and phrases. Enter the words or phrases you are checking in the Find text box. The computer will highlight each instance in which you have used that word or word group. Evaluate each instance of use as it appears. Do the repetitions make your writing more coherent?

Grammar Link

Verbs must agree with indefinite pronoun subjects.

Some indefinite pronouns are singular and require singular verbs.

*One of the racquets **was** mine.*

Other indefinite pronouns are plural and take plural verbs. There are also indefinites whose number depends on the nouns to which they refer.

Write sentences using the following subjects and one of the verbs in the pair that follows.

1. Each neighbor on the cul de sac (know/knows)
2. Nobody on my bus (speak/speaks)
3. Several elected to the commission (watch/watches)
4. Most of the noise (was coming/were coming)
5. Some of the members (nod/nods)

See Lesson 16.7, pages 611–612.

Franz Marc, *Little Blue Horse*, 1912

The Writing Process

Revising: Using Peer Responses

It's hard to be objective about your own work. Often, friends and classmates can offer valuable suggestions on how you can revise your writing.

Using an Extra Pair of Eyes

Writers through the centuries have tried out their new creations on wives, husbands, friends, other writers, and total strangers. They valued the advice of their peers—even if they didn't always like the advice they received.

Peer reviewing is helpful for both the famous and the not-yet-famous. It is difficult to assess your own work because you've labored over the words you've chosen, and you may have become attached to them. You may not see gaps in logic or fact because, as the originator of the idea, your mind tends to fill in those gaps between what you meant and what you actually wrote.

A writer/reviewer relationship is most effective when the partners follow the tips below:

TIPS FOR PEER REVIEWERS

Your goal is to bring out the writer's best work. The writer will respond better if you begin with praise rather than criticism. Ask questions to help you understand the writer's intention and meaning. Direct criticism at the writing, not the writer. Be constructive; suggest specific solutions. "What if you tried . . ." or "Would it be stronger if you . . ." are better than "This doesn't work."

TIPS FOR WRITERS

Another pair of eyes can give you fresh insights into your writing. To make the process most productive, question any comments you don't understand and solicit suggestions for how to fix problems. Take careful notes. Listen with an open mind, but remember that in the end you make your own decisions about what and how much to change.

Play Your Part Well

As a Reviewer If you are asked to review someone's writing, start by reading the piece all the way through—without commenting—to judge its overall effect. Were you excited, bored, saddened, or entertained? Writers can't possibly find these things out on their own.

Next, go through the piece again, jotting down comments in the margins or on a separate piece of paper. Avoid vague remarks such as "This is good" or "This needs a lot of work." Instead, point out specific places where you lost the train of thought or where your interest flagged. If you cannot understand a section or you are unsure why the writer uses certain evidence or language, ask. Questions are often as helpful as comments.

As you read to help the writer revise, don't be concerned with misspelled words or grammar problems. Those issues can be dealt with later. Now is the time to be concerned with content, coherence, and flow of the writing. The checklist on the right reviews some items to look for as you read.

As a Writer When you take notes on your reviewer's comments, keep in mind that every person will react a little differently to what he or she reads. Get a couple of different reactions to your writing. What one person doesn't catch, another might. The very words you're reading now were read and commented on by dozens of readers.

If one peer editor likes your work and another doesn't, consider all the comments and choose those you find helpful. Ultimately, the final decisions are yours.

Peer Reviewer Checklist

1. What are your favorite parts? Why?
2. What do you think is the weakest part? Why?
3. How does the writing make you feel?
4. Does the opening make you want to keep reading?
5. Is the main idea, or thesis, clear? Do all sentences and paragraphs support it? If not, which ones don't?
6. Are there enough details, reasons, facts, and examples to support the thesis? If not, can you ask questions to elicit new supporting details?
7. Are you able to follow the writer's essay easily?
8. Are the word choices effective? Are verbs strong? Are nouns concrete?
9. Is the ending strong?

Journal Writing

Reread the peer reviewer checklist above. Copy the checklist into your journal, grouping together questions about the piece as a whole, questions about specific sections, and questions about language. Refer to the list when evaluating your own or others' writing.

Work Together

In peer reviewing, writer and reviewer have the same goal: to improve the piece of writing. Here's a sample draft complete with written peer responses.

> Is this paragraph necessary? If you could identify Miller as the owner at the end, you might delete it. I think the cobwebs sentence is a stronger opening.

> Do you need "from many years past"? Cobwebs and dust suggest the many years.

> You could go into more detail here. I would like to "see" some of the controls. Nice description of the engine noises!

Driving past a barn in the small New Hampshire town, my friend and I saw a gleam of chrome, so we stopped to find the owner. Mr. Miller was delighted to show us the car as he'd been trying unsuccessfully to sell it for months.

Underneath the cobwebs and the dust from many years past sat the 1958 Cadillac. Faded light blue and white paint covered a slightly rusty body, easy to fix with some fiberglass and Bondo. Above the dirty, flaking front bumper a pair of chrome-bevelled headlights stared, eyes of a once majestic beast. A large gold eagle perched proudly on the hood. Inside, the car smelled musty. The worn white leather interior was home to many of the barn animals that had crawled through the minor floor rot. A large white dashboard housed many perfect, simple controls.

I gave the key a turn and the car turned over, sputtered and finally caught, sending the 503-cubic-inch engine into a frenzy of knocks and pings. The old unused valves made a loud *tick! tick!* After talking to Miller, we settled on a $500 price. It was a bargain for a car that could be restored to look as it did coming off an assembly line in 1958.

General Comments:

This description really makes me picture this old car, but I'm not sure about the thesis. Do you want to emphasize the car's value or its age and decay? You use many strong details that appeal to the senses, and the ending makes me think that you really respect the car. Maybe you could emphasize that. You could also add dialogue for variety.

Revise with a Peer

Now you will work with a partner to evaluate and improve your first drafts. Each of you should follow the same steps as you evaluate each other's papers.

PURPOSE To use peer review to help you revise your first draft

AUDIENCE One or more classmates

LENGTH 1 page of comments

WRITING RUBRICS To use the peer review process, you should

- read your partner's draft all the way through without commenting
- use the Peer Reviewer Checklist on page 87 to write specific suggestions about the content of your partner's draft
- use your partner's comments on *your* draft to help you revise your paper

Using Computers

If you and your peer reviewer have access to computers or word processors with split-screen capabilities, you can use a split screen for more effective peer reviewing. Format the draft onto the left side of the monitor, and use the right side to write comments and suggestions. Don't forget to point out sections you like, as well as those you do not like, and to explain why you think a certain section is or is not effective.

Grammar Link

Use prepositional phrases to add detail to your writing.

Prepositional phrases can add descriptive detail, additional data, or information about location.

> ***Underneath the cobwebs and the dust from many years past*** *sat the 1958 Cadillac.*

Add one or more prepositional phrases to each of these sentences.

1. A vase tumbled and smashed.
2. Energetic march music set the tone.
3. Some spotted deer cast perfect reflections.
4. His old convertible was parked.
5. Who scribbled this grocery list?
6. The train is a local.
7. Which are leaving for college this fall?
8. The horse runs fast.
9. The window shattered into a thousand pieces.
10. Why ask me?

See Lesson 12.1, pages 513–514.

Listening and Speaking

COOPERATIVE LEARNING Ask your partner to read your draft and write a statement about the purpose of your essay. (Is it intended to inform, persuade, explain, describe, or entertain?) Does your partner's response match your intended purpose? If not, how can you revise your essay to better fit your purpose? Then help evaluate your partner's draft.

Editing and Presenting: Completing Your Essay

*W*hen the sports car below came off the assembly line, someone checked it to see that all its parts held together firmly and all its details were just right. When you write, your job is not finished until you check that all the details fit together.

Read for Errors

Attention to the small details applies as much to your writing as to any other product. To produce high-quality work, you've got to think critically about it.

If you assume the work contains errors, you'll find them. If you assume the writing is perfect, you may not notice the mistakes. You might try the approach of the English poet Samuel Butler.

Literature Model

*T*hink of and look at your work as though it were done by your enemy. If you look at it to admire it, you are lost. . . . If we look at it to see where it is wrong, we shall see this and make it righter. If we look at it to see where it is right, we shall see this and shall not make it righter. We cannot see it both wrong and right at the same time.

Samuel Butler, *The Note-Books of Samuel Butler*

Look hard at your own writing: edit and proofread to check the details of grammar, mechanics, and spelling. Editing refers to issues of paragraph and sentence construction, including grammar and transitions. Proofreading means checking capitalization, punctuation, and spelling. Both kinds of quality control are essential to good writing. The checklist on this page covers the kinds of errors writers are most likely to make.

After revising and before presenting any piece of written work, you should read it at least twice, first to edit and then to proofread. You may find that by the second or third reading, you have become so familiar with the writing that your eyes skim over spelling mistakes, mentally correcting them as you go. If this happens to you, try this proofreading trick: read backward, word by word. This will force you to look at each word out of context, and you'll be more likely to see mistakes. Be careful, however; you'll miss errors involving possessives and usage.

To polish your writing, try putting the piece aside for a day or two. When you read your writing after being away from it, you may catch errors you missed earlier. You might also try reading your piece aloud. Often, you will be able to "hear" a mistake that you might not "see."

Just as peer reviewing can help you revise writing, peer editing and proofreading can help you polish your work. Most of us recognize others' errors more quickly than we do our own.

Editing and Proofreading Checklist

Editing

✔ Do all verbs agree with their subjects?

✔ Do pronouns agree with their antecedents?

✔ Are the point of view and tense consistent?

✔ Are there any fragments or run-ons?

✔ Is the writing redundant or wordy?

✔ Are all words used correctly?

Proofreading

✔ Are all necessary words capitalized?

✔ Is punctuation clear and correct: end punctuation, commas, semicolons, apostrophes, quotation marks?

✔ Are numbers treated correctly?

✔ Are all words spelled correctly?

Journal Writing

Start a personal editing and proofreading checklist by reviewing several pieces of writing and noting the errors. List specific words that you commonly misspell or misuse. Keep your checklist handy and add to it as you notice other patterns in your writing.

Use Proofreaders' Marks

When you proofread, use the symbols shown below to mark various kinds of errors. Use a different color ink from that of your draft to make sure the corrections show up. Circle any small punctuation marks you add so that you won't miss them later.

Common Proofreaders' Marks

∧ insert something	∼ reverse letters or words	... let it stand as it was (under something crossed out)
# add a space	⌒ close up space	
¶ begin a new paragraph	M̶ make this letter lowercase	C̲ capitalize
℘ delete		

A sample of a well-edited, well-proofread piece of writing follows. Editing corrections are shown in blue; proofreading corrections in red.

Student Model

¶Watching maggie take her first steps is a "hoot and a holler," as mom would say. First, she hoists herself up to her ~~little~~ tiny feet by pulling with all her ~~its~~ might on the edge of the couch or chair. Once up right, she looked around to make sure you are watching, and then she grins. She turns herself toward the center of the room and takes that first step ~~still~~ with one hand still planted on "home base." Then, she purses her lips and let go, lifting her feet ~~awkwardly~~ and throwing her ~~wait~~ weight toward your outstretched arms. She looks like Frankenstein's monster. and Giggling all the way, hoping she'll make it to you before she tumbles.

Use Correct Format

Study the suggestions below. Try to make your writing look good.

The Writing Process

Name and date in upper right-hand corner

Five-space indent at the beginning of paragraphs

Title centered, no quotation marks

Clear typing (or printing) with erasing done neatly

1-inch margin on left, 1 1/2-inch margins on bottom, top, and right

```
                                        Jazmyne Fuentes
                                        September 22, 1992
                    Unbroken Chains

        I insisted on carrying the basket, which appeared
    to contain some canned food and oatmeal. He carried a
    pail of coffee and led the way through a damp, lumpy
    field toward the unlit barn where he and his fellow
    farmhands were spending the night.
        As he pushed open the door, I asked, "What about
    a can opener for the vegetables?"
        "The cans are empty," he said softly, as the
    scent of animals and men in close quarters smothered
    us. "They're for drinking the coffee."
```

Whether you're writing for your teacher or for a publication, be sure to use whatever format is preferred. If the choice is yours, follow the guidelines above, or come up with creative ideas appropriate to the piece. For longer pieces, you may want to include a cover sheet, dedication page, or other features, such as a table of contents or index. Illustrations, photocopied pictures, charts, and graphs can all contribute to the look and the content of the piece.

These suggestions apply whether you're writing by hand, typing, or using a word processing program. Such a program also lets you

change   type   STYLES   and   type   <u>sizes</u>

to give your paper a professional look. Don't go overboard with clever devices, though; keep the text clean and easy to read.

Journal Writing

Return to one of your earlier journal entries, and practice using proofreaders' symbols to clean it up. Rewrite the journal entry according to the changes you have marked.

Choose a Strong Title

A good title can reach out from the bookshelf and grab you. Some titles are whimsical teasers, like *Zen and the Art of Motorcycle Maintenance,* or Tom Wolfe's *Kandy-Kolored Tangerine Flake Streamline Baby.* The title of Stephen King's thriller *Misery* is simple, true to the content of the book, and hauntingly effective.

Good titles often convey a sense of the content of the work without giving away too much. A twist of language can often be effective if not overdone: alliteration ("The Flower-Fed Buffaloes"), rhyme and rhythm (*Tinker, Tailor, Soldier, Spy*), and word plays (an article on designer baby clothes called "Gucci, Gucci, Goo"). Even among nonfiction works, titles can be grabbers: *50 Simple Things You Can Do to Save the Earth.*

The search for a title, whether it comes at the beginning, middle, or end of the writing process, can cause you to think more deeply about the work and to find its central or main idea. Warning: if a title continues to elude you, it could mean that the piece lacks a strong focus.

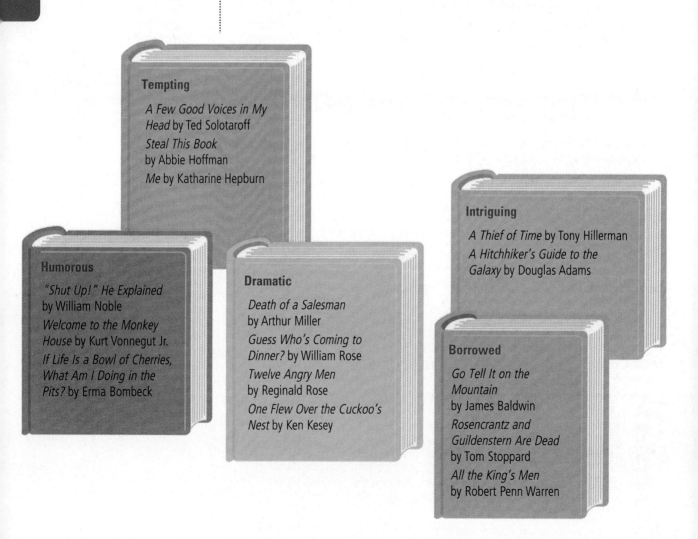

Tempting

A Few Good Voices in My Head by Ted Solotaroff

Steal This Book by Abbie Hoffman

Me by Katharine Hepburn

Intriguing

A Thief of Time by Tony Hillerman

A Hitchhiker's Guide to the Galaxy by Douglas Adams

Humorous

"Shut Up!" He Explained by William Noble

Welcome to the Monkey House by Kurt Vonnegut Jr.

If Life Is a Bowl of Cherries, What Am I Doing in the Pits? by Erma Bombeck

Dramatic

Death of a Salesman by Arthur Miller

Guess Who's Coming to Dinner? by William Rose

Twelve Angry Men by Reginald Rose

One Flew Over the Cuckoo's Nest by Ken Kesey

Borrowed

Go Tell It on the Mountain by James Baldwin

Rosencrantz and Guildenstern Are Dead by Tom Stoppard

All the King's Men by Robert Penn Warren

Edit and Present Your Essay

You're almost finished. Check through your paper one more time, and then make a final copy.

PURPOSE To edit your paper and prepare it for presentation
AUDIENCE Yourself and your intended audience
LENGTH 5–6 paragraphs

WRITING RUBRICS To edit your essay and prepare it for presentation, you should

- use the Editing and Proofreading Checklist on page 91 to correct sentence-level errors
- use proofreading symbols to mark capitalization, punctuation, and spelling errors
- make an error-free, legible copy of your paper, title it, and prepare it for presentation

Using Computers

If you have composed on the computer, run the spell-checking function a final time to find and correct errors. The spell-checking function will recognize misspellings but will not recognize when you have written the wrong word, such as writing "they" when you meant to write "then." Be sure to give your paper a final read-through to catch this type of error.

Avoid sentence fragments in your writing.

Proofread all of your writing for sentence fragments—incomplete sentences punctuated as sentences. Sometimes you will need to add a subject, verb, or both; sometimes you can attach a fragment to a complete sentence nearby.

Correct the sentence fragments in the following items.

1. I volunteered to help. Not wanting to seem uncooperative.
2. In order to buy the running shoes at a sale price.
3. Tawanna, the most talented of our cheerleaders.
4. Raney, change the channel. Before the news comes on.
5. Sometimes, when I work out too hard and don't drink enough water.

See Lesson 13.9, pages 551–552.

Listening and Speaking

COOPERATIVE LEARNING Take twenty minutes to write two paragraphs about a gathering area at school, such as the front steps or lobby. Exchange papers with a partner. Review each other's work for errors in spelling, grammar, and punctuation. Use the checklist on page 91 as a guide. Discuss ways to correct your errors.

The Writing Process

WRITING ABOUT LITERATURE
Analyzing a Character in a Play

If you were asked to write an essay about Laura in the passage below, how would you analyze her character?

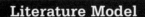

Literature Model

LAURA: Well, I do—as I said—have my—glass collection—
JIM: I'm not right sure I know what you're talking about. What kind of glass is it?

LAURA: Little articles of it, they're ornaments mostly! Most of them are little animals made out of glass, the tiniest little animals in the world. Mother calls them a glass menagerie! Here's an example of one, if you'd like to see it! This one is one of the oldest. It's nearly thirteen.

Oh, be careful—if you breathe, it breaks!

JIM: I'd better not take it. I'm pretty clumsy with things.

LAURA: Go on, I trust you with him! *[She places the piece on his palm.]* There now—you're holding him gently! Hold him over the light, he loves the light! You see how the light shines through him?

JIM: It sure does shine!

LAURA: I shouldn't be partial, but he is my favorite one.

JIM: What kind of a thing is this one supposed to be?

LAURA: Haven't you noticed the single horn on his forehead?

JIM: A unicorn, huh?

LAURA: Mmmm-hmmm!

JIM: Unicorns—aren't they extinct in the modern world?

LAURA: I know!

JIM: Poor little fellow, he must feel sort of lonesome.

Tennessee Williams, *The Glass Menagerie*

Prewrite About the Character

To really understand the character of Laura, it is important to read the play. Then cast your net wide to assemble your own collection of responses and ideas. Begin your analysis of a character by freewriting or by creating a cluster diagram to identify his or her traits. This diagram shows how you might begin thinking about the character of Laura.

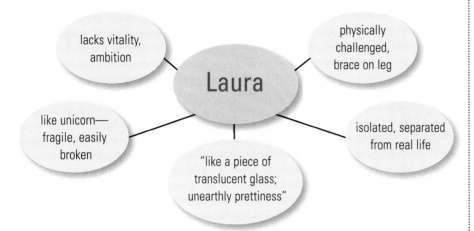

If you want to push your thinking further, you can create another chart, talk about the topic with a friend, or ask yourself questions:

- Do you like the character? Why or why not?
- What adjectives best describe the character?
- What actor or actress might you choose to play the role?
- How is the character related to the theme of the play?

Now study your prewriting notes, and write a one-sentence thesis statement that can guide the organizing and drafting of your analysis. Try to develop your thesis statement from a simple fact to an insight that reveals the function or motivation of the character. For example, your notes about Laura in *The Glass Menagerie* might lead you to this initial thesis: "Laura is like her glass menagerie: fragile, easily broken, and delicate." A more developed thesis might be, "Laura represents the trapped, overprotected woman of her era, fragile and easily broken."

Journal Writing

In your journal, list all the techniques you can think of to generate ideas about a character. Then write down the method you think works best for you and the reasons why.

Draft Your Essay

Once you've formulated a thesis statement, select an appropriate method of organization. Remember to consider your audience: How much do your readers already know? Finally, revise and edit your essay.

Model

Laura, a crippled young woman in *The Glass Menagerie,* embodies the fragility of her family. Like her prized glass collection, Laura is slightly unreal, delicate, and easily broken. Laura cannot survive real life any more than her delicate glass unicorn. Her fate, and the fate of her glass menagerie, parallels the breakdown of her family.

We meet Laura in the first scene, listening to her mother reminisce about past beaus. Amanda, illuminated in the spotlight, describes the myriad of "gentlemen callers" she had as a girl. Laura remains in the dark, too shy and withdrawn to follow in her mother's footsteps.

As the play continues, we see that Laura exists in a fantasy world, doing nothing except take care of her glass animals. She is trailed by a piece of circus music, "The Glass Menagerie," which underscores the unreality of her life. When Laura's brother Tom has a raging argument with Amanda, Laura stands in a bright spotlight, speechless, as if she were watching an act in the ring of a circus. She is only an audience, never a participant, in life.

The fate of Laura and her family mirrors that of the glass menagerie. At first, the glass pieces are in fine condition. Laura cares for her menagerie almost obsessively, and the family clings together in much the same fashion. During Amanda and Tom's fight, a piece of glass breaks, sparking the family's descent. Later, when Jim arrives, Laura looks "like a piece of translucent glass touched by light." She shows him a piece of her collection, really a piece of herself, but as they dance the glass unicorn is accidentally broken. Soon after, Jim, likewise, breaks Laura's heart. This final blow completes the disintegration of Amanda's hopes for her daughter. Laura, the menagerie, and the dream have all been shattered.

Laura's tragedy is the core of the play. Her delicacy, fragility, and shyness symbolize the death of a family.

Jennifer Simon, Newton North High School,
Newton, Massachusetts

How has Jennifer developed the simple thesis on page 97 to deepen her analysis of Laura?

Which of the details in the diagram on page 97 does Jennifer use to support her thesis?

How much does Jennifer assume her audience knows?

Notice that Jennifer uses elements other than the plot, such as lighting and stage directions, to support her position.

2.11 Writing Activities

Write a Character Analysis

Read Annie Dillard's remembrance of her mother beginning on page 104. What is unique about Dillard's mother? What impact does she have on those around her? Write a character analysis of Annie Dillard's mother.

PURPOSE To write a character analysis
AUDIENCE Yourself
LENGTH 3–4 paragraphs

WRITING RUBRICS To write an effective character analysis, you should

- use a cluster diagram to identify the character's traits
- write a one-sentence thesis about the character
- develop your thesis with supporting facts

Using Computers

When you are writing a draft of a character analysis, use the "copy" feature of your word-processing program to preserve your first draft as you work to improve your writing. Try following these steps:

1. Save your first draft when completed.

2. Make a copy of your draft, as a new file.

3. Continue to rework your draft. Each time you complete a new version, save and copy that version as you did the first.

If you follow this procedure, you will always have a record of your initial ideas, as well as a record of the changes you made as you revised.

Grammar Link

Compound subjects linked by *and* generally require a plural verb.

*Laura, the menagerie, and the dream **have** all been shattered.*

In the following sentences, select a verb that agrees with the subject.

1. Amy and her cousin (jog/jogs) in the Maymont Park on Saturdays.

2. Lotsee and the library staff (are/is) ready for questions from patrons.

3. Before buying a painting, the collector and her husband (consider/considers) both value and enjoyment.

4. Early each day, a stray cat and dog (skulk/skulks) down the back alley.

5. During the storm, the computer monitor and printer (were/was) turned off.

See Lesson 16.5, page 608.

Viewing and Representing

VISUAL MEDIA View a movie version of *The Glass Menagerie*. As you watch, jot down the main messages of the play. How are these messages conveyed? How does the director use such techniques as distance and close-up shots, camera angles, and contrasting shots to affect the viewer? How is music used? Discuss your notes and ideas with classmates.

Writing Process in Action

The Writing Process

The Writing Process

In preceding lessons you've learned to follow a process for effective writing. You've had a chance to practice each step in the process: prewriting, drafting, revising, editing/proofreading, and publishing/presenting. In this lesson you're asked to write an essay relating a particular aspect of your childhood to the person you are today. Recalling and developing memories will be an important part of this assignment.

Assignment

Context	An editor sends this notice to your school: *American Childhoods: A Collection of Essays by Young Writers*
	We are seeking essays that recall American childhoods. The memories can be happy or sad, everyday or extraordinary. Your essay should be something that no one else could possibly have written. It should be specific and lively, and give insight into who you have become as a young adult.
Purpose	To write an essay that recalls one aspect of your childhood and shows how that experience helped shape the person you are today
Audience	Teachers, psychologists, parents, teenagers
Length	2 pages

WRITING Online

Visit the Writer's Choice Web site at **writerschoice. glencoe.com**, for additional writing prompts.

The following pages can help you plan and write your essay. Read through them and refer to them as needed. But don't be tied down by them. This is a personal essay. Develop your ideas as you take charge of your own writing process.

Prewriting

What aspect of your childhood will you be writing about? First, open up your imagination and think about possibilities. You can start by flipping through an old photo album to spark your memory. Push yourself to remember as much as you can. Discuss memories with relatives and friends, and compare their recollections with yours. Additional points of view will help you understand incidents from your childhood. Make a list of possible topics.

Now you are ready to limit your topic and define your purpose. Choose the two or three topics that interest you most, and explore them using freewriting or by making a tree chart. Then select one topic and begin to formulate a purpose, or focus, for your essay. The prewriting questions shown here may help you.

Write a one-sentence statement of what your essay is about. This statement is your focus. Reread your notes, highlighting items that support your focus. Now you are ready to begin drafting.

Prewriting Questions

- What details about this topic do I remember most clearly?
- What do they tell me about the child I was?
- How does the topic relate to my present life?
- Would I interpret these experiences in the same way now?
- How would my family and friends view these experiences?

Drafting

Make some written plans to help you begin drafting. Consider the following:

- **Essay beginning.** Get the reader interested. Refer to the one-sentence statement you wrote in the prewriting step.
- **Essay organization.** Decide where your essay will go, how it will get there, how many parts it will have, and how each part will contribute to the whole.
- **Essay ending.** Decide how your essay will end, and how this ending will affect your readers.

Once you've mapped your essay, start writing. Let your writing flow to get your ideas down. Remember that you can always go back to prewriting if you discover gaps.

Consider using dialogue to enliven your essay. In the following model, notice how much mileage author Annie Dillard gets out of just three words.

Drafting Tip

For more information about finding a focus for your essay, and organizing your essay, see Lessons 2.6, pages 72–75, and 2.7, pages 76–81.

Literature Model

"Terwilliger bunts one?" Mother cried back, stopped short. She turned. "Is that English?"

"The player's name is Terwilliger," Father said. "He bunted."

That's marvelous," Mother said. " 'Terwilliger bunts one.' No wonder you listen to baseball. 'Terwilliger bunts one.' "

Annie Dillard, *An American Childhood*

Revising

Ask yourself broad questions to make sure your draft presents the big picture correctly. Then discuss your essay with a partner.

To begin revising, read over your draft to make sure that what you have written fits your purpose and your audience. Then have a **writing conference.** Read your draft to a partner or small group. Use your audience's reactions to help you evaluate your work so far. The checklist questions can help you and your listeners.

Revising Tip

For help with making connections between paragraphs, see Lesson 2.8, pages 82–85.

Revising Checklist

- Does every paragraph serve the larger purpose?
- Does each paragraph flow naturally into the next?
- Is there enough description for the reader to picture and feel my experiences?
- Is the dialogue believable and meaningful?
- Is it clear how this experience helped shape the person I am today?

Editing/Proofreading

Once you are happy with the basic content and setup of your essay, **proofread** it carefully for errors in grammar, usage, mechanics, and spelling. Use the questions at the right as a guide.

In addition to proofreading, use the self-evaluation list below to make sure your essay does all the things you want it to do. When you're satisfied, make a clean, legible copy of your essay, and proofread it one more time.

Self-Evaluation

Make sure your essay—

✔ focuses on a significant aspect of your childhood and shows how you were shaped by that experience

✔ uses specific details, including dialogue, to bring the memory to life

✔ uses organization appropriate to topic and purpose

✔ is unified and coherent with an engaging introduction and powerful conclusion

✔ follows the standards of grammar, usage, and mechanics

Publishing/Presenting

Choose a title that grabs the readers' interest and suggests your essay's purpose. It may help to use one of your best images in the title, one that captures the spirit of your essay.

Remember that the editor of *American Childhoods*—or of any other publication to which you decide to submit your essay—will be swamped with manuscripts. Make yours shine. If you are writing by hand, copy your essay neatly on clean paper. If you are typing or word processing, make the format of your essay pleasing to the eye. Even as the editor picks your piece from the pile, he or she is unconsciously making a judgment based simply on your essay's appearance.

Editing/Proofreading Checklist

- Do my subjects and verbs agree?
- Have I avoided double negatives?
- Have I used commas correctly with clauses?
- Have I avoided sentence fragments?
- Are all words spelled correctly?

Proofreading Tip

For proofreading symbols, see page 92. If you have composed your essay on the computer, try running a check on your spelling and grammar.

Journal Writing

Reflect on your writing process experience. Answer these questions in your journal: What do you like best about your personal essay? What was the hardest part of writing it? What did you learn from peer review? What new things have you learned as a writer?

Literature Model

Memories, especially of childhood, can spark powerful pieces of writing. In this selection from her 1987 book, An American Childhood, *Annie Dillard reflects on her youth by focusing on memories of her mother. As you read, notice the ways in which Dillard effectively organizes her writing and enhances it with dialogue. Then try the activities in Linking Writing and Literature on page 109.*

an AMERICAN Childhood

by Annie Dillard

One Sunday afternoon Mother wandered through our kitchen, where Father was making a sandwich and listening to the ball game. The Pirates were playing the New York Giants at Forbes Field. In those days, the Giants had a utility infielder named Wayne Terwilliger. Just as Mother passed through, the radio announcer cried—with undue drama— "Terwilliger bunts one!"

"Terwilliger bunts one?" Mother cried back, stopped short. She turned. "Is that English?"

"The player's name is Terwilliger," Father said. "He bunted."

"That's marvelous," Mother said. " 'Terwilliger bunts one.' No wonder you listen to baseball. 'Terwilliger bunts one.' "

For the next seven or eight years. Mother made this surprising string of syllables her own. Testing a microphone, she repeated, "Terwilliger bunts one"; testing a pen or a typewriter, she wrote it. If, as happened surprisingly often in the course of various improvised gags, she pretended to whisper something else in my ear, she actually whispered, "Terwilliger bunts one." Whenever someone used a French phrase, or a Latin one, she answered solemnly, "Terwilliger bunts one." If Mother had had, like Andrew Carnegie, the opportunity to cook up a motto for a coat of arms, hers would have read simply and tellingly, "Terwilliger bunts one." (Carnegie's was "Death to Privilege.")

She served us with other words and phrases. On a Florida trip, she repeated tremulously, "That . . . is a royal poinciana." I don't remember the tree; I remember the thrill in her voice. She pronounced it carefully, and spelled it. She also liked to say "portulaca."

The drama of the words "Tamiami Trail" stirred her, we learned on the same Florida trip. People built Tampa on one coast, and they built Miami on another. Then—the height of visionary ambition and folly—they piled a slow, tremendous road through the terrible Everglades to connect them. To build the road, men stood sunk in muck to their armpits. They fought off cottonmouth moccasins and six-foot alligators. They slept in boats, wet. They blasted muck with dynamite, cut jungle with machetes; they laid logs, dragged drilling machines, hauled dredges, heaped limestone. The road took fourteen years to build up by the shovelful, a Panama Canal in reverse, and cost hundreds of lives from tropical, mosquito-carried diseases. Then, capping it all, some genius thought of the word Tamiami: they called the road from Tampa to Miami, this very road under our spinning wheels, the Tamiami Trail. Some called it Alligator Alley. Anyone could drive over this road without a thought.

Hearing this, moved, I thought all the suffering of road building was worth it (it wasn't my suffering), now that we had this new thing to hang these new words on—Alligator Alley for those who liked things cute, for connoisseurs[1] like Mother, for lovers of the human drama in all its boldness and terror, the Tamiami Trail. . . .

When we children were young, she mothered us tenderly and dependably; as we got older, she resumed her career of anarchism.[2] She collared us into her gags. If she answered the phone on a wrong number, she told the caller, "Just a minute," and dragged the receiver to Amy or me, saying, "Here, take this, your name is Cecile," or, worse, just, "It's for you." You had to think on your feet. But did you want to perform well as Cecile, or did you want to take pity on the wretched caller?

During a family trip to the Highland Park Zoo, Mother and I were alone for a minute. She approached a young couple holding hands on a bench by the seals, and addressed the young man in dripping tones: "Where have you been? Still got those baby-blue eyes; always did slay me. And this"—a swift nod at the dumbstruck young woman, who had removed her hand from the man's—"must be the one you were telling me about. She's not so bad, really, as you used to make out. But listen, you know how I miss you, you know where to reach me, same old place. And there's Ann over there—see how she's grown? See the blue eyes?"

And off she sashayed, taking me firmly by the hand, and leading us around briskly past the monkey house and away. She cocked an

---

1 **connoisseurs** (kän′ ə surz′): experts in a special field
2 **anarchism** (an′ ər kiz′ əm): resistance to government or codes of behavior that limit individual liberty

ear back, and both of us heard the desperate man begin, in a high-pitched wail, "I swear, I never saw her before in my life. . . ."

Mother's energy and intelligence suited her for a greater role in a larger arena—mayor of New York, say—than the one she had. She followed American politics closely; she had been known to vote for Democrats. She saw how things should be run, but she had nothing to run but our household. Even there, small minds bugged her; she was smarter than the people who designed the things she had to use all day for the length of her life.

"Look," she said. "Whoever designed this corkscrew never used one. Why would anyone sell it without trying it out?" So she

> She respected the rare few who broke through to new ways.

invented a better one. She showed me a drawing of it. The spirit of American enterprise never faded in Mother. If capitalizing and tooling up had been as interesting as theorizing and thinking up, she would have fired up a new factory every week, and chaired several hundred corporations.

"It grieves me," she would say, "it grieves my heart," that the company that made one superior product packaged it poorly, or took the wrong tack in its advertising. She knew, as she held the thing mournfully in her two hands, that she'd never find another. She was right. We children wholly sympathized, and so did Father; what could she do, what could

anyone do, about it? She was Sampson in chains. She paced.

She didn't like the taste of stamps so she didn't lick stamps; she licked the corner of the envelope instead. She glued sandpaper to the sides of kitchen drawers, and under kitchen cabinets, so she always had a handy place to strike a match. She designed, and hounded workmen to build against all norms, doubly wide kitchen counters and elevated bathroom sinks. To splint a finger, she stuck it in a lightweight cigar tube. Conversely, to protect a pack of cigarettes, she carried it in a Band-Aid box. She drew plans for an over-the-finger toothbrush for babies, an oven rack that slid up and down, and—the family favorite—Lendalarm. Lendalarm was a beeper you attached to books (or tools) you loaned friends. After ten days, the beeper sounded. Only the rightful owner could silence it.

She repeatedly reminded us of P. T. Barnum's dictum: You could sell anything to anybody if you marketed it right. The adman who thought of making Americans believe they needed underarm deodorant was a visionary. So, too, was the hero who made a success of a new product, Ivory soap. The executives were horrified, Mother told me, that a cake of this stuff floated. Soap wasn't supposed to float. Anyone would be able to tell it was mostly whipped-up air. Then some inspired adman made a leap: Advertise that it floats. Flaunt it. The rest is history.

She respected the rare few who broke through to new ways. "Look," she'd say, "here's an intelligent apron." She called upon us to admire intelligent control knobs and intelligent pan handles, intelligent andirons and picture frames and knife sharpeners. She questioned everything, every pair of scissors,

Fairfield Porter, Early Morning, 1966

every knitting needle, gardening glove, tape dispenser. Hers was a restless mental vigor that just about ignited the dumb household objects with its force.

Torpid[3] conformity was a kind of sin; it was stupidity itself, the mighty stream against which Mother would never cease to struggle. If you held no minority opinions, or if you

---

3 **torpid** (tor'pid): sluggish

failed to risk total ostracism[4] for them daily, the world would be a better place without you.

Always I heard Mother's emotional voice asking Amy and me the same few questions: Is that your own idea? Or somebody else's? *"Giant* is a good movie," I pronounced to the family at dinner. "Oh, really?" Mother warmed to these occasions. She all but rolled up her sleeves. She knew I hadn't seen it. "Is that your considered opinion?"

She herself held many unpopular, even fantastic, positions. She was scathingly sarcastic about the McCarthy hearings while they took place, right on our living-room television; she frantically opposed Father's wait-and-see calm. "We don't know enough about it," he said. "I do," she said. "I know all I need to know."

She asserted, against all opposition, that people who lived in trailer parks were not bad but simply poor, and had as much right to settle on beautiful land, such as rural Ligonier, Pennsylvania, as did the oldest of families in the finest of hidden houses. Therefore, the people who owned trailer parks, and sought zoning changes to permit trailer parks, needed our help. Her profound belief that the country-club pool sweeper was a person, and that the department-store saleslady, the bus driver, telephone operator, and housepainter were people, and even in

groups the steelworkers who carried pickets and the Christmas shoppers who clogged intersections were people—this was a conviction common enough in democratic Pittsburgh, but not altogether common among our friends' parents, or even, perhaps, among our parents' friends.

Opposition emboldened Mother, and she would take on anybody on any issue—the chairman of the board, at a cocktail party, on the current strike; she would fly at him in a flurry of passion, as a songbird selflessly attacks a big hawk.

"Eisenhower's going to win," I announced after school. She lowered her magazine and looked me in the eyes: "How do you know?" I was doomed. It was fatal to say, "Everyone says so." We all knew well what happened. "Do you consult this Everyone before you make your decisions? What if Everyone decided to round up all the Jews?" Mother knew there was no danger of cowing me. She simply tried to keep us all awake. And in fact it was always clear to Amy and me, and to Molly when she grew old enough to listen, that if our classmates came to cruelty, just as much as if the neighborhood or the nation came to madness, we were expected to take, and would be each separately capable of taking, a stand.

---

4 **ostracism** (os′ trə siz′ əm): banishment or exclusion from a group

Linking Writing and Literature

Readers Respond to the Model

What makes Annie Dillard's anecdotes so effective?

Explore Dillard's character study by answering these questions. Then read what other students liked about Dillard's anecdotes.

1. How does Dillard use humor to illustrate her mother's complex personality?
2. Which anecdotes reveal the mother's values and the values she instilled in her children?
3. Do you think most people would see qualities similar to those of their own mother in Dillard's mother?

4. Do you think Dillard enjoyed her mother's antics? What passages influenced your response?

What Students Say

"Through everything Dillard said, I was able to visualize what her mother would be like. What I remember most clearly from the selection is the part where the mother plays the joke on that poor couple. Although I sympathized with the couple, the joke did make me laugh. It was a good example of the mother's strange sense of humor. Almost everyone has a mother and can see his or her mother in Dillard's mother. "

David Alonzo

"This literature selection was funny when the writer talked about the things her mother said. I would love to have a mother with that sense of humor. It would be fun to challenge her. The writer didn't seem to enjoy her mother. "

Becky Byer

UNIT 2 Review

Reflecting on the Unit

Summarize what you have learned in this unit by answering the following questions.

1 What are some prewriting techniques?

2 What prewriting technique did you use to develop your topic? Would another technique have been more effective?

3 If you had written for a different audience, what changes would you have made?

4 What kinds of things do you do during the drafting stage of the writing process?

5 How can peer review help you to revise your draft?

6 What revisions were in response to peer comments? What questions could you have asked your peer reviewer so that his or her comments would have been more helpful?

7 What is the purpose of editing and proofreading?

8 When did you go back to a previous stage in the writing process? Which stage did you find most difficult? Most helpful? How would you approach the process differently in the future?

9 In the context of the writing process, what does *presenting* mean?

Adding to Your Portfolio

Look over the writing you did for this unit. Choose a piece of writing for your portfolio. The writing you choose should show one or more of the following:

- a clear central idea
- relevant details
- a logical order
- smooth transitions
- thorough editing and proofreading

REFLECT ON YOUR CHOICE Attach a note to the piece you chose, explaining briefly why you chose it and what you learned from writing it.

SET GOALS How can you improve your writing? What skill will you focus on the next time you write?

Writing Across the Curriculum

MAKE A CIVICS CONNECTION Think of a political figure, either living or dead, whose life you know something about. Plan and write a brief summary of an event that seemed to have a significant effect on the person. Use all the stages of the writing process, including finding an interesting way to present your summary.

TIME

Facing the Blank Page

Inside the writing process with TIME writers and editors

Writing for TIME

ach week, TIME publishes stories that are the work of experienced professionals. The writing is strong; the facts are accurate; the grammar, spelling, and punctuation are error-free (or close!). Behind the scenes, however, there is another story to be told. As these pages reveal, TIME staffers struggle with many of the same challenges that students face in the messy, trial-and-error process that is writing: selecting among topics; finding information; getting organized; starting to draft; and then revising, revising, and revising some more.

What is the secret to the quality of writing in TIME? Beyond experience and hard work, the key lies in collaboration. As the chart on these pages illustrates, writers are assisted at each stage of the process by other members of the staff in a kind of "group journalism" that has become the magazine's hallmark. The writers and editors teach and learn from one another every week; student writers can do the same. Try out and adapt the writing and collaboration strategies in "Facing the Blank Page" to discover what works for you.

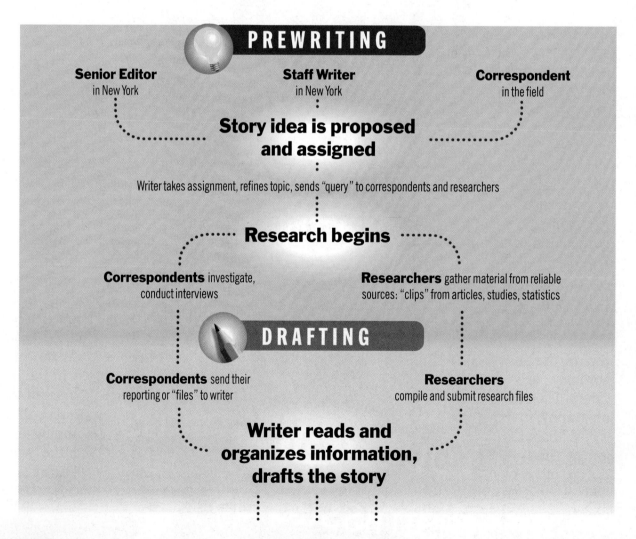

PREWRITING

Senior Editor
in New York

Staff Writer
in New York

Correspondent
in the field

Story idea is proposed and assigned

Writer takes assignment, refines topic, sends "query" to correspondents and researchers

Research begins

Correspondents investigate, conduct interviews

Researchers gather material from reliable sources: "clips" from articles, studies, statistics

DRAFTING

Correspondents send their reporting or "files" to writer

Researchers compile and submit research files

Writer reads and organizes information, drafts the story

REVISING

Editor reads draft, asks for revisions

Correspondents
check interpretation,
make suggestions

◀┈┈┈┈┈▶

Writer revises, resubmits for comments

◀┈┈┈┈┈▶

Researchers
check accuracy,
details

Writer and editor revise again, "green" (edit for length)

EDITING AND PROOFREADING

Checks for conformity to TIME
style and conventions

◀┈┈┈┈▶

Copy Desk

◀┈┈┈┈▶

Checks and corrects grammar,
mechanics, spelling

PUBLISHING AND PRESENTING

Managing Editor chooses to print, hold, or "kill" (omit) story

Circulation of TIME
rises or falls

◀┈┈┈┈▶

Readers respond to published story

◀┈┈┈┈▶

E-mail and letters
to the editor

Prewriting

Finding a Topic: Writing to Discover

Any piece of writing, whether it is personal or expository, begins as an idea. As TIME's Jesse Birnbaum explains, "In writing anything—whether it's a memo to the boss, a piece for TIME, or an essay for your high school English class—you have to know essentially what you want to say. You have to have an idea. There has to be

Jesse Birnbaum: Let one idea lead to another.

something you want to communicate." But discovering what your idea is can take some work. Many writers at TIME put pen to paper (or fingers to the keyboard) to find out what they have to say. They "think" on paper, writing freely until the topic takes shape.

Birnbaum wrote a feature for TIME on left-handedness, a piece that generated an enormous response from readers (see Letters to the Editor on the next page). As with many strong pieces of writing, this one arose out of Birnbaum's personal experience.

Birnbaum describes how he began:

❝ Deciding to write this story was fairly easy. I had read a scientific report carried in the daily papers reporting some findings about left-handed people. I was interested because I am a left-handed person, so I thought it might be fun to take this news story, deal with the actual news, and then go on and play around with the idea of the problems that left-handed people have in the modern world.

As I started writing, one idea led to another. I began with a sort of run-down, a lead about all the various impediments that befall left-handed people. And as I did it, fresher ideas occurred to me. So I just charged forward with it, with the idea that I would get everything down on paper that I could think of, and then go back and reshape it, trim it, organize it, and make it work as a whole. ❞

Writing freely can give you direction. As importantly, it can also show you when you must turn back and begin again. Advises Birnbaum: "If the idea doesn't strike you, if it suddenly doesn't start ringing bells and suggesting ideas immediately, then the topic really isn't for you."

WRITING TIP

"To become a good writer, practice, just as a would-be concert pianist must practice the piano. Write for the wastebasket if necessary; so what? Just keep writing."

—Jesse Birnbaum

The Perils of Being Lefty

Left-handed people are such a sorry lot. Though they are a minority (perhaps 10% of the population), no antidiscrimination laws protect them. They bump elbows with their partners at the dinner table. They are clumsy with scissors and wrenches. In a world designed and dominated by righties, they are condemned to a lifetime of snubs, of fumbling with gadgets and switches and buttons.

Possibly because of a stressful birth or because the left side of the brain sometimes doesn't know what the right side is doing, they suffer disproportionately from migraine headaches and stuttering. Since lefties also tend to be dyslexic, they are forever going right when they want to go left, transposing digits when they punch up phone numbers and, when writing words, getting their letters all mixed up.

Now they have something else to worry about. Two right-handed Ph.D.s, Diane F. Halpern of California State University and Stanley Coren of the University of British Columbia, reported in the *New England Journal of Medicine* last week that righties live longer than lefties.

The California study was quickly attacked by other researchers, who contended that other factors may be more relevant, such as illness or poverty. Still, the report cannot come as a complete surprise to lefties, who have suffered from superstition and suspicion for centuries.

—**Jesse Birnbaum**

DISCUSSION

1. Read the excerpt above from the opening paragraphs of Birnbaum's piece. What evidence is there in the final version of the freewriting Birnbaum did to explore his topic?
2. Birnbaum wanted to write this piece because he is left-handed. Is this an example of personal writing? How can personal experience be useful for other writing forms, such as persuasive or expository writing?
3. Recall a time when you abandoned one writing topic and found another. How did you know that the first topic wasn't for you?

TRY IT OUT
The power of the personal. Use your journal to write freely about a topic from your personal experience, as Jesse Birnbaum did in the process of creating his article on challenges facing left-handed people. Title the entry "The Perils of Being _____."

Letters to the Editor

In response to "The Perils of Being Lefty," TIME heard from more than 80 readers, many of whom quarreled with Jesse Birnbaum for "making us look like blundering, dyslexic idiots." Elina Subero of Houston wrote that she couldn't decide "which is more irritating, the article's flippant tone or the writer's obvious ignorance on the subject."

Lefty Birnbaum responded, "I am convinced that left-handed people are especially gifted, their occasional dyslexia notwithstanding. To those readers who took the story a bit too seriously, I can only urge them to lighten up and heed my call to arms: LEFTIES OF THE WORLD, UNTIE!"

Drafting

The Art of the Essay

Lance Morrow is a master of the essay. In TIME, essays can be satirical or serious, political or personal, light-hearted or impassioned. Morrow's pieces have been all these. He loves the essay for its freedom and for the opportunity it presents for the vigorous expression of an idea or viewpoint. "The point of an essay," says Morrow, "is to try to penetrate the essence of a particular question or controversy."

Lance Morrow: An essay is a dialogue.

Advice from an essayist:
THE ESSAY FORM

❝ An essay has to get at the core of the subject. Clarity is extremely important. What is the core? The irreducible dead core? But essays are great fun, too. Once you know what you want to say, you can play. You can do anything with an essay. ❞

GETTING STARTED

❝ To write an essay, begin with a subject. Make some sort of assertion about it. Then ask what further questions are raised by your initial question.

A good essay follows Newton's laws of motion: for every assertion, you can have an equal and opposite counter-assertion. Be absolutely clear and honest with yourself as a writer in making the assertion, then test it by the counter-assertions. An essay is having an argument with yourself. The more honest and clear the argument, the better the essay. ❞

ANTICIPATING OPPOSING VIEWS

❝ It's important to keep an open mind and constantly put yourself into the mind of others

who might have a different opinion. That doesn't mean I don't have opinions as a writer, but the opinions I express are smarter and more effective if the essay is able to embrace contrary points of view. To me, the interest arises in a truly honest dialogue with myself. ❞

THOUGHTS ON SHAPE
AND STRUCTURE

❝ Every essay has its own shape. I believe that you discover the shape in the process of writing. My essay will take the shape arising from my consideration of it. This is important: the essay has no pre-set, pre-ordained form. Get it out of your mind that you should write: kaboom, one, two, three, four, five. I don't think it works that way.

To me, you write an essay the way you talk to an intelligent friend. I think that to write essays, you should write letters. Like a letter, an essay takes the shape that the subject should take. ❞

Deconstructionist at the Super Bowl

Intellectuals love baseball, and they read sweet meanings into it. The game "has a mythic quality," Bernard Malamud thought—the myths being innocent democracy, recovered childhood, a harmless, universal cast of heroes (from Ruth and DiMaggio long ago to McGwire and Sosa in last year's memorable season) and a sentimental reconciliation, over peanuts and Crackerjacks, between the college-educated and the working man.

Overeducated fans turn baseball into "text." One historian sees the game as an American fertility rite. A professor of English at the University of Rochester, George Grella, has written that "while [baseball] radiates a spiritual transcendence, it also expresses a parallel paradoxical quality of sadness ... it instructs us in two crucial American concepts, the loneliness of space and the sadness of time."

I'm concerned that professional football has no such mythic dimension. I think that explains why football's television ratings have fallen off; ABC's *Monday Night Football*, for example, has just wound up the worst season in its 29 years on the air. I have located the problem. Pro football remains in bad odor among thinkers. It needs a richer intellectual tradition.

I was surprised several weeks ago at dinner when a friend of mine, the writer Ted Morgan, launched into a rhapsody about professional football. Ted, whose Sundays are lost from September to Super Bowl, loves what he calls "the beauty" of pro football—its power, its grace, its intelligence. Ted explains that football is a symbolic re-enactment of America's westward conquest of territory—while baseball is a "post-settlement" enterprise in which each team by turns pacifically yields the field to the other.

You don't run across this sort of profound reading of football every day. Ted inspired me to renew a lapsed relationship with the game, and eventually, as a favor to football, to cast about for an interpretive metaphysics.

I start by embroidering an obvious difference between baseball and football: the role of time. A baseball game may in theory go on forever: it ends only with the last out. Football binds itself to the tragedy of the clock. All mortals play with the clock running. Football faces up to the pressure and poignance of its deadline, the official's fatal, final gunshot. Or something like that.

—**Lance Morrow**

DISCUSSION

1. What question or controversy is the subject of "Deconstructionist at the Super Bowl"? Does Lance Morrow express a clear point of view on this question? What is it?

2. Morrow advises writers to let the subject of an essay suggest its structure. Refer to the table of Organizing Techniques in Lesson 2.7. What technique has Morrow chosen for "Deconstructionist at the Super Bowl"?

TRY IT OUT

Have a "conversation on paper." Identify an important issue in your school, your community, or in the news. Write a letter to a friend about the issue—a "conversation on paper"—in which you assert your own point of view and address the counter-assertions of others. Reread your writing and consider:

a. Did using the letter form help you tackle the issue with "clarity and honesty"?

b. What shape should an essay on this subject take? Select the organizing technique that fits it best.

Revising
The Editor's Role

At TIME, revision is a group project. A writer's completed draft is submitted to an editor who takes the lead in suggesting changes, much as a peer or teacher does in a writing conference. As Assistant Managing Editor Howard Chua-Eoan explains, a good editor can help you:

Revise for order and coherence

❝There is often a lot of revision of stories in TIME. Even the best writers need an editor. For example, sometimes you think you've figured everything out, but you've slid over an essential step in reasoning a story. So an editor will say: 'I know what you are trying to do and I agree with what you're trying to do, but you missed a step explaining how you got from this point to that point.' Then the writer can work on how to fix the problem. ❞

Match tone to purpose

❝Sometimes an editor can hear that a writer is using the wrong tone for the piece. I might tell a writer, 'This is a bit too humorous' or 'The story is too flat—try it again with something livelier.' ❞

Ensure accuracy

❝Researchers are huge contributors; they go through a story to make sure the facts are right. Similarly, the contributing correspondents get to have their say on whether or not the writer's version is accurate. Sometimes you might have a completely factual story, but the implications are all wrong. There is a lot of back and forth, lots of 'this is the opinion of the people here, this is the opinion of the people there,' and you have to work that out somehow. Because that's the process of journalism. We have to make sure we get the right story. Not just the best-told story, because sometimes the best-told stories are not the truest ones. But our stories need to be the truest and the best-told at the same time. ❞

Establish an identity as a writer

❝It used to be that TIME spoke with one voice, but now there are more and more voices in the magazine. Our Managing Editor, Walter Isaacson, is very good about letting individual voices spring to the fore and cultivating those voices so that our readers recognize them and attach a name to them.

Howard Chua-Eoan: Writing as theater.

So it's very important that an editor recognize the writer's tone, what his pacing is, what she brings to a story. There is a particular way of reasoning and talking and writing that editors have to be sensitive to, because that is what constitutes a writer's identity, an identity the readers sense and recognize. Once you start taking off the stylistic elements, then you're basically robbing the writer of his or her identity. 99

Find your voice

66 You should think of every sort of writing as a piece of theater. You are going onstage. One thing I always suggest to young writers is to read your story out loud and find out if this is the way you want it to sound. Then you can pace things. And don't just read your stories out loud, but read other people's stories out loud to see why they sound the way they do and why you like the way they sound.

I sometimes stop and read a paragraph over and over again out loud just to see if that's the way I really want it to sound. You can hear the cadences and syllables that may not be giving you the sound or the pace you want. So you have to hear yourself. 99

Tell powerful stories

66 I like looking for emotion, because I think emotion is what brings us into any kind of story, even those with the driest subject. It could be something very funny, or something really sad. But once you are confronted with emotion, you get drawn into it because it's a very revealing thing. You're seeing someone's heart, and you want to find out more and more. It could be something that drives an economic story, but economics are the lifeblood of our society, and if you can't make that somehow strike an emotional chord, then it won't be compelling. 99

LEARNING FROM THE EDITOR

DISCUSSION

1. How does the revision process used in your classroom compare to the revision process at TIME? If Howard Chua-Eoan were your partner in a writing conference, what questions would he have on his list to guide revision?

2. Recall or review a piece of writing you worked on that required a great deal of research. What were the special challenges of writing and revising this work? Why is it sometimes difficult for research writing to be both accurate and "well told"?

TRY IT OUT

1. Experimenting with tone. Read two pieces in your writing portfolio that are different in tone. What is the subject and purpose of each piece? Select a passage from one piece and rewrite it in the tone of the other. Does the rewritten passage still fit? Why?

2. Listening for "voice." In the library, locate an issue of TIME published before 1975. Read any two articles in the issue. How is the "voice" in each piece similar? What characterizes the voice? Compare that issue to a recent issue of TIME. Look for evidence that TIME writers today are given the freedom to write with distinctive voices. Try rewriting two short pieces from a current issue of TIME in the same voice. What do you have to change?

3. Finding your own "voice." Read a piece of your writing out loud. Underline the sections in which you hear a "voice" (rhythm, word choice, pace) that you like. What characterizes your writing voice? Circle sections that don't sound as you would like them to and revise, using your underlined sections as models.

Editing and Proofreading

Hunting for Errors

In the final stage of the writing process at TIME, every article passes under the sharp eyes of the copy editing staff. The copy editors are charged with finding and correcting errors in usage, style, and spelling.

Deputy Copy Chief Judy Paul identifies persistent problems that can sneak into the writing of even the most seasoned professional.

JAY COLTON FOR TIME

Judy Paul: On the lookout for errors.

Agreement

“We always change a sentence like 'Everyone expressed their opinion.' *Everyone* is singular, so the pronoun should be *his* or *her*, but that is awkward. The easiest way to fix this is to change the noun to a plural and then use the plural pronoun: 'All the students expressed their opinions.'”

Dangling modifiers

“This is an easy kind of mistake to make: 'Floating down the street, I saw a sheet of paper.' Some dangling modifiers are easy to fix. They hit you between the eyes. But sometimes we'll pass around a piece of copy to three or four people and say, 'What do you think? Is this a dangler? Do we need to fix it? Or is it not a dangler?' When in doubt, always change it. You're safer.”

Redundancy

“A lot of writers use the word *recent*, which is a journalistic no-no. If it wasn't a recent confer-

ence, for example, then why are we writing about it? But people use the words *recent* and *recently* all the time instead of pinning down a specific date. It's an easy way out.”

Run-on sentences

“We go through fashions in writing, and right now we are seeing more writers turning in copy that has long, run-on sentences separated by semi-colons. Why give a reader a ten-line run-on sentence when you can express the thought more clearly in two sentences?”

Italics

“A pet peeve of mine is to use italics for emphasis. I think it's a lazy way to write. You shouldn't have to put text in italics to show emphasis. Just rewrite it!”

LEARNING FROM THE EDITOR

TRY IT OUT

1. Spotting errors. What are the most common errors or stylistic weaknesses in your own writing? Punctuation problems? Awkward constructions? To come up with a list, look over a piece of writing you have revised and identify changes you made on your own or with the help of a teacher or peer editor. Did you fix any of the common errors on Judy Paul's list? Can you find any stylistic errors, such as lack of parallel construction, that slipped through the editing process? Fix them.

2. Create a class list of common errors and persistent problems. Provide an illustrating example for each. Post the list on the wall of the classroom and refer to it when you edit your own copy or the work of a classmate.

Publishing and Presenting

Readers and Writers

"How much should you care about people's reactions to the pieces that you write?" asks Staff Writer James Poniewozik:

"I think that a strong writer should pay close attention to the feedback he gets. Did you achieve the goal you wanted? If you write a piece and get responses that indicate that a lot of people thought you meant something the opposite of what you said, then you should go back and think. 'How did I write that? What can I learn from this for the future? How can I make my points better?'

There is a difference between listening to readers and writing to try to please others. That, I think, is ultimately no good for anybody. But it is easy to get arrogant, so you should be willing to take feedback and admit when you've been wrong."

"Tuesdays with Morrie"

For NBC's snarky *Will & Grace*, the book of heartfelt life lessons from dying professor Morrie Schwartz to his ex-student, sportswriter Mitch Albom, has become phenomenon enough to merit a punch line (a wealthy client fires Will, blithely telling him to read Albom's book and appreciate all he still has). But for the unironic masses who've kept this *memento Morrie* a best seller for more than 100 weeks, ABC has needle-pointed an Oprah Winfrey Presents telepic that's as earnest as life is short. However worthy the book, its *carpe diem* aphorisms don't translate well to a film that deploys every tear-jerking stratagem short of a poke in the eye.

—James Poniewozik

Letters to TIME

To the Editors:
Tell me–does James Poniewozik speak the way he writes? I read his review of *Tuesdays with Morrie* twice and I have no idea what he was really saying. Of course, I don't watch prime-time TV, so maybe that's my problem.
—Jeannie Boone

To the Editors:
I am a subscriber and I enjoy reading your magazine, but frequently your writers send me to the dictionary! My query: in James Poniewozik's article on *Tuesdays with Morrie*, I found a word that is not listed in my dictionary. Please define: *unironic!*
—A. O'Connor

LEARNING FROM THE WRITER

DISCUSSION
1. What can James Poniewozik learn from the letters he received about his review?
2. As a student writer, when do you get written feedback on your writing? Look back at written comments on one of your pieces.

What did you learn?
3. What do you think Poniewozik means when he says, "There is a difference between listening to readers and writing to please others"? Think about how pieces you have written would be different if pleasing the audience were

your primary purpose.

TRY IT OUT
Write a letter to the editor of a publication you read regularly. Try to give the writer the kind of feedback that will make his or her next published piece even better.

"*The swamp was thickly grown with great gloomy pines and hemlocks, some of them ninety feet high, . . .*"

—Washington Irving, "The Devil and Tom Walker"

UNIT 3 Descriptive Writing

Writing in the Real World

Descriptive writing requires strong observation skills as well as precise, informative word choices. The following excerpt is from an article written by Dr. Richard MacNeish and several other archaeologists for *American Antiquity,* a professional journal. It describes what he and the others unearthed in a cave near Orogrande, New Mexico, in 1991. Later in the article, the authors explain why those findings have led them to conclude that people have been living and hunting in North America far longer than scientists previously thought.

The Excavation

By Donald Chrisman, Richard S. MacNeish, Jamshed Mavalwala, and Howard Savage

. . . Crew member Aame Vennes . . . completed the excavation of the underlying gray loam of zone I, which contained three large flat rocks and two flat pieces of burned clay that may have indicated a hearth. As she screened the sediments of zone I, Vennes noticed a peanut-sized piece of burned clay that had unusual markings. Cunnar . . . , who supervised the entire excavation of [the cave], suspected that these markings represented a fingerprint. During the daily review of excavation results, MacNeish examined the clay, using tweezers and magnifying glass, and confirmed Cunnar's suspicion. . . . Because of the importance of this find, Cunnar took over excavation of the unit. In the 20-x-25-cm, 3-cm-thick burned clay in the square's northeast corner, he found a fractured middle phalange[1] of *Equus alaskae*[2] impaled by a stone wedge. When he broke up the original clay deposit, he found what seemed to be another print. At the southern edge of this clay slab he found . . . a piece of fractured horse phalange and a small crescentic[3] burned clay fragment with a tiny imprint. . . . A second slab of burned clay had charred oak remains that were dated to 32,000 ± 1200 B.P.[4] . . .

---

[1] A finger or toe bone of a vertebrate.
[2] An extinct species of horse.
[3] Shaped like a crescent moon, or the moon when it's in its first or last quarter.
[4] Before present.

A Writer's Process

Prewriting
Collecting the Evidence

The mystery engaging Richard MacNeish and his associate, Jane Libby, is this: When did people first appear in the New World? For years, archaeologists maintained that human beings migrated across the Bering Strait within the last 14,000 years. But in 1991, under MacNeish's direction, the Massachusetts-based Andover Foundation for Archaeological Research excavated an important site in New Mexico. What MacNeish's crew unearthed at Orogrande cave suggested to them that people may have lived and hunted on this continent as far back as 39,000 years ago.

Libby, a skilled writer and editor, often accompanies MacNeish on his digs. Libby spent her childhood rummaging around the ruins of an old building on her farm, digging up handmade nails and pieces of wooden buckets. Now she scrutinizes clues that as a novice she might have ignored.

"The first day I worked in the field," Libby recalls, "a well-trained archaeologist dumped a pail of dirt onto the screen, shook the screen to get the extra dirt off, and said, 'Look, there's a piece of pottery. There's another—and another.' And I said, 'How can you tell? It all looks like rocks to me.' But after a while, I could do the same thing. The more artifacts you see, the more easily you recognize them."

Finds such as the one at Orogrande illustrate why archaeologists pay strict attention to tiny details. "We got an ancient fingerprint on a piece of clay the size of a peanut," MacNeish explains.

"If somebody hadn't had sharp eyes, this baked clay would have been discarded as dirt. You have to know what you're looking for and, when you recognize it, to realize its significance."

Writing in the Real World

The picture on the upper right shows part of an excavated cave. The chalk-board resting against the cave wall tells the location; tags on the wall identify layers from various time periods. The artifacts shown here are bagged and labeled with identification numbers.

Drafting
Examining the Clues

As they excavate an area, MacNeish and his crew make notes about its soil, digging conditions, and features such as burials and fireplaces. They carefully map and measure each artifact they find before collecting it for later analysis. Back at camp, crew members write detailed descriptions from their notes. "It becomes very important to describe things well," says Libby, since the arti-facts might be studied by other scien-tists months later.

Like police work, archaeology often requires specialized scientific analysis to evaluate the evidence. "To prove our case that people arrived in the New World thousands of years earlier than previous estimates, it is going to take a lot of experts from a number of disciplines," notes MacNeish.

Once the scientific evidence is gathered, documented, and evaluated, MacNeish begins writing his report.

"Long before I sit down and start writing," MacNeish explains, "I make a very thorough outline of exactly what I'm going to write. I start by defining the problem or purpose of the article or monograph. Next I describe the methodology I used to collect and ana-lyze the data. Then I talk about the data and how they relate to the prob-lem." Finally he draws a conclusion from the data. "Either they show that I've solved the problem or that I have other problems still to be solved."

Revising/Editing
Unraveling the Mystery

"My work often takes some pretty heavy editing," the scientist admits. That's where Libby comes in. "I rewrite it and then it gets cor-rected again," MacNeish says, "so there may be two or three versions before the final one goes to the printer."

Publishing/Presenting

News of the Orogrande discovery spread quickly, and many groups and publications called upon MacNeish to share his findings. In writing for fellow archaeologists, he had to follow the strict guidelines used in his profession. Some journals, such as *American Antiquity,* print responses from other scholars challenging the findings of authors.

Writing informal speeches or arti-cles for the popular press challenges the archaeologist. MacNeish explains: "When I think about popular writing, I want a lead paragraph that gives all the sensational and interesting data first. Then, of course, I'm hoping that people will read the rest of it."

Examining Writing in the Real World

Analyzing the Media Connection

Discuss these questions about the article on page 124.

1. Describe the tone of the excerpt from MacNeish's article.

2. MacNeish states his major finding—a human fingerprint in North America dating back 32,000 years—with little fanfare. Why does MacNeish avoid dramatic language to announce this startling discovery?

3. What technical details does MacNeish include to establish the scientific integrity of his findings?

4. To what does MacNeish compare the size of the object that his associate, Vennes, found?

5. What is the significance of the discovery of the fingerprint?

Analyzing a Writer's Process

Discuss these questions about Richard MacNeish's Writing Process.

1. Why is it so important for archaeologists to be good observers?

2. Why is detailed description important in reporting archaeological findings?

3. What five steps does MacNeish follow when he writes his report for fellow archaeologists?

4. Why does MacNeish use the help of a writer/editor?

5. Explain how MacNeish modifies his archaeological writing to grab the attention of a general audience.

Use precise nouns and verbs.

As MacNeish states in his article, to make his writing clear he must "describe things well." One way to do this is to use precise nouns and verbs.

We got an ancient fingerprint on a piece of clay the size of a peanut.

The sentence below is ambiguous. It can be used to describe all the locations on the list below. Use more precise nouns and verbs to write five descriptive sentences.

Description: *This is a building in which people perform activities by themselves or with others.*

1. Apartment
2. Private house
3. School
4. Restaurant
5. Library

See Lesson 10.1, pages 435–441, and Lesson 10.3, pages 449–455.

Creating Vivid Description

Descriptive Writing

By organizing descriptive details effectively, you can bring a scene to life. Notice how writer Tony Hillerman uses this strategy to create an image of the Grand Canyon at twilight.

Literature Model

Here, two hundred feet below the earth's surface, the air moved down-canyon, pressed by the cooling atmosphere from the slopes above. Leaphorn heard the song of insects, the chirping of rock crickets, and now and then the call of an owl. A bullbat swept past him, hunting mosquitoes, oblivious of the motionless man. Once again Leaphorn became aware of the distant steady murmur of the river. It was nearer now, and the noise of water over rock was funneled and concentrated by the cliffs. No more than a mile and a half away, he guessed. Normally the thin, dry air of desert country carries few smells. But the air at canyon bottom was damp, so Leaphorn could identify the smell of wet sand, the resinous aroma of cedar, the vague perfume of piñon needles, and a dozen scents too faint for identification. The afterglow faded from the clifftops.

Tony Hillerman, *Listening Woman*

Hillerman appeals to the senses of touch, hearing, smell, and sight in his description.

Why do you think Hillerman includes so little in the way of visual description?

The order a writer uses to present descriptive details has a great effect on the way a reader perceives a scene. In the model above, Hillerman puts you at the bottom of the Grand Canyon and lets you sniff the air, feel the coolness, and hear the insects from that vantage point. The sensory description is filtered through Leaphorn's senses, and his perceptions help you imagine the scene as he experiences it.

Pick an Approach

Three possible ways of organizing descriptive details are by order of impression, order of importance, and spatial order. The method that you choose depends on what you are trying to emphasize, as the following chart demonstrates.

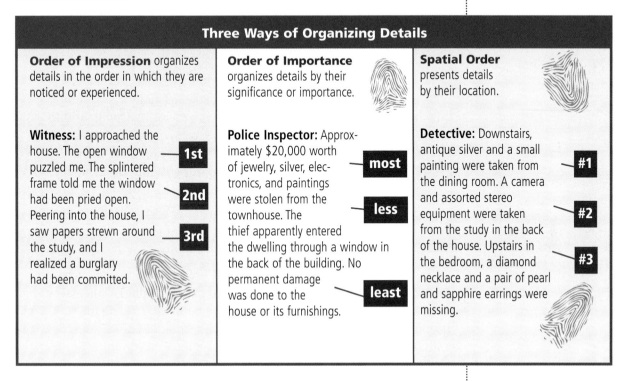

Three Ways of Organizing Details

Order of Impression organizes details in the order in which they are noticed or experienced.

Witness: I approached the house. The open window puzzled me. **1st** The splintered frame told me the window had been pried open. **2nd** Peering into the house, I saw papers strewn around the study, and I **3rd** realized a burglary had been committed.

Order of Importance organizes details by their significance or importance.

Police Inspector: Approximately $20,000 worth of jewelry, silver, electronics, and paintings **most** were stolen from the townhouse. The **less** thief apparently entered the dwelling through a window in the back of the building. No permanent damage was done to the **least** house or its furnishings.

Spatial Order presents details by their location.

Detective: Downstairs, antique silver and a small painting were taken from **#1** the dining room. A camera and assorted stereo equipment were taken **#2** from the study in the back of the house. Upstairs in the bedroom, a diamond **#3** necklace and a pair of pearl and sapphire earrings were missing.

For a witness, it makes sense to describe things in the order in which they were noticed—the order of impression. For the police inspector, using order of importance highlights the value of the stolen items. For the detective, spatial order helps to pinpoint locations of stolen items. Spatial order can also be effective in creating the sense of a room or of an unfolding landscape.

Journal Writing

Reread the model by Tony Hillerman on page 128. List in your journal all the words and phrases that grabbed your attention. Note the method of organization used in this passage.

Revising Tip

In the revising stage, think about the objects in your description and ask yourself questions such as, "What kind?" "What color?" "How big?" "How does it sound/feel/smell?"

Order of Impression

When you want to create a "you are there" feeling in your writing, organize your details by order of impression. Because it presents the narrator's changing reactions, order of impression has greater drama and urgency than does either spatial order or order of importance.

What is the narrator's initial impression as she enters?

The description is organized to reflect the narrator's impression and her reactions in response to the situation.

Model

I knew I was late for rehearsal as I tugged open the heavy metal fire door. But as I entered the theater, I felt like I was entering a tomb. As my eyes adjusted to the darkened auditorium, I realized that no one, absolutely no one, was there. The spotlights lit the vacant stage with a harsh white glare. I squinted up at the empty projection booth. My "Hello?" was met by eerie silence. I ran up on the stage, the wooden boards creaking loudly under my feet. The heavy black curtain was drawn. The freshly painted scenery stood in place. Pages of a script were scattered about the stage.

In the model above, the writer's use of order of impression allows the reader to identify with the narrator and to discover things as the narrator discovers them. At the end of the passage, you may be feeling the same confusion and discomfort as the narrator. This technique engages the reader and makes the reader feel involved in the action. Can you think of other ways this description might have been organized to create different reactions in a reader?

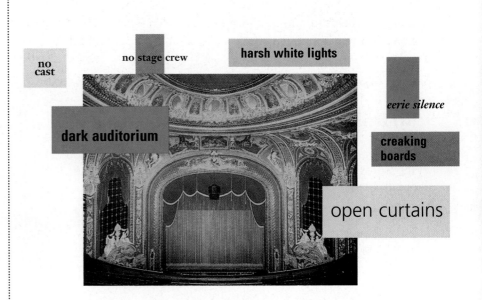

no cast

no stage crew

harsh white lights

eerie silence

dark auditorium

creaking boards

open curtains

Write a Description

Select a painting that you enjoy from this or another book. Imagine that it will be part of a showing of the artist's works. Write a description of the painting for the exhibit guide that will make the painting come alive for its viewers.

PURPOSE   To describe a painting for a museum guide
AUDIENCE   Museum visitors
LENGTH   2–3 paragraphs

WRITING RUBRICS   To write an effective description, you should

- choose an order for your details—order of impression, order of importance, or spatial order—and make sure the order suits your purpose

- as you write your description, ask yourself questions about what you see and experience when you look at the painting

- as you revise your description, substitute concrete nouns and descriptive adjectives to improve the writing

Using Computers

If you have access to a computer scanner, scan a photo of the artwork for your exhibit guide. Then design an illustrated page for the guide. Combine your page with those of other students and create a class exhibit guide.

Grammar Link

Adjectives describe nouns and enliven descriptions.

Adjectives such as *steady, damp,* and *resinous* in Tony Hillerman's paragraph can make a description come to life.

Revise this paragraph, adding precise adjectives to make it more vivid.

[1]As I approached the house, I saw a door and spotted chips of paint on the ground. [2]The sound of a dog barking stopped me. [3]I was about to turn away when I noticed a piece of paper lying in the grass. [4]The writing was hard to read, but the strokes looked familiar. [5]Judging by the note and the condition of the house, I knew my friend needed me to get inside those walls.

See Lesson 10.4, pages 456–461.

Viewing and Representing

RESEARCH   In the exhibit guide, include background information on the artist and how the artwork fits into his or her overall work. Why was the painting created? Was it in response to political or social turmoil? Does it represent a theme or life view that the artist developed in many works over a period of years?

Using Sensory Details

A writer pays special attention to colors, smells, sounds, and textures. Well-chosen words based on those sensations can draw the reader into a description, as in the following model by archaeologist Judith E. Rinard. Pay special attention to the way Rinard contrasts the darkness of the first paragraph with the startling colors in the last paragraph.

Literature Model

Down a dark passageway I slowly descended, groping my way between ancient stone walls. Before me, a guide carried a lamp that bobbed in the gloom and cast flickering shadows on the cold walls. With each hesitating step, I was penetrating farther into the Tomb of the Leopards, an Etruscan crypt deep in a lonely hillside in Italy. . . .

We soon reached the bottom of the passageway, and I blinked in the dim lamplight, peering anxiously ahead while my eyes adjusted to the subterranean darkness. For a moment I could distinguish nothing more than three stone walls of what looked like a plain little chamber. But then, as I stood watching, it happened.

The chamber exploded with color—vivid color. Bright, startling reds and yellows, emerald greens, and deep azure blues swam into view before me. And as I continued to watch, the room magically began to come alive.

Judith E. Rinard, *Mysteries of the Ancient World*

> Rinard's concrete details appeal to senses of touch and sight.

> What sense is emphasized in the final paragraph?

Observe Details

As you see in the model, archaeologist Judith Rinard uses sensory details to draw you into the splendor of the tomb. A less precise writer might have said, "It was a cold, dark tomb until you saw lots of colorful drawings on the walls." But a dedicated archaeologist, like a detective or a writer, constantly practices and develops the art of description. Notice how Rinard contrasts the darkness in the first paragraphs with the startling colors in the last paragraph.

However, you don't have to be an archaeologist to observe and use sensory details in your writing. Imagine for a moment that you are in a large urban bus station and are flooded with sensations. The chart below shows how your perception of such sensations could be translated into words and then transformed into more precise descriptions. What other items could you add under each sense? What words would describe these objects or impressions effectively?

Prewriting Tip

As you take notes for descriptions during prewriting, close your eyes and concentrate on the senses of hearing, taste, smell, and touch.

Sharpening the Focus			
Perception	**Focus**	**Sharper Focus**	**Sharpest Focus**
• Touch	• floor texture	• gritty underfoot	• rough as sandpaper
• Smell	• bus fumes	• noxious odor	• choking odor
• Sound	• PA system	• loud noise	• garbled, blaring voices
• Sight	• fluorescent lighting	• weird, sterile glow	• greenish-looking skin
• Taste	• granola bar	• stale	• hard, tasteless

As you look for settings and incidents to use in your writing, ask yourself questions like the following: What is most striking here? What does this remind me of? How could I express this sensation in my writing?

Journal Writing

Use your journal to record sensory details about objects you observe in your classroom. As you note each impression, sharpen the focus by taking it another step or two, by creating a chart like the one shown above. Include at least two observations for each of your five senses.

Revise for Effect

Noting details is only one part of the writer's job. Equally important is the task of selecting and arranging details to achieve the effects you want.

After reading the first draft of the bus station description below, the writer decided that the beginning was too abrupt. The writer also decided to elaborate on the lighting.

Student Model

As soon as I opened the grimy glass door, the bus station began its assault.

^ The first thing I thought was, "Wow, it smells bad in here!" I thought it was from the bus fumes. ~~Then there was the gritty floor and~~ that weird ~~fluorescent~~ lighting. There were lots of crying babies and little kids running around. I couldn't understand the garbled blare of the P.A. system. The last time I was there, I was eating a ~~stale~~ granola bar, and this guy came up ~~to me~~ and said, "Hey kid, gotta match?" Well, I don't carry matches so he was out of luck. I just shook my head and he walked away to ask someone else. I sat on those lousy wooden benches for about an hour until my bus came. ^ ^

made everyone look green. No one looked cheerful at that bus station. We all looked like victims of some new strain of the flue.

How does the revised beginning improve on the opening of the first draft?

The writer included additional details to emphasize the effects of poor lighting. How does the final sentence of the revision make the paragraph easier to understand?

Be aware that too many strong sensory details can numb your reader. Have you ever been bored because someone couldn't resist showing you every single picture of a recent family vacation? Writers also are tempted to provide too much information. It's smarter to pick a few good details and let these carry the description.

Write a Description

You may want to improve one of these sites in your community: a park, a shopping center, or an empty lot. Using sensory details, describe for the local government planning board the site as it is and as it could be.

PURPOSE To describe a community site
AUDIENCE Local planning board
LENGTH 3–4 paragraphs

WRITING RUBRICS To write an effective description, you should

- choose details that appeal to the senses
- sharpen your details with precise words
- arrange the details to create an effect

Listening and Speaking

COOPERATIVE LEARNING In a group of four, divide the painting shown into four quadrants and observe the painting for one full minute. Then list the details you recall from your section. Look at the picture again. Help one another add to the lists and sharpen your descriptions. Imagine yourselves within the painting and describe any smells, sounds, sights, and textures you perceive. Write a description of the scene, using as many sensory details as possible.

Cross-Curricular Activity

ART Thomas Hart Benton, who painted *July Hay,* was a regionalist artist. Write a research report about this art style and present it to the class.

Avoid double negatives.

Use only one negative word to express a negative idea.

Rewrite the following sentences to eliminate the double negatives.

1. The old dog can't hardly climb up the hill no more.
2. As I turned the corner, I couldn't hear nothing except my heart beating.
3. The student learned the library didn't have no more copies of the book.

See Lesson 18.6, pages 658–659.

Thomas Hart Benton, *July Hay,* 1943

Descriptive Writing

Creating a Mood

The overall feeling, or mood, of a piece of writing depends on the details used in it. Notice the contrast between the mood established in the photo below and the details used to develop the paragraph that follows it.

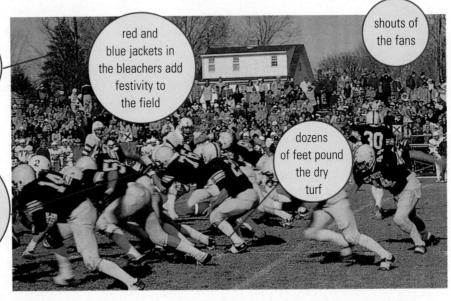

a crisp fall day

red and blue jackets in the bleachers add festivity to the field

shouts of the fans

dozens of feet pound the dry turf

a knot of black-and-yellow players surges forward over the line

Below is a description of the overall feeling, or mood, of another game. How does the mood in the paragraph below differ from the mood established in the photo?

The lack of time, the player's injury, and bad weather establish the mood of this description.

What specific words in this description create the overall mood of despair?

Model

The two-minute warning blared rudely across the field. Our star running back was out with a sprained ankle and we were down by ten points. The gloomy gray sky dropped a chilly rain on the band members, who seemed more intent on keeping their instruments dry than on tuning up for the fight song. I couldn't tell whether the wet, bedraggled cheerleaders were crying or wiping raindrops from their eyes.

Develop a Mood

Writers use mood to create an emotional response. It helps readers interpret what's on the page. When you write, you create mood through the details you choose and the language you use.

Some descriptions create stronger moods than others. Think about your purpose. Do you want your readers to get a sense of excitement as you describe the music during halftime? You can use words like "trill," "crash," and "jumping." Do you want to convey serenity? Words like "gentle," "wafted," and "familiar" may do the job. Here are some of the ways a writer could describe a high school band at halftime to convey different moods. As you read each sample, think about the mood the writer is trying to evoke.

Glee As the bright notes of the march filled the air, sunshine glinted on the golden horns, and the fluffy plumes of the band members' hats dipped and swayed like birds strutting in time to the music.

Disappointment Some winced at the off-key groans of the new French horn player.

Amusement Fans chuckled as a trombone player made a less than graceful turn and knocked the hat off the player in front of him.

Serenity The gentle strains of the Alma Mater, so familiar to the home fans, wafted over the clipped green field.

Excitement With a tremendous trill of the horns and a crash of the cymbals, the crowd jumped to its feet.

Journal Writing

Recall the last event you attended, such as a football game, a concert, or a school play. What was your mood at the time? Jot down descriptive words to portray your mood. Then consider the mood of someone else at the event—spectator or participant. Use descriptive words to capture that person's mood as you envision it.

Shift Moods

Sometimes you want to convey more than one mood in a piece of writing. Changing the mood in a description can alert readers to a change in feeling toward the subject or a shift in the action. In the passage below, N. Scott Momaday creates one mood to describe his grandmother's house when his grandmother was alive; the mood he evokes by his description of her house after her death is quite different. Think about the mood he creates in each paragraph below.

Literature Model

What mood does Momaday establish in the first paragraph?

Once there was a lot of sound in my grandmother's house, a lot of coming and going, feasting and talk. The summers there were full of excitement and reunion. . . . The aged visitors who came to my grandmother's house when I was a child were made of lean and leather, and they bore themselves upright. They wore great black hats and bright ample shirts that shook in the wind. They rubbed fat upon their hair and wound their braids with strips of colored cloth. Some of them painted their faces and carried the scars of old and cherished enmities. They were . . . full of jest and gesture, fright and false alarm. They went abroad in fringed and flowered shawls, bright beadwork and German silver. They were at home in the kitchen, and they prepared meals that were banquets. . . .

What details and language signal the change in mood?

Now there is a funeral silence in the rooms, the endless wake of some final word. The walls have closed in upon my grandmother's house. When I returned to it in mourning, I saw for the first time in my life how small it was. It was late at night, and there was a white moon, nearly full. I sat for a long time on the stone steps by the kitchen door. From there I could see out across the land; I could see the long row of trees by the creek, the low light upon the rolling plains, and the stars of the Big Dipper. Once I looked at the moon and caught sight of a strange thing. A cricket had perched upon the handrail, only a few inches away from me. My line of vision was such that the creature filled the moon like a fossil. It had gone there, I thought, to live and die, for there of all places, was its small definition made whole and eternal. A warm wind rose up and purled like the longing within me.

N. Scott Momaday, *The Way to Rainy Mountain*

Presenting Tip

When you present your writing by reading it aloud, you can create or emphasize a mood with vocal techniques such as a lowered voice, a drawn-out phrase, or increased speed.

3.3 Writing Activities

Write Scene Descriptions

Choose a setting you know well—your school, the street where you live, or someplace near your home. Think about the moods of this place at different times of the day. Mentally re-create for yourself three moods of your chosen place. Then write a paragraph describing each mood and what creates that mood.

PURPOSE To create different moods in writing
AUDIENCE Your classmates
LENGTH 3 paragraphs

WRITING RUBRICS To create different moods in writing, you should

- make a list of words and phrases that describe the different moods
- use descriptive details
- organize your descriptions to build a sense of the mood
- include transitions that show how the moods shift from one into the other

Cross-Curricular Activity

MUSIC Listen to two instrumental pieces of music, each of a different genre. You might select classical, jazz, blues, or folk compositions. As you listen, jot down a list of nouns, verbs, adjectives, and adverbs that characterize the mood evoked by each piece. Think about how tempo, loudness, repetition, phrasing, and sound elicit different sensations. Then describe the mood of each musical selection in one or two paragraphs.

Grammar Link

A subject must agree with its verb even when it follows that verb.

*It was late at night and there **was** a white **moon**, nearly full.*

Add a verb in the present tense to each of these inverted sentences. Make sure the verb agrees with the subject, not with the object of a preposition if there is one.

1. There ____ the most inspiring teachers ever.
2. Into the turbulent winds ____ the eagle.
3. Here ____ the dolphin and a diver.
4. There in the shadows ____ the detective, searching quietly for clues.
5. Outside the door ____ the applicants, hoping to be called for an audition.
6. In the hallway ____ the boy, waiting for his friend's class to end.
7. Which ____ the ones you want to bring home with you?
8. Up the tree trunk ____ the squirrel.

See Lesson 16.3, pages 604–605.

Viewing and Representing

CONVEYING MESSAGES Think of a movie you have recently seen or view a portion of a movie in a small group. Write a journal entry in which you reflect on how the director created mood using music, color, lighting, camera angles, weather conditions, and other factors. Be as specific as possible.

Descriptive Writing

Writing a Character Sketch

A character sketch is a quick profile that reveals personality and physical appearance. Notice how many characteristics are revealed in the model below about a favorite teacher.

Model

Mr. Kowalski should have been a weight lifter or a football player. Instead he's my driver's ed teacher. His frame is so big he can hardly fit behind the teacher's desk. His arms look as hard as metal beams under his pushed-up shirt sleeves. His bristly crew cut adds to the "tough guy" look.

Actually, Mr. Kowalski is a lot of fun. He really likes teaching and has a way of putting things that makes kids remember, like, "Don't brake for the birds; they'll take off on their own." He tells great stories about his days in the Marines. If anyone complains about an assignment, he says, "Lemme tell ya what they do with whiners in boot camp." There are always a bunch of students talking to him about cars or engines or anything. Mr. Kowalski is a friend as well as a teacher.

> Why do you think the writer begins with a physical description?

> How does the writer show that "Mr. Kowalski is a lot of fun"?

Can you really convey the essence of a person in writing? Answer these questions when you are planning a character sketch:

- How does the person look, move, and speak?
- How does the person behave toward others?
- How do others react to this person?
- What character traits does the person have?
- What anecdotes and examples would illustrate these traits?
- What overall impression should my description convey?

Focus on the Person

We know the people around us through their appearance and behavior. Over time, we also learn their values and beliefs. A successful character sketch conveys values, beliefs, and personality through the external evidence of appearance and behavior.

Behavior: friends with Janet M. and Marty B., babysits brother after school, volunteers in literacy program, swims every day, reads mystery novels.

Underlying Personality: adores little brother, wants to attend an all-women's college, believes honesty is her most important trait, can't stand to see animals suffer.

Appearance: curly black hair, gray eyes, big smile, pierced ears, wears pink.

Some parts of your sketch may relate basic information, such as "the man was nearly eighty years old." Other parts may use physical description to reveal behavior or personality. If you tell your readers that someone has "sunburned, muscular arms," for example, you suggest someone who works outside.

Be careful that you don't trap yourself or your readers into easy conclusions, however. To some, a soft voice implies shyness, yet a small voice may mask determination; gray hair can imply old age, or it may simply be a genetic trait. People defy stereotypes. Some football players dance to keep fit; not all grandmothers enjoy needlepoint. If you find yourself stereotyping someone's personality, dig a little deeper.

> **Editing Tip**
>
> When editing a character sketch, refer to Lesson 10.2, pages 442–448, to be sure you have used pronouns correctly.

Journal Writing

How do you appear to others? Brainstorm a list of your physical characteristics, your behaviors, your beliefs, and your attitudes to create a multi-layered diagram of your own character.

Add Clues to Character

You can add to what you know about a person and improve a character sketch by evaluating objects like the ones below.

Grandmother was the youngest of five girls who sang together.

She wore this shawl the day she married Grandfather, a violinist.

She loved opera and musical comedy.

She wrote to her mother every week when she and Grandfather were performing.

Notice how Maya Angelou uses "printed voile dresses," "flowered hats," and "gloves" to convey character in the model below.

Literature Model

> Angelou begins by describing how Mrs. Flowers looked.

Mrs. Bertha Flowers was the aristocrat of Black Stamps. . . . She was thin without the taut look of wiry people, and her printed voile dresses and flowered hats were as right for her as denim overalls for a farmer. She was our side's answer to the richest white woman in town.

> What does Angelou mean by this sentence?

Her skin was a rich black that would have peeled like a plum if snagged, but then no one would have thought of getting close enough to Mrs. Flowers to ruffle her dress, let alone snag her skin. She didn't encourage familiarity. She wore gloves too.

I don't think I ever saw Mrs. Flowers laugh, but she smiled often. A slow widening of her thin black lips to show even, small white teeth, then the slow effortless closing. When she chose to smile on me, I always wanted to thank her. The action was so graceful and inclusively benign.

> What is Angelou's attitude toward Mrs. Flowers? How do you know?

She was one of the few gentlewomen I have ever known, and has remained throughout my life the measure of what a human being can be.

Maya Angelou, *I Know Why the Caged Bird Sings*

Write a Character Sketch

Think of a truly colorful character you have known. Perhaps it's someone you admire or find frightening, dignified, or very funny. Try to understand why this person is so vivid to you. For instance, Maya Angelou remembers Mrs. Flowers as "one of the few gentlewomen I have ever known." Then write a character sketch of the person, letting your description flow from that understanding.

PURPOSE To convey a character
AUDIENCE Someone who has never met the person being described
LENGTH 2–4 paragraphs

WRITING RUBRICS To create a vivid character sketch, you should

- decide on the overall impression you want to convey
- include details showing the person's behavior, appearance, and personality
- describe possessions and other objects that reveal character

Viewing and Representing

INTERPRETING CHARACTER A great deal can be learned and imagined from studying the subject of a portrait. View a portrait in this or another book or check the National Portrait Gallery Web site. How would you describe the subject of the painting? What personality traits do you infer from the subject's expression, position, and body language, and from objects included in the painting? What attitude might the painter have had toward the subject? Write a two- or three-paragraph character sketch based on these factors.

Grammar Link

Watch for subject-verb agreement with collective nouns.

Use a plural verb with a collective noun if the noun is referring to each group member individually:

*There **are** always a **bunch** of students talking to [Mr. Kowalski]. . . .*

Use a singular verb if the collective noun refers to the group as a whole.

Write a pair of sentences for each collective noun listed below. In the first sentence, use the collective noun as a singular subject; in the second sentence use it as a plural subject. Make sure the subject and verb agree.

1. flock of sparrows
2. jury
3. my mother's team
4. school committee
5. population

See Lesson 16.4, pages 606–607.

Using Computers

A word processing program can help you organize your character sketch. If your word processor has an outlining feature, you can use it to lay out the main ideas of the sketch. You can then use cut, copy, and paste commands to experiment with different sequences of text.

Describing an Event

After an accident, many people say, "It all happened so fast!" In the model below, notice how the action is slowed down as every detail is presented from the point of view of the narrator in the front seat of her car.

Literature Model

Behind me, the Dodge had made a U-turn and was now accelerating as it headed straight at me again. I ground at the starter, nearly singing with fear, a terrified eye glued to my rearview mirror where I could see the pickup accumulating speed. The Dodge plowed into me, this time with an impact that propelled the VW forward ten yards with an ear-splitting BAM. My forehead hit the windshield with a force that nearly knocked me out. The safety glass was splintered into a pattern of fine cracks like a coating of frost. The seat snapped in two and the sudden liberation from my seat belt slung me forward into the steering wheel. The only thing that saved me from a half-rack of cracked ribs was the purse in my lap, which acted like an air bag, cushioning the blow.

Sue Grafton, *G Is for Gumshoe*

> How do words like "behind," "straight," "rearview," and "forward," help the reader understand the event?

> Grafton uses strong, active verbs in this passage. Identify some of them.

Choose a Vantage Point

Because events involve time and motion, they are sometimes harder to describe than static scenes. Writers need to place an event into a logical sequence of clearly linked actions and reactions. The vantage point from which those actions are witnessed must be clear and consistent so the reader can follow what's happening.

Descriptive Writing

The chart shows the reactions of three people observing a fire from different vantage points.

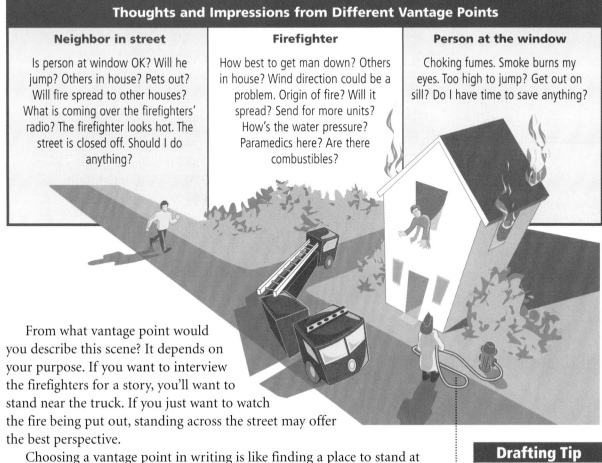

Thoughts and Impressions from Different Vantage Points

Neighbor in street	Firefighter	Person at the window
Is person at window OK? Will he jump? Others in house? Pets out? Will fire spread to other houses? What is coming over the firefighters' radio? The firefighter looks hot. The street is closed off. Should I do anything?	How best to get man down? Others in house? Wind direction could be a problem. Origin of fire? Will it spread? Send for more units? How's the water pressure? Paramedics here? Are there combustibles?	Choking fumes. Smoke burns my eyes. Too high to jump? Get out on sill? Do I have time to save anything?

From what vantage point would you describe this scene? It depends on your purpose. If you want to interview the firefighters for a story, you'll want to stand near the truck. If you just want to watch the fire being put out, standing across the street may offer the best perspective.

Choosing a vantage point in writing is like finding a place to stand at the scene of a fire; it selects and limits the details available to you. Therefore, it is important to determine your purpose in writing before choosing your vantage point.

Drafting Tip

As you draft a piece, be sure to alert the reader when you shift vantage points. Begin a new paragraph, or say something like "Meanwhile, at Sue's house . . ."

Journal Writing

Think of an event you described differently from the way someone else described it. It might have been an accident, a party, an athletic event, or even a scene from a movie. List in your journal some reasons why you think your impressions might have differed from those of other people.

Test Your Description

Keep these questions in mind when you describe an event:

- Is my vantage point clearly defined and consistent?
- Can I see, hear, smell, taste, or touch the things I describe from my vantage point?
- Is the passage of time logical and believable?

Remember that your readers can't ask you questions. Your writing has to stand by itself. Look at this model to see what to avoid.

> **Disarming the burglar alarm should have come at the beginning.**

> **Which part of the model is inconsistent with the vantage point of the rest of the model?**

> **What piece of information do you need to understand this sentence?**

Model

The thief rummaged in the drawers for valuables. Before that, he disarmed the burglar alarm. When he found nothing in the dining room, he went into the back bedroom. When he saw the police car pull up in front of the house, he grabbed the earrings and slithered out the back window, leaving a thin trail of blood on the white carpet.

In this model Diona Haley demonstrates how to use different, yet clearly defined and consistent, vantage points.

> **From what vantage point would someone hear this dialogue?**

> **Where does the vantage point change in this passage? How does Diona alert you to the change?**

Model

As the man lingered between life and death, his wife's cries were drowned out by that word no one wants to hear. "Flatline!" "Get the pads, set it at three hundred. Ready, clear!" A long pause. "Again at five hundred!" Another pause. "We're losing him. Once more, ready, CLEAR!"

The doctors didn't realize what was going on in his seemingly lifeless brain. His sixteenth birthday, the red car. Graduation, college, his job. His wife. Thirty long beautiful years. Where did it go? Why didn't he make his life more meaningful, enjoy it, and not take it for granted? . . . Why didn't he tell his wife how much he really loved her? Wait, it doesn't have to be this way. Fight it! You can do it, fight!

"We got him!" A big sigh of relief, then the bustling resumed. "Good job, Doctor, he gets another chance now."

Diona Haley, Centennial High School, Pueblo, Colorado

Write a News Story

From a history textbook, select a painting illustrating a historical event. Write an account of the event for a local newspaper. Describe the event in three paragraphs, each from a different vantage point within the painting.

PURPOSE To describe an event from different vantage points

AUDIENCE Readers of a newspaper

LENGTH 3 paragraphs

WRITING RUBRICS To describe an event from different vantage points, you should

- select plausible vantage points from which to describe the event

- maintain a consistent vantage point in each paragraph

- make sure that events and passage of time make sense from each vantage point

Viewing and Representing

COMMUNICATING MEANING Locate an exciting, dramatic photograph of an athlete in action. What action is taking place? What emotions show on the face of the athlete? What is the vantage point of the photographer? How does this vantage point affect the photo? What message is the photographer presenting through this image? Write a paragraph about the photo and its possible effect on the viewer.

Grammar Link

Use adjective clauses to make descriptions more interesting.

A *restrictive clause* is needed to make a sentence's meaning clear; it is not set off with commas. A *nonrestrictive clause,* which is set off with commas, is not essential to meaning. Note the clauses in Sue Grafton's sentence:

> The only thing **that saved me from** . . . cracked ribs was the purse in my lap, **which acted like an air bag** . . .

Add a restrictive and a nonrestrictive clause to each sentence below.

1. Mary Nolan pried open the door.
2. The curator hung the painting.
3. The messenger delivered the letter.
4. The child raced through the book.
5. Rico Alvarez squeezed into the shoes.

See Lesson 13.5, pages 542–544.

Listening and Speaking

COOPERATIVE LEARNING In groups of three, observe an event at your school, such as a theatrical production, an athletic competition, or a dance. Each person in the group should assume a different vantage point and make notes to use in describing the event. Discuss and compare your impressions of the event, emphasizing the differences.

Writing About Mood in a Play

Specific elements, such as setting and character description, contribute to the mood of a play. When you write about mood, describe the elements that contribute to it. Then it might be interesting to analyze the effect each element has.

Describe the Mood

The name *Sherlock Holmes* on a book or a play might lead many readers to assume that they are about to experience suspense. As you read the following model, look for elements that help convey suspense.

Edward Gorey,
The Listing Attic, 1954

Literature Model

Pathetic music, very p.p. (pianissimo, or very soft)
   A pause—no one moves.
   [Enter ALICE FAULKNER. *She comes down a little—very weak —looking at* LARRABEE, *then seeing* HOLMES *for first time.]*
   [Stop music.]
   HOLMES *[on seeing* ALICE *rises and puts book on mantel. After a brief pause, turns and comes down to* LARRABEE*]:* A short time since you displayed an acute anxiety to leave the room. Pray do not let me detain you or your wife—any longer.

[*The* Larrabees *do not move. After a brief pause,* HOLMES *shrugs shoulders slightly and goes over to* ALICE. HOLMES *and* ALICE *regard each other a moment.*]

ALICE: This is Mr. Holmes?

HOLMES: Yes.

ALICE: You wished to see me?

HOLMES: Very much indeed, Miss Faulkner, but I am sorry to see— [*placing chair near her*] —you are far from well.

ALICE [*a step.* LARRABEE *gives a quick glance across at her threateningly and a gesture of warning, but keeping it down*]: Oh no— [*Stops as she catches* LARRABEE'S *angry glance.*]

HOLMES [*pausing as he is about to place chair and looking at her*]: No? [*Lets go of his chair.*] I beg your pardon—but—[*Goes to her and takes her hand delicately—looks at red marks on her wrist. Looking up at her.*] What does this mean?

ALICE [*shrinking a little. Sees* LARRABEE'S *cruel glance*]: Oh— nothing.

Arthur Conan Doyle and William Gillette, *Sherlock Holmes*

Prewriting Tip

Music can be one of the strongest elements contributing to mood in a dramatic production. When prewriting an essay on mood in drama, you may want to begin by analyzing the contribution of the music.

To describe the mood in *Sherlock Holmes,* begin with a chart like the one below. Such a chart helps you isolate and analyze elements contributing to the mood of a play.

Mood (Suspenseful)			
Dialogue	**Characters**	**Action**	**Music**
"You are far from well. . . . What does this mean?"	man with threatening glances; fearful woman	Holmes examines marks on Alice Faulkner's wrist	soft, serene, as Alice Faulkner enters

Journal Writing

What kind of mood is set by the theme music or opening credits of a popular television show or movie you have seen? Write about the music, images, lighting, scenes, or other elements that help create the mood of the program or movie.

Analyze the Mood

Jennifer Spiher analyzed mood in "The Final Hour," an episode from the old radio mystery drama series known as *The Shadow*. "The Final Hour" is the dramatic story of the efforts of Lamont Cranston, also known as The Shadow, to save an innocent man from execution.

Analyzing the elements that contribute to mood in a play can help a writer focus and organize an essay. For example, which sound effects have the biggest impact in "The Final Hour"? How do the sound effects make the listener feel? What is the effect of the repetition of these sounds?

Notes like those below helped Jennifer organize her thoughts and decide which elements to emphasize and which to eliminate from her essay. What element seems to be most important?

Student Model

Sound effects--which have biggest impact?
- --footsteps
- --slamming cell door
- --ticking clock...
  - clock ties into title/ Final Hour/passing time
- Emphasize idea of repetition
- ~~Music: mention theme song?~~
- Importance of the word "shadow"

> Where does Jennifer summarize her analysis of the mood of this play? Do you find this effective? Why or why not?

> Jennifer gives examples of each element that she has identified as contributing to mood: character, dialogue, and sound effects.

> Are there any elements that Jennifer does not discuss that you would have included? Which ones?

"The Final Hour" is a dramatic play which was broadcast over radio in 1954. The playwright, Jerry McGill, creates a feeling of suspense for the reader. Defined by Webster as "a state of uncertainty or anxiety," suspense is conveyed through the characters, dialogue, and sound effects of this play. The main character, Lamont Cranston's alter ego, The Shadow, is a good example of suspense as created through characters. The word "shadow" compels the reader to envision dark corners and lurking figures, thus helping to produce a sense of apprehension. Another example is Sam Walker. His frantic actions at Barton's Tavern on the night Jim Martin is to be executed convey to the reader a sense of uncertainty as to Jim's fate. . . . This feeling of urgency is also produced by the constant ticking of the clock in Sam's house. Finally, by repeating the phrase "final hour" in the dialogue, Jerry McGill causes the reader to recall Jim Martin's predicament and to feel anxiety.

Jennifer Spiher
Rangeview High School, Aurora, Colorado

Write a Review

Watch a movie, play, or television show. Then write a review for a local newspaper. Analyze the mood of the production, beginning with a general statement, followed by supporting details.

PURPOSE To describe and evaluate the mood of a dramatic production

AUDIENCE Readers of the local newspaper

LENGTH 3–4 paragraphs

WRITING RUBRICS To evaluate the mood in a dramatic production, you should

- include discussion of mood-creating elements such as setting, dialogue, and music
- emphasize two or three elements
- analyze how the elements make the viewer feel

Using Computers

With a word processor, try using the cut-and-paste feature to organize your review. You might find it effective to build your case by starting with subtle details, or you may find your review works better with the strong details first. The cut-and-paste feature will let you move sentences around to see what works best.

Listening and Speaking

PRESENTATION Check your review to be sure you have supported your interpretation of the mood of the movie, play, or TV show with examples. Then read your review aloud to the class. Involve your listeners by altering your pace, raising and lowering your voice, and pausing appropriately as you read.

Grammar Link

Use adverbs to make meaning more specific.

Precise adverbs, such as *slightly, delicately,* and *threateningly* in the Literature Model, help define action very precisely.

Add adverbs to each sentence to show the kind of emotion listed.

1. *Excitement:* He approached the room, opened the door, and stepped in.
2. *Fear:* He approached the room, opened the door, and stepped in.
3. *Anger:* She glanced at the groom before tossing the bridal bouquet.
4. *Optimism:* She glanced at the groom before tossing the bridal bouquet.
5. *Apprehension:* The child slept during the night as the leaves rustled in the wind.
6. *Serenity:* The child slept during the night as the leaves rustled in the wind.
7. *Anxiety:* The challenger folded her hands as last year's champion completed her dive.
8. *Relief:* The challenger folded her hands as last year's champion completed her dive.
9. *Joy:* Facing an empty nest, the parents prepare for the next stage of their lives.
10. *Sadness:* Facing an empty nest, the parents prepare for the next stage of their lives.

See Lesson 10.5, pages 462–467.

Writing Process in Action

Descriptive Writing

In preceding lessons you've learned how to use descriptive details to paint effective word pictures of events, characters, and moods. You've had the opportunity to write a character sketch and to describe an event in a news story. Now it's time to apply what you've learned. In this lesson you're invited to create an idea for a television screenplay and then describe it.

Assignment

Context	You have an idea for a story that you would like to see produced as a television movie. You have decided to send several producers a brief description that will evoke the setting, paint a portrait of the main character or characters, and reveal something about the central conflict. You are hoping that this sketch will arouse their curiosity and spark their interest in seeing more of what you have in mind.
Purpose	To create a strong and effective description of a character and a setting that establishes personality, mood, and conflict
Audience	Several television producers
Length	1–2 pages

Visit the Writer's Choice web site at **writerschoice. glencoe.com** for additional writing prompts.

You will want to involve your audience so intensely in your description that they want to know more. If an idea for a character, setting, and conflict doesn't immediately occur to you, however, don't be concerned. Subjects for your sketch are all around you—in your everyday experiences, in your hopes and dreams, and in your reading.

The following pages can help you plan and write your description. Read through them and refer to them as you need to. But remember: you're in charge of your own writing process.

Prewriting

To get an idea for your story, tap into your memory by freewriting or clustering, or jump-start your imagination by asking yourself *what if* questions. What if you awoke one day to find that you had turned into an enormous animal? What if there really were time machines that you could travel in? Once you have an idea, use the Prewriting Questions at the right to begin making notes.

As you play with various combinations of setting, character, and conflict, keep your goal in mind. For example, you'll want your setting to serve as more than just background. In "The Signature," author Elizabeth Enright establishes a mood that affects the character and acts as an element of the conflict.

Prewriting Questions

- What kind of conflict does the character experience?
- What does the character look like?
- Where is the action taking place?
- What time of year is it?
- What point of view will I use?

Literature Model

The street was dark, though light was glimmering through the cracks of the closed shutters. What was left of sunset, green as water, lay on the western horizon. Yet was it really western? In a sky of new stars, was it not possible and in fact probable that what I had believed to be the sun was not really Sun at all? Then what were the compass points, what were the easts and wests of this city? And what would I find when once I found myself?

Elizabeth Enright, "The Signature"

Cluster, brainstorm, or freewrite to collect as many concrete details as you can about your own setting.

Now get to know your main character. This person should be so clear in your mind that you understand not only what he or she might think or do in a particular situation, but also how others will react. You will also need to suggest the struggle—inner turmoil or external troubles—experienced by the character. Once you have some workable ideas, generate the details that bring your sketch to life.

Finally, make some decisions about point of view. If you use a first-person narrator, you can establish a sense of immediacy and intimacy. With third-person point of view, you provide an invisible observer.

Drafting

Begin by giving your readers enough information to pull them immediately into the situation. Present the main character engaged in the conflict, create atmosphere by describing the setting, or use dialogue to reveal the situation.

Since you will be concentrating primarily on description to reveal character, conflict, and setting, consider carefully the order in which you will present your descriptive details.

Keep in mind that drafting should be a fluid process in which you get ideas down on paper without pausing to polish. Think also about which details you will use to bring the setting and character to life.

Finally, draft a conclusion that leaves your readers wanting more. Unlike a complete narrative, your sketch might end with a provocative question or a detail that stimulates the imagination.

Revising

To begin revising, read over your draft to make sure that what you've written fits your purpose and audience. Then have a writing conference. Read your draft to a partner or a small group. Use your audience's reactions and the following Revising Checklist to help you evaluate your work.

Drafting Tip

For more information on different ways to organize descriptions, see Lesson 3.1, pages 128–131.

Revising Tip

For suggestions on how to establish mood, see Lesson 3.6, pages 148–151.

Revising Checklist

- Have I established a clear perspective on setting, mood, character, and conflict?
- Are my details concrete and vivid? Have I used all five senses?
- Does my method of organization work with my purpose for writing?
- Have I chosen an effective point of view?

Editing/Proofreading

Once you are happy with the basic content and setup of your description, **proofread** it carefully for errors in grammar, usage, mechanics, and spelling. Use the questions at the right as a guide.

In addition to proofreading, use the Self-Evaluation list below to make sure your description does all the things you want it to do. When you're satisfied, make a clean, legible copy of your description and proofread it one more time.

Self-Evaluation

Make sure your description—

- ✔ creates mood, reveals character, and suggests conflict
- ✔ employs concrete and vivid language to evoke the five senses
- ✔ employs a method of organization appropriate to the purpose
- ✔ uses unity and coherence to create a clear impression
- ✔ follows the standards of grammar, usage, and mechanics

Publishing/Presenting

If you think your sketch is good television-movie material, collect the names of some producers that appear in the credits at the end of shows. Send these producers a copy of your description with a letter explaining why your approach will appeal to the public.

You might also turn the sketch into a screenplay that you and classmates can work on together and videotape.

Editing/Proofreading Checklist

- Do my subjects and verbs agree?
- Have I avoided double negatives?
- Have I used commas correctly with clauses?
- Have I avoided run-on sentences?
- Are all the words spelled properly?

Proofreading Tip

For proofreading symbols, see page 92. Consider using the spellchecking feature if you have composed on the computer.

Journal Writing

Reflect on your writing process experience. Answer these questions in your journal: What do you like best about your descriptive writing? What was the hardest part of writing it? What did you learn in your peer review session? What new things have you learned as a writer?

Literature Model

With a background in art, Elizabeth Enright (1909–1968) established herself as an illustrator of children's books and a writer of short stories. In the following story, "The Signature," Enright draws a striking portrait of a strange city and an alienated character mystified by both her surroundings and her own identity. As you read, look for the descriptive details Enright uses to convey setting and mood.

The Signature

by Elizabeth Enright

The street was wide and sloped gently upward ahead of me. It was paved with hardbaked dust almost white in the early-afternoon light, dry as clay and decked with bits of refuse. On either side the wooden houses stood blind to the street, all their shutters closed. The one- and two-story buildings—some of them set back a little; there was no sidewalk—had door yards with dusted grass and bushes, but many of them stood flush to the road itself with nothing but a powdered weed or two for grace. All of the houses had an old, foreign look, and all were unpainted, weather-scoured to the same pale color, except for the eaves of some which had been trimmed with wooden zigzags and painted long ago, like the crude, faded shutters, in tones of blue or red.

Literature Model

The sky was blanched[1] with light, fronded with cirrus, unemphatic; just such a sky as one finds near the sea, and this, in addition to the scoured, dry, enduring look of the town, persuaded me that an ocean or harbor must be somewhere near at hand. But when I came up over the rise of the road, I could find no furred line of blue at any horizon. All I could see was the great town—no, it was a city—spread far and wide, low lying, sun bleached, and unknown to me. And this was only one more thing that was unknown to me, for not only was I ignorant of the name of the city, but I was ignorant of my own name, and of my own life, and nothing that I seized on could offer me a clue. I looked at my hands: they were the hands of a middle-aged woman, coarsening at the joints, faintly blotched. On the third finger of the left hand there was a golden wedding ring, but who had

1 **blanched** (blanchd): made pale

Giorgio de Chirico, *Piazza d'Italia* (detail), 1912

put it there I could not guess. My body in the dark dress, my dust-chalked shoes were also strangers to me, and I was frightened and felt that I had been frightened for a long time, so long that the feeling had become habitual— something that I could live with, in a pinch, or, more properly, something that until this moment I had felt that I could live with. But now I was in terror of my puzzle.

I had the conviction that if I could once see my own face, I would remember who and what I was, and why I was in this place. I searched for a pane of glass to give me my reflection, but every window was shuttered fast. It was a season of drought, too, and there was not so much as a puddle to look into: in my pocket there was no mirror and my purse contained only a few bills of a currency un- known to me. I took the bills out and looked at them; they were old and used and the blue numerals and characters engraved on them were also of a sort I had never seen before, or could not remember having seen. In the cen- ter of each bill, where ordinarily one finds the pictures of a statesman or a monarch, there was instead an angular, spare symbol: a later- ally elongated diamond shape with a heavy vertical line drawn through it at the center, rather like an abstraction of the human eye. As I resumed my walking I was aware of an impression that I had seen this symbol recently and often, in other places, and at the very moment I was thinking this I came upon it again, drawn in chalk on the side of a house. After that, watching for it, I saw it sev- eral times: marked in the dirt of the road, marked on the shutters, carved on the railing of a fence.

It was this figure, this eye-diamond, which reminded me, by its persistence, that the eye of another person can be a little mirror, and now

with a feeling of excitement, of possible hope, I began walking faster, in search of a face.

From time to time I had passed other peo- ple, men and women, in the street. Their dark, anonymous clothes were like the clothes of Italian peasants, but the language they spoke was not Italian, nor did it resemble any language I had ever heard, and many of their faces had a fair Northern color. I noticed when I met these people that the answering looks they gave me, while attentive, were nei- ther inimical[2] nor friendly. They looked at me with that certain privilege shared by kings and children, as if they possessed the right to judge, while being ignorant of, or exempt from, accepting judgment in return. There is no answer to this look and appeal is difficult, for one is already in a defensive position. Still, I had tried to appeal to them; several times I had addressed the passers-by hoping that one of them might understand me and tell me where I was, but no one could or would. They shook their heads or lifted their empty hands, and while they did not appear hostile, neither did they smile in answer to my pleading smiles. After they had passed I thought it strange that I never heard a whisper or a laugh or any added animation in their talk. It was apparently a matter of complete indiffer- ence to them that they had been approached in the street by a stranger speaking a strange language.

Knowing these things I thought that it might be difficult to accomplish my purpose, and indeed this proved to be the case. The next people I met were three women walking together; two were young and one was middle-aged. I approached the taller of the young women, for her eyes were on a level

---

2 **inimical** (in im′i kəl): unfriendly or hostile

with my own, and looking steadily into them and coming close, I spoke to her.

"Can you tell me where I am?" I said to her. "Can you understand what I am saying?"

The words were a device. I expected no answer and got none of any sort. As I drew close she looked down at the ground; she would not meet my gaze. A little smile moved the corners of her lips, and she stepped aside. When I turned to her companions they also looked away, smiling. This expression on other faces might have been called embarrassment, but not on theirs. The smile they shared seemed noncommittal, secretive, knowledgeable in a way that I could not fathom, and afterward I thought it curious that they had shown no surprise.

For a long time after that I met no one at all. I met no cat, no dog, no cabbage butterfly; not even an ant on the packed, bald dust of the road, and finally rejecting its ugliness and light I turned to the left along another street, narrower and as graceless, and walked by the same monotony of weatherbeaten houses. After a few minutes I heard a sound that halted me and I stood listening. Somewhere not far away I heard children's voices. Though their words were foreign they spoke also in the common tongue of children everywhere: voices high, eruptive, excited, sparked with the universal jokes, chants, quarrels of play; and here, listening to them, my memory stirred for the first time—a memory of memory, in fact. For whatever it was that nearly illuminated consciousness was not the memory itself, but a remnant of light which glowed on the periphery of the obstacle before it: a penumbra.[3]

> ## Where are the children, I thought; where are they?

Where are the children, I thought; where are they? With great urgency and longing I set out in the direction of their voices, determined to find them and in doing so to find something of myself. Their voices chattered, skipped, squabbled like the voices of sparrows, never far away, but though I turned and hunted and listened and pursued I could not find them. I never found them, and after a while I could not hear them either. The ghostly light of memory faded and was extinguished, and my despair rose up in darkness to take its place.

The next person I met was a man, young and dark-browed, and when I confronted him and asked my questions, it was without hope. I knew he would not meet my look, or let his eyes show me my longed-for, dreaded face. Yet here I was wrong; he stood before me without speaking, but the gaze with which he answered mine was so intense and undeviating that it was I who dropped my eyes and stepped aside. I could not look, and soon I heard him going on his way.

I had been walking a long time, and the light was changing; the sun was low and full in my face. West, I said to myself; at least I know west, and I know that I am a woman, and that that is the sun. When the stars come out I will know those, too, and perhaps they will tell me something else.

After a while I sat down on a wooden step to rest. I was struck by the silence of the city around me, and I realized this was because it

---

3 **penumbra** (pi num′ brə): the partly lighted area surrounding the complete shadow of a body during an eclipse; a vague or borderline area

was a city of walkers who walked on dust instead of on pavements. I remembered that I had seen no mark of a wheel on any road, and that nothing had moved in the sky all day except for a few birds in flight.

A breath of dry wind crept along the dust at my feet, and, far away, a noise of knocking started, a sound of stakes being driven into the ground with a wooden mallet. Desolate, reiterated, it sounded as though somewhere in the city they were preparing a gallows or a barricade. Too tired and dispirited to move I sat there listening to the double knock-and-echo of each blow. A few people passed me on their way home, each of them giving me the glance of casual appraisal I had seen so often. Doors opened and doors closed, the sun went down, and soon the street was still again and the knocking stopped. Where would I sleep that night, or find a meal? I neither knew nor cared.

One by one the stars came out on the deepening sky, perfect, still, as if they were really what they seemed to be—calm ornaments for hope, promises of stillness and forever.

I looked for Venus, then Polaris, then for Mars. I could not find them, and as the stars grew in number, coming imperceptibly into their light, I saw with slow-growing shock that these were not the stars I knew. The messages of this night sky were written in a language of constellations I had never seen or dreamed. I stared up at the brand-new Catherine wheels,[4] insignias, and fiery thorn crowns on the sky, and I do not think that I

...and now to all the other fears was added the fear that the trees, too, would magically elude me.

was really surprised when I spied at the zenith, small but bright, a constellation shaped like an elongated diamond, like the glittering abstraction of a human eye. . . .

It was just at this moment, before I could marshal or identify my thoughts in the face of such a development, that I heard a sound of trees, wind in the leaves of trees, and I realized, irrelevantly it seemed, that in all my walking in this city—how many hours, how many days?—I had not seen a single tree, and the sound of their presence was as welcome as the sound of rain is after a siege of drought. As I stood up it occurred to me that neither had I seen one child among all the strangers I had met, that though I had heard the children I had not been able to find them, and now to all the other fears was added the fear that the trees, too, would magically elude me.

The street was dark, though light was glimmering through the cracks of the closed shutters. What was left of sunset, green as water, lay on the western horizon. Yet was it really western? In a sky of new stars, was it not possible and in fact probable that what I had believed to be the sun was not really Sun at all? Then what were the compass points, what were the easts and wests of this city? And what would I find when once I found myself?

I heard the beckoning of trees again and as if they were the clue to sanity, I ran along the street in the direction of their sound. I turned a corner, and there, ah yes, there were the

---

4 **Catherine wheels:** fireworks displaying wheels with projecting spikes

Giorgio de Chirico, *Piazza d'Italia*, 1912

trees: a grove of tall, dry, paper-murmuring trees that grew in a little park or public garden where people were walking together or sitting on the dusty grass. At the center of this park or garden there was a great house of stone, the first stone building I had seen all day. It was lighted from top to bottom; the lights of its long windows twittered in gold among the small leaves of the trees, and a door stood open at the head of a flight of steps.

I passed many people on the path, but now I did not look at them or ask them questions. I knew that there was nothing they could do for me. I walked straight to the steps and up them and through the door into the lighted house. It was empty, as I had expected, a great

Juan Gris, *Face of Harlequin*, 1924

Descriptive Writing

empty ringing house, but there was a splendor about it, even in its emptiness, as if those who had left it—and left it recently—had been creatures of joy, better than people and gayer than gods. But they, whoever they were, had gone. My footsteps sounded on the barren floor, and the talk of the loiterers outside, the foreign talk, came in the windows clearly on the night air.

The mirror was at the end of the hall. I walked toward it with my fists closed, and my heart walked, too, heavily in my chest. I watched the woman's figure in the dark dress and the knees moving forward. When I was close to it, I saw, low in the right-hand corner of the mirror, the scratched small outline of the eye-diamond, a signature, carved on the surface of the glass by whom, and in what cold spirit of raillery? Lifting my head, I looked at my own face. I leaned forward and looked closely at my face, and I remembered everything. I remembered everything. And I knew the name of the city I would never leave, and, alas, I understood the language of its citizens.

Linking Writing and Literature

Readers Respond to the Model

How do Elizabeth Enright's descriptions evoke moods of mystery and suspense?

Explore Elizabeth Enright's descriptions by answering these questions. Then read what other students liked about Enright's story.

1. Enright writes this story in the first person. How does this point of view enhance the descriptions and sense of mystery? How would the mood change if Enright told the story in the third person through a detached observer?
2. Why does the description of the trees and stone building toward the end of the story create a different mood from the description

of the street and houses in the first paragraph?
3. What do you find most disturbing about the world Enright creates? What sensory details in the descriptive passages create this impression?
4. How does Enright's description of the main character's actions in the last paragraph help to build suspense?

What Students Say

"This selection was very metaphorical and very universal. Enright comments that all of us are born as nameless, faceless individuals carving our own identity. If we fail to find this identity, we are doomed to our worst fate—isolation. I found this selection captivating and thought-provoking. I wonder: Have I found my identity?"

Mathew Isaac

"I have always been a sucker for mystery. The scene I remember best is the last scene, when the woman in the story looked into the mirror. The story still has my attention because I'm trying to figure it out! I would recommend this to a friend, mainly to see if my friend could make heads or tails of the ending."

Marsha Novak

Reflecting on the Unit

Summarize what you learned in this unit by answering the following questions.

1 In describing a scene or place, what elements do you need to consider?

2 What questions should you ask yourself when you are trying to capture the essence of a character you are creating?

3 How do the techniques for describing events and the methods used to describe static scenes compare?

4 What elements contribute to dramatic mood?

Adding to Your Portfolio

Follow this procedure to choose a selection for your portfolio.

Look over the descriptive writing you have done during this unit. Select a piece of writing to put into your portfolio. The piece you choose should show some or all of the following:

- descriptive details ordered appropriately for audience and purpose
- a well-defined mood
- precise, vivid nouns, verbs, and modifiers

Reflect on Your Choice

Attach a note to the piece you chose, explaining briefly why you chose it and what you learned from writing it.

SET GOALS How can you improve your writing? What skill will you focus on the next time you write?

Writing Across the Curriculum

MAKE A SCIENCE CONNECTION Someday we may all have the opportunity for space flight. To prepare for someone's first space adventure, write a travel brochure on traveling to another planet, asteroid, moon, or star. Use what you know, or find information in a reference source to help you describe the climate, terrain, and travel time to this destination. Make your description informative and inviting. Order the details to appeal to other travelers.

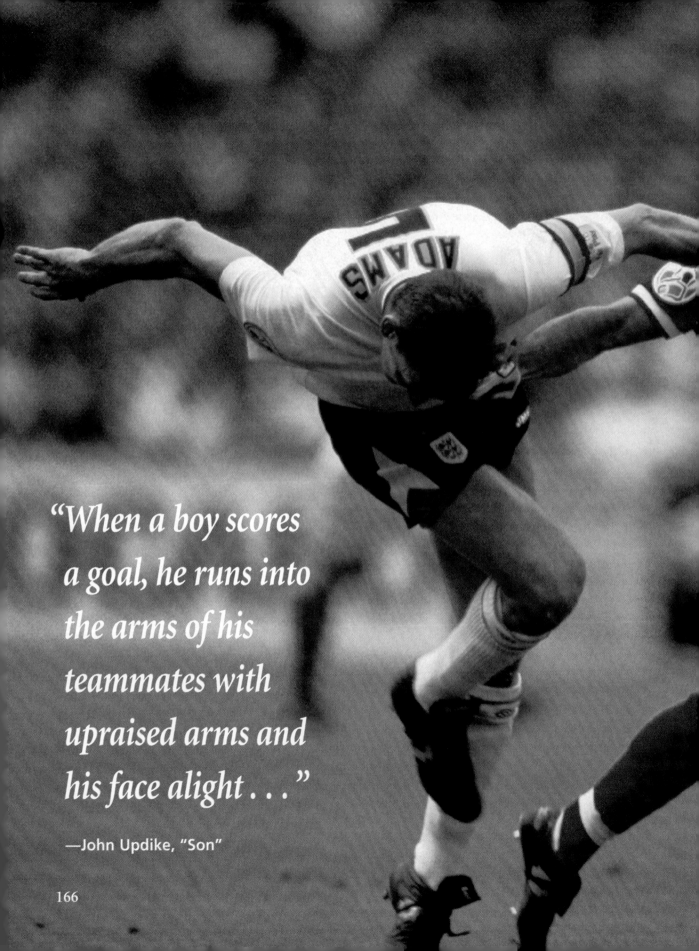

"When a boy scores a goal, he runs into the arms of his teammates with upraised arms and his face alight . . ."

—John Updike, "Son"

Narrative Writing

Writing in the Real World

Narrative writing is writing that tells a story. The following excerpt, an example of narrative nonfiction, contains elements—such as character, setting, and plot—also used in fiction. The author is Samuel Regalado, a professor of history at Washington State University.

from Viva Baseball! Latin Major Leaguers and Their Special Hunger

Samuel O. Regalado

With bag in hand, Tony Oliva bid farewell to his father and sister as he boarded a plane leaving Cuba. Recalling his 1961 departure he wrote, "This was something I had thought about, dreamed about, since I was a little boy playing baseball on the field on my father's farm. And now, here I was, actually going to America to become a professional baseball player." Armed with but a few dollars and no knowledge of the English language, the young ballplayer made his way to the training camp in the hope that his dreams might soon become a reality. In doing so, Oliva joined a growing list of those who migrated to the United States to play professional baseball.

Between 1871 and the mid-1990s, over 500 Latin American–born players joined major league clubs. For most, their love of baseball was rooted in makeshift diamonds amidst the sugarcane fields and jungles of the Caribbean. For others it came from the dusty, windswept dirt farms of northern Mexico, while for still others it emerged from the banana- and coffee-growing regions of Central America and Venezuela. For many, their talents developed despite the limited resources—and scarce athletic equipment—available to them. Hence, the opportunity to play baseball in the United States carried great significance. "Many of us came from families who didn't have the money to send us to college or anything like that. So the only way of bettering ourselves and our families was to make it in baseball," explained Cuban Octavio "Cookie" Rojas. But to "make it," as he and others like him learned, required a "special hunger"—the drive needed to propel them through the pitfalls that they inevitably encountered as they pursued their dreams. That hunger, to be sure, motivated their exodus from regions where the per capita income was often less than a few hundred dollars per year, where "lunch" was as foreign as wealth, where $250 a month was "big money," and where the loss of a ten-dollar bill was a tragedy.

Regalado charts the history of barrio baseball through one player, Manuel "Shorty" Perez (above, second from left).

Writing About History

PREWRITING	DRAFTING/REVISING	REVISING/EDITING

Gathering Material and Planning | Working from an Outline | Soliciting Criticism

A Writer's Process

Prewriting

Gathering Material and Planning

Historian Samuel Regalado's interest in Latin American–born baseball players grew out of his childhood experiences. He and his Mexican American family regularly attended barrio league games, which were popular in the Southwest in the years following World War II. When he was a graduate student in history at Washington State University, he presented a paper on barrio baseball at a sports-history conference. The paper was later published in the magazine *Baseball History.* Regalado's interest in the subject continued, leading to a book titled *Viva Baseball! Latin Major Leaguers and Their Special Hunger.*

Regalado prepared to write by immersing himself in the topic. "I read a variety of secondary materials—materials written after the fact, such as general texts and biographies," he says.

Next, Regalado gathered primary sources. "These are oral histories or contemporary sources such as news-paper articles written without the benefit of hindsight. Other primary sources, such as interviews with people who were there at the time, add a lot of color to what you're writing about."

Regalado's narrative began with a rough outline, which he revised as he conducted his research. "While I'm interviewing somebody," the author points out, "I'm thinking in terms not only of what the person is saying, but also where I am going in my outline. And after I transcribe my interviews, I begin to fuse them into my outline. Pretty soon, I can look at my outline and say, 'OK, this person's interview would be great at this point.'"

Drafting/Revising

Working from an Outline

"To reach an audience, you have to do more than just state facts," says Regalado. "Narrative writing allows you to build a scenario based on the data you've uncovered." In this way you set the stage for a complete understanding of what you're discussing.

TIME

For more about the writing process, see **TIME Facing the Blank Page,** pages 111–121.

Regalado at his campus office. Like many writers, he prefers to write his first draft by hand before transferring it to his computer for revising.

To tell the story of Latin major leaguers, Regalado used his outline to develop narrative elements such as setting and character. He emphasized the personal stories of individual players. Telling the story through a person "adds a human element that makes the writing more effective," says the historian.

Revising/Editing
Soliciting Criticism

Regalado begins writing with pencil and paper. But when he's ready to revise and edit, he works on a computer.

"I realize a lot of people don't have access to computers," the historian notes. "But they make such a big difference in terms of

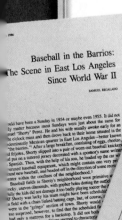

easing the editing process and introducing new ideas."

After writing, Regalado has asked professors and graduate students to critique his writing. He has found their comments "invaluable—exceedingly important," and he has followed many of their suggestions. "Of course, it's up to you to decide whether or not these warrant attention," he notes. "Ultimately, you're the writer; you're the one who knows what you are trying to say."

Publishing/Presenting
Appearing in Print

Regalado's book was published by the University of Illinois Press in 1998.

Today, as a professor himself, Regalado still asks colleagues for constructive criticism of his writing. He says, "I think that everyone's writing can always use improvement. I'm still learning, and I suspect I probably will for a number of years."

Examining Writing in the Real World

Analyzing the Media Connection

Discuss these questions about the excerpt on page 168.

1. Why does Regalado begin his book by describing the experience of one particular baseball player?
2. How does the author use quotations to advance his story?
3. What details does the author include to create a distinctive picture of the way baseball is played in various Latin American countries?
4. What details does the author use to create a vivid impression of the poverty from which Latin American baseball players try to escape?
5. According to Regalado, what do players need to succeed in the major leagues?

Analyzing the Writer's Process

Discuss these questions about Samuel Regalado's writing process.

1. What sources does Regalado use in researching his topic?
2. How does Regalado combine his interviews with his outline?
3. Why does Regalado choose to tell the history of Latin major leaguers through the personal stories of individual players?
4. In your opinion, why might a writer who uses a computer prefer to begin with pencil and paper?
5. How does Regalado incorporate criticism into the writing process?

Grammar Link

Avoid incomplete and illogical comparisons.

Use words such as *else* and *other* to avoid incomplete comparisons:

> . . . *narrative writing is much more effective than any **other** kind of history writing. . . .*

Be sure that your comparisons are between two like things.

Rewrite the following sentences so the comparisons in them make sense.

1. My brother likes reggae more than any type of music.
2. This new ballpoint writes better than any pen on the market.
3. The parks in our city are much smaller than New York.
4. The dirt marks on my legs were harder to wash off than my face.
5. This year's dress lengths are shorter than last year.

See Lesson 18.4, p. 656.

Narrative Writing

Characters in Biographical Narratives

Imagery, vivid description, and realistic dialogue can bring characters to life. Notice how Russell Baker uses these strategies to portray Tennessee senator Estes Kefauver.

Literature Model

He was a big, long, thick log of a man who moved in a dreamy, stiff-jointed walk as though he had no knee joints. His public manner was gentle, folksy, down-home. Getting out of his chartered Greyhound at a central Florida prayer meeting, he stood at the front step, rigid as a cigar-store Indian, and let the people come to him to shake that famous hand, and murmured a little something to each.

"Ah'm Estes Kefauver and Ah'm runnin' for president. Will you he'p me? . . ."

To test my theory that he was punch-drunk with fatigue and so groggy he was running on pure reflex, I got in the handshaking line one day to test his reactions. I had been on the Greyhound with him for three or four days. Earlier that day I had been one of four people who chatted with him over lunch at a Cuban restaurant in Tampa. I thought he might crack wise when he found me waiting for my handshake, but there wasn't a flicker of recognition in those eyes when I laid my hand in his paw and said, "An honor to shake your hand, Senator."

Looking through me at something five thousand miles away, he said, "I hope you're going to he'p me," then dropped my hand and reached for the next one.

Russell Baker, *The Good Times*

Baker brings Kefauver to life with imagery: "big, long, thick log of a man" instead of "tall and solidly built."

Why does Baker use the word "paw" here? What does it tell us about Kefauver?

What does Kefauver's mechanical response indicate?

Reveal Character

Adventure, mystery, humor, heroism—history can be every bit as compelling as a good movie or novel. A fictional narrative is a story from a writer's imagination; it contains events, or plot, and it involves characters. The story is set in a specific place and time, or setting, and told from a particular point of view. Nonfiction narratives, such as histories and biographies, are about events that really happened, but they also contain plot, characters, setting, and point of view.

Real-life characters are at the heart of any historical narrative. They are the people who make history; their actions arise out of their personalities and circumstances, and these actions drive the plot. How you portray these characters can make the difference between a narrative that reads like an encyclopedia and one that is lively and entertaining.

Baker uses several strategies to reveal the character of Estes Kefauver. Each method aids Baker's twin purpose: to show Kefauver's "folksy, down-home manner" and to suggest his grogginess and fatigue. The chart below gives you a menu of strategies you can use for developing characters in a narrative.

Prewriting Tip

Use the observation techniques in Lesson 3.4, pages 140–143, to collect details about characters. Use only those details that will have the most impact.

Strategies for Revealing Character	
PHYSICAL DESCRIPTION	"He was a big, long, thick log of a man who moved in a dreamy, stiff-jointed walk."
CHARACTER'S OWN THOUGHTS OR WORDS	"'Ah'm Estes Kefauver and Ah'm runnin' for president. Will you he'p me?'"
CHARACTER'S ACTIONS	Anecdote about Kefauver's not recognizing Baker after having had lunch with him
WRITER'S OPINION	"He was punch-drunk with fatigue and so groggy he was running on pure reflex."

Journal Writing

Sometimes physical description alone can reveal a great deal about a character. In your journal, list as many elements of physical description as you can, such as clothes, hairstyle, walking, tone of voice, way of dressing, even scent. How could you use each of these physical characteristics to reveal something about a character's personality?

Use Vivid Description

When you describe someone, you can give a general statement: "Bob is soft-hearted and impractical." Or you can demonstrate that person's nature through specific observations: "Bob can't pass a musician on the street without giving away all his change, and so he never has a quarter for the telephone." A description that shows what a character is like can have more impact than one that merely tells you what to think. Consider this description of a famous writer.

Vivid language shows rather than tells: "turns" has become "swivels."

Literature Model

When Louis Auchincloss chooses to be stiff and formal—which is rare—he can be imposing. He is 61 years old, looks 15 years younger, is six feet tall, weighs a trim 170 pounds, has deep-set dark brown eyes and the sort of patrician nose one associates with, say, the American eagle. There is, in fact, something quite birdlike about the way Louis can turn to look at someone. His head swivels leisurely, magisterially, as if his neck were scarved in rich plumage; his eyelids lower slowly, then rise, providing pause enough for feathers to settle, and when he speaks he *pronounces*.

C. D. B. Bryan, "Under the Auchincloss Shell"

Bryan could have simply ended the Auchincloss description at the word "eagle," but that would have told you only how Auchincloss looks. In the extended comparison, Auchincloss actually becomes an eagle.

Showing and telling can work well in combination. Notice how the Auchincloss description uses both.

Ways of Revealing Character	
TELLING	**SHOWING**
"stiff and formal"	"nose [like] the American eagle"
"imposing"	"head swivels leisurely, magisterially"
"birdlike"	"neck … scarved in rich plumage" "eyelids lower slowly, then rise, providing pause enough for feathers to settle"

Use Dialogue

Using conversation, or dialogue, is a good way to bring characters to life. Dialogue lets readers form opinions about characters as they "listen in."

In the model below, Jennifer Beyersdorf introduces the main character of her narrative through dialogue. As the narrator tries to match her Uncle Larry's enthusiasm for his stodgy new car, you almost feel as though you are overhearing a real conversation.

Editing Tip

When you quote from an actual conversation, you may not want to include everything that was said. Use ellipses to indicate the omissions you make. For more information on ellipses, see Lesson 21.9, page 734.

Model

"It's great Uncle Larry, really—great." (Is he serious?)

"Thanks, Jen. It's pretty weird for me, you know. I've never even had a car with a backseat; now I've got room for seven plus a luggage rack. We'll be thankful for the room, though, once the baby arrives."

"Yeah, I guess you're right." (He's serious.) I scan the mini-van's fake wood trim as Uncle Larry rubs the last of the car polish onto the fender. "So what are you gonna do with your sports car?" I ask, casually. "I'll be sixteen next month, you know. I'd really hate to see that car leave the family."

"Nice try, Jen, but your dad would kill me. Besides, I think you should get something bigger for your first car—maybe drive Grandpa's old sedan for a while."

I laugh; Uncle Larry doesn't. "You're serious?"

"Yeah, why not? It's big and safe, and it won't let you go too fast, just what you need."

Jennifer Beyersdorf, Northville High School, Northville, Michigan

Notice the beginning of a second, internal dialogue, the narrator's thoughts.

What does the writer reveal by using the word "casually" here?

After reading this dialogue, you know that Uncle Larry's expecting a baby. You see that he is staid and practical. The writer could have told you these things directly; instead, she lets you find them out through the dialogue.

Journal Writing

Uncle Larry is staid and practical. In your journal write an exchange of dialogue you have had with someone like Uncle Larry—or someone just the opposite. How does your dialogue reveal personality?

Round Out Your Characters

A person's actions can reveal a great deal, and so can the opinions of observers. Here's the rest of the "Uncle Larry" narrative.

I sigh and study my uncle's face. He doesn't look any older, but he surely is acting weird. In fact, ever since he married Aunt Kimberly I've noticed a change in his personality: a gradual loss of coolness accompanied by a rapid increase in nerdiness. In fact, lately he's reminded me of Dad.

Before he got married, Uncle Larry used to pick me up from school in his red sports car. We'd cruise the San Diego Freeway to Grandma and Grandpa's; he always used to blast rock music out the window. Then he'd put the top down and give me an extra pair of sunglasses—"We're cool, Jen, we're cool."

And sometimes we'd walk to Turmaline Hill, the best surfing park in Pacific Beach. Uncle Larry knew everyone's name down there. He "knew how to surf before he knew how to walk" is what he told everyone. Since he hurt his knees skiing last year, he hasn't gone down as much, but I still ask him to take me. I know how he loves the ocean.

We'd sit on the red clay rocks overlooking the beach and watch his wetsuited friends for hours. Once, Grandma came looking to tell us we'd missed dinner. So we went to a fast food place for 39-cent tacos. We tried skipping family meals about four or five times after that, but Grandma caught on.

As I look at him now, waxing his minivan with suburban glee, I wonder what could've happened. Marriage I guess. Grandma's thrilled that "Larry's finally taking responsibility for his life." And Mom and Dad say Aunt Kimberly's really made him grow up. All I know is that I haven't been to Turmaline Hill since the wedding.

Uncle Larry stands up and examines his project. "Looks mighty nice, huh Jen? Finished just in time for dinner."

"Yup—wouldn't want to be late," I mumble, but he's already turned and doesn't hear me. I pick up the spilled can of polish and carefully screw on the lid.

"Hurry up, Jen," he calls back. "After dinner we'll ride out to Turmaline Hill and watch the surfers."

But somehow I know it won't be the same.

The narrator is also a character. What does her opinion of Uncle Larry tell us about her?

What does this anecdote tell us about the "old" Uncle Larry?

The narrator rounds out her character description with other people's opinions of her Uncle Larry.

The writer returns to dialogue to reveal both characters and their current relationship.

Narrative Writing

Write a Narrative That Reveals Character

Write a narrative about someone you know who has faced a high-stress situation or acted bravely during an emergency. Focus on revealing character by describing the person's actions under stress.

PURPOSE To write a narrative that reveals character
AUDIENCE Your teacher and classmates
LENGTH 4–5 paragraphs

WRITING RUBRICS To write an effective narrative that reveals character, you should

- use vivid details to re-create the situation
- establish a link between the situation and your interpretation of character

Cross-Curricular Activity

SOCIAL STUDIES Write a vignette about a real-life person caught up in an event of historical importance. The event could be a dramatic rescue or a battle scene you have read about or seen enacted on film or television. Reveal character by using vivid description and a well-rounded presentation of the person's thoughts and actions.

Listening and Speaking

COOPERATIVE LEARNING In small groups, plan and rehearse dramatic readings of students' vignettes. Some students may assume speaking roles, and some may create sound effects. Have each group choose one reading to share with the class.

Grammar Link

Form possessives of pronouns correctly.

Do not use apostrophes with possessive pronouns *(hers, yours, theirs, ours).* However, do use apostrophes when forming the possessive of indefinite pronouns:

*Uncle Larry knew **everyone's** name. . . .*

Rewrite each sentence, using the correct possessive form of the word in parentheses.

1. (Whose) mobile got the most prizes for motion and color?
2. Joe, (no ones) grandmother bakes better fried pies than (yours).
3. Greta and (somebodys) cousin from Fort Wayne taught line dancing.
4. The raccoon has (its) own way of hunting under logs for food.
5. Officer Akins, I spotted (someones) lost malamute on the cul-de-sac.

See Lessons 10.2 and 21.12, pages 442–448 and 741–743.

Writing a Biographical Sketch

The right details can bring a historical character to life. What does the biographical sketch below reveal about Queen Elizabeth I?

Nicholas Hilliard, *Queen Elizabeth I*, c. 1600

Allegorical portrait of Queen Elizabeth I, English School, c. 1600

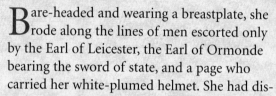

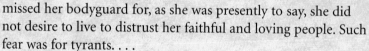

Literature Model

Bare-headed and wearing a breastplate, she rode along the lines of men escorted only by the Earl of Leicester, the Earl of Ormonde bearing the sword of state, and a page who carried her white-plumed helmet. She had dismissed her bodyguard for, as she was presently to say, she did not desire to live to distrust her faithful and loving people. Such fear was for tyrants. . . .

Her dazzled and adoring amateur army did not see a thin, middle-aged woman with bad teeth and wearing a bright red wig perched on the back of an enormous white gelding. Instead they saw the personification of every goddess of classical mythology they had ever heard about, every heroine of their favorite reading, the Bible. They saw Judith and Deborah, Diana the Huntress and the Queen of the Amazons all rolled into one. But they also saw their own beloved and familiar queen.

Alison Plowden, *Elizabeth Regina*

> What does this anecdote reveal about the queen's personality?

> What purpose does this unflattering portrait serve in the narrative?

On this page are three "portraits" of Queen Elizabeth: two in paint and one in words. Each artist chose a certain way to depict the queen. At first glance, the portrayals seem contradictory. Yet each shows a real side of "Good Queen Bess."

Narrow Your Subject

Imagine you are planning a biographical sketch. Before you can write even a short sketch, you need to know a great deal. A good way to begin is by reading about your subject in an encyclopedia or general biographical reference, such as *Current Biography* or *Dictionary of National Biography*.

Next, ask yourself questions that will help you narrow the focus of your biographical sketch. Do you want to cover your subject's whole life? Should you focus on your subject's historical significance? Will you focus on the claims to fame or on the interesting sidelights?

To answer questions such as these, try freewriting or completing a cluster diagram that explores your subject further.

Prewriting Tip

As you research, write notes on index cards. Be sure to record the source on each card.

Narrative Writing

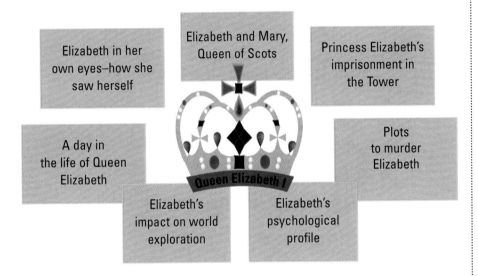

Elizabeth in her own eyes—how she saw herself

Elizabeth and Mary, Queen of Scots

Princess Elizabeth's imprisonment in the Tower

A day in the life of Queen Elizabeth

Queen Elizabeth I

Plots to murder Elizabeth

Elizabeth's impact on world exploration

Elizabeth's psychological profile

After you choose a focus, you need an "angle." As you continue to read, think about what aspect of your subject's character you want to reveal: you may need to examine different sources for each angle. For example, a sketch on Queen Elizabeth as a young woman imprisoned in the Tower of London would require information from an autobiography, childhood diary, or biography. To learn different ways of organizing your information into an essay, see pages 72–75.

Journal Writing

Make a cluster diagram like the one above for someone you know well. What "angle" or character aspect will you focus on? How can you gather facts on different aspects of your subject? Does knowing the subject well help or hinder your writing?

Keep and Discard

When you have narrowed the focus, be ruthless about discarding unnecessary information. Ask yourself questions about each incident and detail you could use: Does it show the side of my subject that I have chosen to reveal? Will it capture my audience's imagination? If you can't answer these questions, you probably haven't fully clarified your focus.

In the model below, the author chose to depict a side of his subject not often seen. He presents a young Richard Nixon in love with his future wife, Pat. Notice how the writer carefully selects just the right details to shed light on the personality of young Nixon.

> **Morris chooses an incident from Nixon's school days to reveal an unknown side of Nixon's character.**

> **Pat's comment makes Nixon more vulnerable and human than most readers would expect.**

> **How does the friend's observation make us feel toward Nixon? How is this detail consistent with the other details Morris presents?**

> **Is this last bit of information surprising? What does it reveal about the older Nixon that we might not have known?**

Literature Model

That spring of 1938 Nixon asked [Pat] repeatedly for dates. Turned down always on weekends and often during the week, he began showing up at her rooms unannounced in the evening to take her on drives or walks through the hillside blocks around the college. Pat thought him "a bit unusual," as she told a friend soon after their meeting, and continued to put him off. When she tactfully excused her own indifference by remarking lightly that she was a vagabond or gypsy, Nixon wrote her affectionate little notes addressed to "Miss Vagabond" or "My Irish Gypsy." When she pointedly arranged a date for him with her roommate, he agreed readily to go, and through the evening talked only about Pat. "He chased her but she was a little rat," said one of her friends who watched it unfold. The notes were soon interspersed with his own romantic poetry, verse she later described as having a "mysteriously wild beauty." Within weeks of their meeting, he even composed a song for her. It was one of the two compositions, along with "Rustle of Spring,". . . that he still knew by heart more than thirty years later—and picked out on the White House grand piano the night he moved in.

Roger Morris, *Richard Milhous Nixon*

Morris could have mentioned Nixon's intense political aspirations or given evidence of Nixon's drive for success, but he does not. He focuses only on Nixon's feelings about Pat. When you write a portrait, try to choose the right details and let them speak for themselves.

Write a Biographical Sketch

Write a biographical sketch of a classmate, friend, or relative for the school paper. Check with the person first to make sure he or she is willing to be your subject.

PURPOSE To write a biographical sketch of a classmate
AUDIENCE Readers of school newspaper
LENGTH 3–4 paragraphs

WRITING RUBRICS To write an effective biographical sketch, you should

- narrow your subject
- reveal one aspect of your subject's character
- discard information that does not shed light on your subject's personality

Cross-Curricular Activity

AMERICAN HISTORY In a small group, brainstorm a list of individuals from American history who you think are appropriate role models for young people. Select one individual, and together gather information about the person's life and accomplishments. Then, individually, select one aspect of your subject, and write a brief narrative that focuses on this aspect. Present your finished biographical narratives to the group, and discuss how they can be "published" in a format for your classmates.

Viewing and Representing

READING A PHOTOGRAPH Every day, newspapers and magazines select photos of famous people—entertainers, sports figures, politicians—for their pages. These photos often convey a subtle message about the subject's personality and character. Locate a photo that you think sends such a message, positive or negative, about the subject and share your interpretation of it with the class.

Use commas with nonrestrictive participles.

Set off nonrestrictive participles—participles not vital to the meaning of a sentence—with commas:

> *Bare-headed and wearing a breast-plate, she rode along the lines of men. . . .*

Do not set off restrictive participles—participles required to make sense of a statement:

The woman **wearing a bright red wig** was the queen.

Punctuate the nonrestrictive participles in the following sentences.

1. Do swimmers coming in first or second get a shot at the trophy?
2. Mrs. Abrams bought a camera weighing only six ounces.
3. Some racks supporting more than two bikes wobble a bit.
4. Leyla limping from fatigue walked through the whole mall in an hour.
5. Singing the state song the trio earned second prize—a trip to Nome.
6. There stood Binny wagging his tail and holding up a paw for me to shake.
7. Harvey and Ted riding their unicycles in circles made ungraceful landings.
8. Mrs. Reber shelving books in a hurry misplaced *Woodsong*.
9. Lou, where is the group carrying the banner?

See Lesson 21.6, page 722.

Structuring the Long Narrative

*H*ow do you show the "big picture" of a person's life? Look for *turning points and significant moments.*

Former slave Sojourner Truth led a life that took many unexpected turns. Here is one such turning point.

What words and phrases does the writer use in the first paragraph to show us that this is a perilous moment in her subject's life?

Notice Sojourner Truth's diction: it is almost biblical and gives power to her speech.

What do the others learn about Sojourner Truth in this incident? What does she learn about herself?

Literature Model

Alone, for none of the others would face the mob of young men, Sojourner walked to the top of a small hill on the meeting ground and began to sing. Her deep, melodious voice carried far, and the troublemakers turned and ran toward her as if to pull her down and silence her. As they approached, she stopped singing and asked them: "Why do you come about me with clubs and sticks? I am not doing any harm to any one." Disarmed by her tranquillity, they answered that they would not hurt her: "We came to hear you sing. Sing to us, old woman. Talk to us, old woman. Tell us your experience."

Surrounded by the roughnecks, Sojourner spoke to them and answered their questions. She even made them laugh. And they evidently enjoyed her singing, for they threatened bodily harm to anyone who might interrupt her. Finally she stopped and said to them: "Children, I have talked and sung to you, as you asked me; and now I have a request to make of you: Will you grant it?" They assured her of their good will, and she asked them to leave in peace after she sang just one more song. True to their word, the men dispersed after hearing her sing, silently and without further trouble.

This experience marked an important stage in Sojourner's life, demonstrating the character traits that would carry her triumphantly through hostile confrontations in future years.

Victoria Ortiz, *Sojourner Truth: A Self-Made Woman*

See the Big Picture

One way to understand the overall direction of Sojourner Truth's—or any famous person's—life is to construct a time line. Start with the beginning and ending dates—birth and death; next, identify the major turning points. Then insert details and look at the big picture.

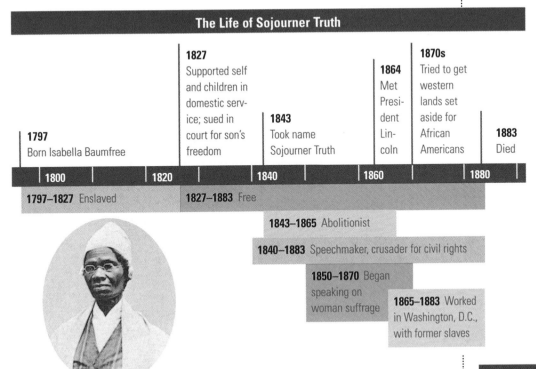

The Life of Sojourner Truth

1797 Born Isabella Baumfree

1827 Supported self and children in domestic service; sued in court for son's freedom

1843 Took name Sojourner Truth

1864 Met President Lincoln

1870s Tried to get western lands set aside for African Americans

1883 Died

1800   1820   1840   1860   1880

1797–1827 Enslaved

1827–1883 Free

1843–1865 Abolitionist

1840–1883 Speechmaker, crusader for civil rights

1850–1870 Began speaking on woman suffrage

1865–1883 Worked in Washington, D.C., with former slaves

The time line for Sojourner Truth tells what happened in her life and gives you a sense of the forces driving her. Before you write a narrative, think about the big picture, or theme, and express it in a thesis statement. This thesis statement will help you give your narrative both unity and coherence.

Presenting Tip

Besides being a prewriting aid, a colorful and well-organized time line can be a thought-provoking illustration for a biographical narrative.

Journal Writing

Develop a time line for the life of someone in your family. Block out the main chapters from birth to the present, and insert important events. Look for patterns in the time line, writing in your journal any insights you gain into forces that have driven your subject's life.

Shape the Narrative

The themes you observe in a person's life will determine how you tell the story. Structure your narrative chronologically, but don't include everything; put in those events and details that best support your image of your subject. When you revise, look for repeated incidents or images to use as connecting threads throughout. Conclude with a particularly characteristic anecdote, image, or perhaps a personal reflection.

In the following excerpts from a narrative, the author uses her grandmother's different styles of dress to shape her story.

What is a "picture bride"? What do you imagine Obāchon wore in the picture sent to her prospective husband?

What remnants of Japanese habit does Obāchon maintain during this period of her life?

In the third chapter of her life, Obāchon wore Western dresses. What other indications of her assimilation into Western culture does the narrator give?

The story comes full circle as Obāchon's granddaughter wears the kimono Obāchon may have worn as a girl.

Literature Model

She came to Hawaii as a "picture bride." In one of her rare self-reflecting moments, she told me in her broken English-Japanese that her mother had told her that the streets of Honolulu in Hawaii were paved with gold coins, and so encouraged her to go to Hawaii to marry a strange man she had never seen. . . . She grew silent after that, and her eyes had a faraway look.

She took her place, along with the other picture brides from Japan, beside her husband on the plantation canefields. . . . I remember her best in her working days, coming home from the canefields at "pauhana" time. She wore a pair of faded blue jeans and an equally faded navy-blue and white checked work shirt. A Japanese towel was wrapped carefully around her head, and a large straw "papale" or hat covered that. . . .

Having retired from the plantation, she now wore only dresses. She called them "makule-men doresu," Hawaiian for old person's dress. They were always gray or navy-blue with buttons down the front and a belt at the waistline. Her hair, which must once have been long and black like mine, was now streaked with gray and cut short and permanent-waved. . . .

She once surprised me by sending a beautiful "yukata" or summer kimono for me to wear to represent the Japanese in our school's annual May Day festival. . . . I have often wondered, whenever I look at that kimono, whether she had ever worn it when she was a young girl.

Gail Y. Miyasaki, "Obāchon"

Write a Biographical Narrative

Write a biographical narrative about a member of your family or a close family friend. Be sure to include your insights into the experiences that have shaped this person's life.

PURPOSE To write a short biographical narrative
AUDIENCE Your teacher, other students
LENGTH 4–5 paragraphs

WRITING RUBRICS To write an effective biographical narrative, you should

- create a chronological time line to organize your material
- choose events and details that support your image and your subject

Listening and Speaking

COOPERATIVE LEARNING To prepare for the Cross-Curricular Activity, draft a list of questions you plan to ask your subject about his or her life, career, and experiences. Working with a partner, review each other's lists and practice asking your questions. Use feedback from your partner to change, add, or delete questions.

Cross-Curricular Activity

ECONOMICS Write a biographical narrative about someone you know in business—a relative, friend, local shopkeeper, or banker. Look for something about the person that intrigues you. Interview the person. Then sketch a time line based on the interview to help you draft the narrative. Remember to depict character and setting and to make effective use of quotations.

Use quotation marks with direct quotes.

Quotation marks indicate when a writer cites a quotation word for word, as when one of the young men tells Sojourner Truth,

"We came to hear you sing."

In an indirect quotation, no quotation marks are used:

They assured her of their good will. . . .

Insert quotation marks in the sentences that contain direct quotes.

1. Lincoln said, A house divided against itself cannot stand.
2. Ramondo reported that lunch would be delayed a few minutes.
3. Grace, did you divulge that you are planning an overnight trip?
4. Andy said that he would help at the neighborhood drugstore.
5. All right, the mayor replied, I heard everybody's views on parking.
6. This is raw weather for sailing, the skipper sang out.
7. Tuning an autoharp, the book implied, requires an expert.
8. Gracious, Luisa, dry off and have some cocoa, Mother ordered.
9. Van and the soccer team chanted, We're number one.
10. Jo asked, Are you sure that Governor Whiteside was in office?

See Lesson 21.10, pages 735–738.

WRITING ABOUT LITERATURE

Identifying Theme in a Narrative

O ften the theme of a story or novel isn't clear until the end. Even then the theme isn't always easy to pin down. In fact, the richer the work, the less likely it is that people will agree on its theme. Just look below at how a number of well-respected literary scholars express the theme of Herman Melville's novel Moby-Dick.

Moby-Dick is a book about man's attempt to understand and interpret his world.

Michael T. Gilmore,
Introduction to *Twentieth Century Interpretations of* Moby-Dick

Moby-Dick . . . is, fundamentally, a parable on the mystery of evil and the accidental malice of the universe.

Lewis Mumford,
"Moby-Dick as Poetic Epic"

Moby-Dick. . . . Of course he is a symbol.
Of what?
I doubt if even Melville knew exactly. That's the best of it.

D. H. Lawrence,
Studies in Classical American Literature

Which of these writers is correct? They all are—as long as they can support their ideas with evidence from the novel.

Determine Theme

Theme is the controlling idea of a story or novel. A particularly rich and complex work may have several complementary themes, all reflecting the author's world view and insight into the human condition. The theme is seldom stated directly; it permeates the entire work. The more familiar you are with a story or novel as a whole, the better your chances of determining its theme(s).

Form First Impressions A conversation about a movie may begin with the question "What did you think of the characters?" and move to "The son: he's a mystery" and "How does the father feel about him?" You can take the same approach to stories you read. Try writing a cluster diagram like the one on the right to help sort out your thoughts.

Gather Evidence When you analyze a narrative to determine its theme, consider all the elements: character, setting, plot, and point of view. All of these should reflect the theme. The questions below suggest some ways you can explore each narrative element to discover and analyze theme.

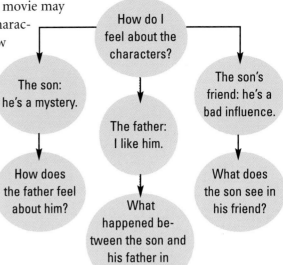

Determining Theme

SETTING	Is it hostile or friendly? What mood does it create?
CHARACTERS	Who are the most likable characters? The least? Why? Who "wins" and who "loses"? Why?
PLOT	What sort of actions lead to success? To failure? Do the characters instigate the action, or do things happen to them?
POINT OF VIEW	Who tells the story? Can you trust the narrator's opinion? Does anyone seem to speak for the author?

Look at your answers. Think about what rules govern the world of this narrative and how these rules could apply to ourselves, to a specific society in time, or to human life in general. Express your understanding of the theme in a sentence or two.

Journal Writing

Set up questions like those in the diagram above for a story or novel you've read recently. You may want to refine the headings in the left column as well as create new questions in the right column.

Drafting Tip

When you write your essay, you will probably state the theme in the opening paragraph. Make sure you have expressed the theme in a full sentence. For information about how to avoid sentence fragments, see Lesson 13.9, page 551.

Support Your Theory

Treat your statement of theme as if it were a hypothesis. Can you support it with evidence from the story? Go back to your notes on plot, character, setting, and point of view. Do your observations of these elements support your theory?

In the model below, notice how the writer presents evidence to support the theme "things are not always what they seem."

Notice how the writer develops her statement of the theme to make it apply to all of us.

Which narrative elements are introduced as evidence in this paragraph?

Why is it important that Mrs. Wang recognize the Japanese soldier's hunger?

Remember that a narrative can have more than one theme. What secondary theme does this analysis of Mrs. Wang's personality suggest?

Model

Though provincial, Mrs. Wang has seen enough of the world to know that things are not always what they seem. In "The Old Demon," Pearl S. Buck reminds us that we must be like Mrs. Wang, open to new things, hesitating to judge until we have seen for ourselves. Perhaps then we can understand our enemies and overcome our ignorant hatred.

The river, which Mrs. Wang first thought was her greatest threat, is actually "full of good and evil together." In the end, it is a weapon capable of saving her country. Similarly, Mrs. Wang learns that the Japanese are not "large, coarse foreigners," but young men, real people who can be hurt and loved. In fact, Mrs. Wang at first thinks the downed soldier is Chinese. When some Chinese soldiers come along and ask her why she is feeding a Japanese soldier, she replies, "I suppose he is hungry too."

Just as the river and the Japanese are not what they first seem to be, neither is Mrs. Wang the ignorant old fool she first appears to be. In the beginning, Mrs. Wang declares that she doesn't believe in the Japanese, that the war "was not real and no more than hearsay since none of the Wangs had been killed." She seems to be a lady rooted in her narrow beliefs, refusing to believe what she hasn't seen. Yet it is this very naiveté that makes her so wise. She does not carry hatred for people and things she does not know. In both her encounter with the soldier and the river, she shows her ability to change. Not only does this sort of attitude open her to new experiences, but ultimately it gives her the courage for her final sacrifice. She understands that the evil river can also contain good, and that she, in her old age, can still serve a vital purpose. She dies a wise, fulfilled woman.

Brenda Marshall,
Newton North High School, Newton, Massachusetts

Write a Paragraph Explaining a Theme

Reread the story "The Signature" on pages 156–163. Write a paragraph explaining the theme of the story.

PURPOSE To identify a theme in a story
AUDIENCE Your peers
LENGTH 1 paragraph

WRITING RUBRICS To write an effective paragraph explaining the theme of a story, you should

- express the theme in a thesis statement
- support your thesis with details
- review your paragraph for subject-verb agreement

Cross-Curricular Activity

ART Locate a photograph or a reproduction of a painting that conveys some kind of message, and think about it as if it were a narrative. What is the setting and mood? Who are the characters? Speculate about the plot. What is happening now? What might happen next? Finally, what is the artist's point of view? Write a statement of the theme, and list at least three examples to support your theory.

Viewing and Representing

CREATE AN EXHIBIT Mount your photo or painting reproduction so it can be displayed for the entire class. Make a legible, grammatically correct copy of your theme statement that your classmates can use to interpret your chosen image. Compile the theme statements into a guide to the class's exhibition.

Make subjects and verbs agree.

A verb must agree with its subject; don't be confused by a predicate nominative that is different in number from the subject.

Moby-Dick **is** several stories in one.

Select a verb in each sentence to agree with the subject.

1. The beach umbrellas (is, are) in the garage.
2. Gray flagstones leading to the gardens (is, are) my only path.
3. The only thing those children talk about (is, are) movies.
4. One of the mail carrier's biggest irritations (is, are) the dogs on the block.
5. The swarming bees (was, were) the worst problem.

See Lesson 16.2, page 603.

Thomas Eakins, *Max Schmitt in a Single Scull,* 1871

WRITING ABOUT LITERATURE
Responding to Narrative Poetry

Narrative poems tell stories. As you read the stanza below from a book-length poem, ask yourself how it is different from prose.

> At late afternoon, light failing, Howard
> Is called, with his brass, to the buffalo robe that
> Lies black against snow. Up from the dry
> Brown gravel and water-round stones of the Eagle,
> Now going snow-white in dryness, and up
> From the shell-churned
> Chaos of camp-site, slowly ascends
> The procession. Joseph, not straight, sits his mount,
> Head forward bowed, scalp lock with otter-skin tied.
>
> Robert Penn Warren, from *Chief Joseph of the Nez Percé*

It's the end of the day.
Winter, too—end of the year. End of
Joseph. Cold, dry, bleak place. No life.
Seems to fit in with what's happening.

What does "water-round" stones
mean? Made smooth by water? How
about "shell-churned"?

The stanza sets the scene for the 1877 surrender of Joseph, chief of the Nez Percé, to Colonel Miles and General O. O. Howard. Their combined forces had chased Chief Joseph's people away from their sacred homeland in Oregon to clear the way for farmers and gold prospectors.

This stanza may seem different from other poetry you've read. In fact, it is part of a book-length narrative poem. Like a narrative in prose, it has characters, setting, point of view—and an amazing story to tell. How does your response to this stanza compare to the response shown in the notes?

Narrative Writing

Listen to the Poem

When you read a narrative poem, start by just enjoying the story. Along the way, try listening to the music of the poem. Listen for rhythm and the repetition of sounds, as in rhyme or alliteration. Poetry is often more concentrated than prose; every word is carefully chosen for its impact. The poet may leave out details that would be considered necessary in a prose story. Below, the story of Chief Joseph's surrender continues.

> *Joseph rises to meet his fate—pride, dignity. Four bullet holes—was he badly hurt? "Straight-flung" sounds defiant, yet he's above it all somehow.*
> *Story shocking and sad, makes me angry. But (strangely) it's also inspiring—he has such grace and stature.*

Joseph draws in his mount. Then,
As though all years were naught in their count, arrow straight
He suddenly sits, head now lifted. With perfect ease
To the right he swings a buckskinned leg over. Stands.
His gray shawl exhibits four bullet holes.

Straight standing, he thrusts out his rifle,
Muzzle-grounded, to Howard. It is
The gesture, straight-flung, of one who casts the world away.

When you respond to a narrative poem, you can respond to any of its various story elements—plot, character, setting, point of view. Consider also responding to its poetic elements—rhythm, word choice, and so on. One way to get ideas flowing is by freewriting in a learning log, such as the ones you see next to these models. See pages 16–19 for hints on writing a learning log.

Journal Writing

Choose a narrative poem. As you read, jot down your impressions in your journal. Write the line numbers from the poem next to your comments.

Revising Tip

If you think that your essay lacks sufficient supporting evidence, go back to your first learning log for your earliest impressions. You may have overlooked a strong detail in your first draft.

Express Your Response

After you have let your thoughts about a poem run freely, try to articulate them. If you have questions about the story, you may want to get more background information. For example, after you read this poem, you might want to do historical research into the flight of the tribe and the events that followed Chief Joseph's surrender. Finally, try to get something on paper. You could recast the narrative into a play or a short story. You might create a painting of one moment of the story, such as the opening scene described on page 190. Or you might write a response essay such as the one below.

Model

Reading Warren's narrative poem, one wonders if it is as much about the deceptiveness of words as it is about Chief Joseph and his people. "But what is a piece of white paper, ink on it?" Chief Joseph says, speaking of the broken treaty between his people and the white settlers. Later, when the extent of the deception has become clear, Chief Joseph cannot speak at all. It is almost as if he has ceased believing in words, or at least in his ability to use them: "Oh, Who will speak! cried the heart in my bosom/Speak for the Nimipu, and speak Truth!"

I guess that is the reason Warren wrote this poem, to speak Truth for the now-silent tribe of the Nez Percé. Warren seems to actually adopt the rhythm of a Native American dialect when he says:

The salmon leaps, and is the Sky-Chief's blessing.
The Sky-Power thus blessed the Nimipu
And blessed them, too, with
The camas root, good to the tongue, in abundance.

Significantly, the language seems very spare, unembellished, as if Warren, like Chief Joseph, does not trust the language he uses: "muzzle-grounded," "straight-flung." Each word shows a careful choice.

Even Warren finally finds words to be inadequate. At the end of the poem, he and a friend visit the site of the Indian warrior's surrender to General Miles over a hundred years ago. "We went," he writes, "and did not talk much on the way."

Unlike an essay on theme, a response essay expresses the personal feelings and thoughts of the reader. What can you see in the first paragraph of this model that shows it is a response essay?

What response do you have to Warren's language?

Write a Response

Many folk songs are actually narrative poems set to music. Select either a classic folk song with narrative lyrics, such as "John Henry" or "Scarlet Ribbons," or a contemporary ballad by Bruce Springsteen or Bob Dylan. Write about your reactions to the song in a short response essay.

PURPOSE   To write a response to a narrative song
AUDIENCE   Your classmates
LENGTH   3–4 paragraphs

WRITING RUBRICS   To write an effective response to a folk song, you should

- respond to the story elements
- respond to the poetic elements

Cross-Curricular Activity

DRAMATIC ARTS   Read a narrative poem, and then choose a part of the poem that would make a good opening for a film. Recast that part of the poem as the opening scene of a film. First, briefly describe the setting, characters, plot, point of view, and theme. Then add details for the set, costume, and makeup designs. Write a short script. Include dialogue, using phrases from the poem if possible. Stay as close to the facts and feelings of the original poem as you can.

Listening and Speaking

COOPERATIVE LEARNING   With a partner or a group of your classmates, perform the script that you prepared in the Cross-Curricular Activity. Invite feedback about whether your adaptation remained faithful to the original while adding new elements of drama or excitement.

Correct run-on sentences.

Avoid run-on sentences—two sentences put together without proper punctuation between them—in any kind of writing that you do.

In the following sentences, correct any run-ons by separating clauses with a semicolon. If a sentence is correct, write "Correct."

1. P. D. James writes thrilling mysteries other books sound flat by comparison.
2. The bakery finished the eclairs and sorted out the macaroons.
3. Do you have tap shoes in an 8 narrow or possibly an 8 slim?
4. Jonas lifted his catch onto the pier crowds admired the size of the tuna.
5. Netta and Bill, plus a few acquaintances, left the game room at noon.
6. Deanie, I hope you and Bill have a terrific holiday I will miss you.
7. Pines make a graceful motion during storms willows also bend and swirl in the wind.
8. Laney ran for secretary the crowd supported her all the way.
9. Icy mornings slow the bus we expect to be later than usual.
10. They didn't join us they had made other plans.

See Lesson 13.10, pages 553–555.

Writing Process in Action

Narrative Writing

Narrative Writing

In preceding lessons you've learned about the kinds of details, writing strategies, and organizational techniques that can bring characters in your narratives to life. You've had the chance to write about contemporary and historical real-life characters. Now it's time to make use of what you've learned. In this lesson, you're invited to write a narrative about a person who astonishes and inspires you.

Assignment

Context	You are entering an essay contest called "The Wonder of Wonders" for high school juniors. You are to write a nonfiction narrative about an astonishing and inspiring person, focusing on the person's character or a particular achievement or event. The narrative must be based on personal experience, research, or a combination of these.
Purpose	To write a narrative about a person you find astonishing and inspiring
Audience	A panel of high school juniors
Length	2 pages

The following pages can help you plan and write your narrative. Read through them, and then refer to them as you wish. But remember: You're in charge of your own writing process.

Prewriting

What or who in your experience has left you full of wonder? As you were reading this assignment, a person or an achievement may have popped immediately to mind. If so, begin exploring your topic right away. If not, try freewriting in response to the following: "The most astonishing person I've ever met is . . ."

Once you have a subject, narrow your focus. Use the prewriting questions to help you.

Search for specifics that will breathe life into your topic. The model below uses specific details that make you feel as if you were part of magician Harry Houdini's astonished audience.

Prewriting Questions

- What do I find wonderful about this person?
- What is truly significant: one achievement or the entire life?
- How wide is the scope of influence of this person?
- What else do I want to know?

Literature Model

On January 7, 1918, Houdini had a ten-thousand-pound elephant led onto the bright stage of the Hippodrome in New York City. A trainer marched the elephant around a cabinet large enough for an elephant, proving there was space behind. There was no trap door in the floor of the Hippodrome, and the elephant could not fly. Houdini ushered the pachyderm into the cabinet and closed the curtains. Then he opened them, and where the elephant had stood there was nothing but empty space.

Daniel Mark Epstein, *The Case of Harry Houdini*

Given your purpose, what structure or organization for your narrative will hook your readers and keep their attention? Before deciding on the most effective structure, formulate a thesis statement and write it down. This is your controlling idea; let it guide you through the decisions that lie ahead. Next, construct a time line, and flesh out this "skeleton" with carefully chosen details, images, and ideas. Include quotes or memorable pieces of dialogue if they are available.

Experiment with two or three structures, choosing the one that best fulfills the promise of your thesis.

TIME

For more about the writing process, see **TIME Facing the Blank Page,** pages 111–121.

Writing Process in Action

Drafting Tip

For help with character development, see Lesson 4.1, pages 172–177, and Lesson 4.2, pages 178–181.

Drafting

Now is the time for pulling together the details you have collected—and others that occur to you as you draft—into a unified and coherent whole. Finally, review the prompt for this assignment, and start writing! Remember, the important object is to get your ideas down, so just let your writing flow.

Once you have everything down on paper, put your draft aside. A few hours' or even a day's time away from it can help you see the strengths and weaknesses of your narrative more clearly.

Revising

To begin revising, read over your draft to make sure that what you've written fits your purpose and audience. Make sure your essay conveys your attitude toward your subject. Do you cite the reasons for your astonishment or inspiration? After you have evaluated the content of your writing, have a **writing conference.** Read your draft to a partner or small group. Use your audience's reactions to help you evaluate your work.

Revising Tip

For examples of how to use dialogue in narratives, see Lesson 4.1, page 175.

Revising Checklist

- Does the narrative flow from my thesis?
- Have I revealed character by using vivid description and presenting dialogue and actions?
- Have I included incidents and details that shed light on my subject's personality?
- Did I structure my narrative chronologically?
- Have I included a personal anecdote or reflection in the conclusion of my narrative?

Editing

Once you are happy with the basic content and organization of your narrative, proofread it carefully for errors in grammar, usage, mechanics, and spelling. Use the questions at the right as a guide.

Use the Self-Evaluation list below to make sure your narrative does all the things you want it to do. When you're satisfied, make a clean copy of your narrative and proofread it one more time.

Editing Checklist

- Have I avoided incomplete comparisons?
- Have I used quotation marks to punctuate dialogue?
- Have I avoided run-on sentences?
- Do my subjects and verbs agree?
- Have I checked spellings of any words of which I'm unsure?

Self-Evaluation

Make sure your narrative—

✔ shows why a particular person or achievement is wonderful and has significance
✔ makes the characters vivid through physical description, believable action, and dialogue
✔ orders the details of plot so as to hold the reader's attention
✔ uses appropriate tone and word choice
✔ is unified and coherent
✔ follows standards of grammar, usage, mechanics, and spelling

Presenting

Consider giving copies of your narrative to family members and friends so that they may share your "wonder." You may also want to create a booklet of your classmates' narratives and display it in the school library.

Proofreading Tip

When you are finished with your narrative, proofread for errors in grammar, usage, mechanics, and spelling. For proofreading symbols, see page 92.

Journal Writing

Reflect on your writing-process experience. Answer these questions in your journal: What do I like best about my narrative? What was the hardest part of writing it? What did I learn in my writing conference? What new things have I learned as a writer?

Literature Model

In "The Case of Harry Houdini," Daniel Mark Epstein brings the early twentieth-century magician Harry Houdini back to life. Epstein had not yet been born when Houdini was dazzling audiences worldwide, yet Epstein tells the magician's story with all the richness of a firsthand account. As you read, pay special attention to how, by placing Houdini in his historical context, Epstein not only narrates but also interprets the famous tricks and escapes. Then try the activities in Linking Writing and Literature on page 206.

The case of Harry Houdini

by Daniel Mark Epstein

As he had done in America and England, Houdini began his tour of Germany with a visit to police headquarters. The Dresden officers were not enthusiastic, yet they could hardly refuse the magician's public invitation to lock him up. A refusal would suggest a crisis of confidence; and like their colleagues the world over, the Dresden police viewed Houdini's news clippings as so much paper in the balance against their locks and chains. Of course the Dresden police had no more success than those of Kansas City, or San Francisco, or Scotland Yard. Their manacles were paper to him. The police chief reluctantly signed the certificate Houdini demanded, but the newspapers gave him little coverage.

So on his opening night at Dresden's Central Theater, Houdini arranged to be fettered in the leg irons and manacles of the Mathildegasse Prison. Some of the locks weighed forty pounds. The audience, packed to the walls, went wild over his escape, and the fact he spoke their language endeared him further. If anything could have held him captive it would have been the adoring burghers of Dresden, who mobbed the theater for weeks. The manager wanted to buy out Houdini's contract with the Wintergarten of Berlin, so as to hold him over in Dresden, but the people of Berlin could not wait to see the magician.

Houdini arrived in Berlin in October of 1900. The first thing he did was march into the police station, strip stark naked and challenge the jailors. They could not hold him. This time Count von Windheim, the highest-ranking policeman in Germany, signed the certificate of Houdini's escape. The Wintergarten was overrun. The management appealed to the theater of Houdini's next engagement, in Vienna, so they might hold him over an extra month in Berlin. The Viennese finally yielded, demanding an indemnity equal to Houdini's salary for one month. When the magician, at long last, opened at the Olympic Theater in Paris, in December of 1901, he was the highest paid foreign entertainer in French history.

But meanwhile there was big trouble brewing in Germany.

But meanwhile there was big trouble brewing in Germany. It seems the police there had little sense of humor about Houdini's peculiar gifts, and Houdini quickly exhausted what little patience they had. In Dortmund he escaped from the irons that had bound Glowisky, a notorious murderer beheaded three days before. At Hanover the police chief, Count von Schwerin, plotted to disgrace Houdini, challenging him to escape from a special straitjacket reinforced with thick leather. Houdini agonized for one and a half hours while von Schwerin looked on, his jubilant smile melting in wonder, then rage, as the magician worked himself free.

The cumulative anger of the German police went public in July of 1901. Inspector Werner Graff witnessed Houdini's escape from all manacles at the Cologne police station, and vowed to end the humiliation. It was not a simple matter of pride. Graff, along with von Schwerin and other officials, feared Houdini was weakening their authority and inviting jailbreaks, if not other kinds of antisocial behavior. So Graff wrote a letter to Cologne's newspaper, the *Rheinische Zeitung*. The letter stated that Houdini had escaped from simple restraints at the police headquarters by trickery; but his publicity boasted he could escape from restraints of *any kind*. Such a claim, Graff wrote, was a lie, and Houdini ought to be prosecuted for fraud.

Though he knew the letter was nonsense the magician could not ignore it, for it was dangerous nonsense. If the police began calling him a fraud in every town he visited,

Houdini would lose his audience. So he demanded that Graff apologize and the newspaper publish a retraction. Graff refused, and other German dailies reprinted his letter. Should Harry Houdini sue the German policeman for libel? Consider the circumstances. Germany, even in 1901, was one of the most authoritarian states in the world. Houdini was an American, a Jew who embarrassed the police. A libel case against Graff would turn upon the magician's claim he could escape from *any* restraint, and the courtroom would become an international theater. There a German judge and jury would try his skill, and should they find it wanting, Houdini would be washed up, exiled to play beer halls and dime museums. Only an artist with colossal pride and total confidence in his methods would act as Houdini did. He hired the most prominent trial lawyer in Cologne, and ordered him to sue Werner Graff and the Imperial Police of Germany for criminal libel.

There was standing room only in the Cologne *Schöffengericht*. The judge allowed Werner Graff to seek out the most stubborn locks and chains he could find, and tangle Houdini in them, in full view of everyone. Here was a hitch, for Houdini did not wish to show the crowd his technique. He asked the judge to clear the courtroom, and in the ensuing turmoil the magician released himself so quickly no one knew how he had done it. The *Schöffengericht* fined the astonished policeman and ordered a public apology. So Graff's lawyer appealed the case.

Two months later Graff was better prepared. In the *Strafkammer*, or court of appeals, he presented thirty letters from legal authorities declaring that the escape artist could not justify his advertisements. And Graff had a shiny new pair of handcuffs. The premier locksmith of Germany had engineered the cuffs especially for the occasion. Werner Graff explained to the judge that the lock, once closed, could never be opened, even with its own key. Let Houdini try to get out of these.

This time the court permitted Houdini to work in privacy, and a guard led the magician

to an adjacent chamber. Everyone else settled down for a long wait, in a chatter of anticipation. They were interrupted four minutes later by the entrance of Houdini, who tossed the manacles on the judge's bench. So the *Strafkammer* upheld the lower court's decision, as did the *Oberlandesgericht* in a "paper" appeal. The court fined Werner Graff thirty marks and ordered him to pay for the trials as well as a published apology. Houdini's next poster showed him in evening dress, his hands manacled, standing before the judge, jurors and a battery of mustachioed policemen. Looking down on the scene was a bust of the Kaiser against a crimson background, and a scroll that read: "The Imperial Police of Cologne slandered Harry Houdini ... were compelled to advertise 'An Honorary Apology' and pay costs of the trials. By command of Kaiser Wilhelm II, Emperor of Germany."

Now this is surely an extravagant tale, and it will seem no less wonderful when we understand the technique that made it come true. When Houdini took on the Imperial Police in 1901, he was not whistling in the dark. By the time he left America at the end of the nineteenth century he had dissected every kind of lock he could find in the new world, and whatever he could import from the old one. Arriving in London, Houdini could write that there were only a few kinds of British handcuffs, "seven or eight at the utmost," and these were some of the simplest he had ever seen. He searched the markets, antique shops, and locksmiths, buying up all the European locks he could find so he could dismantle and study them.

Humankind cannot be held in chains.

Then during his Berlin engagement he worked up to ten hours a day at Mueller's locksmith on the Mittelstrasse, studying restraints. He was the Bobby Fischer of locks. With a chessmaster's foresight Houdini devised a set of picks to release every lock in existence, as well as *any he could imagine.* Such tireless ingenuity produced the incandescent light bulb and the atom bomb. Houdini's theater made a comparable impact on the human spirit. He had a message which he delivered so forcefully it goes without mentioning in theater courses: Humankind cannot be held in chains. The European middle class had reached an impressionable age, and the meaning of Houdini's theater was not lost upon them. Nor was he mistaken by the aristocracy, who stayed away in droves. The spectacle of an American Jew bursting from chains by dint of ingenuity did not amuse the rich. They desperately wanted to demythologize him.

It was not about to happen in the German courtroom. When Werner Graff snapped the "new" handcuffs on Houdini, they were not strange to the magician. He had already invented them, so to speak, as well as the pick to open them, and the pick was in his pocket. Only a locksmith whose knowledge surpassed Houdini's could stop him; diligent study assured him that, as of 1901, there could be no such locksmith.

What else can we understand about the methods of Harry Houdini, né Ehrich Weiss? We know he was a superbly conditioned athlete who did not smoke or take a drop of alcohol. His straitjacket escapes he performed in full view of the world so that everyone could see he freed himself by main force and flexibility.

He may or may not have been able to dislocate his shoulders at will—he said he could, and it seems no more marvelous than certain other skills he demonstrated. Friends reported that his toes could untie knots most of us could not manage with our fingers. And routinely the magician would hold his breath for as long as four minutes to work underwater escapes. To cheapen the supernatural claims of the fakir Rahman Bey, Houdini remained under water in an iron box for ninety minutes, as against the Egyptian's sixty.

Examining Houdini, a physician testified that the fifty-year-old wizard had halved his blood pressure while doubling his pulse. Of course, more wonderful than any of these capabilities was the courage allowing him to employ them, in predicaments where any normal person would panic.

These things are known about Houdini. The same tireless ingenuity when applied to locks and jails, packing cases and riveted boilers—the same athletic prowess when applied at the bottom of the East River, or while dangling from a rope attached to the cornice of the Sun Building in Baltimore— these talents account for the vast majority of

Adolph Friedlander, *Harry Houdini*, 1913

Houdini's exploits. As we have mentioned, theater historians, notably Raymund Fitzsimons in his *Death and the Magician,* have carefully exposed Houdini's ingenuity, knowing that nothing can tarnish the miracle of the man's existence. Their accounts are technical and we need not dwell on them, except to say they *mostly* support Houdini's oath that his effects were achieved by natural or mechanical means. The Houdini problem arises from certain outrageous effects no one has ever been able to explain, though capable technicians have been trying for more than sixty years.

Let us briefly recall those effects. We have mentioned the disappearing elephant. On January 7, 1918, Houdini had a ten-thousand-pound elephant led onto the bright stage of the Hippodrome in New York City. A trainer marched the elephant around a cabinet large enough for an elephant, proving there was space behind. There was no trapdoor in the floor of the Hippodrome, and the elephant could not fly. Houdini ushered the pachyderm into the cabinet and closed the curtains. Then he opened them, and where the elephant had stood there was nothing but empty space. Houdini went on with his program, which might have been making the Hippodrome disappear, for all the audience knew. A reporter for the *Brooklyn Eagle* noted: "The program says that the elephant vanished into thin air. The trick is performed fifteen feet from the backdrop and the cabinet is slightly elevated. That explanation is as good as any." After Houdini stopped

making elephants disappear, nineteen weeks later, the trick would never be precisely duplicated ....

In the Houdini Museum at Niagara Falls, Canada, you may view the famous *Mirror* handcuffs. If you are a scholar you can inspect them. In March of 1904 the London *Daily Mirror* discovered a blacksmith who had been working for five years to build a set of handcuffs no mortal man could pick. Examining the cuffs, the best locksmiths in London agreed they had never seen such an ingenious mechanism. The newspaper challenged Houdini to escape from them. On March 17, before a house of four thousand in the London Hippodrome, a journalist fastened the cuffs on Houdini's wrists and turned the key six times. The magician retired to his cabinet onstage, and the band struck up a march. He did not emerge for twenty minutes. Then he came out to hold the lock up to the light. Remember that most "challenge" handcuffs were regulation, and familiar to Houdini. He studied the lock in the light, and then went back into the cabinet as the band played a waltz.

Ten minutes later Houdini stuck his head out, asking if he could have a cushion to kneel on. He was denied. After almost an hour Houdini came out of the cabinet again, obviously worn out, and his audience groaned. He wanted the handcuffs to be unlocked for a moment so he could take off his coat, as he was sweating profusely. The journalist denied the request, since Houdini had never before seen the handcuffs unlocked, and that might give him an advantage. Whereupon

> ...his effects were achieved by natural or mechanical means.

Literature Model

Houdini, in full view of four thousand, extracted a penknife from his pocket and opened it with his teeth. Turning the coat inside out over his head, he shredded it loose with the penknife, and returned to the cabinet. Someone called out that Houdini had been handcuffed for more than an hour. As the band played on, the journalists of the London *Daily Mirror* could taste the greatest scoop of the twentieth century. But ten minutes later there was a cry from the cabinet and Houdini leapt out of it, free, waving the handcuffs high in the air. While the crowd roared, several men from the audience carried Houdini, crying as if his heart would break, on their shoulders around the theater.

Narrative Writing

Linking Writing and Literature

Readers Respond to the Model

How does Daniel Mark Epstein capture the personality of Harry Houdini?

Explore Epstein's narrative by answering the following questions. Then read what other students liked about Epstein's narrative.

1. From your reading of Epstein's narrative, what words would you use to characterize Houdini and his feats?
2. What response did you have to the *Mirror* handcuffs episode?

3. Which of Houdini's qualities do you admire most? Why?

What Students Say

"The things that Harry Houdini did were phenomenal. I believe that anyone would be interested in a person who was able to accomplish such magic tricks. Houdini's persistence is also an inspiration. A person who gives up when something gets tough could learn a lesson from Houdini. He had the courage to rise to any challenge. That is something that everyone should have. With hard work and strong will, anything can be done. I think that is the message of this reading. It was a joy to read this."

David Alonzo

"I remember the parts about how Houdini unlocked the handcuffs and how all the Germans were trying to prove he was a fraud, but failed. By using words and phrases like "Houdini . . . tossed the manacles on the judge's bench," Epstein makes the accusers look like fools."

Becky Byer

Reflecting on the Unit

Summarize what you have learned in this unit by answering the following questions:

1 What are some ways to reveal character through narrative?

2 What purpose does a time line serve in planning a biographical sketch?

3 What are some of the ways to choose which events to use in a long biographical narrative?

4 Why is it important to formulate a thesis for a biographical narrative?

Adding to Your Portfolio

Look over the narrative writing you have done during this unit. Select a completed piece of writing to put into your portfolio. The piece you choose should show some or all of the following:

- vivid description
- details that reveal character
- events and details that are chosen to focus on one aspect of your subject
- a clear sense of chronological order

REFLECT ON YOUR CHOICE Attach notes to the piece you chose, explaining briefly why you chose it and what you learned from writing it.

SET GOALS How can you improve your writing? What skill will you focus on the next time you write?

Writing Across the Curriculum

MAKE A HISTORY CONNECTION Select a contemporary or historical political figure whose life you know something about. Choose one episode from the person's life that you feel captures the essence of his or her personality. Write a brief narrative account of that episode, organizing your ideas around a thesis statement.

MAKE A LITERATURE CONNECTION Choose a fictional character from literature whom you feel you know well. Choose an event from the character's life to express as a narrative. Write a brief narrative account of that event, including details that reveal what kind of person your character is.

"I smell a river and I am a child again."

—Joyce Orrell, "Song of the River"

Expository Writing

Writing in the Real World

MEDIA Booklet Connection

E ffective expository writing enables readers to understand new and complex information by taking them down a logical step-by-step path. The following is an expository article written by Shelley Lauzon, the director of public information for Woods Hole Oceanographic Institution in Massachusetts.

from R.M.S. *Titanic*

by Shelley Lauzon

Director of Public Information
Shelley Lauzon

T he discovery of the sunken luxury liner R.M.S. *Titanic* September 1, 1985, aboard the Woods Hole Oceanographic Institution's Research Vessel *Knorr* has begun a new era in underwater exploration and scientific research. The *Titanic*, found at a depth of more than 12,000 feet, was first photographed by the new deep-towed sonar and video camera system ARGO, under development in the Institution's Deep Submergence Laboratory (DSL). Additional 35mm photographs were taken by the ANGUS (Acoustically Navigated Geological Underwater Survey), another towed vehicle developed at the Institution.

The discovery of the *Titanic* was a joint French-American effort which began earlier in the summer of 1985 with a cruise aboard the French research vessel *Le Suroit* to test France's new sonar system, SAR (Système Acoustique Remorqué). Dr. Robert D. Ballard, leader of the Woods Hole Oceanographic Institution's Deep Submergence Laboratory, participated in that cruise which ended in early August. Three scientists from the Institut français de recherche pour l'exploitation de la mer (IFREMER) joined the American cruise aboard the *Knorr* August 15 in Ponta Delgada, Azores, for the trip across the Atlantic to the vessel's home port at Woods Hole, Massachusetts. [During this journey, the scientists conducted a search for the *Titanic*.]

Using sonar imagery, the earlier French cruise had ruled out large sections in a 150-square-mile search area, allowing the *Knorr* cruise to concentrate on the remaining areas under a different search strategy. The first visual contact of the *Titanic* was debris including one of the ship's boilers and was made by the ARGO vehicle just after 1:00 A.M. EST September 1, 1985. The seven-member scientific watch which saw the first images included four Institution personnel, two French scientists, and a U.S. Navy officer and was led by Jean-Louis Michel (IFREMER), co-chief scientist with Dr.

Ballard of the expedition. Video filming from ARGO and 35mm filming from ANGUS were conducted throughout the remaining four days of the voyage. R/V *Knorr* returned to the Woods Hole Oceanographic Institution September 9, 1985, to a joyous celebration.

"We are obviously very pleased and excited to have found the *Titanic*," Ballard reported to colleagues at the Institution during the voyage, "But we are also very aware of the significance of the *Titanic* as a maritime disaster." After the elation of the discovery, the remembrance of the tragedy struck home, and some of those aboard the *Knorr* held a brief memorial service on the ship's fantail for those lost in the 1912 disaster.

The importance of the discovery for the Woods Hole Oceanographic Institution, the U.S. Navy and France's IFREMER was proving the capabilities of new camera and sonar systems. Both ARGO and SAR were undergoing sea trials and were not yet in final form. The primary mission of both French and American cruises was to conduct deep-water engineering tests, and finding the *Titanic* was a secondary but dramatic bonus. . . .

"Finding the *Titanic* is a dramatic demonstration of our present capability to explore the ocean depths for scientific purposes," Institution Director John H. Steele said of the *Titanic* discovery. "It has taken years of work by dedicated engineers and will prove its value to science and the nation in the years ahead."

A Writer's Process

Prewriting

Gathering Information

Shelley Lauzon was swamped with requests for information when the public learned that a research ship from Woods Hole had discovered the wreck of the *Titanic* one thousand miles east of Massachusetts. The ill-fated luxury liner had sunk in the North Atlantic in 1912, killing over 1,500 people.

"There were obvious things people wanted to know about," Lauzon recalls. The public especially wanted to see pictures of the sunken ship taken with ARGO. Lauzon decided to publish a booklet twenty to twenty-four pages long.

First Lauzon outlined subjects to include in the booklet. She decided to generate about eleven short articles plus several pages of photographs of the *Titanic* and of the *Knorr's* homecoming.

Lauzon called the Titanic Historical Society for information on the sunken luxury liner. She also spent hours gathering facts about ARGO.

Lauzon's research yielded a stack of papers about two feet high. "I went through it all, read it, and decided what was important for a brief overview of the whole project," she says. In the technical material, she found engineering terms that she didn't understand. She was certain that much of her audience wouldn't grasp the terms either. She had to find a way to simplify the technical language.

Lauzon resolved to ask experts in the field for help. In one instance, she worked with an engineer to find a way to explain the low-light sensitive film used to capture pictures of the *Titanic*.

Writing in the Real World

Writing a Proposal

PREWRITING	DRAFTING/EDITING	PRESENTING

1. Gathering Information

Gathering Information

2. Writing about Technology

Getting the Facts Down

3. Assembling the Booklet

Assembling the Booklet

Drafting/Revising
Getting the Facts Down

Since her office hadn't yet bought computers, Lauzon wrote her first drafts in longhand. "Most of the work went quickly," she says. "The short piece on ARGO, about 350 words, took only a few hours. It went fast because once I understood the technical information, I could translate it into popular English."

Lauzon edited her articles in longhand too. "I edited on the piece of paper I wrote on," she explains. Lauzon moved paragraphs around and worked to make her explanations clear and simple.

Once Lauzon was satisfied with her drafts, she typed the articles and sent them to the appropriate Woods Hole experts—articles on technical subjects, for instance, went to engineers for review. Lauzon then made any changes the experts called for and typed final drafts of the articles.

Publishing/Presenting
Assembling the Booklet

With the text complete, Lauzon was ready to choose photographs and lay out the pages. One of her toughest jobs was narrowing down the fifty-plus

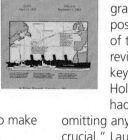

Titanic photos to a representative sample. Lauzon settled on twenty-eight: haunting images such as bedsprings lying on the ocean bottom and the crow's nest from which the fatal iceberg was first spotted.

Lauzon sketched out each page of the brochure on a sheet of 8 1/2-by-11-inch paper. Then she photocopied the photographs and pasted them in position, creating a mock-up of the final product. Lauzon reviewed the brochure with key members of the Woods Hole staff. "At that point we had to make sure we weren't omitting any information that might be crucial," Lauzon says. Once everyone gave the nod, Lauzon sent her layouts to the printer with an order to print 25,000 copies.

In Lauzon's booklet, the visual and verbal elements work together to help the reader understand the subject.

Lauzon was the writer, editor, and designer on the Titanic *project. She laid out her pages in a way that would make the technical information as clear as possible.*

Examining Writing in the Real World

Analyzing the Media Connection

Discuss these questions about the article on pages 210–211.

1. In your opinion, what questions is the article attempting to answer?

2. How does Lauzon make her main points in a way that nonscientists can understand?

3. What facts does Lauzon include to suggest the importance of the *Titanic*'s discovery?

4. How do the quotes by Robert D. Ballard and John H. Steele contribute to the meaning and power of the article?

5. How would you describe the tone of the article? dramatic? matter of fact? What details support your view?

Analyzing a Writer's Process

Discuss these questions about Shelley Lauzon's writing process.

1. How did Lauzon research the subjects she chose to cover?

2. What steps did Lauzon take to ensure that the general public would understand the technical information discussed in her articles?

3. Describe the process Lauzon follows when drafting and revising her articles.

In what ways is it similar to the process you follow?

4. Why did Lauzon feel the need to "translate" technical information into "popular English?"

5. After Lauzon completed her brochure, what steps did she take to publish it?

Use appositives to define unfamiliar terms.

An *appositive* is a word or phrase that is placed next to a noun or pronoun to identify or explain it. If an appositive is not essential to the sentence, it should be set off by commas.

> *The* Titanic*, **the fastest ship in the world in 1912,** sank on its maiden voyage.*

> *Spokeswoman **Shelley Lauzon** integrated information from many sources.*

Put each term below into a sentence, adding appositives to explain or identify the terms.

1. iceberg
2. geologist
3. press kit
4. the *Knorr*
5. *Argo*
6. media
7. Titanic Historical Society
8. Woods Hole
9. low-light sensitive film
10. the crow's nest

See Lesson 12.2, pages 515–516.

LESSON
5.1

Writing Expository Paragraphs

*I*n the model below, Sharon Begley explains how and why chimps at the St. Louis Zoo work for a living. When writing to explain or inform as Begley does, you can choose from several types of expository paragraphs.

> What concrete example does Begley use to bring this topic to life?

Literature Model

The chimps at the St. Louis Zoo . . . work for a living: they poke stiff pieces of hay into an anthill to scoop out the baby food and honey that curators cache away inside. Instead of idly awaiting banana handouts, the chimps get to manipulate tools, just as they do in the wild. . . .

As species become extinct at a rate unparalleled since the Cretaceous era . . . zoos are striving to make their settings match their new role as keepers of the biological flame. Since 1980 the nation's 143 accredited zoos and aquariums have spent more than $1 billion on renovation and construction, much of it going to create habitats that immerse both animals and visitors in the sights, sounds, feel, and smell of the wild.

Sharon Begley, "Wilder Places for Wild Things," *Newsweek*

Choose the Right Kind of Paragraph

Expository paragraphs such as those in the model are the building blocks of longer essays. The kinds of paragraphs you use to develop an essay depend on the topic you select and your purpose for writing. The chart on the next page shows some kinds of expository paragraphs that could be used in writing about the possible extinction of the African elephant.

Ivory Trade		
QUESTION	**TYPE OF EXPOSITORY WRITING**	**STRATEGY**
1. What is the process by which ivory smugglers transport tusks out of Africa?	Process Explanation	uses step-by-step organization to explain how something happens, works, or is done.
2. What has caused the African elephant population to decline?	Cause and Effect	identifies the causes and/or effects of something and examines the relationship between causes and effects
3. How do ivory substitutes compare with ivory in different uses?	Compare and Contrast	examines similarities and differences to find relationships and draw conclusions
4. How can the African elephant be saved from extinction?	Problems and Solutions	examines aspects of a complex problem and explores or proposes possible solutions
5. Would an international ban on the sale of ivory end poaching?	Building a Hypothesis	uses patterns of facts to offer explanations or predictions and then test the hypothesis

The chart shows how different questions lead to different types of expository writing. For example, the first question can lead to a paragraph that explains the process by which ivory is smuggled out of Africa.

Answering many of these questions will involve using the same information but will require different types of organization and writing.

Whichever question you choose, keep in mind the knowledge and interests of your audience in selecting details to support your explanations. This cube shows how the choice of details for two cause-and-effect paragraphs varies depending on the audience.

Topic
Ivory Trade

Audience
Ivory consumers

Details
1. Thousands of elephants are cruelly killed for ivory.
2. Elephant populations are near extinction.
3. Elephants are crucial to African ecosystems.

Audience
Scientists

Details
1. African elephant population dropped from 1.3 million to 500,000 between 1979 and 1995.
2. Seventy-two percent of elephant families in a recent study were lacking adult females.

Journal Writing

In your journal, write a paragraph for U.S. lawmakers about the African ivory trade. What information from the boxes above would you delete? What would you add? Why?

Use Effective Transitions

Use transitional words to show the relationship between details. Simply writing a series of details will result in a choppy, unclear paragraph, even if they are arranged logically. A paragraph like the one below takes your reader on a bumpy ride.

Student Model

That ivory bracelet you just couldn't resist threatens the very existence of elephants in Africa. Mature elephant populations have been virtually wiped out. Poachers kill more and more young adults and juveniles. Elephant families have been destroyed. The killings have disrupted the elephants' breeding patterns.

Transitional words help make the relationships among ideas clear. Note these commonly used transitions and the relationships they show:

Time: *after, always, before, finally, first, immediately, later, meanwhile, now, sometimes, soon, until*

Place: *above, ahead, around, below, down, far, here, inside, near, next to, opposite, outside, over, parallel, there, under, vertically, within*

Order of Importance: *first, former to, latter, primarily, secondarily*

Cause and Effect: *as a result, because, by, so, then, therefore*

Comparison and Contrast: *but, even more, however, just as, like, on the other hand, unlike*

Example: *for example, for instance, namely, that is*

Now read the revised model with transitions added:

Revising Tip

When you revise your paragraph, make sure it is as clear as possible. Weed out information that doesn't contribute to or support the topic sentence.

Student Model

That ivory bracelet you just couldn't resist may be the end of a cruel and illegal process that threatens the very existence of elephants in Africa. In many regions, mature elephant populations have been virtually wiped out by ruthless poachers seeking large tusks for ivory. Consequently, poachers now kill more and more young adults and even juveniles to get the same amount of ivory. Because of the slaughter, the elephants' breeding patterns have been disrupted. As a result, females bear fewer offspring, shrinking the population even more.

Write an Expository Paragraph

A teacher has asked you to explain to a group of small children what a trip to the zoo is like. Before you visit the class, the teacher has asked you to write an expository paragraph that will serve as a basis for your talk. Your paragraph should include an explanation of how the tour of the zoo will be conducted and offer brief examples of what the children will see at the zoo.

PURPOSE To explain what a trip to the zoo is like
AUDIENCE Small children visiting a zoo for the first time
LENGTH 1 paragraph

WRITING RUBRICS To write an effective expository paragraph, you should

- use an appropriate method of organization
- select details that will make sense to your audience
- use transitional words to clarify relationships between ideas

Using Computers

If you use a computer to write your expository paragraph, you may want to triple-space a printout of your first draft. Use the extra space between the lines to write comments and revisions; then input the corrections to your draft.

Grammar Link

Write possessive nouns correctly.

Use an apostrophe and -s to form the possessive of a singular noun.

the **nation's** 143 accredited zoos

Use an apostrophe alone to form the possessive of a plural noun that ends in -s:

the **elephants'** breeding patterns

Make the noun in parentheses in each sentence possessive.

1. The speaker described the (St. Louis Zoo) collection of animals.
2. The (chimps) habitat is being rebuilt at our local zoo.
3. Many (families) entertainment for a Sunday afternoon is visiting the zoo.
4. We are studying the (Cretaceous era) climate in our science class.
5. That (aquarium) manager wants to stop having dolphin shows.
6. The wildlife (populations) grazing area is getting smaller every year.
7. One (species) habitat is not necessarily ideal for another.
8. (Africa) wildlife is some of the most threatened in the world.
9. The (poachers) lack of concern about animals is obvious.
10. (Ivory) value on the world market has actually gone down.

See Lesson 21.12, pages 741–743.

Listening and Speaking

COOPERATIVE LEARNING In small groups, read your expository paragraphs aloud. Critique each presentation, focusing on clarity, specificity, and suitability for the intended audience.

Explaining a Process

I n explaining a process, either how to do something or how something happens, present the steps in order and keep your audience's background knowledge in mind. Different kinds of processes are explained in the two models that follow.

> **Student Model**
>
> O ne of the football player's most important pieces of protective equipment is a mouth guard. This is one piece of equipment that must be made to fit the person who will use it. The first step in making a mouth guard is to select a mouth piece that is the correct size. . . . The next step is to fit the mouth piece to your mouth. To do this, you'll need to heat a pot of water. While the water is boiling, dip the plastic mouth piece in the water for ten to fifteen seconds. Immediately remove the mouth piece from the water and place it in your mouth. The plastic will be warm, but it isn't hot enough to burn your mouth. Bite down on the mouth piece and suck the excess water out of it. Then remove it from your mouth, spit out the water, and run the mouth piece under cold water. . . .
>
> Marcus Romero, Saint Bonaventure High School
> Ventura, California

If you want to make a mouth guard, what is the first thing you do after selecting a mouth piece of the correct size?

If you've ever followed instructions for assembling a kit, sewing a blouse, or operating unfamiliar equipment, you know how important it is that the process be explained clearly and simply. In the model above, Marcus Romero explains how to make an essential piece of football equipment. Romero explains a fairly simple process that requires steps to be performed in a certain order.

In the model on page 219, however, John McPhee presents a far more complex process involving years of interaction between rivers and rock to create the whitewater rapids of the expansive Grand Canyon.

Expository Writing

Literature Model

Rapids and waterfalls ordinarily take shape when rivers cut against resistant rock and then come to a kind of rock that gives way more easily. This is not the case in the Grand Canyon, where rapids occur beside the mouths of tributary creeks. Although these little streams may be dry much of the year, they are so steep that when they run they are able to fling considerable debris into the Colorado [River]—sand, gravel, stones, rocks, boulders. The debris forms dams, and water rises upstream. The river is unusually quiet there—a lakelike quiet—and then it flows over the debris, falling suddenly, pounding and crashing through the boulders. These are the rapids of the Grand Canyon, and there are a hundred and sixty-one of them.

John McPhee, *Encounters with the Archdruid*

> What is the first step in the process McPhee describes?

Use the Writing Process Stages

To explain a process, the writer must first understand the steps involved. The chart below illustrates the writing stages that are used.

PREWRITING	
Research by reading, watching others, or performing the process. Analyze the steps necessary to complete the process.	
DRAFTING	
Arrange the steps in chronological order. Break one step into two if more detail is needed. Leave out unnecessary steps.	
REVISING	
Reread the explanation. Make sure that you've included all necessary details and signaled separate steps with transition words. Reorder steps as needed.	

Journal Writing

Think of a simple process you perform. List in your journal the steps involved in this process.

Know Your Audience

As you plan your composition, consider your audience. What do members already know about the process you are explaining? How much detail are they likely to need? Will you need to define unfamiliar terms? The excerpt below, explaining how bicycle derailleur gears work, comes from a book that describes the workings of machines for people with little technical background.

Literature Model

The chain connecting the pedals of a bicycle to the rear wheel acts as a belt to make the wheel turn faster than the feet. To ride on the level or downhill, the rear-wheel sprocket needs to be small for high speeds. But to climb hills it needs to be large so that the rear wheel turns with less speed but more force.

Derailleur gears solve the problem by having rear-wheel sprockets of different sizes. A gear-changing mechanism transfers the chain from one sprocket to the next.

David Macaulay, *The Way Things Work*

Drafting Tip

As you draft your explanation, use analogies to give a clear picture of a complicated process.

This simple explanation gives readers a basic understanding of a process, using vocabulary that most readers can understand. Notice how the explanation below provides more thorough information, using technical terms such as *chainwheel* and *freewheel* that the first writer found unnecessary. This excerpt comes from a book written for serious cyclists who may want to work on their bicycles.

Literature Model

The basic derailleur system uses a combination of two sprockets (called chainwheels) on the front where the pedals are joined, and five sprockets (called the freewheel) at the rear attached to the wheel. To utilize all of the potential gear variations, a method to move the chain from sprocket to sprocket was developed. Using a control lever, the rider can move the derailleur which in turn forces (derails) the chain to adjacent sprockets.

Denise M. de la Rosa and Michael Kolin
Understanding, Maintaining, and Riding the Ten-Speed Bicycle

Write to Explain a Process

Choose a process that you are familiar with and can explain, such as how to change a bicycle tire or how to balance a checkbook. Write a short explanation for someone who knows little about it.

PURPOSE To explain a process
AUDIENCE People who are unfamiliar with the process
LENGTH 2–3 paragraphs

WRITING RUBRICS To explain a process, you should

- analyze the process to make sure you include all the steps
- arrange the steps in chronological order
- adapt your explanation to the knowledge level of your audience
- proofread and correct misplaced or dangling modifiers

Listening and Speaking

COOPERATIVE LEARNING Work with another student to test the effectiveness of your process paper. Partners should exchange papers and then try to carry out the process, either in class or at home. Evaluate the clarity and thoroughness of your partner's paper. Use the evaluation to revise your process description.

Grammar Link

Avoid dangling or misplaced modifiers.
Put modifiers as close as possible to the words or phrases they are modifying:

Using a control lever, the rider can *move the derailleur. . . .*

Avoid dangling modifiers, modifiers that do not logically seem to modify any word in a sentence.

Rewrite the following sentences, correcting misplaced or dangling modifiers.

1. He rode the bicycle to the mall only.
2. Tom softened a mouth guard for a friend with boiling water.
3. Before playing in the football game, the mouth guard was adjusted to a smaller size.
4. Flowing over the rocks, we watched the powerful river.
5. After sitting in the garage for twenty years, she fixed her bicycle.

See Lesson 18.7, pages 660–665.

Cross-Curricular Activity

Collage is an art form in which the artist assembles paper and other materials to create a work that expresses a new idea. Imagine you are an artist teaching a student how to make a collage. Prepare for this assignment by making a collage of materials you choose. As you work, note the steps you follow. Then write an explanation of the process you used to make the collage.

Analyzing Cause-and-Effect Connections

To explain connections between an event and its causes or consequences, look for real relationships among things that happened. In the model below, John Canemaker shows how several causes led to one event, the resurgence of animation.

Literature Model

> What effect is being discussed in this essay?

What's up, Doc? Animation, that's what. And that wascally wabbit Bugs Bunny, who celebrated his 50th birthday in 1990, is only part of animation's exciting comeback. Animation seems to be everywhere. For the first time in 30 years, many movie theaters are running cartoon shorts before live-action motion pictures. . . . And on television, "The Simpsons," the first prime-time weekly animated TV series on a United States network in 20 years, has consistently ranked among the top-rated programs. . . .

One explanation for the animation boom is the high quality of the artwork in the new cartoons and features. Thanks in part to computers, animation has never looked better. Another reason is the appeal animation has for the large chunk of the U.S. population known as baby boomers—people born between 1945 and 1964—who grew up with TV cartoons and who are now looking for entertainment they can enjoy with their own children.

> The author lists several causes for animation's comeback, saving the most important one for last.

But the biggest reason for the revival of animation, once scarcely seen outside Saturday morning television, is financial reward. . . . When they are successful, . . . [cartoons] can be as profitable as the most popular live-action movies. By late 1990, more than 30 full-length animated motion pictures were in production around the world.

John Canemaker, "Once Again, 'Toons' Are Tops"
The 1991 World Book Year Book

Determine the Precise Relationship

There are several different kinds of cause-and-effect relationships. In the model you just read, several causes led to the comeback of cartoons. The top panel of the diagram below illustrates this pattern of several causes leading to one effect.

In other cases, one event can have several effects. For example, when the Soviet Union launched the first orbiting satellite, *Sputnik,* in 1957, the U.S. government reacted in three ways out of fear of Soviet technical domination. The middle panel of the diagram illustrates the multiple effects of the *Sputnik* launch.

Still another kind of cause-and-effect relationship is the causal chain, in which one event affects the next, as in a line of falling dominoes. The bottom panel of the diagram shows that an increased demand for lobster leads to overfishing. The decrease in the number of lobsters, which are the natural predators of sea urchins, in turn causes an increase in the number of sea urchins.

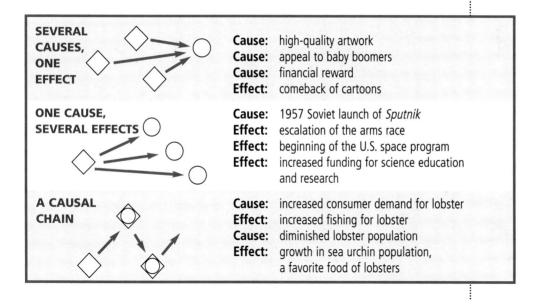

SEVERAL CAUSES, ONE EFFECT

Cause: high-quality artwork
Cause: appeal to baby boomers
Cause: financial reward
Effect: comeback of cartoons

ONE CAUSE, SEVERAL EFFECTS

Cause: 1957 Soviet launch of *Sputnik*
Effect: escalation of the arms race
Effect: beginning of the U.S. space program
Effect: increased funding for science education and research

A CAUSAL CHAIN

Cause: increased consumer demand for lobster
Effect: increased fishing for lobster
Cause: diminished lobster population
Effect: growth in sea urchin population, a favorite food of lobsters

Journal Writing

Think of other examples for each of the three kinds of cause-and-effect relationships shown above. Copy the diagram for each type of relationship into your journal and provide new cause-and-effect labels for each.

Make Legitimate Connections

When you write a cause-and-effect essay, make certain that the events have a true cause-and-effect relationship. Just because one event precedes another (it had been snowing for six hours) doesn't mean that the first event is the cause of the other (the temperature dropped to zero).

Help your audience understand events by explaining their connection to other events. In the model below, William S. Ellis helps readers understand the modern city by combining elements of two of the three basic cause-and-effect relationships shown on page 223.

Literature Model

This is a magical time in the evolution of America's urban landscapes, a time of bold (for better or worse), fresh architecture and computer-driven engineering, and a time too of a new generation of skyscrapers rising to be clad in clouds over major cities across the country—Minneapolis, even, and Los Angeles with its ill-defined downtown.

All of this is happening at a time when, paradoxically, organized opposition to construction of sunlight-blocking towers is stronger than ever before. It is too late, however, to reverse the reality that the skyscraper has become the logo for urban development in America; from King Kong to Donald Trump, it has bridged the 20th century with its indestructible, prodigious presence.

Today's skyscraper is a creation of economics and the need to escape the press of horizontal crowding. With raw land in midtown Manhattan now costing more than entire buildings a few decades ago, it is not surprising that developers are looking upward rather than outward. And (in the right place, in good times) a prestigious new building can attract tenants who will happily pay more than a thousand dollars for each square foot of lofty floor space they occupy.

William S. Ellis, "Skyscrapers: Above the Crowd"
National Geographic

How many causes are discussed in this model? How many effects?

Draw a diagram to represent the cause-and-effect relationships described in this paragraph.

Notice that in his opening discussion of the reasons for the evolution of America's urban landscape, Ellis mentions three causes. Then he takes one of those causes, a new generation of skyscrapers, and discusses it as an effect with several causes of its own. In essence, Ellis presents a causal chain in reverse.

Write a Cause-and-Effect Article

Write an article explaining what causes music videos to be so popular among teenagers.Use the several causes, one effect pattern from the chart on page 223.

PURPOSE To explain the appeal of music videos
AUDIENCE Your teacher and classmates
LENGTH 2–3 paragraphs

WRITING RUBRICS To write an effective cause-and-effect article, you should

- be sure each cause-and-effect relationship is genuine
- use transitional words and other connections between ideas
- use verb tenses correctly

Viewing and Representing

COOPERATIVE LEARNING Taken by Mathew Brady during the Civil War, the photograph on this page shows four members of the Union army. Working in a small group, assign one character in the photograph to each member.

Noting details of posture, facial expression, and dress, create a personal background for your character. Write down the chain of events that caused you to become involved in the war. Then, together write a two- to three-page script for a play that illustrates causes and effects discussed in each character profile.

Culver Pictures, Inc.

Grammar Link

Use verb tenses correctly.

Do not shift tenses when two or more events occur at about the same time.

*Architects **develop** innovative designs while new building sites **disappear.***

Rewrite the following sentences, correcting mistakes in verb tenses.

1. The architect designs skyscrapers that minimized horizontal crowding.
2. It is too late to think that building skyscrapers was a thing of the past.
3. Many animated movies are financially rewarding and were quite profitable.
4. People who attended the movie see a cartoon before the other film starts.

See Lesson 15.6, page 587.

Using Computers

Search the Internet to learn more about Mathew Brady's Civil War photography. In your group, develop a report on Brady's techniques and subjects and his perspective on the war. Have each group deliver its report to the class.

Writing an Essay to Compare and Contrast

Compare-and-contrast essays should be carefully constructed around thesis statements to explain similarities and differences between items or events.

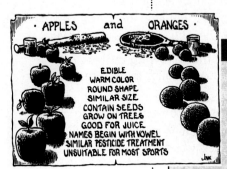

Why do you think Dalia explains American customs before informing her audience about Egyptian practices?

Student Model

American couples celebrate their engagement and marriage differently from couples in my homeland, Egypt. Here in the United States, in most cases, a couple dates for a while until they decide to get married. They then announce their engagement to their families. In the Egyptian culture, men and women cannot date without a chaperon until they decide to marry. To formalize their engagement, the man must ask the woman's parents, while his parents are present, for their daughter's hand in marriage. If the parents do not agree to the engagement, the relationship between the two must end.

In the United States, during the engagement friends and relatives often throw a wedding shower for the bride, while the groom is given a bachelor's party. In Egypt, a wedding shower is held for the couple. Both American and Egyptian showers feature music, food, and gifts, but the Egyptian shower has one special item on the night's agenda. The table where the bride and groom sit has a bowl of mud, placed there by one of their parents, with a candle in it. This bowl is blessed by a priest who then draws a cross with the mud on both the man's and the woman's forehead. This shared cross symbolizes their holy unity.

In each culture, the man and woman marry in a wedding ceremony. An American wedding lasts about half an hour to an hour. The Egyptian wedding lasts anywhere from one to two hours. In both cultures, couples are united by a kiss at the end of the ceremony.

Dalia Bichay, Quartz Hill High School, Quartz Hill, California

Almost any two objects—even apples and oranges—can be compared. Everyone knows that apples and oranges are different; the trick is to find ways in which they are similar. In the compare-and-contrast essay you just read, Dalia Bichay includes both similarities and differences in her discussion of engagement practices in Egypt and the United States.

A compare-and-contrast essay allows you to give more information than an essay that simply defines one subject. For example, you can clearly define frozen yogurt by saying it has the same consistency as soft ice cream but it contains less fat. It would be much more difficult to define frozen yogurt—or almost anything else—without referring to similar or different items.

Shape Your Essay Around a Thesis Statement

The thesis statement of a compare-and-contrast essay expresses the essential differences and similarities between two subjects. The thesis gives the essay a shape, much as the concept of a constellation leads you to see the linkage among some stars but not others. As a result, the thesis statement determines what information belongs in the essay.

The thesis statement of Dalia Bichay's essay, for example, is that Egyptian engagement and wedding customs are more formal than American customs even though they share a common goal. Therefore, Dalia includes only information about dating practices, the process of getting engaged, and the actual marriage ceremony in Egypt and the United States. She does not include information about, for example, schools, styles of dress, or child-rearing practices because information on these topics is not related to her thesis.

Journal Writing

Select two places you know well to compare and contrast. Jot down some ideas for a thesis statement about how these subjects may be compared and contrasted. List some elements that these places have in common; then list some elements that are different.

Sort the Information

In the model below, Joseph Weizenbaum describes two types of computer programmers. Writers rarely follow a rigorous organizational pattern in comparing and contrasting two subjects; Weizenbaum, however, generally discusses first one type of programmer and then a second type.

> **Weizenbaum states his thesis near the beginning of the passage and then proceeds to assemble evidence.**

> **How has the thesis influenced Weizenbaum's choice of details in these paragraphs?**

Literature Model

How may the compulsive programmer be distinguished from a merely dedicated, hard-working professional programmer? First, by the fact that the ordinary professional programmer addresses himself to the problem to be solved while the compulsive programmer sees it mainly as an opportunity to interact with the computer. The ordinary computer programmer will . . . do lengthy preparatory work, such as writing and flow diagramming, before beginning work with the computer itself. . . . He may even let others do the actual console work. . . .

Unlike the professional, the compulsive programmer cannot attend to other tasks, not even tasks closely related to his program, while not actually operating the computer. He can barely tolerate being away from the machine. But when he is forced by circumstances to be separated from it nevertheless, he has his computer print-outs with him. He studies them, he talks about them to anyone who will listen, though no one can understand. Indeed, while in the grip of his compulsion, he can talk of nothing but his program. But the only time he is, so to say, happy is when he is at the computer console.

Joseph Weizenbaum,
"Science and the Compulsive
Programmer," *Partisan Review*

Professional Programmer
- Goal is to solve a problem
- Allows others to operate the computer
- Can attend to other aspects of work

All Programmers
- Work with computers
- Skilled and hard-working

Compulsive Programmer
- Views problem as a chance to interact with computer
- Cannot attend to other aspects of work
- Happy only when working at the computer

This Venn diagram offers one way to explore similarities and differences such as those presented in the model above. Notice that similarities appear in the area where the circles overlap.

Choose a Method of Organization

The chart below illustrates two basic ways of organizing a compare-and-contrast essay.

Feature Approach: Courtship   **Subject Approach:** Computer programmers

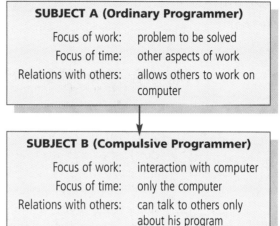

FEATURE 1 (Engagement)

U.S.: occurs after a period of dating
Egypt: begins a dating relationship

FEATURE 2 (Wedding Shower)

U.S.: for woman only
Egypt: for both man and woman

FEATURE 3 (Wedding)

U.S.: lasts 1/2–1 hour, ends with kiss
Egypt: lasts 1–2 hours, ends with kiss

SUBJECT A (Ordinary Programmer)

Focus of work: problem to be solved
Focus of time: other aspects of work
Relations with others: allows others to work on computer

SUBJECT B (Compulsive Programmer)

Focus of work: interaction with computer
Focus of time: only the computer
Relations with others: can talk to others only about his program

Dalia uses the feature approach to organization. First she compares and contrasts engagement practices, then wedding showers, and finally wedding ceremonies. She moves back and forth between subjects—the United States and Egypt.

Weizenbaum organizes his discussion by subject rather than by feature. The subjects of his comparison are ordinary programmers and compulsive programmers. He lays a foundation by describing one subject, and then he describes the second subject in relation to the first. Neither the feature nor subject approach is necessarily better than the other; purpose, topic, thesis, and personal preference determine the best method for each essay.

> **Grammar Tip**
>
> As you begin writing comparisons, you might want to refer to the Usage section of this book for more information on indicating degrees of comparison. See Lessons 18.1–18.4, pages 649–656.

Journal Writing

Create a chart or Venn diagram to compare and contrast two appliances or products you use regularly. For example, you might compare and contrast a car with a bicycle, a softball with a soccer ball, or a television set with a radio.

Achieve Coherence

Carefully choose transitional words and phrases, such as those listed on page 216, to show the relationships between features and to improve the flow of the essay. You can also repeat key words and phrases to create a link between ideas in your essay. Notice how Douglas Adams repeats forms of the words "compete," "survive," and "introduce" in the model below. By repeating certain key ideas, and linking them with transitional phrases, Adams makes it easy to follow his explanation.

Adams begins by explaining what it is he intends to compare and contrast.

Which transitional phrase at the beginning of the second paragraph helps you understand the significance of the information that follows?

Which transitional phrase alerts you that Adams is about to contrast his second subject with his first?

Literature Model

An **endemic species** of plant or animal is **one that is native** to an island or region and is found nowhere else at all. **An exotic species is one that has been introduced** from abroad, and a disaster is usually what results when this occurs.

The reason is this: continental land masses are big. They support hundreds of thousands, even millions, of different species, **each of which is competing** with one another **for survival.** The sheer ferocity **of the competition** is immense, and it means that the species that do **survive** and flourish are mean little fighters. They grow faster and throw out a lot more seeds.

An island, **on the other hand,** is small. There are far fewer species, and **the competition for survival** has never reached anything like the pitch that it does on the mainland. Species are only as tough as they need to be, life is much quieter and more settled, and evolution proceeds at a much slower rate. **This is why** you find on Madagascar, for instance, species like the lemurs that were overwhelmed eons ago on the mainland. Island ecologies are fragile time capsules.

So you can imagine what happens when a mainland species gets **introduced** to an island. **It would be like introducing Al Capone** . . . to the Isle of Wight—the locals wouldn't stand a chance.

Douglas Adams, *Last Chance to See*

Write an Article That Compares and Contrasts

Write an article comparing and contrasting two basically similar things, such as racing bikes and trail bikes, or two other items of your choice. Use a Venn diagram to organize details.

PURPOSE To explain similarities and differences between two items

AUDIENCE Your teacher and classmates

LENGTH 2–3 paragraphs

WRITING RUBRICS To write an effective comparison and contrast, you should

- select only details that are relevant to your thesis statement
- organize details by feature or by subject
- use transitional and repetition to link ideas

Viewing and Representing

COOPERATIVE LEARNING Working in a small group, look at the photograph on this page. Create a large Venn diagram by orally comparing and contrasting the occupational risks, benefits, and responsibilities of the two men in this photograph. Each of you then write one paragraph comparing or contrasting one common feature of the two men's jobs (for example, opportunities for physical exercise or career mobility). Finally,

Alan Berner, *A Day in the Life of America*, 1986

Make sure that subjects and verbs agree in sentences with compound subjects.

In compare-and-contrast writing, you will often use sentences with compound subjects joined by *or* or *nor*. In such sentences, the verb always agrees with the subject nearer the verb.

Neither ordinary programmers nor a compulsive programmer knows how to adapt the new program.

Use each of the following compound subjects in a sentence.

1. Several short weddings or one long wedding
2. Either the bride's relatives or the groom
3. A single amateur programmer or several professional programmers
4. Neither the endemic species nor the exotic species
5. Either the continental land mass or the islands

See Lesson 16.5, page 608.

combine information in the paragraphs into a single compare-and-contrast essay.

Cross-Curricular Activity

SCIENCE Use a Venn diagram to sharpen your understanding of the distinctions between such natural phenomena as primates and amphibians or hurricanes and tornadoes. Explain your diagram in an oral presentation.

Analyzing Problems, Presenting Solutions

When writing about problems and solutions, define the problem carefully and try to present a range of possible solutions. In the model below, Stephen Koepp uses strong images, references to popular culture, and storytelling to describe gridlock.

Expository Writing

How does the writer pull readers into the article?

A colorful example of how a traffic jam affected one man helps readers identify with the problem.

Literature Model

Remember when getting there was half the fun? When driving was a breeze and flying was a cinch? No longer. Gridlock has gripped America, threatening to transform its highways and flyways into snarled barriers to progress. . . .

The congestion, which is certain to grow worse in the coming decade, is hampering Americans' cherished mobility and changing the way they travel and do business. Instead of boasting "I Get Around," the tune they are wailing nowadays is "Don't Get Around Much Anymore." Consider:

The Detroit Tigers baseball team lost an important asset last week when its newly hired outfielder, Fred Lynn, failed to qualify for postseason play. Reason: he got caught in a traffic jam. Lynn was playing in Anaheim, Calif. . . . when he accepted Detroit's offer late Wednesday afternoon. But to qualify for the playoffs under league rules, he had to join the team, then in Chicago, by midnight. The Tigers chartered a jet for Lynn . . . but rush-hour congestion reportedly stretched his 35-minute drive to an hour and 15 minutes. That proved a costly delay: Lynn's plane did not reach Chicago airspace until 12:10 A.M.

Stephen Koepp, "Gridlock!" *Time* magazine

Gather Information

Suppose you want to write about the problem of traffic congestion. Begin by gathering information from several sources to answer such questions as What is the nature and extent of the problem? What are its causes? How does the problem affect people, the environment, and the economy? Library research may help you answer these questions. See Unit 7 for additional information on how to research a topic.

Draw on different kinds of information to explain dimensions of a problem. Use personal anecdotes to help your readers relate a problem to their own lives. Statistics will help you present an overview of a problem, as shown in the chart below.

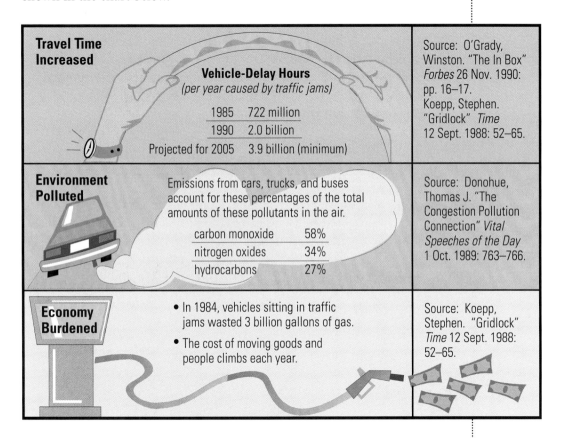

Travel Time Increased	**Vehicle-Delay Hours** *(per year caused by traffic jams)* 1985 722 million 1990 2.0 billion Projected for 2005 3.9 billion (minimum)	Source: O'Grady, Winston. "The In Box" *Forbes* 26 Nov. 1990: pp. 16–17. Koepp, Stephen. "Gridlock" *Time* 12 Sept. 1988: 52–65.
Environment Polluted	Emissions from cars, trucks, and buses account for these percentages of the total amounts of these pollutants in the air. carbon monoxide 58% nitrogen oxides 34% hydrocarbons 27%	Source: Donohue, Thomas J. "The Congestion Pollution Connection" *Vital Speeches of the Day* 1 Oct. 1989: 763–766.
Economy Burdened	• In 1984, vehicles sitting in traffic jams wasted 3 billion gallons of gas. • The cost of moving goods and people climbs each year.	Source: Koepp, Stephen. "Gridlock" *Time* 12 Sept. 1988: 52–65.

Journal Writing

Spend at least ten minutes freewriting in your journal about a social problem that interests you. Then list ways to explain the problem.

Present Solutions

After explaining the problem and its dimensions, your next step is to present solutions. Jennifer Hudgins presents her solution to the problem of traffic congestion in the paragraph below.

Model
The most practical solution to traffic congestion is to reduce traffic by encouraging people to use mass transit and car pools. . . . To encourage people to use mass transit systems, companies that supply employees with company cars and pay for parking fees should instead pay for employees' bus, train, or subway fare. Another incentive is to restrict more freeway lanes to high-occupancy vehicles. During morning rush hour on Interstate 350 in Virginia, two high-occupancy lanes carry about 33,000 commuters, slightly more than four regular lanes, yet in only one-fifth as many vehicles.
Jennifer Hudgins, Penn Manor High School Millersville, Pennsylvania

Most problems have many solutions. Examine the advantages and disadvantages of proposed solutions carefully and systematically. A chart like this might help organize your thoughts.

Table of Solutions		
POSSIBLE SOLUTION	**ADVANTAGES**	**DISADVANTAGES**
1. **Build more highways**	• reduces congestion immediately	• eats up land • encourages more traffic
2. **Improve mass transit**	• transports many people efficiently • reduces pollution • reduces need for parking	• doesn't always take people where they need to go
3. **Give tax or road toll incentives to car pools**	• encourages commuters to car pool, reducing the number of cars	• can be inconvenient

By listing each solution with its advantages and disadvantages, you can see that while each of these solutions offers some relief to the problem of traffic congestion, none of them can solve the problem completely. Be realistic when you explain solutions.

5.5 | Writing Activities

Write a Problem-and-Solution Essay

Think of a problem in your school or community, such as lunchroom overcrowding or a dangerous intersection near an elementary school. Write an essay explaining the problem and proposing solutions.

PURPOSE To explain a problem and propose solutions
AUDIENCE Someone who might be able to solve the problem
LENGTH 2–3 paragraphs

WRITING RUBRICS To write an effective problem-and-solution essay, you should

- use information about the problem from various sources
- explain how the problem affects people
- propose alternative, realistic solutions

Cross-Curricular Activity

SOCIAL STUDIES Working with two or three other students, scan recent newspapers and magazines to learn about a social problem that interests your team. Develop a table of solutions similar to that shown on page 234. Then decide what organizations or people are in a position to bring about change. Each team member should write a letter to one or more of the groups you have identified, briefly outlining the dimensions of the problem and recommending a solution.

Use commas with introductory phrases and clauses.

Adverb clauses and long prepositional phrases or a series of prepositional phrases (except when they directly precede a verb) should all be set off with commas at the beginnings of sentences:

During morning rush hour on Interstate 350 in Virginia, two high-occupancy lanes . . . *To encourage people to use mass transit systems,* companies who supply employees . . .

Complete the following sentences, using commas when appropriate.

1. When driving was a breeze
2. In order to qualify for the team
3. While the outfielder waited in the airport
4. Behind the car in the passing lane
5. Without statistical evidence about local traffic problems
6. On the ramp between the Eisenhower and Kennedy expressways
7. Although no one had witnessed the accident

See Lesson 21.6, pages 722–730.

Listening and Speaking

MAKING A SPEECH After you have completed your problem-and-solution essay, recast it as a speech and deliver it to your classmates. As you revise, check to see that your speech is appropriate for the audience and occasion you have in mind. Get feedback from classmates on ways to make your speech more dramatic and convincing.

Using Time Lines and Process Diagrams

*ime lines and process diagrams are graphic devices used to pre-
sent complex data clearly. Notice how the diagram below helps to
clarify the written explanation that accompanies it.*

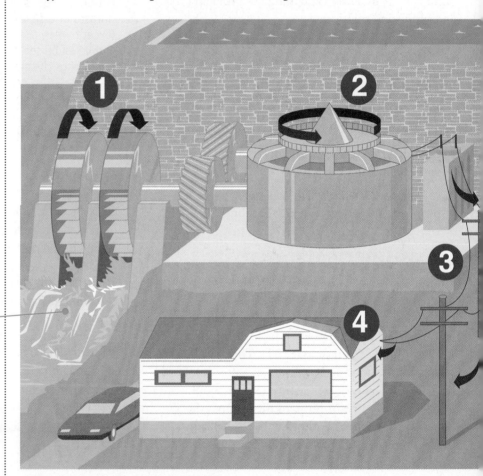

Producing Electricity
1. Flowing water pushes the turbines' panels, forcing them to rotate.
2. Magnets in the generator convert the force of rotation into electrical energy.
3. Transmission lines carry electric current to the house.
4. Switches and outlets provide access to electricity.

Highlight Events and Relationships in a Time Line

You can construct time lines to organize many types of data in many different ways. Often time lines simply highlight important events. Others use arrows to connect events that are linked by cause-and-effect relationships. You can also group events, using brackets or color to illustrate stages. The time line for Sojourner Truth on page 183 illustrates one use of a time line.

A time line can also show comparisons and contrasts. A time line comparing the development of printing in China and in Europe could have one set of dates above the line, the other below. The following time line shows a comparison, but here the dates above the line highlight "firsts" for women in education. The percentages below the line compare the overall enrollment of women and men in colleges and universities.

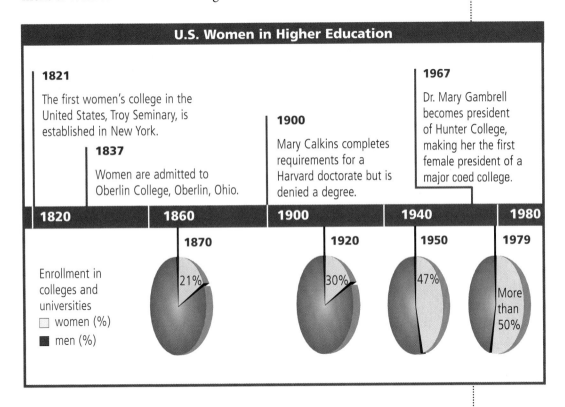

U.S. Women in Higher Education

1821
The first women's college in the United States, Troy Seminary, is established in New York.

1837
Women are admitted to Oberlin College, Oberlin, Ohio.

1900
Mary Calkins completes requirements for a Harvard doctorate but is denied a degree.

1967
Dr. Mary Gambrell becomes president of Hunter College, making her the first female president of a major coed college.

| 1820 | 1860 | 1900 | 1940 | 1980 |

1870 — 21%
1920 — 30%
1950 — 47%
1979 — More than 50%

Enrollment in colleges and universities
☐ women (%)
■ men (%)

Journal Writing

Think of two events that you would like to compare and contrast. Make notes in your journal about the ways that you might use a time line to illustrate some point of comparison or contrast between the events.

Presenting Tip

Consider preparing a poster-sized time line or process diagram to accompany your next oral report or oral presentation of a written report.

Show a Process

A process diagram can help you portray the sequence of activities that make up a process. Notice how the process diagram below supports and enhances the explanation of how to use a flywheel rowing machine.

How to Use a Flywheel Rowing Machine

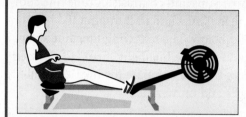

STEP 1

Place feet under straps and adjust for comfortable fit. Grasp handlebar and extend legs. Bring handlebars into chest.

STEP 2

Extend arms, lean forward from hips keeping back straight, and bend knees to pull seat forward.

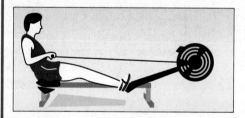

STEP 3

Extend legs to slide seat back. Lean backwards from hips. Pull handlebars into chest.

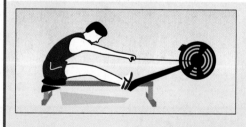

STEP 4

Repeat steps 2 and 3 without stopping. Step 3 should be three times faster than step 2.

The process diagram above combines pictures and text in a step-by-step format to make a fairly complex process comprehensible to a reader, even one who has never before used or seen a flywheel rowing machine.

Create a Time Line or a Process Diagram

Select an event or a process that could be explained with a time line or a process diagram. Possibilities include such topics as turning points in your own or a historical figure's life and a how-to essay.

PURPOSE To create a graphic to explain something
AUDIENCE Your teacher and classmates
LENGTH 1 page

WRITING RUBRICS To create an effective time line or process diagram, you should

- select the appropriate type of graphic—time line or process diagram—for your topic
- assemble the facts into graphic form, labeling and explaining each element of the graphic
- capitalize titles and headings correctly

Using Computers

You can store facts and dates you may want to use for a historical time line in your computer. Type each piece of information, give it a heading, and box it so it looks like a note card. You can then work on and organize your boxed computer notes just as you would note cards, adding, deleting, and rearranging facts and dates. When you've finished collecting information and are ready to prepare your time line, you can simply call up your boxes of data and plug them into the time line as you are constructing it.

Grammar Link

Capitalize words in titles correctly.

Capitalize the first word of a title, the last word, and every word in between except articles (*a, an, the*), prepositions of fewer than five letters, and coordinating conjunctions (*and, but, for, or, nor, yet*):

> "U.S. Women in Higher Education"
> "How to Use a Flywheel Rowing Machine"

Invent titles for articles about these topics and capitalize them correctly. (Enclose titles in quotation marks.)

1. highlights of your community's history
2. how to obtain a driver's license in your state
3. significant dates in space exploration
4. how to cross-country ski
5. how to operate an answering machine
6. roller-blading equipment and accessories
7. advantages and disadvantages of a part-time job at a fast-food restaurant
8. bird-watching in the Midwest
9. ways to amuse young children
10. modern etiquette for teens

See Lesson 20.2, pages 696–701.

Viewing and Representing

COOPERATIVE LEARNING With a group of your classmates, locate a time line in a magazine (popular magazines such as *Time* and *National Geographic* routinely use time lines). Discuss with your group the techniques the magazine used (for example, graphics, captions, dates, colors, and dotted lines) to enhance readers' understanding of the content of the time line.

Building a Reasonable Hypothesis

A hypothesis is a statement of a belief that you assume to be true. The model below discusses Dr. Clara Rising's hypothesis that President Zachary Taylor may have been assassinated by his political enemies.

Literature Model

Rising traces her intense interest in Taylor to a gathering of Civil War enthusiasts she attended in January 1990. Chatting there with Betty Gist, the owner of the Kentucky farm where Taylor lived as a young man, Rising began to realize how much the president's political foes had gained by his death. . . . Rising's strong feelings led her to the library and eventually to a Gainesville-based forensic pathologist, Dr. William Maples. She showed him contemporary accounts of Taylor's five-day death agony, which had been ascribed to cholera morbus, a catch-all phrase then used to describe a variety of intestinal illnesses. Maples said that it sounded more like "a classic case of arsenic poisoning."

Newsweek, July 1, 1991

Develop a Hypothesis

The first step in building a hypothesis is to decide on the issue or question you want to explore. You might build a hypothesis to explain a foreign policy decision in a history paper or a chemical reaction in a lab report. Dr. Rising based her hypothesis on the sudden, inexplicable nature of Taylor's death.

The chart on the next page shows the remaining steps required to build a hypothesis and the way Dr. Rising carried them out.

Building a Hypothesis

STEP 1	STEP 2	STEP 3	STEP 4	STEP 5
Identify what you are trying to explain.	Collect data and consult experts.	Compare and contrast data to identify patterns or trends.	Decide on most reasonable hypothesis based on the data.	Test conclusion for acceptance, modification, or rejection.
Asked what caused Taylor's death.	*Researched historical accounts. Consulted forensic pathologist and historians.*	*Considered arsenic poisoning, stomach ailment, and other explanations.*	*Selected arsenic poisoning as best explanation of data.*	*Had Taylor's remains tested for traces of arsenic.*

After identifying an issue to explore, you will collect facts and expert opinions, either through research, observations, or interviews. Then you can look for patterns or trends in the data. Be alert to any connections between ideas that indicate unseen relationships. When Dr. Rising compared historical records with medical facts, she found that Taylor's death resembled that of someone who has been poisoned. She also noted that Taylor's political opponents benefited from his death.

Analyzing trends will help you decide on a reasonable hypothesis that is supported by data. Finally, you can test your hypothesis. Dr. Rising tested hers by having Taylor's remains analyzed for arsenic. Since no appreciable levels of arsenic were found, it seems that Taylor died of natural causes after all. Dr. Rising, however, did not feel she had wasted her time. She understood that a well-thought-out hypothesis, even if disproved, provides a framework for examining, organizing, and testing evidence.

Prewriting Tip

As you research a tentative hypothesis, keep these two questions in mind: What do you want to prove? What do you need to do to prove it?

Journal Writing

A person returns home to find papers strewn all over his or her living room. The window in the living room is open. In your journal, explain how you would follow the steps outlined above to formulate and test a hypothesis about what happened.

Present Your Data

State your hypothesis in a thesis statement as part of an introductory paragraph that tells how and why your topic and thesis are important.

Develop your explanation in the body of your essay by supporting each point with specific examples, facts, or expert testimony where appropriate. Use transitional words and phrases to direct your readers from one idea to the next. (See pages 216 and 230 in lessons 5.1 and 5.4 for further discussion of transitional words and phrases.)

Finally, summarize your main points in your concluding paragraph. Draw a conclusion by evaluating the evidence you've assembled or by expressing a judgment or a realization. In the example below, Edward T. Hall, an expert in the science of proxemics (how people use the space around them), develops one aspect of his hypothesis that Arabs and Americans have difficulty understanding each other because they have very different ideas about how space should be used.

Literature Model

One mistaken American notion is that Arabs conduct all conversations at close distances. This is not the case at all. On social occasions, they may sit on opposite sides of the room and talk across the room to each other. They are, however, apt to take offense when Americans use what are to them ambiguous distances, such as the four- to seven-foot social-consultative distance. They frequently complain that Americans are cold or aloof or "don't care.". . .

Arabs are involved with each other on many different levels simultaneously. Privacy in a public place is foreign to them. Business transactions in the bazaar, for example, are not just between buyer and seller, but are participated in by everyone. Anyone who is standing around may join in. If a grownup sees a boy breaking a window, he must stop him even if he doesn't know him. Involvement and participation are expressed in other ways as well. If two men are fighting, the crowd must intervene. . . .

Perceiving the world differently leads to differential definitions of what constitutes crowded living, different interpersonal relations, and a different approach to both local and international politics. . . .

Edward T. Hall, "The Arab World," *The Hidden Dimension*

What assumption do Americans make about Arab conversational style?

How may Arabs interpret American conversational patterns?

Write a Hypothesis

Locate a painting or photograph depicting a single person in a scene. Formulate a hypothesis about who the person is and what he or she is doing. Write a short essay explaining the procedure you went through to arrive at this hypothesis.

PURPOSE To present a hypothesis
AUDIENCE Your teacher and classmates
LENGTH 1–3 paragraphs

WRITING RUBRICS To write an effective hypothesis, you should

- state a reasonable hypothesis in the introductory paragraph
- arrange in logical order the steps you followed to form your hypothesis
- explain how details such as dress, posture, and setting support your hypothesis
- provide clear antecedents for pronouns

Cross-Curricular Activity

SCIENCE Recall a proven hypothesis that you have studied in a science class. Write a brief explanation of the hypothesis, the basis on which it was formulated, and some of the steps that were taken to test it.

Viewing and Representing

COOPERATIVE LEARNING In a small group, share the painting or photograph you used in formulating your hypothesis. Before you read your essay to the group, ask members of your group to formulate their own hypotheses about your picture. Then read your essay and compare and contrast your hypothesis with those suggested by others. Did you come to similar conclusions? Were the hypotheses widely varied?

Use clear antecedents for pronouns.

The antecedent of a pronoun or pronouns must be clear:

> *Rising,* strong feelings led **her** to the library. . .

For each of the following sentences, write a new sentence using appropriate pronouns.

1. The social-consultative distance varies greatly from culture to culture.
2. Dr. Clara Rising formed a hypothesis about the death of President Taylor.
3. While gathering related facts, Dr. Rising consulted a forensic pathologist.
4. Enthusiasts from across the country gathered at a symposium to discuss issues related to the Civil War.

See Lesson 17.6, pages 632–636.

LESSON 5.8

WRITING ABOUT LITERATURE
Comparing and Contrasting Two Authors

A comparative analysis should consider such elements as the authors' positions on the subject, word choice, and tone.

Literature Models

> **Can you find and paraphrase Emerson's thesis statement?**

But a man must keep an eye on his servants, if he would not have them rule him. Man is a shrewd inventor and is ever taking the hint of a new machine from his own structure, adapting some secret of his own anatomy in iron, wood and leather to some required function in the work of the world. But it is found that the machine unmans the user. What he gains in making cloth, he loses in general power. . . . The incessant repetition of the same hand-work dwarfs the man, robs him of his strength, wit, and versatility, to make a pin-polisher, a bucklemaker, or any other specialty. . . .

> **What, according to Emerson, is the effect of specialization of labor?**

Ralph Waldo Emerson, "Wealth"

Obviously, computers have made differences. They have fostered the development of spaceships—as well as a great increase in junk mail. The computer boom has brought the marvelous but expensive diagnostic device known as the CAT scanner, as well as a host of other medical equipment; it has given rise to machines that play good but rather boring chess, and also, on a larger game board, to a proliferation of remote-controlled weapons in the arsenals of nations. Computers have changed ideas about waging war and about pursuing science, too. It is hard to see how contemporary geophysics or meteorology or plasma physics can advance very far without them now. . . .

> **How does Kidder's choice of vocabulary reveal his position?**

Tracy Kidder, *The Soul of a New Machine*

Analyze Similarities and Differences

In the model below, the author compares and contrasts Emerson's and Kidder's views.

Model

Technology has always promised a new world. From the first steam locomotive to the latest electronic gadget, industry experts have predicted better, easier, more efficient living. Along with those who glorify the results of technology, however, are those who question the value of better and faster machines. Ralph Waldo Emerson and Tracy Kidder, writing over a century apart, see both the positive and the negative aspects of technological change. Although they view different machines from different perspectives, both urge caution in allowing technology to dominate our lives.

Ralph Waldo Emerson, writing in the second half of the nineteenth century, takes a serious approach to textile machinery in the almost zealous tone of a social reformer. He speaks of machines as servants needing supervision, lest they come to rule their creators. Emerson worries that technology "unmans" users, absorbing their power. Kidder, on the other hand, approaches his subject with the air of an investigator. He questions and observes, comparing what he reads and hears with what he sees. To him it seems that computers have delivered neither the harm they threatened nor the benefits they promised.

> What is the thesis statement in this model?

> How, according to this writer, are Emerson and Kidder similar? How are they different?

Journal Writing

Think about two short stories that are similar in some manner. Write the titles of the stories in your journal and jot down one way in which they are similar and one way in which they are different.

Establish Categories of Comparison

Although Emerson and Kidder treat a common theme, they are writing in different centuries about different technologies. They take very different approaches to their subject, as can be seen in the following chart.

Basis of Comparison or Contrast		
FEATURE	**1ST SUBJECT: EMERSON**	**2ND SUBJECT: KIDDER**
TIME	1876	1981
TECHNOLOGY	textile machinery	computers
POSITION	opposed: criticizes industrialization, sees few advantages	open-minded: presents arguments for and against
TONE	exhorting	reflective
IMAGERY	natural: silk-worms, caterpillars	technological: machines
WORD CHOICE	derogatory: "unmans," "loses," "incessant," "dwarfs," "robs"	qualifying: "marvelous but expensive," "good but . . . boring," some technical: "CAT scanner," "geophysics," "meteorology," "plasma physics"
THEME	Machines should not supersede people.	Machines have advantages and disadvantages but are an indispensable part of everyday life.

You can use the features listed in the chart above to compare and contrast many different pieces of nonfiction writing. Of course, you may add or delete categories of comparison. For example, if you are comparing two pieces of writing composed only a few years apart, "time" may not be an important category. "Where" the author lived—a rural setting, an urban setting, this country, a foreign country—may play an important role, however, as may the author's gender or ethnic identity.

This chart could include an additional feature: "Impact on Reader." In this feature you would answer these questions: How did you react to this piece of writing? Why?

Write a Compare- and-Contrast Article

In magazines or newspapers find two reviews of one movie. Write an article for your school newspaper comparing and contrasting the two reviews.

PURPOSE To compare and contrast two reviews of the same movie

AUDIENCE Readers of the school newspaper

LENGTH 2–3 paragraphs

WRITING RUBRICS To write an effective compare-and-contrast article, you should

- use a thesis statement that summarizes similarities and differences
- refer to comparison categories that are relevant to your topic
- compare both factual details and the writers' style and tone
- proofread the article

Using Computers

Before submitting your compare-and-contrast article, you might want to use your computer's spelling checker to double-check your work. Remember, however, that you cannot rely on an electronic spelling checker to catch all of your errors. If you use a homophone (for example, typing *week* instead of *weak*), your software will not detect the error.

Grammar Link

Use comparative forms correctly.

The comparative form of an adjective or adverb shows two things being compared. Form the comparative by adding the suffix *-er* or by preceding the modifier with *more* or *less*:

> *From the first steam locomotive to the latest electronic gadget, industry experts have predicted* **better, easier, more efficient** *living.*

Use the comparative degree of each of the following modifiers in a sentence.

1. shrewd
2. efficiently
3. happy
4. sad
5. serious
6. angrily
7. cautiously
8. important
9. zealous
10. critical

See Lesson 18.1, pages 649–650.

Viewing and Representing

COOPERATIVE LEARNING Find a partner who has seen a recent movie or television show that you have also seen. Discuss the movie or show with your partner to find out where you agree and disagree about the effectiveness of the production. Make a Venn diagram of your views, showing how they compare and contrast. Then conduct a discussion for the entire class, highlighting the similarities and differences in your opinions of the movie or show.

LESSON 5.9

WRITING ABOUT LITERATURE

Comparing and Contrasting Two Poems

*T*o analyze the poems below, you might first compare your emotional response to the two pieces. You might then consider elements such as imagery, tone, and theme.

Expository Writing

Literature Models

To My Dear and Loving Husband

If ever two were one, then surely we.
If ever man were loved by wife, then thee;
If ever wife was happy in a man,
Compare with me, ye women, if you can.
I prize thy love more than whole mines of gold
Or all the riches that the East doth hold.
My love is such that rivers cannot quench,
Nor ought but love from thee, give recompense.
Thy love is such I can no way repay,
The heavens reward thee manifold, I pray.
Then while we live, in love let's so persevere[1]
That when we live no more, we may live ever.

                                        Anne Bradstreet

In Retrospect

Last year changed its seasons
subtly, stripped its sultry winds
for the reds of dying leaves, let
gelid drops of winter ice melt onto a
warming earth and urged the dormant
bulbs to brave the
pain of spring.
We, loving, above the whim of
time, did not notice.
Alone. I remember now.

                                        Maya Angelou

---

[1] Pronounced "pûr sev' ər" in the seventeenth century

248   Unit 5 Expository Writing

Explore Your Responses

You can use expository writing to explain your reaction to poetry and other forms of literature. A poem may immediately ignite a barrage of feelings and memories or may require additional readings before reactions begin to surface. Here are some basic questions to pose to uncover your likes and dislikes.

Exploring Responses to Two Poems

- Which poem do you prefer? Why?
- What did you like least about either poem?
- Which poem matches your own experiences or observations? In what way?
- Which poem sounds more appealing?
- What is the most memorable image or idea from each poem?
- Which words or phrases in the poems do you find interesting or beautiful?

Having explored your taste in poetry, you can dig deeper for meaning. In the following model, the writer begins to compare and contrast Bradstreet's and Angelou's poetic approaches to love.

Model

Both writers use poetry to explore the nature of love. The speaker in Bradstreet's poem views love as immortal, even transcending the deaths of the lovers. Angelou's speaker, on the other hand, sees love as transient, like the seasons. Ironically, however, it is after love has died that the speaker in Angelou's poem is able to notice the life around her.

Drafting Tip

When drafting an essay about a poem, be sure that you provide quotations from the poem to support the statements you make about it. For information about punctuating quotations, see Lesson 21.10, pages 735–738.

Journal Writing

Do you prefer Bradstreet's formal, rhythmic style or Angelou's less structured modern language? How does the language of these poems affect the way you respond to them? Record your responses to these questions in your journal.

Analyze Devices

Now you can approach the poems from an intellectual perspective. Compare and contrast the variety of devices—meter, rhyme, sound effects, line length, imagery—the poets use to convey their message. When you analyze how the poet uses each device, you increase your understanding of the broad strokes and nuances of the poems.

Basis of Comparison or Contrast		
FEATURES	**1ST SUBJECT: BRADSTREET**	**2ND SUBJECT: ANGELO**
TIME	American colonial	Modernday
FORM AND METER	12 lines, iambic pentameter, rhymed	10 lines, free verse
IMAGERY	Images of wealth: gold, riches of the East	Natural images: changing seasons, dying leaves, melting ice, dormant bulbs
FIGURATIVE LANGUAGE	Metaphors of trade: "prize," "recompense," "repay," "reward" Metaphor of thirst: "rivers cannot quench"	Metaphors of the natural world: changing seasons, melting ice, warming earth, growing bulbs
CHARACTERIZATION OF LOVE	Love is of great value.	Love is changeable, natural.
SPEAKER	Addresses her husband	Speaks to herself
TONE	Intimate, celebratory	Pensive, somewhat sad
CONCLUSION	Perseverence in love while we live will bring us immortality after death.	Love is a state that removes lovers from the concerns of daily life but not forever.
OVERALL EFFECT	Love is the most valuable thing on earth, and one should maintain it at all costs.	Love is transitory, yet the experience of loving and ceasing to love is natural and healing.

Use this chart and the one on page 249 to develop an essay that compares and contrasts two or more poems. Start with your emotional response to help you decide what to look for in your analysis.

Compare and Contrast Two Poems

From a literature textbook or anthology, select two poems that share some common elements. Plan and write an essay comparing and contrasting these two works.

PURPOSE To compare and contrast two poems
AUDIENCE Your teacher and classmates
LENGTH 4–5 paragraphs

WRITING RUBRICS To compare and contrast two poems effectively, you should

- include discussion of literary elements such as tone, speaker, imagery, and overall effect
- include both personal feelings and formal analysis in your essay
- use a logical organization to show the relationships between the two poems
- proofread your essay for correct punctuation with quotations

Using Computers

When writing about poems, there will be times when you will want to paraphrase or describe a poem without quoting from it. Finding the right words to express the subtle variations in meaning used by poets can be difficult. Many word processing programs include an electronic thesaurus that can suggest words with the same general meaning but with subtle differences in connotation, tone, or usage.

Grammar Link

Punctuate quotations correctly.

When quoting lines of poetry in text, put commas and periods inside final quotation marks but put semicolons outside them. Put a question mark or exclamation point outside the quotation marks unless it is part of the quotation.

Rewrite the following sentences, adding punctuation marks where needed.

1. Bradstreet's poem opens "If ever two were one, then surely we"
2. What do you suppose Angelou meant by "pain of spring"
3. Angelou uses vibrant sounds in phrases such as "stripped its sultry winds" she has a good ear for alliteration.
4. Bradstreet wrote "thy love is such I can no way repay" she must have truly adored her husband.
5. After I finished reading the line "I prize thy love more than whole mines of gold" I knew Bradstreet's husband must have been a special man.

See Lesson 21.10, pages 735–738.

Viewing and Representing

COOPERATIVE LEARNING You and a group of classmates are travel agents putting together a travel brochure titled "The Two Faces of _____" (fill in the blank with a country or region). Your goal is to plan for contrasting vacations in the country or region; one plan should emphasize cities, the other the country. Gather background information from print and electronic sources; then design the brochure, using facts, vivid language, and photos to make your "faces" attractive and interesting.

Writing Process in Action

Expository Writing

In the preceding lessons you have learned how to organize expository material, use graphic aids, and form reasonable conclusions. You have had opportunities to explain a process, analyze problems and their solutions, develop a hypothesis, and compare and contrast various subjects.

Your task in the following assignment is to choose a piece of equipment for your school and then analyze the benefits it could bring.

Assignment

Context	A local corporation is donating equipment to your school. Its board of directors wants the students to decide what high-tech equipment would be particularly beneficial. Price—within reasonable limits—is not a concern. The principal has asked everyone to write a proposal.
Purpose	To write an essay explaining how a certain piece of high-tech equipment would benefit the school
Audience	The board of directors of a corporation
Length	2 pages

Visit the Writer's Choice Web site at **writerschoice. glencoe.com**, for additional writing-prompts.

The pages that follow can help you research, organize, and write your essay. Read them carefully and use them as a guide. Keep in mind the purpose of your essay and its audience. However, you are in charge of your own writing.

Prewriting

Brainstorm with your class to list high-tech equipment that would benefit your school. Would students' writing improve with an updated computer lab? Would on-site physical fitness equipment be popular? Does the science department need electron microscopes or the drama department new audiovisual equipment? Evaluate the advantages and disadvantages of each idea. Eliminate the most far-fetched ideas. Make your choice from the remaining ideas.

Once you've made your selection, make brief notes about how the technology works. Do some research, if necessary. Freewrite to focus on the major effects the equipment would have in your school.

After assembling your information, evaluate it in terms of the Prewriting Questions at the right. Then create a thesis statement and select the details that will guide your draft. Finally, consider the organizational method that will best accomplish your purpose.

In the model below, Pamela McCorduck uses clear, precise language to explain why computers are unique, vital technology.

Prewriting Questions

- What do my readers need and want to know?
- What impression do I want to convey about this equipment and our need for it?
- What details can I use to illustrate the importance of this equipment?

Literature Model

By now nearly everyone understands that the computer is no mere calculating device but can manipulate symbols of all kinds. . . .

This new piece of intellectual technology stands in relation to our reasoning powers as written language stands to our memories. The computer has amplified the faculty of reason and will soon automate the process. The computer is dynamic, not static. Like the changes brought about by the proliferation of printed books, the new tool in our kit introduces a qualitative change into our intellectual life.

Pamela McCorduck, "Resolving Shades of Gray," *Columbia*

Writing Process in Action

Drafting Tip

For help in explaining how something works, see Lesson 5.2, pages 218–221.

Drafting

Your opening paragraph should include a thesis statement to focus the attention of your audience immediately on the type of equipment that best suits your school's needs and why. However, you could actually start your paragraph with any of the following:

- A startling statistic
- An anecdote
- A rhetorical question

In the body paragraphs of your essay, define terms your readers may not understand and explain how the equipment works. Don't forget to describe your school and analyze its needs. Use transitional words and phrases to help your readers follow the development of your argument. Don't belabor each word at this stage, but consider the tone you want for your piece.

Your conclusion should reemphasize the main points of your essay, but it should also explore their implications. You may want to save a particularly good anecdote or quotation for last.

Revising Tip

For help in making relationships clear, see Lesson 5.1, page 216, Lesson 5.4, page 230, and Lesson 5.7, page 242.

Revising

To begin revising, read over your draft to make sure that what you've written fits your purpose and audience. Then have a **writing conference.** Read your draft to a partner or small group. Use your audience's reactions to help you evaluate your work.

Revising Checklist

- Do I focus my essay with a thesis statement?
- Have I explained my points clearly and in a logical order?
- Have I explained any technical terms?
- Do I address the weaknesses as well as the strengths of the equipment I've chosen?

Editing

Once you are satisfied with the content and organization of your essay, use the questions to the right as a **proofreading** guide.

Use the Self-Evaluation list below to make sure your persuasive essay achieves your goals. Make your changes and proofread it again.

Self-Evaluation

Make sure your essay—

✔ analyzes and explains how a piece of high-tech equipment would benefit your school

✔ explains how the equipment works

✔ analyzes your school's needs and shows how the equipment would meet those needs

✔ uses vocabulary and organization suitable to the purpose and audience

✔ follows the standards of grammar, usage, and mechanics

Presenting

Many businesses and organizations are extremely supportive of education and even receive tax benefits for donating equipment to schools. Investigate some of the corporations in your area, and send in your proposal. Your recommendations may help to put your school on the cutting edge of technology.

Editing Checklist

- Have I punctuated appositives correctly when defining unfamiliar terms?
- Have I written possessive nouns correctly?
- Do I have any dangling or misplaced modifiers?
- Are my verb tenses consistent?
- Have I checked for spelling, especially of technical terms?

Proofing Tip

For proofreading symbols, see page 92.

Journal Writing

Reflect on the work you did to prepare and write your essay. Answer these questions in your journal: How did the writing process affect my understanding of the issue? What did I find the hardest in preparing and writing the essay? What do I think I did best? What new skill or technique have I learned as a writer?

Literature Model

In this selection, Tracy Kidder and a friend attend a computer fair.
As you read, notice how Kidder expresses his opinions about the
advantages and disadvantages of computerization.

THE SOUL OF A NEW MACHINE

by Tracy Kidder

Norbert Wiener coined the term *cybernetics* in order to describe the study of "control and communication in the animal and the machine." In 1947 he wrote that because of the development of the "ultra-rapid computing machine, . . . the average human being of mediocre attainments or less" might end up having "nothing to sell that is worth anyone's money to buy." Although Wiener clearly intended this as a plea for humane control over the development and application of computers, many people who have written about these machines' effects on society have quoted Wiener's statement as though it were a claim of fact; and some, particularly the computer's

Manuel Neuhaus, *Figure and Globe*, 1994

boosters, have held the remark up to ridicule—"See, it hasn't happened."

Since Wiener, practically every kind of commentator on modern society, from cartoonists to academic sociologists, has taken a crack at the sociology of computers. A general feeling has held throughout: that these machines constitute something special, set apart from all the others that have come before. Maybe it has been a kind of chrono-centrism, a conviction that the new machines of your own age must rank as the most stupendous or the scariest ever; but whatever the source, computers have acquired great mystique. Almost every commentator has assured the public that the computer is bringing on a revolution. By the 1970s it should have been clear that *revolution* was the wrong word. And it should not have been surprising to anyone that in many cases the technology had served as a prop to the status quo. The enchantment seemed enduring, nevertheless. So did many of the old arguments.

"Artificial intelligence" had always made for the liveliest of debates. Maybe the name itself was preposterous and its pursuit, in any case, something that people shouldn't undertake. Maybe in promoting the metaphorical relationship between people and machines, cybernetics tended to cheapen and corrupt human perceptions of human intelligence. Or perhaps this science promised to advance the intelligence of people as well as of machines and to imbue the species with a new, exciting power.

"Silicon-based life would have a lot of advantages over carbon-based life," a young engineer told me once. He said he believed in a time when machines would "take over." He snapped his fingers and said, "Just like that." He seemed immensely pleased with that thought. To me, though, the prospects for truly intelligent computers look comfortably dim.

To some the crucial issue was privacy. In theory, computers should be able to manage, more efficiently than people, huge amounts of a society's information. In the sixties there was proposed a "National Data Bank," which would, theoretically, improve the government's efficiency by allowing agencies to share information. The fact that

David Em, *Transjovian Pipeline*, 1979

such a system could be abused did not mean it would be, proponents said; it could be constructed in such a way as to guarantee benign[1] use. Nonsense, said opponents, who managed to block the proposal; no matter what the intent or the safeguards, the existence of such a system would inevitably lead toward the creation of a police state.

Claims and counterclaims about the likely effects of computers on work in America had also abounded since Wiener. Would the machines put enormous numbers of people out of work? Or would they actually increase levels of employment? By the late seventies, it appeared, they had done neither. Well, then, maybe computers would eventually take over hateful and dangerous jobs and in general free people from drudgery, as boosters like to say. Some anecdotal evidence suggested, though, that they might be used extensively to increase the reach of top managers crazed for efficiency and thus would serve as tools to destroy the last vestiges[2] of pleasant, interesting work.

Dozens of other points of argument existed. Were computers making nuclear war more or less likely? Had the society's vulnerability to accident and sabotage increased or decreased, now that computers had been woven inextricably into the management of virtually every enterprise in America?

Wallach and I retreated from the fair, to a café some distance from the Coliseum. Sitting there, observing the more familiar chaos of a New York City street, I was struck by how unnoticeable the computer revolution was. You leave a bazaar like

> **Computers were everywhere, of course—in the café's beeping cash registers and the microwave oven and the jukebox, in the traffic lights, under the hoods of the honking cars.**

the NCC expecting to find that your perceptions of the world outside will have been altered, but there was nothing commensurate in sight—no cyborgs, half machine, half protoplasm, tripping down the street; no armies of unemployed, carrying placards denouncing the computer; no TV cameras watching us—as a rule, you still had to seek out that experience by going to such places as Data General's parking lot. Computers were everywhere, of course—in the café's beeping cash registers and the microwave oven and the jukebox, in the traffic lights, under the hoods of the honking cars snarled out there on the street (despite those traffic lights), in the airplanes overhead—but the visible differences somehow seemed insignificant.

Computers had become less noticeable as they had become smaller, more reliable, more efficient, and more numerous. Surely this happened by design. Obviously, to sell the devices far and wide, manufacturers had to strive to make them easy to use and, wherever possible, invisible. Were computers a profound, unseen hand?

In *The Coming of Post-Industrial Society,* Daniel Bell asserted that new machines introduced in the nineteenth century, such as the railroad train, made larger changes in "the lives of individuals" than computers have. Tom West liked to say: "Let's talk about bulldozers. Bulldozers have had a hell of a lot

---

1 **benign** (bi nīn´): beneficial
2 **vestiges** (ves´ ti jəz): traces

bigger effect on people's lives." The latter half of the twentieth century, some say, has witnessed an increase in social scale—in the size of organizations, for instance. Computers probably did not create the growth of conglomerates and multinational corporations, but they certainly have abetted it. They make fine tools for the centralization of power, if that's what those who buy them want to do with them. They are handy greed-extenders. Computers performing tasks as prosaic as the calculating of payrolls greatly extend the reach of managers in high positions; managers on top can be in command of such aspects of their businesses to a degree they simply could not be before computers.

Obviously, computers have made differences. They have fostered the development of spaceships—as well as a great increase in junk mail. The computer boom has brought the marvelous but expensive diagnostic device

> **Obviously, computers have made differences. They have fostered the development of spaceships—as well as a great increase in junk mail.**

known as the CAT scanner, as well as a host of other medical equipment; it has given rise to machines that play good but rather boring chess, and also, on a larger game board, to a proliferation of remote-controlled weapons in the arsenals of nations. Computers have changed ideas about waging war and about pursuing science, too. It is hard to see how contemporary geophysics or meteorology or plasma physics can advance very far without them now. Computers have changed the nature of research in mathematics, though not every mathematician would say it is for the better. And computers have become a part of the ordinary conduct of businesses of all sorts. They really help, in some cases.

Not always, though. One student of the field has estimated that about forty percent of commercial applications of computers have proved uneconomical, in the sense that the

job the computer was bought to perform winds up costing more to do after the computer's arrival than it did before. Most computer companies have boasted that they aren't just selling machines, they're selling *productivity*. ("We're not in competition with each other," said a PR man. "We're in competition with labor.") But that clearly isn't always true. Sometimes they're selling paper-producers that require new legions of workers to push that paper around.

Coming from the fair, it seemed to me that computers have been used in ways that are salutary,[3] in ways that are dangerous, banal[4] and cruel, and in ways that seem harmless if a little silly. But what fun making them can be!

A reporter who had covered the computer industry for years tried to sum up for me the bad feelings he had acquired on his beat. "Everything is quantified," he said. "Whether it's the technology or the way people use it, it has an insidious ability to reduce things to less than human dimensions." Which is it, though: the technology or the way people use it? Who controls this technology? Can it be controlled?

Jacques Ellul, throwing up his hands, wrote that technology operates by its own terrible laws, alterable by no human action except complete abandonment of technique. More sensible, I think, Norbert Wiener prophesied that the computer would offer "unbounded possibilities for good and for evil," and he advanced, faintly, the hope that the contributors to this new science would nudge it in a humane direction. But he also invoked the fear that its development would fall "into the hands of the most irresponsible and venal of our engineers." One of the best surveys of the studies of the effects of computers ends with an appeal to the "computer professionals" that they exercise virtue and restraint.

> **Norbert Wiener prophesied that the computer would offer "unbounded possibilities for good and for evil."**

---

3 **salutary** (sal´yoo ter´ē): beneficial
4 **banal** (bān´əl; bə näl´): dull because of overuse; commonplace

Linking Writing and Literature

Readers Respond to the Model

What techniques does Kidder use to make a technical subject interesting?

Consider Tracy Kidder's exposition by answering these questions. Then read other students' opinions of this selection.

1. How does Kidder's use of quotes enliven his article?

2. Do you think the selection would have been more effective if Kidder had offered more of his own opinions on the subject? Why or why not?

3. Is it your impression that Tracy Kidder likes or dislikes computers? Explain how evidence from the selection supports your impression.

What Students Say

&&I disagreed with Kidder's opinion of computers, or what I feel his opinion is. He seemed to dislike them. I felt it was unfair that whenever he mentioned a good quality about computers, he counter-attacked with a bad quality, but not vice-versa. I did like his use of quotes. I found his quotations of Norbert Wiener especially fascinating. 》》

Arthur Housinger

&&I found Kidder's style of writing appealing. He had an upbeat approach to the influence of computer technology. He explained his subject matter as an observer.

If I had written the selection, I might have displayed some more of my own opinion toward the subject. 》》

Michelle Kalski

UNIT 5 Review

Reflecting on the Unit

Summarize what you have learned in this unit by answering the following questions.

1 What are some possible types of expository writing? How do you determine which type you should use?

2 What bearing does your audience have on what you write in explaining the steps in a process?

3 What steps would you use to plan a problem-solution essay?

4 How does the feature approach differ from the subject approach to comparing and contrasting?

5 What steps should you follow to build a hypothesis?

Adding to Your Portfolio

CHOOSE A SELECTION FOR YOUR PORTFOLIO Look over the expository writing you did for this unit. Choose a piece of writing for your portfolio. The writing you choose should show one or more of the following:

• a well-worded thesis statement

• relevant details that support your thesis statement

• appropriateness for a specific audience

• transitions and repetition of key terms to link ideas

Reflect on Your Choice

Attach a note to the piece you chose, briefly explaining why you chose it and what you learned from writing it.

SET GOALS

• How can you improve your writing?

• What skill will you focus on the next time you write?

Writing Across the Curriculum

MAKE A CHEMISTRY CONNECTION Imagine that your chemistry teacher has asked you to explain an experiment to another group of students. Select one that you have performed this year. List the steps involved. Then write an essay that explains the purpose of the experiment and what you learned from it.

MAKE A HEALTH CONNECTION List cause-and-effect relationships in the field of health. For instance, consider the results that occur when one's skin receives too much sun, when one's diet is low in protein or vitamin C, or when one gets too little exercise. Choose a series of causes and effects and explain it in an expository paragraph. Be sure to use transitional words and phrases to guide your audience through your exposition.

"Simplify, simplify. . . . We are determined to be starved before we are hungry."

—Henry David Thoreau, *Walden*

Persuasive Writing

Writing in the Real World

Persuasive essays, letters, and speeches use facts and reasons to support a well-structured argument. Following is an excerpt from a persuasive speech by Walter R. Echo-Hawk, a staff attorney for the Native American Rights Fund in Boulder, Colorado. He leads a nationwide lobbying effort to seek protection of ancestral remains and cultural objects held by museums, universities, and historical societies. He gave this speech to a group of North American archaeologists.

From *Native American Burials: Legal and Legislative Aspects*

By Walter R. Echo-Hawk

[Desecration of burial grounds and public display of Indian remains occur] in major part because society over the years . . . has determined that it is "OK" to treat Indian dead differently from the dead of other races. Hence, until very recently, law and social policy [placed] our dead people into . . . categories which enabled and rationalized such differential treatment. For example, it is commonplace for many citizens and agencies to think of and treat our dead as "archaeological resources," "historical property," "pathological material," "scientific data or specimens," or even "library books." When placed in such non-human categories along with dinosaur bones and insects, it has become possible to treat Native dead in ways society would never tolerate if done to citizens of other races under the statutes which protect the dead. . . .

The differential treatment of Indian burials, the expropriation of Indian dead, and the withholding of these dead and funerary objects from reburial—against the wishes of tribal descendents—all implicate a number of constitutional and other legal rights secured to

Attorney Walter R. Echo-Hawk

Indian people and tribes. First, American common law protections of graves and dead bodies, which so strongly protect the interests of the living in the dead, should serve to protect Indians too. . . .

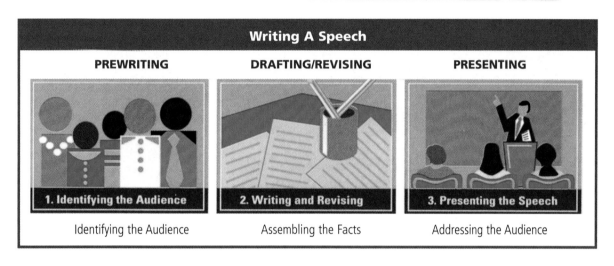

Writing A Speech

PREWRITING	DRAFTING/REVISING	PRESENTING
1. Identifying the Audience	2. Writing and Revising	3. Presenting the Speech
Identifying the Audience	Assembling the Facts	Addressing the Audience

A Writer's Process

Prewriting

Identifying the Audience

Walter R. Echo-Hawk received an invitation from the Montana and Alberta archaeological societies to speak at an annual meeting. Echo-Hawk wanted to persuade his audience that Native ancestral remains and cultural objects be returned to tribal descendents.

In thinking about his speech, Echo-Hawk assumed that his audience of scientists would be opposed to the Native cause. He also concluded that policy makers from the National Park Service would be on hand to hear the Native view as they considered the future of their collections of Native artifacts.

"You have to write for your audience," Echo-Hawk explains. "It directs your whole organization, tenor, and style." After considering his approach, Echo-Hawk constructed an outline "to organize my thoughts and lay out the points I wanted to make." The main points of his argument were these: First, the nation's laws and policies protect graves and cemeteries and guarantee every person a decent burial. Second, these laws had not been applied consistently to Native people, resulting in serious human rights violations. Third, society's attitude toward Native rights was changing fast, and it was time for scientists to join the mainstream.

Writing in the Real World

Drafting/Revising
Assembling the Facts

Now Echo-Hawk was ready to write—to "fill in the outline and create a first draft." Avoiding complex legal issues, he based his appeal on "universal values concerning treatment of the dead to make the point that this was a basic human problem shared by all humanity regardless of race—not a Native American issue but a universal thing."

He began by citing the research of scholars to assign responsibility for mistreatment of the dead. "Historians have documented the many facts and circumstances under which these dead were taken by government agents, soldiers, pot hunters, and other private citizens, museum collecting-crews, and scientists."

Echo-Hawk concluded by naming museums and historical societies that had repatriated human remains and sacred objects and called upon the scientists to "stand up for the human rights of the very people they study."

It took Echo-Hawk about a day and a half to draft his forty-five-minute presentation, editing as he went. "You have to remember that for five years I had been working in this area and I was very versed in the law and facts, so I didn't need to do any independent legal research. I also do a lot of writing in my job, so I write pretty fast."

After setting aside his draft for a day or two, he returned to it with a fresh eye and edited it one last time. "You have to work on it, polish it, fine-tune it, and make it something you can be proud of," he says.

Publishing/Presenting
Addressing the Audience

More than 250 archaeologists, anthropologists, U.S. government officials, and Native tribal leaders from the United States and Canada gathered for the conference at Waterton Lakes National Park in Alberta, Canada. With his speech in hand, Echo-Hawk addressed his audience, reading some parts and improvising others, using his prepared remarks as notes.

Echo-Hawk was surprised by the response of his audience. "People were genuinely receptive to what I had to say," he recalls, saying he thought the historical part of his paper was especially convincing. Later, Echo-Hawk talked one-on-one with people at the conference. "I think we were able to change a few minds."

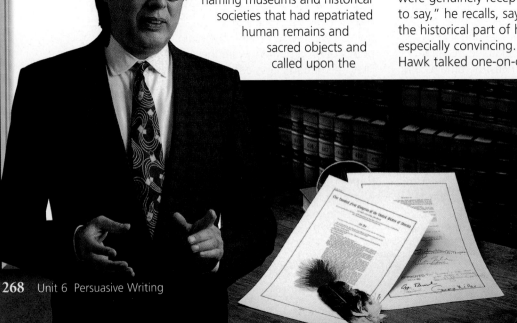

Tourist sites such as the one advertised above are found throughout the country. To many Native Americans, such displays of ancestral remains and sacred artifacts are offensive and sacrilegious.

Examining Writing in the Real World

Analyzing the Media Connection

Discuss these questions about the speech on pages 266–267.

1. What idea does Echo-Hawk present in the opening sentence of his speech? Why might he begin his speech with this idea?

2. How would you characterize the tone of Echo-Hawk's speech? How appropriate is the tone for his audience?

3. What arguments does Echo-Hawk present to convince his audience of his opinion?

4. In what way does Echo-Hawk use his legal background to make his argument?

5. In your opinion, does Echo-Hawk succeed in making the points he set out to make (see p. 267)?

Analyzing the Writer's Process

Discuss these questions about Walter R. Echo-Hawk's writing process.

1. Why was identifying the audience so important to Echo-Hawk as he prepared his speech?

2. Echo-Hawk decided to avoid complex legal issues in his speech. What did he focus on instead and why?

3. Why did Echo-Hawk set the draft of his speech aside for a day or two before working on it again?

4. Why do you think Echo-Hawk decided to improvise parts of his speech rather than read exclusively from a prepared text?

Grammar Link

Adapt your sentence style to your audience.

Adapt each sentence below into two or more simple sentences for a younger audience.

1. Echo-Hawk, a staff attorney for the Native American Rights Fund in Boulder, Colorado, has been a leader of a nationwide lobbying effort to seek protection of Native ancestral remains and cultural objects and to return such items held by museums, universities, and historical societies to tribal descendents.

2. In thinking about his speech, Echo-Hawk assumed that his audience of scientists would be opposed to the Native cause.

3. With his speech in hand, Echo-Hawk addressed his audience, reading some parts and improvising others, using his prepared remarks as notes.

4. "People were genuinely receptive to what I had to say," he recalls, saying he thought the historical part of his paper was especially convincing.

See Lessons 13.3 and 13.4, pages 538–541.

OUR PUBLIC LIBRARY:

LESSON 6.1

Stating Your Case

To make a persuasive argument, you must state your opinion clearly, concisely, and without hesitation. When you do, you focus your reader's attention on your purpose and help to hold his or her interest.

When it came time to choose a national bird, Benjamin Franklin disagreed with the majority, who wanted the eagle. In a letter to a friend more than two hundred years ago, Franklin suggested an alternative, the turkey.

Literature Model

The Turk'y is . . . a true original native of America. Eagles have been found in all Countries, but the Turk'y was peculiar to ours; the first of the Species seen in Europe being brought . . . from Canada, and serv'd up at the wedding table of Charles the Ninth. He is, though a little vain and silly, it is true, but not the worse emblem for that, a Bird of Courage, and would not hesitate to attack a Grenadier of the British Guards, who should presume to invade his Farm Yard with a *red* Coat on.

Benjamin Franklin, letter to Mrs. Sarah Bache, January 26, 1784

Light-hearted as this passage is, it can serve as a model for any effective persuasion. In persuasive writing, the writer tries to make the reader accept a specific claim or opinion. Like Franklin, persuasive writers state their positions clearly. They back up their positions with facts, reasons, and examples, and then choose a presentation that is designed to appeal to their particular audiences.

Construct an Argument

At some time or another you will have your own case to argue—to your teachers, your parents, your boss, or even your children. To make a strong argument, you need to state your opinion clearly, back it up with well-organized evidence, and present it in a way that appeals to your particular audience.

Begin by clearly expressing your opinion in a thesis statement. Compare the thesis statements in the chart below.

Sample Thesis Statements		
NOT SO GOOD	**COMING ALONG**	**RIGHT ON**
In a democracy all citizens are allowed to participate.	Democratic rule requires participation; therefore, everyone should vote.	Low voter turnout is undermining our democracy; we must encourage greater participation through voter information.
Not an opinion, just a statement of fact.	Vague; sounds like a platitude.	Well-defined position, specific solution.

To test your thesis, summarize the opposing view. If you cannot state an opposing view, you probably do not have a strong point to make.

Next gather evidence to support your thesis and develop a strategy for presenting it.

Drafting Tip

Increasing order of importance can fail if you don't hold the audience's attention until the end. A catchy introduction and strong middle are essential to this strategy.

Decreasing Order of Importance

Thesis: The school year should be lengthened to 11 months.

Argument:
✔ **U.S. students are falling behind those in other countries.**
• A longer school year would help parents who work.
• More time in school would keep kids out of trouble.

Increasing Order of Importance

Thesis: Everyone should donate blood regularly.

Argument:
• Donations take very little time.
• Fears of contagion are unfounded.
✔ **Your donation could save someone's life.**

Journal Writing

In your journal, describe a strategy you have used to make a request of your parents, a teacher, or a friend. How well did the strategy work for you? How would you make the same request now?

Know Your Audience

In 1852 the antislavery crusader Frederick Douglass was asked to give a Fourth of July speech. If Douglass had opened with the harshest part of his message, he might have antagonized his audience. Instead, he began with words that most would agree with.

Literature Model

The signers of the Declaration of Independence were brave men. They were great men, great enough to give frame to a great age. It does not often happen to a nation to raise, at one time, such a number of truly great men. . . . They were statesmen, patriots and heros, and for the good they did, and the principles they contended for, I will unite with you to honor their memory.

. . . Washington could not die till he had broken the chains of his slaves. What, to the American slave, is your Fourth of July? I answer: a day that reveals to him, more than all other days in the year, the gross injustice and cruelty to which he is the constant victim. To him, your celebration is a sham; . . . your sounds of rejoicing are empty and . . . heartless; your shouts of liberty and equality, hollow mockery.

Frederick Douglass, Fourth of July Oration, 1852

> Notice how Douglass works to create a sense of community between himself and his audience.

> Gradually, however, Douglass's message shifts to the subject of slavery.

Because Douglass understood his audience, his argument began with statements that his listeners would easily accept and then moved to ones that might challenge their views.

Prewriting Tip

Make a list of your audience's characteristics, their likes and dislikes, their biases. Keep these in mind when crafting your argument.

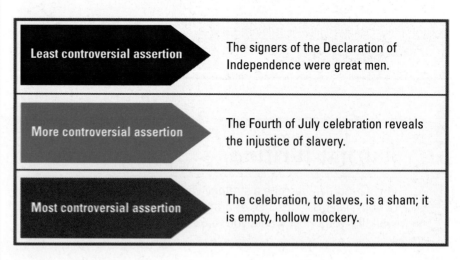

Least controversial assertion	The signers of the Declaration of Independence were great men.
More controversial assertion	The Fourth of July celebration reveals the injustice of slavery.
Most controversial assertion	The celebration, to slaves, is a sham; it is empty, hollow mockery.

Write a Persuasive Note

Your older brother is asleep on a Saturday morning. You decide to borrow his car because you want to visit a friend to hear about last night's rock concert. Knowing that when your brother wakes, he's going to be angry, you need to write him an eloquent note persuading him not to be.

PURPOSE To persuade your audience to accept a controversial position.
AUDIENCE Your older brother
LENGTH 2–3 paragraphs

WRITING RUBRICS To write a persuasive note, you should

- include a simple thesis statement defending what you've done
- organize your supporting evidence in decreasing or increasing order of importance
- show that you understand your audience

Viewing and Representing

HISTORY Watch a rerun of a television show from the 1950s or 1960s. How would you characterize adults' roles in the show? What impression do you get of the children's lives? Write a brief essay stating and supporting your position on whether or not family life then was better than it is now.

Listening and Speaking

GIVE A SPEECH To extend the Viewing and Representing activity, present your opinion as a speech to your classmates. Invite questions and comments. Use classmates' responses as feedback for revising your writing.

Don't overuse commas and capital letters.

Benjamin Franklin's letter to Mrs. Sarah Bache shows the usage of an earlier time.

Eliminate unnecessary commas and capital letters in the paragraph below.

1. The visitors to the Museum included, two company executives and a Secretary.
2. They visited two Historical exhibits, about the growth of the American West.
3. They met with the Curator, and discussed the possibility of setting up a small Exhibit at their company.

See Lessons 20.2 and 21.6, pages 696–701 and pages 722–730.

Persuasive Writing

Sifting Fact from Opinion

A strong persuasive argument backs up opinions with relevant facts. But what happens when opinions are presented as facts? Compare the two sets of statements below.

Jackson refers to "established fact" but offers no proof; this statement is simply opinion.

What is the purpose of these authoritative-sounding phrases?

Ridge lists specific, verifiable facts to support his conclusion that the Cherokee had a right to stay.

Literature Model

It seems now to be an established fact that [the Cherokee] cannot live in contact with a civilized community and prosper. Ages of fruitless endeavor have at length brought us to a knowledge of this principle . . . no one can doubt the moral duty of the Government of the United States to protect and if possible to preserve and perpetuate the scattered remnants of this race which are left within our borders.

President Andrew Jackson, address to Congress, 1835

Literature Model

You asked us to throw off the hunter and warrior state: We did so. You asked us to form a republican government: We did so, adopting your own as a model. You asked us to cultivate the earth, and learn the mechanic arts: We did so. You asked us to learn to read: We did so. You asked us to cast away our idols, and worship your God: We did so.

John Ridge, address to Georgia state officials, 1832

The case of the Cherokee illustrates the importance of evaluating evidence carefully. Sometimes the lives of people are at stake.

Recognize Facts and Opinions

Recognizing the difference between fact and opinion can help bring you closer to the truth as well as guide you in using facts and opinions appropriately in writing.

Follow the guidelines below to help you determine whether the "facts" you read and hear are actually opinions in disguise.

Revising Tip

Using repeated patterns of words can add emphasis in persuasive writing, as Ridge does in the speech on page 274.

Recognizing Facts and Opinions	
RECOGNIZING FACTS	**RECOGNIZING OPINIONS**
Can the statement be verified?	Is the statement based on personal preference or belief?
Facts can be proven or measured; you can check them in an encyclopedia or other reference works compiled by experts. Sometimes you can observe or test them yourself.	Often, although not always, opinions contain phrases such as "I believe" or "in my view" and are open to interpretation.

The following hypothetical situation is typical of many issues that challenge citizens to sift facts from opinion.

"City in Danger of Burning," reads the headline. The head of the city firefighters' union maintains that recent cutbacks in personnel threaten the safety of residents. Fires could burn out of control, he says, if firefighters are not rehired.

Pressed by reporters for a response, the mayor said that the union leader—her opponent in the upcoming mayoral election—is trying to capture the headlines and smear her. The mayor dismisses the claims as mere opinion, not fact.

If you're a reporter covering the uproar, how will you make sense of this situation for your readers? If you're a citizen, how will these claims affect your voting decision?

To resolve the dispute between the two mayoral candidates, you might check city records to measure the firefighters' response time for emergency calls. A sharp drop in the number of calls handled promptly after the layoffs will support the union leader's statement. If no change has occurred, however, you might judge the claims to be scare tactics.

Journal Writing

Clip a newspaper article on a controversial subject. Paste it into your journal. Then use two colored markers, one to indicate facts and the other to indicate opinions.

Evaluate Facts and Opinions

To evaluate the strength of an argument, you need to do more than distinguish between fact and opinion. You also need to determine whether facts are relevant and tell the whole story. Look back at the example of the firefighters on page 275. What if the mayor tried to counter her opponent's claim by citing a poll showing that most city residents supported the layoffs of firefighters? No one can deny the results of the poll. The opinion of city residents about the layoffs, however, has no bearing on whether the city is adequately protected.

Opinions, as well as facts, should be evaluated carefully. Informed opinions, based on facts and on the experiences of eyewitnesses or experts, carry the most weight.

Return once more to the example of the firefighters and evaluate the range of opinions illustrated below.

Prewriting Tip

In researching evidence to support your argument, gather as many facts as you can. You can select the strongest facts later, during drafting.

City Employee:
Statistics show that it takes firefighters an average of two minutes longer to answer calls than it did before the layoffs. But these delays probably were due to the unusually large number of fires this month. I don't see any cause for alarm.

Consultant:
I evaluate fire departments around the country to see whether cities are properly protected. Based on my research and experience, I can say with certainty that the recent layoffs have placed the city at risk. I recommend that at least fifty firefighters be rehired immediately.

City Resident:
Seventy-five firefighters were laid off last month, and I don't see the city going up in smoke. Obviously the layoffs were a good idea.

Write an Opposing Editorial

The thesis statements below come from the editorial page of a high school newspaper. Choose one that you disagree with and write an opposing editorial expressing your opinion.

1. Because of diminishing funds, high school sports programs should be cut and more funds allocated to academics.

2. Young people should be required to spend one year doing community service jobs such as delivering food to the poor, tutoring illiterate adults, or planting new forests.

3. School administrators should have the right to randomly search students' lockers.

PURPOSE To persuade readers using facts and informed opinions

AUDIENCE Your classmates

LENGTH 2–3 paragraphs

WRITING RUBRICS To write an effective opposing editorial, you should

• state an opinion

• support it with relevant facts

• include opinions based on facts or on eye-witnesses' evidence

Listening and Speaking

COOPERATIVE LEARNING In groups of three, role-play a job interview. One student can be the applicant. Another can be the interviewer, who will draft six questions drawing out the applicant's job history, education, and qualifications. The third student can listen carefully and then present a short oral or written recommendation to the company about whether or not to hire the applicant. Each student should have an opportunity to play each role.

Grammar Link

Make verbs agree with nouns of amount.

When a noun refers to an amount that is considered one unit, it takes a singular verb. When a noun refers to a number of individual units, it takes a plural verb.

Write the correct verb to complete each sentence below.

1. Five pounds of potato salad (is, are) more than enough to feed everyone at the picnic.

2. Three months (has, have) gone by since we began planning this outing.

3. Twenty yards of material (was, were) purchased to make the table coverings.

4. Ninety percent of the invited guests (plans, plan) to attend.

5. Six dollars (is, are) the donation requested from each guest.

See Lesson 16.4, page 606.

Using Computers

Newspapers usually state a maximum number of words for a guest editorial. To find the word count of your editorial, learn the appropriate command on your word processing program, often Information, Summary Information, or Tools. If you want to know the word count for only part of a file, highlight that part; then check the word count.

Evaluating Evidence

To support your argument in persuasive writing, you must choose and evaluate a variety of evidence. Your evidence must be relevant and reliable.

Irving B. Harris, in the address below, argues that much of our mental development occurs in early childhood. To make his point, he reveals a surprising fact about our physical development.

The force of gravity is equal to the square root of . . .

Literature Model

Most of a child's growth has occurred before the age of sixteen. As a matter of fact, it's a little awesome to realize that all of us had attained one-half of our mature height by the time we were two-and-one-half years old. That's right. If you're six feet tall now, you were already three feet tall when you were two and one half.

Irving B. Harris, address to City Club of Cleveland,
December 15, 1989

Harris continues his argument by using an analogy between physical and mental development. He asks, "If you wanted to increase children's height, would you spend money to improve the diet of sixteen-year-olds? No. The money would go toward better diets for the very young. . . . Likewise," he says, "to increase children's mental development, we must spend money to improve education at the youngest ages, when mental growth is most rapid."

Choose Relevant Evidence

The more focused your supporting evidence is, the stronger your argument will be. Harris opens with a persuasive analogy, but an analogy alone doesn't give enough strength to his argument. To persuade his listeners, he needs well-substantiated, convincing facts about mental development. In the excerpt on the next page, Harris uses other types of evidence to back up his claim.

Literature Model

Professor Benjamin Bloom, of the University of Chicago, pointed out that human intelligence . . . grows at a decelerating rate. His research showed that by the age of four, more than one-half of our intelligence is in place. . . . T. Berry Brazelton, a respected pediatrician at Harvard, says he can tell by examining a nine-month-old infant whether that infant is likely to make it in school or fail in school, simply by observing how that child approaches very simple tasks, like playing with blocks.

Irving B. Harris

> Harris uses both statistics and expert opinion to bolster his argument.

Both facts and opinions lead to Harris's conclusion: "Programs that attempt to radically improve children's health, education, and overall well-being must start very early."

When you build a persuasive argument, each type of evidence you use adds a different kind of support to your position (see page 73 on types of evidence). Factual information and concrete details, such as statistics, observations, scientific reports, and historical precedents, are convincing because they are verifiable. Opinions are effective if they are from a respected authority. Examples, anecdotes, and analogies can bring your subject to life or illuminate a point. Reasons guide your audience through the logic of your position.

Collecting mountains of evidence, however, doesn't guarantee that you'll have a strong argument. As you gather evidence from authoritative interviews, from texts, or from available technology, you'll need to judge the quality of the information. The questions below can help you analyze your research.

Checklist for Evaluating Evidence

- Does the evidence come from a reliable, qualified, unbiased source?
- Is the evidence consistent with what you know to be true or with what authorities on the subject agree to be true?
- Does the evidence address all sides of the issue, taking all objections into account?
- Is the evidence up-to-date?

Journal Writing

Carefully read an editorial, a letter to the editor, an op-ed article, or an arts review in a newspaper or magazine. State the opinion expressed in the article; then list the evidence used. Refer to the questions above as a guide. Is the evidence sound?

Drafting Tip

Unity is essential for effective persuasive writing. Make sure that every piece of evidence you include is relevant; extraneous data will weaken an argument.

Roosevelt's first statement acknowledges the complaints against the U.N.

Why does Roosevelt begin her argument with facts everyone can agree on?

What evidence does Roosevelt use to make her case?

She concedes "failures," but turns this failure into part of her proposed solution.

Anticipate Opposition

When you write an argument, anticipate objections to your view and try to answer those objections. A good strategy for handling opposition is to make concessions—to admit that some point in your argument is weak or to agree with some part of your opponent's argument. Honesty often strengthens rather than weakens a case.

Eleanor Roosevelt used this strategy effectively in a 1954 speech in support of the United Nations.

Literature Model

You hear people say, "Why hasn't the United Nations done this or that?" The United Nations functions just as well as the member nations make it function, and no better or worse. And so the first thing to look at is, I think, the kind of machinery that was set up, and what it was meant to do.

Now we have to go back in our minds to the time when the [U.N.] was first planned. At that time the war was not over, and this was a dream, and everybody accepted it as a dream—an idea to set up an organization, the object of that organization being to keep peace....

[The founding nations] had co-operated during the war; they believed that they were going to go on co-operating after the war. That was one of the great myths of the centuries.

They also believed that this organization they were setting up was to be an organization to maintain peace, not to make peace. Peace was going to be made, and then this organization would help to maintain it. What happened, of course, was that peace has never been found. And so this organization, which was not set up to meet certain questions, has had questions brought to it that were not in mind at the beginning.

... When we look upon the failures in the United Nations, we should not be disheartened, because if we take the failure and learn, eventually we will use this machinery better and better. We will also learn one important thing, and that is, no machinery works unless people make it work.

Eleanor Roosevelt, speech for the U.N. Seminars
Brandeis University, 1954

Write an Editorial

Write an editorial on a school topic you feel strongly about, such as a mandatory dress code or a minimum grade requirement for athletes. Try to convince your readers to accept your point of view.

PURPOSE To convince others to accept your beliefs about a school topic

AUDIENCE Your classmates

LENGTH 3–4 paragraphs

WRITING RUBRICS To write an effective editorial, you should

- use facts and verifiable opinions as evidence
- show that you have evaluated the quality of your evidence
- anticipate others' objections to your view

Cross-Curricular Activity

ECONOMICS Take a position on the following statement: "The state should fund 100 percent of the tuition cost for any postsecondary student enrolled in one of the state's colleges or universities, trade schools, or technical schools." List points that support your position; then be your own "devil's advocate" and note possible objections to each of your points. You may want to set up a class debate.

Viewing and Representing

Watch a national evening-news broadcast. Focus your attention on possible bias in the reporting. Look for bias in the types of stories selected for coverage, the way in which people are portrayed, or the connotations of words used to report events. Compose and send an e-mail to the network news organization outlining why you thought a report you saw was biased or unbiased.

Grammar Link

Make sure that subjects and verbs agree when a phrase or expression comes between them.

. . . by the age of four, . . . one-half of our intelligence is in place.

Use present-tense verbs in completing the following sentences, maintaining subject-verb agreement.

1. Eleanor Roosevelt, as well as Lady Bird Johnson, _____.
2. Five noted scholars, along with a contemporary writer, _____.
3. The bureau, in addition to Chad's posters, kazoo, and guitars, _____.
4. The tallest girls in the church choir _____.
5. The car behind that huge clump of bushes _____.

See Lessons 16.1 and 16.6, pages 601 and 609.

Persuasive Writing

Inductive and Deductive Reasoning

Inductive and deductive reasoning both involve using facts to arrive at conclusions, but they work in different ways. You must decide which type of reasoning works best for a particular argument.

Literature Model

The scenario is straight out of a science-fiction movie: Giant meteorite strikes earth, setting the planet afire. Volcanoes erupt, tsunamis crash into the continents. . . . In the moments following the impact of an object ten kilometers in diameter, experts believe, a blast wave similar to that of a nuclear explosion would destroy everything within several hundred kilometers, its intense heat and winds combining to set wildfires, perhaps even a global inferno.

National Geographic, June 1989

Based on evidence uncovered in the late 1980s, many researchers conclude that a giant meteorite collided with the earth about 66 million years ago. The meteorite theory has aroused keen interest, yet it is based only on rock samples from around the world. No people witnessed such an event. So how can scientists be sure their conclusions are reasonable?

Use Inductive Reasoning

Scientists often use inductive reasoning. With induction, one assembles a series of facts and finds a relationship between them that can be stated as a conclusion, or generalization. The chart on the next page shows how inductive reasoning led some scientists to conclude that the earth was hit by a meteorite.

Fact: Iridium, a chemical element, is found in layers of rock bed in Italy, Denmark, and New Zealand. **Fact:** Iridium is rarely found on earth, but is found in meteorites. **Fact:** The rock containing the iridium is about 66 million years old.	**Generalization:** A meteorite hit the earth about 66 million years ago.

We rely on inductive reasoning for much of our knowledge. We cannot test whether the sun will rise in the east and set in the west every day, but we can conclude with reasonable certainty that it will do so. You don't have to conduct tests on all ten fingers to figure out that if you place any one of them on a hot stove, you will get burned.

Fortunately, you need experience that sensation only once; you can then generalize about the effect of a hot stove on all fingers. In these examples, the reasoning proceeds logically from limited facts or observations to a general conclusion. An inductive argument will hold up only if the evidence is accurate and the conclusion follows reasonably from the evidence. Check your reasoning by asking whether you could draw another conclusion from the evidence. A correct inductive argument will meet the criteria below.

> **Revising Tip**
>
> Persuasive arguments will seem more objective when presented in the third person. Avoid using the first person unless you are stating an opinion.

Inductive Reasoning Checklist

✓ **Is the conclusion consistent with other known facts?**

For instance, the meteorite collision is thought to have occurred at the precise time that dinosaurs suddenly disappeared from the earth. The conclusion that something wiped out the dinosaurs at the time of the meteorite fits well with the theory of a cataclysmic impact.

✓ **How large was the sample from which the evidence was drawn?**

The iridium was found in several widely separated locations on earth, a fact that scientists say is significant.

✓ **Does the evidence apply to the whole group it claims to represent?**

All of the rock containing the iridium was of the same age. Furthermore, as far as we know, iridium exists in all meteorites.

Journal Writing

Your friend is an excellent basketball player; she is also good at tennis, volleyball, softball, and football. Construct a chart like the one at the top of this page in which you use inductive reasoning to draw a conclusion about your friend.

Avoid the Pitfalls of Inductive Reasoning

Conclusions reached through inductive reasoning are not foolproof. Using evidence improperly can lead to a problem called a hasty generalization. This error in reasoning occurs when your conclusion goes further than the evidence permits.

Hasty generalizations can lead to stereotyping, a form of faulty reasoning that assumes that all members of a group have the same characteristics. Suppose that the only drummers you had ever seen were boys. You might reason inductively that only boys play drums, but your reasoning would be incorrect because you have not examined a large enough sample of drummers. If you looked at a larger sample, you might learn that many girls play drums as well.

Most people wouldn't stereotype drummers in this way. Unfortunately, however, real-life stereotyping does occur, and it can be both harmful and insulting. People sometimes stereotype certain groups, erroneously concluding that all of the members of a particular group behave in a particular way.

You can avoid stereotyping by limiting your generalizations. Unless you are certain that something is true of every member of a group, don't use absolute terms such as *all* or *everyone*. You might say, "*Many* teenagers like going to parties" rather than "*All* teenagers like going to parties." Make your sample as large and as representative as possible. Don't claim, "Most students in our school are good athletes" unless you have measured the athletic ability of more than half the students. Avoid stereotypes that describe all members of a group as being alike.

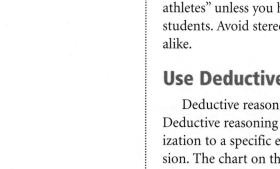

Looking at a small sample, you conclude that all drummers are boys.

Looking at a larger sample, you see that drummers are both boys and girls.

Use Deductive Reasoning

Deductive reasoning is another commonly used thinking process. Deductive reasoning begins with a generalization, then applies that generalization to a specific example, or set of examples, and arrives at a conclusion. The chart on the next pages outlines the deductive reasoning used by the people who left Love Canal, a community in upstate New York, when they discovered it had been built on a toxic waste dump.

Generalization: Toxic chemical waste is dangerous to humans.

 is

Fact: Love Canal is located on top of a layer of toxic waste.

 is

Conclusion: Love Canal is a dangerous place to live.

 is

Editing Tip

During editing, check for pronoun antecedent agreement. To follow your line of reasoning, a reader must know to what pronouns refer. See Unit 17, pages 622–647, on pronoun usage.

You probably use deduction without realizing it. When you decide to eat a banana, how do you know that you will like it? From past experience, you know that you like bananas; you know that this piece of fruit is a banana; so you deduce that you will like this piece of fruit.

In essays or speeches, deduction may be difficult to identify. What deductive argument did Susan B. Anthony use below to make her case in her famous speech for women's suffrage?

Literature Model

The only question left to be settled now is: Are women persons? And I hardly believe any of our opponents will have the hardihood to say they are not. Being persons, then, women are citizens; and no State has a right to make any law, or to enforce any old law, that shall abridge their privileges.

Susan B. Anthony
"On Woman's Right to Suffrage," 1873

Citizens ▶ have the right to vote.

Women ▶ are citizens.

Women ▶ should have the right to vote.

Journal Writing

Construct a chart illustrating correct deductive reasoning for the conclusion *A turkey has wings*.

Find Pitfalls in Deductive Reasoning

When you reason deductively, you start with a general statement about a group—for example: *All dogs have four legs.* You then identify someone or something that belongs to that group: *Rover is a dog.* Finally, by deduction, you attribute the characteristic of the group to that member: *Therefore, Rover has four legs.*

You must be careful, however, in constructing such an argument. The following reasoning would be incorrect: *Dogs have four legs; Rover has four legs; therefore, Rover is a dog.* In fact, Rover could be a hippopotamus or a muskrat or any other four-legged creature.

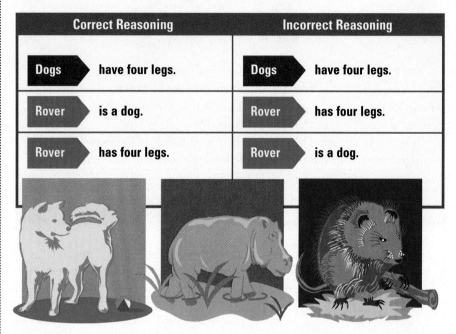

Correct Reasoning	Incorrect Reasoning
Dogs have four legs.	**Dogs** have four legs.
Rover is a dog.	**Rover** has four legs.
Rover has four legs.	**Rover** is a dog.

If any statement in your argument is not true, the entire deduction becomes questionable. Your deduction may be logically constructed, but your conclusion may still be false.

Consider the following line of reasoning: *To attract top-notch students, a school needs a good science program; our school wants to attract top-notch students; therefore, we need to improve our science program.* Not everyone may agree with the first assumption. Must a school have a good science program to attract top-notch students? In this case, the reasoning is well constructed but the conclusion is not necessarily true.

Most arguments use both inductive and deductive logic. For example, if you were trying to dissuade someone from trying a crash diet, you could cite studies linking crash dieting with weight gain, depression, eating disorders, anemia, and an increased incidence of colds to prove inductively that such diets are ineffective. Then you could use the amassed evidence to deduce that crash dieting can threaten one's health.

Write a Persuasive Paragraph

Using deductive reasoning, supply a conclusion for the following argument. Then write a persuasive paragraph expanding on the argument. Use details taken from your own experience to bring your paragraph to life with valid evidence, substantiated facts, and well-supported opinions.

GENERALIZATION: Anyone who claims to be concerned about the use of pesticides and chemical fertilizers on fruits and vegetables should buy only organically grown produce.

FACT: Students at Health High School say they are concerned about the use of pesticides and chemical fertilizers on produce.

CONCLUSION:

PURPOSE To derive and present a logical conclusion
AUDIENCE Your classmates and teacher
LENGTH 1 paragraph

WRITING RUBRICS To write an effective persuasive paragraph, you should

- make sure that the conclusion is valid
- check the argument for faults in logic
- use evidence that is verifiable

Cross-Curricular Activity

ECONOMICS Write an essay for or against requiring all U.S. companies to give their employees at least three weeks of vacation a year. Form an opinion on the issue, and develop an inductive argument. Use well-supported facts, such as the number of hours American workers work per week and how many official holidays and vacation days most U.S. workers get.

Grammar Link

Avoid sentence fragments.

Fragments can often be eliminated by attaching them to complete sentences.

Giant meteorites struck the earth.
Which is why the dinosaurs died.
Giant meteorites struck the earth, which is why the dinosaurs died.

Revise the following, correcting any sentence fragments.

1. A young paleontologist discovered a stratum of iridium. Which is rarely found on earth.
2. Found in layers of bed rock in Italy, Denmark, and New Zealand. Iridium was identified as an element years ago.
3. The iridium was found in rock strata of similar formation. In locations separated by great distances.
4. The stratum of iridium is about sixty-six million years old. Which puts it at the end of the Cretaceous Period. The time of most dinosaur extinctions.

See Lesson 13.9, page 551.

Using Computers

Review your writing portfolio, looking for words that you commonly misspell. Using your computer, create a personal list of correct spellings for those confusing words. Review the spellings frequently and refer to your list whenever you write.

Persuasive Writing

Recognizing Logical Fallacies

Constructing a sound argument requires reasoning that is free from fallacy. There are various types of fallacious arguments that you must learn to recognize and avoid.

Avoid Faulty Reasoning

Intentionally or unintentionally, faulty reasoning creeps into what we write and say. Faulty reasoning involves errors called logical fallacies. Learning to recognize your own and others' logical fallacies will strengthen your skills in persuasive writing. It will also make you more alert to the flaws in advertising and other forms of persuasion directed at you. Here are some of the most common types of logical fallacies.

Red Herring A red herring is a statement that diverts attention from the issue at hand. Red herrings appear frequently in politics. A congressional representative attacked for irregular attendance might, in trying to defend himself, launch into a discourse on his charitable work to prove that he is productive. But this defense does not address the criticism about the missed meetings.

Circular Reasoning An argument that apparently leads to a logical conclusion but actually takes you back to where you started uses circular reasoning. The statement "Shaquille O'Neal is a great basketball player because he has so much talent" sounds true enough. To say, however, that talent makes O'Neal great is just another way of saying that he is a great basketball player. The statement doesn't prove anything; it merely repeats the point in different words.

The danger of circular reasoning is that we can fool our audience—even ourselves—into believing we have supported our position when we have just talked in circles, as shown in this speech by a fictitious secretary of defense.

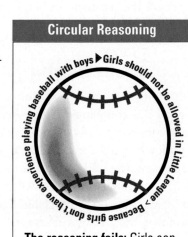

Circular Reasoning

Girls should not be allowed in Little League ▷ Because girls don't have experience playing baseball with boys ▷

The reasoning fails: Girls cannot get that experience unless they're allowed to play.

Model

I have been proud to oversee the administration of our nation's space program, and I believe the Department of Defense should continue directing this program. As you all know, the department has been involved in every aspect of space research and development, from the efforts of the nation's first astronauts in the 1950s to the secret military missions of the space shuttle today. During this period, the Defense Department has been headed by such famous figures as General Buhrl and General Donnelly.

Based on this record, it is clear that research and systems development of our nation's crucial space program should go forward under the direction of the Defense Department.

> The military should direct research and development in the space program because . . .

> . . . the military has always directed research and development in the space program.

Revising Tip

If you or a peer editor finds a passage confusing, always study the logic. Write the key points of evidence in an outline or chart to check for fallacies.

If you are not sure about whether an argument is circular or not, try listing the evidence. Note whether the list contains facts or simply restatements of the original premise.

Bandwagon Reasoning The term "jumping on the bandwagon" means doing (or thinking) something because everyone else is doing it.

This kind of reasoning is fallacious because it provides no hard evidence to support a decision or viewpoint. When you try to persuade your parents to let you go to a party "because everyone else is going," you are using bandwagon reasoning.

Journal Writing

In your journal, write a passage that uses a form of faulty reasoning. Then make a diagram to represent it, and share your diagram with the class.

Watch for Oversimplification

In oversimplification, a few facts are cited and loose connections are made between them.

Cause and Effect The cause-and-effect fallacy assumes that since one event preceded another, the first event causes the second. President Herbert Hoover was blamed for the Great Depression, which began shortly after he took office. However, the conditions for the economic crisis had been brewing long before Hoover's time.

The cause-and-effect fallacy often stems from superstition, ignorance, or wishful thinking. The following time line shows how chronologically related events can lead people to such misguided reasoning.

February 1992: The Springfield Stilts win their twelfth consecutive state high school basketball championship.	**July 1992:** Springfield High completes construction of a new gymnasium.	**September 1992:** Enrollment at Springfield High reaches an all-time high.	**November 1992:** The Stilts get new uniforms.	**February 1993:** The Stilts fail to win a thirteenth championship title.
February	**May**	**August**	**November**	**February**
	1992			**1993**

Springfield was devastated by the Stilts's loss of the thirteenth state title. Some people claimed that replacing the old "lucky" uniforms and gymnasium caused the defeat. Some said it was the unlucky number *thirteen* that was responsible for the loss. Others felt that the increased enrollment brought bigger crowds to the games, heightening the players' nervousness. Few reasoned that the Stilts lost because they were outplayed by a better team.

Either/Or Comedian Groucho Marx, posing as a doctor, takes a patient's pulse and says, "Either this man is dead or my watch has stopped." This scenario illustrates another kind of oversimplification: the either/or fallacy.

Either/or reasoning assumes that there are only two alternatives and ignores other possible explanations. You sometimes hear this fallacy used deliberately, as a form of hyperbole or overstatement: "Come down from that tree or you'll break your neck!" There are certainly more possibilities than the two mentioned, but the speaker is choosing to ignore them to make a point. This kind of hyperbolic use of either/or reasoning is sometimes put in deliberately to intensify an argument. That is, the audience recognizes the fallacy but understands it is being used for emphatic—or dramatic—effect.

Either/or reasoning can be used to express the highest principles. One of the most celebrated examples is the conclusion of Patrick Henry's speech to the Virginia Convention of Delegates in 1775. Urging his fellow citizens to war against the British, he said: "Is life so dear, or peace so sweet, as to be purchased at the price of chains and slavery? Forbid it, Almighty God! I know not what course others may take; but as for me, give me liberty, or give me death!"

Before the United States had decided to enter World War II, Dorothy Thompson, a well-known American journalist, gave a less-often quoted but similarly impassioned speech urging her fellow citizens to enter the war. Notice how she sets up what appears to be an either/or fallacy in order to show that, in this case, it is no fallacy.

Drafting Tip

To avoid oversimplifying, don't be afraid to note other viewpoints in your text. A well-constructed argument will persuade people that your view is superior to others.

Persuasive Writing

Literature Model

Every nation on this globe and every individual on this globe will presently learn what a few have always known: that there are times in history when the business of one is the business of all, when life or death is a matter of choice, and when no one alive can avoid making that choice. These times occur seldom in history, these times of inevitable decisions. But this is one of those times.

   Before this epoch is over, every living human being will have chosen, every living human being will have lined up with Hitler or against him, every living human being will either have opposed this onslaught or supported it. For if he tried to make no choice that in itself will be a choice. If he takes no side, he is on Hitler's side: if he does not act that is an act—for Hitler.

Dorothy Thompson, May 2, 1941

How does Thompson prepare her audience for the choice she feels they have to make?

Thompson asserts that we have only two choices: oppose Hitler or support him.

Thompson refutes those who would object to this logic as a fallacy by arguing that there are no alternatives. Do you agree or disagree? What alternatives could you suggest?

Journal Writing

Think of a time when someone used the either/or fallacy to put pressure on you. Describe it in your journal. How did it make you feel? Was it convincing? Were you able to counter the fallacy with an alternative?

Spot Errors in Reasoning

If you outline your argument and check its validity carefully during prewriting, you can avoid most logical fallacies. It pays to double-check your reasoning as you revise, as did the writer in the model below.

Student Model

Strong introduction— keep.

Compared with people from other nations, Americans know next to nothing about cultures outside their own. This ignorance leads to intolerance and misunderstandings. One place to begin eliminating the problem is in schools. Why not in <u>our</u> school?

Circular reasoning.

I propose that we launch a student exchange program. Such a program will involve the entire student body, ~~because all students will participate.~~ Teachers and parents will also enjoy contact with visiting students.

Faulty cause-and-effect? There may be other reasons for dropout rates in those schools. Besides, it's a red herring.

The chance to study abroad will be an incentive for studying foreign languages and world history. Exchange students will return with stories that will inspire others to participate. ~~In addition, statistics show that in schools that have adopted exchange programs, the dropout rate has not increased, as it has elsewhere.~~

Either/or fallacy: either my proposal or isolation. Not true.

I urge you to adopt my proposal, so we may begin the exchanges next year. *Students deserve the opportunity to learn more about their world.* ~~Without such a program, our students will grow up in isolation.~~

Write a Letter Exposing Logical Fallacies

The following telegram is a response to an invitation to move to California during the gold rush. It contains several logical fallacies. Respond to the telegram in a letter. Note that the word stop stands for a period at the end of a sentence.

NOT SURE WE WILL LIKE CALIFORNIA BECAUSE WE'VE NEVER LIVED THERE STOP WHY WON'T YOU COME HOME STOP HAVEN'T I ALWAYS BEEN A GOOD BROTHER TO YOU STOP DON'T YOU LOVE YOUR FAMILY STOP IF WE MOVE OUT WEST WE'LL NEVER COME BACK STOP MARY'S BROTHER NEVER CAME BACK STOP EVERYONE SAYS GOING TO CALIFORNIA IS BAD LUCK STOP CAROLINE AND JIMMY MOVED TO CALIFORNIA LAST YEAR AND THEIR HOUSE BURNED DOWN STOP YOUR LOVING BROTHER

PURPOSE To expose the logical fallacies
AUDIENCE Your classmates
LENGTH 3–4 paragraphs

WRITING RUBRICS To write an effective letter exposing logical fallacies, you should

- identify the types of logical fallacy in the telegram
- explain why each is an error in reasoning

Cross-Curricular Activity

CURRENT EVENTS Working in a small group, review the editorial pages of one edition of your local newspaper for examples of logical fallacies. These fallacies may appear in the newspaper's own editorials, in articles by syndicated columnists, in letters to the editor, or in editorial cartoons. Make a chart, listing each logical fallacy and categorizing it. Share your list with the class.

All subjects preceded by *each* **and** *every* **take singular verbs.**

Notice how the writer uses a singular form of the verb in this sentence: Each of the cows in this barn is going to be milked now.

Revise the sentences below, checking for subject-verb agreement.

1. Every one of those girls are wearing the same backpack and jeans jacket.
2. Each CD and videotape at that store cost about ten percent more than it should.
3. In those families, each child and each adult have acting ability.
4. Every nation represented in the United Nations have a responsibility toward the whole world.

See Lessons 16.5 and 16.7, pages 608, 611.

Viewing and Representing

Read the informational "blurbs" from two currently popular books, either fiction or non-fiction. Blurbs usually appear on the inside of the dust jacket on hardbound books or on the back cover of paperback books. Remember that a blurb is essentially advertising copy designed to interest you in buying the book. Make a list of the adjectives, adverbs, and other modifiers used to describe each book. Write a two-paragraph essay in which you discuss how the publisher tailors language to appeal to readers.

Persuasive Writing

Persuasive Writing

Writing and Presenting a Speech

*A*n effective speech can persuade an audience in some ways that reading cannot. However, the elements of a memorable speech are based on the same techniques as persuasive writing.

In 1963, President John F. Kennedy visited the Berlin Wall, erected by the communist government of East Germany to keep its people from fleeing to the West. A huge crowd had gathered to hear him speak. Kennedy did not disappoint them.

Literature Model

Two thousand years ago the proudest boast was *Civis Romanus sum.* ["I am a citizen of Rome."] Today, in the world of freedom, the proudest boast is *Ich bin ein Berliner.* ["I am a Berliner."]

There are many people in the world who really don't understand, or say they don't, what is the great issue between the free world and the communist world.

Let them come to Berlin!

And there are some who say in Europe and elsewhere we can work with the communists. . . .

Let them come to Berlin!

. . . When this city will be joined as one . . . the people of West Berlin can take sober satisfaction in the fact that they were in the front lines for almost two decades.

All free men, wherever they may live, are citizens of Berlin, and therefore, as a free man, I take pride in the words *Ich bin ein Berliner!*

President John F. Kennedy, address to the citizens of West Berlin
June 1963

Organize Your Presentation

The president's speech writer, Ted Sorensen, wrote the words that would persuade the people of West Berlin that Kennedy was on their side, and Kennedy knew how to deliver those words. To get from Sorensen's typewriter in Washington to Kennedy's platform in Berlin, however, this great speech had to go through the steps of the writing process.

If you have to give a speech, use prewriting techniques to help you find a topic and position, reflect on audience and purpose, and come up with strong reasons and evidence. When you draft your speech, organize your material in a way that will be persuasive. Decide how much of your speech you want to write down and how much, if any, you want to give spontaneously. Some people enjoy the informality of an improvised speech. Others prefer to deliver a fully written speech. Either way, it's a good idea to have a well-thought-out opening for your talk, so your first words will be powerful.

The chart below presents some pointers for effective speaking.

Revising Tip

Tape record your speech and listen to it, taking notes on tone and rhythm. Use your notes to help you revise your speech; then record the speech again.

Persuasive Writing

Aspects of Speaking		Tips
	Length How much time are you allotted? Have you practiced your speech aloud, timing it?	*Take it easy: People often rush their words when they're nervous.*
	Audience What is the mood of your listeners? Their background? Attitudes?	*Create rapport: Humor is often a good way to win over an audience.*
	Tone Do you want your speech to sound casual, emotional, serious?	*Choose suitable language: In an informal speech you may use contractions and slang.*
I have a dream / I have a dream / I have a dream / I have a dream / I have a dream	**Rhythm** Dr. Martin Luther King Jr. made four words immortal by repeating them: "I have a dream."	*Repetition of words or phrases can make your speech memorable: "Let them come to Berlin!"*

Journal Writing

If you were running for a school government office and had to give a speech to your classmates, which of the aspects above do you think you might use most effectively? In your journal, describe briefly any ideas that immediately come to mind.

Use Graphic Displays

Words are not a speechmaker's only tools of persuasion. You can use visuals to strengthen your point; sometimes you can convey an idea more clearly in a diagram or picture than in words. How do the visuals on this page work with the ideas in the model below?

Revising Tip

Practice delivering your speech before a mirror. Try using gestures and body movements for emphasis at key points in your speech. Make your gestures natural.

Student Model

Many people don't recycle because they think it is just as expensive to recycle goods as it is to make items from new materials. This is not true. Not only is recycling less expensive, but it also provides the recycler with a small profit. And not only does recycling cost less, it saves energy as well. For example, even though bauxite (the material from which aluminum is made) is earth's most abundant metal, it is expensive to mine and refine. It takes 95 percent less energy to make aluminum cans from recycled ones than from aluminum ore. The energy saved from recycling one aluminum can is enough to keep a 100-watt light bulb burning for 3 1/2 hours! Likewise, paper made by recycling consumes half the energy needed to process new paper. And by recycling 43 newspapers, you will save one mature tree.

Darin R. Anderson
Wynford High School, Bucyrus, Ohio

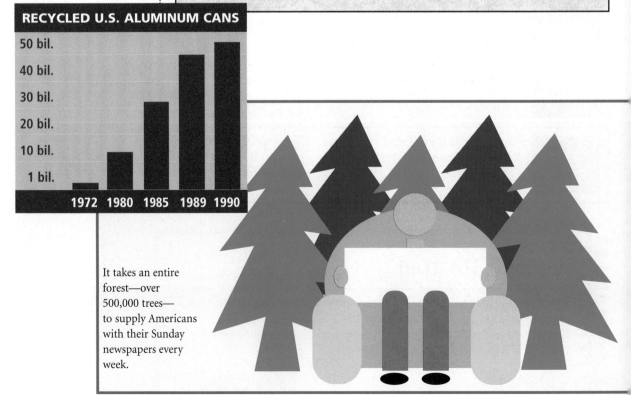

RECYCLED U.S. ALUMINUM CANS

50 bil.
40 bil.
30 bil.
20 bil.
10 bil.
1 bil.

1972 1980 1985 1989 1990

It takes an entire forest—over 500,000 trees—to supply Americans with their Sunday newspapers every week.

Write a Persuasive Speech

Prepare a persuasive speech about a topic you have strong feelings about. You can focus on a community issue, such as preservation of old buildings; a school issue, such as the need to update sports facilities; or a personal issue, such as the amount of responsibility given to each child in a family.

PURPOSE To prepare a persuasive speech on a subject of your choice
AUDIENCE Your classmates
LENGTH 3–5 minutes

WRITING RUBRICS To write an effective persuasive speech, you should

- support your position with strong reasons and convincing evidence
- organize your material in a way that will be persuasive
- decide which parts of your speech to write out and which to outline

Using Computers

Proofreading is especially important in speech writing because you don't want to stumble over misspelled or omitted words. If you're able to prepare your speech with a word processing program, use the spelling checker. Double- or triple-spacing will make your text easier to read out loud. If you choose to write you speech out by hand, be sure that your cursive writing is legible.

Grammar Link

Use the correct case for personal pronouns.

Use *I, we, he, she, they* for subjects and *me, us, him, her, them* for objects.
  Let *them* come to Berlin!

Correct the use of personal pronouns in these sentences.

1. Jake, Jessie, and me went to the gym for a pickup game of basketball.
2. Between Mishio and I, we finished the project in an hour.
3. It was himself who worked harder on the project.
4. The Florios and us have always taken vacations together.
5. These bags were left behind for those boys and I to carry.
6. Who was it who decided on that complicated combination, him or me?

See Lesson 17.1, page 623.

Listening and Speaking

Working with two other students, read aloud your speeches to each other. Discuss how each speech might be recast for a different audience. How would the arguments change? What new facts would be needed? How might the tone of each speech shift?

LESSON 6.7

Writing a Letter to an Editor

To be effective, a letter to the editor must be reasonable, clearly organized, and credibly presented. How does the letter below meet these criteria?

Model

Dear Editor:
Whose idea was it to endorse Joe Graft for reelection? If you had simply walked outside and opened your eyes, you couldn't help but see what's happened here since His Majesty was elected mayor.

Let's take a look at what he's done to help the town of Dillard. The streets are full of holes the size of the Grand Canyon. The playgrounds should have "Danger: Keep Out" signs on them. And how about that eyesore at the end of Nice Street? I'm ready to go out and rent a wrecking ball and rip down that hideous old house myself!

Mayor Graft can't get involved in these matters, of course. He's too busy signing new tax bills and playing golf with his pals at the country club. To his credit, however, he did spend thousands of taxpayer dollars for that so-called sculpture in front of City Hall. That's the ugliest piece of junk I've ever seen!

Graft is the worst mayor Dillard has ever had! Wake up to the facts, Dillard Daily Snooze.

A Concerned Citizen

Where has the writer used name calling and insults? What effect would these have on readers?

Exaggeration and unsupported opinions obscure legitimate issues. What needs to be done that Graft did not do?

Before You Write

If you want to influence or affect a course of events, your letter must be reasonable, well written, and credible, not to mention legible.

Unlike a speech or a debate, a letter depends solely on the strength of written words to express an opinion or to prompt people to action. Most publications have limited space, so there's no room for a long treatise. To compose a convincing letter to an editor, use freewriting, brainstorming, and clustering to explore an issue. Next, develop a thesis statement that identifies the problem and, if appropriate, proposes a solution.

Most importantly, get your facts straight. Using available resources and technology, do a little homework to uncover relevant data. To support your point, use concrete details, facts or statistics, examples, and sound reasons. The notes below show that the writer collected evidence, highlighted the strongest points, and came up with a method for organizing the evidence persuasively.

Grammar Tip

When editing a letter to an editor, make sure you use correct capitalization and punctuation in the heading and inside address. For punctuation of letter parts, see Lesson 21.6, page 729, and Lesson 21.15, page 750.

Thesis
The dilapidated house at the end of Nice Street is an eyesore; it should be restored and turned into a museum of local town history.

Notes
1. House built 1798 by town founder Millard Dillard
2. Quirky: has hidden staircases, secret rooms, unexpected windows and gables; unusual 18th-century architecture
3. Bad shape: weeds, peeling paint, cracked windows
4. Dillard High School Community Service Club is looking for a worthy project
5. Architect and contractor will donate services
6. Vacant since Josephine Dillard died there in 1971
7. Neighbors want it torn down
8. Reports of wails, bangs, and odd noises at night

Strategy
Describe situation: condition of house
Propose solution: restoration
Reasons for restoring: architectural, historic value
Solving obstacles to restoration: donated labor

Journal Writing

In your journal, make a checklist of the features of a good letter to the editor. Then read and evaluate some letters in your local newspaper. Do the letters meet the criteria for effective arguments? Why or why not?

Consider Your Tone

Once you've stated your thesis and assembled and organized your evidence, writing the letter can be fairly straightforward. As you revise your letter, pay attention to your tone. Even the strongest argument can be ineffective if the tone is disrespectful, unpleasant, or too casual. Notice the clear organization and reasonable tone of this letter.

Model

The opening will catch the interest of the editor as well as that of the paper's readers.

Dear Editor:
Hauntingly beautiful, perhaps—but not a haunted house!
Some neighbors claim they hear strange sounds at night from the old Dillard house at the end of Nice Street. Others complain that with the foot-high weeds, teetering fence, and peeling gray paint, the place might just as well be haunted. Now the Nice Street Neighborhood Association is pressuring the city government to bulldoze the old house.

The writer acknowledges the problem and offers a solution. What elements contribute to a reasonable tone?

The house has been empty since 1971, and it certainly has become a dilapidated eyesore. But I don't believe that it is haunted, and I don't believe that tearing it down is the answer. This once-grand house is an important structure in this town's history. It could easily be made into a spacious and beautiful museum.

Many of our citizens recognize that Dillard needs a town museum. In fact, the Clarion Historical Society has been talking about building a town museum for some time now. Why not restore this remarkable old house?

The facts in this paragraph support the writer's opinion, and they are believable because they are based on research.

I have researched the old records at City Hall and discovered that the house was built in 1798 by our town founder, Millard Dillard. The house has a number of unusual architectural features, such as hidden staircases leading to secret rooms, rare amethyst-glass windows, and unexpected gables. It pains me to think of bulldozing the hidden history and quirky charm of this historic eighteenth-century mansion.

Let's preserve the heritage of our city and make Dillard House into a museum we can all be proud of!

Sincerely,
Sam Citizen

Write a Letter to an Editor

A controversy is brewing in your city: state aid to your school district has been cut substantially. This means that some high school programs will be eliminated. The school board has asked the city council for a 10 percent increase in the annual budget. Elderly people on fixed incomes are opposed to an increased budget because their taxes would go up. Write a persuasive letter to the editor of your local paper for or against the proposed increase.

PURPOSE To urge the city council to vote for or against the proposed increase
AUDIENCE Readers of the local paper
LENGTH 4–5 paragraphs

WRITING RUBRICS To write an effective letter to an editor, you should

- state your position on the issue in a thesis statement
- present your case succinctly
- use a pleasant and respectful tone

Cross-Curricular Activity

ART The picture below shows a work considered by some people to be art and by others to be an eyesore. It features ten Cadillacs from the fifties, half buried along Route 66 near Amarillo, Texas. Imagine that *Cadillac Ranch* was created in your town. Draft a letter to the editor of your local paper explaining and arguing your position about whether or not public funds should be used to create such artistic projects.

Ant Farm, *Cadillac Ranch*, c. 1974

Grammar Link

Punctuate letter parts correctly.

When you write a business letter, make sure that you punctuate the various parts correctly.

Rewrite the parts of the business letter below. Add punctuation where needed.

1. 6538 S Hiawatha
   Chicago IL 60613
   October 27 2001
2. Mr. James T Martello
   Quick Time Records
   2300 N Superior Street
   Milwaukee WI 53207
3. Dear Mr Martello
4. Very sincerely yours

See Lessons 21.4, 21.6, and 21.14, pages 718, 729, and 748.

Using Computers

If you use a computer to create any business correspondence, such as a letter to the editor or a job application letter, consider using the Envelope command (usually under Tools) to address the envelope. The Envelope dialogue box allows you to verify the pertinent information for the addressee and also lets you enter your return address. Printing the envelope creates a more professional appearance.

WRITING ABOUT LITERATURE
Evaluating a Speech

Since the purpose of most speeches is to manipulate and persuade, it pays to be especially alert to persuasive strategies when you listen to a speaker's presentation. When you evaluate a speech, consider both the speaker's purpose and delivery.

Saturday Evening Post cover, 1946

When you evaluate a speech, consider these questions: In what frame of mind did the speaker find the audience—expectant, bored, hostile? How did the speaker leave the audience—thoughtful, enthusiastic, yawning? Did the speech accomplish its purpose?

What Is the Speaker's Purpose?

Skilled orators often have rallied their audiences to support worthy causes and high ideals. Other equally persuasive speakers have manipulated public opinion by appealing to emotion instead of reason. You will need to evaluate what you hear before responding to it.

While you are listening to a speech, try to separate the content from the emotional appeal. The chart below can help you.

Analyzing the Text of a Speech	
PURPOSE	Can you identify the main point of the speech?
CREDIBILITY	Are the ideas and arguments well supported and believable?
APPROPRIATENESS	Do the language and ideas suit the audience and occasion?
COHERENCE	Can you easily follow the speaker's ideas or points?
INTEREST	Do the ideas hold your attention?
VARIETY	Does the speech incorporate anecdotes, opinions, and facts?

In 1976 Barbara Jordan, U.S. Representative from Texas, was selected to be the keynote speaker at the Democratic National Convention. She was the first African American to receive this honor. Read this excerpt from the speech that she gave.

Literature Model

A lot of years have passed since [the first Democratic party convention in] 1832, and during that time it would have been most unusual for any national political party to ask that a Barbara Jordan deliver a keynote address—but tonight, here I am. And I feel notwithstanding that past that my presence here is one additional bit of evidence that the American Dream need not forever be deferred.

Now that I have this grand distinction, what in the world am I supposed to say? I could easily spend this time praising the accomplishments of this party and attacking the Republicans, but I do not choose to do that. I could list the many problems which Americans have. . . . and then I could sit down and offer no solutions. But I do not choose to do that either. . . .

We are a people in a quandary about the present. We are a people in search of our future. We are a people in search of a national community. . . . The great danger that America faces [is] that we will cease to be one nation and become instead a collection of interest groups: city against suburb, region against region, individual against individual. . . .

There is no law that can require the American people to form a national community. This we must do as individuals and if we do it as individuals, there is no President of the United States who can veto that decision.

Barbara Jordan
address to Democratic National Convention, 1976

Jordan knows her audience expects her to criticize the Republicans and list the nation's problems, so she begins by stating what she is not going to talk about.

Note the solemn and dignified language and tone, in keeping with the occasion.

Journal Writing

Use the criteria at the bottom of page 302 to evaluate the content of a speech in print, either in a newspaper or in a collection of historical papers.

Does the Delivery Affect Your Response?

A good delivery of a speech can convey qualities that the written text alone cannot. In reviewing Barbara Jordan's address to the Democratic National Convention, reviewers noted that the speaker's personality shone through her words.

Literature Model

It was the second keynote address, by U.S. Rep. Barbara Jordan of Texas, that generated the only excitement. It is almost a pity that the competition was so feeble, because the speech itself was far and away the best political address that any of us are liable to hear in the Bicentennial election year.

Jordan's integrity, sincerity, faith, common sense, and passionate—rather than emotional—commitment to what this country is all about tower so far above the main candidates that it is indeed a pity that she is not a candidate herself. Not since Franklin Roosevelt has either political party had an adherent with more rights to a podium—she is one of the very few Americans who should be allowed to make speeches. Jordan dropped all clichés; she spoke as an American rather than a party hack, and she even quoted a Republican president.

Donald Morris, *Houston Post*, July 15, 1976

As shown in the chart on the left, good speakers use a variety of techniques to enhance their delivery and make their speeches more effective. How important is a good delivery? When Lincoln delivered his Gettysburg Address, many reviews were critical. "Anything more dull and commonplace it would not be easy to produce," wrote the *London Times*. Lincoln was not the most polished of orators, and on that day in November, he spoke after one of the most celebrated orators of the time, Edward Everett. Perhaps Lincoln's delivery seemed unexciting when compared with that of the more dramatic Everett.

We will never be sure why Lincoln's speech was not immediately recognized for its greatness. Ironically, however, Everett's speech is rarely reprinted, while the text of Lincoln's Gettysburg Address has survived as one of the most eloquent speeches in American history.

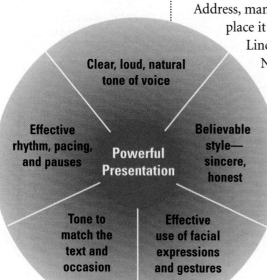

Clear, loud, natural tone of voice

Effective rhythm, pacing, and pauses

Powerful Presentation

Believable style—sincere, honest

Tone to match the text and occasion

Effective use of facial expressions and gestures

Write an Evaluation

Listen to a recording of Martin Luther King Jr.'s "I Have a Dream" or some other famous speech. Many libraries own tapes of well-known contemporary speeches. Then write a few paragraphs evaluating the speech.

PURPOSE To evaluate the content of a speech
AUDIENCE Your classmates
LENGTH 4–5 paragraphs

WRITING RUBRICS To write an effective evaluation, you should

- consider such content elements as purpose, coherence, believability of ideas and arguments, appropriateness to audience, interest, and variety
- evaluate delivery, including pacing and tone

Listening and Speaking

COOPERATIVE LEARNING In groups of four, create a list of contemporary issues that might be interesting topics for a persuasive speech. Then working in pairs, pick a topic on which to write a speech. You may wish to have one person write and the other edit, or both write and edit. The other two members of your group will be your audience.

One partner from each team can deliver the speech to the other team. Teams will take turns delivering speeches and acting as the audience. The audience will take notes and evaluate the speech in a written review.

Viewing and Representing

With the sound turned off, watch a video of a speech given by a religious, civic, or business leader. What does the speaker convey through his or her body language—gestures and facial expressions? Then watch the video a second time, this time with the sound on. Listen to the words while noticing the speaker's gestures. Discuss how the two elements work together to convey the speaker's message.

Use irregular verbs correctly.

You may have to look up the past and past participle forms of irregular verbs.

Jordan . . . spoke as an American . . .

Write the correct form of the verb in the following sentences.

1. He (draw, drew, drawn) a line in the sand, and everyone respected him for his courage.
2. He had (grow, grew, grown) into a legend in the town because people (know, knew, known) and respected his integrity.
3. But Harry had (take, took, taken) the last of the taunts he ever wanted to hear in his life.
4. Big Betty, the brainiest woman on the prairie, (see, saw, seen) a way to nettle him.
5. He never (forgive, forgave, forgiven) her for beating him at chess.

See Lessons 15.1 and 15.2, pages 575–578.

Writing Process in Action

Persuasive Writing

In this unit you have learned about techniques that can make a strong and well-reasoned argument. You've also had an opportunity to evaluate persuasive writings of others as well as your own. Now you will have a chance to put into practice what you have learned. In this lesson, you will prepare a persuasive speech that can help younger students learn from your experiences in high school.

WRITING Online

Visit the Writer's Choice Web site at **writerschoice. glencoe.com**, for additional writing prompts.

Assignment

Context	Your school has started a peer-support group to help first-year students adjust to high school. You have been invited to speak to a small group to persuade them to act in a certain way in order to avoid some common pitfalls. The talk will be based on your own experiences and observations. While you may use humor and irony, your overall tone should be thoughtful.
Purpose	To persuade your audience to avoid or follow some course of action
Audience	First-year students
Length	1 to 2 pages

The ideas on the next few pages can serve as guides in writing your speech. Read them over and refer to them as needed. But remember, you're in charge of the writing process.

Prewriting

What regrettable event comes to mind that could serve as a warning to others? In thinking over various events, remember your audience—ninth graders—and your purpose—to persuade them that what might seem like a good course of action may actually lead to disaster. Choose a pitfall that you believe is significant, and offer compelling reasons to avoid it. Support the reasons with details. The prewriting questions to the right might help you in selecting the experience and in deciding what lesson you want to draw from it.

Likewise, the words of Kai Erikson can help you understand why an act with profound consequences must be discussed and lessons extracted from it. He argues that the question of whether to use atomic force against Japan was never given thorough, "mature consideration."

Prewriting Questions

- What have I done that I regret?
- What was my motivation at the time?
- What were the consequences of my actions?
- What lesson did I learn?

Literature Model

The difficulty . . . as historians of the period all testify, is that the more closely one examines the record, the harder it is to make out where in the flow of events something that could reasonably be called a decision was reached at all . . . it is hard to distinguish those pivotal moments in the story when the critical issues were identified, debated, reasoned through, resolved. The decision, to the extent that one can even speak of such a thing, was shaped and seasoned by a force very like inertia.

Kai Erikson, *Of Accidental Judgments and Casual Slaughters*

Prewriting Tip

For help in judging your audience, see Lesson 6.1, page 272.

Drafting

Because every element of your argument hinges directly or indirectly on your thesis statement, write it down and refer to it often as you draft. Your speech is an amplification of this single idea.

Writing Process in Action

Persuasive Writing

Drafting Tip

For more information on inductive and deductive reasoning, see Lesson 6.4, page 282.

Try mapping out your plan of attack. Make an informal outline or some other kind of list that shows where you're going in your argument and how you're going to get there. Include at least one piece of supporting evidence (a personal observation, an expert opinion, a quotation, an anecdote, a statistic, an example) for every major point you make. Because you will be generalizing from particular facts and opinions, or reasoning inductively, supporting evidence is especially important.

Once you have your entire speech mapped out, decide which parts of it, such as your introductory comments, you will need to write out in detail. Decide also on the tone you will use in order to really connect with your audience. Recall how effectively John F. Kennedy communicated with the people of Berlin through his tone and word choice.

Revising

Revising Tip

For help with logical fallacies, see Lesson 6.5, page 288.

Now is the time to evaluate the strengths and weaknesses of your argument and to check for unity and coherence. If your argument lacks unity and coherence, it will be difficult to follow and unlikely to persuade anyone.

To begin revising, read over your outline and the parts you have written out in detail. Then have a writing conference. Try your speech on an audience—a partner or a small group. Use your audience's reactions to help you evaluate what you've planned so far. The Revising Checklist can help you and your listeners.

Revising Checklist

- Is my opening tantalizing? Do my enthusiasm and conviction come through?
- Is my argument tight, or are there holes that need filling?
- Are all aspects of the essay in line with my audience and purpose?
- Is my reasoning sound? Have I oversimplified?
- Is my organization logical and easy to follow?

In his journal, Ralph Waldo Emerson wrote, "I found when I had finished my new lecture that it was a very good house, only the architect had unfortunately omitted the stairs." What do you think he meant? Check your argument to be sure it has good, sturdy transitions that help the reader get from one part of the structure to the next.

Editing/Proofreading

The last stage your speech must pass through before its presentation is editing. Tape-record your speech, or have a partner listen to it. Check to make sure you've avoided all the errors on the checklist. Then use the list that follows to make sure your persuasive speech says all the things you want it to. When you're satisfied, make a clean copy of your notes or completed draft and proofread one more time.

Editing/Proofreading Checklist

- Do all subjects and verbs agree?
- Are all sentences complete?
- Do all pronouns have clear antecedents?
- Have I checked for spelling errors?

Editing Tip

For last-minute ideas to make your speech more effective, see Lesson 6.6, page 295.

Self-Evaluation

Make sure your persuasive speech—

- ✔ uses a situation from your own experience or observation to persuade the audience to follow a particular course of action
- ✔ captures the audience's attention immediately
- ✔ is logically argued and well supported with evidence
- ✔ uses humor or irony when appropriate
- ✔ follows the standards of grammar, usage, mechanics, and spelling

Proofreading Tip

For proofreading symbols, see page 92.

Publishing/Presenting

Is the issue you tackled one that affects many people at your school or in your community? If so, consider turning your speech into a letter to the editor of your school or local newspaper. Let others benefit from your experience.

Presenting Tip

For help in using graphic displays in your presentation, see Lesson 6.6, page 296.

Journal Writing

Reflect on your writing process experience. Answer these questions in your journal: What do you like best about your persuasive speech? What was the hardest part of writing it? What did you learn in your writing conference? What have you learned as a writer?

Literature Model

Are important decisions always deliberately made, or do things—even terrible things—sometimes " just happen"? In the following excerpt from a 1985 essay, historian Kai Erikson examines the atomic attacks on Japan during World War II and argues that they may be an all-too-real example of the danger of "accidental judgments." After you have read the essay, complete the activities in Linking Writing and Literature on page 320.

OF ACCIDENTAL JUDGMENTS & CASUAL SLAUGHTERS

by Kai Erikson

The bombings of Hiroshima and Nagasaki, which took place forty years ago this month, are among the most thoroughly studied moments on human record. Together they constitute the only occasion in history when atomic weapons were dropped on living populations, and together they constitute the only occasion in history when a decision was made to employ them in that way.

I want to reflect here on the second of those points. The "decision to drop"—I will explain in a minute why quotation marks are useful here—is a fascinating historical episode. But it is also an exhibit of the most profound importance as we consider our prospects for the future. It is a case history well worth attending to. A compelling parable.

If one were to tell the story of that decision as historians normally do, the details arranged in an ordered narrative, one might begin in 1938 with the discovery of nuclear fission, or perhaps a year later with the delivery of Einstein's famous letter to President Roosevelt. No matter what its opening scene, though, the tale would then proceed along a string of events—a sequence of appointees named, committees formed, reports issued, orders signed, arguments won and lost, minds made up and changed—all of it coming to an end with a pair of tremendous blasts in the soft morning air over Japan.

The difficulty with that way of relating the story, as historians of the period all testify, is that the more closely one examines the record, the harder it is to make out where in the flow of events something that could reasonably be called a decision was reached at all. To be sure, a kind of consensus emerged from the sprawl of ideas and happenings that made up the climate of wartime Washington, but looking back, it is hard to distinguish those pivotal moments in the story when the crucial issues were identified, debated, reasoned through, resolved. The decision, to the extent that one can even speak of such a thing, was shaped and seasoned by a force very like inertia.[1]

Let's say, then, that a wind began to blow, ever so gently at first, down the corridors along which power flows. And as it gradually gathered momentum during the course of the war, the people caught up in it began to assume, without ever checking up on it, that it had a logic and a motive, that it had been set in motion by sure hands acting on the basis of wise counsel.

Harry Truman, in particular, remembered it as a time of tough and lonely choices, and titled his memoir of that period *Year of Decisions*. But the bulk of those choices can in all fairness be said to have involved confirmation of projects already under way or implementation of decisions made at other levels of command. Brig. Gen. Leslie R. Groves, military head of the Manhattan Project, was close to the mark when he described Truman's decision as "one of noninterference—basically, a decision not to upset the existing plans." And J. Robert Oppenheimer spoke equally to the point when he observed some twenty years later: "The decision was implicit in the project. I don't know whether it could have been stopped."

In September of 1944, when it became more and more evident that a bomb would be produced in time for combat use, Franklin Roosevelt and Winston Churchill met at Hyde Park and initialed a brief *aide-mémoire*,

---

1 **inertia** (i nur′shə): the tendency to keep moving in the same direction

noting, among other things, that the new weapon "might, perhaps, after mature consideration, be used against the Japanese." This document does not appear to have had any effect on the conduct of the war, and Truman knew nothing at all about it. But it would not have made a real difference in any case, for neither chief of state did much to initiate the "mature consideration" they spoke of so glancingly, and Truman, in turn, could only suppose that such matters had been considered already. "Truman did not inherit the question," writes Martin J. Sherwin, "he inherited the answer."

What would "mature consideration" have meant in such a setting as that anyway?

First of all, presumably, it would have meant seriously asking whether the weapon should be employed at all. But we have it on the authority of virtually all the principal players that no one in a position to do anything about it ever really considered alternatives to combat use. Henry L. Stimson, Secretary of War:

At no time, from 1941 to 1945, did I ever hear it suggested by the President, or by any other responsible member of the government, that atomic energy should not be used in the war.

Harry Truman:

I regarded the bomb as a military weapon and never had any doubt that it should be used.

General Groves:

Certainly, there was no question in my mind, or, as far as I was ever aware, in the mind of

either President Roosevelt or President Truman or any other responsible person, but that we were developing a weapon to be employed against the enemies of the United States.

Winston Churchill:

There never was a moment's discussion as to whether the atomic bomb should be used or not.

And why should anyone be surprised? We were at war, after all, and with the most resolute of enemies, so the unanimity[2] of that feeling is wholly understandable. But it was not, by any stretch of the imagination, a product of mature consideration.

"Combat use" meant a number of different things, however, and a second question began to be raised with some frequency in the final months of the war, all the more insistently after the defeat of Germany. Might a way be devised to demonstrate the awesome power of the bomb in a convincing enough fashion to induce the surrender of the Japanese without having to destroy huge numbers of civilians? Roosevelt may have been pondering something of the sort. In September of 1944, for example, three days after initialing the Hyde Park *aide-mémoire*, he asked Vannevar Bush, a trusted science adviser, whether the bomb "should actually be used against the Japanese or whether it should be used only as a threat." While that may have been little more than idle musing, a number of different schemes were explored within both the government and the scientific community in the months following.

---

2 **unanimity** (ū′ nə nim′ ə tē): complete agreement

One option involved a kind of *benign strike:* the dropping of a bomb on some built-up area, but only after advance notice had been issued so that residents could evacuate the area and leave an empty slate on which the bomb could write its terrifying signature. This plan was full of difficulties. A dud under those dramatic circumstances might do enormous damage to American credibility, and, moreover, to broadcast any warning was to risk the endeavor in other ways. Weak as the Japanese were by this time in the war, it was easy to imagine their finding a way to intercept an incoming airplane if they knew where and when it was expected, and officials in Washington were afraid that it would occur to the Japanese, as it had to them, that the venture would come to an abrupt end if American prisoners of war were brought into the target area.

The second option was a *tactical strike* against a purely military target—an arsenal, railroad yard, depot, factory, harbor—without advance notice. Early in the game, for example, someone had nominated the Japanese fleet concentration at Truk. The problem with this notion, however—and there is more than a passing irony here—was that no known military target had a wide enough compass to contain the whole of the destructive capacity of the weapon and so display its full range and power. The committee inquiring into likely targets wanted one "more than three miles in diameter," because anything smaller would be too inadequate a canvas for the picture it was supposed to hold.

> **THE RISK OF BEING EMBARRASSED BY A DUD WAS MORE THAN MOST OFFICIALS . . . WERE WILLING TO TAKE.**

The third option was to stage a kind of *dress rehearsal* by detonating a bomb in some remote corner of the world—a desert or empty island, say—to exhibit to international observers brought in for the purpose what the device could do. The idea had been proposed by a group of scientists in what has since been called the Franck Report, but it commanded no more than a moment's attention. It had the same problems as the benign strike: the risk of being embarrassed by a dud was more than most officials in a position to decide were willing to take, and there was a widespread feeling that any demonstration involving advance notice would give the enemy too much useful information.

The fourth option involved a kind of warning shot. The thought here was to drop a bomb without notice over a relatively uninhabited stretch of enemy land so that the Japanese high command might see at first hand what was in store for them if they failed to surrender soon. Edward Teller thought that an explosion at night high over Tokyo Bay would serve as a brilliant visual argument, and Adm. Lewis Strauss, soon to become a member (and later chair) of the Atomic Energy Commission, recommended a strike on a local forest, reasoning that the blast would "lay the trees out in windrows[3] from the center of the explosion in all directions as though they were matchsticks," meanwhile igniting a

---

3 **windrows** (wind´ rōz´): rows

Jacob Lawrence, *Hiroshima Series, Family,* 1983

Persuasive Writing

Literature Model

fearsome firestorm at the epicenter. "It seemed to me," he added, "that a demonstration of this sort would prove to the Japanese that we could destroy any of their cities at will." The physicist Ernest O. Lawrence may have been speaking half in jest when he suggested that a bomb might be used to "blow the top off" Mount Fujiyama, but he was quite serious when he assured a friend early in the war: "The bomb will never be dropped on people. As soon as we get it, we'll use it only to dictate peace."

Now, hindsight is too easy a talent. But it seems evident on the face of it that the fourth of those options, the warning shot, was much to be preferred over the other three, and even more to be preferred over use on living targets. I do not want to argue the case here. I do want to ask, however, why that possibility was so easily dismissed.

The fact of the matter seems to have been that the notion of a demonstration was discussed on only a few occasions once the Manhattan Project neared completion, and most of those discussions were off the record. So a historian trying to reconstruct the drift of those conversations can only flatten an ear against the wall, as it were, and see if any sense can be made of the muffled voices next door. It seems very clear, for example, that the options involving advance notice were brought up so often and so early in official conversations that they came to *mean* demonstration in the minds of several important players. If a James Byrnes, say, soon to be named Secretary of State, were asked why one could not detonate a device in unoccupied

territory, he might raise the problem posed by prisoners of war, and if the same question were asked of a James Bryant Conant, another science adviser, he might speak of the embarrassment that would follow a dud—thus, in both cases, joining ideas that had no logical relation to each other. Neither prisoners of war nor fear of failure, of course, posed any argument against a surprise demonstration.

There were two occasions, however, on which persons in a position to affect policy discussed the idea of a nonlethal demonstration. Those two conversations together consumed no more than a matter of minutes, so far as one can tell at this remove, and they, too, were off the record. But they seem to represent virtually the entire investment of the government of the United States in "mature consideration" of the subject.

The first discussion took place at a meeting of what was then called the Interim Committee, a striking gathering of military, scientific and government brass under the chairmanship of Secretary Stimson. This group, which included James Byrnes and Chief of Staff Gen. George C. Marshall, met on a number of occasions in May of 1945 to discuss policy issues raised by the new bomb, and Stimson recalled later that at one of their final meetings the members "carefully considered such alternatives as a detailed advance warning or a demonstration in some uninhabited area." But the minutes of the meeting, as well as the accounts of those present, suggest otherwise. The only exchange on the subject, in fact, took place during a luncheon

> THE MEMBERS "CAREFULLY CONSIDERED SUCH ALTERNATIVES AS A DETAILED ADVANCE WARNING."

break, and while we have no way of knowing what was actually said in that conversation, we do know what conclusion emerged from it. One participant, Arthur H. Compton, recalled later:

Though the possibility of a demonstration that would not destroy human lives was attractive, no one could suggest a way in which it could be made so convincing that it would be likely to stop the war.

And the recording secretary of the meeting later recalled:

Dr. Oppenheimer . . . said he doubted whether there could be devised any sufficiently startling demonstration that would convince the Japanese they ought to throw in the sponge.

Two weeks later, four physicists who served as advisers to the Interim Committee met in Los Alamos to consider once again the question of demonstration. They were Arthur Compton, Enrico Fermi, Ernest Lawrence and Robert Oppenheimer—as distinguished an assembly of scientific talent as could be imagined—and they concluded, after a discussion of which we have no record: "We can propose no technical demonstration likely to bring an end to the war; we see no acceptable alternative to direct military use." That, so far as anyone can tell, was the end of it.

We cannot be sure that a milder report would have made a difference, for the Manhattan Project was gathering momentum as it moved toward the more steeply pitched

> **WE DID NOT THINK EXPLODING ONE OF THOSE THINGS AS A FIRECRACKER OVER THE DESERT WAS LIKELY TO BE VERY IMPRESSIVE.**

inclines of May and June, but we can be sure that the idea of a demonstration was at that point spent. The Los Alamos report ended with something of a disclaimer ("We have, however, no claim to special competence. . . ."), but its message was clear enough. When asked about that report nine years later in his security hearings, Oppenheimer said, with what might have been a somewhat defensive edge in his voice, "We did not think exploding one of those things as a firecracker over the desert was likely to be very impressive."

Perhaps not. But those fragments are telling for another reason. If you listen to them carefully for a moment or two, you realize that these are the voices of nuclear physicists trying to imagine how a strange and distant people will react to an atomic blast. These are the voices of nuclear physicists dealing with psychological and anthropological questions about Japanese culture, Japanese temperament, Japanese will to resist—topics, we must assume, about which they knew almost nothing. They did not know yet what the bomb could actually do, since its first test was not to take place for another month. But in principle, at least, Oppenheimer and Fermi reflecting on matters relating to the Japanese national character should have had about the same force as Ruth Benedict and Margaret Mead reflecting on matters relating to high-energy physics, the first difference being that Benedict and Mead would not have presumed to do so, and the second being that no one in authority would have listened to them if they had.

USAF, *Hiroshima*, 1945

The first of the two morals I want to draw from the foregoing—this being a parable, after all—is that in moments of critical contemplation, it is often hard to know where the competencies of soldiers and scientists and all the rest of us begin and end. Many an accidental judgment can emerge from such confusions.

But what if the conclusions of the scientists had been correct? What if some kind of demonstration had been staged in a lightly occupied part of Japan and it had been greeted as a firecracker in the desert? What then?

Let me shift gears for a moment and discuss the subject in another way. It is standard wisdom for everyone in the United States old enough to remember the war, and for most of those to whom it is ancient history, that the bombings of Hiroshima and Nagasaki were the only alternative to an all-out invasion of the Japanese mainland involving hundreds of thousands and perhaps millions of casualties on both sides. Unless the Japanese came to understand the need to surrender quickly, we would have been drawn by an almost magnetic force toward those dreaded beaches. This has become an almost automatic pairing of ideas, an article of common lore. If you lament that so many civilians were incinerated or blown to bits in Hiroshima and Nagasaki, then somebody will remind you of the American lives thus saved. Truman was the person most frequently asked to account for the bombings, and his views were emphatic on the subject:

It was a question of saving hundreds of thousands of American lives. I don't mind telling you that you don't feel normal when you have to plan hundreds of thousands of complete, final deaths of American boys who are alive and joking and having fun while you are doing your planning. You break your heart and your head trying to figure out a way to save one life. The name given to our invasion plan was "Olympic," but I saw nothing godly about the killing of all the people that would be necessary to make that invasion. I could not worry about what history would say about my personal morality. I made

> **"I SAW NOTHING GODLY ABOUT THE KILLING OF ALL THE PEOPLE THAT WOULD BE NECESSARY TO MAKE THAT INVASION."**

the only decision I ever knew how to make. I did what I thought was right. . . .

Veterans of the war, and particularly those who had reason to suppose that they would have been involved in an invasion, have drawn that same connection repeatedly, most recently Paul Fussell in the pages of *The New Republic.* Thank God for the bomb, the argument goes, it saved the lives of countless numbers of us. And so, in a sense, it may have.

But the destruction of Hiroshima and Nagasaki had nothing to do with it. It only makes sense to assume, even if few people were well enough positioned in early August to see the situation whole, that there simply was not going to be an invasion. Not ever.

For what sane power, with the atomic weapon securely in its arsenal, would hurl a million or more of its sturdiest young men on a heavily fortified mainland? To imagine anyone ordering an invasion when the means were at hand to blast Japan into a sea of gravel at virtually no cost in American lives is to imagine a madness beyond anything even the worst of war can induce. The invasion had not yet been called off, granted. But it surely would have been, and long before the November 1 deadline set for it.

The United States did not become a nuclear power on August 6, with the destruction of Hiroshima. It became a nuclear power on July 16, when the first test device was exploded in Alamogordo, New Mexico. Uncertainties remained, of course, many of them. But from that moment on, the United States knew how to produce a bomb, knew how to deliver it and knew it would work. Stimson said shortly after the war that the bombings of Hiroshima and Nagasaki "ended the ghastly specter of a clash of great land armies," but he could have said, with greater justice, that the ghastly specter ended at Alamogordo. Churchill came close to making exactly that point when he first learned of the New Mexico test:

To quell the Japanese resistance man by man and conquer the country yard by yard might well require the loss of a million American lives and half that number of British. . . . Now all that nightmare picture had vanished.

It *had* vanished. The age of inch-by-inch crawling over enemy territory, the age of Guadalcanal and Iwo Jima and Okinawa, was just plain over.

Linking Writing and Literature

Readers Respond to the Model

What makes Kai Erikson's essay about the "decision to drop" so powerful?

Explore Kai Erikson's essay by answering these questions. Then read what other students found significant in Erikson's essay

1. Did Erikson persuade you to share his viewpoint about the bombing? Identify specific passages that influenced your response.
2. What kind of evidence did Erikson use to argue his points? Why were you convinced or not convinced by this evidence?

3. How is the reference to "accidental judgments and casual slaughters" appropriate to Erikson's argument?

What Students Say

"The point of studying the causes and effects of dropping "the bomb" is not to rehash the horror or play God and dish out blame, but rather to remember these bombings because they remind us of our destructive capabilities. The repercussions from the decision to drop the atomic bomb still ring, and it would benefit everyone to educate themselves about it. Under circumstances of war or confusion, "accidental judgments and casual slaughters" are quite possible. This essay lays out the issues surrounding the bombings and makes an old but important point. We must learn from our mistakes. "

Peter Ivaska

"Erikson claims that a definite decision to drop the atomic bomb was never really made. The people involved in the decision never really weighed all the options. I liked the way Erikson used psychology in talking about history. "

Susannah Levine

UNIT **6** Review

Reflecting on the Unit

Summarize what you have learned in this unit by answering the following questions:

1 In persuasive writing, what is used to support a claim?

2 When evaluating a persuasive argument, what two criteria must be differentiated?

3 What are two valid forms of reasoning that can be used in persuasive writing?

4 How is an effective speech developed?

5 What elements should a strong letter to the editor include?

6 In delivering an effective speech, what, in addition to content, should the speaker consider?

Adding to Your Portfolio

Choose a selection for your portfolio. Look over the persuasive writing you have done during this unit. Select a completed piece of writing to put into your portfolio. The piece you choose should show some or all of the following:

- an ability to form a thesis statement
- relevant facts and informed opinions
- use of inductive and/or deductive reasoning
- avoidance of faulty reasoning
- awareness of audience
- awareness of the opposition's argument

Reflect on Your Choice

Attach a note to the piece you chose, explaining briefly why you chose it and what you learned from writing it.

SET GOALS

- How can you improve your writing?
- What skill will you focus on the next time you write?

Writing Across the Curriculum

MAKE A SCIENCE CONNECTION Suppose that you are a biochemist who believes that you have discovered a vaccine against a rare but lethal disease. The clinical trials to test this vaccine will be very expensive, and many people feel that medical research money should be spent on more common diseases. Still, you feel that your vaccine can save lives and that the information you get from your research might help scientists working on other diseases. Write a persuasive proposal arguing that an important medical institute should fund the trials.

"... take a seat on the top of a gate post and watch the world go by."

—Zora Neale Hurston, *Dust Tracks on a Road*

UNIT 7

Research Paper Writing

Prewriting: Planning and Researching

Your footsteps echo through the cave's musty darkness. Your flashlight probes the rock cavern for passages to explore. Some passages will lead to dead ends, forcing you to backtrack. Others will open to spectacular caverns seen by no one else.

Like exploring a cave, researching a topic can be exhilarating. You're on your own as you explore and choose material to read. You too will make your way along twisting and turning paths as you draft and revise your thoughts, and you can expect to run into dead ends from time to time. The result, however, can be the most satisfying writing that you will do in high school.

Decide Where to Start

Writing a research paper can feel overwhelming. It doesn't have to immobilize you, however. Break down the project into smaller tasks, and then set a schedule to complete each task, as shown below.

The top arrows show how you will spend most of your time, but at any stage, you may need to return to a previous stage to rethink your topic, gather more information, or reorganize your ideas.

Schedule for Research Paper

PLANNING AND RESEARCHING	DRAFTING	REVISING	EDITING AND PRESENTING
2 weeks →	2 weeks →	1 week →	1 week →
• choose topic • research topic • take notes • make outline • create thesis statement	• develop ideas • prepare documentation	• reorganize ideas • delete superfluous information • flesh out details	• clarify concepts • polish wording • proofread • assemble for reader

Investigate and Limit a Topic

The key to enjoying the process of writing a research paper lies in choosing a topic that interests you. To get started, list possible topics. Consider books and television documentaries that you have enjoyed. Classroom discussions may also trigger ideas. Brainstorm ideas with your teacher, family, and friends too. Even if your teacher assigns a general topic, you may be able to narrow the focus and investigate an aspect of it that interests you.

After you choose a topic, determine whether it is too broad for a research paper of the length you are writing. Analyze how your topic can be divided by scanning the indexes and tables of contents of books about your topic. You will need to limit your topic until it is neither so broad that you will be writing in generalities nor so narrow that you can't find adequate resources to use.

Stephanie Murray, a student at Westwood High School in Westwood, Massachusetts, is interested in art. Throughout this unit, you will see examples of notes, outlines, and drafts leading to her finished research paper about the art of Grant Wood and of Edward Hopper. You can read Stephanie's finished paper on pages 350–356.

Compare the topics in the chart below to see the differences between topics that are too broad, too narrow, and appropriately limited.

Narrowing a Topic		
TOO BROAD	**LIMITED**	**TOO NARROW**
Western art	The theme of man against nature in Western art	Telegraph lines in Western art
Art in the Depression era	Depression era artists Wood and Hopper	Cats in Depression era art

Before you begin your own research, you need to know what you are looking for. To clarify your topic and to guide your research, ask yourself questions such as, Why is my topic interesting? What people or events are integral to it? What caused these events to happen? What are some of the effects of my topic? As you learn more, you can refine your research questions and begin to focus on a central idea for the paper.

Find Information

Researching a topic is not a linear process; undoubtedly you will make more than one trip to the library as you develop your view of your topic. Conserve some effort, however, by doing background reading before you plunge into gathering sources. Reading about your topic in its larger context will make you more aware of the significance of your topic. For example, if you are writing a paper about railroads in the American West, you need to know what social and economic factors encouraged their development.

When you gather research resources, you will be looking for important facts, interesting statistics, and revealing quotations. Refer to pages 775–782 for the kinds of sources and references available in libraries. Many references cover specific topics. For example, for sources on American art, literature, and culture, you can consult the *Art Index*, the *Humanities Index*, and the *Media Review Digest*, to name a few.

Evaluate Sources Since you have only a limited amount of time for research, you should carefully evaluate sources before taking notes from them. Some sources may be out of date, reflecting obsolete opinions or old technology. Other sources, such as tabloids and propaganda published by radical groups, are unsuitable because of their slanted treatment of topics.

Some of the information you find will be based more on opinion, and some will be based more on fact. If your topic is a controversial one, such as prison reform, read a variety of viewpoints. A broad perspective will enrich your understanding. Also evaluate how an author presents facts. Although an author will certainly have opinions about the facts, blatant bias will hinder an author's ability to present a clear, analytical evaluation. To detect bias in an author or a source, ask yourself the following questions.

To Detect Author Bias, Ask Yourself . . .

- Does the author fail to give evidence for certain claims?
- Is the author reliable on some points and not others?
- Is the author's scope of vision limited by his or her age, country of origin, or politics?
- Is the author a qualified expert on this subject?
- Does the author's biography indicate a special interest that would prejudice his or her judgment?

As you read further, you may want to review your topic and guiding questions occasionally to be sure that the notes you take are relevant to your paper. While you should be open to taking new directions as you learn more about the subject, don't digress into another area and take notes on material that ultimately you can't use.

Make Bibliography Cards As you find possible sources for your research, record the full publication information on a computer file or on a three-by-five-inch index card for each source. You will use the information twice: once to give credit to your sources in the body of your paper and once to list your sources at the end of your research paper. Number each bibliography card or source entry so that when you take notes, you can write just the number instead of the complete title.

Examples of numbered bibliography cards for Stephanie's research paper are shown at the right.

For a book, record the author's full name (last name first), the complete title (including subtitle), the city of publication, the name of the publisher, and the year of publication.

For a newspaper or magazine article, record the author's name, the title of the article, the title of the periodical, the date of publication, and the inclusive page numbers of the article.

For an online or Internet source, record the name of the author (if there is one), the title of the document, the name of the database, the date of electronic publication or last update, the name of the organization sponsoring the Web site, the date you accessed the site, and the network address or URL.

See the excerpt from Stephanie's works-cited list on page 342 for more information on what to record on your bibliography cards or enter into your electronic file of sources you use during your research. The excerpt shows what to include, for example, if you use a personal interview or a television program as part of your research or if a book has several authors, an editor or translator, or is part of a multivolume work.

"Wood, Grant."
Britannica Online. Vers. 99.1. 1994–1999.
Encyclopaedia Britannica. 7 Nov. 1999
<http://www.members.eb.com /bol/topic?eu=79456&ctn =1&pm=1>. ①

Dennis, James M. *Grant Wood.* Columbia: U of Missouri P, 1986. ②

Hughes, Robert. "Under the Crack of Reality." *Time* 17 July 1995: 54–56. ③

Take Notes from Sources

Keep your thesis statement and research questions in mind as you carefully read your sources, and take notes only on the material that is relevant to your topic. If a source has useful information, take notes on four-by-six-inch index cards, using one card for each distinct piece of information. In the upper right corner of each card, record the number of the corresponding source card, and in the bottom right corner, record the number of the page on which you found the ideas and information. At the top of each card, write the note's main idea. That way, when you're ready to begin drafting, you'll be able to easily group your notes and arrange them in a logical order.

Take Notes in One of Three Ways A **paraphrase** is a restatement of information in your own words. A **summary** is a brief synthesis of a long passage containing only main ideas and key supporting information. A **direct quotation** is the exact wording of a source, set off with quotation marks. Look at the note cards on the following page for examples of the three note-taking methods.

Simply stringing together pages of direct quotations is not the same as writing a research paper. To prepare an insightful paper, you will need to understand your sources and weave them together with your own explanations and analysis. Your distinctive writer's voice will make your research paper flow smoothly from idea to idea.

Prewriting Tip

As you take notes, be alert to how you might convey information using visual aids, such as charts, pictures, and diagrams.

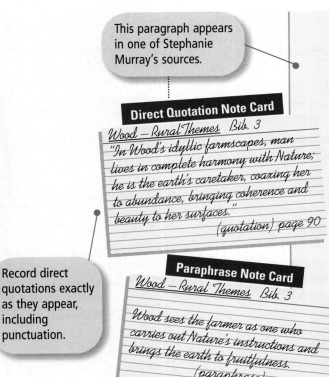

This paragraph appears in one of Stephanie Murray's sources.

Wood's farm landscapes are, without a doubt, the most sensuous and passionate works he painted. Mingling eroticism with ecstasy, Wood made the relationship between the farmer and mother earth into a Wagnerian love duet. While mother earth is always the principal protagonist, overwhelming the farmer in scale and vitality, she is always loving and benevolent. In Wood's idyllic farmscapes, man lives in complete harmony with Nature; he is the earth's caretaker, coaxing her to abundance, bringing coherence and beauty to her surfaces.

Direct Quotation Note Card

Wood – Rural Themes   Bib. 3
"In Wood's idyllic farmscapes, man lives in complete harmony with Nature; he is the earth's caretaker, coaxing her to abundance, bringing coherence and beauty to her surfaces."
(quotation) page 90

Record direct quotations exactly as they appear, including punctuation.

Paraphrase Note Card

Wood – Rural Themes   Bib. 3
Wood sees the farmer as one who carries out Nature's instructions and brings the earth to fruitfulness.
(paraphrase)
page 90

Summary Note Card

Wood – Rural Themes   Bib. 3
Wood's farmscapes his most passionate works
farmer and mother earth "love duet"
man as caretaker of the land
(summary)
page 90

A paraphrase is a restatement of someone else's original idea; in what other ways could you restate this information?

When you summarize, you synthesize key points and important details.

The page number of the source is 90; complete information about the source is on bibliography card #3.

As you take notes, consider how ideas interrelate. Note how certain trends or patterns emerge. As your ideas evolve, you may need to take several trips to the library to gather more data for your paper or to fill in gaps.

Avoid Plagiarism An honest writer avoids plagiarism, the use of another writer's words or ideas without giving credit. The first step in avoiding plagiarism is to indicate on each note card whether an idea is your own, a paraphrase, a summary, or a direct quotation. Without these marks, you will not remember whether an idea was yours or was summarized or paraphrased from a research source.

You can plagiarize unintentionally. If you carelessly treat a direct quotation as a paraphrase or summary, you have plagiarized. You have plagiarized too if your paraphrase is too close to the wording of an idea expressed in the original source. For example, if a source's words are "Successful advertising preys on our fear of rejection" and you paraphrase it as "Successful advertising campaigns pitch to people's fear of rejection," you have plagiarized, even if you name your source.

Be sure to use your own words as you summarize and paraphrase information. Then reread the source to ensure that the words you have used are your own and that they accurately reflect the facts and opinions presented in the original source. Remember always to document, or cite, the source of a paraphrase, summary, or direct quotation. (See Lesson 7.4 for information on how to cite your sources properly.)

7.1 | Writing Activities

Skills Practice

1. For each broad topic below, list three ideas for appropriately limited topics.
- technology in sports
- women in modern art
- the motion picture industry

2. Imagine that you will write a research paper on the work of playwright Thornton Wilder. Which of the following sources do you think will be suitable? Explain.
- a collection of Thornton Wilder's essays: *American Characteristics*
- the *National Enquirer*
- a videotape of Wilder's *Our Town*
- a television documentary about Wilder
- a *TV Guide* summary of a movie version of his novel *The Bridge of San Luis Rey*

3. "The simplified abstract shapes of [Georgia O'Keeffe's] flowers, bones, mountains, and clouds reveal a classic order hidden in nature."

This quotation was taken from a book about American women artists. Tell whether the writer of each sentence below has plagiarized-even if credit to the source has been given.

- Georgia O'Keeffe's subject matter consisted of natural forms such as flowers, bones, and mountains.
- O'Keeffe's flowers, bones, mountains, and clouds reveal a classic order hidden in nature.

Your Research Paper

Begin the process of writing a research paper by following these bulleted directions:

- Select a research paper topic, write five questions about it that you'd like your research to answer, and acquire permission to proceed from your teacher.
- Begin conducting library research and preparing bibliography cards. Use the *MLA Handbook for Writers of Research Papers,* the text and samples on page 327, or the chart on page 341 as a guide to accurate recording of bibliographic data on your source cards.
- Write legibly and follow the conventions of punctuation, capitalization, italics, and quotation marks as laid out in the resources named.
- Begin taking notes from the sources you've gathered.

Prewriting: Developing an Outline

Edward Hopper, *Cape Cod Evening* (sketch), 1939

*P*eople in all fields organize their ideas in a variety of ways. Artists, for example, may make charcoal sketches before beginning to paint on canvas. Computer programmers may create flow charts to show the steps in their programs. Likewise, writers devise outlines to organize their ideas and information.

Now you will create a working outline to help you to organize your research notes. As you learn more, adjust your outline to reflect your increasing knowledge.

Make a Formal Outline

You can use many methods to arrange your note cards into an outline. You may wish to use a combination of methods—one method for main ideas and another method for supporting details.

Use the other units in this book to explore methods of organization. Unit 3, for example, examines order of importance, order of impression, and spatial order (pages 128–130). Unit 4 illustrates chronological order (pages 182–184), and Unit 5 demonstrates how to explain a process (pages 218–220). Collaborating with a partner and sharing your ideas can help you choose the best way to organize your data.

Stephanie Murray used another method of organization illustrated in Unit 5, comparison and contrast (pages 226–230). A portion of her initial outline is shown on the next page. Although she knew that her paper would ultimately begin with an introduction and some background information, she began outlining the section of her paper that would deal with the contrast that exists between the paintings of Grant Wood and the reality of the time period in which he lived. As you will see in the completed research paper on pages 350–355, Murray again uses comparison and contrast to discuss the works of Grant Wood and Edward Hopper.

Evaluation Rubric

By the time you complete Lesson 7.2, you will have

- made a formal outline, tree, or cluster diagram that reveals an appropriate method of organization for your paper
- drafted a thesis statement and revised it until it provides a clear focus for your writing

You may also find that you need to return to the stages covered in Lesson 7.1.

The Art of Grant Wood and of Edward Hopper

I. Wood's time in history

    A. Population moving to cities

        1. Prompted by World War I

        2. Problems with unemployment, etc.

    B. Hard times in rural America

        1. Farm economy depressed ←— *Get more statistics.*

        2. Crash of 1929

        3. Droughts, dust storms, grasshoppers

    C. Economy and national spirit at all-time low

II. Paradox: between Wood's paintings and his era
     ←— *Move down.*

    A. Wood as spokesman for rural America

    B. Paintings *Spring Turning, Stone City*

        1. Awesomeness of American landscape

        2. Man a small element in picture

        3. No signs of industrialization

    C. Realities of dust bowls and rotting crops

    D. Government policies initially ineffective
       ←— *Unnecessary idea. Delete.*

III. Paradox: theme of community spirit

    A. Paintings *Arbor Day, Dinner for Threshers*

        1. Community spirit

            a. People working together

            b. No signs of industrial progress

        2. Role of women ←— *Get more information.*

            a. Dressed in old-fashioned clothes

            b. Feeding the men after work is done

                (1) Establishment of social ritual

                (2) Cooking over wood stove = simplicity

Sidebar notes:

Use Roman numerals for main topics. For subtopics, start with capital letters; continue with Arabic numerals, then lowercase letters, and, finally, Arabic numerals in parentheses.

Research Paper Writing

Historical background information is in chronological order. It gives readers a context in which to understand the information that follows.

Not all ideas need equal development.

Comparison and contrast is used to examine the paradoxes created by the reality shown in the paintings.

The boldface suggestions for changes were made during a conference with a classmate.

When you create a formal outline, you may employ several levels of subheadings. Either use two or more subheadings under a heading or subheading, or use none at all. In addition, all subheadings should be written in parallel grammatical form, either fragments (used in the above outline) or complete sentences.

Drafting Tip

When you choose a method of organizing details, think of how they are most logically related to the main idea and to each other.

Drafting Tip

You may wish to use a computer program to create your outline or to diagram the organization of your paper.

Consider Other Organizing Tools

Depending on your topic, you may find that other ways of organizing your paper are more helpful than the traditional outline. Using a tree or cluster diagram, for example, enables you to map out your information and see how your details are connected. Choose the organization tool that helps you best to manage your information during drafting. Remember that as the bulk of your information increases, so will the need to organize it clearly and in detail. The diagram below shows how the information in Stephanie Murray's paper will be compared and contrasted.

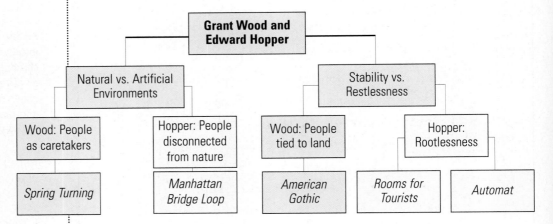

Create and Revise a Thesis Statement

A successful thesis statement does several things: In one sentence it presents the main idea that you will develop in your paper, it explains your perspective on your topic, and it prepares readers to see how you arrived at that perspective. To create a thesis statement, consider the "big picture." Read the Roman numeral headings of your working outline; they will suggest a main idea. Writing answers to the following questions will also help you to formulate a thesis statement.

Questions Leading to a Thesis Statement

1. What was the central idea that guided my research?
2. What questions did I answer in my research?
3. What significant ideas surfaced during my research?
4. How could my research findings be stated in one sentence?

THESIS STATEMENT

Continue to revise your thesis statement and your outline to reflect the insights you gain from your research and writing. The final version of your thesis statement may not emerge until you write the final revision of your paper. Look at how the example thesis statement evolves.

The central idea illustrates the sort of obvious, surface observation that you might develop after doing preliminary reading and research about a topic. It is the cornerstone on which research is based.

The first thesis statement is more specific than the central idea, but it's still just a general statement of the differences in subjects of the two painters. The statement reveals neither the significance of the writer's research nor the writer's approach to the topic. The real value of a first thesis statement is that it can keep a writer from veering off the topic during early planning and drafting.

The first revised thesis statement is more detailed and reveals more of the depth of the writer's research, but the writer's approach to the topic is still not clear. Thus, the thesis statement does not seem to make a point and needs further refinement.

The second revised thesis statement succinctly states the topic and the writer's unique approach to it. This thesis statement makes a point that can be supported in the body of the paper.

Evolution of a Thesis Statement

Central idea Grant Wood and Edward Hopper painted at about the same time, but their paintings were very different.

Thesis statement While Wood painted scenes of rural America, Hopper dealt with city life.

Revised thesis statement While Wood evoked a simpler era, Hopper portrayed an urban world of loneliness and disconnection.

Revised thesis statement The art of Grant Wood and Edward Hopper reflected the conflict between rural and urban views of American life during the Depression.

7.2 | Writing Activities

Skills Practice

Rewrite each of the following into a concise, single-sentence thesis statement.

- The 1960s were a tumultuous time in all aspects of U.S. society. A great deal of artistic energy was devoted to the exploration of nontraditional media. For this reason, it is impossible to identify a single preeminent 1960s novel.

- Motion pictures generally provide a reflection of the political era in which they are made. This is true whether or not the film deals with contemporary issues or stories.

Your Research Paper

Continue working on your own research paper. Complete the following steps:

- Reread your note cards and arrange them in groups according to subject.
- Identify main ideas and use those as the main headings in a formal outline or graphic organizer.
- Complete your outline or graphic, adding subheadings and details.
- Draft a thesis statement that reveals the main idea you will develop in your report.
- Refine your thesis statement so that it reflects your own approach to the topic.

Drafting

Sitting down to write can be hard, even for professional writers. One writer, John McPhee, admits that he once used the belt on his bathrobe to tie himself into his writing chair. You may not relish drafting either, but there are easier ways of creating a draft than tying yourself into a chair.

Draft from an Outline

Before you begin writing, review your outline and note cards, and think about what you want to say. Try arranging your note cards, using various methods of organization, and adjust your outline if one of those methods seems more fitting. Be sure that the sequence of your note cards matches your final outline. If the information on some note cards doesn't fit naturally into your outline, put those note cards aside for now. Never throw any note cards away, even if you think you have finished using the information on them. You may need to refer to them as you revise.

As you write your paper, you will learn more about your topic. You are also likely to formulate new questions about your topic that your research notes don't yet answer. That's OK; just jot down notes in the margins of your paper where you need to find more information. You may conduct additional research and fill in the holes later on. If you need to return to the research stage during your writing process, you're in good company—professional writers continually dig for more information throughout their writing process.

In addition to containing the body paragraphs that your outline suggests, your paper will begin with an introduction that includes your thesis statement and will end with a conclusion. Many writers begin by writing the introduction first; others choose to start with the sections that seem easiest to write. If you have trouble writing anything at all, freewrite a page or two without referring to your note cards. Freewriting may help you to develop a tone and a feel for your paper. You can then go back to your note cards and begin to focus your writing.

As you write each section of your paper, use your outline or graphic organizer as a guide. In the following example, the outline guides the draft without limiting it.

As you write the text for each heading, consider how the main ideas relate to each other and how details support main ideas. Use strong, logical transitions between ideas; a research paper requires more than just "connecting the dots."

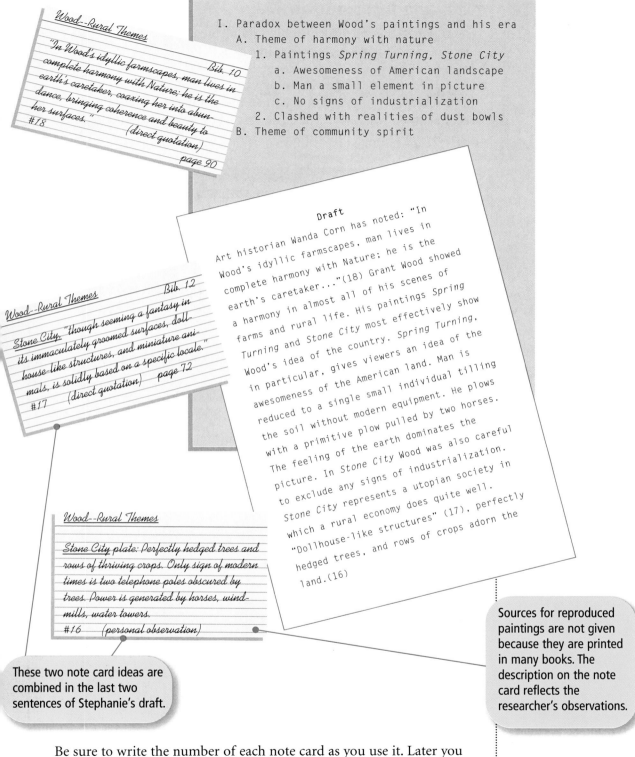

Wood--Rural Themes

Bib. 10

"In Wood's idyllic farmscapes, man lives in complete harmony with Nature; he is the earth's caretaker, coaxing her into abundance, bringing coherence and beauty to her surfaces."
#18 (direct quotation)
page 90

I. Paradox between Wood's paintings and his era
  A. Theme of harmony with nature
    1. Paintings *Spring Turning, Stone City*
      a. Awesomeness of American landscape
      b. Man a small element in picture
      c. No signs of industrialization
    2. Clashed with realities of dust bowls
  B. Theme of community spirit

Wood--Rural Themes

Bib. 12

Stone City, "though seeming a fantasy in its immaculately groomed surfaces, doll-house-like structures, and miniature animals, is solidly based on a specific locale."
#17 (direct quotation) page 72

Draft

Art historian Wanda Corn has noted: "In Wood's idyllic farmscapes, man lives in complete harmony with Nature; he is the earth's caretaker..."(18) Grant Wood showed a harmony in almost all of his scenes of farms and rural life. His paintings *Spring Turning* and *Stone City* most effectively show Wood's idea of the country. *Spring Turning,* in particular, gives viewers an idea of the awesomeness of the American land. Man is reduced to a single small individual tilling the soil without modern equipment. He plows with a primitive plow pulled by two horses. The feeling of the earth dominates the picture. In *Stone City* Wood was also careful to exclude any signs of industrialization. *Stone City* represents a utopian society in which a rural economy does quite well. "Dollhouse-like structures" (17), perfectly hedged trees, and rows of crops adorn the land.(16)

Wood--Rural Themes

Stone City plate: Perfectly hedged trees and rows of thriving crops. Only sign of modern times is two telephone poles obscured by trees. Power is generated by horses, windmills, water towers.
#16 (personal observation)

These two note card ideas are combined in the last two sentences of Stephanie's draft.

Sources for reproduced paintings are not given because they are printed in many books. The description on the note card reflects the researcher's observations.

Be sure to write the number of each note card as you use it. Later you will replace the numbers with full information about your sources.

Revising Tip

You can combine similar ideas from note cards in the same way that you create compound sentences. Review pages 538–539.

Manage Information

As you draft, don't worry about finding the perfect word. Instead, concentrate on sequencing your ideas in a logical, effective order. You will revise your paper for style and usage later.

If the amount of information that you have gathered is overwhelming, draft your paper one section at a time. You can make connections between sections when you revise. The chart that follows contains other hints for overcoming drafting problems.

Drafting Problems and Solutions	
PROBLEMS	**SOLUTIONS**
I can't seem to get a handle on my topic.	Make sure that your thesis statement is clearly focused. Also, try telling someone about your topic to clarify your thinking and to build up your enthusiasm.
I need more information for one section of my paper.	Go back to the library or log onto the Internet to get it. Neither you nor your readers will be satisfied with your work if it's incomplete.
I'd like to change topics.	Be realistic about how much time you have. Don't start over without discussing it with your teacher.
I feel as if I'm just cutting and pasting the words of other people.	Use direct quotations sparingly; summarize and paraphrase more often. Your paper should reflect your thinking and analysis of what other writers have written plus your own insights.

Draft an Effective Introduction

A good introduction announces your topic, presents a clear thesis statement, and grabs the readers' interest. You can begin your paper with a pithy quotation, a vivid description, or a little-known fact. You can also ask your readers a question to draw them into your topic.

You might freewrite several introductions before deciding on the best one. You don't need a long introduction.

Why is this introduction effective? Read another effective introduction on page 350.

A Good Introduction

Have you ever experienced the pleasure of biting into a veggie-nut burger spilling over with guacamole, tomatoes, and sprouts? No? Then you're probably not a vegetarian. Vegetarians are people who choose not to eat meat for political, ecological, biological, or spiritual reasons. These people have changed their lifestyles because of their convictions.

Draft a Conclusion

Your conclusion should recap the main ideas of your paper and create a sense of closure. It might also put your ideas in perspective, describe the significance of your research, or stress the need for further investigation. Make sure it doesn't introduce new or unexplained information that will leave readers dangling.

An Effective Conclusion

Whether for the health of their planet, their fellow creatures, their country, or themselves, vegetarians are setting an example of constructive activism. Vegetarianism may not be for everyone; however, if everyone held the concerns of vegetarians, the results might be more far-reaching than even the most avid vegetarian could hope for.

7.3 | Writing Activities

Skills Practice

1. Freewrite an introduction for the three thesis statements that follow. Your introduction should include a "hook" that engages the reader's interest.

- Because making motion pictures has become a multibillion dollar industry, artistic expression is often sacrificed for big box-office receipts.
- Government support of the arts is increasingly under fire from a public that feels its tastes are not being represented.
- If creative expression in high schools is encouraged through financial and public support, students will create public works of art for all to enjoy. Academic performance is also likely to improve as a result.

2. For each pair of note-card sentences below, write a transitional sentence that connects the ideas.

- Many people prefer live theater to movies because theater is "more real." One attraction of live theater is that it brings together real people—the actors and the audience.

- Many authors become unhappy when they see how their novels have been made into films. The visual nature of film is fundamentally different from the verbal nature of the novel.

Your Research Paper

Now begin drafting your research paper, completing the following steps:

- Begin writing the section with which you feel most comfortable.
- Use the main and subordinate headings in your outline or graphic organizer as a guide. Pull information from your note cards, providing strong transitions from one idea to the next.
- Craft an introduction that captures your readers' attention and includes a thesis statement that reveals the direction your paper will take.
- Write a conclusion that reinforces your thesis and the paper's main points.

LESSON 7.4

Citing Sources

"They're playing my song." That's been the cry of several famous musicians who have recognized their tune in someone else's release. Famous singers are often sued successfully for recording a hit song without paying royalties to its creator. However, creative ideas are often shared in the music industry. Rap stars routinely use parts of other people's songs through electronic sampling and other methods. This use is perfectly legal, as long as the rapper gives credit to and pays royalties to the original artists.

Similarly, when you write a research paper, your readers will expect you to borrow a certain amount of information from other sources. However, you avoid plagiarism when you cite, or name, the sources of the information in your research paper, thus giving credit where credit is due.

Document Sources

When you cite or document sources, you give credit to the author whose original work you use and provide readers with the information they would need to locate a source if they wanted to read more about your topic. In addition to citing books, magazines, newspapers, online sources, and CD-ROM databases from which you take information, you must cite interviews, television programs, song lyrics, letters, and dialogue from plays. If you put into words information that is expressed graphically in tables, charts, and diagrams, also cite these sources.

Generally, you will cite your sources each time you use the exact words, facts and statistics, or opinions and ideas of others. Of course, you don't need to document every sentence in your paper. You need not document your own ideas or common knowledge, information that can be found in a number of sources. For example, it's a well-known fact that Grand Coulee Dam is in Washington State, so you would not need to document that information. The chart on the next page shows what kind of information you do and do not need to document as you draft your research paper.

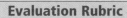

Evaluation Rubric

By the time you complete Lesson 7.4, you will have

- learned what information in your paper does and does not need to be documented

- chosen an appropriate method for citing your sources

- correctly cited your sources in the body of your paper

Type of Information	Is Citation Needed?
"The very long horizontal shape of this picture is an effort to give a sensation of great lateral extent."	**Yes.** Always cite a direct quotation.
The Gothic windows in the background indicate that in the couple's house the values of Christianity are fostered and taught.	**Yes.** Always credit another writer for his or her opinion, even if you agree with it.
Almost every American city would eventually suffer overcrowding, housing shortages, slums, unemployment, pollution, and a lack of recreational facilities.	**Yes.** Always credit an author's generalization or conclusion that is based on his or her own research and analysis.
Wood emphasized the harmonious relationship between people and the landscape.	**No.** This information can be found in many sources. It is considered common knowledge.
By 1920, the bulk of the American population lived in cities with 2,500 people or more.	**Yes.** Always cite statistics that are not well known; doing so enables readers to evaluate the source of the data or to search for further information.
The stock market crashed in 1929.	**No.** The year of the Great Crash is common knowledge.

Prewriting Tip

Make sure that each of your note cards identifies its source and the page number(s) from which the information was taken.

Format Citations

At this stage in your writing process, you will find that the time you spent carefully completing and numbering your source cards and note cards during the prewriting stage has been time well spent. Citing your sources is easy if you have all the information you need at your fingertips. The information you've borrowed from your sources can be cited in one of three ways: footnotes, endnotes, or parenthetical documentation, which is recommended by the Modern Language Association of America (or MLA). Because parenthetical documentation is generally preferred, the instruction and models in this unit conform to the MLA guidelines. Be sure to check with your teacher, however, and use the method that he or she prefers.

Parenthetical Documentation with a Works-Cited List
Your works-cited list is an alphabetized, detailed list of sources that you used in writing your research paper. In the body of your paper, after each quotation, summary, or paraphrase of information from a source, you must include a reference to the source and a page number within parentheses. This citation points readers to the corresponding entry in your works-cited list. The chart on the next page and Stephanie Murray's final draft of her research paper on pages 350–355, provide guidance and models for how to reference your sources in text, giving credit in parentheses.

Editing Tip

To aid your placement of citations, review the structure of clauses on pages 535–549.

Creating parenthetical documentation should be an uncomplicated task. In your draft, you wrote the numbers of the note cards next to the information you used from them. Now, replace the note card numbers with the proper parenthetical documentation. Place the citation as close to the end of the borrowed information as possible so that readers can tell which ideas are being cited. Notice the following example:

The lines in their faces reflect a hard life; their expressions suggest the Puritan values of hard work and thrift (Corn 130).

Source	Parenthetical Documentation
One author (Goodrich 70–71)	Put the author's last name and the page reference in parentheses. If you're using two or more works by different authors with the same last name, be sure to include the author's first name or initial.
Two or three authors (Bar and Burchfield 55)	Put all authors' last names and the page reference in parentheses. If a work has more than three authors, use the last name of the first author, followed by *et al.,* and the page reference: (Jones et al. 35–36).
No author given ("Waiting" 44)	Give the title, or a shortened form of it, and the page reference (if any).
Author of more than one work listed in the works cited (Pratt, *Modern Art* 67)	If you use more than one source by the same author, include the author's last name followed by a comma, the source title or a shortened form of it, and a page reference.
Author's name in text (178)	If you use the author's last name in the sentence that includes the information you need to document, you need only provide a page reference in parentheses, as shown in this example. *Critic John Davidson claims the artist's style is "unconsidered and blobby" (178).*
More than one work in a single parenthetical reference (O'Shea 31; Musick 109)	Cite each work as you normally would, including a semicolon between the entries.
Nonprint sources ("Wood")	The example at the left corresponds to a works-cited entry for an article called "Wood, Grant" that was published by *Britannica Online.* For videocassettes, recordings, interviews, films, and electronic sources that cannot be cited by page number, name the work in running text, or, in parentheses, give readers the information they need to find the complete citation in the works-cited list.

The following chart—as well as Stephanie's works-cited list—shows the proper formats to use for a variety of source types you're likely to include in your works-cited list. If you use a source that is not modeled in this unit, consult your teacher or the *MLA Handbook for Writers of Research Papers*.

Source	Format for Works-Cited Entries
A book with one author	Hobbs, Robert. *Edward Hopper*. New York: Abrams, 1987.
A book with two or three authors	Barr, Alfred H., and Charles Burchfield. *Edward Hopper Retrospective*. New York: Museum of Modern Art, 1933.
A book with no author given	*American Printmakers 1900–1989: Edward Hopper to Jasper Johns*. Chicago: R. S. Johnson Fine Art, 1989.
A book with an editor but no author	McCoubrey, John W., ed. *Modern American Painting*. New York: Time-Life, 1970.
A work included in an anthology	Rosenblum, Robert. "The Primal American Scene." *The Natural Paradise: Painting in America 1800–1950*. Ed. Kynaston McShine. New York: Museum of Modern Art, 1976. 165–178.
A work in a collection of works by one author	Hughes, Robert. "Edward Hopper." *Nothing If Not Critical: Selected Essays on Art and Artists*. New York: Knopf, 1990. 227–230.
An encyclopedia article	"Realism." *World Book Encyclopedia*. 1990 ed.
An article in a magazine	Wooden, Howard E. "Grant Wood: A Regionalist's Interpretation of the Four Seasons." *American Artist* July 1991: 58.
An article in a newspaper	Artner, Alan G. "An American Original: The Unique Midwestern Vision of Grant Wood." *Chicago Tribune* 15 Jan. 1984, sec. 10: 15–19.
A videocassette	*Edward Hopper: The Silent Witness*. Dir. Wolfgang Hastert. Videocassette. Kultur Intl. Films, 1994.
An online information database	"Wood, Grant." *Britannica Online*. Vers. 99.1. 1994–1999. Encyclopaedia Britannica. 7 Nov. 1999 <http://www.members.eb.com/bol/topic?eu=79456&sctn=1&pm=1>.
A professional or personal Web site	Haven, Janet. *Going Back to Iowa: The World of Grant Wood*. U of Virginia American Studies Program. 7 Nov. 1999 <http://www.lib.virginia.edu/etd/theses/ArtsSci/English/1998/Haven/home.html>.
A CD-ROM	Levin, Gail. *Edward Hopper: A Catalogue Raisonné*. CD-ROM. New York: Whitney Museum of American Art; New York: Norton, 1995.

Use this order, as it applies, for book sources: authors' name(s), title of anthologized work, title of book, name of editor, name of edition, city of publication, publisher's name, and publication date.

Use this order, as it applies, for periodical sources: authors' name(s), title of article, name of periodical, series number, date of publication, newspaper edition, and page numbers of the complete article.

This is the correct format for two (or more) publishers.

How to Format a List of Works Cited The excerpt from a works-cited list below shows proper format, indentation, and punctuation. Notice that all entries are alphabetized by authors' names or by title, excluding words such as *A* and *The* at the beginning of titles. Thus, the first entry is a book written by Wanda Corn titled *Grant Wood: The Regionalist Vision*. The title of the book is followed by the city of publication, New Haven (Connecticut); an abbreviation of the publisher, Yale UP, (Yale University Press); and the year of publication, 1983. Consult your teacher or the *MLA Handbook for Writers of Research Papers* for abbreviations of other publishers' names.

Notice that the encyclopedia entry begins with the title of the encyclopedia article because the author is not named. If an encyclopedia article does name an author, treat the name as you would for an author whose work is included in an anthology.

> The first line of an entry is flush left; indent all others five spaces or half inch.

> For a second entry by the same author, instead of the author's name, use three hyphens and a period.

> Double-space all lines and between entries.

> This is the correct format to use for an essay published in a journal. The number *15* represents the volume number.

> This is the correct format to use for a book with two or more editors.

> Use this format for a face-to-face interview, citing the date on which the interview took place. You may also specify *Telephone interview* or *Online interview*, depending on the method you used.

> For a radio or television program, include the title of the episode or segment (if appropriate), the title of the program, the name of the network, the station's call letters and city of the local station, and the broadcast date.

> Your last name and the page number go here.

Murray 7

Works Cited

Corn, Wanda. *Grant Wood: The Regionalist Vision*. New Haven: Yale UP, 1983.

Dennis, James M. *Grant Wood*. Columbia: U of Missouri P, 1986.

- - -. *Grant Wood: A Study in American Art and Culture*. New York: Viking, 1975.

Hobbs, Robert. *Edward Hopper*. New York: Abrams, 1987.

Lewis, Michael J. "Homer, Hopper, and the Critics." *The New Criterion* 15 (Sept. 1996): 74–80.

McCoubrey, John W., ed. *Modern American Painting*. New York: Time-Life, 1970.

Pierson, William H., and Martha Davidson, eds. *Arts of the United States: A Pictorial Survey*. New York: McGraw, 1960.

"Realism." *World Book Encyclopedia*. 1990 ed.

Topaz, Wayne. Personal interview. 7 Nov. 1999.

"Whitney Museum Opens Exhibit of Edward Hopper Paintings." *All Things Considered*. Natl. Public Radio. WBEZ, Chicago. 1 July 1995.

Evaluate Your Treatment of Sources

When you finish your draft, evaluate how well you have represented your sources. First, make sure that you haven't taken a quotation out of context and thus changed its meaning. For example, suppose a critic had written, "While Grant Wood is unsophisticated and sentimental in his subject matter, his compositions reflect a mastery of modern design." You would misrepresent the author's opinion of Wood's skill if you quoted only the first half of the sentence.

If you are writing about a controversial subject, make sure you have included multiple viewpoints. Presenting only statements from one point of view creates a boring and biased paper.

Strive also for a balance of primary and secondary sources. Use primary sources—first-hand accounts, such as newspaper articles, interviews, journals, and original documents—to give your paper a sense of immediacy and authority. Use secondary sources—writings about primary sources, such as biographies, literary criticism, and histories—to enrich your paper with the wisdom of perspective and expert analysis.

7.4 | Writing Activities

Skills Practice

1. For each of the following statements on artist Andy Warhol, state whether documentation is needed and why.

- Andy Warhol worked for many years as a commercial artist.

- Silk-screening allowed Warhol to experiment with repetitive images.

- "Warhol seems concerned about our anesthetized reaction to what is put in front of us."

- Warhol himself wrote, "You live in your dream America that you've custom-made from art and schmaltz and emotions just as much as you live in your real one."

2. Write proper entries for a list of works cited for the following sources.

- An article by Robert Morris in the April 1968 issue of *Artforum* magazine entitled "Anti-Form," on pages 55–58.

- A book, *Art on Trial*, by Lois Miller, published by Viking Press in New York City in 1991.

- An unsigned article, "Surrealism," in the 1990 edition of *The Encyclopedia Americana*.

Your Research Paper

Continue working on your research-paper draft by successfully completing the following steps.

- Insert proper documentation within the body of your paper. If you're using parenthetical documentation, replace the note-card numbers that correspond to your source cards with a proper citation in parentheses.

- Create a draft of your works-cited page.

- Ensure the accuracy of your documentation and of your works-cited list by following the formats outlined in this lesson and in the *MLA Handbook for Writers of Research Papers*.

Revising

Grant Wood, *American Gothic,* 1930

*G*reat works of art, as well as great research papers, do not spring into existence perfect and complete. Artists often make changes in their compositions, by painting out figures, adding more details, and rearranging elements. You should revise the first draft of your paper in the same spirit. Step back from your work, and give it a fresh look as did Grant Wood when he painted American Gothic, *the painting on this page.*

Creating any work, whether a painting or a research paper, involves a rethinking of the path that the work is to take. At the same time, you will need to keep a vigilant eye on your original purpose. As you determine your paper's future, review its past. Read your research questions, all versions of your thesis statement, and your outline, and then evaluate whether you have strayed from your original vision.

Revise in Stages

After you finish your first draft, be sure to allow time to set your draft aside for a day or two before you revise it. By putting some distance between yourself and the drafting process, you'll gain perspective and be better able to notice flaws.

When you revise your paper, you will analyze everything from organization and content to word choices. However, it's nearly impossible to revise both the "big picture" and the details at the same time. It will be faster and easier for you to revise your paper in stages, focusing on only one kind of problem at each stage. First tackle major ideas, next inspect supporting details, and then proofread and polish tone, style, and individual word choices before completing an error-free final draft.

Evaluation Rubric

By the time you complete Lesson 7.5, you will have

- evaluated your research paper draft for both content and mechanics
- analyzed the paper's organization and crafted a new outline or graphic if necessary
- reorganized the content to ensure coherence, logical progression, and support for your ideas
- refined your writing style to suit the requirements of the research paper and to meet the needs of your audience

Use Revision Strategies

Many different strategies can aid you in revision. To check your paper's organization, write a new outline of your first draft. If information is out of order, you will quickly notice. If a method of organization is not apparent, find out why. Chances are you will need either to reorganize information or to create stronger transitions. You can experiment with different methods of organization by physically cutting apart your draft and resequencing elements.

A good way to test your writing style for smoothness and clarity is to read your draft aloud. Mark awkward passages, shifts in tone, inadequate transitions, and wordy or repetitive sentences.

For another perspective on your work, exchange drafts with classmates. Ask them to point out not only what is wrong with your paper but also what they liked about it. After hearing your readers' comments, you will be better able to determine whether you need to provide more information to clarify some points.

When making revisions on paper, try using different-colored pencils or writing on self-sticking removable notes. Just be sure to write legibly! If your draft exists on a computer file, adjust the formats so that the paper is triple-spaced and has extra-wide margins before making a printout. That way, you can write notes to yourself in the margins or make changes between the lines. You can then reformat your paper in the final stages of your revising and editing process.

Revising Tip

If you have drafted your paper on a word processor, you can experiment with organization by cutting and pasting sections of your draft. Remember to save your file under a new name so that you can refer to the original if you wish.

Research Paper Writing

Editing Tip

For information on how to make sure you have clear antecedents for pronouns, see Lessons 17.6–17.7, pages 632–641.

Revision Checklist

Review the following points as you revise your paper.

✓ **Content and Organization:**
Does the thesis statement reflect the paper's main idea?
In what ways could you better organize major ideas?
What irrelevant or repetitious ideas could you delete?
Which of your main points could be better supported?
How could you strengthen transitions between ideas and paragraphs?

✓ **Style:**
Have you varied your sentence structures and used lively verbs?
Have you avoided sophisticated vocabulary that you don't really understand?

✓ **Usage:**
Have you defined technical terms that will be unfamiliar to readers?
For which frequently used words can you substitute synonyms?

✓ **Documentation:**
Have you cited your sources correctly in the body of your paper?
Is your list of works cited accurate, complete, and properly formatted?

Grammar Tip

Review the rules for capitalizing titles of works and proper names on pages 696–699.

The following research paper has been revised in stages. Notice how the major organizational and content elements are examined first, and then the details are considered.

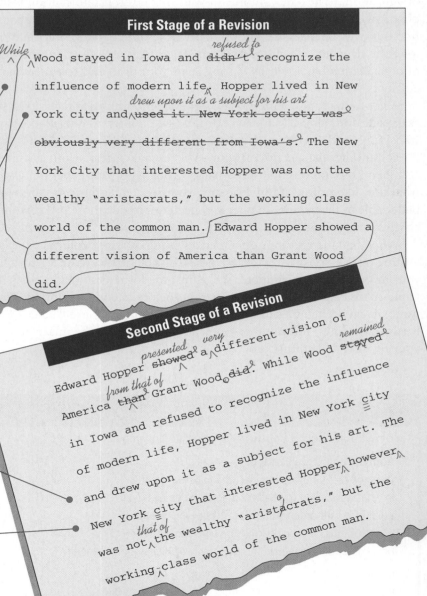

First Stage of a Revision

While Wood stayed in Iowa and ~~didn't~~ *refused to* recognize the influence of modern life. Hopper lived in New York city and ~~used it.~~ *drew upon it as a subject for his art* ~~New York society was obviously very different from Iowa's.~~ The New York City that interested Hopper was not the wealthy "aristacrats," but the working class world of the common man. Edward Hopper showed a different vision of America than Grant Wood did.

Second Stage of a Revision

Edward Hopper ~~showed~~ *presented* a *very* different vision of America ~~than~~ *from that of* Grant Wood ~~did.~~ While Wood ~~stayed~~ *remained* in Iowa and refused to recognize the influence of modern life, Hopper lived in New York city and drew upon it as a subject for his art. The New York city that interested Hopper, *however*, was not, *that of* the wealthy "aristacrats," but the working-class world of the common man.

Wood surely "recognized" the influence, but he made the decision to exclude it from his paintings.

Why are these first two sentences more effective when they are combined?

This wording is more specific about how Hopper used it.

More accurately, the subject is the city or environment of these people.

Why is "however" set off with commas? For a review of conjunctions and coordinating conjunctions, see pages 472–478.

In the first revision, the writer has moved the topic sentence from the end of the paragraph to the beginning, thereby clarifying her main point and providing a framework for the supporting details. In addition, she has deleted an unnecessary detail. In the second revision, the writer has replaced dull verbs with vivid ones and has corrected errors in usage and mechanics.

Consider Special Issues

There may be some special issues to consider as you revise your paper. For example, make sure that you explain any specialized terms or techniques that will be unfamiliar to your readers. You should also anticipate the confusion that may result from words that take on a specialized meaning when they are used in a particular context. For example, there is quite a difference between a romantic composer and a Romantic composer.

Another issue to consider is that of subjective judgment. For example, the merit of a work of art or a social trend is often a matter of opinion. You may state your own opinions, but remember that you are writing a research paper, not an editorial. Words such as *I feel* have no place in an objective analysis. Instead, use the opinions of experts. To be fair to your subject, though, present criticism from more than one source.

7.5 | Writing Activities

Skills Practice

1. Make the following passage clearer, more concise, and better organized. Correct errors in grammar, usage, spelling, and punctuation.

   One subject that for centuries artists have used for inspiration is religion. European art in the Middle Ages was often patronized by the church and people connected with the church. the church of that time had a influence that was pervasive in most aspects of Midieval society. The church has less influence as an institution, in currant times. Many modern artists are exploring relegious themes, event though they may not belong to any formal religion as such. Primitive religious art, has attracted many modern artists. Spiritual questions is being explored by these artists outside of the boundaries of the church's belief system.

2. Revise the following sentence to make it more powerful.

   A legend has grown around Jack Kerouac, the writer, due to his freewheeling lifestyle and rejection of mainstream values current then.

Your Research Paper

Begin revising with the following steps:

- Evaluate the organization of your draft and decide how you can improve the flow of ideas.
- Clarify your thesis, making sure that it sets a purpose and direction for the rest of the paper.
- Conduct additional research if you need to bolster your data.
- Strengthen your transitions and make sure that you've supported your claims with information from your sources.
- Refine your writing style, using vivid words and correcting errors in usage and mechanics.

RESEARCH PAPER WRITING
Editing and Presenting: A Model Paper

Grant Wood, *Stone City, Iowa,* 1930

*O*nce a painting is finished, an artist wants to be sure the painting is shown to its best advantage. The proper frame, position on a wall, and lighting are all part of the presentation. In the same way, you will want to show your writing to its best advantage by preparing a final copy that is free of errors.

Use the Final Edit Checklist

After completing a final revision of your research paper, you should carefully proofread it for errors in grammar, punctuation, spelling, and typing. Use the following final edit checklist as an aid. *The Chicago Manual of Style* is an invaluable reference at this stage in your writing process.

Evaluation Rubric

By the time you complete Lesson 7.6, you will have

- proofread your paper, identifying and correcting errors in logic, grammar, punctuation, and spelling
- confirmed that every summary, paraphrase, or quotation was properly credited to a source and checked that every source you used is listed in a properly formatted works-cited list
- created a clean final copy that is free of errors and ready to present to your audience

Final Edit Checklist

✓ Read your paper from beginning to end, checking to be sure that no information has been omitted or inadvertently missequenced.

✓ Read your paper once just for errors in grammar and usage. Make sure that pronoun references are clear and correct.

✓ Proofread to be sure that all proper nouns in the body of your paper and within your works-cited list are capitalized correctly. Double-check the spellings of foreign words and phrases and make sure you've used accents correctly. If you're using a word processor, run a spell check—but remember that you will still need to proofread for the incorrect use of homophones.

✓ Read your paper yet another time to be sure that all parenthetical documentation is in place and that the works-cited page is complete and properly formatted.

✓ Read your paper a final time for legibility and for punctuation errors. Make sure that periods come after internal citations instead of in front of them.

Present Your Paper

Your final paper will include a title page (or a first page that acts as a title page), a body, a works-cited page, and possibly a separate cover. Visual aids such as copies of works of art, diagrams, time lines, and process charts can give your readers a context in which to consider your information. The model paper from this lesson could include photographs of the Grant Wood and Edward Hopper paintings discussed in the text.

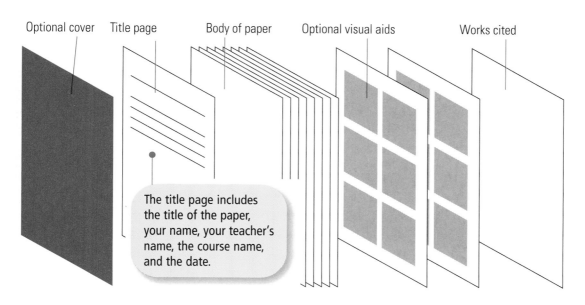

Optional cover   Title page   Body of paper   Optional visual aids   Works cited

The title page includes the title of the paper, your name, your teacher's name, the course name, and the date.

7.6 | Writing Activities

Skills Practice

Rewrite this paragraph correcting errors in spelling, grammar, and punctuation. Rewrite or combine sentences as necessary to improve the flow of ideas.

Architecture is an art form that carries with it an enormus amount of technical requirements. Architects must design structures, that is pleasing to the eye. They must also build structures, that are practical and safe. A third ellement must be considered as well. That is the wishes of the clients who finances the project. Constructing buildings that meet all the necessary use and aesthetic requirements also within the budget, is quite a balancing act. Aesthetics must make compromises with functionality. Sometimes successfully, sometimes not. Sometimes state safety requirements, such as a builsing's being eqrthquake-proof, compromise what an architect consider a good design.

Your Research Paper

Prepare and hand in the final version of your research paper.

Murray 1

Contrasting Images of America:
The Art of Grant Wood and Edward Hopper

The question of the value of nationality in art is perhaps unsolvable. In general, it can be said that a nation's art is greatest when it most reflects the character of its people.

—Edward Hopper (Goodrich 9)

Grant Wood (1892–1942) claimed that all the really good ideas that he had ever had came to him while he was milking a cow (Haven /home.html). This statement contains truth, for many of Wood's paintings portrayed idyllic country scenes of a bygone era. On the other hand, Edward Hopper (1882–1967) focused on the city as the quintessential reflection of American society. Unlike Wood, Hopper did not try to idealize what he saw. Thus, the art of Grant Wood and Edward Hopper reflected not only the conflict between romanticism and reality but also the conflict between rural and urban views of American life that existed in the decades of the 1920s and the 1930s.

According to historian Richard Hofstadter, "The United States was born in the country and has moved to the city" (23). By 1920 "more Americans lived in cities and towns of over 2,500 people than in the countryside" (Blum 549). "Almost every U.S. city would eventually suffer overcrowding, housing shortages, slums, unemployment, pollution and a lack of recreational facilities" (Weisberger 214). Despite these problems, people kept coming to the cities.

While the American city experienced growth during the 1920s, rural America experienced hard times. "In the early twenties the farm prosperity of the war years had rapidly declined and the rural economy was failing" (Dennis 206). The more crops farmers tried to produce, the less profit they made. By 1929 the economic failure had spread to the cities after the stock market crash. This crash brought the reality of the Great Depression to all sectors of the economy: more than 100,000 businesses failed between 1929 and 1932; the annual income of labor fell from $53 billion in 1929 to $31.5 billion in 1933. Western farmers were also hit extremely hard by "droughts, dust storms and plagues of grasshoppers from 1933 to 1936, which drove many families off their farms into tenancy or migrancy" (Dennis 206). The American economy and national spirit had reached an all-time low during the early years of the 1930s.

Research Paper Writing

This research paper was first published by *The Concord Review,* a quarterly review of essays by secondary students of history in the English-speaking world.

A quote from Hopper presents the premise on which the paper is founded.

What is the function of this opening sentence?

Why is this an effective thesis statement?

This sentence incorporates the author's name into the text.

Why is historic background on urban and rural living useful?

Wood emphasized in his art the theme of rural America: the land, community spirit, and pioneer values. A paradox surrounding Grant Wood's works resulted from the contrast between Wood's choice of themes and the times in which he painted. He portrayed an idyllic rural America during an age when America had become the most powerful industrial country in the world; he painted America as a land of bountiful harvests at a time of dust bowls and deprivation. (Haven/drepreg. html).

Art historian Wanda Corn has noted: "In Wood's idyllic farmscapes, man lives in complete harmony with Nature; he is the earth's caretaker . . ." (90). Grant Wood portrayed this sense of harmony in almost all of his farmscapes. His paintings *Spring Turning* and *Stone City* most effectively illustrate Wood's idea of the country. *Spring Turning*, in particular, conveys the awesomeness of the American land. Wood painted lush, rolling hills, evenly plowed fields, and golden light to celebrate the land. The feeling of the earth dominates the picture; man is reduced to a single small individual tilling the soil. The man in the painting does not work with modern equipment but with a primitive plow pulled by two horses. In *Stone City* Wood was also careful to exclude any signs of industrialization in his rural scene. *Stone City* represents a Utopian society in which a rural economy flourishes. "Dollhouse-like structures" (Corn 72), perfectly hedged trees, and rows of thriving crops adorn the land. Wood revealed only a small hint of industrial America by including two thin lines to represent telephone poles. Yet the poles are barely visible, for they are partially hidden by trees. Water tanks, horses, and windmills provide the energy for the people of *Stone City*. Through his paintings of farmers nurturing fecund woods, Wood emphasized the harmonious relationship between man and the land.

Wood's view of rural America clashed with the realities of the times, however. Actual farm conditions included "dustbowls, droughts, rotting crops, and mosquito-infested fields" (Dennis 210).

A second major theme in Wood's work was community spirit. In his paintings *Arbor Day* and *Dinner for Threshers*, Grant Wood portrayed rural America as a community-oriented society. In *Arbor Day* a wood schoolhouse stands proudly elevated on a green plateau. Communal activity centers around the schoolhouse as people work together to plant a tree in the

Use ellipses to indicate that words have been omitted from a direct quotation.

Underline titles of books and works of art or use italic type.

Why is this transition effective?

Research Paper Writing

(continued)

schoolyard. This rural scene shows no signs of industrialization or urbanization. The tracks in the unpaved dirt road were created not by an automobile but by a horse-drawn buggy. No evidence of telephone poles or electric wires appears in this picture. Instead, a hand-operated pump places the scene in a simpler past.

Wood further turned back the clock in his portrayal of women. In *Arbor Day,* for example, he painted the woman with her hair pulled back, dressed in a long dress that hangs below her ankles. Also, in *Dinner for Threshers*, women are again portrayed dressed in late nineteenth-century attire. The feeling of "community" permeates the work as the women graciously serve their men dinner after they have just finished a hard day of work. According to art historian Wanda Corn, "*Dinner for Threshers* rejoices not just in the fullness of agrarian life, but in the establishment of community and social ritual on the frontier" (104). Men comb their hair and wash before eating dinner. The subject matter of the painting presents an image of a simpler America. A horse and wagon rest in front of the barn, in place of a car. The women cook over a wood stove, oblivious to the advantages of electricity. The sense of simplicity is further enhanced by the colors Wood used to paint this picture. He limits his palette to only five colors: the three primary colors—red, yellow, and blue—and black and white. Wood definitely believes that this spirit of community and family which he portrayed in *Arbor Day* and *Dinner for Threshers* could only survive in a simpler, mainly rural America.

Although Wood painted both *Arbor Day* and *Dinner for Threshers* in the early 1930s, he refused to recognize automobiles, electricity, or even the railroad in these paintings. Art historian Robert Hobbs reminds us that "the total number of car registrations almost tripled during the decades of the twenties. A total of over thirty-one million cars were sold . . ." (91). Yet the horse-drawn buggy represented the only means of transportation in Wood's art.

Similarly, Wood's portrayal of women was out of sync with reality. In the decades of the 1920s and 1930s, Wood presented women wearing long dresses and slaving over primitive stoves to serve men, while in reality, the "new woman had revolted against masculine prerogatives . . . against being treated as a species of property" (Leuchtenburg 159). The hemline on women's dresses rose from ankle to midthigh as "flappers" emerged in the 1920s.

Why do you think Murray might want to include photos of some of these paintings in her paper?

This statistic puts the times into focus.

Why is the word "flappers" in quotation marks? If you don't know, review page 736.

Finally, in his most famous painting, American Gothic ("Wood"), Wood exemplified the theme of pioneer values that he felt made America great. In this picture Wood portrayed an elderly Midwestern couple. The man and woman stare straight ahead, sternly. The lines in their faces reflect a hard life; their expressions suggest the Puritan values of hard work and thrift (Corn 130). There is no doubt that they possess strong rural roots and a stable environment. The man's pitchfork reveals that the couple is tied to the land. A hint of religion permeates the picture. The Gothic windows in the background indicate that in the couple's house the values of Christianity are fostered and taught (Corn 130). In fact, Grant Wood once claimed about the couple in *American Gothic,* "I tried to characterize them honestly. . . . To me they are basically good and solid people" (McCoubrey 66).

Edward Hopper presented a very different vision of America from that of Grant Wood. While Wood remained in Iowa and refused to recognize the influence of modern life, Hopper lived in New York City and drew upon it as a subject for his art. The New York City that fascinated Hopper, however, was not that of the wealthy "aristocrats," but that of the working-class world of the common man.

A paradox, however, also existed in Hopper's portrayal of the city in the 1920s and 1930s. Hopper painted at a time when the building of skyscrapers had escalated, especially in New York. All around Hopper, enormous buildings were going up which "represented a radiant, defiant display of American energy and optimism" (Leuchtenburg 182–183). Yet Hopper chose not to paint this side of the city. He looked beyond the spectacular facade of city life, its tall buildings, crowds, excitement, and glamour. "There are never any crowds in Hopper's pictures, never the hurrying tide of humanity . . ." (Goodrich 68).

In *Approaching a City* and *Manhattan Bridge Loop,* Edward Hopper portrayed a realistic view of urban society. The view in *Approaching a City,* for example, is seen from the eyes of a traveler. The painting invites the viewer down into the depths of the railroad tunnel. Stone buildings loom overhead, their windows forming monotonous rows. Hopper painted this picture in cold colors, reflecting the coldness of urban society. He employed cool tans, charcoal grays, brick reds, and dull blues to give the effect of lack of warmth.

In the painting *Manhattan Bridge Loop,* Hopper presented the city as even more uninviting. The sky is painted a slate blue;

Notice how repeating Wood's name makes the transition to Hopper smoother.

A parallel is drawn between the artists: paradoxes exist in both of their works.

Research Paper Writing

(continued)

To emphasize the contrast, readers are briefly reminded of Wood's painting.

Why do you think Murray included this quotation in her paper?

Murray interprets the painting but remains objective in her analysis of it.

Why is this contrast effective?

steel grays are used to indicate buildings. Contrasting with Grant Wood's *Spring Turning* which celebrates the land, this painting depicts the domination of buildings and the conversion of grass to paved sidewalks. A solitary man, hunched over, walks along the street, his figure lost in the shadows cast by the buildings. He appears insignificant in the midst of these colossal structures. Hopper wanted this picture to give the viewer a sense of the vast space of the city: "The very long horizontal shape of this picture," he wrote, "is an effort to give a sensation of great lateral extent" (Goodrich 69).

Hopper tried to reveal a deeper character of urban America: its rootlessness, lack of community, and loneliness. These elements represented a theme in his art. The city's lack of community spirit and the rootlessness of its people is represented in the painting *Nighthawks*. Hopper painted three people sitting at the counter of an all-night diner. The viewer is placed outside the diner, in the dark empty streets, observing people through a glass window. "Many of Hopper's city interiors are seen through windows, from the viewpoint of a spectator looking in at the unconscious actors . . . a life separate and silent, yet crystal clear" (Goodrich 70). *Nighthawks* emphasizes the disconnectedness that exists among people in a city. Although the people in the diner share an intimate environment, they are probably strangers, for they sit looking straight ahead without any signs of communication between them. *Nighthawks* presents a great contrast to Grant Wood's *Dinner for Threshers*. In Wood's painting the viewer sees a warm, personal environment in which people gather together to share food and conversation with one another. The sense of community is as strong in this picture as the sense of separateness is in *Nighthawks*. These two paintings, then, represent not merely differing views of American society, but rather, opposing views.

Along with the theme of lack of community, Hopper also explored the theme of rootlessness in his paintings. In his work *Rooms for Tourists*, for example, Hopper depicted a boarding house, a place where transients could come and go. This house with its advertisement for a room for rent represented a reality about urban life. Many of the people who came to the city were just "passing through" or were people who could not afford to own the kind of homes pictured in Grant Wood's *Stone City*. A room or a tiny apartment was the only "home" the city boarder would ever know.

Finally, loneliness constituted still another major theme in Hopper's art (Hughes 56). In his painting *Automat*, a solitary woman sits at a table. She seems to have no roots, no real home, as she sits drinking a cup of coffee in a strange restaurant. The only light is the artificial light which hangs above her. Hopper almost seems to be implying that this world in which she exists was, in fact, an artificial world, man-made and unnatural. The woman herself has no identity; shadows from her hat conceal her face, yet the viewer can ascertain that she is part of the cheapness of urban society. Critic Robert Hobbs has commented that "in his painting of a lonely female, Hopper emphasizes the new 1920s look of short skirts and silk stockings . . . the girl's legs form the brightest spots on the canvas and the viewer is drawn into the uncomfortable position of staring" (72). Hopper's *Automat*, then, presents a great contrast to Wood's *American Gothic* in which the upright Puritanical values of rural America are proclaimed.

Thus, Edward Hopper's works portrayed not only the realities of urban society in the 1920s and 1930s, but also the changes which had taken place in American life during this period. Unlike Grant Wood, Hopper did not turn away from the "uglier," unpleasant sides of American society. According to one critic, "Hopper's work is most decidedly founded, not on art, but on life . . ." (Goodrich 64).

Through their art Grant Wood and Edward Hopper have presented us with two contrasting views of America in the 1920s and 1930s. Grant Wood's vision of American society as based on simple, solid rural values has survived mainly as a dream. Edward Hopper's vision of American society has, in fact, become a reality. Considered together, Wood and Hopper represent both ends of the spectrum of the Great Depression era.

This contrast summarizes the artists' differences.

Why is this conclusion effective?

Works Cited

Blum, John M. *The National Experience: A History of the United States*. New York: Harcourt, 1985.

Corn, Wanda. *Grant Wood: The Regionalist Vision*. New Haven: Yale UP, 1983.

Dennis, James M. *Grant Wood*. Columbia: U of Missouri P, 1986.

Goodrich, Lloyd. *Edward Hopper*. New York: Abrams, 1976.

Haven, Janet. *Going Back to Iowa: The World of Grant Wood*. U of Virginia American Studies Program. 7 Nov. 1999 <http://www.lib.virginia.edu/etd/theses/ArtsSci/English/1998/Haven/home.html>.

Hobbs, Robert. *Edward Hopper*. New York: Abrams, 1987.

Hofstadter, Richard. *The Age of Reform*. New York: Knopf, 1955.

Hughes, Robert. "Under the Crack of Reality." *Time* 17 July 1995: 54–56.

Leuchtenburg, William E. *The Perils of Prosperity: 1914–1932*. Chicago: U of Chicago P, 1958.

McCoubrey, John W., ed. *Modern American Painting*. New York: Time-Life, 1970.

Weisberger, Bernard A., ed. *The Family Encyclopedia of American History*. New York: Reader's Digest, 1975.

"Wood, Grant." *Britannica Online*. Vers. 99.1. 1994–1999. Encyclopaedia Britannica. 7 Nov. 1999 <http://www.members.eb.com/bol/topic?eu=79456&sctn=1&pm=1>.

Use either italic type or underlining for book, magazine, or newspaper titles or for works of art. Make sure that you are consistent in your use of underscoring and italics.

Abbreviate publishers' names (*University Press* becomes *UP*) or shorten them by omitting unnecessary words (*McGraw-Hill, Inc.* becomes simply *McGraw*).

Include the page range for the entire article found in a newspaper, magazine, or anthology; do not include the page range for books.

Research Paper Writing

Reflecting on the Unit

Summarize what you have learned in this unit by answering the following questions.

1 What are some of the ways you can investigate and limit your research topic?

2 What is the function of a thesis statement?

3 In organizing your research notes, what different methods of outlining can be used?

4 What is the purpose of citing sources in the body of a research paper?

5 What steps should you follow in revising a research paper?

Adding to Your Portfolio

Look over the research paper you have worked on during this unit, and put it into your portfolio. Your research paper should do the following:

- demonstrate your ability to locate and correctly use library and Internet resources
- employ a method of organization best suited to your topic
- contain a succinct thesis statement
- support assertions with information from a variety of sources
- employ proper documentation of sources
- assemble elements in a logical order

REFLECT ON YOUR PROCESS Attach a note to your research paper explaining what you learned from writing it.

SET GOALS How can you improve your research paper writing skills? What skill will you focus on the next time you write?

Writing Across the Curriculum

MAKE A SCIENCE CONNECTION Read an article in a newspaper, magazine, or newsweekly about a scientific subject, discovery, or break-through. Write a one-page report to evaluate the article. Take notes and select quotations to amplify examples or ideas. Develop an outline of your report and include a thesis statement that reveals your position. When you write the report, demonstrate that you have separated fact from opinion.

"This the easy place. This the easy going."

—Eudora Welty, "A Worn Path"

UNIT 8
Sentence Combining

Style Through Sentence Combining

You know the feeling. Hunched over your rough draft, you stare at sentences that look like snarled spaghetti. Should you start over? How will you ever untangle the mess? Is there no hope?

Take heart. One approach that works is sentence combining. By using revising skills such as adding, deleting, and rearranging ideas, you can transform sentences into more readable structures. Research on sentence combining indicates that such practice transfers to your real writing and improves its overall quality.

If you need help in smoothing out your sentences—improving their readability, variety, and style—here's an approach that deserves your attention.

Unlock Your Style

Sentence combining is a research-tested writing strategy that enables students to explore options, make choices, and develop style. This process of combining short sentences into more complex ones is the focus of this unit. Your goal, however, is not to make long sentences, but to make good ones. Sometimes you will find that longer, more complex sentences enable you to express your ideas with precision and clarity. At other times, shorter sentences are more effective.

The point is that sentence combining helps you understand your stylistic options. Instead of being locked into one type of sentence and "playing it safe" with a short, choppy style that reads like a first-grade reader, you can make choices as a writer. Practice in combining unlocks your style by making you aware of writing choices.

Learn the Drill

In sentence combining, you express the same information in different ways by using four combining strategies: (1) deleting repeated words; (2) using connecting words; (3) rearranging words; and (4) changing the form of words. Consider this cluster of short, basic sentences to see how they might be combined differently.

Sentence combining is a writing strategy.
The strategy has been tested by research.
It enables students to explore options.
It enables students to make choices.
It enables students to develop style.

As you scan these sentences, your brain goes to work, drawing upon your built-in knowledge of language. You can use the four combining strategies to express these ideas in fewer words. For example, take a look at one way of combining illustrated below:

Example

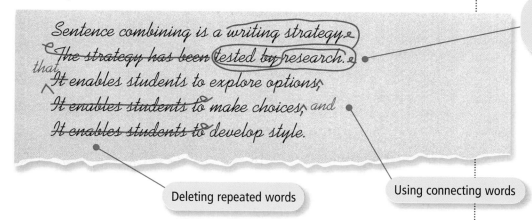

Rearranging words and changing the form of words

Deleting repeated words

Using connecting words

Notice how editing produces the sentence that starts the section headed "Unlock Your Style" on the previous page. But there are other ways to combine these sentences. Read the ones below aloud, listening to differences in style:

1. Sentence combining is a writing strategy that has been tested by research; as options are explored and choices are made, students develop style.

2. Sentence combining, a writing strategy that has been tested by research, enables students to develop style by exploring options and making choices.

3. Enabling students to explore options, make choices, and develop style, sentence combining is a strategy for writing tested by research.

All of these sentences communicate basically the same message, but each one has a different emphasis. Which is "best"? The answer to that question depends on the *context,* your *purposes* as a writer, and your sense of *audience.* Put simply, your choice of the "best" sentence depends on what sounds right for you.

Follow the Hints

Sentence combining is easy and fun. Here are some basic suggestions that have worked for other high school students—suggestions you might try as you explore style.

1. **Whisper sentences to yourself.** As you work with clusters of sentences, try saying them aloud. This process is faster than writing, and it helps you decide on a "best sentence" to write down.

2. **Work with a partner.** By trying out sentences on a partner—and hearing your partner's ideas—you often discover new, interesting ways to solve specific challenges. Feel free to borrow ideas.

3. **Use context when choosing sentences.** Each paragraph has an emerging context—the sentences you have already combined. Reading this context aloud helps you decide on the best sentence option.

4. **Compare your sentences with those of other students.** Seeing how others have solved combining tasks broadens your awareness of sentence options. Keep asking yourself, "Which do I prefer?"

5. **Look for stylistic patterns in your writing.** Calculate the average number of words per sentence; study your sentence openers; listen to rhythms in your style. Try new patterns to stretch yourself.

6. **Take risks.** Learning to make clear, effective sentences also means taking risks and making mistakes. It actually makes *sense* to accept mistakes—even *welcome* them—as you combine sentences. After all, mistakes provide feedback for your language learning. As you learn from them, you develop an expressive style, a voice of personal authority. You come to know yourself as a writer.

As you can see, sentence combining involves the skills of talking to yourself, making judgments, and holding what you say in your short-term memory so that you can transcribe it. These are oral skills as much as they are writing skills. Good writers trust their "inner voices."

Workshop on Style

In this unit you will find two types of sentence-combining exercises. The first type consists of clusters of short sentences that you will combine into longer ones. The second type draws from literature selections in this book.

The first type of combining gives you practice in creating descriptive, narrative, expository, and persuasive paragraphs. You can combine each cluster of short sentences into one single sentence, or you can leave a cluster partially combined—or combine two or more clusters together. The idea, always, is to take risks and create the best sentences you can, writing them in your journal or as your teacher directs.

Exercises on facing pages deal with the same topic or situation. Think of these exercises as "bookends" for the writing you will do. After you have combined sentences into paragraphs, your task is to connect the paragraphs into a longer essay or story. Doing so will help you transfer sentence-combining skills to your own writing.

The second type of exercise, drawn from literary passages, invites you to test your skills against those of a professional writer. As you do these unclustered exercises, you will need to figure out the ideas that are logically connected. After you have completed the sentence-combining exercises, you can check your version against the original in the literature models in this text.

By studying the similarities and differences in the two passages, you will learn a great deal about your own style. Sometimes you will prefer the professional writer's sentences. Why, specifically, are they "better" than yours? Sometimes, however, you will prefer your own style. Can you build on this writing skill, trying it out in your own stories and essays? Either way, you will learn how to write.

Explore Your Own Style

Sentence-combining practice helps when you revise your real writing. Why? Because you know that sentences are flexible instruments of thought, not rigid structures cast in concrete. The simple fact that you feel confident in moving sentence parts around increases your control of the writing process.

To acquire this sense of self-confidence—one based on your real competence in combining and revising sentences—you can try strategies like those shown below.

1. **Vary the length of your sentences.** Work for a rhythmic, interesting balance of long and short sentences, remembering that brevity often has dramatic force.

2. **Vary the structure of your sentences.** By using introductory clauses on occasion—and by sometimes tucking information in the middle of a sentence—you can create stylistic variety.

3. **Use parallelism for emphasis.** Experiment with repeated items in a series—words, phrases, and clauses—to understand how structural patterns work and how you can use them to advantage.

4. **Use interruption for emphasis.** Colons, semicolons, dashes, commas, parentheses—all of these are useful tools in your stylistic tool kit; knowing how to use them well matters.

5. **Use unusual patterns for emphasis.** That you might sometimes reverse normal sentence patterns may never have occurred to you, but such a strategy can work—if you know how.

Of course, the whole point of sentence-combining practice is to improve your revising and editing skills. Therefore, when it comes time to rework a draft, it's important to apply what you have learned about combining and revising.

The same holds true when you are responding to the writing of your peers. If you spot a passage that can be improved with stylistic tinkering, simply write SC (for sentence combining) in the margin. This will provide a cue to apply some of the skills learned in this unit.

8.1 Description

Sandwich Shop

Directions   Combine each cluster of numbered items into one or more sentences. Combine clusters if you wish.

1.1 The sun had faded in the west.
1.2 The air still seemed humid.
1.3 It still seemed thick with heat.
1.4 This was inside the sandwich shop.

2.1 A half-dozen tables jammed the room.
2.2 They had checkered tablecloths.
2.3 They had chrome napkin holders.

3.1 Two boys lounged in a corner booth.
3.2 One ran fingers through his hair.
3.3 His hair was oily.
3.4 The other slouched against red vinyl.
3.5 He sipped a king-size cola.

4.1 A girl stood at the jukebox.
4.2 She chewed pink bubble gum.
4.3 She combed her hair in the reflection.
4.4 Her hair was sun-bleached.
4.5 The reflection was neon.

5.1 Behind a counter were shelves.
5.2 The shelves were cluttered.
5.3 The shelves displayed clever signs.
5.4 The shelves displayed boxes of candy.
5.5 The boxes were dusty.

6.1 The counter itself was glossy white.
6.2 It was worn thin by many elbows.
6.3 It was worn thin by scrubbings.
6.4 The scrubbings were countless.

7.1 A dozen stools stood like sentries.
7.2 The sentries were silent.
7.3 The sentries awaited customers like me.
7.4 The customers might be hungry.

Invitation   How do you handle yourself in such a situation? To link "Sandwich Shop" to "Meatball Sandwich," describe the scene that happens next.

Revising Tip

To create parallel absolutes in cluster 3, change *ran* to *running* and *slouched* to *slouching*.

Exercise B   Meatball Sandwich

Directions   Combine each cluster of numbered items into one or more sentences. Combine clusters if you wish.

1.1   The sandwich arrived in a basket.
1.2   The sandwich was split in half.
1.3   The basket was oval-shaped.
1.4   It was lined with wax paper.
1.5   The wax paper was yellow.

2.1   Meatballs filled a loaf of French bread.
2.2   The meatballs were huge.
2.3   The meatballs were juicy.
2.4   The loaf was freshly baked.

3.1   It was smothered in tomato sauce.
3.2   It was sprinkled with grated cheese.
3.3   It smelled of onions.
3.4   It smelled of garlic.
3.5   It smelled of Italian spices.
3.6   The spices were fragrant.

4.1   It was a culinary triumph.
4.2   It was a work of art.
4.3   The work engaged all the senses.

5.1   I eyed it with anticipation.
5.2   My anticipation was mouthwatering.
5.3   I then made my move.
5.4   My move was swift.
5.5   It was unhesitating.

6.1   The tomato sauce was rich.
6.2   It was deliciously thick.
6.3   It was pungent with Old World flavor.

7.1   Bread complemented the meatballs.
7.2   The bread was crusty.
7.3   It was still warm from the oven.
7.4   The meatballs were succulent.

> ### Revising Tip
>
> Try opening cluster 3 with participial phrases beginning with *smothered* and *sprinkled;* try using a pair of dashes for emphasis in cluster 7.

Invitation   Describe what you notice as you eat the sandwich. Share your text—"Sandwich Shop" plus "Meatball Sandwich"—with a writing partner.

Exercise C   Country Drive

Directions   Combine each cluster of numbered items into one or more sentences. Combine clusters if you wish.

1.1 Cheryl felt nervous.
1.2 She drove into a lane.
1.3 The lane was asphalt.
1.4 The lane was narrow.
1.5 It led to her employer's estate.

2.1 Her headlights swept past lilacs.
2.2 Her headlights swept past chestnuts.
2.3 Her headlights swept past white fences.
2.4 These were below the hilltop house.

3.1 On both sides were acres of fields.
3.2 The fields were grassy.
3.3 Arabian horses ran safe there.
3.4 Arabian horses ran free there.
3.5 The horses were prize-winning.

4.1 The night air was cool along the ridge.
4.2 The night air was soft along the ridge.
4.3 A summer moon blanched the landscape.
4.4 The landscape was rolling.

5.1 The house held a view of the valley below.
5.2 The house was Georgian-style.
5.3 The view was commanding.
5.4 Lights carpeted the darkness.
5.5 The darkness was velvety.

6.1 Luxury sedans lined the driveway.
6.2 Cheryl parked her car there.
6.3 Her car was well used.
6.4 It was built for economy.

7.1 She had never seen such a house.
7.2 She tried to imagine its interior.
7.3 She tried to imagine what to expect.

> **Editing Tip**
>
> Cluster 3 provides an opportunity to use *where* as a connector. Look for other opportunities elsewhere in this exercise.

Invitation   Using a spatial pattern of organization, describe what Cheryl first sees inside. Link this description to "Chief Executive."

Exercise D   Chief Executive

Directions   Combine each cluster of numbered items into one or more sentences. Combine clusters if you wish.

1.1   French doors opened into a dining room.
1.2   The dining room was massive.
1.3   A chandelier hung from the ceiling.
1.4   The chandelier was glittering.

2.1   There stood the company's leader.
2.2   She looked poised.
2.3   She looked regal.

3.1   She was a woman.
3.2   The woman was tall.
3.3   The woman was gaunt.
3.4   She shimmered in a sequin dress.
3.5   The sequins were black.

4.1   One hand was extended in greeting.
4.2   Her mouth was frozen into a smile.
4.3   The smile was waxy.
4.4   She welcomed selected employees.
4.5   Their work was outstanding.

5.1   Her hair was pulled into a knot.
5.2   The knot was tight.
5.3   The knot was smooth.
5.4   This emphasized her diamond earrings.
5.5   The diamonds were emerald-cut.

6.1   Behind her was a table spread with silverware.
6.2   Behind her was a table spread with china.
6.3   Behind her was a table spread with crystal.
6.4   The table was elegant.
6.5   The crystal was imported.

7.1   Everything about her suggested wealth.
7.2   Everything about her suggested power.
7.3   Everything about her suggested privilege.

Invitation   How does Cheryl react now? Is she speechless? Does she use a table napkin to blow her nose? Share the text you create with a writing partner.

> ### Revising Tip
>
> To create parallel modifying phrases in cluster 4, try using *with* as a sentence opener and deleting *was* in sentences 4.1 and 4.2.

8.2 Narration

Con Man

Directions   Combine each cluster of numbered items into one or more sentences. Combine clusters if you wish.

1.1 Dexter carried a backpack.
1.2 It was jammed with books.
1.3 Dexter shuffled into an empty classroom.
1.4 His teacher was correcting papers there.

2.1 She glanced up from her work.
2.2 She smiled at him.
2.3 He made his hesitant approach.
2.4 His forehead was knitted with worry.

3.1 He hunched his shoulders.
3.2 He limped toward her.
3.3 He looked as submissive as possible.
3.4 He looked as deferential as possible.

4.1 She invited him to be seated.
4.2 He folded his hands meekly.
4.3 He studied his running shoes.
4.4 His shoes had untied laces.

5.1 Then he collapsed with a sigh.
5.2 His sigh was audible.
5.3 He bit his lip.
5.4 He watched her conclude a comment.
5.5 He had interrupted the comment.

6.1 His request was well rehearsed.
6.2 It was for a deadline extension.
6.3 He wondered how she would respond.

7.1 She looked up from her work.
7.2 She put down her pen.
7.3 He took a deep breath.
7.4 He returned her gaze.
7.5 He summoned up persuasive skills.
7.6 The skills were from past experience.

Invitation   Narrate the conversation between Dexter and his teacher. Use this dialogue to link "Con Man" to "Act Two."

Revising Tip

To make an absolute in cluster 2, delete *was* in sentence 2.4. Try a participle (*hunching, limping,* or *looking*) in cluster 3.

Directions   Combine each cluster of numbered items into one or more sentences. Combine clusters if you wish.

1.1 Dexter was out of the classroom.
1.2 Dexter sprinted for his locker.
1.3 He would dump his backpack there.
1.4 His backpack was unwanted.

2.1 It thumped his ribs.
2.2 It jostled his ribs.
2.3 He grinned smugly.
2.4 He congratulated himself.

3.1 He slid around one corner.
3.2 He then loped past a teacher.
3.3 The teacher was eagle-eyed.
3.4 The teacher was on hall patrol.

4.1 The bus still stood at the curb.
4.2 It awaited any stragglers.
4.3 Dexter was a straggler.
4.4 Dexter still hoped to make it.

5.1 He slouched against his locker.
5.2 He spun the combination too far.
5.3 He missed the right numbers.

6.1 He muttered under his breath.
6.2 He eyed the dial more carefully.
6.3 He tried once again.

7.1 His friends sauntered by.
7.2 They were urging him to hurry up.
7.3 He jerked the locker open.
7.4 He grabbed a tennis racket.
7.5 He shoved his backpack inside.

8.1 It was then he saw his teacher.
8.2 She was striding down the hall.
8.3 Her hand was lifted to stop him.

Invitation   How does Dexter handle himself? Narrate an effective ending for "Con Man" and "Act Two." Then share your text with a writing partner.

> ### Revising Tip
>
> In clusters 5 and 6, try using participles to vary sentence rhythms. In sentence 8.3 delete *was* to create an absolute.

Exercise C   **Prom Night**

Directions   Combine each cluster of numbered items into one or more sentences. Combine clusters if you wish.

1.1 Kim hobbled from the floor.
1.2 Her eyes were filled with tears.
1.3 Her mouth was clenched tight.

2.1 Her date found her a chair.
2.2 She collapsed.
2.3 She pulled off her shoe.
2.4 Her shoe was scuffed.
2.5 She inspected the damage.

3.1 A bruise had already formed.
3.2 The bruise was purple.
3.3 The bruise was aching.
3.4 It was just above her toes.

4.1 She shook her head.
4.2 She muttered under her breath.
4.3 She knew her prom night was over.

5.1 Then she put ice on the bruise.
5.2 She watched a football player.
5.3 The football player was manic.
5.4 He was still stomping.
5.5 He was still lunging about.
5.6 He was on the dance floor.

6.1 The dancer clapped his hands.
6.2 He cleared a wide swath.
6.3 No one ventured there.
6.4 It was too dangerous to do so.

7.1 Kim rubbed her foot.
7.2 Her foot was injured.
7.3 Kim felt her anger grow stronger.
7.4 The brute had not even apologized.
7.5 The brute was clumsy.

> **Editing Tip**
>
> By opening with *hobbling* in cluster 1, you create a humorous writing error, a *dangling participle*.

Invitation   What does Kim think about on the sidelines? Use her thoughts (or her dialogue with her date) as a link to the "Chaperones" exercise.

Exercise D   Chaperones

Directions   Combine each cluster of numbered items into one or more sentences. Combine clusters if you wish.

1.1   The chaperones shuffled past Kim.
1.2   They shuffled onto the dance floor.
1.3   They were middle-aged.
1.4   The dance floor was crowded.

2.1   The man made a pivot.
2.2   His pivot was sudden.
2.3   The woman followed him.
2.4   Her shoulders bounced in tempo.
2.5   The bounce was light.

3.1   They cocked their heads back.
3.2   They clicked their fingers.
3.3   They snaked through the crowd.

4.1   The man's face was relaxed.
4.2   The man's face was smiling.
4.3   His forehead glistened with sweat.
4.4   His forehead was broad.

5.1   The woman spun beneath his hand.
5.2   The woman followed his lead.
5.3   She then began to improvise.
5.4   She tried a step of her own.
5.5   The step was complicated.
5.6   This caused a small crowd to gather.

6.1   The pair danced in a controlled way.
6.2   They enjoyed each other's company.
6.3   They welcomed each other's steps.

7.1   Off to one side was the football player.
7.2   He had just backed into another girl.
7.3   He crushed her white shoe with his heel.
7.4   Her shoe was slender.
7.5   His heel was wide.

> **Revising Tip**
>
> To create absolutes in clusters 2 and 4, change *bounced* to *bouncing* and *glistened* to *glistening*.

    Invitation   What does Kim do next? Narrate an effective conclusion for "Prom Night" and "Chaperones." Then share it with a writing partner.

Exercise A   **How Animals Navigate**

Directions   Combine each cluster of numbered items into one or more sentences. Combine clusters if you wish.

1.1 Many creatures have senses.
1.2 The creatures migrate.
1.3 The creatures forage for survival.
1.4 The senses are astonishingly acute.

2.1 A salmon uses its sense of smell.
2.2 A salmon migrates thousands of miles.
2.3 A salmon returns to its home to spawn.
2.4 A salmon returns to its home to die.

3.1 Sharks detect electrical fields.
3.2 The electrical fields are faint.
3.3 The fields are generated by prey.
3.4 Sharks use this information to attack.

4.1 A homing pigeon sees ultraviolet light.
4.2 A homing pigeon hears wind sounds.
4.3 The wind sounds have low frequencies.
4.4 The sounds are thousands of miles away.

5.1 Honeybees sense subtle changes.
5.2 Bobolinks sense subtle changes.
5.3 The changes are in the earth's magnetic field.
5.4 They use this information to navigate.

6.1 A black desert ant has a unique compass.
6.2 Each of its eyes has eighty lenses.
6.3 Each lens receives polarized light.
6.4 The light is from different points in the sky.

7.1 Savannah sparrows navigate.
7.2 The sparrows are night flyers.
7.3 They use the stars to navigate.
7.4 They may also use their sense of smell.

Invitation   Is intelligence a "sense" that human beings have developed? If so, what purpose might this sense serve? Write a follow-up paragraph.

> **Editing Tip**
>
> In cluster 6 first try a colon followed by a complete sentence. Then try a dash followed by an *each of which* construction.

Directions   Combine each cluster of numbered items into one or more sentences. Combine clusters if you wish.

1.1   Many animals have remarkable sensory equipment.
1.2   Others apparently have genetic compasses.
1.3   The compasses provide built-in direction.

2.1   One such animal is the monarch butterfly.
2.2   They migrate by the millions from Mexico.
2.3   They spend the winter there.

3.1   Monarchs look like an orange cloud.
3.2   Monarchs flutter northward each spring.
3.3   The journey to Canada is a long one.

4.1   Along the way the monarchs mate.
4.2   Their eggs are laid atop milkweed.
4.3   Along the way the monarchs die.

5.1   Their offspring then take up the journey.
5.2   Their offspring repeat the same life cycle.

6.1   Several generations of monarchs are born.
6.2   Several generations of monarchs breed.
6.3   Several generations of monarchs die.
6.4   A final generation reaches Canada.

7.1   Autumn winds begin to blow.
7.2   The monarchs ingest flower nectar.
7.3   The monarchs get ready to head south.

8.1   The old monarchs are long gone.
8.2   The new monarchs "know" where home is.

9.1   They fly all the way back to Mexico.
9.2   They roost in the trees of their ancestors.

> **Revising Tip**
>
> In cluster 6 try using *after* and *before* as connecting words. Which is preferable if you use *after* in cluster 7?

Invitation   Are human beings "programmed" for language just as monarchs are "programmed" for flight? Consider this idea in a follow-up paragraph.

Directions   Combine each cluster of numbered items into one or more sentences. Combine clusters if you wish.

1.1 English colonists settled North America.
1.2 This was early in the seventeenth century.
1.3 They encountered a great wilderness.
1.4 It was inhabited by many Native American groups.

2.1 The Native American languages contained sounds.
2.2 The settlers had never heard them before.
2.3 They therefore had trouble reproducing them.
2.4 They therefore had trouble spelling them.

3.1 John Smith listened to the Algonquian Indians.
3.2 He tried to capture their word for an animal.
3.3 The animal was small and furry.
3.4 He recorded the sounds as *raughroughcum*.
3.5 He later shortened it to *rarowcun*.

4.1 In 1672 the word was finally printed as *raccoon*.
4.2 This was sixty-five years after Smith's first effort.
4.3 This was a far cry from the native original.

5.1 A similar process occurred for many other names.
5.2 The names included *skunk* (from *segankw*).
5.3 The names included *woodchuck* (from *otchock*).
5.4 The names included *moose* (from *moosu*).

6.1 Others native terms were absorbed intact.
6.2 The terms included *hominy*.
6.3 The terms included *mackinaw*.
6.4 The terms included *moccasin*.
6.5 The terms included *tepee*.
6.6 The terms included *powwow*.

7.1 The colonists learned hundreds of native words.
7.2 They used them to name places and things in their new land.
7.3 They used them to enrich their language.

Invitation   Many of America's landmarks—thousands of places across the land—bear Native American names. How does this use of Native American words reflect upon the character of America in general? Write a paragraph explaining your opinion, and connect it to "Native American Words."

Revising Tip

In cluster 3 try opening with the participle *listening* for sentence variety. In cluster 4 try making an appositive.

Exercise D   Spanish Words

Directions   Combine each cluster of numbered items into one or more sentences. Combine clusters if you wish.

1.1 Many European languages have enriched English.
1.2 Spanish contributed many words.
1.3 This was during the colonization of America.

2.1 Many Americans pushed westward.
2.2 This was after the Mexican War.
2.3 This was during the California gold rush.
2.4 They heard Spanish words of many kinds.
2.5 They adopted them into their vocabularies.

3.1 Among these words were topographical terms.
3.2 The terms included *canyon*.
3.3 The terms included *mesa*.
3.4 The terms included *sierra*.

4.1 They adopted building terms like *adobe*.
4.2 They adopted building terms like *patio*.
4.3 They adopted building terms like *plaza*.
4.4 They also adopted mining words like *bonanza*.
4.5 They also adopted mining words like *placer*.
4.6 They also adopted mining words like *El Dorado*.

5.1 Dozens of ranching words were appropriated.
5.2 These included words like *alfalfa*.
5.3 These included words like *corral*.
5.4 These included words like *bronco*.
5.5 These included words like *stampede*.
5.6 This is not to mention the word *ranch* itself.

6.1 Spanish also gave us the word *cockroach*.
6.2 It is derived from *cucaracha*.
6.3 Spanish also gave us the word *tornado*.
6.4 It is derived from *tronado*.

7.1 Even *California* is a Spanish name.
7.2 It literally means "hot oven."

Invitation   Many other Spanish words are a part of modern American English. Write a paragraph about the ones that spring immediately to mind.

> **Revising Tip**
>
> In cluster 5 put the list of specific examples in the middle of the base sentence, following *words*. Use dashes for emphasis.

8.4 Persuasion

Exercise A   Cheeseburger

Directions   Combine each cluster of numbered items into one or more sentences. Combine clusters if you wish.

1.1 On the grill a hamburger sizzles.
1.2 The hamburger is plump and rare.
1.3 It is in the fast-food tradition.
1.4 The tradition is American.

2.1 The meat bastes in a puddle.
2.2 The puddle is sputtering.
2.3 The puddle sends up hot showers.
2.4 The showers are greasy.

3.1 Its patty is covered by a bun.
3.2 The patty is hefty.
3.3 The bun traps meat juices.
3.4 The bun traps water vapor.

4.1 A slab of cheese assures added fat.
4.2 It assures added cholesterol.
4.3 The cheese melts.

5.1 The meat spatters grease.
5.2 The bun is spread with mayonnaise.
5.3 Mayonnaise is a crowning touch.
5.4 It is rich in egg yolks.
5.5 It is rich in oils.

6.1 A spatula cradles the cheeseburger.
6.2 The spatula is dripping.
6.3 It positions the cheeseburger atop condiments.
6.4 The sandwich is wrapped in foil.
6.5 This is to seal in the juices.
6.6 The flavor is succulent.

7.1 It is then packaged with french fries.
7.2 They have been soaked in more fat.
7.3 This is to provide a dining experience.
7.4 The experience is truly unforgettable.

Invitation   To emphasize the unhealthy nature of the cheeseburger meal, write a paragraph contrasting it with a healthy, low-fat meal consisting of the basic food groups.

Revising Tip

In cluster 1 try a pair of adjectives after *hamburger;* in cluster 5 try a dash—plus an appositive that describes *mayonnaise.*

Sentence Combining

Exercise B   Fat City

Directions   Combine each cluster of numbered items into one or more sentences. Combine clusters if you wish.

1.1   Fast foods are a major source of fat.
1.2   These include hamburgers.
1.3   These include french fries.
1.4   These include milkshakes.
1.5   The fat is in the American diet.

2.1   Health experts suggest twenty grams of fat.
2.2   This would be a daily average.
2.3   The daily average would be reasonable.
2.4   Fewer grams of fat should be a goal.

3.1   Many hamburgers have thirty grams of fat.
3.2   The hamburgers are commercially prepared.
3.3   Some contain more than thirty-five grams.

4.1   Now add a slice of cheese.
4.2   It has eight grams of fat.
4.3   Now add an order of fries.
4.4   It has eleven grams of fat.
4.5   Now add a chocolate shake.
4.6   It has nine grams of fat.

5.1   The total is hardly good nutrition.
5.2   The total approaches sixty grams of fat.
5.3   This is for a single meal.
5.4   It triples the suggested daily quota.

6.1   Such meals are pitched in TV commercials.
6.2   The meals are fat-saturated.
6.3   The commercials are seductive.
6.4   Many of us see them 5,000 times per year.

7.1   Our culture is hooked on a diet.
7.2   The diet emphasizes fast foods.
7.3   Kids today are more overweight than kids twenty years ago.
7.4   Our nation has a high rate of heart disease.

Editing Tip

In cluster 3 try *and* or a semicolon (;) to join sentences 3.1 and 3.3. In cluster 7 try connectors like *because, hence, therefore.*

Invitation   Write a concluding paragraph that proposes a solution to the "Fat City" problem. Then share your text with a writing partner.

Directions Combine each cluster of numbered items into one or more sentences. Combine clusters if you wish.

1.1 December 26 is a peculiar occasion.
1.2 It is the day after Christmas.
1.3 Some Americans go slightly berserk then.

2.1 Parking lots become a snarl.
2.2 Intersections become a snarl.
2.3 The snarl is confused.
2.4 Cars head for shopping malls.
2.5 The malls are jammed with people.

3.1 Shoppers clog the store aisles.
3.2 The shoppers are short-tempered.
3.3 They are trying to return gifts.
3.4 They are trying to find bargains.
3.5 The bargains are discounted.

4.1 Most have received gifts.
4.2 The gifts were useless.
4.3 The gifts were ill-fitting.
4.4 They hope to redeem these for credit.

5.1 Such gifts have little or no meaning.
5.2 They were often purchased under duress.
5.3 The purchase was to fulfill obligations.
5.4 The obligations are social.

6.1 Holidays have been commercialized.
6.2 Much junk is dutifully given.
6.3 Much junk is politely accepted.
6.4 Much junk is exchanged with relief.

7.1 What underlies these rituals is guilt.
7.2 The rituals are strange.
7.3 The rituals are gift giving.
7.4 The guilt is pervasive.
7.5 The guilt is supported by advertising.

Invitation Describe a personal experience with post-holiday shopping that you can use to introduce "Holiday Spirit" and "Shopping Spree."

Revising Tip

In clusters 5 and 6 try causal connectors—*because, since, therefore, consequently,* and *so.* Make sure to check your punctuation.

Directions   Combine each cluster of numbered items into one or more sentences. Combine clusters if you wish.

1.1 Merchants look forward to December 26.
1.2 It is always a day for record sales.
1.3 It is a chance to reduce inventories.
1.4 The inventories are unwanted.

2.1 Typically they discount merchandise.
2.2 They reinforce the desire to spend.
2.3 The reinforcement is through advertising.
2.4 The advertising is relentless.

3.1 A "bandwagon effect" is created.
3.2 Shoppers convene for a single purpose.
3.3 The purpose is to buy for themselves.
3.4 The buying is not for someone else.

4.1 The buying spree intensifies.
4.2 Group behavior supports spending.
4.3 Group behavior encourages spending.
4.4 The spending is mindless.

5.1 Many shoppers are sucked into this vortex.
5.2 The shoppers are undisciplined.
5.3 The vortex is consuming.
5.4 They are like moths.
5.5 The moths are drawn to a candle flame.

6.1 They are no longer buying for others.
6.2 The buying is not out of guilt.
6.3 They are instead spending on themselves.
6.4 The spending is unashamed.

7.1 December 26 is finally over.
7.2 Credit cards are at their limit.
7.3 The shoppers head for home.
7.4 They feel exhausted.
7.5 They feel strangely depressed.

Editing Tip

Try combining groups 3 and 6 into a single sentence.

Invitation   Write a concluding paragraph for "Holiday Spirit" and "Shopping Spree." Then share your text with a writing partner.

Exercise A

Directions   Scan the sentences below. Decide which of the numbered sentences belong together, and combine them in your own way. Then compare your sentences with the originals, from Lorene Cary's *Black Ice*, on pages 40–43.

1. We were in the gymnasium.
2. We heard the commotion in the locker rooms.
3. Fumiko ran to the wall behind the basket.
4. A few balls lay there.
5. She picked one.
6. She dribbled it.
7. She then passed it to me.
8. She ran onto the court.
9. I passed it back to her.
10. She shot the ball.
11. It headed toward the basket.
12. It made a low arc.
13. It dropped through the hoop.
14. She ran hard to retrieve her own rebound.

There could have been four girls after her, as hard as she ran.

15. She snatched the ball out of the air.
16. She then leapt to make a lay-up.
17. It hit the backboard softly.
18. It fell through the hoop.
19. Then she passed me the ball.
20. I hesitated.
21. I passed it back.
22. She thrust it at me.
23. I caught the pass.
24. It was chest-high.
25. She threw it as perfectly as a diagram.
26. She threw it harder than my old gym teacher.
27. She threw it with no effort I could see.
28. I did not want to play.
29. I wanted to watch.
30. She seemed intent on teaching me.

Directions   Scan the sentences below. Decide which of the numbered sentences belong together, and combine them in your own way. Then compare your sentences with the originals, from Annie Dillard's *An American Childhood*, on pages 104–108.

She [Mother] didn't like the taste of stamps so she didn't lick stamps; she licked the corner of the envelope instead.

1. She glued sandpaper to the sides of kitchen drawers.
2. She glued sandpaper under cabinets.
3. She always had a handy place to strike a match.
4. She designed doubly wide kitchen counters.
5. She designed elevated bathroom sinks.
6. She hounded workmen to build them against all norms.
7. She wanted to splint a finger.
8. She stuck it in a lightweight cigar tube.
9. She drew plans for a toothbrush for babies.
10. The toothbrush went over the finger.
11. She drew plans for an oven rack.
12. The rack slid up and down.
13. She drew plans for Lendalarm.
14. Lendalarm was a beeper.
15. You attached it to books (or tools).
16. The books (or tools) were loaned to friends.
17. The beeper sounded after ten days.
18. Only the rightful owner could silence it.

She repeatedly reminded us of P. T. Barnum's dictum: You could sell anything to anybody if you marketed it right. The adman who thought of making Americans believe they needed underarm deodorant was a visionary.

19. So, too, was the hero.
20. The hero made a success of a new soap.
21. A cake of this stuff floated.
22. Soap wasn't supposed to float.
23. Then some inspired adman made a leap.
24. Advertise that it floats.
25. The rest is history.

"*This is my letter to the world....*"

—Emily Dickinson

UNIT 9

Troubleshooter

Use Troubleshooter to help you correct common errors in your writing.

9.1 Sentence Fragment

Troubleshooter

Problem 1

Fragment that lacks a subject

frag   Michael slipped a length of rope into his pack. ~~Thought it might be useful.~~

SOLUTION   Add a subject to the fragment to make it a complete sentence.

Michael slipped a length of rope into his pack. He thought it might be useful.

Problem 2

Fragment that lacks a complete verb

frag   The silence was broken by an eerie sound. ~~A loon out on the lake.~~

frag   Zina pointed toward the west. ~~A golden sun setting on the horizon.~~

SOLUTION A   Add a complete verb or a helping verb to make the sentence complete.

The silence was broken by an eerie sound. A loon out on the lake was calling.

Zina pointed toward the west. A golden sun was setting on the horizon.

SOLUTION B   Combine the fragment with another sentence.

The silence was broken by an eerie sound, for a loon out on the lake was calling.

Zina pointed toward the west, where a golden sun was setting on the horizon.

Problem 3

Fragment that is a subordinate clause

frag Linda returned the novel to the library. Although she had not read the last four chapters.

frag Jorge owns an antique car. Which he has restored himself.

> **SOLUTION A**   Combine the fragment with another sentence.
>
> **Linda returned the novel to the library, although she had not yet read the last four chapters.**
>
> **Jorge owns an antique car, which he has restored himself.**

> **SOLUTION B**   Rewrite the fragment as a complete sentence, eliminating the subordinating conjunction or the relative pronoun and adding a subject or other words necessary to make a complete thought.
>
> **Linda returned the novel to the library. She had not yet read the last four chapters, though.**
>
> **Jorge owns an antique car. He has restored it himself.**

Problem 4

Fragment that lacks both a subject and a verb

frag The chorus sang Kirsten's favorite song. "Misty."

frag Keisha found the kitten. In her dresser drawer.

> **SOLUTION**   Combine the fragment with another sentence.
>
> **The chorus sang Kirsten's favorite song, "Misty."**
>
> **Keisha found the kitten in her dresser drawer.**

If you need more help in avoiding sentence fragments, see Lesson 13.9, pages 551–552.

9.2 Run-on Sentence

Comma splice—two main clauses separated only by a comma

run-on *Andres could not attend the meeting, he had a previous commitment.*

SOLUTION A   Replace the comma with an end mark of punctuation, such as a period or a question mark, and begin the new sentence with a capital letter.

Andres could not attend the meeting. He had a previous commitment.

SOLUTION B   Place a semicolon between the two main clauses.

Andres could not attend the meeting; he had a previous commitment.

SOLUTION C   Add a coordinating conjunction after the comma.

Andres could not attend the meeting, for he had a previous commitment.

Two main clauses with no punctuation between them

run-on *Mariko writes poetry one of her poems was recently published.*

SOLUTION A   Separate the main clauses with an end mark of punctuation, such as a period or a question mark, and begin the second sentence with a capital letter.

Mariko writes poetry. One of her poems was recently published.

SOLUTION B   Separate the main clauses with a semicolon.

Mariko writes poetry; one of her poems was recently published.

SOLUTION C   Add a comma and a coordinating conjunction between the main clauses.

Mariko writes poetry, and one of her poems was recently published.

Problem 3

Two main clauses with no comma before the coordinating conjunction

run-on Last year Julius won the contest easily but this year the competition is stiffer.

run-on We saw several deer and raccoons were everywhere.

SOLUTION   Add a comma before the coordinating conjunction to separate the two main clauses.

Last year Julius won the contest easily, but this year the competition is stiffer.

We saw several deer, and raccoons were everywhere.

If you need more help in avoiding run-on sentences, see Lesson 13.10, pages 553–555.

9.3 Lack of Subject-Verb Agreement

Problem 1

A subject that is separated from the verb by an intervening prepositional phrase

agr The brightness of those colors (please) the baby.

agr The sources of revenue (has) increased.

Do not mistake the object of a preposition for the subject of a sentence.

SOLUTION Make the verb agree with the subject, which is never the object of a preposition.

The brightness of those colors pleases the baby.

The sources of revenue have increased.

Problem 2

A predicate nominative that differs in number from the subject

agr Crossword puzzles (is) his favorite pastime.

SOLUTION Ignore the predicate nominative, and make the verb agree with the subject of the sentence.

Crossword puzzles are his favorite pastime.

Problem 3

A subject that follows the verb

agr At the bottom of the stairs (stand) a statue.

agr Here (comes) the newest members of the cheerleading squad.

SOLUTION   In an inverted sentence look for the subject *after* the verb. Then make sure the verb agrees with the subject.

At the bottom of the stairs stands a statue.

Here come the newest members of the cheerleading squad.

Problem 4

A collective noun as the subject

agr   The audience always (cheer) loudly for that singing group.

agr   The committee (disagrees) on a chairperson.

SOLUTION A   If the collective noun refers to a group as a whole, use a singular verb.

The audience always cheers loudly for that singing group.

SOLUTION B   If the collective noun refers to each member of a group individually, use a plural verb.

The committee disagree on a chairperson.

Problem 5

A noun of amount as the subject

agr   Fifty dollars (seem) high for that radio

agr   Three strikes (makes) an out in baseball.

SOLUTION   Determine whether the noun of amount refers to one unit and is therefore singular or whether it refers to a number of individual units and is therefore plural.

Fifty dollars seems high for that radio.

Three strikes make an out in baseball.

Problem 6

A compound subject that is joined by _and_

agr Sodium and chlorine (combines) to form table salt.

agr Fish and chips (are) on the menu today.

SOLUTION A If the parts of the compound subject do not belong to one unit or if they refer to different people or things, use a plural verb.

Sodium and chlorine combine to form table salt.

SOLUTION B If the parts of the compound subject belong to one unit or if both parts refer to the same person or thing, use a singular verb.

Fish and chips is on the menu today.

Problem 7

A compound subject that is joined by _or_ or _nor_

agr Neither Ed nor the twins (likes) to travel.

agr Either the pasta or the fish (are) excellent.

SOLUTION Make the verb agree with the subject that is closer to it.

Neither Ed nor the twins like to travel.

Either the pasta or the fish is excellent.

Problem 8

A compound subject that is preceded by _many a, every,_ or _each_

agr Many a boy and girl (have) great ambitions.

When _many a, each,_ or _every_ precedes a compound subject, the subject is considered singular.

SOLUTION Use a singular verb when *many a, each,* or *every* precedes a compound subject.

Many a boy and girl has great ambitions.

A subject that is separated from the verb by an intervening expression

agr Carl, as well as Mattie, love to swim.

Certain expressions, such as *as well as, in addition to,* and *together with,* do not change the number of the subject.

SOLUTION Ignore an intervening expression between a subject and its verb. Make the verb agree with the subject.

Carl, as well as Mattie, loves to swim.

An indefinite pronoun as the subject

agr Each of the students are giving a report.

Some indefinite pronouns are singular, some are plural, and some can be either singular or plural, depending upon the noun they refer to. (See page 447 for a list of indefinite pronouns.)

SOLUTION Determine whether the indefinite pronoun is singular or plural, and make the verb agree.

Each of the students is giving a report.

If you need more help with subject-verb agreement, see Lessons 16.1 through 16.8, pages 601–615.

9.4 Lack of Pronoun-Antecedent Agreement

Problem 1

A singular antecedent that can be either male or female

ant *A good doctor treats (his) patients considerately.*

ant *A member may be accompanied by (his) guest.*

Traditionally a masculine pronoun is used to refer to an antecedent that might be either male or female. This usage ignores or excludes females.

SOLUTION A Reword the sentence to use *he or she, him or her,* and so on.

A good doctor treats his or her patients considerately.
A member may be accompanied by his or her guest.

SOLUTION B Reword the sentence so that both the antecedent and the pronoun are plural.

Good doctors treat their patients considerately.
Members may be accompanied by their guests.

SOLUTION C Reword the sentence to eliminate the pronoun.

A good doctor treats patients considerately.
A member may be accompanied by a guest.

Problem 2

A second-person pronoun that refers to a third-person antecedent

ant *Milena and Sean like volunteer work because it gives (you) a chance to help others.*

Do not refer to an antecedent in the third person using the second-person pronoun *you.*

SOLUTION A Use the appropriate third-person pronoun.

Milena and Sean like volunteer work because it gives them a chance to help others.

SOLUTION B Use an appropriate noun instead of a pronoun.

Milena and Sean like volunteer work because volunteers have a chance to help others.

Problem 3

A singular indefinite pronoun as an antecedent

ant   Each of the women finished (their) work quickly.

ant   Neither of the boys remembered to bring (their) lunch.

Each, everyone, either, neither, and *one* are singular and therefore require singular personal pronouns.

SOLUTION Don't be fooled by a prepositional phrase that contains a plural noun. Determine whether the indefinite pronoun antecedent is singular or plural, and make the noun agree.

Each of the women finished her work quickly.
Neither of the boys remembered to bring his lunch.

If you need more help with pronoun-antecedent agreement, see Lesson 16.7, pages 611–612, and Lesson 17.6, pages 632–636.

9.5 Lack of Clear Pronoun Reference

Problem 1

A pronoun reference that is weak or vague

ref My article was poorly written, (which) was the result of careless research.

ref The dry cleaners ruined my new sweater, and (that) annoyed me greatly.

ref The candidates argued for an hour about details of the budget, and so (it) was boring.

Be sure that *this, that, which,* and *it* have clear antecedents.

SOLUTION A Rewrite the sentence, adding a clear antecedent for the pronoun.

My article was poorly written and contained factual errors, which were the result of careless research.

SOLUTION B Rewrite the sentence, substituting a noun for the pronoun.

The dry cleaners ruined my new sweater, and their carelessness annoyed me greatly.

The candidates argued for an hour about details of the budget, and so the debate was boring.

Problem 2

A pronoun that could refer to more than one antecedent

ref Shotaro told David that (he) had missed the deadline.

ref When the chorus performed for the hospital patients, (they) enjoyed themselves.

SOLUTION A Rewrite the sentence, substituting a noun for the pronoun.

Shotaro told David that David had missed the deadline.

SOLUTION B Rewrite the sentence, making the antecedent of the pronoun clear.

The chorus enjoyed performing for the hospital patients.

Problem 3

The indefinite use of *you* or *they*

ref   In many European countries (you) are expected to master English at an early age.

ref   Maria and Suki went to the museum, where (they) have a dazzling display of minerals.

SOLUTION A Rewrite the sentence, substituting a noun for the pronoun.

In many European countries children are expected to master English at an early age.

SOLUTION B Rewrite the sentence, eliminating the pronoun entirely.

Maria and Suki went to the museum, where there is a dazzling display of minerals.

If you need more help in making clear pronoun references, see Lesson 17.7, pages 637–641.

Problem

An incorrect shift in person between two pronouns

> *pro*   They spent their vacation in Glacier National Park, where (you) see remnants of ancient glaciers.
>
> *pro*   I like traveling in the West, where (you) can still find great expanses of unsettled land.
>
> *pro*   One has choices to make in life: (you) can either move ahead or remain in place.

Incorrect pronoun shifts occur when a writer or speaker uses a pronoun in one person and then illogically shifts to a pronoun in another person.

SOLUTION A   Replace the incorrect pronoun with a pronoun that agrees with its antecedent.

They spent their vacation in Glacier National Park, where they saw remnants of ancient glaciers.

I like traveling in the West, where I can still find great expanses of unsettled land.

One has choices to make in life: one can either move ahead or remain in place.

SOLUTION B   Replace the incorrect pronoun with an appropriate noun.

They spent their vacation in Glacier National Park, where vacationers can see remnants of ancient glaciers.

I like traveling in the West, where travelers can still find great expanses of unsettled land.

If you need more help in eliminating incorrect pronoun shifts, see Lesson 17.6, pages 632–636.

9.7 Shift in Verb Tense

Problem 1

An unnecessary shift in tense

shift t Whenever Alice watches the news, she (paid) particular attention to the weather report.

shift t I dropped my menu just as the waiter (arrives.)

When two or more events occur at the same time, be sure to use the same verb tense to describe both events.

SOLUTION Use the same tense for both verbs.

Whenever Alice watches the news, she pays particular attention to the weather report.

I dropped my menu just as the waiter arrived.

Problem 2

A lack of correct shift in tenses to show that one event precedes or follows another

shift t By the time Enrique called, we (left.)

When events being described have occurred at different times, shift tenses to show that one event precedes or follows another.

SOLUTION Shift from the past tense to the past perfect tense to indicate that one action began and ended before another past action began. Use the past perfect tense for the earlier of the two actions.

By the time Enrique called, we had left.

If you need more help with shifts in verb tenses, see Lesson 15.4, pages 583–584, and Lesson 15.6, pages 587–588.

9.8 Incorrect Verb Tense or Form

Problem 1

An incorrect or missing verb ending

tense Three new stores (open) in the mall last week.

tense Have you ever (wish) for a second chance?

SOLUTION Add -ed to a regular verb to form the past tense and the past participle.

Three new stores opened in the mall last week.

Have you ever wished for a second chance?

Problem 2

An improperly formed irregular verb

tense Max (creeped) along behind the hedges looking for the ball.

tense Lawana (lended) me her computer software.

Irregular verbs form their past tense and past participle in some way other than by adding -ed. Memorize these forms, or look them up.

SOLUTION Use the correct past or past participle form of an irregular verb.

Max crept along behind the hedges looking for the ball.

Lawana lent me her computer software.

Problem 3

Confusion between the past form and the past participle

> *tense* Have you ever ⟨rode⟩ on a monorail?
>
> *tense* Karen has ⟨drank⟩ the last of the juice.

SOLUTION Use the past participle form of an irregular verb, not the past form, when you use the auxiliary verb *have*.

Have you ever ridden on a monorail?
Karen has drunk the last of the juice.

Problem 4

Improper use of the past participle

> *tense* To our dismay, it ⟨begun⟩ to rain hard.
>
> *tense* We ⟨sung⟩ all our favorite songs for the guests.

The past participle of an irregular verb cannot stand alone as a verb. It must be used with the auxiliary verb *have*.

SOLUTION A Add the auxiliary verb *have* to the past participle to form a complete verb.

To our dismay, it has begun to rain hard.
We have sung all our favorite songs for our guests.

SOLUTION B Replace the past participle with the past form of the verb.

To our dismay, it began to rain hard.
We sang all our favorite songs for the guests.

If you need more help with correct verb forms, see Lesson 15.1, page 575, and Lesson 15.2, pages 576–578.

9.9 Misplaced or Dangling Modifier

Problem 1

A misplaced modifier

> *mod* The woman in the front row (with the red dress) is our new swimming coach.
>
> *mod* (Cleaned and polished,) Kareem proudly viewed his car.

Modifiers that modify the wrong word or seem to modify more than one word in a sentence are called misplaced modifiers.

SOLUTION Move the misplaced phrase as close as possible to the word or words it modifies.

The woman with the red dress in the front row is our new swimming coach.

Kareem proudly viewed his cleaned and polished car.

Problem 2

The adverb *only* misplaced

> *mod* Juana (only) eats mushrooms on her pizza.

The meaning of your sentence may be unclear if the word *only* is misplaced.

SOLUTION Place the adverb *only* immediately before the word or group of words it modifies. Note that each time *only* is moved in the sentence, the meaning of the sentence changes.

Only Juana eats mushrooms on her pizza.

Juana eats only mushrooms on her pizza.

Juana eats mushrooms only on her pizza.

A dangling modifier

mod *Having lost the directions,* the house was hard to find.

mod *After hiking for hours,* the mountaintop finally came into sight.

mod *Following the recipe carefully,* the soup was easy to make.

Dangling modifiers do not logically seem to modify any word in the sentence.

SOLUTION   Rewrite the sentence, adding a noun to which the dangling phrase clearly refers. Often you will have to add other words, too.

Having lost the directions, we had trouble finding the house.
After hiking for hours, Tasha finally saw the mountaintop.
Following the recipe carefully, Daryl found the soup easy to make.

If you need more help with misplaced or dangling modifiers, see Lesson 18.7, pages 660–665.

Troubleshooter

9.10 Missing or Misplaced Possessive Apostrophe

Problem 1

Singular nouns

poss The (mayors) assistant greeted the delegation.

poss The (actress) dressing room was opulent.

SOLUTION Use an apostrophe and an *-s* to form the possessive of a singular noun, even one that ends in *-s*.

The mayor's assistant greeted the delegation.
The actress's dressing room was opulent.

Problem 2

Plural nouns ending in *-s*

poss The (teachers) lounge is down that corridor.

SOLUTION Use an apostrophe alone to form the possessive of a plural noun that ends in *-s*.

The teachers' lounge is down that corridor.

Problem 3

Plural nouns not ending in *-s*

poss The (mens) tennis team practices at four o'clock.

SOLUTION Use an apostrophe and an *-s* to form the possessive of a plural noun that does not end in *-s*.

The men's tennis team practices at four o'clock.

Problem 4

Pronouns

poss Is ⟨everyones⟩ name correctly spelled?

poss The package on the table is ⟨your's.⟩

> **SOLUTION A**   Use an apostrophe and an *-s* to form the possessive of a singular indefinite pronoun.
>
> **Is everyone's name correctly spelled?**

> **SOLUTION B**   Do not use an apostrophe with any of the possessive personal pronouns.
>
> **The package on the table is yours.**

Problem 5

Confusion between *its* and *it's*

poss A canyon wren was warbling ⟨it's⟩ melodic song.

poss ⟨Its⟩ wise to take an umbrella.

The possessive of *it* is *its*. *It's* is the contraction of *it is*.

> **SOLUTION A**   Do not use an apostrophe to form the possessive of *it*.
>
> **A canyon wren was warbling its melodic song.**

> **SOLUTION B**   Use an apostrophe to form the contraction of *it is*.
>
> **It's wise to take an umbrella.**

If you need more help with apostrophes and possessives, see Lesson 17.1, pages 623–625, and Lesson 21.12, pages 741–743.

9.11 Missing Commas with Nonessential Element

Problem 1

Missing commas with nonessential participles, infinitives, and their phrases

> com Jesse obviously pleased stood admiring the large mural.
>
> com My sister looking a little anxious hesitated before her first dive from the high tower.
>
> com To be sure no one can help you if you will not help yourself.

SOLUTION Determine whether the participle, infinitive, or phrase is truly not essential to the meaning of the sentence. If it is not essential, set off the phrase with commas.

Jesse, obviously pleased, stood admiring the large mural.

My sister, looking a little anxious, hesitated before her first dive from the high tower.

To be sure, no one can help you if you will not help yourself.

Problem 2

Missing commas with nonessential adjective clauses

> com His most recent play which was written in just one week has won every major award.

SOLUTION Determine whether the clause is truly not essential to the meaning of the sentence. If it is not essential, set off the clause with commas.

His most recent play, which was written in just one week, has won every major award.

Problem 3

Missing commas with nonessential appositives

> *com*   Roberto Morales our class president will represent us at the convention.

SOLUTION   Determine whether the appositive is truly not essential to the meaning of the sentence. If it is not essential, set off the appositive with commas.

Roberto Morales, our class president, will represent us at the convention.

Problem 4

Missing commas with interjections and parenthetical expressions

> *com*   My goodness movie tickets have become expensive.
>
> *com*   Elaine said I think that she would be here by seven o'clock.

SOLUTION   Set off the interjection or parenthetical expression with commas.

My goodness, movie tickets have become expensive.
Elaine said, I think, that she would be here by seven o'clock.

If you need more help with commas and nonessential elements, see Lesson 21.6, pages 722–730.

9.12 Missing Commas in a Series

Missing commas in a series of words, phrases, or clauses

s com Yvette packed the basket with enough sandwiches salad soup and fruit for everyone.

s com Manuel carefully turned the knob opened the door and peered into the darkened room.

s com We watched the mouse scamper across the tablecloth down a chair leg and under the refrigerator.

s com Pat saw the sailboat drifting with the tide riding the waves and skimming the blue water.

s com In our trio Neil sings tenor Otis sings baritone and Tom sings bass.

SOLUTION   When there are three or more elements in a series, use a comma after each element, including the element that precedes the conjunction.

Yvette packed the basket with enough sandwiches, salad, soup, and fruit for everyone.

Manuel carefully turned the knob, opened the door, and peered into the darkened room.

We watched the mouse scamper across the tablecloth, down a chair leg, and under the refrigerator.

Pat saw the sailboat drifting with the tide, riding the waves, and skimming the blue water.

In our trio Neil sings tenor, Otis sings baritone, and Tom sings bass.

If you need more help with commas in a series, see Lesson 21.6, pages 722–730.

Proofreading Symbols

Symbol	Example	Meaning
⊙	Lieut. Brown	Insert a period.
∧	No one came to the party.	Insert a letter or a word.
⋀	The bell rang the students left for home.	Insert a semicolon.
≡	I enjoyed paris.	Capitalize a letter.
/	The Class ran a bake sale.	Make a capital letter lowercase.
⌢	The campers are home sick.	Close up a space.
ⓢⓟ	They visited N.Y. ⓢⓟ	Spell out.
∧	Sue please help.	Insert a comma.
∩	He enjoyed feild day.	Transpose the position of letters or words.
#	alltogether	Insert a space.
ℐ	We went to to Boston.	Delete letters or words.
∨ ∨	She asked, Who's coming?	Insert quotation marks.
/=/	mid January	Insert a hyphen.
¶	"Where?" asked Karl. "Over there," said Ray.	Begin a new paragraph.
∨	She liked Sarah's glasses.	Insert an apostrophe.

Business and Technical Writing

Contents

Business Letters

Writing an effective business letter is a valuable skill that you will use in school and throughout your life. People write business letters every day to apply for jobs, complain about poor service, order items, say thanks, request help or information, and express opinions.

The language and tone of a business letter should be conversational but polite. Aim for clarity, and avoid out-dated, overly formal business language, such as "In reference to yours of the fourteenth." The impression the letter makes on the reader will certainly dictate the nature of his or her response. Correct grammar, spelling, and punctuation are essential.

Single-space your business letters and use only one side of a page. You may double-space a very short business letter to fill the page. If the letter extends to more than one page, include the name of the recipient, the date, and the page number, all flush with the left margin on subsequent pages.

```
K. Lasher
10/23/01
Page 2
```

Activity 1

Bring to class three or four examples of business letters. In small groups, evaluate these letters. What do these letters have in common? Which are the most effective? Share the results of your discussion with the rest of the class.

Business Letters

Parts of a Business Letter

A business letter contains the following parts. Examine each part in the model letter on page 411.

Heading The heading includes the sender's complete address and the date. If you use letterhead (stationery with a preprinted return address), simply add the date.

Inside Address The inside address is the name and address of the recipient of the letter. Be sure it is correct and complete.

Salutation The salutation begins with the word *Dear* and is followed by the recipient's title—such as Mr., Ms., or Dr.—and last name, followed by a colon. If you don't know and cannot get the person's name, you may use a title such as "Dear Personnel Officer" or omit the salutation.

Body The body is the main part of the letter. Be sure to place the most important information—usually a call to action—as close to the beginning as possible. Be clear and simple about the purpose of your letter. Do not make your reader search for what you want.

Closing The closing precedes the formal identification of the sender. You may choose among such conventional closings as *Yours truly, Sincerely, Sincerely yours, Best regards,* or *Respectfully.* Do not capitalize the second word of the closing, and follow the phrase with a comma. Type your name four spaces below the closing, allowing room for your signature.

Styles of Business Letters

There are two basic styles of business letters: block style and modified block style.

Block Style The block style is the most commonly used style. In this style, all parts of the letter are aligned with the left margin, and paragraphs are separated with a line space.

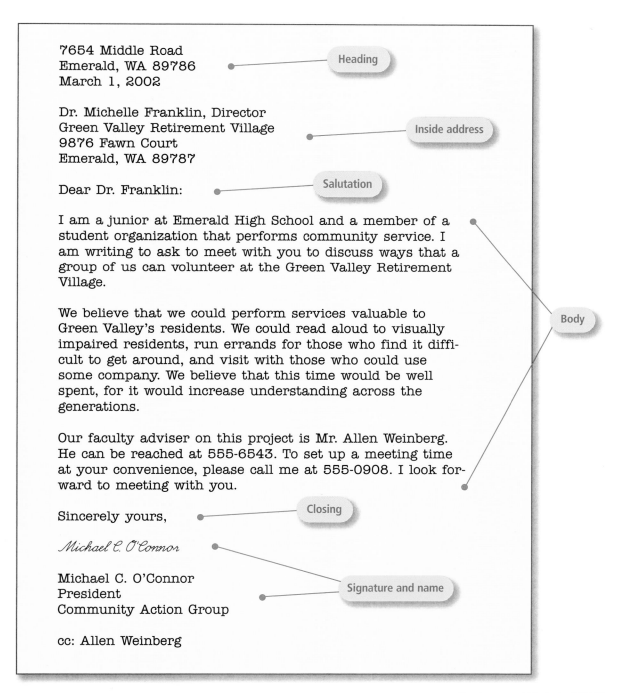

7654 Middle Road
Emerald, WA 89786
March 1, 2002

Heading

Dr. Michelle Franklin, Director
Green Valley Retirement Village
9876 Fawn Court
Emerald, WA 89787

Inside address

Dear Dr. Franklin:

Salutation

I am a junior at Emerald High School and a member of a student organization that performs community service. I am writing to ask to meet with you to discuss ways that a group of us can volunteer at the Green Valley Retirement Village.

We believe that we could perform services valuable to Green Valley's residents. We could read aloud to visually impaired residents, run errands for those who find it difficult to get around, and visit with those who could use some company. We believe that this time would be well spent, for it would increase understanding across the generations.

Body

Our faculty adviser on this project is Mr. Allen Weinberg. He can be reached at 555-6543. To set up a meeting time at your convenience, please call me at 555-0908. I look forward to meeting with you.

Sincerely yours,

Closing

Michael C. O'Connor

Michael C. O'Connor
President
Community Action Group

Signature and name

cc: Allen Weinberg

Business Letters

Modified Block Style Some writers prefer a modified block style, in which the date and closing are indented, and which may include a subject line. Indent both the return address and the closing as well as the body paragraphs. With this style, no extra space is used between paragraphs.

> 7654 Middle Road
> Emerald, WA 89786
> March 1, 2002

Dr. Michelle Franklin, Director
Green Valley Retirement Village
9876 Fawn Court
Emerald, WA 89787

Re: Request for Appointment

Dear Dr. Franklin:

    I am a junior at Emerald High School and a member of a student organization that performs community service. I am writing to ask to meet with you to discuss ways that a group of us can volunteer at the Green Valley Retirement Village.

    We believe that we could perform services valuable to Green Valley's residents. We could read aloud to visually impaired residents, run errands for those who find it difficult to get around, and visit with those who could use some company. We believe that this time would be well spent, for it would increase understanding across the generations.

    Our faculty adviser on this project is Mr. Allen Weinberg. He can be reached at 555-6543. To set up a meeting time at your convenience, please call me at 555-0908. I look forward to meeting with you.

> Sincerely yours,
>
> *Michael C. O'Connor*
>
> Michael C. O'Connor
> President
> Community Action Group
>
> cc: Allen Weinberg

Re is short for *regarding*. This optional subject line tells what the letter concerns.

Personal Letter Style On rare occasions, you may need to use a friendly letter style for business purposes. Use the format of a friendly letter, as shown in the model below.

November 21, 2002

Dr. Michelle Franklin
Green Valley Retirement Village
9876 Fawn Court
Emerald, WA 89787

Dear Aunt Michelle,

    Our community action group would like to volunteer at Green Valley, as we discussed last week at dinner. Representatives of our group would like to meet with you to consider the options. The students were especially interested in reading to the residents and running errands for those who need help. Please give me a call and let me know when we can meet.

      Love,
      Mike

Types of Business Letters

People write business letters to request information or assistance, complain, express opinions, or apologize for an inconvenience. Although the basic form of the letter remains unchanged regardless of the purpose, each type of letter will be organized and structured somewhat differently. Elements of style may also change, depending on your purpose.

Request for Information or Action The key to writing a letter requesting information or action is to ask for what you want in the first paragraph. Clearly describe your expected response in the paragraphs that follow. If you are requesting several items, it is helpful to provide a bulleted list.

Please send the following items:
- one ream of white copy paper
- two 12-packs of black erasable pens
- three yellow legal pads
- two rolls of 1.5-inch strapping tape
- one box of 8.5″ x 11″ manila envelopes

Type your return address clearly and include other helpful information such as a phone or fax number or an e-mail address in case the reader needs clarification.

Request for Personal Assistance Another kind of business letter is a request for personal assistance. To write this sort of letter, follow these three steps.

1. Acquaint the reader with the situation for which you are requesting assistance.
2. Provide details.
3. Suggest a way or ways that the reader can address your request.

The tone of your letter should be respectful but not pleading or demanding.

I am writing to ask if you would write a letter of reference that I can use for college applications. You will recall that I was a student in your freshman biology and junior advanced biology classes. I am planning to major in science or pre-med. Please submit the letter to Mrs. Jander at our college placement office.

Activity 2

Imagine that you have been asked to write a profile of a famous living person. The subject of your profile could be a sports star, a political figure, or the head of an organization. Your goal is to learn as much as you can about the person. One source of information is a "press kit" often put together by organizations (or the individuals themselves) to help writers like you. Write a business letter to the media relations or public relations department of the organization with which the person is affiliated. Request a press kit or other biographical information about the individual.

PURPOSE To write a business letter requesting information

AUDIENCE Public relations office

LENGTH 1 page

Writing Rubrics

To write an effective request letter, you should

- use the correct spacing and alignment for the style chosen
- write clearly and succinctly
- state your request in the first paragraph of the letter
- use polite but conversational language
- check your letter for grammar, spelling, and mechanics

Complaint If you are writing to complain about a product or service, first decide what you want the recipient to do. Do you want an apology, a replacement, a refund, or a change in the product? In the first paragraph, explain the problem and politely express how you would like to have it resolved.

Recently, I and five other students ate at your restaurant after the junior prom. We were treated rudely by our server, even though we were mannerly and left a 15 percent tip. Students deserve the same respect accorded other customers. We would appreciate an assurance that students choosing to dine with you in the future will not be treated in such an unpleasant manner.

Activity 3

Suppose that, during a class trip, you experienced an inconvenience—poor service, canceled reservations, lost luggage, or rude service personnel. Write a letter of complaint to the service provider.

PURPOSE To write a business letter registering a complaint

AUDIENCE Service provider

LENGTH 1 page

Writing Rubrics

To write an effective letter of complaint, you should

- write clearly and succinctly
- state your complaint in the first paragraph of the letter
- use polite but conversational language
- check your letter for grammar, spelling, and mechanics
- use correct business-letter style

Opinion When you write to state your opinion, you want to persuade others to adopt your point of view. If you will disagree with another point of view, you must also state the opposing position clearly and accurately.

I am opposed to most of the new security arrangements proposed for Emerald High School. While I understand the concern about school safety, turning the school into a fortress will only create a prison-like atmosphere. I believe that other steps can be taken to make students and faculty more secure.

Activity 4

Write a letter to your school or local newspaper expressing your opinion about an issue that concerns you. Before you write, take some time to investigate and understand the opposing position or positions. Use either a block or a modified block style.

PURPOSE To express your opinion about an issue

AUDIENCE Readers of your school or local newspaper

LENGTH 1 page

Writing Rubrics

To state your opinion in a business letter effectively, you should

- state your opinion clearly in a reasonable tone
- give a fair picture of the opposing points of view
- provide evidence or reasons to support your opinion
- check the letter for errors

Business Letters

Apology There are two keys to writing an effective apology. First, do not trivialize the concern of the person making the complaint. Too often, people who write apologies say things like "I'm very sorry for any inconvenience you experienced," but to the person who bothered to complain, *inconvenience* is probably much too weak a word to describe the experience. Second, do not make excuses. The person complaining does not want to hear about how "the computer was down" or how "we were really busy."

> We are sorry that you were treated rudely by the server at our restaurant. Please accept our apologies and the enclosed coupon for a free lunch for your party of six, which you can use whenever you wish. I will make sure that our servers are more aware of the need to treat all our patrons with the respect they deserve. Thank you for bringing this problem to my attention.

Notice that the writer takes the complaint seriously and offers no excuses for the error.

Letter of Application When you apply for a job, you usually send a letter of application, or cover letter, along with your résumé. A cover letter presents your qualifications but does not provide the specific details that are found in your résumé. However, you can and should refer to your résumé in your letter. For example, "As my résumé shows, I have substantial experience in retail sales"—and you should mark your résumé as an enclosure at the bottom of your letter. Begin your letter with a reference to the advertisement or job posting.

> I am writing to apply for the sales job advertised in the *Miami Herald*.

If there is no advertisement and you are simply writing to determine whether there is an opening, begin with a relevant statement.

> I am writing to find out if you have an opening for an entry-level sales person.

Then immediately identify yourself and your qualifications for the position.

> As my résumé indicates, I have three years of experience in retail sales and one year of experience as an assistant manager.

In the body of the letter, you can expand on the relationship between your experience and the specific job advertised. You may even want to quote portions of the advertisement to show exactly how your experience matches the company's needs. End your letter by asking for an interview and include your phone number and suggested times for calling. Your final sentence can thank the reader for considering you for the position.

I would like to meet you personally to discuss my qualifications. I can be reached at 444-2234 after 3:00 P.M. to schedule an interview.

Thank you for considering me for your open position.

Activity 5

Write a cover letter to accompany a résumé. Follow a block or modified block style.

PURPOSE To write a cover letter

AUDIENCE The company with the open position

LENGTH 1 page

Writing Rubrics

To write an effective letter of application, you should

- refer to your résumé in the letter
- make sure that the letter is completely error free
- make your interest in the job clear

Memos, E-mail, and Application Forms

Memos and e-mail may be used more frequently than the regular mail in many businesses. Forms of various kinds are also frequently used for business and other purposes.

Memos

Memos are documents that are written for use within a business, school, or other organization. They share many of the characteristics of the business letter but are less formal.

The memo format allows maximum efficiency. Typically, a memo is one page or less, and all the text is flush left. The heading is double-spaced and contains essential information for the reader, including the identity of the writer and the subject. The rest of the memo is single-spaced, with a line space between paragraphs. The content is direct and concise. There is no closing, since the writer is identified in the heading.

One advantage of the memo format is that the recipient can write a response on the memo itself and return it. If you choose, you can end the memo with the word *Response:* or *Comment:* to make it clear that you expect only a quick, handwritten note in response.

To: Alice Suarez

From: Jocelyn Alexander   *JBA*

Date: February 15, 2002

Re: Textbook recommendations

The board of education has asked for our history textbook recommendations for next year by February 25. Has the history text selection committee met? If not, you'll need to call a meeting right away and urge members of the committee to come armed with recommendations. If you have met, have you decided on the texts that you want to recommend? Please let me know the status of this issue as soon as possible.

Thanks.

> The sender need not sign the memo, but he or she may initial it.

Activity 6

Imagine that you are the chairperson of a school committee charged with investigating allegations of unruly student behavior at football games. The committee has been asked to determine whether there is a problem and, if one exists, to make recommendations for solving it. Write a memo to members of the committee asking that they research the issue and gather ideas before the first meeting. Be sure to include the date and time of the meeting.

PURPOSE To write a memo

AUDIENCE Committee members

LENGTH 2–4 paragraphs

Writing Rubrics

To write an effective memo, you should

- use the correct format
- convey the message clearly and concisely
- include all necessary information
- proofread the memo

E-mail

Of all the forms of business communication, e-mail is by far the least formal. E-mail can read like a transcript of a conversation. As e-mail becomes more and more prevalent, however, writers need to analyze their audiences. The use of sentence fragments, colloquial language, and abbreviations may be fine for friends, but they are not appropriate for many business exchanges.

For anyone other than a close friend, an e-mail message should be similar to a memo in format and style. The subject line, in fact, is even more important, since busy readers use the subject line to decide whether to open the message.

Clarity and directness are also important. If you are answering an e-mail message, repeat enough of the original message to remind the recipient of the context.

Because you cannot always format an e-mail as you can a letter, messages that must be somewhat formal should be done in a word processing program and e-mailed as attachments. In most e-mail programs, sending an attachment requires simply that you click on a button marked *attachment*, type in the path and file name, and click *OK*.

Activity 7

Send an e-mail message to a classmate concerning one of the letters or memos written for a previous activity. Explain to your classmate the circumstances that prompted the correspondence and ask for a response to your e-mail message. Send the letter or memo with the e-mail as an attachment.

PURPOSE To send an e-mail message with an attachment

AUDIENCE Classmate

LENGTH 1 paragraph

Writing Rubrics

To send an e-mail message with attachment, you should

- convey your message clearly and concisely
- include all necessary information
- call attention to the attachment
- request a response
- proofread the message

Application Forms

People fill out application forms for a variety of purposes, such as to obtain an apartment, a social security card, a driver's license, or a credit card. Almost every employer requires that job applicants complete an application.

There are four important steps in completing an application form.

1. Read instructions carefully. Read through the entire document before writing anything.

2. Keep in mind that neatness counts. If possible, request more than one copy of the form so you can redo it if necessary.

3. Do not leave blank spaces. If something does not apply, write *n/a* (not applicable) in the space. Blank spaces suggest that you have something to hide or that you did not carefully read the form.

4. Complete the form in ink, preferably black.

Voter Registration Form

Check all that apply: ❏ Name change   ❏ Address change   ❏ New registration

Name _____

       last name   first name   middle initial

Address _____

    street number / street name / apartment number / city or town / ZIP code

Date of Birth _____   Telephone number: (   )   –

       month   day   year

Party Enrollment or Designation (check one): ❏ Democratic   ❏ Republican

❏ Libertarian   ❏ No party (independent)   ❏ Other (identify) _____

Address at which you were last registered to vote:

_____

    street number / street name / apartment number / city or town / ZIP code

I hereby swear (or affirm) that I am the person named above, that the information is true, that I am a citizen of the United States, and that I am not disqualified by law from voting.

Signed _____   **Date** _____

    Sign your name here.   month   day   year

Activity 8

Fill out one or more practice applications. You can obtain blank forms from a bank, a local employer, the Department of Motor Vehicles, the public library, or possibly from your school. Work in a small group to evaluate and critique each other's work.

PURPOSE   To complete a sample application

AUDIENCE   Your classmates

LENGTH   1–2 pages

Writing Rubrics

To prepare an application form, you should

- respond to each request for information
- correctly place information on the form
- write neatly and legibly in ink
- check spelling and punctuation

Business and Technical Writing

Graphic Organizers

Graphic organizers are devices for organizing data pictorially. They are useful in business and technical writing because they help readers to comprehend and compare data.

Charts

Organization Charts Organization charts show how individuals, positions, or departments within an organization are related to one another. Your word processing program may have a function or template to help you create organization charts. Check its Help menu. If your program does not allow you to create them automatically, you can use the drawing tools to make a chart.

Simply click the appropriate icons to create text boxes and lines similar to those shown in the example chart. You can choose either a vertical (portrait) or horizontal (landscape) orientation from Page Setup in the File menu, depending on whether you need greater depth or greater width for your chart. Once you have determined a structure, simply type in the names, titles, or needed information.

Be careful not to show too much information in one chart or one box; your information should be easy to read and understand. Start each box the same way. Be sure to include a title for your chart.

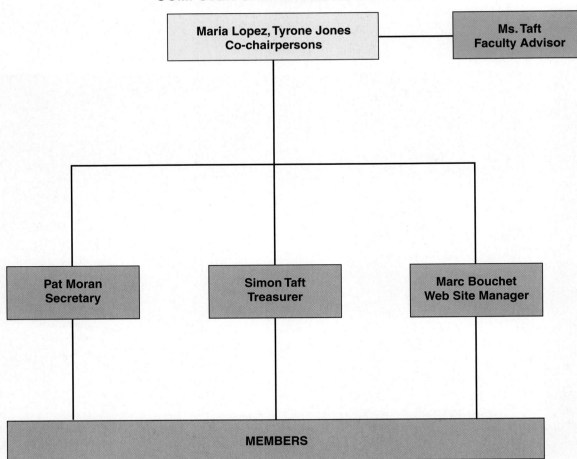

COMPUTER CLUB ORGANIZATION

Maria Lopez, Tyrone Jones
Co-chairpersons

Ms. Taft
Faculty Advisor

Pat Moran
Secretary

Simon Taft
Treasurer

Marc Bouchet
Web Site Manager

MEMBERS

Flow Charts Flow charts highlight a different kind of relationship; they show the stages in a process. They usually use arrows to show progress from one step to the next. In flow charts, be consistent in the kind of information you enter in each box. For example, each box might include a single step or a single action in a process. The example describes how you can use your word processing software to create a flow chart.

How to Create a Flow Chart

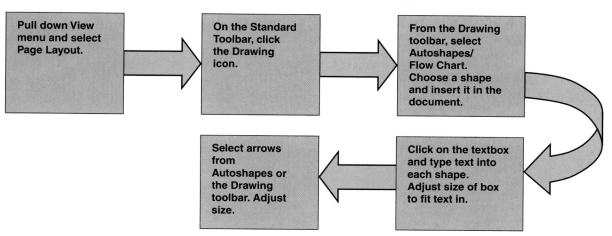

Pull down View menu and select Page Layout. → On the Standard Toolbar, click the Drawing icon. → From the Drawing toolbar, select Autoshapes/ Flow Chart. Choose a shape and insert it in the document. → Click on the textbox and type text into each shape. Adjust size of box to fit text in. → Select arrows from Autoshapes or the Drawing toolbar. Adjust size.

Activity 9

Choose one option:

- Use a computer to make an organization chart showing the structure of your student council or some other school group. Show each level of the organization.
- Use a computer to make a flow chart that explains a process with which you are familiar, such as how to do a physics experiment, how to install a modem for your computer, or how to make a favorite dish. Show all steps in the process.

PURPOSE	To create an organization chart or a flow chart
AUDIENCE	Your teachers and classmates
LENGTH	1 page

Writing Rubrics

To create an effective chart, you should
- write a title for the chart
- use the correct format
- label consistently
- check for accuracy

Graphic Organizers

Graphs

Business and technical writing often includes one or more graphs. A graph highlights data by showing it pictorially. Many word processing and spreadsheet programs include a graphing function. These programs usually refer to graphs as charts. Software specifically for creating graphs and charts is also available. You can create a graph in another type of software and import it into a word processing document.

Bar Graphs Bar graphs usually show numbers or quantities of something. They make it easy to see and compare data. A bar graph plots data along two axes—the vertical axis, or y-axis, and the horizontal axis, or x-axis. The y-axis usually contains a scale of numbers or percentages. The bar graph example shows the amount of annual snowfall in a particular location.

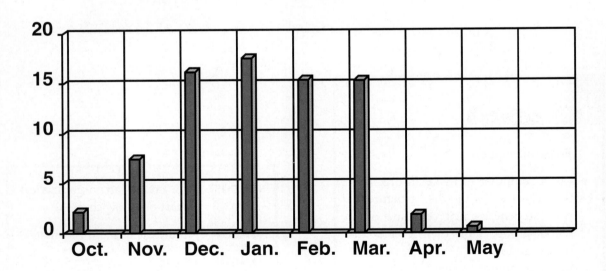

Annual Snowfall, in Inches

Circle Graphs A circle graph (or pie chart) shows the relationship of parts to a whole. The parts can be labeled with either numbers or percentages. The whole circle always represents 100 percent of something. The example circle graph, for instance, using some of the same numbers used in the bar graph on page 424, expresses in percentages the amount of snowfall each month.

Percentage of Yearly Snowfall per Month

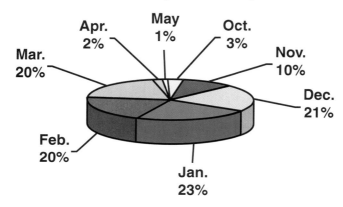

Line Graphs A line graph shows changes in data over time. For example, the line graph here shows changes in the price of a corporation's shares of stock. Line graphs allow you to easily spot changes or trends. XYZ Corporation's stock, for example, is clearly increasing in value following a slight drop in 2000.

Average Share Price
XYZ Corporation, 1998-2002

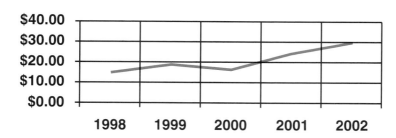

Creating Graphs Most spreadsheet programs include a graphing function. You enter data into a worksheet, and the program converts the information into a graph. Some word processing programs also have a graphing function. After the data is entered into a worksheet, you can choose the kind of graph you want, enter titles and a legend, and click *OK*. The word processor creates the chart for you and inserts it into your document. If you discover a problem with your chart after it has been inserted into the document, simply double-click on the chart to return to the editing function. In some programs, you can switch between one kind of chart and another once the data is entered to see which best conveys the point you wish to make. Use the Help menu of your software if you need additional help.

Activity 10

Use the Internet or print resources to gather statistical data for publication in a student magazine. You may choose any topic that interests you and for which you can find statistics. Research your topic, gather data, and create a graph to show the data pictorially.

PURPOSE   To gather, use, and present data in graphic form

AUDIENCE   Readers of a student magazine

LENGTH   1 graph

Writing Rubrics

To prepare an effective graph, you should

- choose data that can be presented visually
- present the data in the most effective graphic form
- include a descriptive title, labels, and/or legend
- proofread for accuracy

Technical Writing

Elements of Technical Communication

Technical writing is practical and objective, focusing on the technical content of the subject. Technical style is simple and direct. Accuracy, consistency, clarity, and brevity are its most important characteristics.

Accuracy While errors in all kinds of writing are to be avoided, errors can cause a calamity in technical writing. Merely substituting the word *left* for the word *right* in assembly directions can lead to millions of dollars worth of damage if the piece of equipment in question is an aircraft part or an industrial boiler.

Consistency Technical writers and editors must use a uniform style, so that words are consistently capitalized and units of measure are the same throughout the document. In some cases, inconsistencies may be merely annoying, but in other cases they can spell disaster. For example, in 1999 NASA lost a Mars Climate Orbiter worth $125 million dollars because the manufacturer, which was supposed to supply metric measurements, sent English measurements instead. That small error caused the orbiter to hurtle past Mars, which it was supposed to orbit, and to spin into orbit around the Sun.

Most companies that issue technical documents and reports have a style manual to help writers maintain a consistent style. These manuals deal with such issues as capitalization, abbreviations, punctuation, and methods of writing numbers and equations. You can use such manuals as *The Chicago Manual of Style* or the *MLA Handbook for Writers of Research Papers,* or the *Publication Manual of the American Psychological Association.*

Clarity In technical writing, the writer's goal is to translate scientific or technical information into language that is easy to read and understand. Thus, technical writers must be particularly aware of their audiences. Language appropriate for an audience of engineers may baffle nontechnical readers. On the other hand, if a document is intended for engineers, translating technical jargon into everyday language will unnecessarily complicate the writing.

Brevity People who read technical writing want to be able to gather the relevant information as quickly as possible, so technical writers often use short sentences, bulleted lists, and brief paragraphs to convey information. They divide the text into multiple sections that make it easy to find information.

The abstract at the beginning of many technical reports and papers summarizes the document in one tightly written paragraph. Many readers rely on abstracts not only to get the information they need but also to help them decide if the document is one they need to read in its entirety.

Technical writers are careful to organize reports so that readers can easily find the sections that are relevant to their needs. Tables of contents guide the reader, and chapters are divided into sections. Abstracts provide a quick summary, and appendixes include details too cumbersome to be included in the body of the report.

Technical writers also help their readers by presenting as much information as possible in charts, graphs, tables, or other graphic forms.

Technical Instructions

In order to write instructions well, you must thoroughly and completely understand the process you are describing. Then you must travel backward in time to recall what it was like not to understand the process so that you can explain it to others.

You should also divide the process into clearly delineated logical steps. Then explain the steps in the correct order so that the person performing the process does not have to repeat steps or backtrack.

Following are some key recommendations from technical writers of "how-to" manuals.

- Show or describe the finished product so that the reader knows the goal.
- List all required parts and tools. You do not want to send the reader to the store in the middle of a project because you forgot to mention that your process requires a blank disk.
- Label each step clearly: _Step One: Make a backup copy of the master disk._
- Write imperative sentences. _Insert a working copy of the master disk, metal end first and label side up, in your internal disk drive._
- Spell out even those steps that you think ought to be obvious: _Start up your computer._
- Check for errors or omissions by following your directions exactly as they are written. Then have someone else follow the steps to help you identify instructions that may be confusing or difficult to understand.

Activity 11

Write a brief "how-to" manual to teach your classmates to perform a step-by-step process. Select a process that you know well but which others may not know. Consider such processes as setting up a tent, playing a card game, assembling a toy, scanning a photograph, or refinishing a piece of furniture.

PURPOSE   To write a "how-to" manual

AUDIENCE   Your teacher and classmates

LENGTH   2–4 pages

Writing Rubrics

To write effective instructions, you should

- list tools and equipment
- place steps in chronological order
- label each step
- use visuals effectively
- write clearly
- test for omissions
- consider the audience
- proofread for grammatical errors and vague language

Making Tables

Tables present facts and figures in an easy-to-read format. Information is organized into columns and rows. Columns are the vertical elements in a table, and rows are the horizontal elements. Cells are the individual boxes that contain data.

To make a table in a word processing program, use the Tables pull-down menu. Select the number of rows and columns you think you will need. An empty table will appear, and you can fill in the data. If necessary, you can insert or delete rows and columns after you have created your table. You can also add borders, shading, and color. For further help, see your software's Help menu.

Notice that each column has its own title.

The title explains what the table is about.

CURRENCIES OF SELECTED COUNTRIES			
Country	Name	Symbol	Subdivision
Greece	drachma	Dr	100 lepta
Iceland	krona	KR	100 aurar
Nigeria	naira	₦	100 kobo
Poland	zloty	ZI	100 groszy
Venezuela	bolivar	B	100 centimos

Borders help show the columns and rows.

Using Spreadsheets

A spreadsheet looks like a table. A spreadsheet, however, allows you to group fields and sort within a category; you can also analyze data and perform math operations.

Spreadsheets are helpful at home and school as well as in business. Most spreadsheet programs have a variety of options: You can change the size of columns and rows, add borders and fill, change how the numbers appear in the cells, and tell the program that the numbers in cells are dates or times.

You can also use spreadsheets to sort text and numerical data. To sort a column of data, highlight the data, click the sort option, and then indicate whether you want to sort in ascending or descending order, alphabetically or numerically.

The spreadsheet below is a list of expenditures for a school chemistry lab. The spreadsheet does the math work for you. The benefit of using a spreadsheet like this one is that if the cost of an item changes or if there is a change in the number of items ordered, the program automatically recalculates the total cost.

Name of Item	Cost per Item	Number of Items Ordered	Total Cost
Test tubes	$0.75	74	$55.50
Beakers	$3.95	12	$47.40
Calcium chloride	$4.95	4	$19.80
		Total	$122.70

Activity 12

Imagine that you are the class treasurer and that part of your job is planning the junior prom. Using spreadsheet software, identify the various expenses the prom will entail, such as a band, decorations, and the printing of tickets. Then revise the spreadsheet on the assumption that the original band canceled and you have to hire another, more expensive one.

PURPOSE To create a spreadsheet

AUDIENCE Yourself and classmates

LENGTH At least 1 page

Writing Rubrics

To create an effective spreadsheet, you should

- identify the categories useful to you and label them
- sort the data to produce different reports
- proofread to make sure the data is accurate

Writing Scientific Reports

You may be familiar with technical reports. Many science and social science teachers require students to produce such reports. Often they will outline a specific format for these reports. If not, the following format will probably be acceptable.

Every report needs a title page, followed by an abstract. The text should be divided into sections, each with its own heading. Number pages consecutively and include a header with your name and a brief version of the title on each page.

Jones, dress code
p. 1

Abstract
This report demonstrates that students surveyed at Emerald High School favor the establishment of a limited dress code. The majority of students feel that banning hats and tattoos would limit the influence of gangs while still allowing students to express individuality in other forms of dress.

The first section of the report should be an introduction that includes the purpose of the survey or experiment, relevant background information, and your hypothesis. This section may also include a review of the literature of similar experiments.

Introduction
The purpose of this report is to discover whether students favor a uniform dress code, limited clothing regulations, or no dress code at all.

The second section should cover materials and methods used.

Materials and Methods
A twenty-item questionnaire was administered to one hundred Emerald High students. The sample was evenly divided by grade. All one hundred questionnaires were returned.

The third section details the result of the experiment and may include tables and graphs to showcase the data collected.

Results
As the following chart indicates, the opinions expressed by juniors closely matched the overall student response. Seniors were more inclined to favor liberal dress policies, and freshmen were more interested in uniformity.

In the fourth section, the writer should discuss the results and draw conclusions.

Conclusions

While students in general favor establishing a limited dress code, the overall concern seems to be one for safety rather than morality.

If necessary, you may include appendixes including raw data or references. For example, a copy of the questionnaire you used to gather data might be included as an appendix. The model that follows can be used as a guide as you develop your own questionnaire.

Sample Questionnaire

1. Should Emerald High School have a dress code?
   ❏ Yes   ❏ No   ❏ No opinion

2. A dress code would enhance the learning environment at Emerald High School. (Check one.)
   ❏ True   ❏ False

3. If you favor a dress code, which of the following items should it include?
   ❏ Clothing   ❏ Shoes   ❏ Hats
   ❏ Jewelry   ❏ Tattoos

4. Who do you think should make the decision about a dress code? (Check one.)
   ❏ School board   ❏ Parents
   ❏ Principal   ❏ Faculty
   ❏ Student Council   ❏ All of the
                           above

   ❏ None of the above

Activity 13

Work with five or six classmates to design, administer, and then report on a survey of high school students. Each group should select one of the following topics:

- school security
- school dress codes
- a twelve-month school calendar
- preferences for extracurricular activities
- ideas for reducing student absenteeism

Develop a questionnaire that includes at least twenty questions. Use the questionnaire to collect data from everyone in your class, including members of your own group. Be sure to write questions that can be easily scored—multiple-choice questions or rankings rather than open-ended questions.

Analyze your data and present it in a report, using the report format outlined above.

PURPOSE   To write a technical report

AUDIENCE   Your teacher and classmates

LENGTH   4–5 pages

Writing Rubrics

To write an effective technical report, you should

- use the proper format
- draw reasonable conclusions from the data
- include charts, tables, or graphs
- write clearly and simply

"*The months grew cold, November, December.*"

—Julia Alvarez, "Snow"

Claude Monet,
Haystack in Winter,
1891

PART 2

Grammar, Usage, and Mechanics

433

10.1 Nouns

■ A **noun** is a word that names a person, a place, a thing, or an idea.

PERSON	aunt, astronaut, Ramón, daughter-in-law, child
PLACE	universe, village, bedroom, North Carolina
THING	shark, eagle, oak, foot
IDEA	pride, honor, dignity, hope, 1992

■ A **concrete noun** names an object that occupies space or that can be recognized by any of the senses.

stone   lightning   shout   air   salt

■ An **abstract noun** names an idea, a quality, or a characteristic.

sadness   hope   anger   clarity   dissonance

Nouns are singular or plural. A singular noun names one person, place, thing, or idea. A plural noun names more than one.

SINGULAR	mask, briefcase, fly, loaf, woman
PLURAL	masks, briefcases, flies, loaves, women

Nouns have a possessive form, which is used to show possession, ownership, or the relationship between two nouns.

SINGULAR POSSESSIVE	PLURAL POSSESSIVE
a **boy's** hat	the **boys'** hats
the **country's** laws	those **countries'** laws
a **woman's** smile	**women's** smiles
a **mouse's** whiskers	**mice's** whiskers

Exercise 1   Identifying Nouns

On your paper, write the nouns in each sentence. Identify each noun as a person, place, thing, or idea.

SAMPLE	Inventions are the products of creativity and determination.
ANSWER	Inventions—thing creativity—idea
	products—thing determination—idea

1. Alfred Nobel experimented with explosives in a laboratory in Sweden.
2. In his research, Nobel worked with an explosive compound called nitroglycerin.
3. He mixed nitroglycerin with other chemicals to create dynamite.
4. At his death, Nobel left most of his fortune in a trust for international awards called Nobel Prizes.
5. The first Nobel Prizes were for outstanding work in science, literature, and peace.

Exercise 2   Identifying Nouns

On your paper, write each of the twenty nouns that appear in the following paragraph.

Lucy Terry, Poet

The American poet Lucy Terry was born in Africa about 1730. Terry was brought to America at a very young age as an enslaved worker. When she married, she was given her freedom. After her marriage, the poet and her husband settled in Vermont. Terry was known as a storyteller, activist, and orator. However, only one of her poems survived. It is the earliest existing poem by an African American.

Exercise 3   Supplying Abstract and Concrete Nouns

For each concrete noun in items 1–10, write an abstract noun that names an idea with which the concrete noun can be associated. For each abstract noun in items 11–20, write a concrete noun that has the quality of the abstract noun.

SAMPLE ANSWERS   astronaut—fearlessness
                 darkness—cave

1. athlete
2. thunder
3. roses
4. honey
5. toothache
6. storm
7. criminal
8. mountain
9. lion
10. explosion

11. authority
12. truth
13. tranquillity
14. respect
15. guilt
16. concentration
17. ability
18. kindness
19. cooperation
20. gentleness

Exercise 4   Completing Sentences with Nouns

On your paper, complete each sentence by filling in the blanks with nouns. Be sure that your completed sentences make sense.

1. We discovered four _____ in the dusty _____.
2. Ramón's _____ to help others wins my _____.
3. A(n) _____ destroyed the _____.
4. The _____ soared high over the _____.
5. The _____ reminded us of _____.
6. We didn't find any _____ in the _____.
7. The _____ at the _____ didn't look fresh.
8. When I go to the _____, I usually take _____ along.
9. The _____ looked different after the _____.
10. _____ came into the _____ and asked for a _____.

Exercise 5 · Identifying Singular, Plural, and Possessive Nouns

Identify the underlined nouns in each sentence as *singular, plural, singular possessive,* or *plural possessive.*

Angelina Grimké

1. Angelina Grimké was born in <u>1805</u> in the South.
2. Although she was born into a life of privilege, by 1835 she had moved north to join the <u>abolitionists</u>.
3. Ironically, she was a prominent <u>slaveholder's</u> daughter.
4. In 1836 she wrote an appeal to white southern <u>women</u> supporting the abolition of <u>slavery</u>.
5. One year later, <u>Grimké's</u> abolitionist appeal to <u>northerners</u> was published.
6. The <u>abolitionist's</u> writings appeared in <u>pamphlets</u> and <u>journals</u>.
7. This <u>woman's</u> <u>suggestions</u> were not well received in the South.
8. <u>Grimké</u> urged all women to work together as <u>sisters</u> to fight for social <u>justice</u>.
9. When Grimké gave <u>speeches</u>, huge <u>audiences</u> came to listen.
10. The <u>abolitionists'</u> <u>views</u> were effectively disseminated by a woman who could have benefited from slavery but chose to reject it.

Exercise 6 · Correcting Singular and Plural Possessive Nouns

Decide whether each underlined possessive noun is written correctly. If it is correct, write *correct* on your paper. If it is incorrect, write the correct form.

SAMPLE Before storing information on a computer, always learn about the <u>systems'</u> backup program.

ANSWER system's

1. Information is stored in a <u>computers'</u> hard drive.
2. A floppy <u>disk's</u> memory is considered external, or secondary.
3. Four <u>worker's</u> computers went down this morning.
4. One of the <u>worker's</u> disks contained records that cannot be duplicated.
5. A <u>technicians'</u> warning about backing up information went unheeded.

Exercise 7 · Using Possessive Nouns in Sentences

Write a sentence for each noun, using the form indicated in parentheses.

1. man (plural possessive)
2. writer (singular possessive)
3. teacher (plural possessive)
4. child (plural possessive)
5. student (singular possessive)

Proper and Common Nouns

■ A **proper noun** is the name of a particular person, place, thing, or idea.

■ A **common noun** is the general—not the particular—name of a person, place, thing, or idea.

Proper nouns are capitalized; common nouns are generally not.

	PROPER NOUNS
PERSON	Richard Wright, Connie Chung, Dr. Jonas Salk, Eric the Red
PLACE	Pasadena, Bering Sea, Nicaragua, White House, Saturn
THING	Society of Friends, Titanic, Native Son, Memorial Day, Ford Motor Company
IDEA	Augustan Age, Islam, Romanticism, Jazz Age

Exercise 8   Matching Proper Nouns with Common Nouns

On your paper, match the proper nouns on the left with the common nouns on the right.

1. San Antonio
2. Iroquois
3. Mark McGwire
4. Clara Barton
5. December
6. *Time*
7. Hawaii
8. *Star Wars*
9. George Washington
10. Statue of Liberty

a. month
b. president
c. people
d. landmark
e. athlete
f. author
g. state
h. city
i. movie
j. magazine

Exercise 9   Identifying Proper and Common Nouns

On your paper, write each of the twenty-five nouns that appear in the following passage. Identify each noun as proper or common.

Martin Luther King Jr.

Dr. Martin Luther King Jr., civil rights leader and president of the Southern Christian Leadership Conference, led a demonstration in Birmingham, Alabama, in protest of segregationist practices in the city. The response of the local government was the arrest of many nonviolent marchers. King, who was also arrested, believed in the power of nonviolent resistance. While in jail, he wrote a letter explaining his views on nonviolence. King's direct-action efforts eventually resulted in the passage of the Civil Rights Act of 1964.

Collective Nouns

■ A **collective noun** names a group.

class	(the) faculty
crew	(the) cast
team	(a) herd (of cows)
congregation	(a) swarm (of bees)

A collective noun may be considered either singular or plural. When a collective noun refers to a group as a whole, it is regarded as singular. When a collective noun refers to the individual members of a group, it is regarded as plural.

SINGULAR	The **jury** has reached a verdict. The **cast** includes a small chorus.
PLURAL	The **jury** were unable to agree. The **cast** are staying at different hotels.

Exercise 10   Identifying Collective Nouns

On your paper, list the five collective nouns in the following paragraph.

A Nature Study

[1]Unloading their gear, the band of naturalists set up their tents along the river by the entrance to the cave. [2]Nearby a flock of mallards rests quietly in the shallows while a swarm of gnats reels overhead. [3]The party are eager to conduct their separate studies of different aspects of this cave, which is noted for its numerous bats. [4]As they begin their exploration, the naturalists are not disappointed to discover a thriving colony of insect-eating mammals.

Exercise 11   Distinguishing Between Singular and Plural Collective Nouns

On your paper, write the collective noun in each sentence, and label it as *singular* or *plural.*

1. The cast begins rehearsal next week.
2. The Wilson family were discontented with their seating arrangements.
3. After the play, the audience always calls for an encore.
4. A group of people are waiting in line for tickets.
5. After school the faculty plans to hold a meeting about the school play.
6. Since tomorrow is a half-day of school, the stage crew have agreed to go out for lunch somewhere.
7. The audience was disappointed at the replacement of the star by his understudy.
8. In the school yard, the class talk among themselves about the upcoming play.
9. An unruly group of children were running in all directions.
10. A crowd often gathers outside the theater for autographs.

Review: Distinguishing Nouns from Other Parts of Speech

On your paper, identify the underlined word in each sentence as *noun* or *not a noun*.

1. There is a vast amount of <u>work</u> required in running a restaurant.
2. Waiters and waitresses depend on <u>tips</u> as a major part of their salaries.
3. Deciding on the <u>tip</u> for a waiter or waitress can be a complicated process.
4. Usually, the <u>tip</u> should be between 15 percent and 20 percent of the bill before taxes.
5. The success of any restaurant depends a great deal on the talents of the <u>cook</u>.
6. Customers who patronize restaurants are often fussy about the way the chef <u>cooks</u>.
7. Some diners prefer that the cook <u>roast</u> their meat.
8. In addition to a talented chef, a successful restaurant will usually have a unique yet <u>comfortable</u> atmosphere.
9. Most people prefer to dine in <u>quiet</u> surroundings.
10. Many restaurants will specialize in a particular meal on which they can <u>build</u> their reputation.
11. It is not unusual for an eating <u>establishment</u> to be open only for dinner.
12. Other restaurants prefer to serve <u>breakfast</u> and lunch and then to close for dinner.
13. The <u>number</u> of specialty restaurants continues to grow.
14. Fast-food establishments <u>top</u> the list of popular places for the teenage crowd to eat.
15. Restaurants that serve fast foods usually have a <u>light</u> and airy atmosphere.
16. For formal dinners, the waiter will <u>light</u> a candle on the table.
17. Usually restaurants that serve ethnic foods can be found in cities throughout the <u>country</u>.
18. Going to Illio's Italian Restaurant is like taking a <u>step</u> into Italy.
19. When seated by a window, I always ask for a table in the <u>shade</u>.
20. Because of the sunlight, the customer seated next to me asked for the <u>shade</u> to be drawn.

Review: Proper and Common Nouns

For each common noun, write an example of a proper noun. For each proper noun, write an example of a common noun.

SAMPLE	city	Hawaii
ANSWERS	San Francisco	island

Common nouns
1. mountain
2. president
3. organization
4. country
5. actor
6. friend
7. ocean
8. teacher
9. planet
10. holiday

Proper nouns
11. Central High School
12. Empire State Building
13. California
14. Elvis Presley
15. John P. Gordon, M.D.
16. Christine
17. Professor Washington
18. Dr. Martin Luther King Jr.
19. *Titanic*
20. Barracudas Swim Team

Parts of Speech

Review: Creating Sentences with Nouns

Write five sentences about a close friend. Rely especially on concrete nouns to convey a vivid picture of the person.

Exercise 15   **Review: Nouns**

On your paper, complete the sentences by filling in the blanks with the kinds of nouns specified in italics. Be sure that your completed sentences make sense.

1. *proper* saw a *common* near the *concrete*.
2. The *abstract* of *common* has always intrigued the *collective*.
3. The *collective* left their *concrete* at *proper*.
4. Two *concrete* stalked a *collective* of *common*.
5. The young *collective* spent a long, lazy *common* on their *concrete*.
6. *proper* was the best *common* of his *collective*.
7. *abstract* is a(n) *abstract*.
8. *plural possessive* thoughts sometimes wander.
9. *proper* brought *singular possessive* books into the house.
10. The *collective* decided to go to the *common* after all.
11. We saw the *plural* on our *concrete*.
12. Have you seen *singular possessive plural*?
13. *Proper* wants to become a(n) *common* in the *abstract*.
14. A(n) *singular* flew over the *concrete*.
15. *Proper* was a(n) *common* of the *collective* in *proper*.
16. *Plural* and *plural* make good *common*.
17. The last *singular* in the *concrete* is a(n) *common*.
18. Do you ever dream of *abstract*?
19. The *plural possessive* new *concrete* is the talk of the *common*.
20. *Abstract* is the *abstract* of the *abstract*.
21. Did the *collective* of the *proper* win the *common*?
22. The *singular* was broken for three *plural*.
23. The *concrete* talked to the *plural possessive* club about *abstract*.
24. *Proper* found *singular possessive singular* in the *concrete*.
25. The *collective* spent their *common* in *proper*.
26. The *proper* is famous for its *concrete*.
27. The *plural* of two famous *concrete* are celebrated in February.
28. Many *plural* are fascinated by the *concrete* in the *proper*.
29. The *abstract* of a hurricane can damage *concrete*, *concrete*, and *concrete*.
30. The *collective* that plays in *proper* is called the *proper*.
31. A *common* is a *common* that names a *concrete*, *concrete*, *concrete*, or *abstract*.
32. What is your favorite musical *collective*?
33. Did *singular possessive concrete* ask you to give the *concrete* a *common*?
34. Our *abstract* is important to me.
35. I tried to help the *proper* with their *plural*.

10.2   Pronouns

■ A **pronoun** is a word that takes the place of a noun, a group of words acting as a noun, or another pronoun. The word or group of words that a pronoun refers to is called its **antecedent.** A pronoun must agree with its antecedent in number and gender.

> Ralph Bunche received the Nobel Prize for Peace in 1950 while **he** served as director of the United Nations Trusteeship Division. [The pronoun *he* takes the place of the noun *Ralph Bunche.*]
>
> Both Benito Juárez and Emiliano Zapata affected Mexican history. **Each** is regarded as a national hero. [The pronoun *each* takes the place of the nouns *Benito Juárez* and *Emiliano Zapata.*]
>
> **Few** remembered to bring **their** notebooks to the lecture. [The pronoun *their* takes the place of the pronoun *few,* which stands for an unidentified group of people.]

There are about seventy-five pronouns in the English language. They fall into one or more of the following categories: personal pronouns, possessive pronouns, reflexive and intensive pronouns, demonstrative pronouns, interrogative pronouns, relative pronouns, and indefinite pronouns.

Personal and Possessive Pronouns

■ A **personal pronoun** refers to a specific person or thing by indicating the person speaking (the first person), the person being addressed (the second person), or any other person or thing being discussed (the third person).

Like nouns, personal pronouns are either singular or plural.

Personal Pronouns		
	SINGULAR	**PLURAL**
FIRST PERSON	I, me	we, us
SECOND PERSON	you	you
THIRD PERSON	he, him she, her, it	they, them

FIRST PERSON	**We** sent Angela a get-well card. [*We* refers to the people speaking.]
SECOND PERSON	Tell Otis to give **you** the key. [*You* refers to the person being addressed.]
THIRD PERSON	**They** told **her** the good news. [*They* and *her* refer to the people being discussed.]

Pronouns in the third-person singular have three **genders:** *he* and *him* are masculine; *she* and *her* are feminine; *it* is neuter (neither masculine nor feminine).

Among the personal pronouns are forms that indicate possession or ownership. These are called **possessive pronouns,** and they take the place of the possessive forms of nouns.

Possessive Pronouns		
	SINGULAR	**PLURAL**
FIRST PERSON	my, mine	our, ours
SECOND PERSON	your, yours	your, yours
THIRD PERSON	his her, hers its	their, theirs

Where there are two possessive forms shown, you use the first before a noun and the second alone, in place of a noun.

USED BEFORE A NOUN   Where is **their** house?
USED ALONE   That house is **theirs**.

Exercise 16	Using Personal and Possessive Pronouns

Replace the thirty underlined words or phrases with personal or possessive pronouns. Write your answers on your paper.

Karen lent a tennis racket to John; [1] John returned [2] the racket to [3] Karen one week later.

Each time Dan visits Mrs. Wagner at the nursing home, [4] Dan brings a different book for [5] Mrs. Wagner to read; last time [6] the book was *To Kill a Mockingbird.*

Amy looked at the alarm clock; [7] the alarm clock was buzzing, telling [8] Amy that [9] Amy was going to be late for school if [10] Amy didn't hurry.

Most of the books Tom reads are from the library; some of [11] the books, however, are [12] Tom's. [13] Tom's four-year-old sister, Candy, likes to look at [14] Candy's brother's books and pretend [15] the books are [16] Candy's.

Susan left [17] Susan's book bag in [18] Susan's English classroom. When [19] Susan returned to the classroom, the book bag was no longer there. [20] Susan learned from the teacher, Mr. Brown that [21] the teacher had sent [22] the book bag to Lost and Found. At Lost and Found Susan identified which book bag was [23] Susan's.

"Save a muffin for [24] Brian," Brian said to [25] Brian's sister, Sarah. "There are three of [26] the muffins left," [27] Sarah remarked. "Don't worry."

Donna knocked on Mrs. Kraft's door and asked Mrs. Kraft, "Is this kitten [28] Mrs Kraft's? [29] The kitten was meowing on [30] Donna's back porch."

Exercise 17   Identifying Personal and Possessive Pronouns

On your paper, write the pronouns in each sentence. Identify each as *personal* or *possessive*.

1. He left their books on our porch.
2. She could not tell whether the briefcase was hers.
3. They had no idea how he would react to it.
4. A majority of them would have to be convinced before they would agree.
5. Since they stopped using high-quality materials, we have no longer carried their products.

Exercise 18   Using Personal and Possessive Pronouns

On your paper, fill in the blanks with pronouns that make sense in each sentence. There may be more than one right answer for each blank.

1. _____ went over to _____ school.
2. _____ put _____ basketballs in the bus.
3. _____ wondered when _____ would come to basketball practice.
4. Why did _____ bring _____ books to practice?
5. When did _____ teammates decide to buy _____?

Reflexive and Intensive Pronouns

To form the reflexive and intensive pronouns, add *-self* or *-selves* to certain personal and possessive pronouns.

Personal Pronouns		
	SINGULAR	**PLURAL**
FIRST PERSON	myself	ourselves
SECOND PERSON	yourself	yourselves
THIRD PERSON	himself, herself, itself	themselves

■ A **reflexive pronoun** refers, or reflects back, to a noun or pronoun earlier in the sentence.

We considered **ourselves** honored to be invited.

■ An **intensive pronoun** adds emphasis to another noun or pronoun.

They built that cabin **themselves.**

Demonstrative Pronouns

A **demonstrative pronoun** points out specific persons, places, things, or ideas.

Demonstrative Pronouns		
SINGULAR	this	that
PLURAL	these	those

Is **this** the guitar you like?

Let me do **that** today.

These are the only drums left.

Bring **those** to me.

Exercise 19   Using Reflexive, Intensive, and Demonstrative Pronouns

Supply the appropriate reflexive, intensive, or demonstrative pronoun for each blank. On your paper write the pronoun, and identify whether it is *reflexive, intensive,* or *demonstrative.*

Bette Bao Lord

1. After I read *Spring Moon* by Bette Bao Lord, I wanted to discover for _____ how she came to write this novel about her family's past.
2. The novel _____ is a masterpiece of research into the complex and tumultuous history of China in the twentieth century.
3. _____ is Lord's first novel; her first book was a biography of her sister.
4. _____ are books that touch the reader through rich characterization and absorbing situations.
5. Lord _____ has had an eventful life, both as a child in Shanghai during World War II and as the wife of the American ambassador to China.
6. The three events that led to Lord's meeting her future husband in economics class were _____ : emigrating, skipping two grades, and failing at chemistry.
7. When the Communists took control of China, the Baos suddenly found _____ immigrants in Brooklyn, New York.
8. In the United States, young Bette Bao faced problems that were very different from _____ she had encountered in China.
9. Just learning English _____ must have been a struggle, for Lord has said that to Chinese ears "English sounds like somebody gargling water."
10. Lord's description of _____ as an immigrant child gave me a fresh insight into the courage that people must have as they face the challenges of living in a strange new land.

Interrogative and Relative Pronouns

■ An **interrogative pronoun** is used to form questions.

> who?   whom?   whose?   what?   which?

> **Who** were the winners?
> **Whom** did the drama coach praise?
> **Whose** are these?
> **What** does this mean?
> **Which** of these songs do you like?

Whoever, whomever, whosoever, whichever, and *whatever* are the intensive forms of the interrogative pronouns.

> **Whatever** do you want?

■ A **relative pronoun** is used to begin a special subject-verb word group called a subordinate clause (see Unit 13).

> who   whose   whomever   that   whoever
> whom   what   whichever   which   whatever

Roots, **which** was filmed for television, was written by Alex Haley. [The relative pronoun *which* begins the subordinate clause *which was filmed for television.*]

| Exercise 20 | Distinguishing Between Interrogative and Relative Pronouns |

On your paper, list the interrogative and relative pronouns that appear in the following sentences, and label each of them as *interrogative* or *relative.*

Cleopatra, an Extraordinary Queen

1. Which Egyptian queen was one of the most fascinating women in history?
2. At eighteen Cleopatra, who was of Macedonian descent, became queen of Egypt.
3. The coins that were minted during her reign do not portray her as the beautiful woman of legend.
4. Cleopatra, who could be ruthless at times, also cared for her subjects' welfare and won their loyalty.
5. Julius Caesar first met Cleopatra in Alexandria, which was Egypt's capital in the first century B.C.
6. Caesar fell in love with Cleopatra, whose intelligence and charm were captivating.
7. According to history, which other famous Roman leader loved Cleopatra?
8. Do you think Mark Antony, whom Cleopatra married, wished to be Rome's sole ruler?
9. Which of Shakespeare's plays tells the story of Cleopatra and Antony?
10. Shakespeare's *Antony and Cleopatra* (1607) is one of several well-known literary works that dramatize the extraordinary story of Mark Antony, the legendary leader of ancient Rome.

Indefinite Pronouns

■ An **indefinite pronoun** refers to persons, places, or things in a more general way than a noun does.

> Do you know **anyone** who can run as fast as Jackie? [The indefinite pronoun *anyone* does not refer to a specific person.]
>
> **Many** prefer this style of jacket. [The indefinite pronoun *many* does not refer to a specific group of people.]
>
> When we opened the box of pears, we found that **each** was perfectly ripe. [The indefinite pronoun *each* has the specific antecedent *pears.*]

Some Indefinite Pronouns			
all	either	much	others
another	enough	neither	plenty
any	everybody	nobody	several
anybody	everyone	none	some
anyone	everything	no one	somebody
anything	few	nothing	someone
both	many	one	something
each	most	other	

Exercise 21   Using Indefinite Pronouns

On your paper, fill in the blanks with indefinite pronouns so that the sentences make sense. There is more than one correct answer for each blank.

SAMPLE _____ has ever seen a more dedicated actor than Michael.
ANSWER   No one

1. _____ knows how hard it is to get the leading part in a play.
2. _____ of us tried to help Marcia improve her acting skills.
3. There was _____ about the producer's tone of voice that let _____ know he was angry.
4. _____ thought the play was wonderful.
5. Jim thanked _____ for supporting him after he won the award for best playwright.
6. Unfortunately, _____ could be done after the tickets were sold out.
7. Connie was surprised that _____ of her friends had come to see her in the play.
8. _____ bothered to stay for the whole performance.
9. _____ agreed that the play should be held over for another month.
10. _____ of the actors would admit to forgetting the lines.

Exercise 22   Review: Personal and Possessive Pronouns

Improve the following paragraph by replacing the underlined words with personal or possessive pronouns. Write your answers on your paper.

Christopher Columbus

You may already know a great deal about the explorations of Christopher Columbus. But how much do you know about [1] Columbus's early days, before Ferdinand and Isabella gave [2] Columbus [3] Ferdinand and Isabella's support for the four voyages to the New World? Columbus was born in 1451 in Genoa, Italy, an important port and trading center. [4] Columbus was the eldest of five children; two brothers helped [5] Columbus on later projects. Columbus's father was a wool weaver, and young Columbus worked in [6] Columbus's father's shop. In 1476 [7] Columbus and his brother Bartholomew lived in Lisbon, where [8] Columbus and his brother worked as chartmakers. What is not known is when Columbus made his first sea voyages.

Exercise 23   Creating Sentences with Pronouns

Write ten sentences about a sport that you enjoy watching or playing with friends. Try to use pronouns from the following categories you studied in this lesson:

personal	demonstrative
possessive	interrogative
reflexive	relative
intensive	indefinite

Exercise 24   Review: Pronouns

(a) On your paper, list in order the twenty pronouns that appear in the following paragraphs. (b) Identify each pronoun as *personal, possessive, reflexive, intensive, demonstrative, interrogative, relative,* or *indefinite.*

A Visit to a Tropical Rain Forest

[1]Everyone on our tour enjoyed the last stop best—El Yunque, which means "The Anvil" in Spanish. [2]This is the second highest mountain in Puerto Rico, and it is only a short drive from San Juan. [3]It is special, however, because of the tropical rain forest that covers its slopes. [4]According to the tour guide, the pre-Columbian natives of the island believed El Yunque was the home of the creator god, Yukiyú, who lived on the mist-enshrouded summit. [5]None of us could imagine a better home for him.

[6]Everyone was amazed to learn about the forest's annual rainfall. In excess of 180 inches, the amount is conducive to growing a profuse variety of plant and animal life. [7]The guide claimed she herself has identified many of the 240 varieties of trees known to exist in the forest. [8]Walking the trails, we saw cascading waterfalls, orchids, thirty-foot ferns, and flocks of colorful chattering parrots. [9]Whoever said an earthly paradise does not exist? [10]If you ever visit Puerto Rico, you should spend an afternoon at El Yunque.

10.3 Verbs

■ A **verb** is a word that expresses action or a state of being and is a necessary part of a sentence.

Students **concentrate.**	The test **is** tomorrow.
The teacher **reviewed** the story.	The class **became** noisy.

A verb expresses time—present, past, and future—by means of various *tense* forms.

PRESENT TENSE	We **see** the waves.
PAST TENSE	We **saw** the waves.
FUTURE TENSE	We **will see** the waves.

Exercise 25   Identifying Verb Tense

On your paper, write the verb in each sentence. Then label it as *present, past,* or *future.*

1. Pollution is one of the world's most serious problems.
2. It affects all parts of the earth, including the land, sea, and air.
3. Oil spills caused the death of numerous sea animals in the oceans.
4. Unfortunately, people's carelessness will destroy many of our country's natural resources.
5. In time people will surely realize the effects of their carelessness.
6. Eventually tourists will avoid public beaches and the surrounding areas.
7. At some point, companies will find better means of disposal for toxic wastes than landfills.
8. According to some scientists, chlorofluorocarbons contributed to the formation of a hole in the ozone layer of the earth's atmosphere.
9. In our town, civic groups constantly organize rallies against pollution.
10. Heavy traffic areas suffer from both air and noise pollution.

Exercise 26   Adding Verbs to Make Sentences

On your paper, write ten complete sentences by supplying a verb for each of the blanks in the items below.

The Excitement of Hot-Air Balloons

1. The hot-air balloons _____ over the countryside.
2. They _____ colorful against the white clouds.
3. Noticing the balloons, villagers _____ outside.
4. Moving with the wind, the balloons _____ silently.
5. The gathering villagers _____ mesmerized.
6. Do you want to watch us _____ a hot-air balloon?
7. First, you _____ the balloon on the ground.
8. A large fan _____ air into the balloon until it is about half full.
9. The pilot _____ a propane burner, heating the air inside the balloon.
10. Gradually the balloon _____, lifting the basket aloft.

Action Verbs

- An **action verb** tells what someone or something does.

  Action verbs can express action that is either physical or mental.

  PHYSICAL ACTION The baker **prepared** the cake.

  MENTAL ACTION The baker **studied** the recipe closely.

- A **transitive verb** is an action verb that is followed by a word or words that answer the question *what?* or *whom?*

  The athletes **obey** their coach. [The action verb *obey* is followed by the noun *coach*, which answers the question *obey whom?*]

- An **intransitive verb** is an action verb that is *not* followed by a word that answers the question *what?* or *whom?*

  The athletes **obey** immediately without protest. [The action verb is followed by words that tell *when* and *how*.]

| Exercise 27 | Recognizing Action Verbs |

Write on your paper the action verb in each of the following sentences. Indicate whether each action verb is used as a *transitive* or an *intransitive* verb.

SAMPLE The Anasazi lived in the southwestern part of the United States.
ANSWER lived—intransitive

The Anasazi

1. The Anasazi lived in parts of Colorado, Arizona, New Mexico, and Utah.
2. They first settled there almost two thousand years ago.
3. The ruins of one of their most spectacular settlements survive high on the Mesa Verde, a plateau in Colorado.
4. The earliest Anasazi hunted game for much of their food.
5. Later generations also cultivated the land.
6. We know these Native Americans by another name: the Pueblo, from the Spanish word for "town."
7. In time the name Pueblo identified the Anasazi themselves and their descendants.
8. The height of the development of the Anasazi culture occurred between the years 1050 and 1300.
9. Sometime during the fourteenth century, the Anasazi left their homes for reasons still unknown.
10. The Navajo word *Anasazi* means "Ancient One."

Creating Sentences with Transitive and Intransitive Verbs

For each of the following action verbs, write two sentences. First, use the verb as a transitive verb. Then use it as an intransitive verb.

1. ride   **2.** spin   **3.** plunge   **4.** fly   **5.** rush

Linking Verbs

■ A **linking verb** links, or joins, the subject of a sentence (often a noun or pronoun) with a word or expression that identifies or describes the subject.

Be in all its forms is the most commonly used linking verb. Forms of *be* include *am, is, are, was, were, will be, has been,* and *was being.*

The hiker **is** an expert.   The noise **was** loud.
These trees **are** rare.   The bus **will be** late.

In addition, several other verbs can act as linking verbs.

Other Linking Verbs			
appear	grow	seem	stay
become	look	smell	taste
feel	remain	sound	

Understanding Linking Verbs

On your paper, write the linking verb in each sentence. Next to each verb, write the subject and the word or expression to which it was linked.

SAMPLE   My cousin is a writer.
ANSWER   is–cousin-writer

1. Surprisingly, the damage appeared inconsequential.
2. The stolen vehicle will become a statistic on the list.
3. Thankfully, Timothy remains my best friend to this day.
4. The recovered automobile was unrecognizable after the accident.
5. Since the first day of his release from the hospital, the accident victim has been cautious.

Exercise 30   Identifying Action and Linking Verbs

On your paper, write the verb that appears in each of the following sentences. Then identify each verb as either an *action verb* or a *linking verb*.

SAMPLE   For her outstanding talent, Virginia Hamilton won many literary awards.
ANSWER   won—action verb

Virginia Hamilton, Novelist

1. Yellow Springs, Ohio, was the childhood home of the author Virginia Hamilton.
2. The southern Ohio area became part of the Underground Railroad system.
3. Runaway enslaved persons used the Underground Railroad system on their way to freedom in the North.
4. Virginia Hamilton set her novel *The House of Dies Drear* in a southern Ohio community.
5. The large old houses of Hamilton's own community were hideouts on the Underground Railroad during the Civil War.
6. The *House of Dies Drear* tells a present-day mystery story with connections to the Underground Railroad.
7. Virginia Hamilton studied at both Antioch College and Ohio State University.
8. Hamilton's husband works as an author, too.
9. Her husband's name is Arnold Adoff.
10. Before her return to Yellow Springs, Hamilton lived for many years in New York City.

Exercise 31   Using Action and Linking Verbs in Sentences

On your paper, fill in each blank with an example of the kind of verb indicated in parentheses.

SAMPLE   At first, writing a résumé may _____ easy. (linking verb)
ANSWER   seem

Finding a Job

1. Not knowing where to begin, most job seekers _____ the want ads. (action verb)
2. From an inexperienced person's point of view, job hunting _____ a difficult task. (linking verb)
3. Until a full-time position materialized, part-time work _____ a good substitute. (linking verb)
4. Job searchers _____ on interviews. (action verb)
5. Most employers _____ prospective employees for a résumé. (action verb)
6. In an effective interview a job seeker's attitude _____ focused and positive. (linking verb)
7. Just as an actor auditions for a part, job searchers _____ for a job. (action verb)
8. Often an employer _____ several interviews with the prospective employee before a job offer is made. (action verb)
9. Each job interview _____ a learning experience. (linking verb)
10. After going on several interviews, a job searcher _____ an expert interviewee. (linking verb)

Verb Phrases

- The verb in a sentence may consist of more than one word. The words that accompany the main verb are called **auxiliary,** or helping, **verbs.**
- A **verb phrase** consists of a main verb and all its auxiliary, or helping, verbs.

Auxiliary Verbs	
FORMS OF *BE*	am, is, are, was, were, being, been
FORMS OF *HAVE*	has, have, had, having
OTHER AUXILIARIES	can, could
	do, does, did
	may, might
	must
	shall, should
	will, would

The most commonly used auxiliary verbs are the forms of *be* and *have.* They enable the main verb to express various tenses.

She **is talking.**

Exercise 32   Distinguishing Between Main Verbs and Auxiliary Verbs

On your paper, make two columns labeled *Auxiliary Verbs* and *Main Verbs.* Write the words in the following verb phrases in the correct columns. (Words that interrupt a verb phrase are not considered part of the verb phrase and should not be listed in either column.)

SAMPLE   would never have expected
ANSWER   **Auxiliary verbs**   **Main verbs**
          would have   expected

1. may have brought
2. might still appear
3. has never been told
4. had been running
5. does not require
6. should have been approached
7. could still enjoy
8. must surely have been notified
9. should be acquired
10. shall unexpectedly bring

Exercise 33   Identifying Verb Phrases

On your paper, write each verb phrase that appears in the following sentences. (Five of the sentences have more than one verb phrase.) Put parentheses around the auxiliary verbs in each phrase. (Words that interrupt a verb phrase are not considered part of the verb phrase.)

SAMPLE   Law books have been written about the opinions of Justice Holmes.
ANSWER   (have been) written

Justice Holmes

1. "The life of the law has not been logic: it has been experience."
2. The above words were spoken by Supreme Court Justice Oliver Wendell Holmes Jr. in 1899.
3. Holmes was still expressing eloquent ideas thirty-two years later, when he was approaching the age of ninety.
4. In 1871, five years after he had graduated from Harvard Law School, Holmes was appointed university lecturer on jurisprudence at that same institution.
5. After he had spent a year in the law office of George Shattuck, Holmes could have chosen a number of jobs.
6. Holmes had by then expressed interest in the position of chief justice of Massachusetts.
7. In 1902 Justice Holmes would move to Washington, D.C., as a member of the Supreme Court.
8. Generations of law students have read, and undoubtedly will read, Justice Holmes's Supreme Court opinions.
9. You might enjoy Francis Biddle's biography, *Mr. Justice Holmes.*
10. Holmes had also written on the preconceptions of judges themselves.

Exercise 34   Creating Sentences with Vivid Verbs

Write five sentences that describe how a particular animal moves. Choose very specific action verbs and verb phrases to convey a vivid sense of movement.

Exercise 35   Review: Identifying Action, Linking, Transitive, and Intransitive Verbs

On your paper, write the verb in each sentence in this passage. Identify each verb or verb phrase as an *action* or a *linking verb*. Also identify each action verb as *transitive* or *intransitive.*

All About Broccoli

[1]Broccoli originally grew in Asia Minor. [2]In ancient times, it was one of the favorite vegetables of the Romans. [3]Since then it has had an enduring place in many cuisines. [4]By the early 1900s, cultivation of broccoli had extended to the United States. [5]Broccoli gained popularity with people in the United States in the early 1900s. [6]A member of the cabbage family, this bright green vegetable is nutritious and versatile. [7]It can serve as a side dish or as the principal ingredient of a main dish. [8]For example, you might serve broccoli with pasta and oil and garlic. [9]At the grocery store, shoppers should choose only heads with unopened flowers. [10]This flavorful vegetable should be available year round.

Review: Verb Phrases

On your paper, write an answer to each question, using a main verb and at least one auxiliary verb.

SAMPLE   When did you last speak on the phone?
ANSWER   I may have spoken on the phone last night.

1. How long have you been going to this school?
2. Before leaving home in the morning, what must you do?
3. What should you do if you cannot attend a party you are invited to?
4. What would you do if you were having an important test but felt too ill to take it?
5. What might a dog do if it were trying to protect its domain?
6. What should have been done to the lawn when it grew too high?
7. How many people were in your class last year?
8. When should you be going on your next vacation?
9. If you could travel anywhere in the world, where would you go?
10. How long has it been since you last went to the movies?
11. What was your father doing the last time you saw him?
12. Do most dogs like people?
13. What are your plans for the future?
14. What might the weather be like tomorrow?
15. How many pounds can you lift without straining?
16. What should you have said to someone whose feelings you hurt?
17. Did you agree with the outcome of the election?
18. What were the fans doing at the last sporting event you attended?
19. What is being done to promote recycling in your school?
20. How old will you be in three years?
21. What has your favorite entertainer been doing lately?
22. Does your grandmother live with you?
23. When is the package being delivered?
24. How could you have prevented the accident?
25. What had you been doing before you began this assignment?

Exercise 37   **Review: Types of Verbs**

Complete each sentence with an example of the type of verb indicated in parentheses.

1. Last week a suspicious fire completely _____ the store on the corner of Front Street. (transitive action verb)
2. Firefighters _____ to the scene of the fire within ten minutes, but the flames were already out of control. (intransitive action verb)
3. The store owner _____ despondent over the incident. (linking verb)
4. Neighbors were reluctant to inform him that all of his inventory _____ destroyed. (helping verb)
5. Fortunately, the arsonist who started the fire _____. (verb phrase)

10.4 Adjectives

■ An **adjective** is a word that modifies a noun or a pronoun by limiting its meaning.

quiet song	**two** dollars	**that** house
baby turtles	**Korean** cooking	**these** shoes
blue sky	**official** documents	**few** people
windy day	**every** student	**any** problems

An adjective's position in relation to the word it modifies may vary.

How **green** the *leaves* are!

The **green** *leaves* shook in the breeze.

The *leaves* are **green.**

Sunlight makes the *leaves* **green.**

The *leaves,* **green** as emeralds, shook in the breeze.

Green as emeralds, the *leaves* shook in the breeze.

Exercise 38	Identifying Adjectives

On your paper, write the adjectives in each sentence. Next to each adjective, write the word it modifies. Do not count the words *a, an,* and *the.*

Helen Keller and Her Teacher, Anne Sullivan

1. She was born a normal child, but Helen Keller suffered a serious illness when she was nineteen months of age.
2. After the unknown illness, no one was able to communicate a clear message to Helen because she was now deaf and blind.
3. The physical body continued to develop normally; however, because she needed language in order to learn, the mind did not grow strong.
4. The Perkins Institution for the Blind in Boston helped the parents with a difficult problem.
5. The Institution sent a recent graduate, Anne Sullivan, to educate Helen.

Exercise 39	Using Adjectives in Sentences

On your paper, write an adjective that will complete each of the sentences.

1. How _____ the waves were at the beach last night!
2. Today the ocean, _____ as the sky, appears to have lost its fury.
3. The _____ winds blew the sand into dunes along the fence.
4. As rain falls throughout the day, the beach becomes _____.
5. Sun worshipers flock back to the _____ shore the moment the clouds depart.

Possessive Nouns and Pronouns as Adjectives

Possessive pronouns—such as *my, our,* and *your*— function as adjectives because they modify nouns in addition to serving as pronouns: *my* dog, *our* dream, *your* accomplishments. Similarly, possessive nouns function as adjectives: *Tanya's* vacation.

Exercise 40   Identifying Possessive Nouns and Pronouns as Adjectives

On your paper, list each possessive noun or pronoun that is used as an adjective. Then identify the word it modifies.

1. Sarah reluctantly turned in her math homework, which wasn't very legible on its crumpled paper.
2. Sarah realized her work was unacceptable and hoped Mrs. Ono would give her a chance to redo it.
3. Mrs. Ono reviewed Sarah's homework and then took two books off the shelf to examine their contents.
4. After Mrs. Ono found a new math exercise, she asked Sarah, "Will you give this your best effort?"
5. Thankful for the second chance, Sarah replied, "This time I'm sure my work will meet your expectations."
6. Sarah went home with her friend Emily, took out the math book, borrowed Emily's pencil, and started working.
7. She studied the new assignment, examining the problems and thinking about their solutions.
8. Within an hour, Sarah completed the evening's homework.
9. Sarah reviewed her calculations and carefully checked their accuracy.
10. Sarah looked forward to Mrs. Ono's reaction during Friday's class.

Exercise 41   Using Adjectives

For each blank, write an example of the type of adjective indicated in the parentheses.

1. _____ contestants (adjective that describes how many)
2. _____ pets (possessive noun used as an adjective)
3. _____ furniture (possessive pronoun used as an adjective)
4. _____ performance (adjective that describes what kind)
5. _____ traffic (adjective that tells which "traffic")
6. _____ vehicle (possessive noun used as an adjective)
7. _____ appointment (possessive pronoun used as an adjective)
8. _____ clients (adjective that describes how many)
9. _____ weather (adjective that describes what kind)
10. _____ briefcase (possessive noun used as an adjective)

Adjectives That Compare

Many adjectives have different forms to indicate their degree of comparison.

POSITIVE	COMPARATIVE	SUPERLATIVE
fast	faster	fastest
happy	happier	happiest
beautiful	more beautiful	most beautiful
good	better	best
bad	worse	worst
sad	sadder	saddest
fine	finer	finest
large	larger	largest

Exercise 42   Identifying Adjective Forms

On your paper, write the adjective of comparison in each sentence. Label each adjective *comparative* or *superlative*.

1. Selling a home is often more inconvenient than buying a home.
2. Because of the emotional ties inherent in home ownership, every homeowner believes his or her domicile is the best.
3. Although there are many decisions to be made when selling your home, the most difficult task is deciding on a fair price.
4. A buyer is more suspicious of an inflated price when the home is in disrepair.
5. The worst part of selling is having to allow strangers to roam through your home.

Exercise 43   Finding Adjectives

On your paper, list the twenty adjectives in the following passage. Count possessive nouns and pronouns as adjectives in this exercise, but do not count the words *a*, *an*, and *the*.

Literature: Rainy Mountain

[1]A single knoll rises out of the plain in Oklahoma, north and west of the Wichita Range. [2]For my people, the Kiowas, it is an old landmark, and they gave it the name Rainy Mountain. [3]The hardest weather in the world is there. [4]Winter brings blizzards, hot tornadic winds arise in the spring, and in summer the prairie is an anvil's edge. [5]The grass turns brittle and brown, and it cracks beneath your feet. [6]There are green belts along the rivers and creeks, linear groves of hickory and pecan, willow and witch hazel. [7]At a distance in July or August the steaming foliage seems almost to writhe in fire. [8]Great green and yellow grasshoppers are everywhere in the tall grass, popping up like corn to sting the flesh, and tortoises crawl about on the red earth, going nowhere in the plenty of time. [9]Loneliness is an aspect of the land. . . . [10]To look upon the landscape in the early morning, with the sun at your back, is to lose the sense of proportion.

From *The Way to Rainy Mountain* by N. Scott Momaday

Articles

■ **Articles** are the adjectives *a, an,* and *the. A* and *an* are called indefinite articles. *The* is called a definite article.

INDEFINITE	I wrote **a** poem.
	Luisa wrote **an** essay.
DEFINITE	I wrote **the** poem.
	Luisa wrote **the** essay.

Proper Adjectives

■ A **proper adjective** is formed from a proper noun and begins with a capital letter.

Federico García Lorca was a **Spanish** writer.
They believe in the **Jeffersonian** ideals of democracy.
Russian is written in the **Cyrillic** alphabet.

The suffixes *-an, -ian, -n, -ese,* and *-ish,* along with others, are often used to create proper adjectives. Check the spelling in a dictionary.

PROPER NOUNS	PROPER ADJECTIVES
Augustus Caesar	Augustan
Brazil	Brazilian
America	American
China	Chinese
Finland	Finnish
Greece	Greek
Hercules	Herculean
England	English

Exercise 44   **Using Articles in Sentences**

For each blank, write an article and label it *indefinite* or *definite.*

Dr. Martin Luther King, Pacifist

1. Although many disagreed with him, Dr. Martin Luther King believed nonviolence was _____ best way to achieve his goal.
2. King knew this approach would be difficult, but he did not believe in taking _____ easy way out.
3. In April 1963, Dr. King led _____ series of civil rights marches in Birmingham, Alabama.
4. The purpose of _____ marches was to make Americans aware of the problems that faced African American and other minorities.
5. History was made as Dr. King led his people to freedom and simultaneously became famous around _____ world.

Exercise 45 Forming Proper Adjectives

Write a proper adjective formed from each of the following proper nouns. Consult a dictionary if you need help.

1. India
2. Laos
3. Albert Einstein
4. Norway
5. Scotland

6. Nigeria
7. Chile
8. Japan
9. Bali
10. Peru

Exercise 46 Creating Paragraphs with Adjectives

Write a paragraph about a place you have always wanted to visit. Describe the place as vividly as you can. Use a variety of adjectives, including those that describe, classify, identify, and qualify.

Exercise 47 Review: Possessive Nouns and Pronouns Used as Adjectives

On your paper, write a sentence using each of the following possessive nouns and pronouns as an adjective. Underline the noun or pronoun that each adjective modifies.

1. my
2. the dog's
3. Korea's
4. his
5. your

6. their
7. the school's
8. our
9. its
10. the family's

11. the Smiths'
12. the operator's
13. California's
14. her
15. the visitors'

Exercise 48 Review: Adjectives of Comparison

For each blank write an adjective in the form of the comparison indicated in parentheses.

SAMPLE   _____ newspaper (comparative adjective that uses the word *more*)
ANSWER   more popular newspaper

1. _____ people (comparative adjective that uses the word *more*)
2. _____ program (superlative adjective ending in *-est*)
3. _____ manager (positive adjective ending in *-y*)
4. _____ recommendation (comparative adjective ending in *-er*)
5. _____ situation (any positive adjective)
6. _____ computer (comparative adjective that uses the word *more*)
7. _____ voyage (superlative adjective that uses the word *most*)
8. _____ representative (comparative adjective that uses the word *more*)
9. _____ crime (superlative adjective that ends in *-est*)
10. _____ incident (superlative adjective that uses the word *most*)

Parts of Speech

Review: Adjectives

On your paper, write the twenty adjectives, including articles, that appear in the following paragraph.

Marianne Moore, American Poet

[1]Some critics consider Marianne Moore the most delightful American poet. [2]Her witty, sharp poems quickly grasp the attention of readers. [3]Her vision is original and precise but rather eccentric. [4]The brilliant and oblique surfaces of her poems are filled with observations of animals and nature. [5]Often she cryptically tosses in mysterious but appropriate quotations from her extensive reading.

Review: Using Adjectives in Writing

For each blank, write an example of the type of adjective indicated in parentheses.

SAMPLE _____ (proper adjective) patrons of the arts have long admired the work of Leonardo da Vinci.

ANSWER American

European Artists

1. Leonardo da Vinci was a famous and inventive _____(proper adjective) painter.
2. One of his _____(superlative adjective) paintings is *Mona Lisa.*
3. This painting caused great controversy because of the _____(positive adjective) smile on the face of the woman in the painting.
4. _____(article) painting resides at the Louvre, in France.
5. The Louvre is a _____(proper adjective) museum that houses many other famous and valuable paintings.
6. _____(possessive noun used as an adjective) painting of Mona Lisa served as a model for other painters.
7. England has made _____ (positive adjective) contributions to the literary arts.
8. The _____(proper adjective) playwright William Shakespeare was born in this European country.
9. _____(possessive pronoun used as an adjective) plays have become known the world over.
10. _____(proper adjective) actors are those actors who excel in performing the plays of Shakespeare.
11. _____(article) woman named Charlotte Brontë was born in 1816 amid the lonely moors of Yorkshire in England.
12. She had two older sisters, a brother, and two _____(comparative adjective) sisters, Emily and Anne.
13. Charlotte, Emily, and Anne became famous for _____(possessive pronoun) novels, *Jane Eyre, Wuthering Heights,* and *Agnes Grey.*
14. _____(possessive noun) four sisters died of tuberculosis.
15. Charlotte lived _____(comparative adjective) than any of her siblings.

Parts of Speech

10.5 | Adverbs

■ An **adverb** is a word that modifies a verb, an adjective, or another adverb by making its meaning more specific.

In the following sentence, you can see how adverbs are used to modify an adjective *(intelligent)*, a verb *(leap)*, and an adverb *(high)*:

Surprisingly intelligent dolphins leap **very high.**

Adverbs tell *when, where, how,* and *to what degree.*

My uncle paid me a visit **yesterday.**
Many birds fly **south** for the winter.
The judge ruled **fairly**.
You have been **exceedingly** kind.

Positions of Adverbs

An adverb that modifies a verb may be placed in different positions in relation to the verb. An adverb that modifies an adjective or another adverb must immediately precede the word it modifies.

MODIFYING A VERB	**Usually** we will dine there.
	We **usually** will dine there.
	We will **usually** dine there.
MODIFYING AN ADJECTIVE	That restaurant is **very** fine.
MODIFYING AN ADVERB	**Only** seldom do we dine elsewhere.

Exercise 51   **Identifying Adverbs in Sentences**

On your paper, write the adverb in each sentence. Then write whether the adverb tells *when, where, how,* or *to what degree.*

Traveling by Train

1. Traveling by train is quite exhausting.
2. I bought my tickets at the station today.
3. The seat I was assigned is very close to the restaurant car.
4. The train streaked quickly past the towns.
5. I decided to travel west for a change.

Exercise 52   Distinguishing Adverbs from Other Parts of Speech

Write whether each italicized word is an *adverb* or *not an adverb*.

1. *old* man
2. *most* unusual
3. *exceptionally* talented
4. opened *suddenly*
5. moved *down*

6. *finally* stopped
7. *unusual* film
8. *her* bicycle
9. *fast* race
10. questioned *intermittently*

Exercise 53   Identifying Adverbs in a Paragraph

Write the adverb(s) that appear in each of the following sentences. Then write the word or words each adverb modifies.

Traditional Dances of Africa

[1]Though traditional dances are usually designed to entertain, they frequently have religious purposes. [2]For example, tribal priests sometimes dance themselves into a trance. [3]In many cultures dancers have traditionally used masks to represent the spirits of the gods, animals, or ancestors. [4]The Yao and Maku people of Tanzania, for instance, use complex masks of cloth and bamboo, which they gradually elongate to truly astonishing heights to suggest the power of animal spirits.

[5]Dance styles may also be linked to occupational skills, and frequently gestures from daily life may be incorporated into dance movements. [6]For example, the Nupe fisherman of Nigeria, known for their net throwing, ingeniously stylize into a dance pattern a fisherman's motion as he flings his net skyward. [7]Other cultures may use gestures that imitate a farmer's bend of the knees as he gracefully swings his machete. [8]So that they may clearly emphasize the discipline required of warriors, Zimbabweans sometimes dance in teams using a linear formation.

Exercise 54   Positioning Adverbs

(a) Rewrite each of the following sentences, using the verb-modifying adverb that appears in parentheses. (b) Then rewrite each sentence again, placing the same adverb in a different position.

Brasília, a Modern Capital for Brazil

1. The idea of building a new capital for Brazil was proposed in 1789. (originally)
2. At the time construction began in the 1950s, Brazilians looked forward to having a modern capital city. (eagerly)
3. The Chamber of Deputies, an immense bowl-shaped building, sits on a huge concrete platform with two skyscrapers nearby. (boldly)
4. The parabolically shaped cathedral is considered by many to be the most impressive structure in the city. (actually)
5. Brasília's architecture and city planning are among the most original in the modern world. (certainly)

Adverbs That Compare

Some adverbs, like adjectives, take different forms to indicate the degree of comparison.

POSITIVE	COMPARATIVE	SUPERLATIVE
sat **near**	sat **nearer**	sat **nearest**
walks **slowly**	walks **more slowly**	walks **most slowly**
sings **badly**	sings **worse**	sings **worst**
ran **fast**	ran **faster**	ran **fastest**
plays **well**	plays **better**	plays **best**
arrived **early**	arrived **earlier**	arrived **earliest**
drives **carefully**	drives **more carefully**	drives **most carefully**

Exercise 55   Identifying Adverb Forms

On your paper, list the adverb in each sentence, and label it as *positive, comparative,* or *superlative.*

SAMPLE   Home fitness equipment is more widely used than ever before.
ANSWER   more widely—comparative

1. Exercise equipment is the most popularly advertised product in sports magazines.
2. Some experts believe exercise is most effective when it is done slowly.
3. Last week one of the trainers badly injured her knee.
4. In our gym the step machine is the most consistently used piece of equipment.
5. The physical fitness center I used to attend moved closer to my home.
6. One hour of exercise each day is time well spent.
7. Losing weight can be most quickly achieved through a combination of exercise and a sensible diet.
8. Some joggers run faster than others.
9. Many people claim that they run better in the morning than later in the day.
10. A serious athlete will most often choose to eat a healthful diet.

Exercise 56   Using Adverbs That Compare

Write a sentence using each of the following as an adverb.

1. worst
2. more excitedly
3. quicker
4. loudest
5. more carefully
6. most energetically
7. gracefully
8. cautiously
9. more vigorously
10. most calmly

Negative Words as Adverbs

The word *not* and the contraction *-n't* are considered adverbs. Certain adverbs of time, place, and degree also have a negative meaning.

The dolphin **didn't** leap.   It is **nowhere** near here.
That dolphin **never** leaps.   That fish can **barely** swim.
That dolphin **hardly** leaps.   Some fish can**not** swim fast.

Exercise 57   Finding Negative Words as Adverbs

For each sentence, write the negative word that is used as an adverb.

1. It wasn't long after the first of October, 1957, that the Soviet Union put a satellite into orbit.
2. Dr. Wernher von Braun, a leading rocket engineer, and his team of scientists could not succeed in launching a satellite before the Soviets did.
3. The Soviet satellite *Sputnik* had barely been launched into orbit when the United States entered the race for space.
4. Since 1957 America's interest in outer space has never ceased.
5. Many people can hardly imagine the ways that space exploration has benefited society.

Exercise 58   Review: Adding Adverbs to Expand Sentences

Rewrite each sentence, adding an example of the kind of adverb indicated in parentheses. Add any other words or phrases to make your expanded sentences make sense.

SAMPLE   We walked to the restaurant. (adverb that indicates a comparative degree)
ANSWER   We walked more cautiously to the restaurant than we had the night before.

An Evening Out with a Friend

1. The performance by the band at last night's concert was superb. (adverb that tells to what degree)
2. The guitar player strummed. (adverb that tells how)
3. As I listened, I became enthralled. (adverb that tells to what degree)
4. The flutes sounded melodious. (adverb that indicates a comparative degree)
5. My companion for the evening paid attention during the entire show. (negative word used as an adverb)
6. We went to a restaurant. (adverb that tells when)
7. The waiter served the food. (adverb that tells how)
8. We did stay for dessert. (negative word used as an adverb)
9. We walked two blocks and returned to our car that was parked in front of a jewelry store. (adverb that tells where)
10. We drove home. (adverb that indicates a superlative degree)

Review: Adverbs in Different Positions

For each sentence, write the adverb and the word or words it modifies.

Beards

1. In early times men greatly prized the hair that grew on their faces.
2. The Egyptians were actually known to weave gold threads through their beards.
3. Then Alexander the Great began a tradition that is with us to this day.
4. He believed that an enemy in battle could easily grab a soldier by the beard and kill him.
5. Alexander immediately gave the order for his soldiers to shave.
6. Records show that the practice of shaving or cutting beards spread quickly through Rome, and Roman barbers were busy by 300 B.C.
7. Despite the custom begun by Alexander the Great, beards remained quite popular.
8. Eventually, men grew specific types of beards.
9. Abraham Lincoln is well remembered as the first president to wear a beard.
10. Famous men such as Sigmund Freud and Bernard Shaw also wore beards.

Exercise 60   **Review: Using Adverbs in Writing**

Write an appropriate adverb for each numbered blank.

Every spring Pablo _____(1)_____ anticipates the first professional basketball game of the season. He can _____(2)_____ wait for the tickets to go on sale. Pablo _____(3)_____ buys a season ticket every year in order to ensure a seat at each game. _____(4)_____ the opening game will be played. Pablo __(5)_____ counts the minutes to tip off. He joins the __(6)_____ cheering fans as they __(7)_____ applaud their favorite players.

_____(8)_____ the announcer introduces the starting players. As they __(9)_____ march onto the court, the crowd continues to ___(10)___ applaud each team member.

Exercise 61   **Review: Writing Sentences with Adverbs**

Write a sentence illustrating the use of each kind of adverb indicated. Underline the adverb.

SAMPLE   An adverb that tells how
ANSWER   Because he was uncertain of the answer, the contestant answered the question slowly.

1. An adverb that modifies an adjective
2. An adverb that indicates a comparative degree
3. An adverb that modifies a verb
4. A negative word used as an adverb
5. An adverb that indicates a superlative degree
6. An adverb that modifies an adverb
7. An adverb that tells where
8. An adverb that tells how
9. An adverb that tells when
10. An adverb that tells to what degree

Review: Adverbs in a Paragraph

On your paper, write the five adverbs in the paragraph below.

Chinese New Year

Anyone who lives in a Chinese American neighborhood will surely hear firecrackers each January or February. This traditional event always heralds the Chinese New Year. People excitedly await this holiday, which begins the lunar year. Families eagerly share foods that are symbols of good luck. Children anticipate this holiday because they often receive gifts of money in red envelopes.

Exercise 63 Review: Finding Adverbs in Sentences

On your paper, write the adverb in each sentence and the word or words the adverb modifies.

SAMPLE   Often a government agency creates a unique solution to a problem.
ANSWER   often creates

Burros in the Desert

1. The Federal Bureau of Land Management is now offering wild burros for adoption.
2. The fee for the animals is very reasonable.
3. Amazingly, these burros will eat weeds and carry heavy equipment on their backs.
4. Burros traveled here with Spanish settlers.
5. As the burros found their way to freedom, their numbers increased alarmingly.
6. They relentlessly travel through the deserts, trampling tiny plants and animals.
7. They most certainly pose a threat to the desert's ecosystem.
8. The government could not allow this destruction to continue.
9. Without government intervention the problem would certainly grow worse.
10. The adoption solution was a very unusual, yet effective, solution.

Modern Mail Delivery

11. Mail delivery may change drastically in the future.
12. Many homeowners in established neighborhoods conveniently receive their mail through a slot in the front door.
13. Other people living in older homes step outside to remove their mail from a box attached to the house.
14. Apartment dwellers often have a locked box near the front entrance of the building.
15. People living in the country and in newer subdivisions must sometimes walk to the end of their driveways to get their mail.
16. Now all of that may change.
17. Residents of new subdivisions may have to walk farther to retrieve their mail.
18. All mailboxes may be placed centrally at a single location in the subdivision.
19. Some people say this method will serve customers more efficiently.
20. One prospective user of the new mailbox locations said angrily, "I think people are going to be bothered by the inconvenience."

10.6 Prepositions

■ A **preposition** is a word that shows the relationship of a noun or a pronoun to another word in a sentence.

> The cat is **under** the desk. [*Under* shows the spatial relationship of the desk to the cat.]
>
> I saw my counselor **before** my first-period class. [*Before* expresses the time relationship between the meeting and the class period.]
>
> I read your poem **to** them. [*To* relates the verb *read* to the pronoun *them*.]

COMMONLY USED PREPOSITIONS

aboard	beside	into	through
about	besides	like	throughout
above	between	near	to
across	beyond	of	toward
after	but*	off	under
against	by	on	underneath
along	concerning	onto	until
amid	despite	opposite	unto
among	down	out	up
around	during	outside	upon
as	except	over	with
at	excepting	past	within
before	for	pending	without
behind	from	regarding	
below	in	respecting	
beneath	inside	since	

*in the sense of "except"

■ A **compound preposition** is a preposition that is made up of more than one word.

COMPOUND PREPOSITIONS

according to	because of	next to
ahead of	by means of	on account of
along with	in addition to	on top of
apart from	in front of	out of
aside from	in spite of	owing to
as to	instead of	

Using Prepositions in Sentences

Write a preposition or compound preposition that would make sense in each sentence below.

1. The exterminator was reluctant to spray insecticide _____ the confines of the room.
2. _____ the infestation, the tenants decided to move.
3. There was little disagreement _____ the tenants and the landlord.
4. The infestation was found to have originated _____ the window of the first-floor apartment.
5. _____ next month, everyone will be able to return home.

Identifying Prepositions

On your paper, list the prepositions that appear in each of the following sentences. Remember that some prepositions are made up of more than one word. (The numeral in parentheses at the end of each item indicates the number of prepositions in that sentence.)

Jackson Hole Valley

1. Scenic Jackson Hole Valley lies at the foot of the Teton Mountains. (2)
2. Towering above Jackson Hole, the Tetons have many peaks that are more than ten thousand feet high. (1)
3. According to reports, the first white trapper in Jackson Hole was John Colter. (2)
4. With the exception of hardy mountaineers who hunted game, early pioneers stayed outside the valley during the harsh winter. (3)
5. In the 1880s some homesteaders became concerned about the survival of Jackson Hole elk. (3)
6. As a result, in 1912 the National Elk Refuge was established within the valley. (3)
7. In addition to the elk problem, there was the question of conservation. (2)
8. By 1929 Congress had established the Grand Teton National Park along the eastern slopes of the Tetons. (3)
9. In the meantime, John D. Rockefeller Jr. had acquired acres of Jackson Hole land for public use. (3)
10. Through the intervention of Franklin D. Roosevelt, Jackson Hole National Monument, which included over 200,000 acres, was established in 1943. (3)
11. The monument was abolished in 1950, and most of it was added to the Grand Teton National Park. (3)
12. Some Jackson Hole residents opposed outsiders' coming into the valley. (1)
13. Very little of Teton County's land is now in private hands. (2)
14. Visitors come to the Grand Teton National Park throughout the year. (2)
15. Flying above Jackson Hole, you see vistas of truly breathtaking splendor. (2)
16. Beyond a doubt, Jackson Hole's lakes and mountains are spectacular. (1)
17. Because of the many clear streams, the fishing alone draws a host of visitors. (2)
18. Along the shore of Jackson Lake, a campground overlooks the marina of Colter Bay. (3)
19. Amid the soaring peaks of Mount Moran, Grand Teton, and South Teton lies little Jenny Lake. (2)
20. Throughout Jackson Hole, wildflowers carpet summer foothills with a riot of color. (3)

Object of the Preposition

Prepositions are found at the beginning of phrases that usually end with a noun or a pronoun called the **object of the preposition.**

Eli told me **about the fire.**   Sook came here **from Korea.**

Owen sat **opposite me.**   All **but Jane** agreed.

They read the report **concerning him.**   All waited **outside the door.**

The birds flew **beyond the clouds.**   The books were thrown **upon the bed.**

Everyone arrived **except Bill.**   The house remained **in the family.**

He left **without notice.**   She parked **between the signs.**

Exercise 66   Finding the Object of the Preposition

For each phrase, write the preposition and its object.

1. a seat in the last row
2. ventured through the night
3. the presentation of the award
4. riding on the early train
5. the man without a name
6. crashing down the mountain
7. soaring high above the clouds
8. all of them
9. running against the wind
10. anyone besides you
11. the grass on the front lawn
12. lasted for an hour
13. a bird outside my window
14. reading to all the children
15. hiding behind the old tree
16. a rabbit running over a bridge
17. impressed by the hard work
18. walking past the fence
19. far beyond the tracks
20. the wheel above the deck

Exercise 67   Creating Sentences with Prepositions

Choose five prepositions from the lists on page 468. Use each preposition in a sentence.

Exercise 68   Using Prepositions and Their Objects in Sentences

Write a sentence for each pair of words listed. Use the first word as a preposition in the sentence and the second word as its object, adding adjectives and adverbs wherever necessary.

SAMPLE   outside, town
ANSWER   The travelers decided to stay outside the town.

1. from, sister
2. without, money
3. about, accident
4. of, page
5. pending, agreement
6. during, show
7. before, appointment
8. over, land
9. at, top
10. through, glass

Exercise 69 — Review: Compound Prepositions

Write the compound preposition in each of the following sentences.

SAMPLE   This is not the right tool according to the instruction book.
ANSWER   according to

Mickey Mouse

1. Next to toys, cartoons are probably the most popular means of childhood amusement.
2. Walt Disney is certainly on top of the list of contributors to childhood fantasies.
3. Walt Disney, along with his brother Roy, set up a studio producing animated cartoons.
4. Disney first thought of making his new character a mouse because of field mice that came into his studio.
5. In spite of his initial idea to name the mouse Mortimer, Disney decided to name the new character Mickey Mouse.
6. Disney's cartoon *Steamboat Willie* was a worldwide success, owing to its use of a sound track.
7. Mickey and Minnie Mouse appeared on movie screens in front of audiences around the world.
8. Disney created a succession of cartoon movies in addition to the Mickey Mouse movies.
9. Walt Disney continued to build on his dream in spite of many difficult times.
10. Because of his determination and foresight, Walt Disney overcame the monetary setbacks he encountered over the years.

Exercise 70 — Review: Expanding Sentences with Prepositions

Expand each sentence by adding the preposition indicated in the parentheses, plus an object for the preposition.

SAMPLE   The chemist developed a new antidote. (in)
ANSWER   The chemist developed a new antidote *in the laboratory.*

Health Care

1. The operation was a success. (in spite of)
2. The patient phoned the doctor's office. (for)
3. Emergencies seem to occur most often at home. (during)
4. As a paramedic, she understands emergency procedures. (for)
5. As the ambulance sped, cars dashed out of its path. (along)
6. The nurse decided to work three hours overtime. (instead of)
7. Caring for patients requires dedication and sympathy. (because of)
8. Difficult decisions are commonplace in the life of a doctor. (despite)
9. Medical insurance has become a necessity. (on account of)
10. Preventive medicine is the best insurance. (against)
11. Nursing homes provide care. (for)
12. Patients in the hospital often complain. (about)
13. Some people should visit a hospital emergency room. (with)
14. Patients should not have to sit for long periods. (in)
15. The patient is recovering. (from)

10.7 Conjunctions

■ A **conjunction** is a word that joins single words or groups of words.

Coordinating Conjunctions

■ A **coordinating conjunction** joins words or groups of words that have equal grammatical weight in a sentence.

> They stand **and** wait.
> Put the boxes in the kitchen **or** in the garage.
> We planted tulips, **but** they did not grow.
> The door was open, **yet** nobody was home.

Coordinating Conjunctions						
and	but	or	nor	for	yet	so

Exercise 71   **Identifying Coordinating Conjunctions**

Read the paragraph. Then, on a separate sheet of paper, write the coordinating conjunction(s) that appear in each sentence.

Kareem Abdul-Jabbar

[1]At the time of his birth in 1947, Ferdinand Lewis Alcindor Jr. was over twenty-two inches long and weighed twelve pounds eleven ounces. [2]By the time he was in sixth grade, the six-foot Lew Alcindor was already playing basketball, but he was too clumsy to be good. [3]The school coach coaxed Lew to stay for practice at the gym until six or seven o'clock most evenings. [4]When he was in the seventh grade, Lew was tall enough (six feet eight inches) to dunk the basketball, and other students grew proud of his ability. [5]Lew won a scholarship to Power Memorial Academy, for the coach there recognized his potential. [6]Lew joined the varsity basketball team as a freshman, yet he was still awkward. [7]With much practice he acquired considerable grace, and he was hailed as the most promising high school player in the country. [8]Lew's basketball career at UCLA was lonely, but it brought many offers from professional recruiters. [9]At the age of twenty-four, Lew Alcindor was a renowned basketball star and was named Most Valuable Player of the National Basketball Association. [10]Now, of course, Lew Alcindor is known as Kareem Abdul-Jabbar, for he changed his name to acknowledge his African heritage.

Exercise 72   **Creating Sentences with Coordinating Conjuctions**

Write an original sentence using each of the coordinating conjunctions listed in the chart above. Remember, the words that each conjunction joins must have equal grammatical weight in the sentence.

Correlative Conjunctions

■ **Correlative conjunctions** work in pairs to join words and groups of words of equal weight in a sentence.

Correlative Conjunctions	
both . . . and either . . . or just as . . . so	neither . . . nor not only . . . but (also) whether . . . or

Correlative conjunctions can make the relationship between words or groups of words somewhat clearer than coordinating conjunctions can.

COORDINATING CONJUNCTIONS	CORRELATIVE CONJUNCTIONS
He **and** I should talk.	**Both** you **and** I should talk.
He **or** I should talk.	**Either** he **or** I should talk.
	Neither you **nor** I should talk.
I speak French **and** Chinese.	I speak **not only** French **but also** Chinese.

Exercise 73   Identifying Correlative Conjunctions

On your paper, write both parts of the correlative conjunctions that appear in the following sentences.

Finding Shelter

1. Whether you are lost on a hike or stuck in a disabled car, your life may depend upon finding shelter.
2. Both the severe cold of a snow-capped mountain and the burning heat of a desert require some kind of shelter.
3. In either hot or cold locations, it is important to protect oneself from the elements.
4. Tarpaulin shelters are not only quick and easy to put up but also light to carry.
5. A triangular tent can be formed either by leaning a pole into the crook of a tree branch or by lashing two poles together in an **X**.
6. Just as strong trees can help provide shelter, so can dense brush.
7. A dense stand of either willows or sagebrush makes a fine shelter when their tops are tied together.
8. Should you have neither tarpaulin nor brush, you may be able to find a protected spot along a river bank.
9. Whether a river bank provides safe shelter or presents risks depends upon the incidence of flash floods in the area.
10. In deep snow, a simple trench roofed with evergreen branches provides both shelter and insulation from the cold.

Subordinating Conjunctions

■ A **subordinating conjunction** joins two clauses, or ideas, in such a way as to make one grammatically dependent upon the other.

A subordinating conjunction introduces a subordinate, or dependent, clause, one that cannot stand alone as a complete sentence.

The audience applauded **when** Aretha Franklin appeared on the stage.

Franklin smiled **as** the audience cheered.

Wherever she appears, people flock to see her perform.

As soon as I heard she was coming, I rushed to buy tickets for my whole family.

Common Subordinating Conjunctions			
after	as though	provided (that)	until
although	because	since	when
as	before	so long as	whenever
as far as	considering (that)	so that	where
as if	if	than	whereas
as long as	inasmuch as	though	wherever
as soon as	in order that	unless	while

Exercise 74   **Identifying Subordinating Conjunctions**

Write the subordinating conjunction that appears in each sentence below. Remember that some subordinating conjunctions are made up of more than one word.

An Wang, a Pioneer of the Electronic Age

1. Born in China, An Wang came to the United States in 1945 to study and decided to stay when the Chinese Communists took power soon after.
2. Because he was brilliant and had had practical experience, he breezed through his doctoral studies in applied physics.
3. His breakthrough came when he devised a way to store electronic information on the tiny magnetized iron doughnuts that were used in primitive computers.
4. Although he had only six hundred dollars, An Wang used his savings to set up a small business in 1951.
5. In 1956 his ferrite magnetic memory core brought him a small fortune after IBM began using it in computers.

Conjunctive Adverbs

■ A **conjunctive adverb** is used to clarify the relationship between clauses of equal weight in a sentence.

Conjunctive adverbs are usually stronger than coordinating conjunctions because they more precisely explain the relationship between the two clauses.

COORDINATING CONJUNCTION	The office was cold, the noise was intolerable, **and** he resigned.
CONJUNCTIVE ADVERB	The office was cold, and the noise was intolerable; **consequently,** he resigned.

The uses of conjunctive adverbs are illustrated by the following:

TO REPLACE *AND*	also, besides, furthermore, moreover
TO REPLACE *BUT*	however, nevertheless, still
TO STATE A RESULT	consequently, therefore, so, thus
TO STATE EQUALITY	equally, likewise, similarly

Exercise 75   **Using Conjunctive Adverbs**

Rewrite each of the following sentences, filling in the blank with an appropriate conjunctive adverb that makes the sentence meaningful. There may be more than one correct answer.

The Police Laboratory

1. Every case that comes to a police laboratory is different; _____, all cases require two basic steps.
2. In criminal cases, physical evidence must be identified; _____, it must be matched to an individual.
3. Everybody's fingerprints are unique; _____, the bullets fired by every firearm are marked with unique grooves.
4. Each chemical compound absorbs different wavelengths of light; _____, police scientists can identify the contents of a pill or a liquid.
5. Modern police laboratories make use of computers; _____, the matching of fingerprints takes only minutes.
6. Forged documents are frequently involved in fraud cases; _____, police laboratories employ document examiners.
7. Professional document examiners can usually match handwriting samples; _____, they can often match typewriting to a specific typewriter.
8. With ultraviolet and infrared light, document examiners can decipher invisible writing; _____, they can spot erasures and alterations.
9. Police laboratory workers may be most at home behind the scenes; _____, an important part of their job often involves testifying in court.
10. Scientific analysis has helped convict many guilty people; _____, it has also prevented many people from being convicted of crimes they did not commit.

Write each sentence, changing the coordinating conjunction so the sentence makes better sense.

SAMPLE	Incorrect: Harry Nelson Pillsbury was famous for his photographic memory yet for his talent at playing chess.
ANSWERS	Rewrite: Harry Nelson Pillsbury was famous for his photographic memory and for his talent at playing chess.

Harry Nelson Pillsbury, Photographic Memory

1. Harry Nelson Pillsbury played twenty-two games of chess at the same time but remembered all the moves everybody made.
2. Pillsbury began playing chess in 1887 at the age of fifteen, for he did not become U.S. champion until 1898.
3. Pillsbury succeeded at winning at chess, but his opponents were champion players.
4. He would give public performances displaying his powers of memory nor his skill as a player.
5. In one performance, Pillsbury memorized a twenty-nine-word list of tongue twisters, for he was able to recite the list word for word.

Exercise 77   Review: Correlative Conjunctions

Complete the blanks with a pair of correlative conjunctions that make sense in the sentence.

SAMPLE	_____ we complete this project _____ I quit.
ANSWERS	Either, or

The Performance

1. _____ students _____ teachers from the local high school were invited to attend the college performance of *Hamlet*.
2. The college theater group _____ performed the play and designed the costumes _____ made the scenery.
3. _____ you bought the tickets through the mail ____ you purchased them at the theater in person, you were assured of a good seat.
4. _____ professional actors require attention, _____ did the college players.
5. At the end of the performance, the audience _____ applauded _____ stood up and cheered.
6. _____ you enjoy Shakespeare ____ not, you will be impressed with this production of the famous play.
7. _____ the director _____ the producer had major roles in the play in addition to their other responsibilities.
8. _____ did this performance sell out, _____ next week's performance is sold out as well.
9. When attending a play, it is proper etiquette to be _____ too late ____ too early.
10. Next year the play will be _____ *Romeo and Juliet* ____ *A Midsummer Night's Dream*.

Exercise 78   Review: Subordinating Conjunctions

Write the subordinating conjunction that appears in each sentence below. Remember that some subordinating conjunctions are made up of more than one word.

More About An Wang

1. An Wang's invention served as the standard memory-storage device in computers until it was replaced by the semiconductor chip twenty years later.
2. Although it sold for sixty-five hundred dollars, his first electronic calculator for scientists cost much less than a mainframe computer and was easier to operate.
3. His name became well-known in business after the Wang electronic word processor, the first "thinking typewriter," was used successfully in offices.
4. An Wang knew his company would prosper as long as he could design useful machines for science and business.
5. As one of twelve outstanding naturalized American citizens, Wang was awarded the Medal of Liberty when the centennial of the Statue of Liberty was celebrated in 1986.

Exercise 79   Review: Conjunctive Adverbs

Complete each sentence with a conjunctive adverb that makes the sentence meaningful. In most cases there can be more than one correct answer.

SAMPLE   John Harvey Kellogg ate a bland diet mostly consisting of grains and vegetables; _____, food became a major influence on his life.

ANSWER   nevertheless

John Harvey Kellogg

1. The Western Health Reform Institute of Battle Creek, Michigan, sent Kellogg to medical school; _____, he returned to become the institute's medical superintendent in 1876.
2. Kellogg renamed the institute the Medical and Surgical Sanitarium; _____, he introduced a number of refinements, such as musical concerts.
3. In the late nineteenth century, Kellogg created a precooked, ready-to-eat health food that he named *Granula;* _____, he learned that this name had already been used.
4. Kellogg was eventually sued for using the name *Granula;* _____, he changed the name of his health food to *Granola.*
5. John Kellogg and his brother, William, ran the Sanitas Food Company, which manufactured health food; _____, they produced exercise equipment as well.

Exercise 80   Review: Using Conjunctive Adverbs in Sentences

Write an original sentence using each of the conjunctive adverbs listed below. Check that the adverb shows the appropriate relationship between the clauses in your sentences.

1. consequently   3. besides   5. likewise
2. however   4. nevertheless

Exercise 81   Creating Sentences with Conjunctions

Think of a favorite motion picture or television program that you have seen. Write several sentences about the typical characters, events, or setting of the movie or show, using as many conjunctions as possible.

Exercise 82   Review: Conjunctions

On your paper, replace the blank or blanks that appear in each of the following sentences with a conjunction that makes sense. The kind of conjunction to use is stated in parentheses at the end of each sentence.

The Lost City Meteorite

1. An Oklahoma farmer went looking for a calf; _____, he found a meteor fragment. (conjunctive adverb)
2. _____ the Lost City Meteorite descended over Oklahoma, it was seen as far away as central Nebraska. (subordinating conjunction)
3. _____ the meteorite was descending, a sonic boom was heard all the way from Tulsa to Tahlequah. (subordinating conjunction)
4. _____ was the Lost City Meteorite tracked photographically, _____ its landing place was accurately predicted. (correlative conjunction)
5. The first meteorite fragment was found quickly _____ flown to the Smithsonian Institution. (coordinating conjunction)
6. _____ the photographic tracking was accurate, many airborne meteor particles could be recovered. (subordinating conjunction)
7. _____ the meteor entered the earth's atmosphere at nine miles per second, it slowed to two miles per second at an altitude of eleven miles. (subordinating conjunction)
8. The fireball dropped the 9.85-kilogram meteorite on December 28, 1970; _____, it was not found until six days later. (conjunctive adverb)
9. _____ the original meteorite _____ three others found later by investigators formed a total mass of 17.3 kilograms. (correlative conjunction)
10. _____ scientists tracked the Oklahoma fireball, they had tracked only one meteor by means of photography. (subordinating conjunction)

Ty Cobb

11. _____ he was just a country boy from Georgia, Ty Cobb became the first superstar of baseball. (subordinating conjunction)
12. His father wanted him to go to college, _____ Ty was determined to try his luck in baseball first, and finally his father agreed. (coordinating conjunction)
13. The other Detroit Tigers tormented Cobb and made his life miserable; _____, in his first full year with Detroit, he won the batting championship with a .350 average and began to practice his aggressive base running. (conjunctive adverb)
14. For twelve out of thirteen years, Cobb led the American League in hitting, _____ his lifetime average was .367. (coordinating conjunction)
15. _____ Babe Ruth _____ Honus Wagner, two other great players of the era, ever came close to Cobb's impressive base stealing. (correlative conjunction)

10.8 Interjections

■ An **interjection** is a word or phrase that expresses emotion or exclamation. An interjection has no grammatical connection to other words.

Well, such is life.
Ouch! That hurts.
Ah, that's delicious!
Sh! Be quiet.

Exercise 83   Using Interjections

On your paper, fill in the blank in each sentence below with an appropriate interjection from the following list:

oh no	wow	bravo	oh well	hooray
whew	oops	ouch	gee	my

1. _____, I'm sorry I forgot your birthday.
2. _____! You just stepped on my foot.
3. _____! That was the finest performance of that play I have ever seen.
4. _____, how you've grown!
5. _____! I spilled the milk.
6. _____! José Canseco has just hit his second home run of the game.
7. _____! That is the tallest building I have ever seen.
8. _____, we burned the meat loaf, but now we can go out to dinner.
9. _____! It looks as though there has been a serious accident down the road.
10. _____! I'm relieved that the exam is over.

Exercise 84   Correcting Interjections

In the following sentences, replace each interjection that does not make sense with one that does. If the interjection that is used makes sense, write *correct*.

SAMPLE   Hooray! I lost my only copy of my book report.
ANSWER   Oh no!

1. Aha! The valuable vase crashed to the floor.
2. Alas! It's freezing outside.
3. Ouch! That's the greatest news I've heard today.
4. Wow! Did you draw that freehand?
5. Oh no! My sister is arriving a day early, and I don't have her room ready.
6. Oh no! My sister is arriving a day early, and I can hardly wait to see her.
7. Gee, I never thought you would eat spinach for lunch.
8. Sh! The baby might awaken.
9. Well, I was only trying to help.
10. Oops! The coach has finally arrived.

Grammar Review

PARTS OF SPEECH

Set in a coastal town in Colombia, Gabriel García Márquez's novel is about an unrequited love that endures for more than fifty years. In this episode the hero, Florentino Ariza, then a young boy, contemplates sending a letter to Fermina Daza, the girl who becomes the great love of his life but whom he admires from afar. This passage, translated from the Spanish, has been annotated to show the parts of speech covered in this unit.

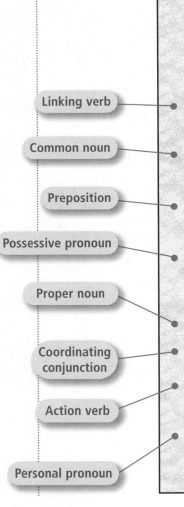

Literature Model

from Love in the Time of Cholera

by Gabriel García Márquez

translated from the Spanish by Edith Grossman

It was in this innocent way that Florentino Ariza began his secret life as a solitary hunter. From seven o'clock in the morning, he sat on the most hidden bench in the little park, pretending to read a book of verse in the shade of the almond trees, until he saw the impossible maiden walk by in her blue-striped uniform, stockings that reached to her knees, masculine laced oxfords, and a single thick braid with a bow at the end, which hung down her back to her waist. She walked with natural haughtiness, her head high, her eyes unmoving, her step rapid, her nose pointing straight ahead, her bag of books held against her chest with crossed arms, her doe's gait making her seem immune to gravity. At her side, struggling to keep up with her, the aunt with the brown habit and rope of St. Francis did not allow him the slightest opportunity to approach. Florentino Ariza saw them pass back and forth four times a day and once on Sundays when they came out of High Mass, and just seeing the girl was enough for him. Little by little he idealized her, endowing her with improbable virtues and imaginary sentiments, and after two weeks he thought of nothing else but her. So he decided to send Fermina Daza a simple note written on both sides of the paper in his exquisite notary's hand. But

Labels (left margin):
- Linking verb
- Common noun
- Preposition
- Possessive pronoun
- Proper noun
- Coordinating conjunction
- Action verb
- Personal pronoun

he kept it in his pocket for several days, thinking about how to hand it to her, and while he thought he wrote several more pages before going to bed, so that the original letter was turning into a dictionary of compliments, inspired by books he had learned by heart because he read them so often during his vigils in the park. . . .

By the time the letter contained more than sixty pages written on both sides, Florentino Ariza could no longer endure the weight of his secret, and he unburdened himself to his mother, the only person with whom he allowed himself any confidences. Tránsito Ariza was moved to tears by her son's innocence in matters of love, and she tried to guide him with her own knowledge. She began by convincing him not to deliver the lyrical sheaf of papers, since it would only frighten the girl of his dreams, who she supposed was as green as he in matters of the heart.

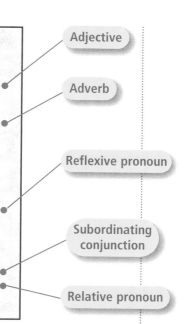

- Adjective
- Adverb
- Reflexive pronoun
- Subordinating conjunction
- Relative pronoun

Review: Exercise 1   Identifying Nouns

On your paper, identify each of the nouns in the following sentences. After each noun identify its use as *common, proper,* or *collective.*

1. In Spain and South America in those days, adults supervised young people in public.
2. Escolástica was the chaperone of her niece, a schoolgirl named Fermina Daza.
3. Fermina and her aunt walked more rapidly than the other women in the group going to the academy.
4. Because of a vow, Escolástica dressed in the brown clothes of a Franciscan.
5. In former times, the school Fermina attended, the Academy of the Presentation, had accepted only the daughters of aristocratic families.

Review: Exercise 2   Using Nouns in Sentences

The following nouns are contained in the excerpt from *Love in the Time of Cholera.* Label each noun as *common, proper,* or *possessive,* and as *singular* or *plural.* Then write an original sentence for each noun.

SAMPLE   Florentino Ariza
ANSWER   proper, singular

Florentino Ariza confided in his mother about his love for Fermina Daza.

1. eyes   2. St. Francis   3. books   4. notary's   5. time

Parts of Speech

Grammar Review

Review: Exercise 3 Using Pronouns Effectively

The following sentences elaborate on ideas suggested by the passage from *Love in the Time of Cholera*. On your paper, write the pronoun that makes sense in each blank. Follow the directions in parentheses.

1. Florentino pretended to read so that _____ could catch sight of Fermina. (Use a third-person singular personal pronoun.)
2. _____ was that woman walking with Fermina? (Use an interrogative pronoun.)
3. _____ was Aunt Escolástica, the sister of Fermina's father. (Use a demonstrative pronoun.)
4. Escolástica was a stalwart chaperone _____ would not allow any man to approach Fermina. (Use a relative pronoun.)
5. Fermina _____ walked so haughtily that no one could easily approach her. (Use an intensive pronoun.)
6. Florentino had not finished the letter, _____ told of his love for Fermina. (Use a relative pronoun.)
7. Perhaps he felt he had listed _____ of Fermina's virtues but not all of them. (Use an indefinite pronoun.)
8. Florentino asked _____ how he could hand Fermina the letter. (Use a reflexive pronoun.)
9. Florentino thought, "I will ask _____ mother what to do." (Use a first-person singular possessive pronoun.)
10. His mother told him _____: a passionate love letter might frighten Fermina. (Use a demonstrative pronoun.)

Review: Exercise 4 Identifying Pronouns

The following sentences paraphrase some of the ideas contained in the passage from *Love in the Time of Cholera*. On your paper, write each pronoun and identify it as *personal, possessive, demonstrative, reflexive, interrogative, relative,* or *indefinite.*

SAMPLE   Her cousin would walk with Fermina each day.
ANSWER   Her, possessive

1. Florentino Ariza waited patiently each morning until he saw the woman, Fermina.
2. His love, though still a secret, continued to grow.
3. Fermina Daza allowed herself the pleasure of a daily stroll with Escolástica.
4. This was the highlight of Florentino's day.
5. Who would expect a one-sided romance to blossom eventually into true love?
6. No one but Tránsito Ariza knew of Florentino's passion for Fermina.
7. Fermina would never allow herself to think of such ideas as love.
8. What was Florentino to do with a sixty-page love letter?
9. Florentino knew his mother was wise in matters of the heart.
10. She advised Florentino to keep the love letter from Fermina.

Review: Exercise 5   Identifying Transitive and Intransitive Verbs

The following sentences contain verbs that appear in the passage from *Love in the Time of Cholera*. For each item, write *transitive* or *intransitive* on your paper, depending upon the way the italicized verb is used in the sentence. Then write your own sentence using the verb in the same way it is used in the item.

SAMPLE   Couples often *sit* on park benches.
ANSWER   intransitive
            Elena sits gracefully on the sofa.

1. Young men and women *see* one another at dances.
2. Sometimes the men *walk* with the women for hours.
3. The women *hold* garlands of flowers.
4. They *keep* small gifts that they give each other.
5. The couples *pass* one another in the park.

Review: Exercise 6   Using Verbs in Sentences

The following is a list of verbs in the passage from *Love in the Time of Cholera*. Write a sentence using each verb in the form indicated in parentheses.

SAMPLE   was (present tense)
ANSWER   There is no excuse for failing the test.

1. saw (future tense)
2. kept (present tense)
3. deliver (transitive)
4. written (add an auxiliary verb)
5. tried (present tense)

Review: Exercise 7   Writing Sentences with Adjectives

The following sentences are adapted from *Love in the Time of Cholera*. First, identify the adjectives in each sentence. (Do not include articles.) Then, for each sentence write a sentence of your own with an identical structure. Place your adjectives in the same position in which they appear in the sentence in this exercise. Each of your sentences may be about a different subject.

SAMPLE   Florentino began his secret life in an innocent way.
ANSWER   his, secret, innocent
            Gemma drew an imaginary winter scene on the frosty window.

1. Fermina wore her long hair in a single braid.
2. Her doelike gait made her seem immune to gravity.
3. The innocent love and romantic longings of her son touched Tránsito Ariza.
4. Would the lyrical sheaf of papers frighten the haughty girl?
5. Fermina might be as innocent as Florentino in tender matters of the heart.

Grammar Review

Review: Exercise 8 — Using Adverbs

The following sentences describe the courtship customs that would have been practiced in the social and historical setting of *Love in the Time of Cholera*. Rewrite each sentence, substituting an appropriate adverb for the phrase in italics. The adverb should express the same idea as the prepositional phrase.

SAMPLE   Courtship had to be handled *with delicacy.*
ANSWER   Courtship had to be handled delicately.

1. By custom young women did not speak *in public* to men.
2. Chaperones guarded their charges' honor *with* ferocity.
3. A wealthy young woman would *in all probability* have many suitors.
4. *According to tradition,* marriages were arranged by the parents of the young people.
5. A young man who acted *with imprudence* might lose his chance to win a young lady.

Review: Exercise 9 — Using Prepositions

The following sentences elaborate on ideas suggested by the García Márquez passage. Rewrite each sentence, filling in the blanks with a preposition that completes the word or phrase in italics and makes sense in the sentence. There may be more than one preposition that makes sense.

1. Florentino sat _____ *a shady almond tree.*
2. Once again he saw Fermina walking _____ *Escolástica,* her chaperone.
3. Fermina's natural haughtiness was evident _____ *the way* she held her head.
4. Her oxfords looked _____ *shoes* a man might wear.
5. Her eyes did not wander _____ *the left or right.*
6. She had woven her hair _____ *a thick braid.*
7. She wore a lace mantilla _____ *church* on Sundays.
8. _____ *Florentino's calm manner,* his heart was pounding.
9. _____ *several days,* he kept adding to his letter.
10. He could recite _____ *memory* every compliment and lofty sentiment in the letter.

Review: Exercise 10

Proofreading

This passage describes the artist Patricia Gonzalez, whose painting appears below. Rewrite the passage, correcting the errors in spelling, capitalization, grammar, and usage. Add any missing punctuation. There are ten errors.

Patricia Gonzalez

[1]Patricia Gonzalez was born in 1958 in Cartagena, Colombia she moved to London when she was eleven. [2]There she studied art, recieving a degree in fine arts from the Wimbledon School of Art in 1980. [3]Gonzalez returned to Cartagena to teach but she had trouble adapting to her new life. [4]"I could hardly paint at all," she has say of that time. [5]She returned to England in 1981 and later moved to Texas her home today.

[6]Gonzalez's imagery, which recalls Latin american landscapes, is inspired partly by memory and partly by imagination. [7]Her dream-like paintings, as you can see from the example here, is rich in color and texture. [8]The woman in *Sleep* who is barefoot and dressed in red, sleeps amid a tropical landscape. [9]Gonzalez creates the sense that the landscape exists only in the womans' dreams. [10]The hero of *Love in the Time of Cholera,* who also lives in a fantasy world dreams that the girl he adores will become the love of his life.

Patricia Gonzalez, *Sleep,* 1985

Exercise 11

Mixed Review

Read the brief biography of Gabriel García Márquez. On your paper rewrite the ten sentences that follow it, filling in the blanks with an appropriate word. Use the directions in parentheses and the biography text as a guide.

SAMPLE Gabriel García Márquez was _____ a newspaper reporter _____ a novelist. (Add a correlative conjunction.)

ANSWER Gabriel García Márquez was not only a newspaper reporter but also a novelist.

Gabriel García Márquez

Gabriel García Márquez is one of the writers credited with awakening world interest in contemporary Latin American literature. A newspaper reporter turned novelist, García Márquez was born in 1928 in Aracataca, Colombia. He transformed this small Caribbean town into Macondo, the setting for his highly acclaimed novel *One Hundred Years of Solitude,* published in 1967. Told with a journalist's regard for detail, the book is both a family chronicle and a mythical history of a century of turmoil and change in Latin America. It has been praised as one of the great novels of the twentieth century for its imaginative blend of fantasy, fable, and fact. Subsequent major works include *The Autumn of the Patriarch* (1975), *Chronicle of a Death Foretold* (1981), and *The General in His Labyrinth* (1989). One of the highest honors a novelist can receive is the Nobel Prize for literature. This award, first given in 1901, is awarded to the person who has made the most outstanding contribution in the field of literature. The Nobel Prize committee chose Gabriel García Márquez as the recipient of its Noble Prize for literature in 1982.

1. The novels of García Márquez _____ world interest in Latin American literature. (Add an action verb.)
2. García Márquez was a reporter who _____ a novelist. (Add a linking verb.)
3. Aracataca, the novelist's _____, is a small town on the Caribbean coast of Colombia. (Add a common noun.)
4. His masterpiece, *One Hundred Years of Solitude,* received _____ acclaim from critics around the world. (Add an adjective.)
5. A native of Colombia who now lives in Mexico City, he writes in _____, but his novels have been translated into numerous languages. (Add a proper noun.)
6. _____ *One Hundred Years of Solitude* has been translated into many languages, its author has become famous worldwide. (Add a subordinating conjunction.)
7. This novel _____ blends fantasy, fable, and fact. (Add an adverb.)
8. García Márquez published four novels _____ 1975 and 1985. (Add a preposition.)
9. In 1982 Gabriel García Márquez won the coveted _____. (Add a proper noun.)
10. Carlos Fuentes of Mexico _____ Julio Cortázar of Argentina have also published world-renowned novels. (Add a coordinating conjunction.)

Writing Application

TIME

For more about the writing process, see **TIME Facing the Blank Page**, pp. 111–121.

Conjunctions in Writing

In this passage from his novel *The Autobiography of an Ex-Colored Man*, James Weldon Johnson uses conjunctions effectively to link ideas. Read the passage, focusing especially on the italicized conjunctions.

> At a very early age I began to thump on the piano alone, *and* it was not long *before* I was able to pick out a few tunes. *When* I was seven years old, I could play by ear all of the hymns *and* songs that my mother knew. I had also learned the names of the notes in both clefs, *but* I preferred not to be hampered by notes. About this time several ladies for whom my mother sewed heard me play, *and* they persuaded her that I should at once be put under a teacher, *so* arrangements were made for me to study the piano with a lady who was a fairly good musician. . .

Techniques with Conjunctions

Try to apply some of James Weldon Johnson's writing techniques when you write and revise your own work.

❶ Whenever possible, use a coordinating conjunction other than *and* to clarify the relationship between ideas.

COORDINATING CONJUNCTION AND I had also learned the names of the notes in both clefs, and I preferred not to be hampered by notes.

JOHNSON'S VERSION I had also learned the names of the notes in both clefs, but I preferred not to be hampered by notes.

❷ Use subordinating conjunctions to clarify time relationships.

COORDINATING CONJUNCTION I was seven years old, and I could play by ear. . . .

JOHNSON'S VERSION When I was seven years old, I could play by ear. . . .

❸ Try replacing some coordinating conjunctions with conjunctive adverbs.

COORDINATING CONJUNCTION . . . I should at once be put under a teacher, and arrangements were made for me to study. . .

JOHNSON'S VERSION . . . I should at once be put under a teacher, so arrangements were made for me to study. . .

Practice   Practice these techniques by revising the following passage, using your own paper. Pay particular attention to the italized words.

A bonsai tree is considered a work of art, *and* unlike a painting or a symphony the bonsai is alive. Bonsai artists create what look like miniature trees, *and* they are actually training young trees to resemble old ones. To train the tree, the bonsai artist must begin to work in winter *and* new spring growth has not yet begun. The artist carefully prunes off some of the branches *and* twists the remaining ones *and* the plant begins to resemble an older tree. The art of bonsai originated in Japan, *and* it is now popular all over the world. My aunt Mioshi is an expert on bonsai, *and* she speaks at garden clubs throughout the country.

UNIT 11 Parts of the Sentence

11.1 Simple Subjects and Simple Predicates

■ A **sentence** is a group of words expressing a complete thought.
The *subject* and the *predicate* are the two basic parts of every sentence.

■ The **simple subject** is the key noun or pronoun (or word or group of words acting as a noun) that tells what a sentence is about.

■ The **simple predicate** is the verb or verb phrase that expresses the essential thought about the subject of the sentence.

SIMPLE SUBJECT	SIMPLE PREDICATE
Nikki Giovanni	wrote.
Senators	will attend.
Everything	has been discussed.
Traffic	slowed.

The way to find the simple subject is to ask *who?* or *what?* about the verb. For example, in the first sentence above, the noun *Nikki Giovanni* answers the question *who wrote?*

Conversely, asking *what is the action of the simple subject?* often helps determine the simple predicate—except in sentences in which the simple predicate is a linking verb or a verb phrase consisting of only linking verbs. In sentence two, *will attend* answers *what is the action of the senators?*

Exercise 1   Locating Simple Subjects and Simple Predicates

In sentences 1–5, locate and write the simple subject in each sentence. In sentences 6–10, locate and write the simple predicate in each sentence.

Poet's Tools

1. *Alliteration* means repetition of consonant sounds at the beginning of words.
2. One example is *Peter Piper picked a peck of pickled peppers.*
3. Concrete poems form visual shapes.
4. The ballad is a story in verse.
5. We acquired haiku, a short kind of poetry, from the Japanese.
6. Writers of haiku must observe the seventeen-syllables rule.
7. Limericks include five lines.
8. Some poets employ personification in their poems.
9. Personification gives human qualities to non-human things.
10. *Dancing leaves* and *angry clouds* are examples of personification.

11.2 Complete Subjects and Complete Predicates

You can usually expand or modify the meaning of both a simple subject and a simple predicate by adding other words and phrases to the sentence.

- The **complete subject** consists of the simple subject and all the words that modify it.

- The **complete predicate** consists of the simple predicate and all the words that modify it or complete its meaning.

COMPLETE SUBJECT	COMPLETE PREDICATE
The celebrated Mark Twain	wrote humorous stories.
The two senators from Ohio	will attend a local caucus.
Everything on the agenda	has been discussed by her.
The rush-hour traffic	slowed to a snail's pace.

Exercise 2   Identifying Subjects and Predicates

Copy each of the following sentences and indicate with a vertical line the division between the complete subject and the complete predicate. Then underline the simple subject once and the simple predicate twice.

The National Park Service

1. Delighted visitors flock each year to the more than three hundred sites in the national park system.
2. The national park system consists of areas of great natural beauty, historic importance, scientific interest, or recreational interest.
3. Yellowstone Park became the first national park in the United States in 1872.
4. Yellowstone is famous worldwide for its hot springs, geysers, and mud cauldrons.
5. The national parks, among them the Grand Canyon, are administered today by the National Park Service, a bureau of the Department of the Interior.
6. The National Park Service has developed different categories of national areas of special interest through the years.
7. Areas of historic interest in the system include national monuments, battlefield sites, historic sites, and memorials.
8. The recreational opportunities of future generations of Americans are guaranteed by the National Park Service's national seashores and national lakeshores.
9. Thousands of workers—such as rangers, naturalists, landscape architects, archaeologists, and historians—maintain the parks.
10. The rangers have the most contact with visitors.

Identifying Verbs

On your paper, write the complete predicate from each sentence. Then underline the verb within each predicate. Remember that a verb may include auxiliary verbs.

Hairstyling

1. People spend much money and time on their hair.
2. Reasons for such expenditures include the desire for beauty or for status.
3. Hairstylists arrange hair in various styles.
4. Some people add false hair or ornaments to their hair.
5. Wigs or hair pieces have always been popular.
6. In some eras, men braided their beards.
7. They also added gold dust or ornaments to their beards.
8. Men wore their hair short during the Middle Ages and into the Renaissance.
9. Fashionable women of the thirteenth and fourteenth centuries contained their hair in braids either over their ears or at the back of their heads.
10. A common hair treatment today for women and for some men is the permanent wave.

Identifying Complete Subjects and Complete Predicates

On your paper, write whether each phrase below would be used as a *complete subject* in a sentence or as a *complete predicate*.

1. a long string of natural pearls
2. expertly lengthened the dough with her hands
3. were hurt in a freak accident
4. fiercely attacked the wild boar
5. sweet, juicy oranges
6. a veteran quarterback with a sprained ankle
7. an enthusiastic spectator in the stands
8. the orange glow over the lake
9. floated into the room
10. often works from daylight until dark
11. tennis players in multicolored sportswear
12. green salad and sweet potatoes
13. reported on the research to the committee
14. spent millions for the new sports arena
15. sometimes traveled across country
16. many fans in the upper balcony
17. bankers and politicians in three-piece suits
18. granted my request for an interview
19. applauded the remarks of the speaker
20. marched through the rain triumphantly

Parts of the Sentence

11.3 Compound Subjects and Compound Predicates

■ A **compound subject** is made up of two or more subjects that are joined by a conjunction and have the same verb.

> Both **experience** and adequate **training** are necessary.
> Neither the **bus** nor the **subway** goes there.
> **Crimson, cerise,** and **vermilion** are shades of red.

■ A **compound predicate** (or **compound verb**) is made up of two or more verbs or verb phrases that are joined by a conjunction and have the same subject.

> Holograms **amaze** and **fascinate**.
> Jerome **will** either **call** or **write**.
> The helicopter **hovered** briefly but **landed** almost at once.
> Our guests **will arrive** early, **eat** a light meal, and **retire** by ten.

Sentences can have both a compound subject and a compound predicate.

>   S   S   P   P
> **Crocuses** and **daffodils** both **herald** and **symbolize** spring.

Exercise 5 — Locating Compound Subjects and Compound Predicates

On your paper, write and label any *compound subjects* or *compound predicates* you find in each sentence.

1. Hawks and vultures are loosely considered members of the eagle family.
2. The golden eagle is found through most of the northern hemisphere and has been regarded as a symbol of courage and power.
3. In history, Poles, Austrians, and Russians have used representations of eagles on military equipment, banners, and flags.
4. The female golden eagle attains a length of about one meter and has a wingspread of about two meters.
5. The golden eagle and the sea eagle are not closely related.
6. The sea eagle inhabits coastal regions, lakes, and streams and feeds heavily on fish.
7. The bald eagle ranges widely in North America and is the only eagle found on that continent.
8. The term *bald* does not imply a lack of feathers but is derived from the bird's white-feathered head.
9. The powerful harpy eagle and the hawk eagle inhabit tropical and subtropical regions of the world.
10. Most eagles hatch and rear only a few nestlings.

Exercise 6   Identifying Subjects and Predicates

On your paper, copy the following sentences. Then for each sentence, underline the simple subject(s) once and the simple predicate(s) twice. Some subjects and predicates are compound.

Tourist Attractions in Atlanta

1. Tourists and local residents enjoy the rich historic sites in Atlanta, Georgia.
2. The birthplace and final resting place of Dr. Martin Luther King Jr. are in Atlanta.
3. Dr. King was born and raised in a house on Auburn Avenue.
4. For many years, Dr. King and his father shared the pulpit at Ebenezer Baptist Church.
5. Tourists can leave Dr. King's birthplace and walk to the Martin Luther King Center for Nonviolent Social Change.
6. Visitors can view Dr. King's tomb and think about the accomplishments of this great man.
7. The Hammonds House and the Herndon Home are also among the city's interesting attractions.
8. In 1910 Alonzo Franklin Herndon not only designed but also built the Herndon Home, a mansion in the Beaux Arts style.
9. The Hammonds House is now a museum of African American art.
10. Atlanta's African American Panoramic Experience Museum treats visitors to a replica of an old Atlanta streetcar.

Exercise 7   Expanding Subjects

(a) Write five sentences. In each one, use a simple subject and a simple predicate.
(b) Expand each sentence by making the subject compound.

SAMPLE ANSWER   (a) Jackie Joyner-Kersee ran in the Olympics.
                            (b) Jackie Joyner-Kersee and Carl Lewis ran in the Olympics.

Exercise 8   Expanding Predicates

(a) Write five sentences, each with one subject and one predicate.
(b) Expand each sentence by making the predicate compound.

SAMPLE ANSWER   (a) The mechanic balanced the car's tires.
                            (b) The mechanic balanced and aligned the car's tires.

Exercise 9   Expanding Subjects and Predicates

(a) Write five sentences, each with one subject and one predicate.
(b) Make the subject and the predicate of each sentence compound.

SAMPLE ANSWER   (a) Television provides entertainment.
                            (b) Television and radio provide entertainment and disseminate information.

Exercise 10   Locating Subjects and Predicates in Narrative

Read the following passages from *Crime and Punishment* by Fyodor Dostoevsky, a Russian writer born in Moscow in 1821. Divide your paper into four columns: *simple subject, complete subject, simple predicate,* and *complete predicate.* Look at the underlined words in the passage and write them under the appropriate column heading.

[1]The lady in mourning had done at last, and got up. All at once, with some noise, an [2]officer [3]walked in very jauntily, with a peculiar swing of his shoulders at each step. He [4]tossed his cockaded cap on the table and sat down in an easy-chair. [5]The smart lady [6]positively skipped from her seat on seeing him, and fell to curtsying in a sort of ecstasy; but the officer took not the smallest notice of her, and she did not venture to sit down again in his presence. He [7]was the assistant superintendent. He had a reddish moustache that stood out horizontally on each side of his face, and extremely small features expressive of nothing much except a certain insolence. He [8]looked askance and rather indignantly at Raskolnikov; he was very badly dressed, and in spite of his humiliating position, his [9]bearing was by no means in keeping with his clothes. Raskolnikov [10]had unwarily fixed a very long and direct look on him, so that he felt positively affronted.

• • •

When Raskolnikov got home, his [11]hair was soaked with sweat and he was breathing heavily. He [12]went rapidly up the stairs, [13]walked into his unlocked room and at once [14]fastened the latch. Then in senseless terror he rushed to the corner, to that hole under the paper where he had put the thing; put his hand in, and for some minutes felt carefully in the hole, in every crack and fold of the paper. Finding nothing, he [15]got up and drew a deep breath. As he was reaching the steps of Bakaleyev's, he suddenly [16]fancied that something, a chain, a stud or even a bit of paper in which they had been wrapped with the old woman's handwriting on it, might somehow have slipped out and been lost in some crack, and then might suddenly turn up as unexpected, conclusive evidence against him.

He stood as though lost in thought, and a strange, humiliated, half senseless smile [17]strayed on his lips. He [18]took his cap at last and [19]went quietly out of the room. [20]His ideas [21]were all tangled. He [22]went dreamily through the gateway.

• • •

The [23]sentence however [24]was more merciful than could have been expected, perhaps partly because the criminal had not tried to justify himself, but had rather shown a desire to exaggerate his guilt. [25]All the strange and peculiar circumstances of the crime were taken into consideration. There [26]could be no [27]doubt of the abnormal and poverty-stricken condition of the criminal at the time. The fact that he had made no use of what he had stolen was put down partly to the effect of remorse, partly to his abnormal mental condition at the time of the crime. Incidentally [28]the murder of Lizaveta served indeed to confirm the last hypothesis: a man commits two murders and forgets that the door is open! Finally, the [29]confession, at the very moment when the case was hopelessly muddled by the false evidence given by Nikolay through melancholy and fanaticism, and when, moreover, there were no proofs against the real criminal, no suspicions even (Porfiry Petrovitch fully kept his word)—all this did much to soften the sentence. [30]Other circumstances, too, in the prisoner's favor came out quite unexpectedly.

Parts of the Sentence

Order of Subject and Predicate

In English the subject comes before the verb in most sentences. Some exceptions to this normal word order are discussed below.

1. *You* as the subject is understood rather than expressed in the case of commands or requests.

   [You] **Listen!**   [You] **Carry** it home.   [You] Please **see** me.

2. In order to add emphasis to the subject, a sentence can be written in **inverted order,** with the predicate coming before the subject.

PREDICATE	SUBJECT
Beneath the waves **lay**	an ancient **shipwreck.**
Over the years **had arisen**	many improbable **tales.**

3. When the word *there* or *here* begins a sentence and is followed by a form of the verb *to be,* the predicate usually comes before the subject. (The sentence appears in inverted order.) Be aware that *there* and *here* are almost never the subject of a sentence.

PREDICATE	SUBJECT
Here **is**	the **quilt** for my friend.
There **were**	new **books** on the shelf.

Exercise 11   **Identifying Commands**

On your paper, write the command found in the sentences below. If a sentence does not contain a command, write *no command*. Some sentences will have more than one command.

Taking Orders

1. Almost everyone hears commands nearly every day of the year.
2. Around your home, you may hear statements such as "Run these errands for me this afternoon" or "Please keep an eye on your brother."
3. "Please start dinner," a parent may say.
4. Family members express commands for various reasons.
5. A parent may say, "Find a job," because he or she knows you will soon need money for college or trade school.
6. The same parent may implore you to wear a seat belt while driving a car or a helmet while riding a motorcycle.
7. These commands are given out of concern for your health.
8. A younger sibling may beg, "Let me borrow your blue shirt."
9. Similarly, school is a place where commands are often heard.
10. "Read chapters two through five by tomorrow," your American literature teacher may say.

Exercise 12   Recognizing the Order of Subject and Predicate

Copy each of the following sentences; draw a vertical line between the complete subject and the predicate, and label each. Then indicate with the letter *C* or *I* those sentences that either express a command (*C*) or are written in inverted order (*I*). (Not all sentences will be labeled *C* or *I*.)

SAMPLE ANSWERS

                                    P
| Look at that cherry blossom tree. **C**

            P   S
On the tour is | the Senate. **I**

       P   S
There are | many reasons for thinking of Washington, D.C., as one of this country's most beautiful cities. **I**

Washington, D.C.

1. Washington, D.C., has a distinctive atmosphere.
2. Of course, there is the monumental quality of many of its huge and impressive government buildings.
3. Notice the distinctive shape of the Washington Monument.
4. Among the best of the contemporary architectural structures in the city is the stunning East Building of the National Gallery of Art.
5. Within this historic city are many broad, tree-lined avenues.
6. Ask the tour guide for directions to the Capitol.
7. With 1,750 forested acres, Rock Creek Park offers miles of bicycle-riding paths and hiking trails.
8. A lack of skyscrapers reinforces the city's sense of openness.
9. Look at the lovely colonial-style houses in the attractive residential district of Georgetown.
10. The city has left a memorable impression on millions of visitors.

Exercise 13   Locating Subjects in Inverted Sentences

On your paper, write the simple subject from each sentence.

John Chapman

1. In the pages of history lives a man with an unusual nickname.
2. Born in Leominster, Massachusetts, in 1774 was John Chapman, or Johnny Appleseed.
3. On the road with the pioneers traveled Johnny.
4. In the ground along his path were apple seeds from cider presses in Pennsylvania.
5. Indistinguishable from legend are facts about this man.
6. Atop his head rested a tin pot.
7. Between him and the weather stood only an old set of clothing.
8. Famous everywhere are stories about his deeds.
9. In his heart were Johnny's deeply religious convictions.
10. In Ohio and other Midwestern states are the results of Johnny's labors.

11.5 Complements

■ A **complement** is a word or group of words that completes the meaning of a verb.

There are four kinds of complements: *direct objects, indirect objects, object complements,* and *subject complements.*

Direct Objects

■ A **direct object** answers the question *what?* or *whom?* after an action verb.

The subject of the sentence usually performs the action indicated by the verb. A direct object—someone or something—is the recipient of that action. Nouns, pronouns, or words acting as nouns may serve as direct objects. Only transitive verbs have direct objects.

Estela sold her **typewriter.** [Estela sold *what?*]

Everyone watched the **diver.** [Everyone watched *whom?*]

They understood **what I had said.** [They understood *what?*]

Estela sold her **typewriter** and **radio.** [Estela sold *what?*]

Marguerite enjoyed Domingo's **singing.** [Marguerite enjoyed *what?*]

Pao painted a remarkable **likeness** of his grandmother. [Pao painted *what?*]

Exercise 14   **Identifying Direct Objects**

On your paper, write the action verb that appears in each of the following sentences. Then list the direct object(s).

Faith Ringgold, Contemporary Artist

1. In the 1950s, Faith Ringgold studied art and education at the City College of New York.
2. After graduation she taught art classes for many years.
3. Ringgold gained a position as a professor of art at the University of California at San Diego.
4. Much of Ringgold's work reveals her interest in civil rights and feminism.
5. She sometimes uses very interesting and unusual media, such as life-sized portrait masks of famous people.
6. Her stuffed fabric masks portray politicians, athletes, and other famous African Americans.
7. She uses these masks as props in dramatic presentations.
8. Ringgold wrote stories for a series of "narrative quilts."
9. These unusual artworks contain both text and images on quilt-like panels.
10. Ringgold adapted one of her quilts into a children's book, *Tar Beach.*

Indirect Objects

■ An **indirect object** answers the question *to whom? for whom? to what?* or *for what?* after an action verb.

In most cases, in order for a sentence to have an indirect object, it must first have a direct object. The indirect object always appears between the verb and the direct object.

> Airlines give **passengers** bonuses. [Airlines give bonuses *to whom?*]
>
> The owner reserved **us** a table. [The owner reserved a table *for whom?*]
>
> The committee gave my **project** top priority. [The committee gave top priority *to what?*]
>
> Airlines give **passengers** and **employees** bonuses. [Airlines give bonuses *to whom?*]
>
> Adrienne made **her report** a cover. [Adrienne made a cover *for what?*]
>
> Nikoli left **Tonya** a message. [Nikoli left a message *for whom?*]

| Exercise 15 | Identifying Indirect Objects |

First write on your paper the direct object in each of the following sentences. Then list any indirect objects. (There may be more than one indirect object in a sentence, or there may be none at all.)

The Art of Collage

1. Collage offers the beginner and the professional an especially flexible art form.
2. The maker of a collage simply glues material to a "ground."
3. The use of diverse materials can lend this genre an unusual effect.
4. For example, different types of paper give artists the opportunity to experiment with various textures.
5. Some artists create vivid sensory detail through the imaginative use of multiple textures and layered effects.
6. Some artists give their collages more interest with three-dimensional objects.
7. The use of paint and ink virtually guarantees both the experienced artist and the novice various effects.
8. Photographs of famous persons often lend collages social or political import.
9. Abstract works, however, can also evoke powerful feelings.
10. The technique of collage has attracted many famous artists, including Pablo Picasso and Georges Braque.

Object Complements

■ An **object complement** answers the question *what?* after a direct object. That is, it *completes* the meaning of the direct object by identifying or describing it.

Object complements occur only in sentences that contain a direct object *and* only in sentences with action verbs that have the general meaning "make" or "consider," such as the following:

appoint	declare	make	prove
call	elect	name	render
consider	find	proclaim	think

An object complement may be an adjective, a noun, or a pronoun. It usually follows a direct object.

> The accident rendered her car **useless.** [adjective]
> I called the dog **Dusty.** [noun]
> Jeanine considers our house **hers.** [pronoun]
> The board named Cho **president** and **treasurer.** [nouns]

Exercise 16   Identifying Object Complements

On your paper, write the object complement(s) that appear in the following sentences. (One sentence has two object complements, and one sentence has none.)

A Mexican–Cooking Contest

1. For my class's midyear cooking contest, the teacher named Mexican food the theme.
2. At a neighborhood restaurant, several students researched unusual appetizers and main courses.
3. Kim judged the restaurant's menu quite good.
4. With a few bold, inventive changes, Juana made a cookbook's recipe hers.
5. Flour made Hank's tomato sauce thicker and paler.

Exercise 17   Providing Object Complements

Complete each sentence by adding an object complement. Label your object complement *adjective, noun,* or *pronoun.*

1. Shoppers consider neighborhood malls _____.
2. Unfortunately, Miki found bargains _____.
3. Mark called the shopping ordeal _____.
4. For sportswear choices, we appointed Miki the _____.
5. Gradually, I made her suggestions _____.

Subject Complements

■ A **subject complement** follows a subject and a linking verb and identifies or describes the subject.

There are two kinds of subject complements: *predicate nominatives* and *predicate adjectives.*

■ A **predicate nominative** is a noun or pronoun that follows a linking verb and points back to the subject to identify it further.

Cellists are **musicians.**

The soloist for this concert is **someone** from Dallas.

Predicate nominatives usually appear in sentences that contain a form of the linking verb *be.* Some other linking verbs (for example, *become* and *remain*) can also be followed by a predicate nominative.

Those two may be **thieves.**

When did he become **treasurer?**

The candidates remained **rivals** but **friends.**

The woman who phoned you is **she.**

The man you have been trying to locate is **he.**

| Exercise 18 | Recognizing Predicate Nominatives |

On your paper, write the subject complements from the following sentences. Then label each subject complement as a *noun* or *pronoun*. If a sentence has no subject complement, write *no complement.*

Commercial Aspects of Horticulture

1. Horticulture is the science and art of growing plants.
2. The two main branches of horticulture are the cultivation of food plants and the cultivation of ornamental plants.
3. The nursery industry is one of the specialized commercial areas of horticulture.
4. Another area of the horticulture business is the plant-growing industry.
5. The third division of the commercial side of horticulture is the seed-production enterprise.
6. The nursery industry grows fruit trees for fruit farmers and decorative trees for the ornamental gardener.
7. Every year, the plant-growing industry is the source of annual, biennial, and perennial plants.
8. The division of horticulture responsible for seeds remains the seed-growing industry.
9. Europe, the Netherlands, Germany, France, Belgium, Great Britain, and the United States are some of the many countries with modern methods of horticulture.
10. The most advanced countries in this field are also they.

■ A **predicate adjective** follows a linking verb and points back to the subject to further describe it.

That cellist is **talented.**

The soloist seemed **thoughtful.**

Any linking verb may precede a predicate adjective.

Rachel's tale sounded **preposterous** to all of us.
The runners looked **exhausted** but **happy.**
We became quite **impatient** with the long wait.

Exercise 19   Recognizing Adjectives as Subject Complements

Write the subject complements and label each by writing *predicate adjective* or *predicate nominative.*

1. Abigail Van Buren is a newspaper advice columnist.
2. Van Buren's identical twin sister, Ann Landers, is also an advice columnist.
3. The names of Ann Landers and Abigail Van Buren are pen names for the twins who were born Esther Pauline and Pauline Esther Friedman.
4. Landers started her column in 1955; Van Buren later felt motivated to follow in her sister's footsteps.
5. The *San Francisco Chronicle* was interested in her articles.
6. Her efforts were immediately successful.
7. Van Buren's advice column, "Dear Abby," is sometimes sarcastic but practical.
8. Ann Landers's suggestions are sometimes humorous and lighthearted.
9. Van Buren and Landers answer many letters.
10. Both columnists are popular with their readers.

Exercise 20   Identifying Subject Complements

On your paper, write all the subject complements that appear in the following sentences. Identify each as a predicate nominative or a predicate adjective. (Two sentences have more than one predicate nominative or predicate adjective; three sentences have none.)

[1]Monks returning from studying Zen Buddhism in Chinese monasteries brought the practice of drinking green tea to Japan. [2]Today the tea ceremony has become a traditional Japanese custom. [3]A teahouse may be a detached structure or a special room in the host's house. [4]The design of a teahouse is simple. [5]Bowing to enter through the three-foot doorway, guests feel humble. [6]A scroll, a flower arrangement, and fragrant incense greet visitors. [7]The host serves a light meal before the ceremony. [8]During the ceremony one feels calm and aware of the surroundings. [9]An admiring examination of the host's teapot and utensils is an important part of the ritual. [10]The *wabi* style of these utensils, plain and simple, has been traditional in Japan since the sixteenth century.

Exercise 21   Review: Identifying Parts of the Sentence

On your paper, identify the underlined portion of each sentence as a *simple subject, simple predicate, complete subject,* or *complete predicate.* If the underlined portion contains a compound subject or a compound predicate, write *compound.*

SAMPLE   <u>Argentina, Brazil, and Chile</u> are three South American countries.
ANSWER   complete subject—compound

ABC Powers

1. <u>The ABC Powers</u> was an early 1900s designation for Argentina, Brazil, and Chile.
2. These three countries <u>struggled to preserve peace in South and Central America.</u>
3. They also <u>endeavored</u> to help all Latin American countries.
4. Finally, <u>Argentina, Brazil, and Chile</u> developed a series of treaties.
5. The agreements <u>granted arbitration of disputes and provided mutual support against aggression.</u>
6. The alliances <u>were</u> principally <u>directed</u> against several policies of the United States.
7. The ABC Powers <u>were particularly dissatisfied with policies in the Monroe Doctrine.</u>
8. <u>The Monroe Doctrine</u> was a statement to the U.S. Congress by President James Monroe in 1823.
9. The doctrine <u>basically granted the United States the right to intercede in any Latin American country's internal or external affairs.</u>
10. One significant <u>effort</u> of the ABC Powers was their offer to arbitrate a 1914 dispute between the United States and Mexico.

Exercise 22   Review: Recognizing Subjects in Exceptional Positions

On your paper, write the simple subjects from each of the following sentences. If the subject is understood *you,* write *you* in parentheses. Then label the sentence *C* for command or *I* for inverted order.

1. Emerging from the tepid earth are daffodils and tulips.
2. Growing daily in blossoming trees are masterfully constructed birds' nests.
3. Help me mow the lawn.
4. Let's drive to the shore and lie in the sun.
5. Here were once trees barren of leaves and yards.
6. Bursting open are the flowers of azalea plants.
7. Heating the earth and the air are longer days of brilliant sunshine.
8. Growing dimmer are the memories of ice and snow.
9. Here is everyone's favorite time of year.
10. Here is the splendor of springtime.

Exercise 23   Review: Creating Sentences with Direct Objects

Write five sentences describing how to make or do something. Use action verbs. Identify all subjects, verbs, and direct objects.

Review: Recognizing Direct and Indirect Objects

(a) For each of the following sentences without a direct object, rewrite the sentence on a separate sheet of paper, adding a direct object. (b) For each sentence that already has a direct object, rewrite the sentence, adding an indirect object. (c) Write a *D* above each direct object and an *I* above each indirect object.

Using Computers for Writing

1. The use of computers for schoolwork offers many advantages.
2. With computers students often write more carefully.
3. From time to time, they check for errors.
4. Computers have also allowed greater ease in the correction process.
5. Students can even e-mail teachers their work electronically.

Exercise 25   Review: Writing Sentences with Complements

Write four sentences about a natural phenomenon. In each sentence, use at least one of the four kinds of complements. Label the complements.

Exercise 26   Review: Complements

On your paper, write the complements that appear in the following sentences. Next to each complement write the kind of complement it is.

American Sign Language

1. American Sign Language (ASL) is the language of hearing-impaired people.
2. Like spoken languages ASL has its own grammar.
3. Nonetheless, in the past many linguistic experts gave ASL short shrift.
4. They called the language primitive.
5. In fact, users of ASL are capable of great precision and subtle expression.
6. Signed English is a simple system of conventional signs.
7. ASL affords hearing-impaired people an efficient means of communication.
8. A hearing learner of ASL can eventually become competent.
9. Only after years of practice, however, can hearing learners achieve proficiency.
10. Today ASL is the fourth most common language in the United States.

Another Composition

11. I must write another composition.
12. I consider composition entertaining.
13. I am becoming a composition robot.
14. My parents and my sister sometimes give me ideas.
15. This composition must be imaginative.
16. It must also have a surprise ending.
17. It could be a science fiction story or a mystery.
18. It should be interesting and exciting.
19. I might become the next Stephen King.
20. I will title my composition "Weird."

PARTS OF THE SENTENCE

The setting of *Main Street* is Gopher Prairie, Minnesota, but as Sinclair Lewis says in his introduction to the novel, the town could be any American town, and "its Main Street is the continuation of Main Streets everywhere." In this excerpt, the heroine, a young woman named Carol Kennicott, glumly surveys the little town. The passage has been annotated to show some of the parts of the sentence covered in this unit.

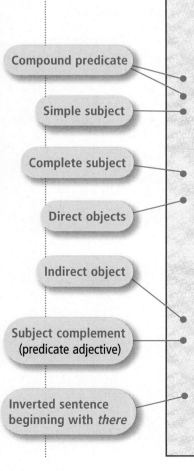

Compound predicate
Simple subject
Complete subject
Direct objects
Indirect object
Subject complement (predicate adjective)
Inverted sentence beginning with *there*

Literature Model

from Main Street

by Sinclair Lewis

When Carol had walked for thirty-two minutes she had completely covered the town, east and west, north and south; and she stood at the corner of Main Street and Washington Avenue and despaired.

Main Street, with its two-story brick shops, its story-and-a-half wooden residences, its muddy expanse from concrete walk to walk, its huddle of Fords and lumber-wagons, was too small to absorb her. The broad, straight, unenticing gashes of the streets let in the grasping prairie on every side. She realized the vastness and the emptiness of the land. The skeleton iron windmill on the farm a few blocks away, at the north end of Main Street, was like the ribs of a dead cow. She thought of the coming of the Northern winter, when the unprotected houses would crouch together in terror of storms galloping out of that wild waste. They were so small and weak, the little brown houses. They were shelters for sparrows, not homes for warm laughing people.

She told herself that down the street the leaves were a splendor. The maples were orange; the oaks a solid tint of raspberry. And the lawns had been nursed with love. But the thought would not hold. At best the trees resembled a thinned woodlot. There was no park to rest the eyes. And since not Gopher Prairie but Wakamin was the county-seat, there was no court-house with its grounds.

> She *glanced* through the fly-specked windows of the most pretentious building in sight, the one place which welcomed strangers and determined their opinion of the charm and luxury of Gopher Prairie—the Minniemashie House. It was a tall lean shabby *structure*, three stories of yellow-streaked wood, the corners covered with sanded pine slabs purporting to symbolize stone. In the hotel office she could see a stretch of bare unclean floor, a line of rickety chairs with brass cuspidors between, a writing-desk with advertisements in mother-of-pearl letters upon the glass-covered back. The dining-room beyond was a jungle of stained table-cloths and catsup bottles.
>
> She *looked no more at Minniemashie House*.

- Simple predicate
- Subject complement (predicate nominative)
- Complete predicate

Review: Exercise 1   Writing Sentences with Complete Subjects and Complete Predicates

Each of the following partial sentences elaborates on an idea suggested by the passage from *Main Street*. Make each sentence complete by writing on your paper either a complete subject or a complete predicate. Do not repeat the exact wording from the novel. Although there is no single right answer, your sentence should make sense within the context of the passage.

1. _____ depressed Carol.
2. The town, east and west, north and south, _____.
3. _____ had both shops and homes.
4. _____ brought to life Carol's worst fears.
5. The vast and empty prairie _____.
6. _____ looked at the muddy distance from concrete walk to concrete walk.
7. The streets with their broad, straight lines _____.
8. _____ felt engulfed in a never-ending sea of prairie.
9. An abandoned iron windmill _____.
10. _____ would huddle together against the fierce winter weather.
11. _____ would roar through the town in winter.
12. Homes barely large enough for birds _____.
13. The bright orange leaves of the maple trees _____.
14. _____ tinted the oaks.
15. _____ had been carefully tended by their owners.
16. With Wakamin as the county seat, no courthouse _____.
17. The tall, shabby Minniemashie House _____.
18. _____ offered a barren, uninviting appearance.
19. _____ made Main Street unattractive.
20. Carol, depressed and unable to gaze at the ugliness, _____.

Grammar Review

Review: Exercise 2	Writing Sentences with Compound Subjects and Compound Predicates

Write on your paper a complete sentence answering each of the following questions about the passage from *Main Street*. Do not repeat the exact wording from the novel. Begin your sentence with the subject. When composing your answer, follow the directions in parentheses. Then underline and label the simple or compound subject and the simple or compound predicate. Finally, draw a line separating the complete subject from the complete predicate.

SAMPLE   What two streets met at one corner of Gopher Prairie?
            (Use a compound subject.)

                      COMPOUND SUBJECT   SIMPLE PREDICATE
ANSWER   <u>Main Street</u> and <u>Washington Avenue</u> | <u>met</u> at one corner of Gopher Prairie.

1. What did Carol do at the corner of Main Street and Washington Avenue?
   (Use a compound predicate.)
2. What kinds of buildings lined Main Street?
   (Use a compound subject.)
3. What kinds of vehicles were parked close together along Main Street?
   (Use a compound subject.)
4. What struck Carol about the land around Gopher Prairie?
   (Use a compound subject.)
5. What characteristics of the houses made them unfit to stand up to winter storms?
   (Use a compound subject.)
6. What trees down the street were turning color?
   (Use a compound subject.)
7. According to Carol, which missing elements of the town would improve its appearance?
   (Use a compound subject.)
8. What did the Minniemashie House do for visitors?
   (Use a compound predicate.)
9. What added to the shabbiness of the hotel office of the Minniemashie House?
   (Use a compound subject.)
10. What gave the dining room of the Minniemashie House an uninviting look?
    (Use a compound subject.)

Review: Exercise 3	Identifying Simple and Compound Subjects and Predicates

The following sentences describe the winter storms of Minnesota, the same ones Carol was concerned about in the passage from *Main Street*. Write each sentence, drawing a line to separate the complete subject from the complete predicate. Then underline the simple subject once and the simple predicate twice.

Minnesota Winters

1. Minnesota usually experiences frigid temperatures and heavy snowfall during the winter.
2. Sleet occurs early in the season and presents a danger for motorists.

3. The first snow can arrive as early as September.
4. Inhabitants face winds of over thirty-five miles per hour in blizzard conditions.
5. Late-season storms are not uncommon in Minnesota.
6. Weather reports provide snow predictions.
7. Traffic tie-ups and accidents are typical features of the morning commute.
8. Blizzards and ice storms often close schools for days.
9. Farmers must round up their livestock and herd them into the barn.
10. Warm gloves and woolen scarves are essential during the winter months.

Review: Exercise 4   Writing Inverted Sentences

The following sentences describe a typical small town of the early twentieth century, the time in which *Main Street* is set. On your paper, rewrite each sentence in inverted order, following the directions given in parentheses.

SAMPLE   The American small town is of great interest to many historians.
            (Begin the sentence with *Of great interest*.)
ANSWER   Of great interest to many historians is the American small town.

1. The similarities among the small towns of turn-of-the-century America were often striking.
   (Begin the sentence with *There were.*)
2. A railroad depot was usually right in the center of town.
   (Begin the sentence with *There was.*)
3. The railroad tracks ran alongside the main street.
   (Begin the sentence with *Alongside the main street.*)
4. The railroad was vital to most towns of that time.
   (Begin the sentence with *Vital to most towns of that time.*)
5. Freight and travelers came through the railroad station.
   (Begin the sentence with *Through the railroad station.*)
6. Businesses and hotels sprang up near the station.
   (Begin the sentence with *Near the station.*)
7. Little effort was expended in matching the architecture of the various buildings.
   (Begin the sentence with *There was.*)
8. Attractive displays of merchandise were in many storefront windows.
   (Begin the sentence with *In many storefront windows.*)
9. Many kinds of stores were found in a typical town.
   (Begin the sentence with *There were.*)
10. The offices of dentists, doctors, and lawyers were located above these stores.
    (Begin the sentence with *Above these stores.*)

Grammar Review

Review: Exercise 5   Writing Sentences with Predicate Nominatives and Predicate Adjectives

The pairs of words that follow are derived from the passage from *Main Street.* For each pair, write a sentence that uses the first word as the subject and the second word as a subject complement. Do not use Lewis's exact words. Then indicate whether the second word of the pair is acting as a *predicate adjective* or a *predicate nominative.*

1. Carol, woman
2. Gopher Prairie, town
3. Main Street, uninteresting
4. streets, gashes
5. prairie, vast
6. houses, weak
7. trees, woodlot
8. Minniemashie House, building
9. floor, dirty
10. tablecloths, stained

Review: Exercise 6   Writing Sentences with Direct and Indirect Objects

Each of the following groups of words elaborates on an idea suggested by the passage from *Main Street.* Each word is labeled *S* (for *subject*), *DO* (for *direct object*), or *IO* (for *indirect object*). Write a sentence using each group of words, but do not use Lewis's exact wording. Add modifiers and prepositional phrases to your sentences.

SAMPLE   Carol (S), Gopher Prairie (IO), look (DO)
ANSWER   Carol gave Gopher Prairie a long, disappointing look.

1. town (S), Carol (IO), feeling (DO)
2. mud (S), streets (DO)
3. windmill (S), ribs (DO)
4. houses (S), people (IO), protection (DO)
5. trees (S), Carol (IO), comfort (DO)
6. Minniemashie House (S), strangers (IO), lodging (DO)
7. windows (S), view (DO)
8. corners (S), stone (DO)
9. dining room (S), guests (IO), atmosphere (DO)
10. hotel (S), Carol (IO), impression (DO)

Proofreading

The following passage describes the artist Gustave Moeller, whose painting is reproduced on this page. Rewrite the passage, correcting the errors in spelling, grammar, and usage. Add any missing punctuation. There are ten errors.

Gustave Moeller

¹The United States has a rich tradition of regional art and the Midwest has been both home and subject for many artists. ²Many Wisconsin painters of German heritage. ³Among them were Gustave Moeller. ⁴Born in New Holstein, Wisconsin, in 1881 and educated at art schools in Milwaukee, Moeller refines his technique in New York and Munich. ⁵His paintings, carefully composed and extravagantly colored depict everyday scenes in his native state.

⁶*Main Street, Alma* gives us a view of an unimpresive Wisconsin town on a summer day. ⁷The street seems deserted the figures blend inconspicuously with the scene. ⁸It is not hard to imagine Carol the heroine of *Main Street,* wandering through a town such as this, with it's modest shops unpaved streets, and battered Fords.

Gustave Moeller, *Main Street, Alma,* **1925**

Review: Exercise 8

Mixed Review

Part A: Rewrite each sentence on your paper, according to the directions that appear after each item. Make sure your answers are complete sentences.

Sinclair Lewis

1. Born in 1885, Sinclair Lewis grew up in Sauk Centre, Minnesota.
   (Add *and later modeled Gopher Prairie after his hometown* to the complete predicate.)
2. To Lewis the atmosphere of Sauk Centre seemed smug.
   (Add *and repressive* to create a second predicate adjective.)
3. Different from any of Lewis's previous works, *Main Street* (1920) was a success.
   (Add *great* as a modifier of the subject complement.)
4. Lewis wrote about various segments of society.
   (Add *novels* so that it functions as a direct object.)
5. In Lewis's novel *Babbitt*, the pressures of conformity in the business world allow no room for idealistic pursuits.
   (Add *the title character* so that it functions as an indirect object.)
6. In his novel *Arrowsmith* is found a portrait of corruption among doctors.
   (Rewrite the sentence so that it begins with the complete subject.)
7. In 1926 *Arrowsmith* earned Lewis the Pulitzer Prize, which he declined.
   (Rewrite the sentence so that *Lewis* becomes the subject and *Pulitzer Prize* becomes the direct object.)
8. While at work on these and other books, Lewis became a hermit.
   (Add *virtual* as a modifier of the subject complement.)
9. Few famous authors were as uneven in their writing as Sinclair Lewis.
   (Rewrite the sentence so that it begins with *There were.*)
10. Nevertheless, Lewis's exceptional ability as a satirist helped him win the coveted Nobel Prize for literature in 1930.
    (Add *and his powerful talent for mimicry* to the complete subject.)

Part B: Use your new rewritten sentences from Part A to answer the questions below.

1. In sentence one, what is the simple subject?
2. In sentence two, what is the simple predicate?
3. In sentence three, what is the subject complement?
4. In sentence four, what is the complete subject?
5. In sentence five, what is the complete predicate?

Writing Application

TIME

For more about the writing process, see **TIME Facing the Blank Page,** pages 111–121.

Sentences in Writing

Varying sentence length and word order is a good way to make your writing interesting. Notice how Maxine Hong Kingston varies sentence length and word order in this fantasy sequence from her book *The Woman Warrior.*

> I leapt onto my horse's back and marveled at the power and height it gave me. Just then, galloping out of nowhere straight at me came a rider on a black horse. The villagers scattered except for one soldier, who stood calmly in the road. I drew my sword. "Wait!" shouted the rider, raising weaponless hands. "Wait. I have traveled here to join you."
>
> Then the villagers relinquished their real gifts to me—their sons. Families who had hidden their boys during the last conscription volunteered them now. I took the ones their families could spare and the ones with hero-fire in their eyes, not the young fathers and not those who would break hearts with their leaving.

Techniques with Sentences

Try to apply some of Kingston's techniques when you write and revise your own work.

1 Vary the length of your sentences. Notice that the length of Kingston's sentences varies from one to thirty words.

SENTENCE LENGTHS NOT VARIED I leapt onto my horse's back. I marveled at the power and height it gave me. I drew my sword.

KINGSTON'S VERSION I leapt onto my horse's back and marveled at the power and height it gave me. I drew my sword.

2 Occasionally use a very short sentence to stress a point, indicate a change of thought, or clinch an idea.

KINGSTON'S SHORT, CLINCHING SENTENCE I drew my sword.

3 To help achieve variety, try inverting the word order of a sentence sometimes.

NOT INVERTED A rider on a black horse came straight at me just then, galloping out of nowhere.

KINGSTON'S VERSION Just then, galloping out of nowhere straight at me came a rider on a black horse.

Practice Practice these techniques by revising the following passage adapted from *The Woman Warrior.* Imagine how Kingston would have combined ideas to create a pleasing variety of sentence lengths. Also decide which sentence would be most effective in inverted order. (Note: An ideograph is a symbol in the Chinese writing system.)

A white horse stepped into the courtyard. I was polishing my armor. The gates were locked tight. It came through the moon door anyway. It was a kingly white horse. It wore a saddle and bridle. The saddle and bridle had red, gold, and black tassels dancing. The saddle was just my size. It had tigers and dragons tooled in swirls. The white horse pawed the ground. It wanted me to go. The ideograph "to fly" was on the hooves of its near forefoot and hindfoot.

UNIT 12 Phrases

12.1 Prepositional Phrases

- A **phrase** is a group of words that acts in a sentence as a single part of speech.

- A **prepositional phrase** is a group of words that begins with a preposition and usually ends with a noun or a pronoun, called the object of the preposition.

> I am going **to the river.** [*River* is the object of the preposition *to.*]
>
> That river is challenging **for the canoeists.** [*Canoeists* is the object of the preposition *for.*]

Adjectives and other modifiers may appear between the preposition and its object, and a preposition may have more than one object.

> He looked **across the broad, serene river.** [adjectives added]
>
> The view was **to the east and the south.** [two objects]

Prepositional phrases may also occur in a sequence.

> The door **of the car with the skis on top** is scratched. [series of prepositional phrases]

A prepositional phrase usually functions as an adjective or an adverb. When it is used as an adjective, it modifies a noun or a pronoun. When used as an adverb, it modifies a verb, an adjective, or an adverb.

> Please use the door **in the rear.** [adjective phrase modifying the noun *door*]
>
> One **of these doors** is locked. [adjective phrase modifying the pronoun *one*]
>
> Open the door **at the head of the stairs.** [adjective phrase modifying the noun *door* followed by an adjective phrase modifying the noun *head*]
>
> **After work** I will return this faulty lock **to the store.** [adverb phrases modifying the verb phrase *will return*]
>
> Automatic doors are commonplace **in supermarkets.** [adverb phrase modifying the adjective *commonplace*]
>
> The old door swings easily **for its age.** [adverb phrase modifying the adverb *easily*]

Exercise 1   Identifying Prepositional Phrases

Write each prepositional phrase that appears in the following sentences. (Some of these sentences have more than one prepositional phrase.)

Thurgood Marshall, Supreme Court Justice

1. In the late 1920s Thurgood Marshall pursued a law career.
2. He was denied admission by one law school because he was an African American, but then he was admitted to Howard University's new law program.
3. Marshall graduated at the top of his class.
4. In 1936 he was hired as an assistant counsel to the NAACP.
5. He filed lawsuits challenging discrimination against African Americans in graduate programs and professional schools.
6. When he argued the case *Brown v. Board of Education,* Marshall challenged the practice of separate-but-equal education for African Americans and whites in the public schools.
7. The Court's 1954 agreement with Marshall's arguments changed the educational system throughout America.
8. Thirteen years later, during the administration of Lyndon Johnson, Marshall became a Supreme Court justice.
9. Throughout his years on the Court, Justice Marshall showed concern for the unempowered.
10. After twenty-four years of service, he resigned in 1991.

Exercise 2   Identifying Adjective and Adverb Phrases

Write the word or words each prepositional phrase in Exercise 1 modifies. Indicate whether each phrase is acting as an *adjective* or an *adverb*.

Exercise 3   Expanding Sentences with Prepositional Phrases

Expand the following sentences by adding at least one adjective phrase and one adverb phrase to each.

1. The revelers set off fireworks.
2. Four nurses received awards.
3. Anyone could have seen it.
4. The spaceship transmitted messages.
5. The ruler was broken.
6. The mayor made a speech.
7. The train was crowded.
8. The students organized a meeting.
9. The new coach met the players.
10. The manager installed a computer system.

12.2 | Appositives and Appositive Phrases

■ An **appositive** is a noun or pronoun that is placed next to another noun or pronoun to identify or give additional information about it.

■ An **appositive phrase** is an appositive plus any words that modify the appositive.

> My sister **Amelia** sells computer software. [The appositive *Amelia* identifies the noun *sister.*]
>
> She works for Softwarehouse, **a new retail outlet.** [The appositive phrase, *a new retail outlet,* identifies *Softwarehouse.*]

If an appositive is not essential to the meaning of a sentence, it should be set off by commas.

Exercise 4   Identifying Appositives and Appositive Phrases

Write the appositive or appositive phrase.

Notable Sports Figures

1. Tara Lipinski, an Olympic figure skater, turned pro in 1998.
2. Walter Payton, star running back of the Chicago Bears, was nicknamed Sweetness.
3. Over his career, St. Louis Cardinals pitcher Bob Gibson won seven World Series games and lost only two.
4. Tracie Ruiz, a swimmer in the 1984 Olympics, won gold medals in the solo synchronized event and, with her partner, Candy Costie, in the duet synchronized event.
5. One of the most versatile athletes ever was the Native American Jim Thorpe, who won gold medals in the pentathlon and the decathlon in the 1912 Olympics.
6. The golf star Nancy Lopez has been setting records since the 1970s.
7. Rebecca Lobo, a former college basketball star, began playing in the Women's National Basketball Association in 1997.
8. Sammy Sosa, the powerful Cubs outfielder, hit sixty-six home runs in 1998.
9. Wilma Rudolph, a track star, had been sickly as a child and could not walk without an orthopedic shoe until age eleven.
10. In 1999 baseball players Tony Gwynn and Wade Boggs each reached the three-thousand mark in hits.
11. In 1995 Miguel Indurain of Spain won the Tour de France, the most prestigious bicycle race in the world, for the fifth year in a row.
12. Pitcher Tom Seaver won 311 major league games.
13. Bonnie Blair, a double gold medal winner in speed skating, was the United States hero of the 1992 Winter Olympics.
14. Barry Sanders, a great running back, played football for the Detroit Lions.
15. Babe Ruth, one of baseball's greatest home run hitters, was also a great pitcher.
16. Joe DiMaggio, one of the greatest outfielders in baseball history, played with the Yankees.

17. Jim Ryun, an American track star, was born in Wichita, Kansas.
18. Babe Didrikson Zaharias, a track, golf, and basketball star, set many world records.
19. One-time manager of the Cleveland team Frank Robinson had been a star outfielder.
20. On one day in 1935, Olympic star Jesse Owens set four world records and tied another.

Exercise 5   **Expanding Sentences with Appositive Phrases**

On your paper expand the following sentences by adding an appositive phrase to each one. Be sure to use commas where necessary.

SAMPLE   Mr. Díaz hired me to paint his fence.
ANSWER   Mr. Díaz, my neighbor, hired me to paint his fence.

1. My friend mailed me a postcard from Madrid.
2. The movie we saw last night starred two fine actresses.
3. Mei Ying went to a concert featuring a new rock group.
4. The announcer reported that our team had won the game.
5. Daryl had no trouble winning the race.

Exercise 6   **Combining Sentences by Using Appositive Phrases**

Combine each pair of sentences into one sentence by using an appositive or an appositive phrase. Use commas where necessary.

SAMPLE   The Wright brothers built their planes in a bicycle shop and a factory.
                 They were the inventors of the first successful airplane.
ANSWER   The Wright brothers, inventors of the first successful airplane, built their planes in a bicycle shop and a factory.

1. Charles Goodyear invented vulcanized rubber when he spilled some rubber and sulfur.
   Charles Goodyear was a nineteenth-century American inventor.
2. Jack Kilby invented the first integrated circuit.
   An integrated circuit is the fundamental component of computers.
3. The Chinese or Babylonians probably invented the abacus.
   The abacus was one of the earliest adding machines.
4. Blaise Pascal was a French philosopher and mathematician.
   In 1642 he built an adding and subtracting machine.
5. The transistor was invented in the 1940s.
   The transistor is a device that amplifies electronic signals.
6. In 1901 Marconi succeeded in using radio waves to communicate across the Atlantic.
   Radio waves are pulses of electrical energy.
7. Thomas Edison designed the phonograph.
   The phonograph was one of the most important inventions in sound recording.
8. The kinetoscope was another invention of Edison's.
   Film in a kinetoscope gave the impression of a moving picture.
9. Clarence Birdseye was a member of a U.S. government survey team in Labrador.
   He invented a way of freezing foods quickly.
10. Every inventor should apply for a patent.
    A patent is a document giving an inventor an exclusive right to make or sell an invention.

Phrases

12.3 | Verbals and Verbal Phrases

■ A **verbal** is a verb form that functions in a sentence as a noun, an adjective, or an adverb.

■ A **verbal phrase** is a verbal plus any complements and modifiers.

Verbals include *participles, gerunds,* and *infinitives.* Each of these can be expanded into phrases.

Participles and Participial Phrases

■ A **participle** is a verb form that can function as an adjective.

Present participles always have an *-ing* ending. *Past participles* often end in *-ed*, but they can take other endings as well. Many commonly used adjectives are actually participles.

Rising prices are inevitable.

I cut my finger on the **broken** glass.

The **opening** speech detailed many **needed** changes.

A participle that is part of a verb phrase is not acting as an adjective.

PARTICIPLE AS ADJECTIVE   The **lost** ship has been recovered.
PARTICIPLE IN VERB PHRASE   The warehouse **had lost** a big shipment.

■ A **participial phrase** contains a participle plus any complements and modifiers.

A participial phrase can function as an adjective, and therefore, like an adjective, it can appear in various positions in a sentence. When it appears at the beginning of a sentence, a participial phrase is followed by a comma.

Preparing for the lunar eclipse, we set our alarm clocks.

The full moon, **suspended in the sky,** was brilliant.

Badly needing sleep but **delighted by the spectacle,** we maintained our vigil.

A past participle may be used with the present participle of the auxiliary verb *have* or *be.* (For more on the *-ing* form of a verb, see Unit 15.)

Having read about the eclipse, we were anxious to see it.

We watched the moon **being consumed by shadow.**

Identifying Participles and Participial Phrases

Write the participle or the participial phrase that acts as an adjective in each of the following sentences. Then write the word each one modifies.

George Lucas, an Influential Filmmaker

1. George Lucas achieved international fame in 1977 with his stunning science fiction movie *Star Wars.*
2. Celebrated for its superb special effects and suspenseful story, *Star Wars* has become a classic.
3. Raised in California, Lucas developed an interest in movies.
4. Having competed against other students, he won a national film competition in 1967 at the age of twenty-three.
5. Lucas's first major success was the popular *American Graffiti* (1973), a film portraying the lives of California teenagers in the 1960s.
6. Lucas worked on *American Graffiti* in two capacities, serving as both coauthor and director of the film.
7. By 1983, having produced *The Empire Strikes Back* and *The Return of the Jedi,* Lucas again proved his great versatility.
8. That year Lucas produced the highly successful adventure film *Raiders of the Lost Ark,* directed by his longtime friend Steven Spielberg.
9. Many people in the film industry marveled at the huge profits of *Raiders* and the two films succeeding it—*Indiana Jones and the Temple of Doom* (1984) and *Indiana Jones and the Last Crusade* (1989).
10. Freed from dependence upon film studios through his wealth and influence, Lucas can continue to pursue his personal artistic vision.

Exercise 8   **Expanding Sentences with Participial Phrases**

On your paper expand the following sentences by adding a participle or participial phrase to each one. Use commas where necessary.

SAMPLE	The campfire kept us warm.
ANSWER	The blazing campfire kept us warm.

1. The driver slammed on his brakes.
2. The strong wind knocked down power lines.
3. The candidate finally acknowledged defeat.
4. Huge crowds gathered around the astronauts.
5. The skater completed her routine for the judges.

Gerunds and Gerund Phrases

■ A **gerund** is a verb form that ends in *-ing* and is used in the same way a noun is used.

Training is essential. [gerund as subject]
We considered **flying.** [gerund as direct object]
We should give **speaking** more attention. [gerund as indirect object]
Do all of us get credit for **trying?** [gerund as object of a preposition]
Their passions were **sailing** and **sculling.** [gerunds as predicate nominatives]
Two skills, **reading** and **writing,** are basic. [gerunds as appositives]

■ A **gerund phrase** is a gerund plus any complements and modifiers.

Actively participating in sports has many benefits.
This suit shows **expert tailoring.**

Although both a present participle and a gerund end in *-ing,* they serve as different parts of speech. A present participle is used as an adjective in its sentence, whereas a gerund is used as a noun.

Waiting in line, we grew impatient. [participial phrase]
Waiting in line made us impatient. [gerund phrase]

| Exercise 9 | Identifying Gerunds and Gerund Phrases |

List the gerunds and gerund phrases.

A History of Sports

1. Hieroglyphics show that boxing was popular in Egypt's Nile Valley as early as 4000 B.C.
2. Early inhabitants of Ireland are known for holding the first organized sports competition, the Tailltean Games, around 1800 B.C.
3. In Mexico, around 1000 B.C., the Olmecs enjoyed playing a game much like soccer.
4. The playing of soccer was outlawed in England in A.D. 1363.
5. In the 1400s, people in Italy and Germany began to enjoy fencing as a competitive sport.

Exercise 10   Distinguishing Between Participles and Gerunds

Each of the following sentences has a verbal or a verbal phrase. Copy the verbal (or verbal phrase) and tell whether it is a gerund (or gerund phrase) or a participle (or participial phrase).

Hurricane Andrew

1. One of the most devastating natural disasters in American history, Hurricane Andrew struck Florida and Louisiana in August 1992.
2. Beginning as a patch of thunderstorms over western Africa, it moved across the Atlantic as a low-pressure wave.
3. About one thousand miles from Florida, the wind shear began slackening, and a high-pressure zone to the north grew stronger.
4. Winds blowing at hurricane strength soon grew to 164 miles an hour.
5. At the National Hurricane Center in Coral Gables, Florida, the instruments for measuring wind were knocked down.
6. A weatherman at a Miami television station had long warned Floridians about the necessity of preparing for a major hurricane.
7. Remaining on the air nonstop for 22 hours, the Miami weatherman, Bryan Norcross, became a local hero.
8. He informed listeners about the progress of the hurricane and gave them advice on protecting themselves and their homes from damage.
9. Heeding emergency and evacuation warnings, thousands of people fled their homes.
10. People gave the efforts of the media and local government credit for keeping the number of casualties fairly low.
11. Residents of Dade County, Florida, saw their property destroyed by the hurricane.
12. Residents of some of the rural regions described losing acres of fruit trees.
13. The total damage from the storm in Florida, including the destruction of more than sixty-three thousand homes in Dade County alone, reached about 30 billion dollars.
14. Mangled beyond repair by the hurricane winds, many planes were hauled off from an airfield and sold for parts or scrap.
15. Surging ashore in southern Louisiana, the hurricane inflicted more casualties.
16. Finding themselves homeless after the hurricane, many Floridians sought shelter in temporary "tent cities."
17. The suffering of Florida's residents moved the rest of the nation, and volunteers arrived.
18. Hundreds of people cooked meals, provided medical assistance, and found shelter for the stricken residents.
19. Contributing large amounts of aid in Andrew's aftermath, all branches of the military worked together in the relief effort.
20. Although weary from their fierce battle with Andrew, Florida's residents soon began the massive job of rebuilding their state.

Exercise 11   Creating Sentences with Gerunds

Select five of the gerunds that you identified in Exercise 10, and write an original sentence for each one. Make sure you use the *-ing* word as a gerund, not as a present participle.

Infinitives and Infinitive Phrases

■ An **infinitive** is a verb form that is usually preceded by the word *to* and is used as a noun, an adjective, or an adverb.

The word *to* used before the base form of a verb is part of the infinitive form of the verb, not a preposition.

To exercise at least twenty minutes each day is healthful. [infinitive as subject]

No one wishes **to volunteer.** [infinitive as direct object]

Their decision was **to merge.** [infinitive as predicate nominative]

I felt a need **to call.** [infinitive as adjective]

Everyone was prepared **to sacrifice.** [infinitive as adverb]

■ An **infinitive phrase** contains an infinitive plus any complements and modifiers.

The lawyers want **to continue working on the case** as long as possible.

Would you prefer **to sleep until noon?**

To speak clearly and slowly is most important.

Occasionally an infinitive may have its own subject. Such a construction is called an *infinitive clause.*

Circumstances forced **the gentlemen to duel.**
[*Gentlemen* is the subject of the infinitive *to duel.* The entire infinitive clause *the gentlemen to duel* acts as the direct object of the sentence.]

The teacher asked **Maria to give a speech.**
[*Maria* is the subject of the infinitive *to give.* The entire infinitive clause *Maria to give a speech* acts as the direct object of the sentence.]

Note that the subject of the infinitive phrase comes between the main verb and the infinitive. The subject of an infinitive phrase always follows an action verb.

Sometimes the word *to* is dropped before an infinitive.

We could have heard **a pin [to] drop.**

They watched **the troupe [to] dance.**

Phrases

Exercise 12   **Identifying Infinitive Phrases**

Write the infinitive phrase that appears in each of the following sentences. (One sentence has two infinitive phrases.)

Art in Winston-Salem

1. Art has come to play a major role in the life of Winston-Salem, North Carolina.
2. The city has two famous museums known to attract visitors from all over the country.
3. For those who wish to see nineteenth-century southern decorative art, the Museum of Early Southern Decorative Arts is the place to explore thoroughly.
4. Over the years art lovers who have wanted to learn more about American painting have visited Reynolda House.
5. The Southeast Center for Contemporary Arts (SECCA) was founded to encourage new southern artists.
6. Thus, what people come to view in this gallery is almost exclusively the work of unrecognized artists.
7. Exhibits change often, perhaps because SECCA never intended to acquire a permanent collection.
8. Each year, to foster talent, SECCA awards fellowships to seven artists from the southeastern United States.
9. To win one of these fellowships is a great honor.
10. To judge the works of the Southeast Seven artists is the job of a group of experts.

Exercise 13   **Recognizing the Function of Infinitive Phrases**

Write the infinitive phrase and tell whether it functions as a noun, an adjective, or an adverb. If the phrase is used as a noun, identify its function by writing *subject, direct object, predicate nominative,* or *object of a preposition.*

Mountains Under the Sea

1. To measure the depths of the oceans has long been a challenge to scientists.
2. About a century ago, scientists began to unlock the secrets of the ocean floor.
3. One technological breakthrough was sonar, which used sound waves to measure ocean depths.
4. The limitations of this new technique spurred scientists to develop even better measures.
5. By the years after World War II, oceanographers could use sonar to chart the ocean's depths with great accuracy.
6. At that time, scientists created machines to record sonar signals automatically and continuously.
7. A stylus recorded sonar signals on a moving strip of paper to chart a continuous profile of the ocean floor.
8. Oceanographers produced maps to show the world our undersea landscape.
9. Brude T. Heezen and Marie Tharp were among the first to develop these new maps.
10. One important result of the new maps was to show underwater mountains higher than the tallest peaks on continental land.

Exercise 14   **Creating Sentences with Infinitives**

Write five action verbs. Then make up a sentence using each verb in an infinitive phrase. Underline the infinitive phrases.

12.4 Absolute Phrases

- An **absolute phrase,** also known as a nominative absolute, consists of a noun or a pronoun that is modified by a participle or a participial phrase. An absolute phrase has no grammatical relation to the rest of the sentence.

An absolute phrase belongs neither to the complete subject nor to the complete predicate of a sentence. It stands "absolutely" by itself in relation to the rest of the sentence.

Its wings being damaged by the storm, the aircraft crashed.

In some absolute phrases the participle *being* is understood rather than stated.

We took off on schedule, **the weather [being] perfect.**

Exercise 15   Identifying Absolute Phrases

Write on your paper the absolute phrase in each of the following sentences.

1. I spend many hours in the backyard, gardening being my favorite activity.
2. The soil rich in nutrients, everything grows quickly.
3. The radishes and beans having been planted a week ago, I now await the first growth.
4. The plan of my vegetable garden is strictly geometric, everything laid out in neat rows.
5. The flower bed is more informal, the plants arranged mainly by color.
6. The climate mild and rainy, many wild plants bloom beautifully.
7. I planted a bog garden, one corner of my yard being somewhat low and wet.
8. My hose already leaking, I punched more holes in it and used it as a soaker hose for the shrubs in front.
9. I conserve as much water as I can, drought being a problem in the summer.
10. His roses overtaken by wild ferns, my neighbor has become enthusiastic about collecting different kinds of ferns.
11. The begonias now thriving, I no longer regret the shady front yard.
12. The soil retains moisture for a long time, the ground covered with leaves and grass.
13. It's easy to get the whole family involved in gardening, children showing great interest in their own plantings.
14. The yard having been cleared of weeds, most of the hard work was behind us.
15. I decided against a new lawn, mowing grass not being one of my favorite pastimes.
16. Our apple trees loaded with fruit, we picked as many as we could and made cider.
17. My luck with roses running out, I tried lilac and hydrangea bushes against our side fence.
18. We decided not to plant daylilies, our garden being somewhat formal.
19. A late frost sure to come, we covered the shrubs with tarps.
20. Potted plants need a regular supply of nutrients, their roots trapped in limited soil.

Phrases

Write each of the verbal phrases and absolute phrases. (Five sentences have more than one verbal phrase or a verbal and an absolute phrase.) Write *participial phrase, gerund phrase, infinitive phrase,* or *absolute phrase* to identify each phrase. (Remember: An absolute phrase has within it a participle or a participial phrase.)

The Hmong

1. Have you ever seen *paj ntaub,* the beautiful cloths stitched by Hmong women?
2. Cutting material in intricate designs and embroidering bold patterns with fine stitches, the Hmong women make their beautiful needlework.
3. From an early age, Hmong girls learn the art of needlework, sewing without pins or patterns.
4. Serving more than decorative purposes, some of the cloths record village scenes, celebrations, and ceremonies of Hmong culture.
5. Over the past two thousand years, the Hmong people have migrated from China, their ancestral home, to settle in the mountains of Vietnam, Laos, and Thailand.
6. The strategic location of their mountain homeland, overlooking North Vietnam, forced the Hmong into the conflict between communist and anticommunist forces.
7. During the Vietnam War, the United States government gave the Hmong military supplies and financial assistance to fight the North Vietnamese.
8. Unfortunately, supporting the Americans in the Vietnam War cost many Hmong their homes and lives.
9. Their allies having withdrawn from Vietnam, the Hmong fled the area.
10. Their traditional economy destroyed, many Hmong left their villages for the security of refugee camps.
11. Attacked even in Laotian refugee camps, the Hmong made their way toward Thailand.
12. One possible means of escape was the trek hundreds of miles to the Mekong River, crossing it in rafts.
13. The United States began to admit thousands of Hmong refugees during the 1970s, initially resettling them in various cities across the country.
14. Building a new life in the United States has not been easy for a people with an alien language and culture.
15. Hearing of the prosperous agriculture of California's Central Valley, many Hmong took up farming there.
16. In large cities, the Hmong experienced the greatest possible contrast to their agricultural way of life, but the efforts of the Hmong to settle in smaller cities have been more successful.
17. One means that the Hmong have used for preserving their traditions has been the telling of age-old Hmong stories and legends.
18. Still placing special emphasis on traditional dress and fabrics, many Hmong see clothing as an important symbol of ethnic identity.
19. At street fairs and in small shops, some Hmong sell their own *paj ntaub* as well as needlework sent from relatives still in Asia.
20. Today the directors of Hmong craft centers work to keep the ancient and beautiful art of *paj ntaub* alive in a new country.

Identifying Verbal Phrases and Absolute Phrases

Copy two absolute phrases and three verbal phrases from the passage below. Write *absolute phrase, participial phrase, gerund phrase,* or *infinitive phrase* to identify each.

adapted from *A Tale of Two Cities* by Charles Dickens

With drooping heads and tremulous tails, they mashed their way through the thick mud, floundering and stumbling between whiles, as if they were falling to pieces at the larger joints. As often as the driver rested them and brought them to a stand, with a wary "Wo-ho! so-ho then!" the near leader violently shook his head and everything upon it—like an unusually emphatic horse, denying that the coach could be got up the hill. . . .

The mist steaming in all the hollows, it had roamed in its forlornness up the hill, like an evil spirit, seeking rest and finding none. A clammy and intensely cold mist, it made its slow way through the air in ripples that visibly followed and overspread one another, as the waves of an unwholesome sea might do. It was dense enough to shut out everything from the light of the coach-lamps but these its own workings and a few yards of road; and the reek of the laboring horses steamed into it, as if they had made it all.

Two other passengers, besides the one, were plodding up the hill by the side of the mail. All three were wrapped to the cheek-bones and over the ears, and wore jack-boots. Each hidden under almost as many wrappers from the eyes of the mind, as from the eyes of the body, not one of the three could have said, from anything he saw, what either of the other two was like.

Exercise 18   Using Phrases in Sentences

Follow the directions below for writing sentences of your own.

1. Use *running quickly* as an adjective in a sentence.
2. Use *the skies becoming darker each minute* as an absolute phrase in a sentence.
3. Use *to win first prize* as the predicate nominative in a sentence.
4. Use *to play basketball* as an adverb in a sentence.
5. Use *the alarm having stopped ringing* as an absolute phrase in a sentence.
6. Use *dancing in the school musical* as a direct object in a sentence.
7. Use *to increase our stamina* as an adjective in a sentence.
8. Use *the last of the tourists having left* as an absolute phrase in a sentence.
9. Use *to find a job* as the subject in a sentence.
10. Use *finding the building empty* as an adjective in a sentence.
11. Use *carefully drawn* as an adjective in a sentence.
12. Use *learning another language* as the subject in a sentence.
13. Use *eating in a hurry* as an adjective in a sentence.
14. Use *eating in a hurry* as the direct object in a sentence.
15. Use *covered with snow* as an adjective in a sentence.
16. Use *the fog reducing visibility to almost zero* as an absolute phrase in a sentence.
17. Use *waiting for the train* as the direct object in a sentence.
18. Use *waiting for the train* as an adjective in a sentence.
19. Use *prepared for a long delay* as an adjective in a sentence.
20. Use *to signal their need for help* as an adverb in a sentence.

Grammar Review

Phrases

PHRASES

The following passages are taken from a classic American novel, *The Red Badge of Courage*. Each passage has been annotated to show how Stephen Crane used the kinds of phrases taught in this unit. The novel is the story of a young man who finds himself caught up in the violence of the Civil War and who faces up to his feelings of self-doubt.

Literature Model

from The Red Badge of Courage
by Stephen Crane

Participial Phrase

Prepositional Phrase

A house standing placidly in distant fields had to him an ominous look. The shadows of the woods were formidable. He was certain that in this vista there lurked fierce-eyed hosts. The swift thought came to him that the generals did not know what they were about. It was all a trap. Suddenly those close forests would bristle with rifle barrels. Ironlike brigades would appear in the rear. They were all going to be sacrificed. The generals were stupids. The enemy would presently swallow the whole command. He glared about him, expecting to see the stealthy approach of his death.

Infinitive Phrase

He thought that he must break from the ranks and harangue his comrades. They must not all be killed like pigs; and he was sure it would come to pass unless they were informed of these dangers. The generals were idiots to send them marching into a regular pen. There was but one pair of eyes in the corps. He would step forth and make a speech. Shrill and passionate words came to his lips.

The line, broken into moving fragments by the ground, went calmly on through fields and woods. The youth looked at the men nearest him, and saw, for the most part, expressions of deep interest, as if they were investigating something that had fascinated them. One or two stepped with overvaliant airs as if they were already plunged into war. Others walked as upon thin ice.

Prepositional Phrase

The greater part of the untested men appeared quiet and absorbed. They were going to look at war, the red animal—war, the blood-swollen god. And they were deeply engrossed in this march.

Some one cried, "Here they come!"

There was rustling and muttering among the men. They displayed a feverish desire to have every possible cartridge ready to their hands. The boxes were pulled around into various positions, and adjusted with great care. It was as if seven hundred new bonnets were being tried on.

The tall soldier, having prepared his rifle, produced a red handkerchief of some kind. He was engaged in knitting it about his throat with exquisite attention to its position, when the cry was repeated up and down the line in a muffled roar of sound.

"Here they come! Here they come!" Gun locks clicked.

When the woods again began to pour forth the dark-hued masses of the enemy the youth felt serene self-confidence. He smiled briefly when he saw men dodge and duck at the long screechings of shells that were thrown in giant handfuls over them. He stood, erect and tranquil, watching the attack begin against a part of the line that made a blue curve along the side of an adjacent hill. His vision being unmolested by smoke from the rifles of his companions he had opportunities to see parts of the hard fight. It was a relief to perceive at last from whence came some of these noises which had been roared into his ears.

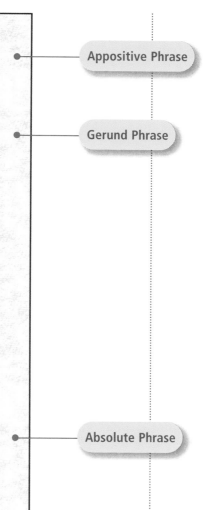

Appositive Phrase

Gerund Phrase

Absolute Phrase

Phrases

Review: Exercise 1   Elaborating Sentences with Prepositional Phrases

The following sentences describe an imaginary battle scene. Read through the sentences quickly to get an idea of the scene, and then rewrite each sentence, adding at least one prepositional phrase—an adjective phrase or an adverb phrase—to each sentence. You do not have to describe a scene from the Civil War, as Stephen Crane did; you can imagine any scene that you wish.

SAMPLE   The struggle was over quickly.
ANSWER   The struggle between the soldiers was over quickly.

1. The attack began early.
2. Mist enveloped the valley.
3. Only a few rays penetrated the fog.
4. The men advanced silently.

(continued)

Grammar Review

5. The leader signaled a halt.
6. Suddenly they heard a shout.
7. The enemy had seen them.
8. The men raced forward.
9. They met fierce resistance.
10. Several men fell wounded.
11. Others ran desperately.
12. The enemy outnumbered the men.
13. The men thought they were doomed.
14. The leader shouted.
15. Never had they seen such confusion.
16. The noise was deafening.
17. Fear paralyzed some.
18. Three men led the assault.
19. They fought a pitched battle.
20. The leader was wounded.

Review: Exercise 2   Elaborating Sentences with Appositives

Rewrite each sentence, incorporating the words in parentheses so that they form an appositive phrase. Be sure to use commas where necessary.

SAMPLE The battle was indecisive. (a brief skirmish)
ANSWER The battle, a brief skirmish, was indecisive.

1. The soldier saw the house.
   (an island of calm in the midst of chaos)
2. The house had an ominous look.
   (a dilapidated clapboard building)
3. Dark shapes obscured the building.
   (the shadows of giant elms)
4. Perhaps the enemy lurked within those shadows.
   (grim soldiers in gray)
5. The soldier felt trapped.
   (a young boy named Henry Fleming)
6. Never in all his life had he felt so frightened.
   (a mere sixteen years)
7. He had a flash of insight.
   (an awful premonition)
8. He and all his fellow soldiers were going to be sacrificed.
   (the entire regiment)
9. Anger swelled within him.
   (an uncontrollable tide)
10. The line advanced through the fields.
    (an unwavering column of blue)

Review: Exercise 3   Elaborating Sentences with Participial Phrases

Each of the sentences below elaborates upon an idea suggested by the passages from *The Red Badge of Courage*. Combine the sentences, changing the sentence in parentheses into a participial phrase. Be sure to place the participial phrase close to the word in the first sentence that it modifies.

SAMPLE   The boy feared the troops.
(The troops were hiding in the woods.)
ANSWER   The boy feared the troops hiding in the woods.

1. The house had an ominous look.
(The house was bordering the woods.)
2. The shadows were dense and foreboding.
(The shadows were engulfing the house.)
3. The boy feared the enemy.
(The enemy was lurking in the shadows.)
4. He imagined the woods.
(The woods were bristling with artillery.)
5. The boy shivered.
(The boy was disturbed by the thought.)
6. He was filled with anger.
(He was convinced of the futility of his situation.)
7. The generals were going to sacrifice their troops!
(The generals were commanding the Union Army.)
8. He advanced through the woods.
(He was casting baleful glances around him.)
9. He resolved to warn his comrades.
(He was rousing his courage.)
10. He decided he would make a speech to stir the men.
(He was setting his fears aside.)
11. His comrades would realize the folly of the assault.
(His comrades were shaken by his words.)
12. His brave resolve soon disappeared.
(His resolve was diminished by his fears.)
13. The line of Union soldiers advanced steadily toward their opponents.
(The line was unwavering in the dim light.)
14. Some men marched jauntily.
(The men were putting on a show of valor.)
15. Others walked stealthily.
(They were glancing fearfully from side to side.)
16. The men seemed subdued and serious.
(The men were untested in battle.)

(continued)

Phrases

17. The enemy looked like a dull gray river.
    (The enemy was pouring out of the woods.)
18. Suddenly the boy felt a wave of calm.
    (The calm was breaking over him.)
19. His eyes took in the entire scene.
    (His eyes were unobscured by the dust and smoke of battle.)
20. The sounds of battle brought him a curious sense of relief.
    (The sounds were surging toward him.)

Review: Exercise 4 — Creating Sentences with Gerund Phrases

For each item write a sentence that answers the question, using the words in parentheses as a gerund phrase.

SAMPLE What is patriotic? (defending one's country)
ANSWER Defending one's country is patriotic.

1. What is part of every soldier's life? (being afraid)
2. What is essential in battle? (having courage)
3. What do few soldiers find easy? (being brave)
4. What is the boy's goal? (warning his fellow soldiers)
5. What do soldiers dread? (being slaughtered)

Review: Exercise 5 — Elaborating Sentences with Infinitive Phrases

For each item write a sentence that answers the question, using the words in parentheses as an infinitive phrase.

SAMPLE What is the goal of every soldier? (to fight bravely and steadfastly)
ANSWER The goal of every soldier is to fight bravely and steadfastly.

1. What has war often threatened? (to destroy nations)
2. What did the Civil War almost manage to do? (to divide our country)
3. What was a goal of the Confederates? (to maintain the Southern way of life)
4. What was the aim of the North? (to preserve the Union)
5. What do most history books tend to do? (to side with the North)

Review: Exercise 6 — Elaborating Sentences with Absolute Phrases

Rewrite each of the following sentences, making the words in italics into an absolute phrase.

SAMPLE *Because war is common,* many children are forced to endure it.
ANSWER War being common, many children are forced to endure it.

1. *Since their experience is limited,* children understand little about war.
2. Nevertheless, *because they have few choices,* many children live in war zones.
3. Children are strongly affected by conflict, *as their minds are impressionable.*
4. *Because turmoil has filled their lives,* the children are forced to adapt.
5. *Since their resilience is great,* these children often survive remarkably well.

Proofreading

The following passage describes the artist Winslow Homer, whose painting appears on this page. Rewrite the passage, correcting the errors in spelling, grammar, and usage. Add any missing punctuation. There are ten errors.

Winslow Homer

¹Winslow Homer (1836–1910) one of America's greatest artists, was born in Boston, Massachusetts. ²Having reached the age of six Homer, along with his family, moved to the nearby town of Cambridge, where the boy learned to love the outdoors.

³Homer worked as a magazene illustrator for seventeen years. ⁴Trained as an illustrator he bringed a clear and unsentimental eye to his famous illustrations of the Civil War. ⁵Photography still being a primitive art at the time illustrators like Homer played a valuable role in relaying images of the war to the public.

⁶Homer receives wide recognition in 1866 for *Prisoners from the Front* the painting shown here. ⁷Homer witnessing the war firsthand painted what he saw; Stephen Crane, on the other hand, born after the war ended, relied on secondary reports and his powerful imagination in writing *The Red Badge of Courage.*

Winslow Homer, *Prisoners from the Front,* 1866

Phrases

Review: Exercise 8

Mixed Review

Below is a brief biographical sketch of Stephen Crane followed by ten sentences. Use the facts in the sketch to expand the ten sentences, following the guidelines that appear in parentheses. Be sure to place the phrases you add close to the word they modify.

Stephen Crane

Stephen Crane was born in Newark, New Jersey, in 1871. When he was a young man, he was restless and rebellious. He studied briefly at Syracuse University. Then he moved to New York City and became a reporter. He worked for several syndicates. When he wrote *The Red Badge of Courage,* he was only twenty-one, and he finished it within ten days. The novel describes a young Union soldier's disillusionment with war. Critics praised *The Red Badge of Courage.* They applauded its unflinching realism.

Later Crane was a war correspondent. He covered the Cuban front of the Spanish-American War and won praise for his courage. War provided an ideal context for the drama of testing oneself in situations of extreme danger or violence. Crane looked for the meaning of life in such situations. In this respect, he resembles other modern writers.

In 1895 Crane went on a trip to the far West. There he wrote two of his best stories. These stories were "The Blue Hotel" and "The Bride Comes to Yellow Sky." The West made a superb backdrop for Crane's mixture of fantasy and realism. Crane also wrote two volumes of poetry. His poetry is remarkably original. Few critics have tried to assess Crane's poetry in the context of poetic tradition.

Crane died in Germany in 1900. The cause of his death was tuberculosis. His clear and ironic prose influenced a generation of American authors, among them Ernest Hemingway.

1. Stephen Crane wrote a powerful novel. (Add an appositive phrase.)
2. Crane studied at Syracuse University. (Add an adverb phrase.)
3. He later became a reporter. (Add an adjective phrase.)
4. He wrote *The Red Badge of Courage.* (Add an adverb phrase.)
5. The novel describes the disenchantment. (Add an adjective phrase.)
6. Critics praised *The Red Badge of Courage.* (Add an adverb phrase.)
7. Crane went to Cuba. (Add an infinitive phrase.)
8. Crane was not afraid. (Add an absolute phrase.)
9. Crane died in 1900. (Add an adverb phrase.)
10. His prose influenced many writers. (Add a participial phrase.)

Writing Application

TIME

For more about the writing process, see **TIME Facing the Blank Page**, pages 111–121.

Phrases in Writing

By using a variety of phrases, writers can create sentences that are vividly detailed and rhythmically expressive. In this excerpt from *The Women of Brewster Place*, Gloria Naylor uses modifying phrases to expand the statement "Kiswana could see." As you read the passage, notice how Naylor underscores the steady bustle of the scene by piling phrase atop phrase in long, rhythmic sentences.

> From the window of her sixth-floor studio apartment, Kiswana could see over the wall at the end of the street to the busy avenue that lay just north of Brewster Place. The late-afternoon shoppers looked like brightly clad marionettes as they moved between the congested traffic, clutching their packages against their bodies to guard them from sudden bursts of the cold autumn wind. A portly mailman had abandoned his cart and was bumping into indignant window-shoppers as he puffed behind the cap that the wind had snatched from his head. Kiswana leaned over to see if he was going to be successful, but the edge of the building cut him off from her view.

Techniques with Phrases

Try to apply some of Gloria Naylor's writing techniques when you write and revise your own work.

❶ Use phrases to create vivid detail. Compare the following.

LACKING DETAIL Kiswana could see the busy avenue that lay just north of Brewster Place.

NAYLOR'S VERSION From the window of her sixth-floor studio apartment, Kiswana could see over the wall at the end of the street to the busy avenue that lay just north of Brewster Place.

❷ Use phrases to give your sentences a smooth rhythm.

CHOPPY RHYTHM They clutched their packages against their bodies. They were guarding themselves from sudden bursts of the cold autumn wind.

NAYLOR'S VERSION ...clutching their packages against their bodies to guard them from sudden bursts of the cold autumn wind. . .

Practice Revise the following passage on a separate sheet of paper. Combine choppy, awkward sentences by turning some of them into phrases that give the passage a smooth rhythm. Use a variety of phrases: prepositional, participial, infinitive, appositive, gerund, and absolute.

It was March. The year was 1513. Ponce de Leon boldly entered Florida's waters. His hopes were as high as the tall ship's mast. The mast was casting its shadow over him. He had been appointed governor of Puerto Rico several years before. He had heard legends. The legends described a fountain. The fountain had miraculous healing powers. He was dreaming of glory. He had left Puerto Rico and sailed far. He had crossed treacherous seas. He had journeyed to Florida's waters. His purpose was that here he would find the Fountain of Youth.

Phrases

UNIT 13

Clauses and Sentence Structure

13.1 | Main Clauses

- A **clause** is a group of words that has a subject and a predicate and that is used as a part of a sentence.

The two kinds of clauses are *main clauses* (also called *independent clauses*) and *subordinate clauses* (also called *dependent clauses*).

- A **main clause** has a subject and a predicate and can stand alone as a sentence.

Every sentence must contain at least one main clause. Each sentence below contains two main clauses: clauses that have both a subject and a verb and would express a complete thought if they appeared individually.

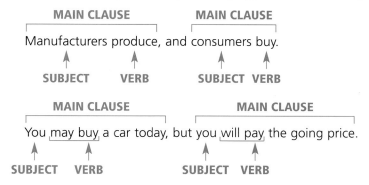

Exercise 1   Identifying Subjects and Verbs in Main Clauses

On your paper, write the main clause or clauses in each sentence. Then underline the subject and circle the verb.

Henry Ford, Automobile Manufacturer

1. Henry Ford was the founder of one of the first and most successful automobile manufacturing companies in the world.
2. He was born in Dearborn, Michigan, in 1863.
3. From an early age, Henry Ford displayed a mechanical aptitude.
4. Because of his interests and talents, he went to Detroit and became an apprentice in a machine shop.
5. He worked as a machinist and engineer at the Edison Illumination Company of Detroit but began building a car in his spare time.
6. In 1899 he founded the Detroit Automobile Company, but it failed because of numerous disagreements among partners.
7. With the financial backing of Alexander Malcolmson, Henry Ford organized the Ford Motor Company in 1903.
8. By 1906 Henry Ford had purchased all available stock from his various partners, and he became president of his own company.
9. Ford Motor Company adapted the conveyor belt and assembly line for car production.
10. As a result, Henry Ford outdistanced his competitors in the American automobile market.

13.2 Subordinate Clauses

■ A **subordinate clause** has a subject and a predicate, but it cannot stand alone as a sentence.

A subordinate clause is dependent upon the rest of the sentence because it does not make sense by itself. A subordinate clause needs a main clause to complete its meaning. Subordinating conjunctions or relative pronouns usually introduce a subordinate clause.

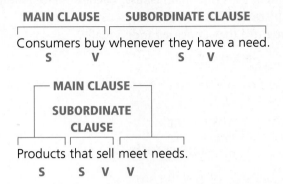

In the first sentence the subordinating conjunction *whenever* introduces the subordinate clause *whenever they have a need*. Even though this subordinate clause has a subject and a predicate, it does not express a complete thought.

In the second sentence the relative pronoun *that* introduces a subordinate clause that comes between the subject and the verb of the main clause. In this case *that* also functions as the subject of the subordinate clause.

Exercise 2   Identifying Subordinate Clauses

On your paper, write the subordinate clause from each sentence, and underline either the subordinating conjunction or the relative pronoun that introduces the clause.

SAMPLE   Mystery books that interest me have intriguing titles.
ANSWER   <u>that</u> interest me

1. The *Model T* Ford, which people loved, was discontinued as a model in 1928.
2. The peace efforts that Henry Ford organized during World War I failed.
3. Henry Ford lost the Senate election in his home state of Michigan although he campaigned hard.
4. Ford automobile workers who were unhappy joined the union.
5. When he retired, Henry Ford was a familiar name across the United States and Europe.

Each of the following sentences has a clause that appears in italics. On your paper indicate whether it is a *main clause* or a *subordinate clause*. (Remember that a subordinate clause cannot stand alone as a sentence.)

Shirley Chisholm, Political Pioneer

1. Shirley Chisholm was a congresswoman from New York *who sought the presidential nomination in 1972.*
2. *Chisholm's campaign was notable* because she was the first African American woman to seek this high office.
3. *Even though her presidential campaign had little chance of success,* Shirley Chisholm considered her bid a serious one.
4. *Because her activities focused attention on important issues,* Chisholm was satisfied.
5. *Four years earlier Chisholm had established another first* when she became the first African American woman to be elected to Congress.
6. Her congressional election followed four years of service in the New York State Assembly, *where Chisholm had gained a reputation for independent thinking.*
7. This independent thinking became obvious to all in Congress *as soon as the freshman representative began her first term in office.*
8. Although she represented an urban district, *Chisholm was assigned to the Agriculture Committee.*
9. After she strongly objected to the inappropriate assignment, *the Democratic leadership reassigned her to a more suitable committee.*
10. Incidents like this exemplified Chisholm's strength of character, *which earned her the fond nickname Fighting Shirley.*
11. *Because she held strong convictions,* Fighting Shirley spoke out against the House seniority system.
12. The Congressional Black Caucus, *of which Chisolm was a founding member,* fought for the rights of the urban poor, including those in her home district.
13. As a tireless spokesperson for the rights of women, *she supported the Equal Rights Amendment.*
14. *Because she considered her gender more of a handicap than her race,* Chisolm founded the National Women's Political Caucus.
15. Before Shirley Chisholm's term in the House ended, *Americans knew her views well.*
16. Young people will find out about Shirley Chisholm *whenever they seek the strong voices of Congress from the past.*
17. *When she wanted to explain her views to the public,* she sometimes wrote books.
18. *If people are interested in learning more about her views,* they may read *The Good Fight.*
19. As her service in Congress shows, *Shirley Chisholm was a strong-minded representative.*
20. *After she retired from Congress in 1982,* she continued to be active in politics.

13.3 Simple and Compound Sentences

■ A **simple sentence** has only one main clause and no subordinate clauses.

Keep in mind that as long as a sentence has only one main clause, it is a simple sentence. Nevertheless, a simple sentence may have a compound subject, a compound predicate, or both. The subject and the predicate of a simple sentence may also be expanded in many ways, such as with the addition of adjectives, adverbs, prepositional phrases, appositives and appositive phrases, and verbal phrases.

> Consumers buy. [simple sentence]
>
> Consumers and investors buy. [simple sentence with compound subject]
>
> Consumers compare and buy. [simple sentence with compound predicate]
>
> Consumers and investors compare and buy. [simple sentence with compound subject and compound predicate]
>
> Most serious investors carefully consider alternative uses for their money. [simple sentence expanded]

■ A **compound sentence** has two or more main clauses.

Although all of the main clauses of a compound sentence are part of the same sentence, each clause has its own subject and its own predicate. Typically, a comma, together with a coordinating conjunction (*and, but, or, nor, yet,* or *for*), is used to join the main clauses, as in the examples that follow.

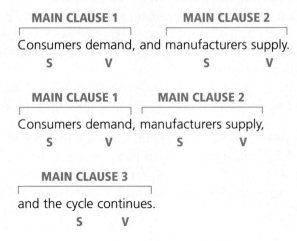

MAIN CLAUSE 1		MAIN CLAUSE 2	
Consumers demand, and manufacturers supply.			
S	V	S	V

MAIN CLAUSE 1		MAIN CLAUSE 2	
Consumers demand, manufacturers supply,			
S	V	S	V

MAIN CLAUSE 3

and the cycle continues.
    S   V

Main clauses may also be joined by a semicolon in place of the comma and the coordinating conjunction.

MAIN CLAUSE 1

First, demand for a specific product increases;

     S   V

MAIN CLAUSE 2

then the price of the product rises.

     S   V

Exercise 4   Identifying Simple and Compound Sentences

On your paper, indicate whether each item is a *simple sentence* or a *compound sentence*. (Remember that a single main clause can have a compound subject and a compound predicate.)

Crocodiles

1. Crocodiles and dinosaurs are related to each other, but crocodiles have survived extraordinary climate changes to the present day.
2. Crocodiles' tails propel them through water, and only their eyes and nostrils are exposed.
3. Full-grown crocodiles can range in length from five to twenty-five feet and can sometimes weigh more than two thousand pounds.
4. A crocodile can kill a large water mammal but can also carry its newly hatched babies between its jaws.
5. Most crocodiles hunt at night; hungry crocodiles, however, hunt during the day too.
6. Crocodiles usually live in remote places, but greedy hunters easily discover them.
7. Crocodiles were once valuable to hunters but are now protected by law.
8. Crocodiles were valued for leather for shoes, belts, and bags, and, as hatchlings, were sold as pets.
9. This led to near extermination in many areas and resulted in their being protected by many governments; the state of New York forbids the sale of crocodilian products.
10. Crocodiles have survived for millions of years and, with new protection, may survive much longer.

Exercise 5   Writing Simple and Compound Sentences

On your paper, write original sentences about crocodiles, using the information in Exercise 4 and the sentence structure indicated.

SAMPLE   Simple sentence with a compound predicate
ANSWER   Laws protect crocodiles and ensure their survival.

1. Simple sentence with a compound subject
2. Compound sentence
3. Simple sentence with a compound subject and a compound predicate
4. Compound sentence with two main clauses
5. Compound sentence with three main clauses

13.4 Complex and Compound-Complex Sentences

■ A **complex sentence** has one main clause and one or more subordinate clauses.

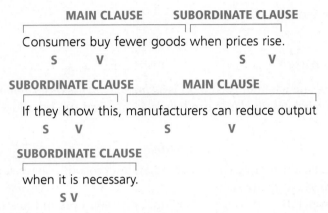

| MAIN CLAUSE | SUBORDINATE CLAUSE |
Consumers buy fewer goods when prices rise.
S   V   S   V

SUBORDINATE CLAUSE | MAIN CLAUSE
If they know this, manufacturers can reduce output
S   V   S   V

SUBORDINATE CLAUSE
when it is necessary.
S V

■ A **compound-complex sentence** has more than one main clause and at least one subordinate clause.

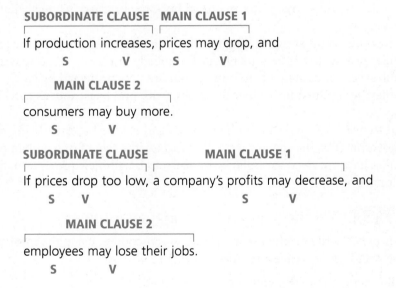

SUBORDINATE CLAUSE | MAIN CLAUSE 1
If production increases, prices may drop, and
S   V   S   V

MAIN CLAUSE 2
consumers may buy more.
S   V

SUBORDINATE CLAUSE | MAIN CLAUSE 1
If prices drop too low, a company's profits may decrease, and
S   V   S   V

MAIN CLAUSE 2
employees may lose their jobs.
S   V

| **Exercise 6** | **Creating Sentences with Various Structures**

On a separate sheet of paper, write a simple sentence. Then rework it, making it into a compound sentence. Now go back to the simple sentence, and rework it to make it part of a complex sentence. Finally, rework your compound sentence, making it into a compound-complex sentence. Refer to the examples on pages 538–539 and this page, as necessary.

Clauses and Sentence Structure

540 Unit 13 Clauses and Sentence Structure

Write on your paper the subordinate clause that appears in each of the following sentences. Indicate whether each sentence is *complex* or *compound-complex.*

Plaza of the Three Cultures

[1]When the ancestors of the Aztecs migrated to the western region of Lake Texcoco during the fourteenth century, they founded two different cities—Tenochtitlán and Tlatelolco—on neighboring islands. [2]The occupants of the two cities gradually filled in the shallow lake surrounding their islands until the two landmasses were joined. [3]Although Tenochtitlán eventually became the capital of the Aztec Empire, Tlatelolco maintained its independence from the empire. [4]Nevertheless, while the Spanish conquistadors were crushing the Aztec Empire, they destroyed much of Tlatelolco, and the area was eventually absorbed into what is now Mexico City. [5]The Spanish constructed their own buildings on the site where the Aztecs had worshiped their gods.

[6]In 1960, over three centuries later, the government of Mexico City began a redevelopment plan that brought new apartment complexes and office buildings to the Tlatelolco area. [7]Construction workers cleared away neglected, dilapidated structures and began to dig the foundations for brand-new buildings, but they soon were greatly surprised by the discovery of ancient stone platforms that were clearly Aztec in origin. [8]Because modern Mexican citizens appreciate the culture and achievements of their Aztec ancestors, the Mexican government has preserved the ancient Aztec ruins for all to appreciate. [9]Today a tourist to Tlatelolco can stand in one place and see evidence of the three cultures—Aztec, Spanish, and modern Mexican—that illustrate Mexico's varied and fascinating history. [10]If you visit Mexico City, you should include in your trip a visit to the Plaza of the Three Cultures.

Exercise 8 Writing with Complex and Compound-Complex Sentences

On your paper, answer the following questions about the passage above. Use the sentence structure indicated in parentheses.

SAMPLE When were Tenochtitlán and Tlatelolco built? (complex)
ANSWER Tenochtitlán and Tlatelolco were built when early Aztecs filled in the water of Lake Texcoco during the fourteenth century.

1. Why did the Spanish destroy Tlatelolco? (complex)
2. What did the Spanish build at Tlatelolco? (complex)
3. What happened in the Tlatelolco area in 1960? (complex)
4. How does the Mexican government view the Tlatelolco area? (compound-complex)
5. What does a person experience at Tlatelolco today? (compound-complex)

13.5 Adjective Clauses

■ An **adjective clause** is a subordinate clause that modifies a noun or a pronoun.

An adjective clause normally comes after the word it modifies.

Periodicals **that inform and entertain** often make good reading.

Several writers **whom I admire** contribute to excellent magazines.

Kim enjoys a magazine **whose style is distinctive and modern.**

Both relative pronouns (*who, whom, whose, that,* and *which*) and the subordinating conjunctions *where* and *when* may begin adjective clauses.

I cannot remember a time in my life **when I did not enjoy reading.**

Libraries are places **where many kinds of periodicals can be found.**

The store **where I buy magazines** sponsors readings by contributors.

The relative pronoun may sometimes be dropped at the beginning of an adjective clause.

The article in this magazine is one **I am sure you will enjoy.** [The relative pronoun *that* has been omitted.]

The writer **you may well remember** won an award for her article. [The relative pronoun *whom* has been omitted.]

An adjective clause is sometimes needed to make the meaning of a sentence clear. Such an adjective clause is called an *essential clause,* or a *restrictive clause.* Without the essential adjective clause, the complete meaning of the sentence would not be expressed.

Magazines **that have no photographs** bore me. [essential clause]

Smithsonian is the magazine **that I like best.** [essential clause]

There is just one store in our town **that sells only magazines and periodicals.** [essential clause]

When an adjective clause is not absolutely needed in order to express the complete meaning of a sentence, it is called a *nonessential clause*, or a *nonrestrictive clause*. Always use commas to set off a nonessential clause.

Newspapers, **which I often read,** are interesting. [nonessential clause]

Also informative are newsletters, **which are widely distributed by many organizations.** [nonessential clause]

Sheryl Kosak, **who won a national journalism award,** recently read at our local magazine store. [nonessential clause]

The relative pronoun *that* usually introduces an essential clause; the relative pronoun *which* introduces a nonessential clause.

Newsmagazines, **which are published weekly,** provide excellent coverage of current events. [nonessential clause]

World events **that have major significance** are thoroughly reported. [essential clause]

| Exercise 9 | Identifying Adjective Clauses |

On your paper, write the adjective clause that appears in each of the following sentences. Then write the word that the clause modifies. (In one sentence the relative pronoun has been dropped.)

Pueblo Ceremonial Dances

1. The Pueblo people celebrate various occasions with ceremonial dances they have been performing in the same way for centuries.
2. Many of the dances are performed by men who sing and dance simultaneously.
3. Women, who perform as featured dancers in front of the men in winter dances, participate in couples dances and group dances in summer
4. The musical instruments that players use include wooden drums, hand-held gourd rattles, and strung rattles of deer hooves and turtle shells.
5. Ceremonial days are occasions for feasts, which the Pueblo people provide for relatives, friends, and visitors.
6. Some ceremonies are open to outsiders who respect the religious aspects of the events and behave accordingly.
7. One famous ceremony is the Hopi Snake Dance, which is performed every other summer.
8. An important festivity that celebrates the harvest is the San Ildefonso Corn Dance.
9. Masks, which have always been an important part of Pueblo culture, are worn by participants in the Zuni Shalako, a winter dance.
10. The dances, which express and reinforce group beliefs, are an important part of Native American culture.

Clauses and Sentence Structure

| Exercise 10 | Recognizing Essential and Nonessential Clauses |

For each sentence in the pairs below, write the adjective clause, and then identify it as an *essential* or a *nonessential* clause.

Rhinos

1. a. We learned a lot about rhinos at the zoo that we visited last week.
    b. The class enjoyed an interesting field trip to the zoo, which has several species of rhino on display.
2. a. The rhinos that exist today have one or two horns on the upper surface of the snout.
    b. One of the rhino's relatives was the Woolly rhinoceros, which survived until the last Ice Age in Europe, about 15,000 years ago.
3. a. The species that is largest and most impressive is undoubtedly the white rhino.
    b. White rhinos, which can tip the scales at two tons, are larger than any other land mammal except for elephants.
4. a. The animal's name, which literally means "nose-horn," derives from its most prominent feature.
    b. Together with elephants and hippos, rhinos represent a life form that was far more abundant in past epochs: the megaherbivores, or giant plant-feeders.
5. a. Rhinos do not depend much on their vision, which is relatively poor.
    b. The senses that are most acute in this species are smell and hearing.
6. a. Few animals can be as dangerous as rhinos, which fortunately do not attack humans often.
    b. A charging rhino that is headed straight for you at over thirty miles an hour is an awesome threat.
7. a. Rhinos, which are native to Africa and Asia, are often prey to poachers.
    b. The poachers who pursue these huge animals should have an easy time finding them because of the rhino's size and relatively predictable movements.
8. a. The valuable appendage that is the poachers' target is the rhino's horn.
    b. Rhino horns, which are prized for their supposed medicinal qualities as well as for their ornamental value, are sold on the international black market.
9. a. Rhino horn that is ground into powder is used as a fever-reducing agent in several countries in the Far East.
    b. In Yemen, which is located on the Arabian peninsula, rhino horn has been traditionally used to make handles for ornamental daggers.
10. a. Perhaps the most severely endangered species is the black rhino, which is native to East Africa.
    b. The poachers who slaughter these prehistoric-looking beasts are hastening the slide of all five species of rhino into extinction.

An **adverb clause** is a subordinate clause that modifies a verb, an adjective, or an adverb. It tells *when, where, how, why, to what extent,* or *under what condition.*

> **Wherever I go,** I take a magazine. [The adverb clause modifies the verb *take.* It tells *where.*]
>
> I am happy **as long as I can read.** [The adverb clause modifies the adjective *happy.* It tells *under what condition.*]
>
> I enjoy magazines more **than I usually enjoy a book.** [The adverb clause modifies the adverb *more.* It tells *to what extent.*]
>
> **As a new month approaches,** you should look for new editions of your favorite monthly magazines. [The adverb clause modifies the verb *should look.* It tells *when.*]
>
> **So that your own copy is assured,** you may subscribe to your favorite magazine by mail. [The adverb clause modifies the verb *may subscribe.* It tells *why.*]
>
> The local bookstore owner greeted me immediately **as if I were the world's greatest magazine consumer.** [The adverb clause modifies the verb *greeted.* It tells *how.*]

Subordinating conjunctions, such as those listed on page 474, introduce adverb clauses. An adverb clause can come either before a main clause or after it.

> I take a magazine **wherever I go.**
>
> **As long as I can read,** I am happy.
>
> You should look for new editions of your favorite monthly magazines **as a new month approaches.**
>
> You may subscribe to your favorite magazine by mail **so that your own copy is guaranteed.**

On occasion, words may be left out of an adverb clause in order to avoid repetition and awkwardness. The omitted words can easily be supplied by the reader, however, because they are understood, or implied. Such adverb clauses are called *elliptical adverb clauses.*

> Few enjoy reading more **than I [enjoy reading].**
>
> Reading makes me more relaxed **than [it makes] her [relaxed].**

Exercise 11   **Identifying Adverb Clauses**

On your paper, write the adverb clause that appears in each of the following sentences. (Three sentences have more than one adverb clause.)

SAMPLE   Whenever I read about Annie Oakley, I admire her spirit.
ANSWER   Whenever I read about Annie Oakley

Annie Oakley, Sharpshooter

1. Until Annie Oakley came along, sharpshooting had been a rather tame affair.
2. Since Annie's widowed mother was very poor, Annie provided for the family by shooting game birds and selling them to hotels and restaurants.
3. When Annie was visiting her sister in Cincinnati, she entered a contest against a champion sharpshooter so that she could earn extra money.
4. After he lost in a close match, the sharpshooter, Frank Butler, fell in love with Annie, and they eventually were married.
5. Frank taught Annie his sharpshooting tricks so that she could join his stage act.
6. Wherever they went, Frank's act was a big success as long as Annie was featured.
7. After Annie was established as a star, Frank retired from the act, though he continued as her manager.
8. Annie attracted many fans because she was entertaining as well as skillful.
9. Probably because she remembered her own unhappy childhood, Annie befriended orphans, staged charity shows, and paid the bills of many poor families.
10. Although Annie Oakley established sharpshooting records, perhaps her greatest feats were her kind deeds.

Exercise 12   **Creating Sentences with Adverb Clauses**

On your paper, combine each pair of sentences by using an adverb clause introduced by one of the subordinating conjunctions below. You may use each subordinating conjunction more than once or not at all.

SAMPLE   The city built additional stands. Rodeo fans can find seats easily.
ANSWER   The city built additional stands *so that rodeo fans can find seats easily.*

while	as	as if
because	so that	as long as
even though	before	although

1. Teenagers across Texas work with their young cattle all year. They hope to win awards at the Houston Livestock Show and Rodeo in March.
2. Some of the contestants are rather small. They still can win a contest in which they wrestle calves to the ground.
3. An old-fashioned trail ride passes by. People line the streets of small towns and cities throughout Texas to watch this parade from the past.
4. The rodeo is especially popular in Texas. People there appreciate regional traditions.
5. The rodeo exhibits are vast and scattered throughout the rodeo grounds. A first-time visitor may not see them all.

Noun Clauses

- A **noun clause** is a subordinate clause used as a noun.

You can use a noun clause in the same ways that you can use a noun or a pronoun: as a subject, a direct object, an indirect object, an object of a preposition, a predicate nominative, or an object complement.

PRONOUN

Someone left these magazines.
S

NOUN CLAUSE

Whoever was here last left these magazines.
S

NOUN

Magazines reflect the values of a society.
DO

NOUN CLAUSE

Magazines reflect **whatever a society values.**
DO

In the examples above, notice that each noun clause forms an inseparable part of the main clause of the sentence. In the second sentence, for example, the noun clause is the subject of the main clause. In the last sentence the noun clause is the direct object in the main clause.

Here are some words that can be used to introduce noun clauses:

how	when	who, whom
that	where	whoever
what	which	whose
whatever	whichever	why

Here are more examples of sentences that contain noun clauses:

Do you know **which magazine is my favorite?** [noun clause as a direct object]

This article is about **how microchips work.** [noun clause as the object of a preposition]

This is **where I get most of my up-to-date information.** [noun clause as a predicate nominative]

At times the relative pronoun is dropped from the beginning of a noun clause.

Hector thinks **PC Computing is the best computer magazine on the market.** [The relative pronoun *that* has been omitted.]

Exercise 13   **Identifying Noun Clauses**

On your paper, write the noun clauses that appear in each of the following sentences. (Three of the sentences have two noun clauses each. In one sentence the relative pronoun has been dropped.)

Fireworks

1. Tradition says the Chinese invented fireworks, but this tale has not been proved.
2. What is known by historians today is that explosives were in military use in many countries around the world during the Middle Ages.
3. Later, military victories were celebrated with fireworks, and these fireworks were set off by whoever was brave enough to ignite the explosives.
4. That fireworks continue to be extremely dangerous cannot be denied.
5. Today whoever manufactures or presents fireworks must observe numerous safety procedures.
6. Still, anyone can understand why fireworks of many different kinds are popular.
7. Traditionalists prefer whatever explodes in a radial burst, like the spread of a chrysanthemum.
8. Modern viewers are usually more interested in how loud the explosion is and in how many bursts are included in a cluster of shells.
9. Whoever loves fireworks will want to keep track of when fireworks are displayed in celebrations around the world.
10. For example, the best time for fireworks displays in Mexico is when the country celebrates its National Independence Day.

Exercise 14   **Writing Sentences with Noun Clauses**

On your paper, write original sentences about fireworks, using your own ideas or those in Exercise 13. Each sentence should include a noun clause that functions as indicated.

SAMPLE   Direct Object
ANSWER   Fireworks have always amazed <u>whoever saw them</u>.

1. Subject
2. Subject
3. Direct Object
4. Object of a Preposition
5. Predicate Nominative

Exercise 15   Using Subordinate Clauses in Sentences

Write four original sentences. In the first, use an adverb clause. In the second, use an adjective clause. In the third, use a noun clause as a subject. In the fourth, use a noun clause as a direct object.

Exercise 16   Review: Clauses

On your paper, write the subordinate clause that appears in each sentence. Then indicate whether the subordinate clause is (a) an adverb clause, (b) an adjective clause, or (c) a noun clause.

Tulsa, Oklahoma

1. Tulsa, Oklahoma, is called the Oil Capital of the World because hundreds of petroleum companies have headquarters there.
2. The city, which is on the Arkansas River, is the second largest in the state.
3. Although many visitors to the city do not at first realize it, Tulsa is a thriving center of both art and distinguished architecture.
4. Philbrook Art Center, which was an estate given to the city by an oil entrepreneur, houses an outstanding art collection.
5. Museum goers must decide how they can best spend their time at Tulsa's Thomas Gilcrease Institute of American History and Art.
6. Although Tulsa has a great many new and distinctive buildings, it has also successfully preserved carefully selected older buildings.
7. The civic center and a unique skyscraper church are only two of the structures that have received widespread acclaim.
8. The campus of nearby Oral Roberts University is remembered by all who visit it.
9. That the fountains and shade trees of the extensive park system in Tulsa are special attractions in themselves is quite clear.
10. Many surprises await whoever visits this fascinating and progressive city.

Exercise 17   Review: Writing with Clauses

On your paper, rewrite the paragraph below and add variety by using adjective clauses, adverb clauses, and noun clauses to combine sentences.

In the center of Oklahoma City lies an oil field. The oil field provides the city with a major industry. Livestock and meat production are also large industries in this city. They are second in importance to aircraft manufacturing and repair. All of these industries help to support Oklahoma City as the state capital of Oklahoma. The city itself was settled overnight. Land rushers settled the city. They settled it when the area was opened to homesteaders on April 22, 1889. The city grew. It is one of the largest cities in the United States. It measures six hundred and thirty square miles in size. It covers five counties. It also has many parks within its boundaries. In 1910 it became the state capital. Today, visitors come to Oklahoma on a regular basis. They come to enjoy its many sights and activities. One popular visitors' sight is the Cowboy Hall of Fame and Western Heritage Center.

Four Kinds of Sentences

■ A **declarative sentence** makes a statement.

> It is already light outside.
> I wake up with the sunrise.

The declarative sentence is the kind of sentence used most frequently. A declarative sentence usually ends with a period.

■ An **imperative sentence** gives a command or makes a request.

> Get up, and take a walk with me.
> Please close the door quietly.
> Wake up and smell the roses.

The subject "you" is understood in an imperative sentence. It, too, usually ends with a period, unless it expresses strong emotion. Then it ends with an exclamation point.

■ An **interrogative sentence** asks a question.

> Is anyone else awake?
> Do you think we should wait for the others?
> Will you wake me at dawn?

A question mark appears at the end of an interrogative sentence.

■ An **exclamatory sentence** expresses strong emotion.

> I will *not* hurry!
> What a glorious sunrise that is!

An exclamation point appears at the end of an exclamatory sentence.

Exercise 18   Identifying Kinds of Sentences

On your paper, rewrite the sentences using correct punctuation. Label each sentence as *declarative, imperative, interrogative,* or *exclamatory.*

1. Will you wake me at dawn
2. That's when the sun rises
3. I, also, wake with the sunrise
4. Wake up now
5. I won't wake up now
6. What time is it
7. Tell me the day, please
8. I refuse to wake up
9. No one likes sleepyheads
10. Ask me about waking up

Exercise 19   Creating Four Kinds of Sentences

Write four sentences about a favorite vacation. Use one declarative, one imperative, one interrogative, and one exclamatory sentence.

Sentence Fragments

■ A **sentence fragment** is an error that occurs when an incomplete sentence is punctuated as though it were a complete sentence.

In general, avoid sentence fragments in your writing. Look for three things when reviewing your work to detect sentence fragments. First, check for a group of words without a subject. Then look for a group of words without a verb, especially a group that includes a verbal rather than a complete verb. Finally, check to see that a subordinate clause is not punctuated as though it were a complete sentence.

Many times you can correct a sentence fragment by attaching it to a main clause that comes before the fragment or after it. Other times you may need to add words in order to make the sentence complete.

FRAGMENT	Levar and Juanita started hiking on the main trail. **Wanted to explore a remote area of the park.** [lacks subject]
COMPLETE SENTENCE	Levar and Juanita started hiking on the main trail, but they wanted to explore a remote area of the park.
FRAGMENT	They were tired. **The two weary hikers walking for hours.** [lacks complete verb]
COMPLETE SENTENCE	They were tired. The two weary hikers had been walking for hours.
FRAGMENT	To their left they found a faint trail. **Which they followed to the river.** [has subordinate clause only]
COMPLETE SENTENCE	To their left they found a faint trail, which they followed to the river.
FRAGMENT	**When they stopped to rest.** They checked their compass and trail guide. [has subordinate clause only]
COMPLETE SENTENCE	When they stopped to rest, they checked their compass and trail guide.

There are times when many professional writers use sentence fragments to create a special effect. They might want to emphasize a particular point or portray realistic dialogue. Keep in mind that professionals use sentence fragments carefully and intentionally. In most of your writing, however, including your writing for school, you should avoid sentence fragments.

Exercise 20   Identifying Sentence Fragments

Indicate on your paper whether each of the following numbered items is a *complete sentence* or a *sentence fragment*.

Jazz Pioneers

[1]Louis Armstrong, known as Satchmo, one of the most famous and beloved figures in American music. [2]Growing up among the brass bands of New Orleans, Louisiana, in the twentieth century's first decade. [3]Armstrong began his musical career singing in a barbershop quartet. [4]As a teen-ager played cornet on riverboats and in New Orleans clubs called honky tonks. [5]Armstrong joined the band of his hero, the jazz cornetist King Oliver, in Chicago in 1922. [6]Switching to the trumpet, Armstrong later formed his own band, the Hot Five (later the Hot Seven), and made a series of recordings between 1925 and 1928. [7]Which had a profound effect on musicians and jazz enthusiasts alike. [8]After appearing in many films in the late 1930s, Armstrong quickly became an international star. [9]By the 1950s his winning personality and great talent making him one of the best-known entertainers in the world. [10]When he died on July 6, 1971, the entire world mourned the loss of this great entertainer.

[11]New Orleans jazz, the kind of music Louis Armstrong played, also called Dixieland. [12]Played by small bands with cornets, trumpets, clarinets, trombones, bass, drums, guitars, and sometimes pianos. [13]The piano and bass were often not included; instead, a tuba was used in place of the larger instruments because it could be carried as the band marched along the streets of New Orleans. [14]Today, you can hear New Orleans jazz played, especially during February Mardi Gras celebration. [15]Also as a traditional part of a New Orleans funeral procession. [16]Billy Bolden formed the first African American New Orleans jazz band. [17]By the 1920s, King Oliver and the musicians like Louis Armstrong and Jelly Roll Morton, who all once played on Mississippi riverboats.

[18]Other cities, including Chicago, the musical home for jazz pioneer Bix Beiderbecke. [19]Beiderbecke, born in Davenport, Iowa, in 1903, could play the cornet and piano, as well as write original compositions. [20]His lyrical, smooth style and use of musical understatement contrasted with Louis Armstrong's strong, bluesy style of playing. [21]When playing the cornet, original phrasing of popular jazz compositions and clarity of tone. [22]Made him stand out as a brilliant jazz pioneer among other jazz and blues musicians. [23]Unhappy and restless but with great ambition to achieve musical success. [24]The classical music of the French composer Debussy influenced a composition by Beiderbecke entitled "In a Mist." [25]After a series of illnesses and bouts with depression, Bix Beiderbecke died in 1931.

Exercise 21   Correcting Sentence Fragments

Revise the preceding paragraphs by correcting each fragment. Wherever possible, combine the fragments with other sentences in the paragraph rather than making them into separate sentences.

13.10 Run-on Sentences

■ Avoid run-on sentences in your writing. A **run-on sentence** is two or more complete sentences written as though they were one sentence.

The following are the three basic kinds of run-on sentences:

1. A **comma splice** is perhaps the most common kind of run-on sentence. It occurs when two main clauses are separated by a comma rather than by a semicolon or a period. In order to correct a comma splice, you can add a coordinating conjunction. Another option is to replace the comma with an end mark of punctuation, such as a period or a question mark, and begin the new sentence with a capital letter.

RUN-ON	Mari and Victor went on a picnic yesterday, they had a wonderful time until it began to rain.
CORRECT	Mari and Victor went on a picnic yesterday, **and** they had a wonderful time until it began to rain.
CORRECT	Mari and Victor went on a picnic yesterday. They had a wonderful time until it began to rain.

2. Another kind of run-on sentence is formed when there is no punctuation between the two main clauses. In order to correct this kind of run-on, you can separate the main clauses with a semicolon, or you can add an end mark of punctuation after the first clause and begin the second one with a capital letter. You can also correct the error by placing a comma and a coordinating conjunction between the two main clauses.

RUN-ON	They brought a large amount of food with them nothing was left over.
CORRECT	They brought a large amount of food with them. Nothing was left over.
CORRECT	They brought a large amount of food with them; nothing was left over.
CORRECT	They brought a large amount of food with them, **yet** nothing was left over.

3. Still another kind of run-on sentence is formed when there is no comma before a coordinating conjunction that joins two main clauses. In order to correct the error, just insert the comma before the coordinating conjunction.

RUN-ON	They were looking for a shady spot but they could not find one.
CORRECT	They were looking for a shady spot, but they could not find one.

Clauses and Sentence Structure

Exercise 22   Identifying Run-on Sentences

Label each sentence as either *run-on* or *correct*. If it is run-on, rewrite it.

1. According to Chinese legends, a man named Yü drained away flood waters during the first millennium B.C. and made China's land livable he established the first Chinese dynasty, known as the Hsia.
2. The Shang dynasty, which began about 1760 to 1520 B.C., is considered to be the successor to the Hsia dynasty.
3. Because of its well developed writing and record keeping, the Shang dynasty is considered the first historic dynasty.
4. The Shang dynasty acquired many musical instruments from preceding societies these instruments included stone chimes, bronze bells and drums, and clay ocarinas, or flute-like instruments.
5. During the Shang dynasty, the people used a calendar system similar to the one used today it had 360 days in a year, 12 months, and 30 days in each month.
6. At that time, the Chinese began using the same symbol for "moon" as they used for "month."
7. The Shang and the Chou lived together peacefully until the Chou decided to conquer the Shang and, after fighting for three years, established the Chou dynasty, which lasted from around 1122–256 B.C.
8. About 475–221 B.C. Chi'in was a small kingdom or feudal state in China, Ch'in conquered other areas and established the Ch'in dynasty.
9. The Ch'in dynasty dates from 221–206 B.C., and it is from this dynasty that China's name originated.
10. The Great Wall was built during the brief Ch'in dynasty yet this monument is one of the longest lasting symbols of Chinese culture.

Exercise 23   Correcting Run-on Sentences

Rewrite each of the following sentences, correcting the run-ons. You may choose from among the several ways of correcting run-ons that you have learned.

1. The Great Wall of China stretches almost four thousand miles and it is considered one of the greatest construction projects in history.
2. Its average height ranges from fifteen to fifty feet the structure is fifteen to thirty feet wide along the base and twelve feet wide at the top.
3. Shih Huang-Ti founded the Ch'in dynasty he was known as Chao Cheng when he was a boy king.
4. He conceived of the Great Wall as a defensive barrier against nomadic tribes but he probably underestimated the cost and danger of the project.
5. In 214 B.C., Shih Huang-Ti formed the Great Wall by linking many existing walls, these smaller walls had been built earlier by various local Chinese leaders.
6. The wall features many forty-foot watchtowers these structures facilitated communication across great distances with signals of smoke by day and fire by night.
7. Behind the wall, the Chinese established small agricultural settlements, these settlements supported the many troops that defended the wall from enemy attack.
8. Today the Great Wall of China remains a symbol of ancient Chinese history and visitors to China continue to marvel at this extraordinary monument.

Exercise 24   Review: Sentence Completeness

Rewrite the following paragraph, correcting all sentence fragments and run-on sentences.

Carlos Fuentes, Contemporary Author

[1]According to many literary critics, Carlos Fuentes stands as Mexico's most important contemporary author, much of his work deals with the consequences of the Mexican Revolution. [2]Has written such books as *Where the Air Is Clear* and *The Good Conscience*, which criticize aspects of Mexican society. [3]Fuentes has had several careers during his lifetime he has worked as a diplomat, novelist, playwright, film critic, editor, publisher, lecturer, and university administrator. [4]Because his father was a career diplomat, the family traveled widely and Fuentes learned to speak English at the age of four. [5]After attending law school at the University of Mexico, helped found an important Mexican literary journal, *Revista mexicana de literatura*. [6]Which he edited for four years. [7]Although master of the short story, essay, and drama, has best displayed his talent in his novels. [8]Many of his novels—notably *The Death of Artemio Cruz* and *Terra Nostra*—show his profound interest in Mexican history and they explore how the nation's past relates to its present. [9]His novel *The Old Gringo* was made into a movie, it is an imaginative examination of the death of the American author Ambrose Bierce. [10]Who disappeared mysteriously in Mexico in 1913, fifteen years before the birth of Carlos Fuentes.

Exercise 25   Review: Identifying Sentence Fragments and Run-on Sentences

On your paper, label each sentence as *fragment, run-on,* or *correct.* If it is a fragment or run-on, correct it.

Octavio Paz, Contemporary Author

1. Many people know Octavio Paz from his work or from the Nobel Prize for Literature he won in 1990.
2. If it is true that every nation has more than one favorite author, some Mexicans would cast their vote for Octavio Paz and cite the titles of many of his books.
3. *The Bow and the Lyre, Alternating Current,* and *Configurations* are some of his books but there are many others.
4. Born in 1914 in a suburb of Mexico City, well educated and involved in political and artistic movements in Europe and the United States as well as Mexico.
5. Paz published his first book of poems in 1933, when he was 19 years old.
6. He was a poet, a critic, a reviewer, and a biographer, as well as a politician who served as Mexican ambassador to India from 1962 to 1968.
7. In English, translations of his poetry by American poets Elizabeth Bishop and William Carlos Williams and a recent translation of his essays by Eliot Weinberger.
8. After his first book of poems was translated into English, he became popular with English audiences, who have followed his work with enthusiasm ever since.
9. His images out of the mythology of Mexico and Latin America.
10. His later poetry blends symbolism and surrealism, attempts to link the individual and society.

Grammar Review

CLAUSES AND SENTENCE STRUCTURE

The novel from which the following passage is taken is about an unscrupulous social climber, Jay Gatsby, who changes his name, invents a privileged background, and gains admission to an exclusive world. While an army officer during World War I, Gatsby has a brief romance with a southern society girl named Daisy Fay. Years later he tells the story of that romance to his friend Nick Carraway, who is Daisy's cousin. The passage has been annotated to show the types of clauses covered in this unit.

Literature Model

from The Great Gatsby
by F. Scott Fitzgerald

Noun clause

"I can't describe to you how surprised I was to find out I loved her, old sport. I even hoped for a while that she'd throw me over, but she didn't, because she was in love with me too. She thought I knew a lot because I knew different things from her . . . Well, there I was, 'way off my ambitions, getting deeper in love every minute, and all of a sudden I didn't care.

Interrogative sentence

What was the use of doing great things if I could have a better time telling her what I was going to do?"

Declarative sentence

On the last afternoon before he went abroad, he sat with Daisy in his arms for a long, silent time. It was a cold fall day, with fire in the room and her cheeks flushed. Now and then she moved and he changed his arm a little, and once he kissed her dark shining hair. The afternoon had made them tranquil for a while, as if to give them a deep memory for the long parting the next day promised. They had never been closer in their month of love, nor communicated more profoundly one with another, than when she brushed silent lips against his coat's shoulder or when he touched the end of her fingers, gently, as though she were asleep.

He did extraordinarily well in the war. He was a captain

Adverb clause

before he went to the front, and following the Argonne battles he got his majority and the command of the divisional machine-guns. After the Armistice he tried frantically to get home, but some complication or misunderstanding sent him to Oxford instead. He was worried now—there was a quality of nervous despair in Daisy's letters. She didn't see why he couldn't come. She was feeling the pressure of the world outside, and she wanted to see him and feel his presence beside her and be reassured that she was doing the right thing after all.

For Daisy was young and her artificial world was redolent of orchids and pleasant, cheerful snobbery and orchestras which set the rhythm of the year, summing up the sadness and suggestiveness of life in new tunes. All night the saxophones wailed the hopeless comment of the Beale Street Blues while a hundred pairs of golden and silver slippers shuffled the shining dust. At the gray tea hour there were always rooms that throbbed incessantly with this low, sweet fever, while fresh faces drifted here and there like rose petals blown by the sad horns around the floor.

Through this twilight universe Daisy began to move again with the season; suddenly she was again keeping half a dozen dates a day with half a dozen men, and drowsing asleep at dawn with the beads and chiffon of an evening dress tangled among dying orchids on the floor beside her bed. And all the time something within her was crying for a decision. She wanted her life shaped now . . .

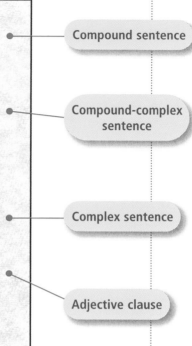

Compound sentence

Compound-complex sentence

Complex sentence

Adjective clause

Clauses and Sentence Structure

Review: Exercise 1 Identifying Main and Subordinate Clauses

Each sentence below contains a clause in italics. Indicate whether the italicized clause is a *main clause* or a *subordinate clause*.

1. *Gatsby was surprised* when he recognized his love for Daisy.
2. *Daisy loved Gatsby, too,* although he came from a different world.
3. Gatsby didn't head home right after the war *because unexpected events forced him to go to Oxford.*
4. *After she had waited for Gatsby for a while,* she felt the pressures of her social world.
5. *While Gatsby remained in England,* Daisy danced the evenings away with other men.

Grammar Review

Review: Exercise 2   Identifying Compound, Complex, and Compound-Complex Sentences

The following sentences are based on the passage from *The Great Gatsby*. On your paper indicate whether each is a *compound, complex,* or *compound-complex sentence.*

SAMPLE   Acquaintances may flatter you, but friends will usually tell you the truth.
ANSWER   compound

1. Gatsby was surprised to discover that Daisy loved him.
2. Whenever he thought of her, he began to question his ambition.
3. Gatsby spent the last afternoon before he left for the war with Daisy, and he and Daisy had never felt closer.
4. Gatsby was upset when he couldn't return home immediately after the war.
5. Daisy wrote to Gatsby, but her letters, with their sense of despair, only made him worry.
6. The cheerful world of Daisy's society called to her, and Daisy was soon part of it again.
7. Music, dancing, and social pleasantries cannot forever distract a woman who is in love.
8. Daisy's attention was momentarily captured, and her life was filled with splendid events and extraordinary people.
9. Disappointment was kept at arm's length whenever it appeared.
10. Something inside her said that she would not be able to wait for Gatsby's return.

Review: Exercise 3   Writing Sentences with Adjective Clauses

The sentences that follow elaborate on ideas from the passage from *The Great Gatsby*. Rewrite each sentence, adding an adjective clause that answers the question in parentheses. Your clause must begin with one of the words listed below, and it must contain a verb. Your sentence should make sense within the context of the passage, but do not use the exact wording from the passage.

RELATIVE PRONOUNS	who	whom	whose	which	that
SUBORDINATING CONJUNCTIONS	when	where			

SAMPLE   Gatsby was a social climber.
                (What did Gatsby create for himself?)
ANSWER   Gatsby was a social climber who created an imaginary background for himself.

SAMPLE   Daisy wanted to see Gatsby.
                (What were major character traits of hers?)
ANSWER   Daisy, who was young and needed reassurance, wanted to see Gatsby.

1. Gatsby told his story to Nick Carraway.
   (Who was Nick Carraway?)
2. Gatsby well remembered a particular fall day.
   (What had happened on that day?)
3. Daisy sat close to Gatsby and felt calm and at peace.
   (What were Daisy's feelings toward Gatsby?)
4. War took Gatsby away from Daisy.
   (What did the war do to their romance?)
5. After the war Gatsby was forced to go to Oxford.
   (What was Gatsby's real desire?)
6. Daisy's letters made Gatsby anxious.
   (What were the letters like?)
7. Daisy desperately needed Gatsby's presence.
   (What would his presence do?)
8. Daisy's world was an artificial place. (What could be found in this artificial place?)
9. Every night people in Daisy's world would listen to orchestras.
   (What did the orchestras do?)
10. Daisy sometimes woke at dawn with her evening dress on the floor beside her.
    (Which evening dress was this?)

Review: Exercise 4   Writing Sentences with Adverb Clauses

The sentences that follow elaborate on ideas from *The Great Gatsby*. Rewrite each sentence, adding an adverb clause that answers the question in parentheses. Your clause must begin with one of the subordinating conjunctions listed below, and it must contain a verb. The sentence should make sense within the context of the passage, but do not use the novel's exact wording. There may be more than one correct answer for each item.

SUBORDINATING CONJUNCTIONS

after	as long as	because	if	than	wherever
as	as though	before	so that	when	while

1. Gatsby lied about his background. (Why?)
2. Gatsby and Daisy had a romance. (When?)
3. Gatsby loved Daisy more deeply. (To what extent?)
4. Gatsby became a machine-gun commander. (When?)
5. After the war Gatsby couldn't return home. (Why?)
6. In her letters Daisy sounded nervous. (To what extent?)
7. She might have married Gatsby. (Under what condition?)
8. Daisy saw a cheerful but snobbish world. (Where?)
9. The orchestras played. (When?)
10. Daisy could be faithful to Gatsby. (Under what condition?)

Grammar Review

Review: Exercise 5   **Identifying Noun Clauses**

The following sentences describe life during the 1920s, the period in which *The Great Gatsby* is set. On your paper write the noun clauses that appear in the sentences. Two of the sentences have two noun clauses each. In one sentence the relative pronoun before the noun clause has been dropped.

SAMPLE   My friend sympathizes with whatever crisis occurs in my life.
ANSWER   whatever crisis occurs in my life

1. In the 1920s the automobile radically changed where Americans went and what they did.
2. Americans could drive their cars to whatever places they pleased.
3. What made the lives of many Americans easier was the widespread availability of electricity.
4. Whoever enjoyed music could now listen to it on electric phonographs.
5. What had once been regarded as shocking behavior became more widely accepted in the 1920s.
6. How men and women dressed showed their new sense of freedom.
7. That many women were wearing shorter dresses and more makeup made the more staid members of society think that the old decorum was gone for good.
8. Whoever had leisure time might attend sports events.
9. Many Americans thought athletes such as Babe Ruth and Jack Dempsey were heroes.
10. That advertising became widespread was an additional reason for the rapid changes of the 1920s.

Review: Exercise 6   **Writing Four Kinds of Sentences**

On your paper, identify each of the following sentences as either *declarative, imperative, interrogative,* or *exclamatory.* Then rewrite each sentence in the form noted in parentheses.

SAMPLE   Gatsby told Daisy to wait for him. (Rewrite in the imperative form.)
ANSWER   declarative
         "Daisy, wait for me."

1. Nick asked Gatsby to tell the story. (Rewrite in the imperative form.)
2. How surprised Gatsby was to find himself in love with Daisy! (Rewrite in the interrogative form.)
3. Was Gatsby a great success during the war? (Rewrite in the declarative form.)
4. Daisy saw other men and tried to forget about Gatsby. (Rewrite in the interrogative form.)
5. Daisy wore a beautiful chiffon dress. (Rewrite in the exclamatory form.)

Review: Exercise 7 Correcting Sentence Fragments and Run-ons

The following paragraph describes Nick Carraway, the narrator of *The Great Gatsby.* Revise the paragraph, correcting any sentence fragments and any run-ons.

¹Convinced by a friend to settle on Long Island, Nick renting the bungalow next to Gatsby's mansion. ²Daisy Fay was Nick's second cousin once removed, lived with her husband in a fashionable area nearby. ³One day Nick drove to her house for dinner, he met her husband, Tom Buchanan. ⁴Who was extremely wealthy but unfeeling and arrogant. ⁵For Nick this was an important dinner, for it marked the beginning of one of the most momentous summers of his life.

Review: Exercise 8

Mixed Review

Revise each item below as indicated in parentheses.

1. F. Scott Fitzgerald was born in 1896 in Saint Paul, Minnesota. As a teen-ager he was already writing stories, poems, and plays. (Rewrite as a compound sentence.)
2. Fitzgerald met and fell in love with Zelda Sayre, an Alabama belle. He was serving in the army at the time. (Combine the sentences by turning the second sentence into an adverb clause beginning with *while.*)
3. Fitzgerald published his first novel, *This Side of Paradise,* in 1920, the novel described the new style of life of the time. (Eliminate the run-on by creating two sentences.)
4. The novel was a spectacular success. Fitzgerald suddenly became an important man who had both money and reputation. (Rewrite as a compound-complex sentence.)
5. Fitzgerald married Zelda Sayre after the book's publication. She resembled many of Fitzgerald's heroines. (Combine the sentences by turning the second sentence into an adjective clause beginning with *who.*)
6. *The Great Gatsby* (1925) is regarded as Fitzgerald's masterpiece. Did not long support the Fitzgeralds' lavish life style. (Eliminate the sentence fragment.)
7. By the late 1920s Zelda was suffering from a serious mental illness. (Rewrite as an interrogative sentence.)
8. In 1937 Fitzgerald moved to Hollywood. He worked there as a screenwriter in order to pay his debts. (Combine the sentences by turning the second sentence into an adjective clause beginning with *where.*)
9. Fitzgerald died at age forty-four. He was working on *The Last Tycoon,* a novel about Hollywood and America in the 1930s. (Rewrite as a complex sentence.)
10. Fitzgerald once said something. "There are no second acts in American lives." (Combine by turning the second sentence into a noun clause beginning with *that.*)

Grammar Review

Review: Exercise 9

Proofreading

This passage describes the artist Guy Pène du Bois, whose painting appears on this page. Rewrite the passage, correcting the errors in spelling, grammar, and usage. Add any missing punctuation. There are ten errors.

Guy Pène du Bois

¹Born in Brooklyn, New York, Guy Pène du Bois (1884–1958) from a family of artists. ²He studied painting at the New York School of Art and later he studied on his own in Paris

³Du Bois worked as an art critic, he also taught painting at a school in New York City. ⁴He depicted realistic scenes of everyday life focusing on café society in New York. ⁵The painting reproduced on this page portrays a small number of people and they have been stylized as if they were mannequins or objects in a still life.

⁶The people in this picture has a staid formality in both dress and pose. ⁷The figures of the woman and the men appears to be carved out of marble. ⁸The painting vividly depicts the elegant society that Jay Gatsby, the hero of F. Scott Fitzgerald's novel *The Great Gatsby* sought so assiduously. ⁹The woman could be Daisy or any other society woman who reveled in her "twilight universe."

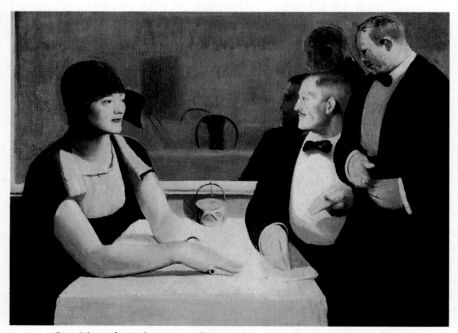

Guy Pène du Bois, *Mr. and Mrs. Chester Dale Dining Out,* 1924

Clauses and Sentence Structure

Writing Application

TIME

For more about the writing process, see **TIME Facing the Blank Page**, pp. 111–121.

Variety of Sentence Structure

In the following passage from her short story "The Signature," Elizabeth Enright uses a variety of sentence structures. As you read, observe how the changing sentence structures develop a rhythm that helps build suspense.

> The mirror was at the end of the hall. I walked toward it with my fists closed, and my heart walked, too, heavily in my chest. I watched the woman's figure in the dark dress and the knees moving forward. When I was close to it, I saw, low in the right-hand corner of the mirror, the scratched small outline of the eye-diamond, a signature, carved on the surface of the glass by whom, and in what cold spirit of raillery? Lifting my head, I looked at my own face. I leaned forward and looked closely at my face, and I remembered everything. I remembered everything. And I knew the name of the city I would never leave, and, alas, I understood the language of its citizens.

Techniques with Variety of Sentence Structures

Try to apply Elizabeth Enright's technique to your own writing.

❶ Vary the length and structure of your sentences to enliven your writing and to create subtle rhythmic effects. Simple sentences are usually short and can have a quick-paced, abrupt effect. Compound, complex, and compound-complex sentences are often longer and may have a slow, meandering quality. Notice that Enright's passage consistently alternates simple sentences with more complicated structures: simple, compound, simple, complex, simple, compound, simple, compound-complex. The alternating rhythm supports the paragraph's mood of mounting tension and gradual realization.

❷ Sometimes the use of an interrogative sentence can heighten dramatic effect. Notice that Enright ends her long fourth sentence as a question. The question not only adds variety but also underscores the narrator's puzzled feelings.

Practice   Apply these techniques by revising the following paragraph on a separate sheet of paper. Combine sentences to create a paragraph in which alternating sentence structures achieve a rhythm that builds suspense. Use at least one compound, one complex, one compound-complex, and three simple sentences. Also make one sentence interrogative, exclamatory, or imperative.

In 1916 an explosion swept through a tunnel. The tunnel was part of the Cleveland Waterworks. Many workers were trapped inside. Poisonous gases began seeping through the tunnel. Rescue parties could not enter. The trapped workers were in terrible danger. Then someone remembered Garrett Morgan. Morgan had invented a device called a gas mask. Few people had been interested in buying it. Now his assistance was sought. Morgan brought some of his gas masks to the site of the explosion. Rescuers gingerly donned them. Morgan's device might allow them to enter the tunnel safely.

UNIT 14 Diagraming Sentences

14.1 Diagraming Simple Sentences

■ **Diagraming** is a method of showing how the various words and parts of a sentence function and relate to the sentence as a whole.

You begin to diagram a sentence by finding the simple subject. Next find the action or linking verb that goes with the subject. Write the subject and the verb on a horizontal line, called a baseline. Separate the subject and verb with a vertical line.

Trees grow.

subject	action verb

Trees	grow

Adjectives and Adverbs

To diagram a sentence with adjectives and adverbs, follow the model diagram below. Note that you diagram adverbs used to modify verbs in the same way that you diagram adjectives used to modify nouns. Diagram adverbs used to modify adjectives or other adverbs on a separate line, as shown.

The young pine trees grow quite fast.

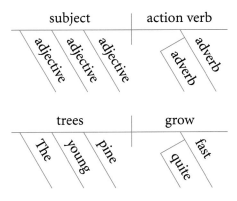

Direct Objects and Indirect Objects

To diagram a sentence with objects, follow the model.

Trees give us medicines.

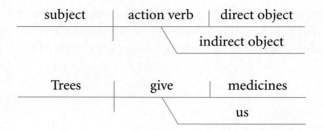

Object Complements

To diagram a simple sentence with a compound subject, a direct object, and an object complement, follow the model.

Designers and carpenters consider hardwoods unsurpassed.

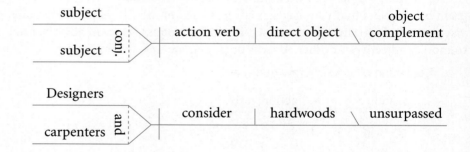

Subject Complements

To diagram a simple sentence with a subject complement (a predicate nominative or a predicate adjective), follow the model.

Trees become timber.

subject	linking verb \ predicate nominative

Trees	become \ timber

To diagram a simple sentence with a compound predicate and two subject complements, follow the model.

Conifers are numerous and will remain plentiful.

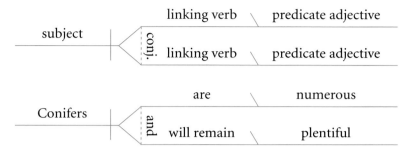

Exercise 1   Diagraming Simple Sentences

Using the models in the lesson as a guide, diagram the following sentences.

1. The gray forest gradually awakened.
2. New buds tinted the branches green.
3. Hikers and campers considered the weather superb.
4. The longer days gave us more useful hours.
5. The spring breezes were fresh.
6. We pitched our tent and unpacked our gear.
7. My friends consider long hikes restorative.
8. Tall trees surrounded our campsite.
9. The clear stream was very cold.
10. My friend lent me an especially warm jacket.

Exercise 2   Completing a Diagram

Study the sentence below and the accompanying diagram "skeleton." Next, number from 1 to 10 on a separate sheet of paper, and copy the word corresponding to each number. Indicate where each word should appear in the diagram by writing the matching letter.

Many diseases kill pine trees or reduce their growth rate.
  1   2   3   4   5 6   7   8   9   10

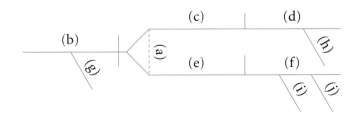

Diagraming Simple Sentences with Phrases

Prepositional Phrases

Place the preposition on a diagonal line that descends from the word the prepositional phrase modifies. Place the object of the preposition on a horizontal line that extends from the diagonal.

Lovers of old buildings spend millions of dollars on renovations.

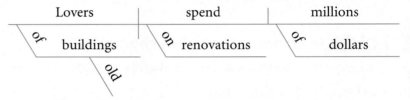

Appositives and Appositive Phrases

Place an appositive in parentheses after the noun or pronoun it identifies. Beneath it add any words that modify the appositive.

Monticello, the home of Thomas Jefferson, was restored by a private organization.

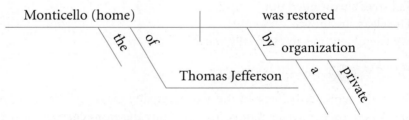

Participles and Participial Phrases

Curve the participle as shown. Add modifiers and complements.

Researching, one may encounter surprises, discovering scandal in a building's history.

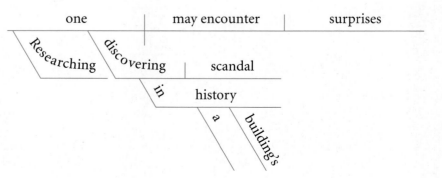

Gerunds and Gerund Phrases

Place a gerund on a "step," and add complements and modifiers. Then set the gerund or the gerund phrase on a "stilt" and position the stilt in the diagram according to the role of the gerund in the sentence.

Finding original plans is a restorer's dream.

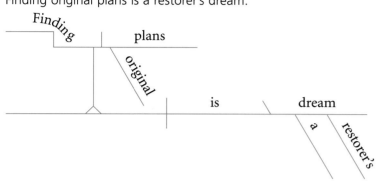

Infinitives and Infinitive Phrases

When an infinitive or an infinitive phrase is used as an adjective or an adverb, it is diagramed like a prepositional phrase. When an infinitive or an infinitive phrase is used as a noun, it is diagramed like a prepositional phrase and then placed on a "stilt" in the subject or complement position.

To perform a restoration project well, you must attempt to re-create something authentically.

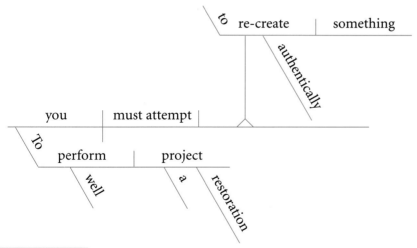

Exercise 3   Diagraming Simple Sentences with Phrases

Using the preceding models as a guide, diagram the following sentences.

1. During restoration you should preserve the beams of old buildings.
2. The University of Virginia, an architectural gem, was designed by Thomas Jefferson.
3. A staircase, rising from the street, reached the building's main door.
4. Architects based the restoration on researching the original appearance of the house.
5. After the application of gold leaf, the cupola seemed to catch fire in the evening light.

Absolute Phrases

An absolute phrase is placed above the rest of the sentence and is not connected to it in any way. Place the noun or pronoun on a horizontal line. Place the participle and any modifiers on descending lines.

Its exterior freshly painted, the house looked almost new.

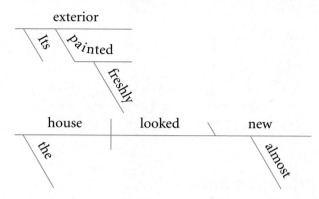

Exercise 4   **Completing Sentence Diagrams**

Number from 1 to 20 on a separate sheet of paper, copying the word in the sentence corresponding to each number. Then indicate the place where each word should appear in the diagram by writing the matching letter.

Faneuil Hall, in Boston, the historic meeting place of colonial revolutionaries,
     1   2   3   4   5   6   7   8   9   10

is now the center of a large, thriving commercial area.
11   12   13   14   15 16   17   18   19   20

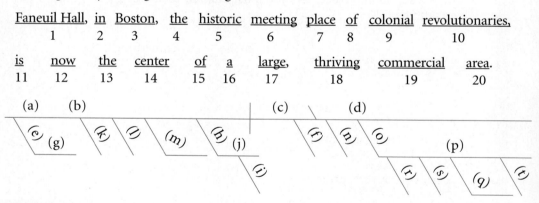

Exercise 5   **Diagraming Sentences with Phrases**

Using the preceding models as a guide, diagram the following sentences.

1. The Jefferson Market Courthouse, a Victorian structure, was completed in 1877.
2. American architects praised the building, voting it one of the most beautiful buildings in the country.
3. A familiar sight to New Yorkers, an enormous clock tower dominates the building.
4. Originally built as a courthouse, the building served various functions throughout its history.
5. By 1946 the building was vacant, its architectural style no longer in favor.

14.3 | Diagraming Compound and Complex Sentences

Compound Sentences

Diagram each main clause separately. If the clauses are connected by a semicolon, use a vertical dotted line to connect the verbs of each main clause. If the main clauses are connected by a conjunction, place the conjunction on a solid horizontal line, and connect it to the verbs of each main clause by vertical dotted lines.

Trial lawyers argue their cases, and juries consider the evidence.

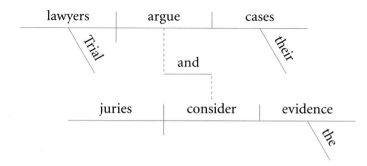

Complex Sentences with Adjective Clauses

Place the main clause in one diagram and the adjective clause beneath it in another diagram. Use a dotted line to connect the relative pronoun or other introductory word in the adjective clause to the modified noun or pronoun in the main clause.

A judge, who presides over trials, rules on procedural matters that may arise.

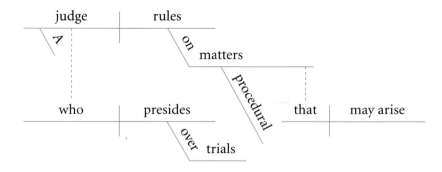

Complex Sentences with Adverb Clauses

Place the main clause in one diagram and the adverb clause beneath it in another diagram. Place the subordinating conjunction on a diagonal dotted line connecting the verb in the adverb clause to the modified verb, adjective, or adverb in the main clause.

Before witnesses testify, they must take an oath.

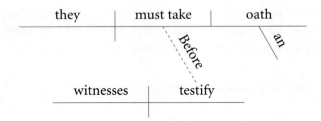

Complex Sentences with Noun Clauses

First decide what role the noun clause plays within the main clause. Is it the subject, direct object, predicate nominative, or object of a preposition? Then diagram the main clause, placing the noun clause on a "stilt" in the appropriate position. Place the introductory word of the clause in the position of the subject, object, or predicate nominative within the noun clause itself. If the introductory word merely begins the noun clause, place it on a line of its own above the verb in the noun clause, connecting it to the verb with a dotted vertical line.

NOUN CLAUSE AS SUBJECT

Whatever the witnesses say will influence the jury.

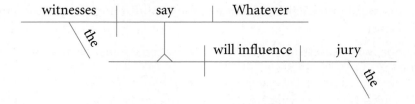

NOUN CLAUSE AS DIRECT OBJECT

Both plaintiffs and defendants hope that juries will believe them.

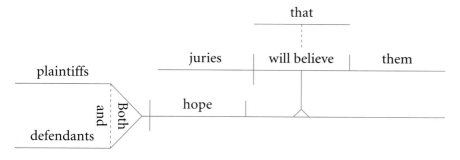

NOUN CLAUSE AS OBJECT OF A PREPOSITION

The jury awards money to whoever wins the case.

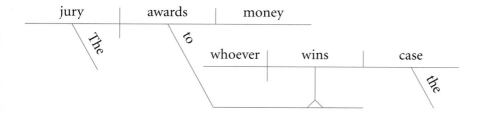

Exercise 6 | **Diagraming Sentences with Clauses**

Using the preceding models as a guide, diagram the following sentences.

1. The jury did not believe the final witness's story, or they did not care.
2. Several witnesses whom the attorneys questioned told stories that seemed contradictory.
3. Until sworn statements are introduced, the facts might exist only in written records.
4. That two witnesses contradict each other is extremely common.
5. The oddity is that people see different things in what is a single event.
6. Jury selection is often time-consuming, since lawyers can reject potential jurors.
7. Lawyers want jurors who seem sympathetic to their side.
8. Some people think that jurors are easily swayed by emotional arguments.
9. Few people believe that the jury system should be abolished.
10. Lawyers for each side summarize the case, and the judge explains applicable law to the jury.

UNIT 15

Verb Tenses, Voice, and Mood

15.1 Principal Parts of Verbs

■ All verbs have four principal parts—a *base form*, a *present participle*, a *simple past form*, and a *past participle*.

Base Form	Present Participle	Past Form	Past Participle
walk	walking	walked	walked
fall	falling	fell	fallen
try	trying	tried	tried
speak	speaking	spoke	spoken
be	being	was, were	been

The base forms (except for *be*) and the past forms can be used alone as main verbs; the present participle and the past participle must be used with one or more auxiliary verbs.

> Dolphins **splash.** [base or present form]
>
> Dolphins **splashed.** [past form]
>
> Dolphins **are splashing.** [present participle with the auxiliary *are*]
>
> Dolphins **have splashed.** [past participle with the auxiliary *have*]

Exercise 1   Identifying Principal Parts of Verbs

On your paper, write the verbs in the following sentences. Then identify each verb as *base form* (b), *present participle with auxiliary verb* (pp), *simple past form* (past), or *past participle with auxiliary verb* (past p). Some sentences have two verbs.

Today's Computers

1. Because early computers used vacuum tubes for memory, they were bulky and slow.
2. Processor chips in desktop computers contain hundreds of thousands of miniature circuits that have been fitted into a space the size of a quarter.
3. Networks are connecting thousands of computers around the world so that they share information.
4. Many household appliances now include computer chips.
5. Stephen Hawking, who was paralyzed by Lou Gehrig's disease, speaks with the aid of a computer.
6. Some computer games teach and entertain.
7. The software industry is demanding programmers and graphic designers.
8. Laptop computers run on batteries for several hours.
9. CD-ROM drives store still pictures and video movies that the computer displays on a monitor screen.
10. The cost of a good basic computer is decreasing.

15.2 Regular and Irregular Verbs

■ A **regular verb** forms its past and past participle by adding *-ed* to the base form.

Base Form	Past Form	Past Participle
watch	watched	watched
laugh	laughed	laughed

With some regular verbs, there is a spelling change when a suffix beginning with a vowel is added to the base form.

study + **-ed** = stud**ied**   skim + **-ed** = skim**med**

■ An **irregular verb** forms its past and past participle in some way other than by adding *-ed* to the base form.

Base Form	Past Form	Past Participle
be	was, were	been
beat	beat	beaten
become	became	become
begin	began	begun
bite	bit	bitten *or* bit
blow	blew	blown
break	broke	broken
bring	brought	brought
catch	caught	caught
choose	chose	chosen
come	came	come
do	did	done
draw	drew	drawn
drink	drank	drunk
drive	drove	driven
eat	ate	eaten
fall	fell	fallen
feel	felt	felt
find	found	found
fly	flew	flown
freeze	froze	frozen
get	got	got *or* gotten

Base Form	Past Form	Past Participle
give	gave	given
go	went	gone
grow	grew	grown
hang	hung *or* hanged	hung *or* hanged
have	had	had
know	knew	known
lay*	laid	laid
lead	led	led
lend	lent	lent
lie*	lay	lain
lose	lost	lost
put	put	put
ride	rode	ridden
ring	rang	rung
rise*	rose	risen
run	ran	run
say	said	said
see	saw	seen
set*	set	set
shrink	shrank *or* shrunk	shrunk *or* shrunken
sing	sang	sung
sink	sank *or* sunk	sunk
sit*	sat	sat
speak	spoke	spoken
spring	sprang *or* sprung	sprung
steal	stole	stolen
swim	swam	swum
take	took	taken
tear	tore	torn
tell	told	told
think	thought	thought
throw	threw	thrown
wear	wore	worn
win	won	won
write	wrote	written

*For more detailed instruction on *lay* versus *lie,* see Unit 19.

*For more detailed instruction on *raise* versus *rise* and *set* versus *sit,* see Unit 19.

Verb Tenses, Voice, and Mood

Exercise 2   Changing Principal Parts

For the italicized verb below, write the form indicated in parentheses.

1. *sink* (past)

2. *fly* (past participle)

3. *took* (base)

4. *swam* (past participle)

5. *think* (past)

Exercise 3 **Supplying the Correct Principal Part**

Complete these sentences by writing the principal part indicated in parentheses.

Planning Cities

1. Throughout history cities often _____ as small villages surrounded by farms. (past form of *begin*)

2. As agriculture improved or trade increased, some villages spontaneously _____ larger. (past form of *grow*)

3. Enterprising people have always _____ ways to accelerate urban growth. (past participle of *find*)

4. For example, Alexander the Great (356–323 B.C.) _____ seventy new cities in great detail. (past form of *plan*)

5. In modern times, the nation of Israel has _____ many new towns on land reclaimed from the desert by means of irrigation. (past participle of *develop*)

6. A number of nations today are _____ urban experiments, new types of cities that meet specific needs. (present participle of *create*)

7. In Europe, Great Britain has _____ one of the leaders in planning new cities. (past participle of *be*)

8. The British have _____ new towns in order to relieve housing shortages and traffic jams. (past participle of *design*)

9. In some instances, planned cities have _____ popular with their inhabitants only after many years. (past participle of *become*)

10. Architects and city planners have _____ of many excellent new ways of solving old problems. (past participle of *think*)

Exercise 4 **Using the Present Participle**

Write ten sentences that might be spoken by a TV or radio sports announcer at a game. Use the present participle forms of the following verbs with auxiliaries in your sentences.

1. pass
2. jump
3. block
4. catch
5. run

6. shoot
7. look
8. throw
9. kick
10. win

SAMPLE ANSWER   Rogers is passing the ball to Smith. Touchdown!

Exercise 5 **Using the Simple Past and Past Participle**

Write a paragraph that describes something you have read about in a newspaper or have seen on the news. Use three simple past verb forms and two past participles with auxiliaries in your paragraph. Underline them.

15.3 Tense of Verbs

- The **tenses** of a verb are the forms that help to show time.

The six tenses in English are the *present, past,* and *future* and the *present perfect, past perfect,* and *future perfect.*

Present Tense

The present-tense form of any verb other than *be* is the same as the verb's base form. Remember, however, that *-s* or *-es* is added in the third-person singular.

	Singular	Plural
First Person	I **help.**	We **help.**
Second Person	You **help.**	You **help.**
Third Person	She, he, or it **helps.** Juanita **helps.**	They **help.** The children **help.**

	Singular	Plural
First Person	I **am** honest.	We **are** honest.
Second Person	You **are** honest.	You **are** honest.
Third Person	She, he, or it **is** honest. Juanita **is** honest.	They **are** honest. The children **are** honest.

- The **present tense** expresses a constant, repeated, or habitual action or condition. It can also express a general truth.

> Water **erodes** rock. [not just now but always: a constant action]
> Lian **drives** defensively. [now and always: a habitual action]
> Steel **is** an alloy. [a condition that is always true]

- The **present tense** can also express an action or condition that exists only now.

> Clara **seems** interested. [not always but just now]
> I **agree** with you. [at this very moment]

- The **present tense** is sometimes used in historical writing to express past events and, more often, in poetry, fiction, and reporting (especially in sports) to convey to the reader a sense of "being there."

The applause **continues** as each cast member **steps** forward and bows.

The basketball **hovers** on the rim and finally **slips** through the net.

Exercise 6 **Expressing the Present Tense in Sentences**

Write a sentence using each of the following verb forms. The content of your sentence should express the kind of present time indicated in parentheses.

SAMPLE   speaks (now and always)
ANSWER   She speaks Spanish fluently.

1. plays (now and always)
2. tastes (just now)
3. are (always true)
4. accepts (at this moment)
5. walk (always)

Past Tense

■ Use the **past tense** to express an action or condition that was started and completed in the past.

Everyone on the team **swam** well.

We **won** by a big margin.

The victory clearly **was** ours.

With one exception, all regular and irregular verbs have only one past-tense form, such as *talked* or *wrote*. The exception—the verb *be*—has two past-tense forms: *was* and *were*.

	Singular	Plural
First Person	I **was** strong.	We **were** strong.
Second Person	You **were** strong.	You **were** strong.
Third Person	She, he, or it **was** strong.	They **were** strong.

Exercise 7 **Expressing the Past Tense in Sentences**

Write a paragraph using the correct past tense of each of the following verbs:

1. drive
2. begin
3. climb
4. enjoy
5. find

Future Tense

■ Use the **future tense** to express an action or condition that will occur in the future.

The future tense of any verb is formed by using *shall* or *will* with the base form: *I shall paint; you will sing.*

> Hector **will buy** a car.
> I **shall finish** my homework.

Other ways of expressing future time do not involve the use of *will* or *shall*. Consider the following options:

1. Use *going to* along with the present tense of *be* and the base form of a verb.

   > Hector **is *going to* buy** a car.
   > I'm ***going to* do** my homework later.

2. Use *about to* along with the present tense of *be* and the base form of a verb.

   > Hector **is *about to* buy** a car.
   > I'm ***about to* do** my homework, Mom.

3. Use the present tense with an adverb or an adverb phrase that shows future time.

   > Monique **graduates *tomorrow*.**

Exercise 8	**Expressing the Future Tense**

Complete the following sentences by supplying the missing part of the future tense for the verb.

A Trip to Mars

1. Some day in the future, people _____ travel to Mars in a spaceship launched from a station circling the earth.
2. They are _____ to find a world that is both similar to and different from our own.
3. We are _____ to take the next big step for humankind, the president told a cheering audience at the Space Center.
4. The journey to Mars and back _____ probably take about three years, with about a year spent on the Martian surface.
5. The spaceship _____ return to Earth loaded with soil samples—and perhaps evidence of Martian life!

Exercise 9   **Using Expressions of Future Time**

Change each sentence below so that the verb or verbs are in the future tense. Try to use at least two ways of expressing future time in addition to *shall* and *will*.

Navajo Sandpainting

1. On Tuesday the director of the Museum of Ceremonial Art in Santa Fe began a three-day demonstration of the Navajo people's use of sandpaintings in healing ceremonies.
2. During the demonstration, a medicine man performed a healing ceremony for a Navajo woman.
3. The ceremony involved the creation of a different sandpainting each day for three days.
4. The healer and his assistants prepared various shades of red, yellow, and white powder by grinding sandstone on a stone slab.
5. They ground root charcoal for black and blue pigments and cornmeal, petals, and leaves for other colors.
6. With trays of colored sand, the painters worked together each day on an abstract painting from traditional Navajo mythology.
7. Each worker carefully rubbed sand between the thumb and forefinger and deposited one thin line of color after another onto the painting.
8. Then the patient sat on the finished painting, and the medicine man recited an appropriate chant.
9. A successful ceremony brought the patient a sense of peace and harmony.
10. At the demonstration's conclusion, the medicine man gathered the sandpainting into a blanket and scattered it to the winds.

Exercise 10   **Using Alternate Expressions of Future Time**

Replace each verb in italics with a different form of the verb in the future tense.

Announcing a Meeting

1. Next Tuesday, our school *will have* a special meeting of students, parents, teachers, and administrators.
2. The participants at the meeting *are going to discuss* the purchase of a new computer network.
3. Because the new budget *is about to be decided*, it is important that everyone attend.
4. Representatives from IBM and Apple *are going to demonstrate* their latest systems.
5. Refreshments *will be served* following the meeting.

Exercise 11   **Expressing Future Time in Sentences**

Write five statements or predictions about the future. Your sentences may be as realistic or as imaginary as you wish. Remember to vary the ways in which you express future time.

SAMPLE ANSWER   Before too long, every home in the nation is going to have a computer.

Perfect Tenses

Present Perfect Tense

■ Use the **present perfect tense** to express an action or condition that occurred at some *indefinite* time in the past.

Use *has* or *have* with the past participle of a verb to form the present perfect tense: *has lived, have eaten.**

> She **has fished** in the Atlantic.
> The birds **have migrated** south.

*Do not be confused by the term *present perfect;* this tense expresses past time. *Present* refers to the tense of the auxiliary verb *has* or *have*.

The present perfect tense is used to refer to past time only in an indefinite way. With this tense, adverbs such as *yesterday* cannot logically be added to make the time more specific.

> Richard **has seen** that movie.
> The Ressners **have** often **flown** to Denver.

To be specific about completed past time, you usually use the simple past tense.

> Richard **saw** that movie on Friday.
> The Ressners **flew** to Denver on their vacation.

The present perfect tense can also be used to show that an action or a condition that *began* in the past *continues* into the present. When a verb is used in this way, it is normally accompanied by adverbs of time or adverb phrases.

> Rafael **has studied** art **for many years.**
> The studio **has been** open **since eleven o'clock.**

Past Perfect Tense

■ Use the **past perfect tense** to indicate that one past action or condition began *and* ended before another past action started.

The past perfect tense is formed with *had* and the past participle of a verb: *had lost, had danced.*

PAST PERFECT   **PAST**
Bernice **had earned** ten thousand dollars before she **resigned.** [She earned the money; then she stopped earning it; then she resigned.]

PAST   **PAST PERFECT**
By the time Ravi **arrived,** all the other guests **had left.** [The other guests began to leave and then finished leaving; Ravi arrived.]

Future Perfect Tense

■ Use the **future perfect tense** to express one future action or condition that will begin *and* end before another future event starts.

The future perfect tense is formed with *will have* or *shall have* plus the past participle of a verb: *will have met, shall have met.*

> In two more laps she **will have run** four hundred meters. [The four hundred meters will be run by the time another future event, the completion of two more laps, occurs.]

Exercise 12   Identifying the Perfect Tenses

On your paper, write the perfect-tense verb that appears in each of the following sentences. Then identify the verb as *present perfect, past perfect,* or *future perfect.*

Seattle

1. In 1853 the city of Seattle was named for Chief Seattle of the Duwamish and Suquamish nations, who had agreed to allow settlers to live on their land.
2. Today, with its diverse cultural offerings and its beautiful scenery, Seattle has become a mecca for visitors.
3. Pike's Place Market has sold produce, seafood, and all kinds of imported and hand-crafted goods to visitors from far and near since it opened in 1906.
4. The Seattle Space Needle, a 606-foot tower constructed for the 1962 World's Fair, houses a revolving restaurant that has served awestruck tourists for years.
5. The Pacific Northwest Dance Ballet Company will have opened its spring season by the first of March.

Exercise 13   Expressing the Present Perfect Tense in Sentences

(a) Rewrite each of the following sentences, changing the tense of the verb from the past to the present perfect. (b) Add appropriate adverbs or adverb phrases to each of your new sentences to communicate the idea that an action or condition began in the past and continues into the present.

SAMPLE   We wrote term papers.

ANSWER   (a) We have written term papers.

                  (b) We have written term papers for the past four years.

1. Otis was away on business.
2. The drama club presented skits.
3. I studied Portuguese.
4. Our senators opposed the bill.
5. We visited Yosemite National Park.

15.5 Progressive and Emphatic Forms

■ Each of the six tenses has a **progressive** form that expresses a continuing action.

The progressive forms consist of the appropriate tense of the verb *be* plus the present participle of the main verb.

PRESENT PROGRESSIVE	They *are* thinking.
PAST PROGRESSIVE	They *were* thinking.
FUTURE PROGRESSIVE	They *will be* thinking.
PRESENT PERFECT PROGRESSIVE	They *have been* thinking.
PAST PERFECT PROGRESSIVE	They *had been* thinking.
FUTURE PERFECT PROGRESSIVE	They *will have been* thinking.

■ The present and past tenses have additional forms, called **emphatic,** that add special force, or emphasis, to the verb.

The emphatic forms consist of *do* (and *does*) or *did* plus the base form of the verb.

PRESENT EMPHATIC	I *do* agree with you.
	He *does* agree with you.
PAST EMPHATIC	I *did* agree with you.
	They disagreed with your choice of words, but they *did* agree with your idea.

Exercise 14   Using the Progressive and Emphatic Forms

For each of the following sentences, replace each verb in parentheses with the progressive or the emphatic form of the verb that makes sense in the sentence. (Only one of the sentences requires the emphatic form.)

The Progress of Mapmaking

[1]Today I (begin) a study of the history of mapmaking. [2]Did you know that when you refer to a modern weather or road map, you (look) at the latest example of a skill that is thousands of years old? [3]For some time now, scientists (suspect) that in certain rock paintings in Africa, Asia, Europe, and South America, ancient peoples used patterns of lines to represent rivers and roads. [4]The earliest known maps were made in the Middle East before 2200 B.C.; these clay tablets show rivers, mountain ridges, and cities that (stand) at the time. [5]Chinese mapmakers of about 500 B.C. believed that they (live) in a land that covered most of a square world. [6]Although we no longer have their maps, we (have) reliable accounts of them. [7]In the far north, the Inuit of Greenland (carve) relief maps of icy coasts out of wood blocks for many years. [8]Until Europeans first landed on the Marshall Islands in the South Pacific, generations of native islanders (make) maps of sticks, shells, and fibers. [9]These maps represented

(continued)

the wave patterns that local navigators needed to watch for when they (travel) between the islands. [10]As changing technology provides map makers with new tools, we (see) increasingly detailed and accurate records of our world.

Exercise 15 — Understanding the Uses of Verb Tenses

Explain the difference in meaning between the sentences in each of the pairs below. Name the tense(s) used in each sentence.

SAMPLE   (a) He stopped in Juárez to visit his sister.
(b) He has stopped in Juárez to visit his sister.

ANSWER   In sentence *a*, the action occurred and has ended (past).
In sentence *b*, the action occurred at an indefinite time in the past (present perfect).

1. **a.** Kim and I are planning our visit to Juárez.
   b. Kim and I will be planning our visit to Juárez.
2. **a.** We stayed in El Paso, Texas, just across the river from Juárez.
   b. We have been staying in El Paso, Texas, just across the river from Juárez.
3. **a.** Kim did enjoy the trip to El Paso.
   b. Kim has enjoyed the trip to El Paso.
4. **a.** We were traveling for three weeks.
   b. We have been traveling for three weeks.
5. **a.** Soon we will visit all the nearby Mexican cities.
   b. Soon we will have visited all the nearby Mexican cities.

Exercise 16 — Using the Emphatic Form

Complete these sentences by writing the form of the verb indicated in parentheses.

Testimony in a Courtroom

1. I _____ to take Ms. Michaels to the store. (past emphatic of *agree*)
2. I _____, however, that I intended to help her rob anyone. (present emphatic of *deny*)
3. She _____ that she didn't tell me of her plans. (present emphatic of *admit*)
4. Yes, I believe she _____ the store, but I had nothing to do with it. (past emphatic of *rob*)
5. You must believe that I _____ the truth. (present emphatic of *tell*)

Exercise 17 — Expressing Past Time in a Paragraph

Write a paragraph of at least five sentences about an important event in your past. Underline five verbs or verb phrases that you have used. (Remember that the perfect tenses, as well as the past tense, can be used to express past action.)

- Do not shift, or change, tenses when two or more events occur at the same time.

INCORRECT	Teresa **dived** into the pool and **swims** to the other side. [The tense needlessly shifts from the past to the present.]
CORRECT	Teresa **dived** into the pool and **swam** to the other side. [Now it is clear that both events happened in the past.]

- Shift tenses only to show that one event precedes or follows another.

INCORRECT	After we **hiked** three miles, we **stopped** for a rest. [The two past-tense verbs give the mistaken impression that both events happened at the same time.]
CORRECT	After we **had hiked** three miles, we **stopped** for a rest. [The shift from the past perfect tense (*had hiked*) to the past tense (*stopped*) clearly indicates that the hiking of three miles happened before the hikers stopped to rest.]

Exercise 18 | Shifting Verb Tenses Appropriately

In each of these sentences, supply the appropriate form of the verb in parentheses. Shift tenses if one event precedes or follows another; otherwise, use the same tense.

The Hundred Year Flood

1. The radio had warned them, but many people _____ anyway. (stay)
2. As the rain continued for days without stopping, the water in the river _____ steadily. (rise)
3. Boats drifted down the river and a frightened cow _____ by. (swim)
4. After the river _____ its banks, people found it was too late to escape. (overflow)
5. Some store owners _____ sandbags in front of their businesses to protect them, but now the current was too strong to be stopped. (pile)
6. It was the kind of flood that _____ only once in a hundred years. (happen)
7. People across the nation watched the TV news that _____ incredible scenes of devastation. (show)
8. Once the governor _____ a state of emergency, the National Guard was called. (declare)
9. Helicopters hovered and _____ people from the roofs of their homes. (pluck)
10. After the flood had finally ended, people _____ to rebuild their lives. (begin)

Exercise 19   Making Tenses Compatible

First find the two verbs that appear in each of the following sentences. Then rewrite each sentence, making the second verb compatible with the first verb.

Alice Walker, Prizewinning Writer

1. Alice Walker was born in 1944 in rural Georgia, where, as the eighth child of sharecroppers, she had endured the hardships of poverty.
2. When her brother accidentally shot her with a BB gun, Alice becomes blind in one eye.
3. Because Alice was feeling depressed as a result of the injury, she turns to her journal and books as outlets for her emotions.
4. By the time Walker participated in the Civil Rights movement, she enrolled in Spelman College in Atlanta.
5. When she published her first book, a volume of poetry, she taught at Jackson State University in Mississippi.
6. In this book, Walker wrote some poems about Africa, where she traveled as a college junior.
7. Her book *In Search of Our Mothers' Gardens,* pays tribute to the strong, creative African American woman and is encouraging women to safeguard their own creative legacy.
8. Long after the African American writer Zora Neale Hurston had died poor and forgotten, Walker discovers her own spiritual kinship with that woman.
9. Before Walker found Hurston's unmarked grave in Florida, she made up her mind to place a tombstone on the site and to write about the experience.
10. Walker has written many novels, including *The Color Purple,* which has won the Pulitzer Prize in 1983.

Exercise 20   Understanding the Compatibility of Tenses

For each sentence below, write the two verbs and identify their tenses. Explain why the tenses are, or are not, compatible.

1. At first, people picked up food with their hands or stabbed it with a handy knife.
2. A new invention, the fork, became fashionable in Italy around 1100, and English nobles started using forks by the 1600s.
3. Early forks had only two tines, so food often falls off before reaching the mouth.
4. Proper table manners become a requirement when people dined in public.
5. In the 1890s, one silverware company offered a set of 131 different pieces of tableware, but most people today considered this to be excessive.

Exercise 21   Using Compatible Tenses in a Paragraph

Write a paragraph of five sentences or more in which you describe how a new invention (such as the computer or VCR) has changed everyday life. Use sentences containing two or more verbs that are compatible. Underline these verbs.

15.7 Voice of Verbs

■ An action verb is in the **active voice** when the subject of the sentence performs the action.

The coach **encouraged** the team.

■ An action verb is in the **passive voice** when its action is performed on the subject.

The team **was encouraged** by the coach.

Generally the active voice is the stronger voice. Sometimes, however, the passive voice is preferred or even necessary. For instance, if you do not want to call attention to the performer of an action or you do not know who the performer is, you would use the passive voice.

The book **was returned.** [You may not know who returned it.]
The glass **was broken.** [You may not want to identify the person who broke the glass.]

You form the passive voice by using the auxiliary verb *be* together with the past participle of the verb. The tense of the auxiliary verb determines the tense of the passive verb.

The team **is encouraged** by the coach. [present tense, passive voice]
The team **was being encouraged** by the coach. [past progressive tense, passive voice]
The team **will have been encouraged** by the coach. [future perfect tense, passive voice]

Exercise 22   Identifying Active and Passive Voice

In each of the following sentences, write the verb and then identify its tense and voice.

A Street Scene

1. She looks out her window at a brilliant spring day.
2. Hot dogs were being sold from a push cart.
3. A small boy with a knit cap and a basketball jacket was kicking a can along the sidewalk.
4. The bus stop had been blocked by an inconsiderate driver.
5. A meter minder is slapping a parking ticket on the car.

| Exercise 23 | **Exercise 23 Changing the Voice of Verbs** |

In each of the following sentences, change the active voice to the passive or the passive voice to the active.

Confucius and His Teachings

1. People throughout the world study the teachings of the Chinese philosopher Confucius.
2. A doctrine of consideration for others, similar to the golden rule, was taught by Confucius as the basis for all social and political conduct.
3. Followers of Confucius regard duty to parents as one of the basic foundations for social order.
4. Moderation in all things, the doctrine of the golden mean, is emphasized in Confucian philosophy.
5. Confucius welcomed students from all social classes.
6. The aristocracy's control over the government was not respected by the philosopher's open-minded policies.
7. Confucius was made provincial governor by the duke of Lu.
8. The nobility of Lu resented many of Confucius's ideas.
9. Before long the men in power forced Confucius into a thirteen-year exile.
10. The *Analects,* a collection of Confucian proverbs and anecdotes, was compiled by Confucius's disciples after his death.

| Exercise 24 | **Strengthening Writing by Using the Active Voice** |

The sentences below were written in the passive voice. If you think a sentence would read better in the active voice, rewrite it that way. If you believe a sentence should remain in the passive voice, explain why.

Unearthing a Giant

1. In 1801 a pond on a New England farm was being drained.
2. A treadmill was turned by twenty-five sweating men.
3. The project was being supervised by Charles Willson Peale, a remarkable American saddle-maker, painter, soldier, inventor, and scientist.
4. In this unusual research project, the skeleton of a strange, giant beast was being searched for by Peale.
5. This beast would later be known as the mastodon.
6. Little was known about the mastodon by scientists, so it was difficult to assemble its skeleton.
7. By the end of the year, the gigantic skeleton was being displayed in a museum in Philadelphia.
8. The mastodon was described by Peale in an advertisement as being the largest of terrestrial beings.
9. Fifty cents each was paid by many people eager to see this strange creature from prehistoric times.
10. Eventually, the display was moved to Independence Hall.

15.8 Mood of Verbs

In addition to tense and voice, verbs also express mood.

■ A verb expresses one of three **moods:** the **indicative mood,** the **imperative mood,** or the **subjunctive mood.**

The indicative mood—the most frequently used—makes a statement or asks a question. The imperative mood expresses a command or makes a request.

> **INDICATIVE MOOD**   She takes the bus home.
> **IMPERATIVE MOOD**   Take the bus home.

The subjunctive mood, although often replaced by the indicative mood in informal English, has two important uses in contemporary formal English.

1. To express, indirectly, a demand, recommendation, suggestion, or statement of necessity.

   > We demand [*or* recommend *or* suggest] that she **take** the bus home. [The subjunctive mood drops the *-s* from the third-person singular.]
   >
   > It is necessary that you **be** home before dark. [The subjunctive mood uses *be* instead of *am, is,* or *are.*]

2. To state a condition or a wish that is contrary to fact. Notice that this use of the subjunctive always requires the past tense.

   > If she **were** late, she would take the bus home. [The subjunctive mood uses *were,* not *was.*]
   >
   > I wish that I **were** a genius.

Exercise 25   Expressing the Imperative Mood in Sentences

The verb in each sentence below expresses the indicative mood. Rewrite the sentence to express the imperative mood.

1. She leaves right away.
2. He always drives carefully.
3. She practices the piano every day.
4. He leaves nothing to chance.
5. She prepares herself mentally to succeed.

Using the Indicative and Subjunctive Moods

For each of the following sentences, first determine whether the verb should express the indicative or the subjunctive mood. Then write the sentence, supplying the appropriate form of the verb in parentheses.

A Tennis Lesson

1. My sister Antonia's tennis instructor (teach) people of all ages and levels of ability.
2. Antonia, who practices for an hour a day six times a week, wishes that she (be) an expert player like Steffi Graf or André Agassi.
3. I told her, "If I (be) you, I would consider working at least an hour a day on my serve alone."
4. Antonia has learned that in order to hit the ball with a good forehand stroke, it is important that she (prepare) for the ball.
5. Good players (shift) their weight forward during the stroke.
6. If my sister is to play her very best game of tennis, it is vital that she (play) on a clay court rather than on a grass court.
7. It (be) important that a player (have) a good sense of balance.
8. If the net (be) six inches high instead of the regulation thirty-six inches, it would be much easier for me to serve effectively.
9. Antonia (want) me to take tennis lessons from her tennis instructor too.
10. She thinks if I (be) willing to apply myself, which I am, we would make a formidable doubles team.

Exercise 27   Supplying the Correct Subjunctive Form

Rewrite each sentence so that at least one verb expresses the subjunctive mood and the idea indicated in parentheses. You may need to change the pronoun for the sentence to make sense.

SAMPLE   I go to the store and buy a notebook. (statement contrary to fact)
ANSWER   If I were to go to the store, I would buy a notebook.

1. She gets extra practice in math. (recommendation)
2. We shot better in the second half and made four more points and won the game. (condition contrary to fact)
3. I am skiing in the Alps. (wish)
4. He completes the training program. (statement of necessity)
5. People walk on Mars and weigh only about a third of what they do on Earth. (condition contrary to fact)
6. We receive a pay raise of 5 percent per year for the next three years. (demand)
7. I can find time to do my homework. (wish)
8. He keeps his eye on the ball without getting distracted by the other players. (suggestion)
9. She spends more time helping and less time complaining. (wish)
10. Three football fields placed end to end are still shorter than the length of the aircraft carrier *Abraham Lincoln*. (condition contrary to fact)

Exercise 28   Understanding the Use of Verb Moods

Explain the difference in purpose between the sentences in each pair below. Identify the mood (*indicative, imperative,* or *subjunctive*) used in each sentence.

SAMPLE   (a) He waited until Saturday.   (b) Wait until Saturday.
ANSWER   Sentence *a* makes a statement. (indicative)
                Sentence *b* gives a command. (imperative)

1. **a.** I am going to the beach for a week.
   b. I wish I could go to the beach for a week.
2. **a.** If you were to break a complicated problem down into simpler parts, it would be easier to solve.
   b. Break a complicated problem down into simpler parts, and it will be easier to solve.
3. **a.** If I didn't have to do this homework now, I could go to the movies tonight.
   b. I don't have to do this homework now, so I can go to the movies tonight.
4. **a.** She passes the ball to the player who can make the shot.
   b. Pass the ball to the player who can make the shot.
5. **a.** If we had more time, we could do a better job.
   b. We had more time, so we could do a better job.
6. **a.** We recommend that you don't take this medicine with meals.
   b. Don't take this medicine with meals.
7. **a.** This computer has a large amount of memory that can store all of our data.
   b. If this computer had a larger amount of memory, it could store all of our data.
8. **a.** It is necessary that you follow these directions exactly.
   b. Follow these instructions exactly.
9. **a.** José watched carefully so that he could give an accurate report.
   b. If José had watched carefully, he could have given an accurate report.
10. **a.** Letitia wished that the dog would stop barking.
    b. Stop barking, right now!
11. **a.** Would you like to leave now?
    b. Please leave now.
12. **a.** The company demands that everyone arrive on time.
    b. Everyone always arrives on time.
13. **a.** Dad suggested that Tony give the dog a bath.
    b. Tony often gives the dog a bath.
14. **a.** Try to improve your handwriting.
    b. If I were you, I would try to improve my handwriting.
15. **a.** The bus driver refuses to wait more than two minutes for stragglers.
    b. The principal recommended that the bus driver refuse to wait for stragglers.

Exercise 29   Using the Imperative Mood in Writing Instructions

Write a set of instructions that explains how to do something, step by step. (For example, you can explain how to start a computer, program a VCR, or drive to a particular destination.) Include at least five steps. Use the imperative mood in writing each instruction.

Grammar Review

VERB TENSES, VOICE, AND MOOD

Verb Tenses, Voice, and Mood

Roots is one man's attempt to reconstruct the history of seven generations of his family. The book begins with the birth in 1750 of Alex Haley's great-great-great-great-grandfather, Kunta Kinte, who was kidnapped from his home in the Gambia in West Africa and brought to Maryland as a slave, and ends with the death of Haley's father.

Roots has inspired Americans of all races to celebrate their family heritage. In this excerpt, Kunta Kinte's mother and other women of the village of Juffure are canoeing down a *bolong*, or canal, to their rice fields. The passage has been annotated to show some of the verb tenses and voices covered in this unit.

Literature Model

from **Roots**
by Alex Haley

Past perfect tense

It was the planting season, and the first rains were soon to come. On all their farming land, the men of Juffure had piled tall stacks of dry weeds and set them afire so that the light wind would nourish the soil by scattering the ashes. And the women in their rice fields were already planting green shoots in the mud.

Past progressive form

Past tense of an irregular verb

The air was heavy with the deep, musky fragrance of the mangroves, and with the perfumes of the other plants and trees that grew thickly on both sides of the bolong. Alarmed by the passing canoes, huge families of baboons, roused from sleep, began bellowing, springing about and shaking palm-tree fronds. Wild pigs grunted and snorted, running to hide themselves among the weeds and bushes. Covering the muddy banks, thousands of pelicans, cranes, egrets, herons, storks, gulls, terns, and spoonbills interrupted their breakfast feeding to watch nervously as the canoes glided by. Some of the smaller birds took to the air—ringdoves, skimmers, rails, darters, and kingfishers—circling with shrill cries until the intruders had passed.

As the canoes arrowed through rippling, busy patches of water, schools of minnows would leap up together, perform a silvery dance, and then splash back. Chasing the minnows, sometimes so hungrily that they flopped right into a moving canoe, were large, fierce fish that the women would club with their paddles and stow away for a succulent evening meal. But this morning the minnows swam around them undisturbed.

The twisting bolong took the rowing women around a turn to a wider tributary, and as they came into sight, a great beating of wings filled the air and a vast living carpet of seafowl—hundreds of thousands of them, in every color of the rainbow—rose and filled the sky. The surface of the water, darkened by the storm of birds and furrowed by their flapping wings, was flecked with feathers as the women paddled on.

As they neared the marshy faros where generations of Juffure women had grown their rice crops, the canoes passed through swarming clouds of mosquitoes and then, one after another, nosed in against a walkway of thickly matted weeds. The weeds bounded and identified each woman's plot, where by now the emerald shoots of young rice stood a hand's height above the water's surface.

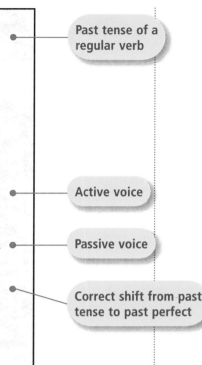

> Past tense of a regular verb

> Active voice

> Passive voice

> Correct shift from past tense to past perfect

Verb Tenses, Voice, and Mood

Review: Exercise 1   Identifying Principal Parts

The following sentences are based on the passage from *Roots*. Each sentence contains a verb in one of four forms: (a) the base form, (b) the past form, (c) the present participle, or (d) the past participle. At the end of the sentence is a second verb in parentheses. First, identify the form of the verb in italics. Then rewrite the sentence, substituting the verb in parentheses for the italicized verb.

1. After the men of Juffure had *piled* dried weeds into stacks, they set them afire. (throw)
2. The women were *starting* their work in the fields. (begin)
3. The villagers always *return* to the same place to plant their rice crops. (go)
4. Kunta Kinte's mother and the other women *journeyed* in their canoes to the rice paddies. (ride)
5. Flocks of birds *sailed* away as the canoes passed. (fly)
6. The canoes are *arrowing* through rippling, busy patches of water. (dart)
7. Large, fierce fish were *chasing* the minnows. (pursue)
8. The twisting bolong *took* the rowing women around a turn. (bring)
9. They neared the marshy faros where generations of Juffure women had *grown* their crops. (raise)
10. The canoes *passed* through swarming clouds of mosquitoes. (glide)

Grammar Review

Review: Exercise 2   Using the Perfect Tenses

Each of the following sentences describes village life in West Africa, the setting for this workshop's passage. On your paper, rewrite each sentence, adding the appropriate form of the italicized verb in the place indicated by the caret. Write the verb in the tense indicated in parentheses, using the past participle of the main verb and the appropriate form of the helping verb *have*.

SAMPLE   Village life in West Africa ∧ the same patterns for generations. (present perfect tense of *follow*)

ANSWER   Village life in West Africa has followed the same patterns for generations.

1. Traditionally villages ∧ many generations of an extended family. (present perfect tense of *encompass*)
2. Many West African nations ∧ Islam for centuries before European colonists arrived. (past perfect tense of *practice*)
3. By early adulthood, women ∧ the duties of raising a family and working on a farm. (present perfect tense of *assume*)
4. By the advent of the dry season, the village ∧ adequate food supplies. (future perfect tense of *collect*)
5. By the time the rains end, children and young people already ∧ crops for food. (future perfect tense of *harvest*)

Review: Exercise 3   Using the Progressive and Emphatic Forms

The following sentences are based on passages from *Roots* not reproduced in this textbook. On your paper, rewrite each sentence, adding the appropriate form of the italicized verb in the place indicated by the caret. Write the verb in the form indicated in parentheses. Use the present participle of the main verb and the appropriate tense of the auxiliary verb *be* or the base form of the main verb and the appropriate form of *do*.

SAMPLE   In 1767 Kunta Kinte ∧ in the Gambia. (past progressive form of *live*)

ANSWER   In 1767 Kunta Kinte was living in the Gambia.

1. Kunta ∧ the arts of hunting and fighting for many years, and he had become a fine young warrior. (past perfect progressive form of *learn*)
2. In the most dramatic episode of *Roots*, Kunta ∧ from sentry duty in the village fields when four slave traders capture him. (present progressive form of *return*)
3. Kunta was shipped to Maryland in the fall of 1767; at that time, slave ships ∧ thousands of Africans to America each year. (past progressive form of *carry*)
4. For the rest of his life, Kunta Kinte ∧ to see his beloved home and family in the Gambia. (future progressive form of *yearn*)
5. Kunta never ∧, however; he remained on plantations in Virginia for the rest of his life. (past emphatic form of *return*)

Review: Exercise 4 Making Tenses Compatible

These sentences are based on the passage from *Roots*. Each sentence has an error in verb tense. On your paper, rewrite each sentence, changing the tense of the italicized verb so that the tenses are compatible.

SAMPLE   By the time the rains arrived, the villagers *began* to plant their crops.
ANSWER   By the time the rains arrived, the villagers had begun to plant their crops.

1. As soon as the dry weeds *burned*, the wind scattered the ashes.
2. The women planted rice in the marshy faros, as their ancestors *did* for centuries.
3. Animals *watch* nervously as the women's canoes glided by.
4. Flocks of birds took to the air when the passing canoes *frighten* them.
5. The rice shoots *grew* far above the water's surface by the time the dry season ended.

Review: Exercise 5 Voice of Verbs

The following sentences describe the writing of *Roots*. First, identify each sentence as being in the *passive voice* or the *active voice*. Then rewrite the italicized portion, changing the active voice to the passive or the passive voice to the active.

SAMPLE   *The book was written* by Alex Haley to memorialize the lives of his ancestors.
ANSWER   passive voice; Alex Haley wrote the book to memorialize the lives of his ancestors.

1. When young, *he was told stories by his grandmother about his ancestor Kunta Kinte.*
2. *Only a few facts were known by Haley;* he knew, for instance, that Kunta Kinte had said he lived by a river called "Kamby Bolongo."
3. *Linguists told Haley* that "Kamby Bolongo" might mean "the Gambia River."
4. *Haley was intrigued by the idea,* so he flew to the Gambia and traveled to a village where members of the Kinte clan still lived.
5. *There he was told this tale by an elderly storyteller:* a boy named Kunta Kinte had disappeared from the village around 1765, soon after the first slave traders had arrived.

Review: Exercise 6

Proofreading

The following passage tells about the Senufo people and the carved Senufo door that appears on the next page. Rewrite the passage, correcting the errors in spelling, grammar, and usage. Add any missing punctuation. There are ten errors.

The Art of the Senufo

[1]The West African peoples known as the Senufo lives in the grassy savannas of the northern Ivory Coast and in southern Mali. [2]The Senufo tribes speak four different languages, raise corn and millet, living in thatched mud houses, and are reknowned marimba players and sculptors.

(continued)

Grammar Review

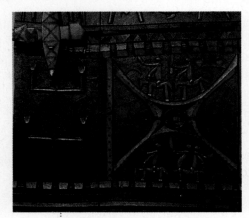

Senufo artists, West Africa, carved wood door (detail)

³The art of the Senufo is considering stylized and elegant. ⁴The Senufo are famous for their carved wooden masks which are wore during ceremonial dances.

⁵The door shown here once barring the entrance to the shrine of a Senufo secret society. ⁶A symbol of the Sun attended by five figures on horseback dominates the central panel, and carvings of animal spirits, including a crocodile, have decorated the side panels. ⁷The sculptors who will have carved this work were clearly proud of their African heritage Alex Haley, the author of *Roots*, was equally proud of his.

Review: Exercise 7

Mixed Review

The following sentences describe the life of Alex Haley. Rewrite each sentence, following the directions in parentheses.

SAMPLE Alex Haley inspired many African Americans to trace their family history. (Change the verb to the present perfect tense.)

ANSWER Alex Haley has inspired many African Americans to trace their family history.

Alex Haley

1. Born in Ithaca, New York, Alex Haley studied education and joins the U.S. Coast Guard in 1939. (Correct the error in the use of verb tense.)
2. During his twenty years with the Coast Guard, Haley writes many adventure stories about the sea. (Change the verb to the past tense.)
3. In 1963 Haley was asked by the African American politician Malcolm X to work on a book. (Rewrite the sentence in the active voice.)
4. *The Autobiography of Malcolm X* was praised by critics, and the book is still required reading in many African American studies programs. (Change the first verb to the present perfect tense.)
5. Haley had planned to write a book about school segregation in the South but instead spent ten years researching and writing *Roots*. (Change the first verb to the past progressive form.)

Verb Tenses, Voice, and Mood

Writing Application

TIME

For more about the writing process, see **TIME Facing the Blank Page**, pp. 111-121.

Using the Active Voice for Clearer Writing

Good writing is clear, precise, and graceful. One way to achieve a good writing style is to avoid using the passive voice. Consider the following sentence written in the passive voice:

> When what was wanted done by him to his shoes was finished being described by Max, they were marked by Feld, both with enormous holes in the soles which he pretended not to notice, with large white-chalk x's, and the rubber heels, thinned to the nails, were marked with o's, though he was troubled the letters might have been mixed up.

It is very hard to follow what is going on in this sentence. The author, Bernard Malamud, actually used the active voice when he wrote the sentence in the short story "The First Seven Years."

> When Max finished describing what he wanted done to the shoes, Feld marked them, both with enormous holes in the soles which he pretended not to notice, with large white-chalk x's, and the rubber heels, thinned to the nails, he marked with o's, though it troubled him he might have mixed up the letters.

Notice how much clearer the sentence is when written in the active voice.

TECHNIQUES WITH ACTIVE VOICE Try to apply some of Bernard Malamud's writing techniques when you write and revise your own work.

1 Whenever possible, use the active voice to make the action clear and direct. Compare the following items:

PASSIVE When what was wanted done by him to his shoes was finished being described. . .

ACTIVE When Max finished describing what he wanted done to his shoes. . .

2 Use the active voice to focus on the subject (the doer of the action) rather than on what is being done.

PASSIVE they were marked by Feld

ACTIVE Feld marked them

Practice Practice these techniques by revising the following passage. Pay particular attention to the underlined words.

Have you watched a game of catch <u>being played</u> by seals in a zoo? Many animals seem to enjoy playing games. In the National Zoo in Washington, D.C, a basketball <u>is pushed</u> around by the snout of a giant African soft-shell turtle for several hours each afternoon. In your own home, the dog may fetch a ball while bits of paper <u>are pounced</u> on by the cat.

It <u>has been found</u> by scientists that play <u>is needed</u> by young animals. Animals use play as a way to learn about their environment. When play <u>is being done</u> by a kitten, it is learning how to hunt for food. But animals don't just play to learn. <u>In highly developed animals such as dogs, cats, monkeys, and dolphins, a very human quality seems <u>to be possessed</u> by their play. Sometimes, it seems, animals may play just for fun.

Subject-Verb Agreement

16.1 Intervening Prepositional Phrases

■ A verb must agree with its subject in person and number.

With most verbs, the only change in form to indicate agreement takes place in the present tense. You add an *-s* (or *-es*) to the base verb when the subject is in the third-person singular. The linking verb *be* is an exception, however. It changes form in both the present and the past tense.

SINGULAR	PLURAL
She **advises.**	They **advise.**
He **is** there.	They **are** there.
It **was** mysterious.	They **were** mysterious.

When the auxiliary verbs *be*, *have*, and *do* appear in verb phrases, their forms change to show agreement with third-person subjects.

SINGULAR	PLURAL
She **is advising.**	They **are advising.**
She **has left** work.	They **have left** work.
Does he **speak** there?	**Do** they **speak** there?

■ Do not mistake a word in a prepositional phrase for the subject of a sentence.

The object of a preposition is never the subject of a sentence. Be certain that the verb agrees with the actual subject of the sentence and not with the object of a preposition.

The *islands* near the Equator off South America **are** the Galápagos. [The subject, *islands,* is plural; *near the Equator* and *off South America* are prepositional phrases; the verb, *are*, is plural.]

The giant *tortoise* of the Galápagos Islands **weighs** more than five hundred pounds. [The subject, *tortoise,* is singular; *of the Galápagos Islands* is a prepositional phrase; the verb, *weighs*, is singular.]

Baby *tortoises* around an adult **have** to be careful. [The subject, *tortoises,* is plural; *around an adult* is a prepositional phrase; therefore, the verb, *have*, is plural.]

This *archipelago* of thirteen large and several smaller islands is also the home of flightless cormorants. [The subject, *archipelago*, is singular; *of thirteen large and several smaller islands* is a prepositional phrase; the verb, *is*, is singular.]

Exercise 1   **Making Subjects and Verbs Agree When Prepositional Phrases Intervene**

Find the simple subject in each sentence. Then write on your paper the verb that agrees with each subject.

Chinese American Scientists

1. Chinese Americans in the field of science (has/have) excelled in many areas.
2. The winner of the 1962 Albert Lasker Medical Research Award and of several other prestigious awards (was/were) the notable biochemist Dr. Choh Hao Li, one of the world's foremost authorities on the pituitary gland.
3. In the tenth edition of *American Men of Science,* the list of names (includes/include) not only that of Dr. Li but also those of his three brothers, each distinguished in his own right.
4. Dr. Frances Sze-Ling Chew's work on the interactions between plants and insects (consists/consist) of determining the poisons that plants produce to protect themselves from insects.
5. Perhaps the best-known Chinese American scientists of the twentieth century (is/are) Dr. Tsung Dao Lee and Dr. Chen Ning Yang, winners of the 1957 Nobel Prize for physics.
6. Through their research, these two physicists (was/were) able to disprove a universally accepted law of nature.
7. Dr. Chien Shiung Wu and others confirmed the theories of Lee and Yang, so textbooks in science no longer (teaches/teach) that elementary particles in nature are always symmetrical.
8. The discoverer of the subatomic particles known as J and psi (was/were) Dr. Samuel C. C. Ting, who along with Burton Richter won the Nobel Prize for physics in 1976.
9. Katherine Hsu, among other Chinese American physicians, (has/have) also received special recognition.
10. These considerable contributions to the field of science (has/have) enhanced our understanding of the world.

Exercise 2   **Using the Correct Verb Form**

Find the simple subject in each sentence, and identify it as singular or plural. Then write the correct form of the verb given in parentheses.

The Fiction of Flannery O'Connor

1. The stories of the southern writer Flannery O'Connor often _____ violent plots, religious themes, and vivid local color. *(feature)*
2. O'Connor's skill at depicting eccentric characters _____ her to her readers. *(endear)*
3. Her concern in her fiction with extremes of emotion _____ her plots an air of melodrama. *(give)*
4. O'Connor's view of life and its strange twists, however, scarcely _____ to sentimentalism. *(amount)*
5. A distinctive relish for comedy and paradox _____ through nearly all O'Connor's work; one notable example is her story "The Life You Save May Be Your Own." *(run)*

Agreement with Linking Verbs

■ Do not be confused by a predicate nominative that is different in number from the subject. Only the subject affects the number of the linking verb.

The **footprints** in the **mud** were the only clue. [The plural verb, *were,* agrees with the plural subject, *footprints,* not with the predicate nominative, *clue.*]

My favorite **breakfast is** eggs scrambled with onions. [The singular verb, *is,* agrees with the singular subject, *breakfast,* not with the predicate nominative, *eggs.*]

Exercise 3   Making Linking Verbs Agree with Their Subjects

Find the simple subject in each of the following sentences. Then write on your paper the form of the verb in parentheses that agrees with the subject of each sentence.

Inuit Carvings

1. As evidenced by Inuit art, the central element in the life of the Inuit people (is/are) the splendors of nature.
2. The lifelike carvings of animals such as birds, seals, and bears (is/are) a popular art form.
3. A popular theme in Inuit art (has been/have been) creatures from the spiritual world.
4. A favorite medium for carvings (is/are) ivory tusks from walruses.
5. The smooth surfaces of each ivory carving (seems/seem) an invitation to hold each object.
6. Chunks of wood, too, (becomes/become) a delight to the senses.
7. Carved by a skilled Inuit artist, even ordinary combs or fish hooks (is/are) something beautiful and graceful.
8. A more exotic kind of carving (is/are) the masks used in ceremonial dances.
9. Inuit artifacts from the ancient past (remains/remain) a beautiful and mysterious treasure today.
10. Elegant carvings (has become/have become) part of the proud heritage of the Inuit people.

Exercise 4   Correcting Errors in Agreement

Rewrite the paragraph below, correcting the five errors in subject-verb agreement.

The Magic of the Rain Forest

[1]According to many scientists, tropical rain forests is nature's greatest achievement. [2]The closely linked lives of rain forest plants and animals seems like an intricate mechanism. [3]Each layer of the forest, with its different proportions of light, moisture, and warmth, have become a distinctive niche for certain plants, animals, birds, and insects. [4]The processes of decomposition on the forest floor holds the secret of how trees receive nutrients. [5]Rain forests remains a treasury of the diversity of life.

16.3 Agreement in Inverted Sentences

■ In an **inverted sentence**—a sentence in which the subject follows the verb—take care in locating the simple subject, and make sure that the verb agrees with the subject.

Inverted sentences often begin with a prepositional phrase. As a result, the object of the preposition may be mistaken for the subject of the sentence. In an inverted sentence, the subject always follows the verb.

SINGULAR	Beyond the Milky Way **lies** the Andromeda *galaxy.*
PLURAL	Beyond the Milky Way **lie** countless *galaxies.*
SINGULAR	Above our heads **twinkles** a vast, glittering *array* of stars.
PLURAL	Above our heads **twinkle** vast, glittering *arrays* of stars.

The words *there* and *here* may also begin inverted sentences. They are almost never the subject of a sentence.

SINGULAR	There **is** one possible *explanation.*
	Here **comes** my best *friend.*
PLURAL	There **are** two possible *explanations.*
	Here **come** my *friends.*

In an interrogative sentence, an auxiliary verb often precedes the subject. Thus, the subject appears between the auxiliary and the main verb.

SINGULAR	**Does** that *man* **teach** in this school?
PLURAL	**Do** those *schools* **offer** Latin?
SINGULAR	When **does** *Thanksgiving* **fall** this year?
PLURAL	When **do** the spring *holidays* **fall** this year?

Exercise 5 Making Subjects and Verbs Agree in Inverted Sentences

Find the simple subject in each sentence. Then write the form of the verb that agrees with each subject.

Computer Games

1. (Does/Do) your friend from school own any of these new computer games?
2. There (is/are) thousands of computer games available from software developers and amateur programmers.
3. In even the simplest games (lies/lie) the challenge of outwitting a "smart" machine.
4. There (is/are) more complex games with both challenge and colorful, high-resolution graphics.
5. Here (is/are) a list of adventures in some of the most popular commercial games.
6. Before you (stretches/stretch) a valley full of magical hazards that your character must master.
7. Down a well (is/are) falling shapes that you must catch and position on a grid.
8. Within a maze of clues (hides/hide) the identity of the time-traveling thief who has stolen Napoleon's hat.
9. (Does/Do) these games sound familiar to you?
10. With the advent of new technology, there (is/are) a strong probability that games will become even more exciting.

Exercise 6 Using the Correct Verb Form

Find the simple subject in each sentence, and identify it as singular or plural. Then write the correct form of the verb given in parentheses.

Cyberspace: Fact or Fiction?

1. _____ the term *cyberspace* ring a bell with you? (do)
2. Where _____ cyberspace exist? (do)
3. Beyond every glowing computer screen _____ a landscape of virtual reality. (stretch)
4. According to the science fiction writer William Gibson, there _____ an actual territory called cyberspace. (be)
5. Here _____ the setting for Gibson's fiction, including his novel *Neuromancer* (1984). (lie)
6. How _____ Gibson describe this setting in his novel? (do).
7. Around constellations and clusters of data _____ three-dimensional warehouses of all the information in every computer in existence. (rise).
8. There _____ other names for Gibson's cyberspace, including the matrix, the datasphere, the electronic frontier, and the information superhighway. (be)
9. Among the newly coined terms with the prefix *cyber-* _____ the words *cyberphilia,* *cyberphobia,* and *cyberwonk.* (be)
10. There _____ one hands-on definition of cyberspace: the place you're in when you're talking on the telephone. (be).

16.4 Agreement with Special Subjects

Collective Nouns

■ A **collective noun** names a group. Consider a collective noun singular when it refers to a group as a whole. Consider a collective noun plural when it refers to each member of a group individually.

SINGULAR	The *orchestra* **plays.**
PLURAL	The *orchestra* **tune** their instruments.
SINGULAR	The *family* **loves** to travel.
PLURAL	My *family* **take** turns choosing places to visit.
SINGULAR	The *jury* **decides** guilt or innocence.
PLURAL	The *jury* **debate** their views on the evidence.

Special Nouns

■ Certain nouns that end in -s, such as *mathematics, measles,* and *mumps,* take singular verbs.

SINGULAR	*Measles* **is** now an epidemic in my city.
	The *news* about their health **was** good.

■ Certain other nouns that end in -s, such as *scissors, pants, binoculars,* and *eyeglasses,* take plural verbs.

PLURAL	These *binoculars* **are** a bargain.
	The *scissors* **were made** in France.

■ Many nouns that end in -ics may be singular or plural, depending upon their meaning.

SINGULAR	*Ethics* **is** the branch of philosophy that most interests me. [one subject of interest]
PLURAL	His *ethics* in this matter **are** questionable. [more than one ethical decision]

Nouns of Amount

■ When a noun refers to an amount that is considered one unit, it is singular. When it refers to a number of individual units, it is plural.

SINGULAR	Two *dollars* **is** the fee. [one amount]
PLURAL	Two *dollars* **are** in his pockets. [two individual dollar bills]
SINGULAR	Five *days* **is** an average work week. [one unit of time]
PLURAL	Five *days* **have flown** by. [five individual periods of time]

Titles

■ A title is always singular, even if a noun within the title is plural.

SINGULAR **The Adventures of Huckleberry Finn is** perhaps Mark Twain's greatest novel.

Exercise 7   **Making Verbs Agree with Special Subjects**

Find the subject in each sentence, and write on your paper the form of the verb in parentheses that agrees with the subject.

Basketball Superstars

1. The audience (roars/roar) as its favorite player steps onto the court.
2. The star player's statistics (justifies/justify) the fans' reaction.
3. Ten years (was/were) the number of years the star player had spent with the team.
4. "Gold Medal Winners" (is/are) the title of an article that describes how Michael Jordan led the U.S. team to a gold medal in the 1984 Olympic Games.
5. Thirty-five points per game (makes/make) an impressive year-end average.
6. The basketball team (depends/depend) upon one another for inspiration during their grueling season.
7. Five million dollars (is/are) a great deal of money, but many think an athlete with great talent deserves that salary.
8. Binoculars (helps/help) fans see brilliant athletes pass and shoot.
9. The crowd (marvels/marvel) at each team member's ability to leap into the air.
10. The public always (enjoys/enjoy)their predictions about which team will win the championship.

Exercise 8   **Writing Sentences with Special Subjects**

Use each of the italicized words in the following phrases as the simple subject of an original sentence. Make sure that the verb in each of your sentences agrees with the subject. Remember that some special subjects may be singular or plural, depending on their meaning in context.

1. my new *sunglasses* in their sleek, elegant case
2. Walt Whitman's *Leaves of Grass*
3. *three-quarters* of the entire junior class
4. one hundred and ninety *miles*
5. that rock group's fanatically loyal *public*
6. Antonio Vivaldi's orchestral work *The Four Seasons*
7. the *statistics*
8. The *Los Angeles Times*
9. our badly demoralized soccer *team*
10. fifty-five *percent* of our school

16.5 Agreement with Compound Subjects

Compound Subjects Joined by *And*

A compound subject that is joined by *and* or *both . . . and* is plural unless its parts belong to one unit or they both refer to the same person or thing.

PLURAL   The **librarian** *and* the **student** **read** in different parts of the library.

Both **duck** *and* **chicken** **are found** in local markets.

SINGULAR   **Macaroni** *and* **cheese** **is** a delicious late-night snack. [The compound subject is one unit.]

Her **teacher** *and* **counselor** **meets** with her daily. [One person is both the teacher and the counselor.]

Compound Subjects Joined by *Or* or *Nor*

With compound subjects joined by *or* or *nor* (or by *either . . . or* or *neither . . . nor*), the verb always agrees with the subject nearer the verb.

PLURAL   *Either* the **violinists** *or* the **cellists** **need practice**.

Either **Pedro's father** *or* his **sisters** **are listening**.

Neither the **adult** *nor* the **children** **listen**.

SINGULAR   *Neither* the **violinists** *nor* the **cellist** **needs practice**.

Either the **adult** *or* the **child** **is listening**.

Neither the **adults** *nor* the **child** **listens**.

Many a, Every, and *Each* with Compound Subjects

When *many a, every,* or *each* precedes a compound subject, the subject is considered singular.

SINGULAR   *Many a* **cook** *and* **waiter** **works** late.

Every **man, woman,** *and* **child** **was** safe.

Each **adult** *and* **child** **is listening**.

Each **father** *and* **son** **enjoys** the dinner.

16.6 Intervening Expressions

Intervening expressions such as *accompanied by, as well as, in addition to, plus,* and *together with* introduce phrases that modify the subject without changing its number. These expressions do not create compound subjects even though their meaning is similar to that of the conjunction *and.*

■ If a singular subject is linked to another noun by an intervening expression, such as *accompanied by,* the subject is still considered singular.

SINGULAR	The **actress,** *accompanied* by her boyfriend, **attends** the benefit.
	Loyalty, *in addition to* common interests, **is** necessary for a lasting friendship.
	The **cook,** *as well as* the waiter, **works** hard at that restaurant.
	Deep in the jungle the **tigress,** *together with* her cubs, **is resting** quietly.

Exercise 9 Making Verbs Agree with Their Subjects

On your paper, write the simple subject of each of the following sentences, and write the appropriate form of the verb in parentheses.

Kitchen Utensils

1. Every chef and gourmet cook (knows, know) the importance of the appropriate kitchen implements.
2. Preparation and service often (depends, depend) upon conveniently placed, high-quality cookware.
3. Many an inexperienced cook and homemaker (needs, need) advice from established cooks about the best brands of utensils.
4. Ham and eggs (is, are) fairly simple to prepare with nothing more than a frying pan and a fork.
5. A food processor, often accompanied by a wide variety of handy accessories, (makes, make) everything from juices to garnishes.
6. For carving meats, a fork and a sharp knife (is, are) essential for smooth, even slices.
7. A kitchen scale, together with measuring cups of various standard sizes, (promotes, promote) accuracy.
8. A strainer, plus colanders of different sizes, (sifts, sift) flour.
9. Many a lover of fudge or boiled eggs (finds, find) a timer or stopwatch not only handy but indispensable.
10. A grater and a blender (is, are) useful for making delicious soups and sauces quickly and efficiently.

Exercise 10   **Creating Sentences with Compound Subjects**

Write ten sentences, each using one of the following items as the compound subject. Make the compound subject agree with a present-tense verb.

1. ham and cheese
2. neither the CD nor the tape
3. both the radio and the television
4. Cousin Jaime or my grandmother
5. many a bird and beast
6. the mother, together with her children,
7. either the lawns or the hedge
8. bacon and sausage
9. every teacher and coach
10. both seniors and juniors

Exercise 11   **Subject-Verb Agreement**

On your paper, write the form of the verb that agrees with the subject in each sentence.

New York, New York

1. You may travel all over the world, but a city with the many diverse attractions of New York (is/are) still rare.
2. The individual neighborhoods of this cosmopolitan city (contains/contain) a wide variety of restaurants, shops, and museums.
3. The sounds of Little Italy, with its festivals and friendly spirit, (fills/fill) the air.
4. An interesting place to visit (is/are) the streets of Chinatown, one of the largest Chinese communities outside Asia.
5. The variety of art styles in Soho (seems/seem) rich indeed.
6. Soho's granite and cast-iron buildings, dating mostly from the nineteenth century and the first decades of the twentieth, (is/are) an example of handsome urban architecture.
7. Among the city's successful urban redevelopment projects (is/are) the South Street Seaport Museum.
8. Here (is/are) eleven blocks of maritime history.
9. Among the marvels of New York Harbor (stands/stand) the Statue of Liberty.
10. Our drama club (visits/visit) New York as a group every year.
11. Fifty cents (was/were) not too much to pay for a ride on the Staten Island Ferry, yet the fare has been eliminated.
12. Neither my friends nor my family (shares/share) my fascination with subway maps.
13. Many a tourist (takes/take) the elevator to the 102nd floor of the Empire State Building.
14. Each store front and apartment building on this block of Chelsea (has/have) been restored.
15. Times Square, in addition to Rockefeller Center, (attracts/attract) millions of tourists each year.
16. A group of Dutch colonial buildings, along with other old structures, (stands/stand) near the financial district.
17. The Metropolitan Opera, as well as the New York City Ballet, (performs/perform) at Lincoln Center.
18. An attraction of the Upper West Side (is/are) the new and diverse restaurants there.
19. Every tourist and resident (is/are) well served by the open spaces of Central Park.
20. America's financial center and fashion and theater capital (is/are) New York.

16.7 Indefinite Pronouns as Subjects

■ A verb must agree in number with an indefinite pronoun subject.

Indefinite pronouns generally fall into three groups.

Indefinite Pronouns			
Always Singular			
each	everyone	nobody	anything
either	everybody	nothing	someone
neither	everything	anyone	somebody
one	no one	anybody	something
much			
Always Plural			
several	few	both	many
Singular or Plural			
some	all	most	none
any	enough	more	plenty

SINGULAR	***Everyone* wants** a ticket to the concert.
	No one in the group **seems** eager to leave.
	Does *anything* in the chapter **confuse** you?
PLURAL	***Many*** of the best runners **eat** pasta the night before a race.
	Few of us **believe** in magic.
	Are *several* of your friends musicians?

As you can see from the preceding chart, certain indefinite pronouns can be either singular or plural, depending upon the nouns to which they refer.

SINGULAR	***Some*** of his music **was** quite sophisticated. [*Some* refers to *music*, a singular noun.]
PLURAL	***Some*** of his songs **were** fun to sing. [*Some* refers to *songs*, a plural noun.]
SINGULAR	***Most*** of the house **was** painted white. [*Most* refers to *house*, a singular noun.]
PLURAL	***Most*** of the rooms **were** spacious and airy. [*Most* refers to *rooms*, a plural noun.]

Exercise 12   Correcting Errors in Subject-Verb Agreement

Rewrite the sentences below, correcting any errors in subject-verb agreement. If a sentence is correct, write *Correct*.

1. Everybody in our class are expected to present a ten-minute report on an American writer.
2. Most of my friends has chosen a novelist or a poet as the subject for their presentations.
3. After every report, anyone are free to make comments or pose questions during the discussion period.
4. When my turn came to choose a subject, I found that both of my favorite writers, Frederick Douglass and Carl Sandburg, were already taken.
5. Each of these authors seem popular with other students in my class.
6. Many of the choices was still available, however, and I selected Eudora Welty.
7. Much of Welty's fiction, like that of her fellow novelist William Faulkner, are set in her native Mississippi.
8. Several of the writers who will be subjects for reports is unfamiliar to me, and I am looking forward to learning more about these authors.
9. Most of Raul's report, for example, discuss the poetry of Sylvia Plath.
10. When enough of my notes suggests a thesis for my paper, I'll begin to write a rough draft.

Exercise 13   Making Verbs Agree with Indefinite Pronoun Subjects

Write ten sentences, each using one of the following indefinite pronouns as the subject. Make each subject agree with a present-tense verb.

SAMPLE   several
ANSWER   Several of the students play piano.

1. everyone
2. many
3. one
4. everything
5. each

6. few
7. anyone
8. both
9. neither
10. something

Exercise 14   Creating Sentences with Indefinite Pronoun Subjects

For each indefinite pronoun listed below, write two sentences. Use the pronoun as the subject of both sentences. In the first sentence of each pair, use a singular present-tense verb. In the second sentence, use a plural present-tense verb.

SAMPLE   Most
ANSWER   Most of the water rushes through the canyon.
                Most of the rocks show the smoothing effect of the rushing water.

1. some
2. all
3. any

4. most
5. none

16.8 | Agreement in Adjective Clauses

■ When the subject of an adjective clause is a relative pronoun, the verb in the clause must agree with the antecedent of the relative pronoun.

The subject of an adjective clause is often a relative pronoun. The number of the relative pronoun is determined by the number of its antecedent in the main clause.

> The Mexican grizzly is one of the **bears that were thought to be extinct.**

In the preceding example the antecedent of *that* is *bears,* not *one,* because *all* the bears, not just the Mexican grizzly, are thought to be extinct. Since *bears* is plural, *that* is considered plural, and the verb in the adjective clause, *were,* must also be plural.

> The whalebone whale is the only **one** of the whales **that has two rows of baleen (whalebone) instead of teeth.**

In this example the antecedent of *that* is *one,* not *whales,* because only one kind of whale (the whalebone whale) has two rows of baleen. Since *one* is singular, *that* is considered singular, and the verb in the adjective clause, *has,* must also be singular.

If the expression *one of* appears in the main clause, you must take care to determine whether the antecedent of the relative pronoun is *one,* as in the second example above, or whether it is the following noun, such as *bears* in the first example. When *one of* is modified by *the only,* as in the example about the whales, the antecedent of the relative pronoun is *one.*

Exercise 15 | Making Subjects and Verbs Agree in Adjective Clauses

On your paper, write the correct form of the verb in parentheses.

1. The Asian tree shrew is one of the mammals that (is/are) difficult to classify.
2. Charlotte Brontë was the only one of the Reverend Patrick Brontë's daughters who (was/were) married.
3. Celia Thaxter was one of the few nineteenth-century American poets who (was/were) better known then than now.
4. Rocky Mountain spotted fever is one of the diseases that (is/are) spread by ticks.
5. Mark McGwire was the only one of the professional baseball players who (was/were) able to hit seventy home runs in 1998.
6. Gloria Estefan is one of the contemporary music stars who (has/have) successfully combined pop and Latin rhythms.
7. In 1986 Dwight Gooden became the only one of the major-league pitchers who (was/were) able to strike out at least two hundred batters in each of his first three seasons.

(continued)

Subject-Verb Agreement

8. Cary Grant was one of the classic Hollywood film actors who (was/were) successful in both comic and dramatic roles.
9. Ella Fitzgerald was one of the great jazz singers of our time who (has/have) popularized scat singing.
10. Martha Graham was one of the innovative choreographers who (was/were) enormously influential in the development of modern dance.

| Exercise 16 | Using the Correct Verb Form |

For each sentence, write the correct form of the verb given in parentheses.

1. New York City is one of the nation's cities that _____ over six million inhabitants. (boast)
2. The lion is one of the few members of the cat family that _____ a social existence rather than a comparatively solitary lifestyle. (enjoy)
3. Quincy Jones is one of the American musicians who _____ received dozens of Grammy Awards. (have)
4. The sequoia seems to be the only tree name that _____ all five vowels in the alphabet. (contain)
5. The green flag of Libya is one of the few national ensigns that _____ only one color. (display)
6. Australia is the only one of the continents that _____ a large, diverse population of marsupials. (support)
7. Is the elusive Giant Panda one of the mammals that _____ hardest to study in the wild? (be)
8. Luciano Pavarotti is one of the few opera singers who _____ acquired superstar status on an international scale. (have)
9. During the 1930s, the clarinetist and band leader Benny Goodman was one of the few white musicians who _____ courageous enough to break the color line of segregation and perform side by side with black artists. (be)
10. The United Nations is one of the few international bodies that _____been successful in mediating disputes between nations. (have)
11. Isak Dinesen, the Danish writer whose real name was Karen Blixen, is one of the authors who vividly _____ the sights, sounds, and smells of East Africa. (describe)
12. Malayalam, the language of Kerala in southwestern India, is one of the words that _____ spelled the same way backward and forward and _____ called *palindromes*. (be)
13. Restaurants with postmodern décor and delicious menus are one of the many attractions that _____ tourists to San Francisco. (draw)
14. The Academy Awards is one of Hollywood's star-studded occasions that _____ to attract so many celebrities. (continue)
15. Saul Bellow is one of several American novelists who _____ won the Nobel Prize for Literature. (have)
16. Ostriches, cassowaries, and emus are among the few species of bird that _____ unable to fly. (be)

17. Israel, Great Britain, France, Turkey, and Sri Lanka are some of the countries in the world that _____ been led by female prime ministers. (have)
18. A kite is one of the few birds of prey that _____ able to hover in the air like a helicopter. (be)
19. Is Spencer Tracy the only star who _____ been awarded an Oscar for best actor in two consecutive years? (have)
20. Costa Rica is one of the countries in the world that _____ set aside a large proportion of land for conservation. (have)
21. Sara is the only person I know who _____ stewed tomatoes. (like)
22. She is one of those people who _____ all kinds of food. (like)
23. Bud is one of those boys who always _____ too loudly. (talk)
24. He is the only boy in the class who _____ to everyone. (talk)
25. The Ruizes are the only people on our street who _____ a pink house. (have)

Exercise 17   **Review: Subject-Verb Agreement**

Read each sentence below, correcting errors in subject-verb agreement. If a sentence is correct, write *correct*.

Puerto Rican Celebrations

1. Puerto Rico, along with many other Caribbean islands, reflect a varied cultural heritage in national and local celebrations.
2. Among the most popular of the Puerto Rican celebrations are Le Lo Lai, a year-round festival that celebrates Puerto Rico's Indian, Spanish, and African heritage.
3. Every man, woman, and child visiting Puerto Rico find some event to enjoy during this celebration.
4. One major tradition handed down from the Spanish culture is the fiestas, or religious festivals, that celebrates each town's patron saint.
5. The music, dancing, parades, and partying connected with a fiesta lasts from one to three days.
6. At these fiestas, many a tourist and resident join in dancing late into the night.
7. My family always enjoys the lively spirits and good food found at Puerto Rican fiestas.
8. One of these fiestas, the festival of San Francisco de Asis, take place in the town of Loíza Aldea.
9. Masks and costumes have been a part of this particular celebration since it originated in Spain.
10. There is also seventy-five to eighty other fiestas celebrated in towns across the island.
11. Twelve days is the traditional length of the Christmas celebration in Puerto Rico.
12. Three Kings' Day (January 6), as well as Christmas Day, is celebrated with feasting and gift giving.
13. Some of the more recent Puerto Rican celebrations includes those associated with national holidays, such as Constitution Day, Luís Muñoz Rivera's Birthday, and Día de la Raza, or Heritage Day.
14. Muñoz Rivera is one of the few Puerto Rican statesmen who is honored with a national holiday.
15. Do these descriptions make you want to attend a Puerto Rican celebration?

Grammar Review

SUBJECT-VERB AGREEMENT

The Country of the Pointed Firs, a novel by Sarah Orne Jewett, is one woman's reflection on a summer spent in a Maine seaside village called Dunnet Landing. In this passage, annotated to show examples of subject-verb agreement covered in this unit, the woman says farewell to the place she has come to love.

An inverted sentence introduced by *there* showing agreement between the singular noun subject, *hour,* and a singular past form of *be*

An inverted sentence introduced by a prepositional phrase showing agreement between the plural noun subject, *houses,* and the plural past form of *be*

Literature Model

from The Country of the Pointed Firs
by Sarah Orne Jewett

There **was** still an **hour** to wait, and I went up to the hill just above the schoolhouse and sat there thinking of things, and looking off to sea, and watching for the boat to come in sight. I could see Green Island, small and darkly wooded at that distance; below me **were** the **houses** of the village with their apple-trees and bits of garden ground. Presently, as I looked at the pastures beyond, I caught a last glimpse of Mrs. Todd herself, walking slowly in the footpath that led along, following the shore toward the Port. At such a distance, one can feel the large, positive qualities that control a character. Close at hand, Mrs. Todd seemed able and warm-hearted and quite absorbed in her bustling industries, but her distant figure looked mateless and appealing, with something about it that was strangely self-possessed and mysterious. Now and then she stooped to pick something—it might have been her favorite pennyroyal—and at last I lost sight of her as she slowly crossed an open space on one of the higher points of land, and disappeared again behind a dark clump of juniper and the pointed firs.

As I came away on the little coastwise steamer, there was an old sea running which made the surf leap high on all the rocky shores. I stood on deck, looking back, and watched the busy gulls agree and turn, and sway together down the long slopes of air, then separate hastily and plunge into the waves. . . . The little town, with the tall masts of its disabled schooners in the inner bay, stood high above the flat sea for a few minutes, then it sank back into the uniformity of the coast, and became indistinguishable from the other towns that looked as if they were crumbled on the furzy-green stoniness of the shore.

The small outer islands of the bay were covered among the ledges with turf that looked as fresh as the early grass; there had been some days of rain the week before, and the darker green of the sweet-fern was scattered on all the pasture heights. It looked like the beginning of summer ashore, though the sheep, round and warm in their winter wool, betrayed the season of the year as they went feeding along the slopes in the low afternoon sunshine. Presently the wind began to blow, and we struck out seaward to double the long sheltering headland of the cape, and when I looked back again, the islands and the headland had run together and Dunnet Landing and all its coasts were lost to sight.

> Agreement between the plural noun subject, *islands,* and the plural past form of *be;* the intervening prepositional phrase, *of the bay,* does not change the number of the subject.

> Agreement between a compound subject, *Dunnet Landing* and *coasts,* and the plural past form of *be*

| Review: Exercise 1 | Making Subjects and Verbs Agree When Prepositional Phrases Intervene |

Each of the following sentences describes the scene from the passage from *The Country of the Pointed Firs.* Rewrite each sentence on your paper, following the directions in parentheses. In some cases, you will need to change the form of the verb to make the sentence correct; in other cases, the verb will remain the same.

SAMPLE   The magical time of summer is ending. (Change *time* to *times.*)
ANSWER   The magical times of summer are ending.

1. The summer visitor to Maine is departing. (Change *visitor* to *visitors.*)
2. Waiting for the steamer, a woman with a suitcase stands on the wharf. (Change *a suitcase* to *suitcases.*)
3. The houses with the apple trees are especially attractive. (Change *houses* to *house.*)
4. Above the houses, a gentle hill provides a perfect view. (Move the prepositional phrase so that it comes directly after the subject.)
5. The pastures beyond the houses are visible from the hill. (Change *pastures* to *pasture.*)
6. A walker on the path moves slowly out of sight behind a dark clump of trees. (Change *A walker* to *Walkers.*)
7. Chugging sounds from the rippling waters announce the arrival of the steamer. (Change *waters* to *water.*)
8. The surf on the rocky shore leaps high, shooting spray and salt into the air. (Change *shore* to *shores.*)
9. Near the boat, hungry gulls fly noisily back and forth. (Move the prepositional phrase so that it comes directly after the subject.)
10. On a small outer island, woolly sheep on the hills graze lazily. (Change *hills* to *hill.*)

Subject-Verb Agreement

Grammar Review

Review: Exercise 2 — Making Linking Verbs Agree with Their Subjects

The following sentences describe Sarah Orne Jewett's writing. Rewrite each sentence, following the directions in parentheses. If necessary, change the form of the linking verb.

SAMPLE   Jewett's portraits of Maine are treasures. (Change *treasures* to *a treasure.*)
ANSWER   Jewett's portraits of Maine are a treasure.

1. The most important elements in Jewett's stories and books are her characters. (Change *elements* to *element.*)
2. Jewett's best work is a collection of character sketches. (Change *a collection* to *several collections.*)
3. These engaging sketches have become records of a disappearing culture. (Change *records* to *a record.*)
4. The character depiction in *The Country of the Pointed Firs* is masterful. (Change *depiction* to *depictions.*)
5. Her favorite subject is the picturesque villager of coastal Maine. (Change *villager* to *villagers.*)
6. An observer from the outside world frequently appears in Jewett's writing. (Change *An observer* to *Observers.*)
7. In *The Country of the Pointed Firs,* the subject is the reaction of a summer visitor. (Change *reaction* to *reactions.*)
8. The most interesting aspects of the book are the visitor's observations about the residents of Dunnet Landing. (Change *aspects* to *aspect.*)
9. Such small coastal villages are becoming relics of the past. (Change *relics* to *a relic.*)
10. The provincial life of Dunnet Landing remains a reality only in Jewett's book. (Change *life* to *ways.*)

Review: Exercise 3 — Making Subjects and Verbs Agree in Inverted Sentences

Each of the following sentences is based on an idea suggested by the passage from *The Country of the Pointed Firs.* First, write each sentence on your paper, choosing the proper form of the verb in parentheses. Then rewrite each of your sentences in inverted order, making adjustments to the form of the verb if necessary.

SAMPLE   The ships (was/were) beside me on the wharf.
ANSWER   The ships were beside me on the wharf.
                  Beside me on the wharf were the ships.

1. The village buildings (clusters/cluster) near the sea.
2. A gentle hill (rises/rise) above the houses.
3. Green pastures (stretches/stretch) beyond the village.
4. The little steamer (sails/sail) on the clear blue waters.
5. Sad farewells (comes/come) with summer's end.

Review: Exercise 4 — Making Verbs Agree with Compound Subjects

On your paper, rewrite each sentence, following the directions in parentheses and making any necessary adjustments to the form of the verb.

1. The Maine coast is the setting for the novel. (Add *and a small village* to the complete subject.)
2. The town and its people are described by an unidentified summer visitor. (Delete *and its people* from the complete subject.)
3. Her landlady, Mrs. Todd, and a sea captain tell charming tales. (Delete *and a sea captain* from the complete subject.)
4. Every adult in the town tells interesting stories. (Add *and child* to the complete subject.)
5. Each story adds to the reader's appreciation of these characters. (Add *and remembrance* to the complete subject.)

Review: Exercise 5 — Making Verbs Agree with Indefinite Pronoun Subjects

Rewrite each sentence, replacing the indefinite pronoun in italics with the pronoun in parentheses. If necessary, change the number of the verb.

1. *Several* in the group watch the sunrise from Cadillac Mountain. (No one)
2. *Everybody* strolls along the carriage trails. (Many)
3. *Some* of the shoreline is edged with pinkish rocks. (Most)
4. *One* of the boats pulls up lobster traps. (Some)
5. *None* of the lobsters in the trap are undersized. (Each)

Review: Exercise 6

Proofreading

The following passage describes the artist Edward Hopper, whose work appears on the next page. Rewrite the passage, correcting the errors in spelling, grammar, and usage. Add any missing punctuation. There are ten errors.

Edward Hopper

¹Edward Hopper (1882–1967) was born in Nyack a town twenty-five miles north of New York City. ²By the time he was a teenager, he has developed a keen interest in art. ³When he was seventeen, he enrolled in the New York School of Art, where painting and illustration was his main feilds of study.

⁴Hopper first made a living as a magazine illustrator, but oil painting, along with the New England coast, were his real love. ⁵Hopper took the advice of his art teachers and paints scenes of New England life. ⁶Many a cityscape and seascape appear in his work.

(continued)

⁷Much of Hopper's work contrast vivid colors and dramatic lighting with a moody, subdued scene. ⁸He was one of a number of artists who was skilled at painting lonely, melancholy figures. ⁹Like the woman in *The Country of the Pointed Firs,* the woman in Hopper's painting survey the view from her window.

Edward Hopper, *Cape Cod Morning,* **1950**

Review: Exercise 7

Mixed Review

The following sentences describe the life of Sarah Orne Jewett. For each sentence, write the appropriate form of the verb in parentheses.

Sarah Orne Jewett

1. Among highly regarded American regional writers (is/are) Sarah Orne Jewett.
2. Neither Jewett's verses nor her tales for children (is/are) as well known as her sketches about provincial life.
3. One of her favorite activities as a child (was/were) to accompany her father, a physician, on his rounds.
4. From this early experience (comes/come) Jewett's portrayals of rural characters.
5. Many a Midwesterner and Southerner (has/have) learned about Maine from Jewett's works.

Writing Application

TIME

For more about the writing process, see **TIME Facing the Blank Page,** pp. 111–121.

Subject-Verb Agreement in Writing

Carefully study the following brief extracts from literary works, noting the agreement between subjects and verbs in italics.

1 A long black *column* of bats *looks* like a tornado spinning far out across the Texas sky.
From "Bats" by Diane Ackerman

2 From the fertile fields of Rota, particularly its gardens, *come* the *fruits* and *vegetables* that fill the markets of Huelva and Seville.
From "The Stub-Book" by Pedro Antonio de Alarcón

3 Upon the rebel this *crowd stares,* and the rebel stares back.
From "The Splendid Outcast" by Beryl Markham

The *mass* of men *lead* lives of quiet desperation.
From *Walden* by Henry David Thoreau

4 . . . What though the field be lost? *All is* not lost . . .
From *Paradise Lost* by John Milton

All are gone, the old familiar faces.
From "The Old Familiar Faces" by Charles Lamb

Techniques with Subject-Verb Agreement

When revising your work, always check for correct subject-verb agreement. Keep these guidelines in mind.

1 When a prepositional phrase or another expression falls between a subject and its verb, mentally block out the intervening material when checking for agreement.

2 Remember that a sentence is in inverted order when the subject follows the verb.

3 When the subject is a collective noun, decide whether the noun refers to the group as a whole or to each member of the group individually. The former case is singular; the latter case is plural.

4 When the subject is an indefinite pronoun that can be either singular or plural, decide whether the pronoun refers to a single entity or to several individual entities.

Practice Apply these guidelines in revising the following paragraph. Make your revision on your own paper, and be sure to check for subject-verb agreement.

Cornfields in my part of rural Pennsylvania is plowed in spring. In the newly turned earth occasionally appears arrowheads, scrapers, and spear points once used by Native American groups who inhabited the area. Some of the objects comes from many centuries ago; some was carved more recently. The best stones for carving is made of flint or a similar hard but neatly flaking substance. Most arrowheads and other artifacts found today show some damage, since damaged tools and weapons were usually discarded. Near the shores of a local stream sit a cornfield where the Delaware once camped. The Delaware no longer lives in the area, but some of their history remains recorded in the earth's surface.

Using Pronouns Correctly

17.1 Case of Personal Pronouns

- Pronouns that are used to refer to persons or things are called **personal** pronouns.
- Personal pronouns have three **cases**, or forms, called **nominative**, **objective**, and **possessive**. The case of a personal pronoun depends upon the pronoun's function in a sentence (whether it is a subject, a complement, an object of a preposition, or a replacement for a possessive noun).

Personal Pronouns			
CASE	**SINGULAR PRONOUNS**	**PLURAL PRONOUNS**	**FUNCTION IN SENTENCE**
NOMINATIVE	I, you, she, he, it	we, you, they	subject or predicate nominative
OBJECTIVE	me, you, her, him, it	us, you, them	direct object, indirect object, or object of preposition
POSSESSIVE	my, mine, your, yours, her, hers, his, its	our, ours, your, yours, their, theirs	replacement for possessive noun(s)

You can avoid errors in choosing the case of personal pronouns if you keep the following rules in mind:

1. For a personal pronoun in a compound subject, use the nominative case.
   Gloria and **I** repaired the fence.   **She** and Julius fixed the gate.
   He and **I** mowed the lawn.

2. For a personal pronoun in a compound object, use the objective case.
   Samuel brought Julius and **me** some lemonade.
   Gary refused to tell **them** and Morgan.

Hint: A good way to check for pronoun errors in compound subjects or objects, is to drop the conjunction and the other subject or object. Does the sentence sound correct?

Chris and (me or I?) went bowling last night.
Say to yourself: Me went bowling last night.
I went bowling last night.

3. Use the nominative case of a personal pronoun after a form of the linking verb *be.*

The most skillful gardener was **he.**

Gloria said that the best supervisor was **I.**

I said that the best gardeners were **they.**

The most respected store manager is **she.**

The silliest students are **we.**

This rule is now changing, especially in informal speech. When speaking informally, people often use the objective case after a form of the linking verb *be;* they say, *It's me* or *It was him.* Some authorities suggest using the objective case in informal writing as well, to avoid sounding pretentious. To be strictly correct, however, you should use the nominative case after forms of *be,* especially in your writing.

4. Do not spell possessive pronouns with an apostrophe.

The lawnmower is **hers.**   The rake is **theirs.**

The lawn is **ours.**   The hedgecutter is **yours.**

It's is a contraction of *it is.* Be careful not to confuse *it's* with the possessive pronoun *its.*

It's her book.   ***Its*** cover is torn.

5. Use a possessive pronoun before a gerund (*-ing* forms used as nouns).

Your working late will be helpful.

We were grateful for **his** playing the piano.

Our singing didn't seem to bother the neighbors.

The shy little boy enjoyed **my** talking to him.

Her hammering disturbed the landlord.

Exercise 1   Identifying Forms of Pronouns

Write the pronouns contained in each sentence. Identify each as *singular* or *plural* and as *nominative, objective,* or *possessive.*

SAMPLE   Leonard Bernstein was the first professional musician in his family.
ANSWER   his—singular possessive

1. Leonard Bernstein learned to play the piano when he was ten.
2. His piano teacher likely encouraged him to become a great pianist.
3. Leonard's father had ambitions for his son to enter the family business, but Leonard had a different idea.
4. In 1943 the New York Philharmonic Orchestra acquired its new assistant conductor: twenty-five-year-old Leonard Bernstein.
5. Among his many talents was the ability to teach difficult music concepts and make them seem simple.

Exercise 2 — Choosing the Correct Case Form

For each of the following sentences, choose the correct personal pronoun from each pair in parentheses.

1. Since Carlos wanted to report on a contemporary West Indian author, (he/him) and (I/me) decided to write about Jamaica Kincaid, who grew up in Antigua.
2. It was (she/her) who wrote *At the Bottom of the River, Annie John,* and *Lucy*—three autobiographical novels about her childhood.
3. (Its/It's) the author's childhood experiences in Antigua that provide the background for each book.
4. (She/Her) and her mother had a very close relationship until Jamaica was nine, when the first of her three brothers was born.
5. What excites Carlos and (I/me) about Kincaid is that lyrical, highly poetic writing style of (hers/her's).
6. An article about Kincaid described for Carlos and (I/me) her move to New York at the age of sixteen to work as an au pair, or live-in housekeeper and baby-sitter.
7. Many interesting facts came to light as a result of (me/my) reading Kincaid's novel *Lucy,* which describes this period of her life.
8. After Kincaid became good friends with George Trow, a writer for the *New Yorker,* (he/him) and (she/her) attended a West Indian Day parade in Brooklyn.
9. It was (I/me) who found Kincaid's first *Talk of the Town* essay, a discovery that was helpful to Carlos and (I/me).
10. Kincaid's career as a staff writer for this highly respected magazine got (its/it's) start with the publication of this article.

Exercise 3 — Using Correct Pronouns in Sentences

Replace each italicized noun with an appropriate pronoun.

SAMPLE George Washington owes *George Washington's* life to the daughter of a tavern keeper.

ANSWER his

1. Thomas Hickey, a member of the guard protecting Washington, plotted to kill *Washington* with poison.
2. *Thomas Hickey* befriended young Phoebe Fraunces, who was Washington's housekeeper in New York.
3. Hickey gave *Fraunces* green peas to serve to Washington at dinner—peas that Hickey had poisoned.
4. Hickey believed Fraunces would be an unknowing participant in the plot when *Fraunces* served Washington his dinner.
5. However, Fraunces apparently was suspicious of *Hickey's* actions.
6. Instead of serving the poisoned peas to the general, Fraunces threw *the peas* to the chickens in the yard.
7. Even though some of the chickens died from Hickey's peas, *Hickey* managed to escape.
8. Later in 1776, the Americans jailed *Hickey* for trying to pass counterfeit notes.
9. While Hickey was in jail, *Hickey* talked about his failed plot to kill General Washington.
10. The army had *the army's* own way of punishing treason in those days, and Hickey was executed on June 28, 1776.

17.2 Pronouns with and as Appositives

■ Use the nominative case for a pronoun that is in apposition to a subject or a predicate nominative.

The first contestants, **she** and **Ramón,** debated well.
[*Contestants* is the subject.]

They were the runners-up, **Ramón** and **she.**
[*Runners-up* is the predicate nominative.]

■ Use the objective case for a pronoun that is in apposition to a direct object, an indirect object, or an object of a preposition.

The principal congratulated the winners, **Shiro** and **her.**
[*Winners* is the direct object.]

The judge gave the funniest speakers, **Tom** and **her,** a special award.
[*Speakers* is the indirect object.]

He had some good words for the scorers, **Grace** and **me.**
[*Scorers* is the object of the preposition *for.*]

■ When a pronoun is followed by an appositive, choose the case of the pronoun that would be correct if the appositive were omitted.

We sisters love skiing. [*We* is the correct form because *we* is the subject of the sentence.]

Uncle Paul gave **us sisters** a set of skis. [*Us* is the correct form because *us* is the indirect object.]

Hint: To choose the correct pronoun, say the sentence aloud without the noun.

Exercise 4   Using Pronouns and Appositives in Sentences

Write an original sentence using the appositives indicated.

SAMPLE   subject: *applicants*; words in apposition: *George and I*
ANSWER   The only applicants, George and I, were asked to return the next day.

1. direct object: *guests*; words in apposition: *Jack and me*
2. indirect object: *heroes*; words in apposition: *Miller and her*
3. object of a preposition: *teachers*; words in apposition: *Mr. Lotus and him*
4. subject: *students*; words in apposition: *she and Larry*
5. predicate nominative: *losers*; words in apposition: *Wilma and I*

Exercise 5   Using Pronouns Correctly with and as Appositives

For each of the following sentences, choose the correct personal pronoun from the pair in parentheses.

SAMPLE   The only English majors in our class, Ken and (I/me), look forward to our next unit on the origin of newspapers.

ANSWER   I

Early Newspapers

1. (We/Us) student journalists have little sense of the history of the newspaper.
2. Our English and journalism teachers, Mr. Gonzalez and (she/her), assigned a joint report on the history of the newspaper industry.
3. It came as a surprise to (we/us) students to learn that the modern newspaper has its roots in an ancient Roman publication *Acta diurna*, which was posted every day.
4. It was the members of our research group—Jolie, Casey, and (I/me)—who reported on the importance of printing in the development of the modern newspaper.
5. Before the invention of printing, news was disseminated orally or by letters, a fact that fascinated (we/us) researchers.
6. It was two friends from another school, Tomoko Mizumoto and (he/him), who told us that the earliest printed newspapers were really just published newsletters.
7. A reference book found for us by those two librarians, Mr. Biello and (she/her), said that the first modern newspaper was the *Avisa Relation oder Zeitung*, published in Germany in 1609.
8. (We/Us) Americans were surprised to learn that the first newspaper in the colonies was *Publick Occurrences, Both Foreign and Domestick*, which was published in Boston as early as 1690.
9. My uncle, a reporter for his village paper, gave (we/us) researchers a pamphlet on the history of newspaper journalism.
10. Two people knowledgeable about publishing, (he/him) and Mr. Gonzalez, said we had collected valuable information for our report.

Exercise 6   Using Pronouns Correctly with and as Appositives

For each sentence in the following paragraph, choose the correct pronoun from the pair in parentheses.

Oscar Arias Sánchez, Spokesperson for Peace

[1]In the History Club's discussion of peace in Central America, the first speakers were two classmates, Kareem and (she/her). [2]After praising the stabilizing influence of the former Costa Rican president Oscar Arias Sánchez, they introduced the next two speakers, Manuel and (I/me). [3]First, we informed everyone in the audience, fellow club members and (they/ them), of Dr. Arias Sánchez's impressive academic career. [4]Then (we/us) enthusiasts elaborated on Dr. Arias Sánchez's efforts to restore economic stability in Costa Rica and to serve as a peace-maker in Central America. [5]All present, (they/them) and (we/us), agreed that Dr. Arias Sánchez was a worthy recipient of the 1987 Nobel Peace Prize.

17.3   Pronouns After *Than* and *As*

In an elliptical clause, some words have been omitted but are understood. An elliptical adverb clause often begins with *than* or *as*. For the pronoun following *than* or *as*, choose the case of the pronoun that you would use if the missing words were fully expressed.

> They arrived at the party earlier than **she.** [The nominative pronoun *she* is the subject in the complete adverb clause *than she arrived.*]
>
> The play amused our guests as much as **us.** [The objective pronoun *us* is the direct object in the complete adverb clause *as much as it amused us.*]

Exercise 7   Using Pronouns After *Than* and *As*

Expand each of the following expressions into a complex sentence containing an elliptical adverb clause. End each sentence with a personal pronoun other than *you* or *it*.

SAMPLE   more delighted than
ANSWER   No one at the play reading was more delighted than he.

1. more helpful than
2. as attractive as
3. less amiable than
4. as athletic as
5. sterner than
6. as unusual as
7. sillier than
8. less disruptive than
9. more careless than
10. as quiet as

Exercise 8   Choosing the Correct Pronoun After *Than* and *As*

Choose the correct pronoun in each sentence.

SAMPLE   Lynn left for work later than (we, us).
ANSWER   we

Going to the Doctor

1. Margaret arrived for her appointment later than (he, him).
2. The examination upset Greg as much as (she, her).
3. The bill surprised the other patients as much as (he, him).
4. Doctor Juarez is unquestionably more knowledgeable than (they, them).
5. This receptionist responds less calmly than (she, her).
6. The medicine helped the Riveras as much as (we, us).
7. All of the patients were as tired of waiting as (I, me).
8. Filling out all the forms annoyed Mr. Douglas as much as (he, him).
9. After seeing the examination instruments, Dan felt as nervous as (we, us).
10. Richie understood the procedure better than (I, me).

Reflexive and Intensive Pronouns

Observe the following rules in the use of reflexive and intensive pronouns.

1. Use *himself* and *themselves*. Do not use *hisself* or *theirselves*; they are incorrect forms.

   Paul corrected the error **himself.**

   My parents **themselves** put out the fire.

2. Use a reflexive pronoun when a pronoun refers to the person who is the subject of the sentence.

INCORRECT	I bought ~~me~~ a book.
CORRECT	I bought **myself** a book.

INCORRECT	He found ~~him~~ a comfortable chair.
CORRECT	He found **himself** a comfortable chair.

3. Do not use a reflexive pronoun unnecessarily. Remember that a reflexive pronoun must refer to the person who is the subject.

INCORRECT	Elsa and ~~myself~~ are going to the mall.
CORRECT	Elsa and **I** are going to the mall.

INCORRECT	Carlos and ~~yourself~~ are invited to the performance on opening night.
CORRECT	Carlos and **you** are invited to the performance on opening night.

Exercise 9   **Correct Use of Reflexive and Intensive Pronouns**

On your paper, correct the underlined pronoun in each sentence. If the pronoun is correct, write *correct.*

Apartment Living

1. I finally found <u>me</u> an apartment I could afford.
2. My friends always make <u>theirselves</u> at home when they come to visit me.
3. The neighbors next door bought <u>themselves</u> a watchdog to deter any potential criminals from breaking into their apartment.
4. The tenant in the top floor apartment found <u>himself</u> locked out of his apartment.
5. The apartment manager and <u>myself</u> disagree about the condition of the hallways.
6. She has convinced <u>herself</u> that the tenants are responsible for maintaining the rugs throughout the hallways in the building.
7. The tenants <u>theirselves</u> have written to the owners complaining about the disagreement.
8. Jane and <u>myself</u> plan to attend a tenants association meeting at the end of next week.
9. I <u>myself</u> believe that such a meeting will have little or no effect.
10. Last week my neighbor found <u>hisself</u> vacuuming the rug in front of his apartment.

17.5 | *Who* and *Whom* in Questions and Subordinate Clauses

In questions, use *who* for subjects and *whom* for direct objects, indirect objects, and objects of a preposition.

> **Who** called me yesterday morning? [*Who* is the subject of the verb *called*.]
>
> **Whom** are you photographing? [*Whom* is the direct object of the verb *are photographing*.]
>
> To **whom** did you send the invitation? [*Whom* is the object of the preposition *to*.]

In questions with interrupting expressions, such as *did you say* or *do you think,* it is often helpful to drop the expression in order to determine whether to use *who* or *whom.*

> **Who** do you think will arrive first? [Think: *Who* will arrive first? *Who* is the subject of the verb *will arrive*.]

Use the nominative pronouns *who* and *whoever* for subjects and predicate nominatives in subordinate clauses.

> Tell me **who** is in charge here. [*Who* is the subject of the noun clause *who is in charge here*.]
>
> She knows **who** her supervisor is. [*Who* is the predicate nominative of the noun clause *who her supervisor is*.]
>
> The prize will be given to **whoever** deserves it. [*Whoever* is the subject of the noun clause *whoever deserves it*.]

Use the objective pronouns *whom* and *whomever* for direct objects, indirect objects, and objects of a preposition in subordinate clauses.

> They asked her **whom** she saw at the party. [*Whom* is the direct object of the verb *saw* in the clause *whom she saw at the party.*]
>
> Harding is a president about **whom** I know little. [*Whom* is the object of the preposition *about* in the adjective clause *about whom I know little.*]
>
> The winner will be **whomever** the people select. [*Whomever* is the direct object of the verb *select* in the noun clause *whomever the people select.*]

In informal speech, many people use *who* in place of *whom* in sentences such as *Who did you ask?* In writing and in formal speech, however, it is best to make the distinctions between *who* and *whom.*

Exercise 10   Using *Who* or *Whom* in Sentences

On your paper complete the passage below by filling each blank with *who* or *whom*.

Midori, a Prodigious Musical Talent

[1] _____ do you think the critics have hailed as one of the greatest talents in classical music in the last twenty years? [2]Midori, a young violinist born in Japan, has excited everyone _____ has heard her. [3]Taught by her mother, Setsu Goto, _____ was a professional violinist herself, Midori began playing a tiny violin when she was only three. [4]Dorothy DeLay, _____ musicians worldwide respect as a violin teacher, heard a tape recording of the young violinist and was instrumental in bringing the ten-year-old girl to New York to study at the Juilliard School of Music.

[5]The famous violinist Pinchas Zuckerman, _____ Midori impressed with her playing soon after her arrival in the United States, said that such artists come along only once or twice in a century. [6]During her first year at Juilliard, Midori was heard by the conductor of the New York Philharmonic Orchestra, Zubin Mehta, with _____ she played a brilliant concert on New Year's Eve. [7]_____ do you suppose was more thrilled that night—Midori or her audience? [8]Playing with the New York Philharmonic when she was fourteen, Midori broke a string; she then walked over to the concert master, _____ handed her another violin; she broke a string on that violin as well, and she finished the piece on a third instrument. [9]After this performance, critics knew _____ the next great musical star would be. [10]When I asked my grandparents _____ we were going to hear at the concert on Wednesday evening, I was excited to hear them respond with Midori's name.

Exercise 11   Choosing *Whoever* or *Whomever*

For each of the following sentences, choose the correct pronoun from the pair in parentheses.

> **SAMPLE**   In addition to talent, (whoever, whomever) chooses music as a professional career also requires determination.
>
> **ANSWER**   whoever

1. (Whoever/Whomever) performs best at the auditions will be offered a summer internship with the orchestra.
2. The orchestra will provide food, lodging, travel expenses, and master classes for (whoever/whomever) the judges choose.
3. The judges will consider (whoever/whomever) they feel is qualified.
4. (Whoever/Whomever) misses the Friday deadline, however, will have to wait another year.
5. The winner will be (whoever/whomever) has played the best.
6. The auditions will be worthwhile to (whoever/whomever) wins.
7. The music director will present a plaque to (whoever/ whomever) excels.
8. A reporter for our school newspaper will interview (whoever/whomever) she feels will be the most interesting subject for an article about the auditions.
9. Of course, an article will appear in the local newspaper about (whoever/whomever) the judges select.
10. The local newspaper will also photograph (whoever/whomever) wins the competition.

17.6 Pronoun-Antecedent Agreement

■ An **antecedent** is the word or group of words to which a pronoun refers. A pronoun must agree with its antecedent in number, gender, and person.

Agreement in Number and Gender

A pronoun must agree with its antecedent in number (singular or plural) and gender (masculine, feminine, or neuter).

A noun, another pronoun, or a phrase or clause acting as a noun may be the antecedent of a pronoun. In the examples that follow, the antecedents appear in boldface italic type and the pronouns appear in boldface type.

> *George Eliot* published **her** masterpiece, *Middlemarch*, in installments in 1871–1872. [singular feminine pronoun]
>
> Claude's *sisters* sailed **their** catamaran out on the bay. [plural pronoun]
>
> *I. M. Pei* constructed many of **his** innovative buildings in the Northeast. [singular masculine pronoun]
>
> Rita's *brothers* are respected in **their** business. [plural pronoun]
>
> We should consult this *magazine* for **its** comprehensive article on whales. [singular neuter pronoun]
>
> *Dogwoods* and *azaleas* are admired in spring for the beauty of **their** blossoms. [plural pronoun]

Traditionally, a masculine pronoun has been used when the gender of the antecedent is not known or when the antecedent may be either masculine or feminine.

> A good *diver* must practice **his** routines daily.

This usage has changed, however. Today many people prefer using gender-neutral language. If you wish to avoid using a masculine pronoun, you can usually reword your sentence in one of the following three ways: (1) by using *he or she, his or her,* and so forth, (2) by making both the antecedent and the pronoun a plural, or (3) by eliminating the pronoun altogether.

> A good *diver* must practice **his or her** routines daily.
>
> Good *divers* must practice **their** routines daily.
>
> Good *divers* must practice routines daily. [no pronoun]

Agreement with Collective Nouns

When the antecedent of a pronoun is a collective noun, the number of the pronoun depends upon whether the collective noun is meant to be singular or plural.

The **group** boarded **its** bus promptly at eight. [The collective noun *group* is being used in the singular sense of one unit of persons. Therefore, the singular pronoun *its* is used.]

The **group** bought **their** souvenirs before leaving. [The collective noun *group* is being used in the plural sense of several persons performing separate acts. Therefore, the plural pronoun *their* is used.]

The **orchestra** played **their** instruments with passion. [The collective noun *orchestra* is being used in the plural sense of several people performing separate actions. Therefore, the plural pronoun *their* is used.]

The **orchestra** gave **its** best performance. [The collective noun *orchestra* is being used in the singular sense of one single group of persons. Therefore, the singular pronoun *its* is used.]

Exercise 12   **Making Pronouns and Antecedents Agree**

On your paper, complete the following sentences by filling each blank with an appropriate possessive pronoun. Then write the antecedent of each pronoun that you supply.

1. Anyone who knows my friend Helen will understand _____ devotion to the theater.
2. In ninth grade Mr. Rodriguez, our English teacher, gave her a small part in one of _____ plays, and she performed the part brilliantly.
3. The entire cast showed _____ enthusiasm for Helen's performance by presenting her with a bouquet of roses on the last day of the show.
4. Since then both she and her boyfriend seem to spend all _____ free time in the theater, either acting or working backstage.
5. Helen has come to believe that an actor must take _____ profession seriously, and she has been studying acting every summer.
6. Helen has developed an interest in set design and lighting because of _____ impact on the overall effect of a performance.
7. The three of us have made drama the center of _____ extracurricular lives.
8. Helen prepares carefully for each of _____ roles so she can be true to the writer's intent.
9. We often noticed that the audience had diverse reactions to a performance and would loudly declare _____ opinions as soon as the curtain had fallen.
10. When I was recently offered the chance to direct a one-act play, I told Helen I would do it only if she agreed to be in _____ cast.

Exercise 13 **Making Pronouns and Antecedents Agree**

In each of the following sentences, find the personal possessive pronoun and its antecedent. Then revise the sentence to correct the problem in pronoun-antecedent agreement.

SAMPLE So much of the music in America has their roots in other cultures.
ANSWER So much of the music in America has its roots in other cultures.

1. A Texan of Mexican descent who enjoys dancing may count the *conjunto* and the *orquesta*, two styles of Tex-Mex music, among their favorite types of dance music.
2. Many people find the relaxed folk style and prominent accordion accompaniment of the *conjunto* to his liking.
3. Influenced by American swing, *orquesta* music is especially popular with the sophisticated city dweller who enjoys stylistic diversity in their music.
4. A student of popular music trying to discover who created the *orquesta* will find their answer in the person of Beto Villa, who made many popular recordings in the late 1940s.
5. Fans of Tex-Mex music and of Beto Villa may also count among his favorite performers Little Joe Hernández, who later revitalized the *orquesta* with infusions of American jazz and rock music.

Exercise 14 **Making Pronouns Agree with Collective Noun Antecedents**

On your paper, complete the following sentences by filling the blank with an appropriate possessive pronoun. Then write the antecedent of each pronoun that you supply.

SAMPLE Most lawyers prefer to meet _____ clients several times before the trial begins.
ANSWER their, lawyers

1. The defendant's family found _____ way to the courthouse easily.
2. A group of people left _____ cars in the parking lot behind the courthouse.
3. The audience in the courtroom expressed _____ opinion loudly and clearly.
4. The jury retired to determine _____ verdict.
5. The legal team beamed over _____ victory.
6. The defendant's family invited _____ friends to a victory party.
7. A class in criminal law wrote _____ term papers on different aspects of the case.
8. Soon a swarm of reporters told the world _____ exciting story.
9. A crew of photographers made _____ way through the crowd.
10. Later the crowd voiced _____ various opinions about the verdict.

Exercise 15 **Using Pronouns and Collective Nouns in Sentences**

Use each pair of words in a sentence. Be sure the collective noun is used so that the pronoun agrees with it.

1. family—its
2. crowd—their
3. team —its
4. class—their
5. jury—their

Agreement in Person

■ A pronoun must agree in person with its antecedent.

Do not use the second-person pronoun *you* to refer to an antecedent that is in the third person. In order to fix an error in which the second-person pronoun is misused in this way, either change *you* to an appropriate third-person pronoun or replace it with a suitable noun.

POOR	John and Angela are going to Ravenna, in northern Italy, where ~~you~~ can admire the Byzantine mosaics.
BETTER	John and Angela are going to Ravenna, in northern Italy, where **they** can admire the Byzantine mosaics.
BETTER	John and Angela are going to Ravenna, in northern Italy, where **tourists** can admire the Byzantine mosaics.

When the antecedent of a pronoun is another pronoun, be sure that the two pronouns agree in person. Do not illogically shift pronouns, as between *they* and *you*, *I* and *you*, and *one* and *you*.

POOR	**They** love to walk along the beach, where ~~you~~ can feel the salt spray.
BETTER	**They** love to walk along the beach, where **they** can feel the salt spray.
POOR	**I** went to Williamsburg, Virginia, where ~~you~~ can learn about life in colonial times.
BETTER	**I** went to Williamsburg, Virginia, where **I** learned about life in colonial times.

Exercise 16   Making Pronouns and Antecedents Agree in Person

Rewrite each of the following items, eliminating the inappropriate use of *you* by substituting a third-person pronoun or a suitable noun.

English Medieval Plays

1. Audiences watched English medieval plays outdoors, where you could enjoy the fine weather.
2. The spectators gathered in the streets and squares of the towns. You would often be celebrating a holiday.
3. Each guild provided actors for the plays. You would circulate through the town in a wagon, which would serve as a movable stage.
4. Residents of the towns of Wakefield, Chester, York, and Coventry were very fond of medieval plays. You might see many short dramas in the course of a single day.
5. This summer we will travel to England, where you can learn about the actors of long ago.

Agreement with Indefinite Pronoun Antecedents

In general, use a singular personal pronoun when the antecedent is a singular indefinite pronoun and use a plural personal pronoun when the antecedent is a plural indefinite pronoun. (See page 447 for a list of indefinite pronouns.)

Neither of the boys in our group wrote **his** own sonnet.

Each of the girls wrote **her** own speech.

Either of the girls can bring **her** parents.

One of the boys forgot **his** notes in the car.

Several of my friends presented **their** work.

Few of the speakers had practiced **their** speeches.

The plural nouns in the prepositional phrases—*of the boys*, *of the girls*, and so on—do not affect the number of the personal pronouns. *His* and *her* are singular because their antecedents, *neither*, *each*, *either*, and *one*, are singular. In informal speech, people often use the plural pronoun *their* in such sentences.

INFORMAL *Neither* of the boys presented **their** speeches.

Each of them decided on **their** own topic.

Either of the speakers can use **their** notes.

One of them decided not to use **their** notes.

When no gender is specified, use gender-neutral language.

Everyone should write **his or her** own research paper.

If you find the sentence above awkward, a better solution may be to reword the sentence. You might use a plural indefinite pronoun or a suitable noun (such as *people*) to replace the singular indefinite pronoun. You might even eliminate the personal pronoun entirely.

All the students should prepare **their** own preliminary outlines.

Everyone should prepare a preliminary outline. [no pronoun]

Many of the participants invited **their** friends to the show.

Each of the participants invited friends to the show.

17.7 | Clear Pronoun Reference

Make sure that the antecedent of a pronoun is clearly stated and that a pronoun cannot possibly refer to more than one antecedent.

Vague Pronoun Reference

You should not use the pronouns *this*, *that*, *which*, and *it* without a clearly stated antecedent.

VAGUE Gwendolyn Brooks is a talented and accomplished writer, and **this** is apparent from her poetry. [What is apparent from Brooks's poetry? Her writing ability is apparent, but *writing ability* is not specifically mentioned in the sentence.]

CLEAR Gwendolyn Brooks is a talented and accomplished writer, and **her writing ability** is apparent from her poetry.

VAGUE In 1906 many buildings in San Francisco burned, **which** was caused by the great earthquake of April 18. [What was caused by the earthquake? A fire was caused, but the word *fire* does not appear in the sentence.]

CLEAR In 1906 a fire, **which** was caused by the great earthquake of April 18, burned many buildings in San Francisco.

Exercise 17 | Correcting Vague Pronoun References

On your paper, rewrite each sentence so that the pronoun reference is clear.

Preventing Home Burglaries

1. The police checked the entrances and exits to see how the burglar entered the house, and then they discussed it with the homeowner.
2. In one town, burglary decreased by twenty-three percent, which was attributed to the installation of home burglar alarms.
3. Police give homeowners advice about preventing burglaries, but this often goes unheeded.
4. In one neighborhood, several homes on the same block were burglarized, which has been blamed on poor security.
5. Some people leave their valuables lying in open places; that has caused additional losses.

Using Pronouns Correctly

Ambiguous Pronoun Reference

If a pronoun seems to refer to more than one antecedent, either reword the sentence to make the antecedent clear or eliminate the pronoun.

UNCLEAR ANTECEDENT	When the large dogs approached the small cats, **they** were intimidated. [Which word is the antecedent of *they*? Were the dogs intimidated or the cats?]
CLEAR ANTECEDENT	The large dogs were intimidated when **they** approached the small cats.
NO PRONOUN	When the large dogs approached the small cats, **the dogs** were intimidated.
UNCLEAR ANTECEDENT	When Mr. Morris forbade Jason to take the algebra test, **he** was upset. [Which word is the antecedent of he? Is Mr. Morris upset or is Jason?]
CLEAR ANTECEDENT	Mr. Morris was upset when **he** forbade Jason to take the algebra test.
NO PRONOUN	When Mr. Morris forbade Jason to take the algebra test, **Mr. Morris** was upset.

Indefinite Use of Pronouns

The pronouns *you* and *they* should not be used as indefinite pronouns. Instead, you should name the performer of the action. In some cases, you may be able to reword the sentence in such a way that you do not name the performer of the action and you do not use a pronoun.

INDEFINITE	When the national anthem is played at a baseball game, **you** should rise.
CLEAR	When the national anthem is played at a baseball game, **the crowd** should rise.
INDEFINITE	In some neighborhoods, **they** pick up the garbage twice a week.
CLEAR	In some neighborhoods, **the sanitation department** picks up the garbage twice a week.
CLEAR	In some neighborhoods, the garbage **is picked up** twice a week.

Exercise 18   Correcting Improper Use of Indefinite Pronouns

On your paper, rewrite each sentence by eliminating the use of *you* or *they* as indefinite pronouns.

SAMPLE   In some classes, they teach about the works of Edgar Allan Poe.
ANSWER   The works of Edgar Allan Poe are taught in some classes.

Edgar Allan Poe's Stories

1. In some bookstores, they have enough horror books for an entire horror section.
2. When reading a story by Poe, you should expect horror as part of the plot.
3. Reading "The Tell-Tale Heart" will give you a taste of the suspense and terror contained in so many of Poe's works.
4. Many libraries hold used book sales where you can find some of Poe's earlier works.
5. In the school library, they limit the number of books a student can borrow.

Exercise 19   Making Pronoun Reference Clear

On your paper, rewrite each of the following sentences, making sure that all pronoun references are clearly stated. In some cases, you may choose to eliminate the pronoun entirely.

SAMPLE   When students must choose only one specific extracurricular activity, it can be a difficult decision.
ANSWER   Choosing only one specific extracurricular activity can be a difficult decision.

1. In most American high schools, they offer students a wide range of extracurricular activities, and one of the most popular of these is sports.
2. Rigorous academic classes make heavy demands on students, and this can affect their health and well-being.
3. Girls as well as boys take part in team sports, and they benefit both physically and mentally from a vigorous workout at the end of the day.
4. Unfortunately, in some schools they no longer have a budget for extracurricular sports programs, and the students themselves must meet the expenses of any such programs.
5. Participation in sports also teaches students how to get along with one another; when my sister Bernice beat her best friend, Marta, in a race, for example, she succeeded in maintaining their friendship.
6. As field-hockey teammates, Bernice and Marta cooperate rather than compete, which suits them both.
7. When hardworking students play a tough game against another school's team, it can boost each team's self-esteem.
8. Playing on a team also helps you learn how to work together for the good of the group.
9. When coaches urge players to work as a team instead of playing as separate competing individuals, they know this advice is sound.
10. Sports should be an integrated part of the school experience, and this is evident from the many benefits afforded students.

Exercise 20   Review: Choosing the Correct Pronoun

On your paper, write the correct pronoun for each sentence.

SAMPLE   Some people have difficulty throwing a ball with (his, their) left hand.

ANSWER   their

1. Each of the players on the team pitches with (his or her, their) left hand.
2. All of the doors to the stadium have (its, their) handles on the right side.
3. Several left-handed ticket collectors had problems holding the door open with (his or her, their) right hands.
4. Neither of the players could catch with (their, his or her) right hand.
5. In the past, teachers attempted to force left-handed pupils to write with (his or her, their) right hands.

Exercise 21   Review: Finding and Correcting Pronoun Mistakes

Rewrite each of the following sentences, eliminating any mistakes in the use of pronouns. Each sentence has one error.

1. In Ulysses S. Grant, Abraham Lincoln found him an ally on the issue of allowing African Americans to fight in the Civil War.
2. Both of these men expressed his personal beliefs that African Americans would make good soldiers.
3. Frederick Douglass, whom had campaigned tirelessly for the recruitment of African Americans by the Union Army, encouraged President Lincoln to make Emancipation an issue in the Civil War.
4. Even after the United States Congress allowed African American men to enlist in the Union Army, it was not popular among some Northerners.
5. African American troops repulsed the attacking Confederates in October, 1862, at the battle of Island Mount, Missouri, which silenced their critics.
6. African Americans showed his or her courage by making up nearly ten percent of the Union Army by the end of the war.
7. When Colonel Robert Gould Shaw attacked Fort Wagner, South Carolina, he was leading African American soldiers whom proudly made up the entire Fifty-fourth Massachusetts Regiment.
8. Respect for the courage of these soldiers is redoubled when you think of the dangers of capture; unlike white soldiers, captured African American soldiers were usually either returned to slavery or immediately shot.
9. The Congressional Medal of Honor is presented to whomever has shown gallantry and courage in conflict with the enemy, at the risk of life and above and beyond the call of duty.
10. No one was more delighted than me to discover that African American soldiers were awarded the Medal of Honor for their bravery during the Civil War.

Exercise 22   Review: Correcting Vague or Unclear Pronoun References

On your paper, indicate which sentences have clear pronoun references by writing *clear*. Rewrite sentences with vague or unclear pronoun references so that the sentences are clear.

SAMPLE   The camp owners have restricted the number of applicants, which the counselors appreciate.

ANSWER   The counselors appreciate that the camp owners have restricted the number of applicants.

Camp Days

1. When the campers first met the counselors, they were friendly.
2. The new campers complained about the food, which made the counselors laugh.
3. The counselors organized the First Day Race, which Lola won.
4. Jim fell into the pool, which surprised him.
5. The campers slept in the blue tent or the red tent; it had a hole in the top.
6. It had rained heavily the first night, which is why all their sleeping bags were hanging on the clothesline.
7. Lisa braided this belt for her sister the summer she was ten.
8. As Sam dunked the ball, his head butted Eric in the ribs, which meant Eric had to drop out of the relay race that afternoon.
9. Everyone roasted marshmallows and told scary stories around the campfire, and it gave Elaine indigestion and nightmares.
10. Tom filled his counselor's sneakers with syrup, and he laughed when he saw them.

Exercise 23   Review: Rewriting Sentences to Clarify Ideas

On your paper, rewrite each sentence so that the pronoun references and antecedents are correct and clear.

A Driver's License

1. Last week I waited two hours for a license at the Motor Vehicle Bureau, which was too long.
2. The young man knew the road test would be hard, which worried him.
3. You should study a driving guide before taking the test; it may be found on the Internet.
4. License plates can be specially ordered, which cost extra.
5. Some states let drivers renew their license by telephone, but they charge an extra fee.
6. The students in drivers education paid close attention to their instruction, and it paid off.
7. Motor vehicle agencies are located throughout some states, which is convenient.
8. If an applicant fails the written test for a driver's license, which is required, it usually can be retaken a limited number of times.
9. Mitch drove his brother to the road test, and he was late.
10. The testers give each new driver applicant an eye test, and this is required.

Grammar Review

USING PRONOUNS CORRECTLY

Though Langston Hughes made his name as a poet, he also wrote many fine works of nonfiction. In this passage from a memoir, Hughes recalls a trip he made to Mexico City in the mid-1930s and the time he spent there with three aging sisters, the Patiños. The passage has been annotated to show some of the kinds of pronouns covered in this unit.

Literature Model

from I Wonder As I Wander
by Langston Hughes

Pronoun in the possessive case

Pronoun in the nominative case used as a subject

Pronoun in the objective case used as an indirect object

The pronoun *they* in the nominative case used as a subject. The pronoun agrees in number with its antecedent, *sisters*.

My last few weeks in Mexico I spent at the Patiño home, because I knew they would feel hurt if I didn't. I went to vespers with them every night in the old church just across the street, lighted by tall candles and smelling of incense. Sometimes I even got up early in the morning to attend mass. And I still cherish the lovely old rosaries they gave me. These sisters were very sweet, kindhearted women. But sometimes I thought their kindness was a little misspent. I was then all in favor of working to change the *basic* economics of the world, while they were engaged in little charities widely dispersed to help various indigents *a little*. From their small income they gave, in proportion, generously—five pesos here, ten there, two to this brotherhood, three to that sisterhood, one peso to one organization, a peso and a half to another—and regularly each week to the church. Then from their home they had their own little private dispensation every seventh day to the poor of the neighborhood.

This weekly ritual seemed touching, but very futile to me. There were literally thousands of poor people in the neighborhood, since the Patiños lived in the heart of Mexico City, not far from the Zócalo. In our block alone there were perhaps two or three hundred shoeless or nearly shoeless folks. Personal charity for a handful, I felt, was hardly a drop in the bucket for so great a need. But these elderly women had been doing this for years, so I said nothing to discourage them. Every Monday, early in the

morning they would busy themselves, these three sisters, pack-
aging in separate cones of newspapers little cups of beans, a tiny
scoop of sugar, perhaps two or three onions, a bunch of grapes
or an orange, and a small slice of laundry soap. Several dozen
such little packets of each thing they would make. Then from
eleven to twelve, just before mid-day dinner, the poor of the
neighborhood would come to receive their gifts. To each who
asked, a set of these tiny packets would be given at the door,
with a "Bless you, Marianita! . . . Bless you, Luz!" as each filed
past with open hands. But the food each got was not enough for
even one good meal. And the tiny piece of soap would hardly
wash anyone's hands and face more than a day.

But there was among the deserving poor in the neighborhood one woman who must have felt as I did—concerning this
small donation—because she always stayed to dinner. After she
got her tiny packages, she would squat on the floor just inside
the dining-room door, and no one could move her until the
three sisters sat down to eat their noonday meal and she was
served on the floor, too.

Reflexive pronoun *themselves* referring to the *three sisters*

Pronoun-antecedent agreement between *their* and the collective noun *poor*

The pronoun *who* in the nominative case used as the subject of *asked* in an adjective clause

Agreement in number and gender between the pronoun *she* and its antecedent, *woman*

Using Pronouns Correctly

Review: Exercise 1   **Choosing the Correct Pronoun Case**

The following sentences are based on the passage from *I Wonder As I Wander*. For each
sentence, determine whether the italicized pronoun is used correctly. If it is not, write
the pronoun as it should appear. If it is used properly, write *correct*.

1. The house in which Hughes was staying was *their's*.
2. Hughes observed that the kindest people must be *they*.
3. *Him* and the Patiños had different ideas about charity.
4. Although the sisters' generosity was sincere, Hughes wondered about *it's* effectiveness.
5. *Them* distributing little packets of food each week could hardly ease the suffering in the neighborhood.
6. The food that Marianita or Luz received was *hers* alone.
7. The packets did not contain even one meal's worth of food for *they* or their families.
8. Hughes decided that *him* and one of the poorest women had the same feelings about the small gifts of food.
9. If a truly determined person ever lived, it was *her*.
10. Despite *them* trying to move her out of the dining room, the sisters were forced to serve this woman a meal.

Grammar Review

Review: Exercise 2   Using Pronouns Correctly with and as Appositives

The following sentences are based on a passage from *I Wonder As I Wander* that is not reprinted in this textbook. For each sentence, determine whether the italicized pronoun appears in the proper form. If it does not, write the pronoun as it should appear. If it is used properly, write *correct*.

1. The Patiños' house was at times home to both men, Hughes's father and *him*.
2. Of the small gathering, *he* and the Patiño sisters, only he was not dressed in mourning.
3. The will pertained to the four people, the Patiños and *him*, who sat together silently.
4. The Patiños told Hughes, "*Us* sisters wish to share the estate with you."
5. The Patiños generously suggested to Hughes that the estate be divided among four people, the three sisters and *he*.

Review: Exercise 3   Using Pronouns Correctly After *Than* and *As*

The following sentences are based on a passage from *I Wonder As I Wander* that is not reprinted in this textbook. Each sentence contains an italicized word or group of words. Rewrite each sentence, substituting the correct pronoun for the word or words in italics.

SAMPLE   Hughes enjoyed no one more than *his Mexican friends*.
ANSWER   Hughes enjoyed no one more than them.

1. These writers and artists relished life as much as *Hughes*.
2. Diego Rivera was probably more famous than *other artists*.
3. Many people love few works of art more than *Rivera's murals*.
4. Hughes had never seen anyone as huge as *Rivera*.
5. Hughes also knew Rivera's ex-wife, Lupe; no one was more colorful than *Lupe*.

Review: Exercise 4

Proofreading

The following passage describes the artist María Izquierdo. A reproduction of one of her paintings appears on the following page. Rewrite the passage, correcting the errors in spelling, grammar, and usage. Add any missing punctuation. There are ten errors.

María Izquierdo

¹Born in a small village in the state of Jalisco, María Izquierdo (1906–1955) became one of Mexicos outstanding modern painters. ²Her had little formal training she studied briefly at the Academy of San Carlos in Mexico City. ³Herself did, however, have an intuitive grasp of form and color.

⁴Painting in jewel-like tones of blue, rose yellow, and magenta, Izquierdo depicted scenes of everyday Mexican life. ⁵Peasant women, handmade toys, and circus scenes appears frequently in her work.

⁶The women in *Dos Mujeres con Papaya* (*Two Women with Papaya*) seem strong, capeable, and content. ⁷Whom might them be? ⁸Its possible to imagine them as the generous Patiño women in Langston Hughes's *I Wonder As I Wander*.

María Izquierdo, *Dos Mujeres con Papaya*, 1936

Review: Exercise 5

Mixed Review

The following sentences describe aspects about the author (Langston Hughes) and setting (Mexico City) of the memoir *I Wonder As I Wander*. For each sentence, choose the proper pronoun from the pair in parentheses and write it on your paper.

(continued)

Langston Hughes and Mexico

1. Langston Hughes, (who/whom) many associate with the writers of the Harlem Renaissance, was born in 1902.
2. Although (he/him) and the other Harlem Renaissance writers are often regarded as New Yorkers, Hughes himself was born in Missouri.
3. When Hughes was young, his family consisted of three people: his mother, his grand-mother, and (he/him).
4. Because of (him/his) leaving his wife soon after their son's birth, Hughes's father was some-thing of a stranger to his son.
5. His father, (who/whom) Hughes saw only occasionally, lived in Mexico for many years.
6. Langston Hughes traveled widely and held many jobs, from busboy to war correspondent; few people have led a more varied life than (he/him).
7. He toured Latin America, Europe, Africa, and Asia, and each of these voyages had (its/their) effect on his writing.
8. Few writers were as versatile and prolific as (he/him).
9. Each poem, novel, story, memoir, play, translation, and feature article he wrote has con-tributed to (his/their) reputation.
10. Of all the Harlem Renaissance poets, it was (he/him) who captured the widest readership outside this country.
11. The central core of Mexico City traces (its, their) history to Aztec times.
12. The Aztecs chose islets in Lake Texcoco on which to build (its, their) principal city, Tenochtitlán.
13. Aztec culture found (its, their) greatest expression in the construction of Tenochtitlán, now known as Mexico City.
14. The streets around the Zócalo, a grand plaza, retain (its, their) role as the hub of the city.
15. At the Zócalo, an Aztec emperor built glorious temples for (himself, hisself).
16. The Spaniards replaced the Aztec temples with a palace and a church of (its, their) own.
17. Diego Rivera, who is one of Mexico's greatest artists, decorated the National Palace with (his, their) murals.
18. Today this city has grown far beyond (its, their) original borders.
19. Manufacturing has brought with (them, it) both revenue and pollution.
20. Many families in Mexico City find that (them, they) most enjoy their Sundays in Chapultepec Park, listening to music and watching the traditional riding demonstrations of the *charros*.

Using Pronouns Correctly

Writing Application

TIME

For more about the writing process, see **TIME Facing the Blank Page,** pages 111–121.

Pronouns in Writing

In this passage from her novel *The Living Reed*, Pearl S. Buck uses pronouns effectively to clarify ideas and relationships within sentences. Read the passage, focusing especially on the italicized pronouns.

> "It is better if *we* face danger together," Yul-han said.
>
> At this moment a voice spoke from the door. It was the girl, *who* had grown weary of waiting. *She* stood there, *her* two feet planted widely apart, *her* bare arms hanging at *her* sides, *her* hair neat and *her* sun-browned face red with scrubbing.
>
> "What do you want *me* to do next, mistress?" *she* demanded.
>
> Yul-han and Induk parted and Yul-han turned *his* back properly on the girl.
>
> "What shall *we* do with *you*?" Induk countered. "Shall *we* not send *you* home again to *your* parents?"

Techniques with Pronouns

Try to apply some of Pearl S. Buck's writing techniques when you write and revise your own work.

❶ When using personal pronouns as subjects, be sure to use the nominative case. When using personal pronouns as objects, be sure to use the objective case.

INCORRECT CASE USE "What do you want I to do next, mistress?" her demanded.

BUCK'S VERSION "What do you want me to do next, mistress?" she demanded.

❷ Always use *who* for subjects and *whom* for objects.

INCORRECT CASE USE "... whom had grown weary of waiting."

BUCK'S VERSION "... who had grown weary of waiting."

❸ Remember to make pronouns agree in number with their antecedents.

INCORRECT AGREEMENT She stood there, their two feet planted widely apart.

BUCK'S VERSION She stood there, her two feet planted widely apart.

Practice Practice these techniques with pronouns by revising the following passage, using a separate sheet of paper. Pay particular attention to the underlined words.

The actress Madhur Jaffrey, <u>who</u> television viewers may know from <u>her</u> cooking show, has published many fine cookbooks over the years. <u>My</u> mother and <u>me</u> especially like *Madhur Jaffrey's Indian Cooking,* with <u>it's</u> excellent recipes and interesting background information. <u>Everyone</u> in the family has <u>their</u> favorite Jaffrey dish, and for Mom <u>its</u> Tandoori-style chicken. Vegetable dishes, more to the liking of <u>my</u> father and <u>I</u>, include potatoes with sesame seeds and sweet-and-sour okra. Madhur Jaffrey, <u>who</u> grew up in Delhi, India, provides a variety of dishes from many regions of <u>her</u> homeland. For <u>each, she</u> includes information about <u>their</u> origins and any unusual ingredients.

Using Pronouns Correctly

UNIT 18 Using Modifiers Correctly

18.1 The Three Degrees of Comparison

Most adjectives and adverbs have three degrees: the positive, or base, form; the comparative form; and the superlative form.

- The **positive form** of a modifier cannot be used to make a comparison. (This form appears as the entry word in a dictionary.)
- The **comparative** form of a modifier shows two things being compared.
- The **superlative** form of a modifier shows three or more things being compared.

POSITIVE	Abby is **fast.**
	I ran **slowly.**
COMPARATIVE	Abby runs **faster** than the other runners.
	I ran **more slowly** than my friend.
SUPERLATIVE	Of the three runners, she is the **fastest.**
	I ran **most slowly** of all.

Use the following rules as a guide:

In general, for one-syllable modifiers add *-er* to form the comparative and *-est* to form the superlative.

small, small**er,** small**est**
The pianist's hands are **smaller** than mine.
That is the **smallest** dog I have ever seen.

Spelling changes occur in some cases when you add *-er* and *-est.*

white, whit**er,** whit**est**
flat, flat**ter,** flat**test**
merry, merr**ier,** merr**iest**

With certain one-syllable modifiers, it may sound more natural to use *more* and *most* instead of *-er* and *-est.*

brusque, **more** brusque, **most** brusque
He is **more brusque** than she.

For most two-syllable adjectives, add *-er* to form the comparative and *-est* to form the superlative.

friendly, friendl**ier,** friendl**iest**
That kitten is **friendlier** than this one.
The Siamese kitten is the **friendliest** of the three.

If *-er* and *-est* sound awkward, use *more* and *most.*

prudent, **more** prudent, **most** prudent

For adverbs ending in -ly, always use *more* and *most* to form the comparative and superlative degrees.

> sweetly, **more** sweetly, **most** sweetly
> Of all the birds, the nightingale sings the **most sweetly.**

For modifiers of three or more syllables, always use *more* and *most* to form the comparative and superlative degrees.

> talented, **more** talented, **most** talented
> This actor is more talented than that one.

Less and *least,* the opposite of *more* and *most,* can also be used with most modifiers to show comparison.

> Earl is **less reflective** than Suki.
> Mark is the **least reflective** person I know.

Less and *least* are used before modifiers of any number of syllables.

Some adjectives, such as *unique, perfect, final, dead,* and *square,* cannot be compared because they describe an absolute condition. However, you can sometimes use *more nearly* and *most nearly* with these adjectives.

> Clara's rug is **more nearly square** than Paul's is.
> That painting is the **most nearly perfect** I have ever seen.

Exercise 1   **Making Correct Comparisons**

Complete the following sentences with the correct degree of comparison of the modifier in parentheses. (The positive degree is also used.)

SAMPLE   I think Aretha Franklin sings soul _____ than any other recording artist. (powerfully)

ANSWER   more powerfully

Aretha Franklin, the Queen of Soul

1. Aretha Franklin may be the _____ female vocalist of all time. (popular)
2. Franklin is well known for her _____ voice. (powerful)
3. Because her father was a successful minister, Franklin's interest in gospel music became _____ than another child's might have. (strong)
4. Of all the children in her father's choir, Aretha sang the _____. (loudly)
5. After four years of recording only gospel songs, Franklin decided to switch to a genre that would be _____ than church music. (profitable)
6. Franklin spent six _____ years with Columbia Records. (disappointing)
7. It was with Atlantic Records that she recorded some of her _____ songs, including "Respect" and "Natural Woman." (popular)
8. Franklin then rose to fame _____ than anyone could have imagined. (quickly)
9. Franklin, _____ known for her soul music, has achieved more million-selling singles than any other woman singer. (widely)
10. Even so, some people still think she sings the _____ of all when performing gospel songs. (sweetly)

18.2 Irregular Comparisons

A few commonly used modifiers have irregular forms.

MODIFIERS WITH IRREGULAR FORMS OF COMPARISON

POSITIVE	COMPARATIVE	SUPERLATIVE
good	better	(the) best
well	better	(the) best
bad	worse	(the) worst
badly	worse	(the) worst
ill	worse	(the) worst
far (distance)	farther	(the) farthest
far (degree, time)	further	(the) furthest
little (amount)	less	(the) least
many	more	(the) most
much	more	(the) most

Exercise 2	**Identifying Irregular Comparisons**

In each of the following sentences, write the irregular comparison and then label it as *positive*, *comparative*, or *superlative*.

SAMPLE Of the two girls, Sue is the better pitcher.
ANSWER better, comparative

Sibling Rivalry

1. She is also good at fielding and hitting.
2. In fact, Sue can hit the ball the farthest of anyone on the team.
3. She can hit it farther than her older brother, Stan.
4. Stan doesn't mind since he is better at basketball than Sue is.
5. Sue has less time for basketball than she does for softball.
6. She has the least amount of time for soccer.
7. She is busier than her older sister, Sharon.
8. Sharon spends the most time in dance class.
9. All the Stone children are good at something.
10. Of the three, Stan is the worst singer!
11. Stan sings so badly, the choir master asked him to mouth the words.
12. But Stan is not the worst singer in the choir.
13. That distinction belongs to Benny, who spends less time practicing than anyone else.
14. Benny is so bad, Mr. Russo considered asking him to resign.
15. But no matter how little talent a person has, everyone gets to be a part of choir.
16. The worst thing of all is to be left out.
17. Benny, however, is the best cook I've ever met in person.

(continued)

18. Each pizza creation is more delicious than the last.
19. This recipe requires the least flour of all.
20. How many talents you develop is up to you.

On your paper write the correct form of the irregular comparison in parentheses to correctly complete each sentence.

SAMPLE   Kevin Connelly is the _____ writer in our class. (good)
ANSWER   best

Class Compositions

1. He tried to write a _____ composition with each assignment. (good)
2. At first, he spent the _____ amount of time on the first draft. (little)
3. Then he began to realize that _____ time could be saved if he worked harder on the first draft. (much)
4. Kevin doesn't always do the _____ research of anyone in class. (much)
5. He feels his time is _____ spent working on his sentences and transitions. (good)
6. _____ of his classmates like to write fiction. (many)
7. Even _____ of them, however, enjoy writing ads. (many)
8. As a project Kevin's class is teaching sixth-grade students to write _____ letters. (good)
9. Kevin's individual student has written some of the _____ letters Kevin has ever seen. (bad)
10. Kevin hasn't had _____ trouble finding improvements to suggest. (much)
11. He has found, though, that he needs to be _____ critical so that the sixth grader is not discouraged. (little)
12. Now Kevin tries to find something to praise in each piece of writing before he begins to make suggestions that will make the piece _____. (good)
13. To Kevin's surprise, the sixth grader's work is really getting _____. (good)
14. Even _____ surprising to Kevin is the fact that his own writing is also improving. (many)
15. Perhaps *Have them teach what you want them to learn* is not a _____ idea, at that. (bad)
16. Suki Lee writes _____ poetry than Kevin. (good)
17. Don writes the _____ fiction stories, especially mysteries. (good)
18. But Kevin is the _____ by far at nonfiction articles, especially sports stories. (good)
19. Someday he may move _____ away to get a job at a newspaper. (far)
20. We all wish him _____ luck because he's a great guy. (good)

Using Modifiers Correctly

Creating Sentences That Make Comparisons

Select five of the irregular modifiers from the list on page 651. Write a sentence for each, using the positive and comparative degrees of the modifier. Underline each modifier.

SAMPLE   well
ANSWER   Susan speaks Spanish well, but Marie speaks it better.

Review: Making Correct Comparisons

Complete the following sentences with the correct degree of comparison of the modifier in parentheses. (The positive degree is used in two sentences.)

SAMPLE   Lewis believes that James Joyce is _____ to read than any other writer. (difficult)
ANSWER   more difficult

James Joyce, Imaginative Author

1. Many knowledgeable people consider James Joyce the _____ writer of English fiction in the twentieth century. (imaginative)
2. James Joyce utilized _____ new techniques in writing the novel than virtually any other writer of his generation. (many)
3. His short stories are generally _____ than his novels, although some of the stories make difficult reading, too. (accessible)
4. One of his great short stories, "The Dead," explores some of the conflicts in Irish society that arise because the older generation is _____ than the younger generation. (traditional)
5. In this story, Joyce _____ presents a number of character types—boisterous, reserved, belligerent, generous, and more—based on real people he knew while he was living and writing in Dublin. (skillfully)
6. The novel *Ulysses* is considerably _____ in style and narrative technique than Joyce's short stories. (complex)
7. The main character of *Ulysses*, Leopold Bloom, feels that he is one of the _____ men in Dublin. (isolated)
8. Although *Ulysses* is epic in scope, Bloom wanders no _____ than the city limits of the capital. (far)
9. Bloom _____ meets the young Stephen Dedalus, who becomes a surrogate son to him. (finally)
10. Joyce used Homer's epic the *Odyssey* as a prototype for his novel, although the total effect is far different from that of the _____ work. (early)

18.3 Double Comparisons

Do not make a double comparison by using both *-er* or *-est* and *more* or *most*.

INCORRECT	Chimpanzees are more smaller than gorillas.
CORRECT	Chimpanzees are smaller than gorillas.
INCORRECT	That is the most saddest song on the album.
CORRECT	That is the saddest song on the album.
INCORRECT	She is the most luckiest girl in school.
CORRECT	She is the luckiest girl in school.

Exercise 6   **Correcting Double Comparisons**

Rewrite each of the following sentences, correcting the double comparisons.

Gandhi, a Great Leader

1. Many historians judge Mohandas Karamchand Gandhi the single most greatest leader India has ever produced.
2. Because Gandhi's native town could provide only a limited education, he was fortunate that his family moved to the town of Rājkot, where the educational facilities were more better.
3. During Gandhi's teenage years, he was more shier than most of the boys in his age group.
4. While studying in England, Gandhi found that adapting to Western culture was more harder than his studies.
5. After accepting a job in South Africa, Gandhi found the treatment of Indians there more harsher than anything he had previously encountered.
6. To fight injustice, Gandhi used the principles of civil disobedience and nonviolence, which are more peacefuller than conventional weapons.
7. In South Africa, Gandhi turned his attention to the fact that the most mightiest nation of that era, Great Britain, maintained his homeland of India as a colony of second-class citizens.
8. Gandhi wanted to dismantle India's caste system and to help the most weakest class of Indians, the untouchables.
9. After being imprisoned by the British government for his civil disobedience, the great spiritual leader found that one of the most clearest ways to communicate his protest was to cease eating.
10. Although Gandhi did live to see India achieve its independence in 1947, one of the least happiest days of Gandhi's life was the day India was divided into the dominions of India and Pakistan.

Correcting Double Comparisons

Rewrite each of the following sentences, correcting the double comparisons.

The Coldest Explorers

1. The North Pole was reached two years more earlier than the South Pole.
2. Robert Peary, an American, reached the North Pole more sooner than Norwegian Roald Amundsen.
3. Amundsen, wanting to be first at something, decided to take the more difficulter trip to the South Pole.
4. Robert Scott, the most best-known of all explorers, was also aiming for the South Pole at that time.
5. Which of these two men had planned his trip more better, Amundsen or Scott?
6. Which of the two would be the more successfuler?
7. Robert Scott's expedition sailed in the most best-equipped ship available.
8. But Amundsen felt his dogs were the most strongest.
9. These dogs could survive even in the most coldest weather.
10. Which team could withstand the most worst of the Arctic storms?
11. Scott had the most worst luck of any explorer.
12. Seeing the Norwegian flag when he finally came to the South Pole was the most harshest blow to Scott.
13. He knew his team could have gone no more faster.
14. Scott could not understand how Amundsen had traveled more faster in the terrible weather.
15. Scott's party was more sicker than ever when they saw the Norwegian flag.
16. Each day their food supplies grew more smaller.
17. The storms outside the tent were the most worst Scott had ever experienced in his many years as an Arctic explorer.
18. Scott watched his men grow more weaker with each day.
19. Their frostbitten feet were not the most severest of their problems.
20. On March 29, 1912, Scott entered the most painfulest entry in his diary.
21. In 1956 the United States set up a permanent scientific base more nearer to the South Pole than any other and called it the Amundsen-Scott South Pole Station.
22. The south geographic pole is most best explained as the point where all the earth's lines of longitude meet.
23. The south geographic pole is what we most oftenest call the South Pole.
24. The south magnetic pole is the place to which compass needles point most strongliest.
25. The pole may move up to five miles in a year and so is stationary much less oftener.
26. Both south poles are in Antarctica, the most coldest and most iciest place on Earth.
27. Antarctica is even more colder than the area around the North Pole.
28. Antarctica is more larger than Europe or Australia if Antarctica's icecap is included.
29. The ice enlarges Antarctica's surface and also makes it the most highest continent if average elevation is considered.
30. Its average elevation is 7,500 feet above sea level—more higher than many mountains!

18.4 Incomplete Comparisons

Do not make an incomplete or unclear comparison by omitting *other* or *else* when you compare one member of a group with another.

UNCLEAR	New York has more skyscrapers than any city in America.
CLEAR	New York has more skyscrapers than any **other** city in America.
UNCLEAR	Juanita received more prizes than anyone.
CLEAR	Juanita received more prizes than anyone **else.**

Be sure your comparisons are between similar things.

UNCLEAR	The salary of a teacher is lower than a lawyer. [The salary of a teacher is being compared illogically with a person, namely, a lawyer.]
CLEAR	The salary of a teacher is lower than **that of a lawyer.**
CLEAR	The salary of a teacher is lower than **a lawyer's.** [The word *salary* is understood after *lawyer's*.]

| Exercise 8 | **Making Complete Comparisons** |

Rewrite each of the following sentences to correct the incomplete comparison in each.

An African Safari

1. On safari in Africa, Henry saw more cheetahs than anyone.
2. Cheetahs are often difficult to spot, since they are rarer than many animals.
3. The cheetah can run faster than any mammal.
4. Its speed of over seventy miles per hour on short runs is greater than the lion or the jaguar.
5. The tails of cheetahs are more distinctive than any large cat.
6. Cheetahs were only one of the many splendors of our African journey, which was more exciting than any trip I've ever taken.
7. Among other facts, we learned that the area of Sudan is greater than Texas and Alaska combined.
8. The area of the African island of Mahé in the Seychelles, however, is less than New Orleans.
9. All across North Africa lies the awesome Sahara, which is vaster than any desert.
10. Africa is also the home of the mighty Nile, which at four thousand miles is longer than any river in the world.

Using Modifiers Correctly

Always use *good* as an adjective. *Well* may be used as an adverb of manner telling how ably something is done or as an adjective meaning "in good health."

Hiroshi is a **good** violinist. [adjective]

Hiroshi feels **good** today. [adjective after a linking verb]

Hiroshi plays the violin **well.** [adverb of manner]

Hiroshi is not **well** this week because he has a cold. [adjective meaning "in good health"]

Always use *bad* as an adjective. Therefore, *bad* is used after a linking verb. Use *badly* as an adverb. *Badly* almost always follows an action verb.

The player made a **bad** throw. [adjective]

The skunk smelled **bad.** [adjective following a linking verb]

I felt **bad** about my mistake. [adjective following a linking verb]

Her nose is bleeding **badly.** [adverb following an action verb]

Exercise 9 **Choosing the Correct Modifier**

On your paper, complete the following sentences correctly by filling the blank with *good, well, bad,* or *badly.*

Studying for an Examination

1. A person who studies _____ can be confident of earning good grades on examinations in college.
2. Doing poorly on an examination can make anyone feel _____.
3. _____ organization is essential to studying effectively.
4. A _____ organized study schedule can cause anyone to lose a great deal of precious time.
5. A _____ schedule allows enough time for the ideas and the subjects that you find difficult to grasp.
6. Even a student who is doing _____ should give some thought to structuring study time more efficiently.
7. If you start out _____ in one of your courses, budgeting additional time for studying that subject is especially important.
8. Most people feel _____ when they go into an exam knowing that they have devoted sufficient time to studying.
9. If you do not feel _____ on the day of an examination, your grade might be adversely affected.
10. Some students perform _____ on examinations if they are unduly nervous during the test.

In general, do not use a **double negative**, two negative words in the same clause. Use only one negative word to express a negative idea.

INCORRECT	I didn't hear no noise.
CORRECT	I did**n't** hear **any** noise.
INCORRECT	She hasn't had no visitors.
CORRECT	She has**n't** had **any** visitors.
CORRECT	She has had **no** visitors.
INCORRECT	He never reads no magazines.
CORRECT	He **never** reads **any** magazines.
CORRECT	He reads **no** magazines.
INCORRECT	He never eats no ice cream.
CORRECT	He **never** eats **any** ice cream.
CORRECT	He eats **no** ice cream.

Exercise 10   **Avoiding Double Negatives**

On your paper, rewrite the following sentences, eliminating the double negative in each. (Most sentences can be corrected in more than one way.)

The Great Lakes

1. My younger brother hasn't visited none of the Great Lakes.
2. I told him that unlike the other four lakes, Lake Michigan doesn't share no boundary with Canada.
3. Except for the Caspian Sea in Asia, there isn't no inland body of water in the world larger than Lake Superior.
4. I have never seen no lake as impressive as Lake Superior.
5. My brother could not name none of the four states—Michigan, Wisconsin, Illinois, and Indiana—that border Lake Michigan.
6. There isn't no way to describe how much I loved the fishing and hiking on my camping trip to Lake Huron.
7. Although Lake Ontario is the smallest of the Great Lakes, it isn't no insignificant body of water.
8. Pollution problems in Lake Erie are not by no means as bad as they were two decades ago.
9. If not for the Great Lakes, hundreds of towns and cities in several states would be without no decent water supply.
10. These days my brother and I cannot think of nothing except planning an autumn trip to Lake Superior.

Avoiding Double Negatives

On your paper, rewrite the following sentences, correcting the double negative in each. (Most sentences can be corrected in more than one way.)

INCORRECT   I have never seen no ocean.
CORRECT   I have never seen an ocean.
CORRECT   I haven't ever seen an ocean.

The Great Oceans

1. I haven't never seen any of the world's great oceans.
2. I don't have no knowledge of oceans.
3. The books I own didn't have no information about them.
4. There isn't no way to describe my intense desire to swim and surf in the great and wonderful Pacific Ocean.
5. I can't think of no better way to spend a summer vacation than to lie on a sunny beach beside the Pacific Ocean.
6. Although quite large in area, the Atlantic is not by no means as large as the magnificent Pacific Ocean.
7. The Indian Ocean isn't no small ocean either.
8. Scientists today don't not consider the Arctic and Antarctic true oceans anymore.
9. The Arctic is not considered a separate ocean no more, but an arm of the Atlantic.
10. Except for the Arctic Ocean at 5,440,000 square miles, there isn't no sea larger than the Arabian Sea at 1,492,000 square miles.
11. Compared to the Arabian Sea, the Gulf of Mexico isn't not very big at a total of 615,000 square miles.
12. Unlike the Atlantic and Indian oceans, the Pacific doesn't have no seas smaller than the Sea of Japan at 389,000 square miles.
13. There just isn't no way to put into words the beauty of the world's oceans and the way I feel about them.
14. I cannot think of nothing I would like better than to see one of the oceans.
15. I haven't not nearly enough money saved, but someday I will get to an ocean.
16. I can't think of no better career than one in oceanography.
17. Oceanographers don't not study just the oceans.
18. They wouldn't never limit themselves to a general study.
19. Oceanographers don't not study just the biology of the world's bodies of water, but also the geology and chemistry.
20. There isn't no way to describe how much this subject interests me.

Not I

21. Nobody is never going to get me to do the dishes tonight.
22. I just don't never like doing the dishes.
23. I can't hardly stand putting my hands in that greasy water.
24. I don't know why we haven't got no dishwasher.
25. There wasn't no reason for Dad to say, "*You're* the dishwasher."

18.7 Misplaced and Dangling Modifiers

Place modifiers as close as possible to the words they modify in order to make the meaning of the sentence clear.

■ **Misplaced modifiers** modify the wrong word, or seem to modify more than one word, in a sentence. You can correct a sentence with a misplaced modifier by moving the modifier as close as possible to the word that it modifies.

MISPLACED **Running at great speed,** the spectators watched the racers. [participial phrase incorrectly modifying *spectators*]

CLEAR The spectators watched the racers **running at great speed.** [participial phrase correctly modifying *racers*]

MISPLACED The beaches of Martinique are favored by many tourists **with their beautiful, calm surf.** [prepositional phrase incorrectly modifying *tourists*]

CLEAR The beaches of Martinique, **with their beautiful, calm surf,** are favored by many tourists. [prepositional phrase correctly modifying *beaches*]

Sometimes a misplaced modifier can be corrected by creating a subordinate clause or by rephrasing the main clause.

MISPLACED **Blowing from the north,** the pines were tossed by the wind. [participial phrase incorrectly modifying *pines*]

CLEAR The pines were tossed by the wind, **which blew from the north.** [participial phrase recast as a subordinate clause correctly modifying *wind*]

CLEAR **Blowing from the north,** the wind tossed the pines. [participial phrase correctly modifying *wind*]

Taken logically, a **dangling modifier** seems to modify no word in the sentence in which it appears. You can correct a sentence with a dangling modifier by supplying a word or phrase the dangling phrase can sensibly modify.

DANGLING   **Using high-powered binoculars,** the lost girl was found. [participial phrase logically modifying no word in the sentence]

CLEAR   **Using high-powered binoculars,** the rescuers found the lost girl. [participial phrase modifying *rescuers*]

CLEAR   The rescuers found the lost girl **because they used high-powered binoculars.** [subordinate clause modifying *found*]

DANGLING   **After searching for hours,** the girl was happily found safe and sound. [prepositional phrase logically modifying no word in the sentence]

CLEAR   **After searching for hours,** the rescuers were happy to find the girl safe and sound. [prepositional phrase modifying *rescuers*]

DANGLING   **Feeling elated,** a celebration with my friends lasted well into the night. [participial phrase logically modifying no word in the sentence]

CLEAR   **Feeling elated,** I celebrated with my friends well into the night. [participal phrase modifying *I*]

Exercise 12   Correcting Misplaced and Dangling Modifiers

On your paper, rewrite the following sentences, correcting the misplaced or dangling modifier in each.

Blue Jeans

[1]Created in California during the gold rush, people all over the world now wear blue jeans. [2]Guaranteed not to rip, gold prospectors liked their durability. [3]With a design perfect for rough conditions, only prospectors and laborers wore these denim pants at first. [4]Wearing them for work and dress, jeans gained popularity among cowboys in the West. [5]No longer associated with bucking broncos, men and women alike now consider jeans to be high fashion.

Exercise 13   Correcting Misplaced and Dangling Modifiers

On your paper, rewrite the following sentences, correcting the misplaced or dangling modifiers in each.

INCORRECT   My brother spent a semester at a university in Mexico City, known for his love of intriguing new places.

CORRECT   My brother, known for his love of intriguing new places, spent a semester at a university in Mexico City.

The Aztec Empire

[1]Presenting a lecture on ancient Aztec civilization, we strolled through the museum exhibit and listened to the curator. [2]After traveling into central Mexico, the city of Tenochtitlán was founded in 1325. [3]Eventually leading the Aztec Empire in terms of population, we studied an elaborate chart that showed the capital city, Tenochtitlán. [4]Reclaiming swamps and irrigating arid land, agricultural techniques were vital to the Aztecs' survival. [5]Resulting in high productivity, these methods only allowed the area to become rich and populous. [6]Illustrating Aztec domination over millions of people and thousands of square miles of the North American continent, our class watched a fascinating film. [7]In a section of central Mexico, another student and I learned that the Aztec language, Nahuatl, is still spoken. [8]In Aztec society, I was surprised to learn that there was an elaborate caste system. [9]Ranging from religious and government leaders at the top to serfs and slaves at the bottom, one means of advancement in the caste system was a military career. [10]The arrival of Hernando Cortés and other Spanish explorers only stopped the Aztec Empire from thriving and expanding into the sixteenth century.

Exercise 14   Modifiers

The following contains ten errors in the use of modifiers. Rewrite the paragraph, correcting all the errors.

Nikki Giovanni, Poet

[1]Were she to look back over her career, Nikki Giovanni would not have nothing to feel badly about. [2]After spending a happy childhood in Knoxville and Cincinnati, her first books were published when she was in her twenties. [3]Her writing of that time reflects her interest in the civil rights movement. [4]It was one of Giovanni's most earliest volumes of poetry, *My House,* that brought her critical acclaim. [5]Many people erroneously think Giovanni writes only for adults. [6]Writing books for young adults, readers of all ages can appreciate her poetry. [7]Some of Giovanni's strikingest poems convey pride in the poet's racial heritage. [8]By the time Giovanni was in her thirties, her outlook changed. [9]Her poetry became personaler and less political and social. [10]She continued to write about the African American identity, but from a personal not a racial standpoint. [11]More than any book, *The Women and the Men* shows Giovanni exploring questions of personal identity. [12]The most good poems in this book deal with the family. [13]The fact that many Americans know how good Giovanni writes is illustrated by her having been given keys to several cities. [14]Giovanni often gives free readings of her work, in an effort to give back to the community.

Correcting Misplaced and Dangling Modifiers

On your paper, rewrite the following sentences, correcting the misplaced or dangling modifier in each.

Gregor Mendel, Botanist

1. Recording all the results carefully, tall plants and short plants were first crossbred by Gregor Mendel.
2. After crossbreeding many times, the offspring of the tall and short plants were all tall, Mendel noticed.
3. Mendel continued to observe that one quarter of the grandchildren plants, with his meticulous notekeeping, were short.
4. Mendel next crossbred plants with white and red flowers with his usual care.
5. Growing excited by his discoveries, offspring of the white and red flowers were always red.
6. Always keeping careful tabulations, one quarter of the grandchildren of the white and red flowers were white.
7. Mendel finally concluded that some traits—such as tallness and redness—after careful consideration, were dominant, or stronger, than other traits.
8. Rushing to summarize his findings, the report was not taken seriously by the scientific community.
9. Dying in 1884, genetic scientists never acknowledged their founder.
10. Rediscovering the report in 1900, Mendel was finally given his due credit by scientists.

Exercise 16 **Identifying Correctly Placed Modifiers**

On your paper, write the letter of the correct sentence from each pair.

1. **a.** Visiting Florida, Cape Canaveral is fascinating.
   b. Visiting Florida, tourists find Cape Canaveral fascinating.
2. **a.** Cape Canaveral, with its impressive space center, attracts a huge crowd.
   b. Cape Canaveral attracts a huge crowd with its impressive space center.
3. **a.** Looking out the window, Munson had witnessed the crime.
   b. Munson had witnessed the crime, looking out the window.
4. **a.** Seeing her leap, joy filled the room
   b. Seeing her leap, I felt joy fill the room.
5. **a.** After arriving in Miami, the beach is the first destination.
   b. After arriving in Miami, most visitors head for the beach first.
6. **a.** Watching the horizon, the sunset presented a bright orange sky.
   b. Watching the horizon, we saw a bright orange sunset.
7. **a.** Florida, with its many tourist attractions, is an ideal vacation spot for the family.
   b. Florida is an ideal vacation spot for the family with its many tourist attractions.
8. **a.** The woman was a diner in the restaurant in the pink hat.
   b. The woman in the pink hat was a diner in the restaurant.
9. **a.** The chef raced out of the restaurant, waving and shouting wildly.
   b. Waving and shouting wildly, the chef raced out of the restaurant.
10. **a.** Before leaving for Europe, the house was rented to another couple.
    b. Before leaving for Europe, the owner rented the house to another couple.

On your paper, rewrite the following sentences, correcting the misplaced or dangling modifier in each.

Education in America

1. Learning the alphabet, the hornbook was used by colonial children.
2. McGuffey's Readers gave schoolchildren a shared background, eventually adopted in thirty-seven states.
3. Sitting on backless wooden benches, the three R's were learned in rustic schoolhouses.
4. Promoting a national spirit, many leaders supported the establishment of public schools.
5. Today's students might look down on the one-room schoolhouse, viewing its limitations as primitive.
6. Colonial students wrote on slates, lacking paper and pencil.
7. Providing many with their only opportunity for an education, some prominent leaders were educated in one-room schoolhouses.
8. In the 1870s and 1880s, laws were passed by the federal government designed to assimilate Native Americans into the mainstream culture.
9. Day and boarding schools were opened for Native American children, operated by the federal government.
10. Showing reluctance to send their children away from home, boarding schools met with objections from Native American parents.
11. Changed by education, some parents feared that their children would lose their traditional values.
12. Church-supported colleges in the mid-1800s enrolled many students less concerned with education than with shaping character.
13. Coupled with educational reform, Harvard philosopher William James popularized a new way of thinking.
14. Providing public land to finance state colleges, many students profited from the Morrill Act of 1862.
15. Begun in 1874 to train Sunday school teachers, enthusiasm for general education was sparked by the Chautauqua Institute in western New York.
16. Remaining the exception rather than the rule in the 1920s, few students could look forward to high school graduation.
17. Championed by John Dewey, some religious groups felt threatened by his views on education.
18. Giving direct federal aid to public and parochial schools, Americans profited from the Elementary and Secondary Education Act of 1965.
19. Helping economically disadvantaged children prepare for school, many parents appreciated Project Head Start.
20. Instruction in today's schools aims at preparing young citizens for new challenges, enhanced by computer technology.

On your paper, rewrite the following sentences, correcting the misplaced or dangling modifier in each.

Birds of North America

1. The birds of North America are some of the most beautiful in the world, with colorful plumage and interesting calls.
2. Inexpensive, relaxing, and fun, people of all ages all over the world enjoy bird-watching.
3. Organized into clubs or simply grouped at the seashore, you can ask bird lovers for information if you are just starting out.
4. Mallards may be seen throughout the day, so getting up early in the morning isn't always necessary, with their distinctive blue wing patch.
5. Having a pair of eyes, the equipment for bird-watching is minimal.
6. As well as carrying a guide book and a pocket notebook, good ears help too.
7. Binoculars can be expensive for the average beginner, with their ability to bring the birds closer to you.
8. Often longed for from the very beginning, most bird enthusiasts invest in a good camera too.
9. Saltwater marshes are not the only place to find birds, with their dense, watery environment.
10. Situated in the middle of big cities, intrepid bird-watchers find wooded parks excellent places to find birds during migration periods.
11. Rushing through the woods, most birds will be frightened away by the beginning watcher.
12. Sitting quietly in one spot, birds will not be able to pick up on your presence.
13. Flying overhead year-round, most bird-watchers will admit they enjoy the sight of birds in the sky.
14. The records of an avid bird-watcher are of interest to local naturalists, with a careful tabulation of numbers and types of birds.
15. Sometimes refuges can be established by area bird enthusiasts, with their safe places to nest and feed.
16. After their initial introduction to bird-watching, bird feeders are built by many beginners.
17. A pair of binoculars stationed by the kitchen window with its familiar black strap is a sure sign of a bird lover.
18. National bird counts are sometimes conducted by amateur bird-watchers important to national bird censuses.
19. Making a count in a specific spot each year on Christmas Day, the fluctuating winter bird population of a particular place can be calculated by a local bird club.
20. After spending time and money in helping endangered species, bird counts help bird lovers know their efforts have been worthwhile.

Using Modifiers Correctly

Grammar Review

USING MODIFIERS CORRECTLY

A Moveable Feast is Ernest Hemingway's memoir of his years in Paris in the 1920s. A poor, struggling writer then, he often had to forgo meals. The following passage has been annotated to show some of the kinds of modifiers covered in this unit.

Literature Model

from A Moveable Feast
by Ernest Hemingway

Positive form of the adjective *good*

Superlative form of the adjective *good*

Comparative forms of the adjectives *clear* and *beautiful*

Comparative form of the adverb *well*

Correct placement of the modifier *only*

Correctly placed participial phrase modifying *shops*

You got very hungry when you did not eat enough in Paris because all the bakery shops had such good things in the windows and people ate outside at tables on the sidewalk so that you saw and smelled the food. When you had given up journalism and were writing nothing that anyone in America would buy, explaining at home that you were lunching out with someone, the best place to go was the Luxembourg gardens where you saw and smelled nothing to eat all the way from the Place de l'Observatoire to the rue de Vaugirard. There you could always go into the Luxembourg museum and all the paintings were sharpened and clearer and more beautiful if you were belly-empty, hollow-hungry. I learned to understand Cézanne much better and to see truly how he made landscapes when I was hungry. I used to wonder if he were hungry too when he painted; but I thought possibly it was only that he had forgotten to eat. It was one of those unsound but illuminating thoughts you have when you have been sleepless or hungry. Later I thought Cézanne was probably hungry in a different way.

After you came out of the Luxembourg you could walk down the narrow rue Férou to the Place St.-Sulpice and there were still no restaurants, only the quiet square with its benches and trees. There was a fountain with lions, and pigeons walked on the pavement and perched on the statues of the bishops. There was the church and there were shops selling religious objects and investments on the north side of the square.

> From this square you could not go further toward the river without passing shops selling fruits, vegetables, wines, or bakery and pastry shops. But by choosing your way carefully you could work to your right around the gray and white stone church and reach the rue de l'Odéon and turn up to your right toward Sylvia Beach's bookshop and on your way you did not pass too many places where things to eat were sold. The rue de l'Odéon was bare of eating places until you reached the square where there were three restaurants.
>
> By the time you reached 12 rue de l'Odéon your hunger was contained but all of your perceptions were heightened again. The photographs looked different and you saw books that you had never seen before.
>
> "You're too thin, Hemingway," Sylvia would say. "Are you eating enough?"
>
> "Sure."

Review: Exercise 1 **Making Correct Comparisons**

The following sentences are about some of Ernest Hemingway's friends in Paris in the 1920s. Rewrite each sentence on your paper, substituting the proper comparative or superlative form of the modifier in parentheses for the word or phrase in italics.

SAMPLE   In the 1920s, Paris was perhaps the *most beautiful city* in Europe. (lively)
ANSWER   In the 1920s, Paris was perhaps the liveliest city in Europe.

1. Of all Hemingway's contemporaries, the poet Ezra Pound went *most clearly* in the direction of establishing a new literary style. (far)
2. Few of Hemingway's writer friends in Paris were *more widely* known than F. Scott Fitzgerald. (well)
3. After *The Great Gatsby* was published in 1925, Fitzgerald was often acclaimed as the *finest* American writer. (good)
4. Scott and Zelda Fitzgerald lived a *more glamorous* life than that of many other literary couples. (flamboyant)
5. One of Hemingway's *best* advisers was the innovative American writer Gertrude Stein. (helpful)

Grammar Review

Review: Exercise 2 | **Correcting Incomplete Comparisons**

The following sentences are about Paris. Rewrite the sentences, correcting any errors of incomplete comparison. Some of the sentences can be revised in more than one way.

1. To struggling artists and writers, Paris in the 1920s was more attractive than any city.
2. Many artists in the 1920s believed that Paris's cultural life was more inspiring than New York.
3. The beauty and the variety of the architecture in Paris are not rivaled anywhere.
4. Paris has historical riches that surpass any American city.
5. Few cities can claim a heritage of beauty and culture that matches Paris.

Review: Exercise 3 | **Choosing the Correct Modifier**

The following sentences are about Sylvia Beach and the bookstore she owned in Paris. For each sentence choose the correct form of the modifier in parentheses, and write it on your paper. Then indicate whether the modifier you have chosen is being used as an *adjective* or an *adverb*.

1. Sylvia Beach, who owned a bookstore in Paris, always treated her customers (good/well).
2. Writers such as Hemingway felt (good/well) about visiting the store, which was called Shakespeare and Company.
3. The store provided a cheerful, warm haven when the weather in Paris turned (bad/badly).
4. Sylvia Beach was confident that Hemingway could write (good/well).
5. Beach knew how (bad/badly) Hemingway wanted to succeed.

Review: Exercise 4

Proofreading

The following passage describes the artist Kees van Dongen, whose painting appears on page 669. Rewrite the passage, correcting the errors in spelling, grammar, and usage. Add any missing punctuation. There are ten errors.

Kees van Dongen

¹Born in Rotterdam, Kees van Dongen (1877–1968) studied art in his native Holland, but in 1897 he decided to make Paris his permenent home. ²There he soon became associated with a group of artists known as the fauves who were famous—or, in the eyes of conservative critics, infamous—for their vibrant colors and fluid brushwork.
³Van Dongen is most best known for his witty portraits of actors, writers, and politicians. ⁴Regarded at the time as the capital of modern culture, he also painted many scenes of Paris.

Kees van Dongen, *Avenue du Bois, Paris*, c. 1925

⁵*Avenue du Bois, Paris* is typical of his mature work, the painting's simplified forms and washes of color clearly show the artist's debt to fauvism.

⁶The art world of the time didn't approve of no use of brilliant colors and primitive forms. ⁷The popularity of the primitive art of indigenous peoples had a more strong influence on the fauvists than on any group.

⁸The influences of fauvism is apparent in the works of Paul Cézanne, Vincent van Gogh, and Paul Gauguin. ⁹Although fauvism had lost its momentum by 1908, it is believed to have paved the way for cubism and more later, abstract expresionism.

Review: Exercise 5

Mixed Review

Read the following biography of Ernest Hemingway. Then rewrite the sentences below it, correcting any errors in the use of modifiers. If you need additional information for your sentences, consult the biography.

Ernest Hemingway

One of the greatest modern novelists, Ernest Hemingway was born in Oak Park, Illinois, in 1899. After he graduated from high school, he volunteered as an ambulance driver in World War I and was wounded in Italy. In 1920 he went to Paris as a correspondent for the *Toronto Star*. *A Moveable Feast* recalls his struggle to become a serious writer. Hemingway wrote many short stories, some inspired by his experiences in Spain. Other short stories feature Africa as their setting. "The Short Happy Life of Francis Macomber" and "The Snows of Kilimanjaro" are two of Hemingway's finest short stories, featured in many short-fiction anthologies. Many consider Hemingway the best short story writer in English.

Hemingway combined his training as a journalist with his love for bullfighting to produce a work of nonfiction, *Death in the Afternoon* (1932). A careful study of his work reveals Hemingway's fascination with violence, be it voluntary, as in the safari or the bullfight, or involuntary, as in war.

Hemingway's experiences as a journalist during the Spanish civil war inspired the novel *For Whom the Bell Tolls* (1940), which many consider his masterpiece. After World War II, he settled in Cuba. He won the Pulitzer Prize in 1953 for his short novel *The Old Man and the Sea* and was awarded the Nobel Prize in 1954. He died in 1961.

1. Of all twentieth-century American novelists, Hemingway may have garnered the greater fame.
2. After graduating from high school, journalism was Hemingway's first choice as a career.
3. Rejected by the United States Army because of an eye injury, the Red Cross gave Hemingway a job as an ambulance driver in Italy during World War I.
4. He was wounded bad in Italy during the war and returned home, a decorated hero.
5. After returning to Michigan to recuperate, a job offer took him to Europe as a foreign correspondent.
6. Tiring of journalism as a career choice, in Paris Hemingway only decided to write fiction.
7. He soon began to turn out novels and short stories that received more acclaim than his contemporaries.
8. Curiouser than many reporters, Hemingway traveled to Spain in 1936 to cover the civil war there.
9. His novel *For Whom the Bell Tolls* captures better than any work of fiction the tragedy of the Spanish civil war.
10. Several Hollywood movies have been made from Hemingway's novels featuring major stars.

Writing Application

TIME

For more about the writing process, see **TIME Facing the Blank Page,** pp. 111–121.

Modifiers in Writing

The correct placement of modifiers is essential if a writer wishes to insure clarity. Notice, for example, the position of the italicized modifiers in the following passage from Julio Cortázar's "Text in a Notebook," translated by Gregory Rabassa:

> *Having reached this conclusion,* I found the rest obvious. *Except at dawn and very late at night,* the Anglo trains are never empty because Buenos Aires people are night owls and there are always a few passengers coming and going before the station gates are closed.

Now think how this passage would read with a dangling participle in the first sentence and a misplaced prepositional phrase in the second sentence.

> *Having reached this conclusion,* the rest was obvious. The Anglo trains are never empty because Buenos Aires people, *except at dawn and very late at night,* are night owls and there are always a few passengers coming and going before the station gates are closed.

Techniques with Modifiers

Keep these guidelines in mind as you write and revise your own work:

❶ A dangling modifier seems to modify no word in the sentence in which it appears. Avoid dangling modifiers by making certain to include the word or phrase being modified.

UNCLEAR VERSION Having reached this conclusion, the rest was obvious.

CORTÁZAR'S CLEAR VERSION Having reached this conclusion, I found the rest obvious.

❷ Decide whether moving a modifier or other words will make the meaning of your sentence clearer. Often the closer a modifier is to the word it modifies, the clearer the meaning of the sentence will be.

UNCLEAR VERSION The Anglo trains are never empty because Buenos Aires people, except at dawn and very late at night, are night owls. . .

CORTÁZAR'S CLEAR VERSION Except at dawn and very late at night, the Anglo trains are never empty. . .

Practice Practice these techniques by revising the following passage, using a separate sheet of paper.

Born during the Depression, poverty haunted Arthur Mitchell's early life. He nevertheless dreamed of becoming a dancer, and he studied as a teenager at New York City's High School of Performing Arts. Then after he graduated from high school, the noted choreographer George Balanchine invited Mitchell to study with the New York City Ballet. Invited to join the ballet troupe in 1955, many of the company productions became Mitchell's star vehicles. He left the New York City Ballet to found the Dance Theater of Harlem and help fulfill the dreams of aspiring dancers at the height of his career.

UNIT
19 Usage Glossary

672

Usage Glossary

The following glossary describes some particularly troublesome matters of preferred usage. It will help you choose between two words that are often confused. It will also point out certain words and expressions that you should avoid completely in formal speaking and writing.

a, an   Use the article *a* when the word that follows begins with a consonant sound, including a sounded *h: a rocket, a helicopter.* Use *an* when the word that follows begins with a vowel sound or an unsounded *h: an endowment, an heir.* Use *a* before a word that begins with the "yew" sound: *a eucalyptus, a union.*

a lot, alot   You should always write this expression as two words. It means "a large amount." Some authorities suggest avoiding it altogether in formal English.

INFORMAL   **A lot** of people attended the final game of the season.

FORMAL   **Many** people attended the final game of the season.

a while, awhile   *A while* is made up of an article and a noun. *In* or *for* often precedes *a while*, forming a prepositional phrase. *Awhile*, a single word, is used only as an adverb.

The musicians paused for **a while**.

The musicians will pause in **a while**.

The musicians paused **awhile**.

accept, except   *Accept*, a verb, means "to receive" or "to agree to." *Except* may be used as a preposition or as a verb. As a preposition it means "but." As a verb it means "to leave out."

Please **accept** my apologies.

Everyone **except** Paul can attend the meeting. [preposition]

If you **except** the planet Earth, you can consider the Solar System uninhabited. [verb]

adapt, adopt   *Adapt* means "to change something so that it can be used for another purpose" or "to adjust." *Adopt* means "to take something for one's own."

It was difficult to **adapt** the play for a young audience.

Some people think that dinosaurs became extinct because they could not **adapt** to the changing environment.

The general must **adopt** a new strategy to win this battle.

advice, advise   *Advice*, a noun, means "helpful opinion." *Advise*, a verb, means "to give advice" or "to counsel."

> Cheryl asked her guidance counselor for **advice** in choosing a college and hoped he would **advise** her well.

affect, effect   *Affect*, a verb, means "to cause a change in," or "to influence." *Effect* may be a noun or a verb. As a noun it means "result." As a verb it means "to bring about" or "accomplish."

> This information will certainly **affect** our decision.
> What **effect** will this information have on your decision? [noun meaning "result"]
> What could **effect** such a change in her outlook? [verb meaning "bring about"]

ain't   *Ain't* is unacceptable in formal speaking and writing. Use *ain't* only when quoting somebody's exact words or when writing dialogue to create a particular effect. Otherwise use *I am not*; *she is not*; *he is not*; and so on.

all ready, already   *All ready* means "completely ready." *Already*, an adverb, means "before" or "by this time."

> The boys were **all ready** to take the test, but by the time they arrived, the test had **already** begun.

all right, alright   Always write this expression as two words. Although it is sometimes spelled as one word, *alright*, most authorities prefer that it be spelled *all right*.

> Is it **all right** for the baby to have ice cream?

Exercise 1	Making Usage Choices

For each sentence choose the correct word or expression from the pair in parentheses.

1. Ragtime played (a/an) important role in the development of American music.
2. First popular in the early 1900s, it enjoyed a revival for (a while/awhile) in the 1970s.
3. Americans quickly (adapted/adopted) ragtime as one of their favorite kinds of music.
4. The popularity of ragtime greatly (affected/effected) the sales of phonographs and records.
5. The music of the ragtime composer Scott Joplin was not merely (all right/alright) but quite enjoyable and sometimes even extraordinary.
6. Joplin's "Maple Leaf Rag," (all ready/already) well known by 1900, helped popularize ragtime throughout the United States.
7. The public quickly (accepted/excepted) a later piece by Joplin, "The Entertainer."
8. (A lot/Alot) of ragtime pieces were reproduced on piano rolls for player pianos.
9. I wonder what (advice/advise) Joplin would offer a young piano player today.
10. Although ragtime compositions (ain't/aren't) easy to play, they remain highly popular.

all together, altogether   The two words *all together* mean "in a group." The single word *altogether* is an adverb meaning "completely" or "on the whole."

> They decided to leave **all together**, but it was **altogether** impossible for them to fit in one car.

allusion, illusion   An *allusion* is "an indirect reference." An *illusion* is "a false idea or appearance."

> The candidate made a disparaging **allusion** to his rival's plan for lowering taxes.

> It is an **illusion** that taxes can be lowered this year.

anywheres, everywheres   Write these words and others like them without a final -*s*: *anywhere, everywhere, somewhere.*

bad, badly   See Unit 18.

being as, being that   Many people use these expressions in informal conversation to mean "because" or "since." In formal writing and speaking, use *because* or *since.*

> **Since** the weather is bad here in the winter, they have decided to stay at home.

> **Because** the weather is bad there in the winter, we have decided not to go.

beside, besides   *Beside*, a preposition, means "at the side of" or "next to." *Besides*, an adverb, means "moreover" or "in addition to."

> Who is that little girl sitting **beside** Joanne?

> **Besides** Carlos, I am inviting James, Lloyd, and Luz.

> Lian is too busy to attend the play at the new theater; **besides**, she is feeling ill.

between, among   *Between* and *among* are prepositions that are used to state a relationship. Use *between* to refer to two persons or things or to compare one person or thing with another person or thing or with an entire group. Use *between* to refer to more than two persons or things when they are considered equals in a close relationship or are being viewed individually in relation to one another.

> Lucinda sat down **between** Tamara and Geraldo. [*Between* establishes a relationship involving two persons—Tamara and Geraldo.]

> What is the difference **between** this novel and the author's previous books? [*Between* is used to compare one book with an entire group—all of the author's previous books.]

ANZUS is a treaty **between** Australia, New Zealand, and the United States. [*Between* establishes a relationship in which each country individually has made an agreement with every other country.]

Use *among* to show a relationship in which more than two persons or things are considered as a group.

The four women talked **among** themselves.

This soprano is **among** the finest singers in the world.

borrow, lend, loan *Borrow* and *lend* have opposite meanings. *Borrow* is a verb meaning "to take something with the understanding that it must be returned." *Lend* is a verb meaning "to give something with the understanding that it will be returned." *Loan* is a noun. It may also be used as a verb, but most authorities prefer that *lend* be used instead.

May I **borrow** your car? [verb]

Will you **lend** me your car if I return it with a full tank of gas? [verb]

Florence will ask the bank for an automobile **loan** so she can buy a new car. [noun]

| Exercise 2 | Making Usage Choices |

For each of the following sentences, choose the correct word or expression from the pair in parentheses.

Patchwork Quilts

1. People (everywhere/everywheres) are rediscovering the beauty and practicality of quilted coverlets.
2. During colonial days, when cloth was needed (bad/badly), quilts were pieced together from scraps of wool and linen.
3. (Being that/Since) these quilts had beautiful designs, they looked quite extraordinary as bed covers.
4. The pattern of a patchwork quilt can create an (allusion/illusion) of a three-dimensional image.
5. For my last quilting bee, or quilting party, I needed to (borrow/lend) a tracing wheel and chalk.
6. (Beside/Besides) being useful household items, quilts are often considered works of art.
7. Many quilters are happy to (borrow/lend) their patchwork quilts for exhibitions.
8. Of the three-hundred quilts I saw at the exhibition, this one is (all together/altogether) my favorite.
9. (Among/Between) these two patchwork patterns associated with frontier life—Lone Star Log Cabin and Wedding Ring—which do you prefer?
10. I would feel (bad/badly) if you spilled your drink on my antique quilt.

bring, take   Use *bring* to mean "to carry from a distant place to a closer one." Use *take* to mean "to carry from a nearby place to a more distant one."

> Will you **bring** me a pineapple when you come back from Maui?

> Don't forget to **take** your camera when you go to Hawaii.

can, may   Use *can* to indicate the ability to do something. *May* indicates permission to do something or the possibility of doing it.

> Carrie **can** speak several different languages.

> You **may** keep my camera till Monday.

can't hardly, can't scarcely   These terms are considered double negatives because *hardly* and *scarcely* by themselves have a negative meaning. Do not use *hardly* and *scarcely* with *not* or the contraction *-n't*.

> That story is so outlandish that I **can hardly** believe it actually happened.

> It is so dark I **can scarcely** see the path.

continual, continuous   *Continual* describes action that occurs over and over but with pauses between occurrences. *Continuous* describes an action that continues with no interruption in space or time.

> The **continual** banging of the door and the **continuous** blare from the TV made it difficult to concentrate.

could of, might of, must of, should of, would of   Do not use *of* after *could, might, must, should,* or *would.* Instead, use the helping verb *have* or its contraction, *-ve.*

> I **would have** gone to the meeting if I had known it would be so important and interesting.

> I **should have** listened to my assistant and gone to the meeting with him.

different from, different than   In general, the expression *different from* is preferred to *different than.*

> A canoe is **different from** a rowboat.

doesn't, don't   *Doesn't* is the contraction of *does not* and should be used with *he, she, it,* and all singular nouns. *Don't* is the contraction of *do not* and should be used with *I, you, we, they,* and all plural nouns.

> Margie **doesn't** like sweet apples.

> I **don't** like them either.

emigrate, immigrate   Use *emigrate* to mean "to move from one country to another." Use *immigrate* to mean "to enter a country to settle there." Use *from* with *emigrate* and *to* or *into* with *immigrate.*

Many people **emigrated** from Europe during the first two decades of the twentieth century.

My grandparents **immigrated** to the United States during Ireland's Great Potato Famine of 1845–1849.

farther, further   *Farther* should be used to refer to physical distance. *Further* should be used to refer to time or degree.

My house is five blocks **farther** from the high school than your house is.

I cannot give you **further** information about the course because the details have not been published.

fewer, less   In comparisons use *fewer* to refer to nouns that can be counted. Use *less* to refer to nouns that cannot be counted. Also use *less* to refer to figures used as a single amount or quantity.

The store sells **fewer** ice-cream cones during the winter than during the summer.

People usually eat **less** ice cream during the winter than during the summer.

The flight from New York to Amsterdam took **less** than seven hours. [*Seven hours* is treated as a single period of time, not as individual hours.]

good, well   See Unit 18.

had of   Do not use *of* between *had* and a past participle.

I wish I **had** seen him before he left the United States for a vacation in Europe.

hanged, hung   Use *hanged* to mean "to put to death by hanging." Use *hung* in all other cases.

The soldier who had deserted was caught and **hanged**.

Phil **hung** the picture above his desk.

in, into, in to   Use *in* to mean "inside" or "within" and *into* to indicate movement or direction from outside to a point within. *In to* is made up of an adverb (*in*) followed by a preposition (*to*) and should be carefully distinguished from the preposition *into*.

The president was working **in** his office.

An assistant walked **into** the office and gave him his mail and several messages.

The assistant takes the day's agenda **in to** the president.

Making Usage Choices

For each of the following sentences, choose the correct word or expression from the pair in parentheses.

United States Immigrants

1. Many people have (emigrated/immigrated) to the United States over the course of the country's history.
2. Although the flow of immigrants to the United States did slow down at various times, it has been (continuous/continual).
3. During the last twenty years of the nineteenth century, no (fewer/less) than nine million immigrants entered the United States, hoping to make better lives for themselves and their families.
4. These people (might of/might have) chosen other countries in which to settle, but they hoped the opportunities would be better in the United States.
5. When they come to the United States, some people (can hardly/can't hardly) wait to find work in the fields in which they are most interested.
6. The film director Billy Wilder, for example, (emigrated/immigrated) from Austria to the United States, where he found fame directing comedies such as *Some Like It Hot*.
7. Can you believe that some people (doesn't/don't) realize that the actresses Ingrid Bergman and Marlene Dietrich were not born in the United States?
8. George Balanchine came to the United States from Russia and created ballets in a style that was (different from/different than) the style of other choreographers.
9. Any physicist knows how (good/well) Chen Ning Yang and Tsung Dao Lee, two Chinese immigrants, did in their field; they won the Nobel Prize for physics in 1957.
10. (Farther/Further) evidence that immigrants have contributed to the culture of this country can be found in the work of many foreign-born writers, such as Lucha Corpi, a poet who moved to the United States from Mexico when she was nineteen years old.

irregardless, regardless   Always use *regardless*. The prefix *ir-* and the suffix *-less* both have negative meanings. When used together, they form a double negative.

> Maria maintains an optimistic outlook **regardless** of unfavorable circumstances or events.

this kind, these kinds   Because *kind* is singular, it is modified by the singular form *this* or *that*. Similarly, *this* and *that* should be used to modify the nouns sort and type (*this type, that type, this sort, that sort*). Because *kinds* is plural, it is modified by the plural form *these* or *those*. Similarly, *these* and *those* should be used to modify *sorts* and *types*.

> **This kind** of dog is easy to train.
> **These kinds** of dogs are difficult to train.
> **That sort** of film is entertaining.
> **Those sorts** of films are rare these days.

lay, lie   *Lay* means "to put" or "to place," and it takes a direct object. *Lie* means "to recline" or "to be positioned," and it never takes an object.

Please **lay** the book on the table.

The cat loves to **lie** in the sun.

To avoid confusion in using the principal parts of these verbs, study the following chart:

BASE FORM	lay	lie
PRESENT PARTICIPLE	laying	lying
PAST FORM	laid	lay
PAST PARTICIPLE	laid	lain

Daryl **laid** the packages on the chair.

The cat **lay** next to the fireplace.

learn, teach   *Learn* means "to gain knowledge or understanding" or "to acquire skill in." *Teach* means "to impart knowledge or instruction."

Many young children easily **learn** a second language.

These instructors **teach** Spanish.

leave, let   *Leave* means "to go away." *Let* means "to allow" or "to permit."

The plane to Phoenix will **leave** in two hours.

Please **let** us help with the dishes.

like, as   *Like* is a preposition and introduces a prepositional phrase. *As* and *as if* are subordinating conjunctions and introduce subordinate clauses. Many authorities say that *like* should never be used before a clause.

He looks **like** a nervous person.

He felt nervous, **as** he does before every performance.

He looks **as if** he's nervous.

loose, lose   The adjective *loose* means "free," "not firmly attached," or "not fitting tightly." The verb *lose* means "to misplace" or "to fail to win."

That bracelet is so **loose** that you might **lose** it.

passed, past   *Passed* is the past tense and the past participle of the verb *to pass*. *Past* can be an adjective, a preposition, an adverb, or a noun.

The time **passed** quickly. [verb]

Kyong has grown very tall and strong during the **past** eight months. [adjective]

The newspaper truck drove **past** our house very early this morning. [preposition]

The truck shifted gears as it went **past**. [adverb]

All of that happened in the **past**. [noun]

For each of the following sentences, choose the correct word or expression from the pair in parentheses.

Gary Soto, Author and Teacher

1. I wonder if author Gary Soto still (teaches/learns) English, creative writing, and ethnic studies at the University of California.
2. (Regardless/Irregardless) of the kind of class, Soto sometimes uses his own life experiences to help relate the subject matter to his students.
3. Soto (had/had of) learned about poetry when he took a class that was taught by Philip Levine at California State University.
4. (This kind/These kinds) of class can inspire young writers to work hard to perfect their craft.
5. People sometimes need to (leave/let) go of their old ideas about poetry in order to develop their own style.
6. Soto once felt inspired to write a poem after he went (in/into/in to) his kitchen and spotted a black widow spider.
7. Much time has (past/passed) since the days when Soto lived in poverty in Fresno, California.
8. In one of his books for children, Soto writes about a cat that doesn't (lay/lie) around the house the way other cats do.
9. I liked one of his poems so much that I framed it and (hanged/hung) it on the wall in my room.
10. As an avid reader of Gary Soto's poetry, short stories, and nonfiction essays, I hope he never (looses/loses) his desire to write.

precede, proceed   *Precede* means "to go before" or "to come before." *Proceed* means "to continue" or "to move along."

An elegant dinner **preceded** the concert.

The speaker **proceeded** to the dais and began her lecture on contemporary architecture.

raise, rise   *Raise* means "to cause to move upward," and it always takes an object. *Rise* means "to get up"; it is intransitive and therefore never takes an object.

Many people **raise** their voices when they become angry.
Antonio **rises** every morning at six and runs two miles.

reason is because   Do not use this expression. Since *because* means "for the reason that," it is repetitious. Use either *the reason is that* or *because.*

The **reason** Jane cannot come to the party **is that** she will be away visiting relatives.

Jane cannot come to the party **because** she will be away visiting relatives.

respectfully, respectively   *Respectfully* means "with respect." *Respectively* means "in the order named."

> The audience listened **respectfully** to the Nobel laureate as she delivered her speech.

> Peggy and Michael are, **respectively**, author and editor of the book.

says, said   *Says* is the present tense, third-person singular form of *say*. *Said* is the past tense of *say*.

> Yesterday he **said** that he would meet us outside the theater before the play began.

> He always **says** he will be on time, but he never is.

sit, set   *Sit* means "to place oneself in a seated position." It rarely takes an object. *Set* means "to place" or "to put" and usually takes an object. When it is used with *sun* to mean "the sun is going down" or "the sun is sinking out of sight," *set* is intransitive.

> Mother and Father **sit** at opposite ends of the table during the main meal of the day.

> Please **set** this casserole on the table.

> We watched as the sun **set**, leaving the sky streaked with orange and red.

than, then   *Than* is a conjunction that is used to introduce the second element in a comparison; it also shows exception.

> Yesterday was busier **than** today.

> We have had no visitors other **than** Mrs. Peterson, who came early in the morning.

Then is an adverb that means "at that time," "soon afterward," "the time mentioned," "at another time," "for that reason," "in that case," or "besides."

> Ana was in high school **then**.

> The musicians tuned their instruments and **then** played the symphony by Mozart.

> By **then**, they had already left town.

> Renee has been to Europe twice; she visited England and Scotland, and **then** she toured France and Italy.

> She found a pleasant hotel and **then** felt contented.

> The down payment is one thing, but **then** there's the interest to be paid.

this here, that there   Avoid using *here* and *there* after *this*, *that*, *those*, or *these*.

> Debbie visited several stores in the mall and then decided to buy **this** sweater.

> Please hand me **that** pencil on the desk.

who, whom   See Unit 17.

Making Usage Choices

In each sentence, choose the correct word or expression from the pair in parentheses.

The Invention of the Automobile

1. There are many people (who/whom) we could name as having contributed significantly to the invention of the automobile.
2. Descriptions of a steam-powered cart dating back to the Chou dynasty in China (preceded/proceeded) the development of a self-propelled vehicle by about two thousand years.
3. By the late eighteenth century, inventors such as army officer Nicolas Cugnot hoped to create a steam-powered vehicle in which one could (sit/set) and ride.
4. Cugnot found some success in 1769 when he turned (this/this here) idea into a reality.
5. The reason Cugnot's first steam-powered vehicle was not a complete success is (because/that) it could not be maneuvered, and it overturned after barely reaching a speed of 2.5 miles per hour.
6. Today, people (raise/rise) few objections when two men, Gottlieb Daimler and Karl Benz, are named as the true fathers of the modern automobile.
7. Never having met each other, both men (preceded/proceeded) to work independently on a gasoline-powered vehicle in 1885.
8. Later, after making successful trial runs with their inventions, each (said/says) that he was the inventor of the automobile.
9. Was Daimler's contribution, the internal-combustion engine, more important (then/than) Benz's three-wheeled vehicle?
10. In 1926 Daimler's and Benz's companies, named (respectfully/respectively) Daimler-Motoren-Gesellschaft and Benz & Co., joined to form a new company, Daimler-Benz, maker of the Mercedes-Benz automobiles.

Exercise 6   Identifying Incorrect Usage

For each of the following sentences, find and correct the improper usage.

1. Henry Ford preceded to found his automotive company on a revolutionary idea: the automobile would become a necessity for every American family, not simply a luxury item for the wealthy few.
2. Most historians agree that this here concept led to the motor age, which changed people's lives, stimulated the economy, and enabled cities and suburbs to grow.
3. Ford was a visionary, able to dismiss the concepts of the passed.
4. Ford treated his workers well, rising the wage and reducing the length of the workday.
5. The price of a Model T automobile fell to $290 in 1924, and by than, many people who wanted to buy a car could afford to do so.

Exercise 7	Making Usage Choices

For each of the following sentences, choose the correct word or expression from the pair in parentheses.

SAMPLE There are (less/fewer) seashells on the beach today than there were yesterday.
ANSWER fewer

Lacrosse

1. Lacrosse is a popular sport (between/among) both men and women in the United States.
2. At the beginning of the game, the referee (sets/sits) the ball in the center of the field.
3. The attackers are supposed to get the ball (in/into/in to) the net of the opposing team.
4. As the defenders try to stop them, the attackers (bring/take) the ball toward the defenders' net.
5. Dodging the defending players, the attackers make (continual/continuous) attempts to score.
6. Skill and speed are especially important at (this/this here) point in the game.
7. In their attempts to score, the players on the attacking team must be careful not to (loose/lose) the ball to the defenders, who are trying their best to get it.
8. An attacker who is (anywhere/anywheres) near the goal may attempt to score.
9. None of the players (accept/except) the goalies may touch the ball with their hands.
10. (Beside/Besides) needing speed and agility, lacrosse players must be strong and able to judge distance.

Exercise 8	Correcting Usage

Rewrite the following sentences, correcting the improper usage or usages.

SAMPLE Some people cannot except the facts, no matter how clearly they are presented.
ANSWER accept

1. It's an historical fact that the game of lacrosse originated with Native Americans.
2. Today, lacrosse is all together different than the original game played by the Iroquois and the Cherokee.
3. The pace of the game is still fast, however, and players ain't allowed to set the ball down on the ground.
4. The sport might never of become popular if lacrosse enthusiasts in Baltimore had not actively promoted the game.
5. College teams that do good are competing for the Wingate Trophy.
6. In men's lacrosse, it is alright for players to block one another with their bodies.
7. Players must be careful not to leave go of the ball too soon.
8. Being that a lacrosse game lasts sixty minutes, players must have endurance.
9. Some people know that ice hockey is not very different than lacrosse.
10. Those football players whom also play lacrosse find that the game enables them to develop their speed and agility.

Making Usage Choices

For each of the following sentences, choose the correct word or expression from the pair in parentheses.

SAMPLE Terry ran (farther/further) than Chris at Tuesday's track meet.
ANSWER farther

Restored Villages

1. A person who (doesn't/don't) find history interesting might be persuaded to think differently after visiting a restored village.
2. History books describe how people in the (past/passed) probably lived.
3. Some restored villages show people actually living (like/as) they did many years ago.
4. I'm sure that historians often (advice/advise) the people who are carrying out the restorations.
5. The oldest European settlement in North America (can/may) be found in Saint Augustine, Florida.
6. Near the James River in Virginia (lay/lie) the restored buildings from the Jamestown settlement.
7. At Plimoth Plantation in Massachusetts, restorers (respectfully/respectively) use the original spelling of the town's name.
8. Walking through the streets of restored Williamsburg, Virginia, some visitors (can hardly/can't hardly) believe their eyes.
9. Do you suppose the artisans at the recreated Cherokee village of Tsa-La-Gi, Oklahoma, are concerned about the (affect/effect) of modern civilization on their heritage?
10. I'd like to know whether (a lot/alot) of these artisans speak the Cherokee language.

Correcting Usage

Rewrite the following sentences, correcting the improper usages.

1. I almost forgot to bring my camera when I went to visit Williamsburg.
2. Your job application might be excepted if you know how to make beeswax candles or weave cloth.
3. I would of applied for a position if I didn't already have a summer job as an intern at the bank.
4. Joe was offered an intern position also, but he don't like working indoors during the summer.
5. I have to admit, an indoor job in a bank is very different than a job at Williamsburg!
6. Someone is going to be learning Joe how to do the work of an eighteenth-century blacksmith.
7. I asked Joe if he would leave me make a few horseshoes.
8. "Absolutely not," he says.
9. The reason is because it's very dangerous work.
10. I wonder what affect this summer job will have on Joe's future career choices.

Usage Glossary

Exercise 11   Making Usage Choices

For each of the following sentences, choose the correct word or expression from the pair in parentheses.

SAMPLE   In the (passed/past) many eloquent people have spoken out for freedom.
ANSWER   past

Maria Tallchief, Prima Ballerina

1. For (a while/awhile) Maria Tallchief, a young girl growing up on the Osage Indian Reservation in Oklahoma, studied both piano and ballet.
2. By the time she was a teenager, she decided she would rather concentrate her efforts on ballet (than/then) on anything else.
3. She knew that she wanted (bad/badly) to be a ballerina.
4. At the age of fifteen, she was (all ready/already) dancing a solo part in a ballet choreographed by Nijinska, the sister of the famous dancer Nijinsky.
5. While she was with the Ballet Russe de Monte Carlo, she had to (adapt/adopt) to rigorous discipline and practice.
6. Members of this ballet company were initially skeptical about Tallchief's abilities, but the dancer soon (learned/taught) them to think of her in a new way.
7. Tallchief was able to go (farther/further) in her career after George Balanchine took over the Ballet Russe.
8. I once read an article that (says/said) Balanchine made Tallchief his protégée and created starring roles for her.
9. (Regardless/Irregardless) of the many roles she danced, she became best known for her title role in the ballet *The Firebird*.
10. The reason Maria Tallchief was so successful as a prima ballerina is (because/that) she was able to display not only great emotion but also superb technique in her dancing.

Exercise 12   Correcting Usage

For each sentence find and correct the improper usage.

1. The word *ballet* is adopted from the Italian word *ballare*, which means "to dance."
2. Ballet developed from a elaborate kind of Italian Renaissance pageantry.
3. After Catherine de Médicis, an Italian, emigrated to France and became queen, she invited many Italian musicians and dancing masters to her court in Paris.
4. The reason Catherine de Médicis is given credit for bringing ballet to France is because the first ballet, the *Ballet comique de la reine*, was performed in her court in 1581.
5. These kind of performances, however, were confined to European courts for many years to come.

Making Usage Choices

For each of the following sentences, choose the correct word or expression from the pair in parentheses.

Reptiles

1. Reptiles have been living on Earth (continuously/continually) for about 280 million years.
2. (Can/May) you decide whether you want a snake or a turtle for a pet?
3. If I had to choose (between/among) a snake or a turtle, I would definitely choose a turtle.
4. Reptiles are (different from/different than) amphibians in many ways.
5. (Fewer/Less) people seem to be afraid of amphibians than of reptiles.
6. (Irregardless/Regardless) of these fears, people should learn more about reptiles and amphibians and do what they can to help conserve them.
7. Many animals are killed (because/being that) belts, shoes, handbags, and other goods are made from their skins.
8. Reptiles have successfully adapted to deserts, forests, grasslands, swamps, and rivers; in fact, they can live almost (anywhere/anywheres).
9. My little sister (doesn't/don't) know that lizards and snakes make up the largest group of reptiles.
10. (Being that/Since) reptiles are cold-blooded and their body temperature fluctuates with the temperature of their environment, they must avoid extreme heat and cold in order to stay alive.

Exercise 14 **Correcting Usage**

For each sentence, find and correct the improper usage.

SAMPLE   I can't hardly read the small print.
ANSWER   can hardly

1. Mrs. Russo learned us that living forms of reptiles include turtles, lizards, snakes, alligators, crocodiles, and tuatara.
2. Irregardless of the species, all reptiles have lungs and breathe air.
3. Many of the reptiles and amphibians of the passed are now extinct.
4. Some scientists believe that at the end of the Mesozoic Era, Earth's climate changed, and plants that could not adopt to the new environment died.
5. One current theory said that plant-eating dinosaurs died as a result, leaving flesh-eating dinosaurs with nothing to eat.
6. Don't you think that lizards look more like dinosaurs then snakes do?
7. Lizards are for the most part harmless, accept for the Gila monster, which is venomous.
8. If you come upon a Gila monster in a southwestern desert, keep walking until you are passed it.
9. Take my advise: if you see an alligator, stay away.
10. Beside alligators and crocodiles, what other reptiles can be found in the southeastern United States?

Grammar Review

USAGE GLOSSARY

The following quotations, which have been annotated to show some of the usage items covered in this unit, deal with the paramount importance of freedom to human existence.

Literature Model

Quotations About Freedom

> What woman needs is not as a woman to act or rule, but as a nature to grow, as an intellect to discern, as a soul to live freely and unimpeded, to unfold such powers as were given her when we left our common home.
>
> From *Woman in the Nineteenth Century* by Margaret Fuller

The articles *a* used before words beginning with consonants and *an* used before a word beginning with a vowel

> I would rather sit on a pumpkin and have it all to myself than be crowded on a velvet cushion.
>
> From *Walden* by Henry David Thoreau

The conjunction *than* used in a comparison

> The cost of liberty is less than the price of repression.
>
> From *John Brown* by W. E. B. DuBois

Less used to modify a noun (*cost*) that cannot be counted

> My first and greatest love affair was with this thing we call freedom, . . . this dangerous and beautiful and sublime being who restores and supplies us all.
>
> From "One Man's Meat" by E. B. White

The relative pronoun *who* in the nominative case as the subject of a clause

> And so, my fellow Americans, ask not what your country can do for you—ask what you can do for your country. My fellow citizens of the world, ask not what America will do for you, but what together we can do for the freedom of man.
>
> Inaugural Address, January 20, 1961, by John F. Kennedy

The verb *can* to indicate the ability to do something

Review: Exercise 1   Making Usage Choices

The following sentences are about political independence. For each one, choose the correct word or expression in parentheses, and write it on your paper.

1. Toussaint L'Ouverture is (a/an) hero in Haiti, where he helped to lead the nation to freedom.
2. (Accept/Except) for French Guiana, an overseas department of France, the South American continent is composed of independent nations.
3. Formerly known as Ceylon, Sri Lanka is one of many countries that have (adapted/adopted) new names since declaring independence.
4. Simón Bolívar, the nineteenth-century freedom fighter, (affected/effected) great change in Latin America.
5. The rest of Central America was (all ready/already) independent when Belize achieved independence in 1981.
6. The United States has been (a/an) independent country for more than two hundred years.
7. (Many/A lot of/Alot of) independent countries are part of the British Commonwealth.
8. Many former dependencies in Africa have been divided (in/into/in to) smaller nations.
9. In India, independence (preceded/proceeded) at a slow pace.
10. Today more countries are independent (than/then) not.

Review: Exercise 2

Proofreading

The following passage describes the artist George Benjamin Luks, whose painting appears on the next page. Rewrite the passage, correcting the errors in spelling, grammar, and usage. Add any missing punctuation. There are ten errors.

George Benjamin Luks

[1]George Benjamin Luks (1867–1933) was born in Williamsport, Pennsylvania, he attended the Pennsylvania Academy of Fine Arts. [2]After having lived in Europe for awhile, Luks returned to the United States in 1894 and excepted a position as an artist-reporter for the *Philadelphia Press*. [3]Later he worked for the *Philadelphia Bulletin* as a war correspondant in Cuba.

[4]After he began to paint in 1897, he preceded to make rapid progress. [5]His subjects were New York, colorful characters and social outcasts. [6]These kind of realistic canvases were painted in a dark, aggressive style. [7]As time past, his works grow more colorful, and his style became much more vivacious.

[8]Luks's painting *Armistice Night* captures the booming festivities that marked the end of World War I and conveys the joyous affect of freedom.

George Benjamin Luks, *Armistice Night*, 1918

Review: Exercise 3

Mixed Review

MAKING USAGE CHOICES   For each of the following sentences, choose the correct word or expression in parentheses.

1. (A lot/Alot) of people have studied the view of Athenian democracy expressed in Pericles' famous funeral oration.
2. As leader of a newly independent Kenya, the skillful orator Jomo Kenyatta told disagreeing factions that (all together/altogether) they could help the nation.
3. The Declaration of Independence makes (allusions/illusions) to some of John Locke's ideas.
4. England's Magna Carta was among the first documents (anywheres/anywhere) that limited the power of kings.
5. America's Declaration of Independence (borrowed/lent/loaned) strength to fighters for independence in many other countries.
6. Thomas Jefferson, (who/whom) we know wrote the Declaration of Independence, saw democracy as a way of life.
7. The American patriot Nathan Hale made a memorable speech before the British (hanged/hung) him.
8. The Fifteenth Amendment gives all citizens the right to vote, (irregardless/regardless) of their race.
9. After becoming Senegal's first president, Léopold Sédar Senghor (preceded/proceeded) to make many eloquent speeches concerning the rights of developing nations.
10. Few speeches are better known (than/then) Martin Luther King's "I Have a Dream" speech.

Writing Application

TIME

For more about the writing process, see **TIME Facing the Blank Page,** pages 111–121.

Troublesome Words in Writing

For some, the English language can be a difficult language to master. Even native English speakers make mistakes, using troublesome words and phrases incorrectly. Read the following passage, focusing especially on the italicized words and phrases.

Benny couldn't sleep. *Except* for a few hours catnapping in an airport thousands of miles away, he hadn't slept in over twenty-eight hours. He wouldn't *advise* changing time zones as often or as capriciously as his job required. How would his sleeplessness *affect* his performance tomorrow? *Among* jet pilots it was an often-discussed job hazard. Benny *rose* and dressed. Then he *borrowed* a jacket from his roommate and left the house, thinking a walk in the fresh air would be better than tossing and turning. His next flight *left* in ten hours. *Regardless* of how he felt, Benny was flying to Hong Kong tomorrow.

Techniques for Troublesome Words

Here are some guidelines for using these troublesome expressions in your own writing:

❶ *Except*, when used as a preposition, means "but." If you can substitute the word *but*, use except, not *accept*.

❷ Always use the preposition *among* to show a relationship in which more than two persons (in this case, pilots) are considered as a group.

❸ Use the verb *rise* when you want to say "to get up," as out of bed. Rise never takes an object: *The sun rises; Rickie rose this morning at seven o'clock*. The verb *raise*, however, always takes an object: *I'm going to raise tomatoes.*

❹ *Borrow*, a verb, means "to take something with the understanding that it must be returned." Clearly, Benny intends to return his roommate's jacket.

❺ *Irregardless* is a double negative. Always use *regardless*.

Usage Glossary

Practice   Practice using some of the troublesome words and phrases you learned about in this unit by revising the following paragraph on a separate sheet of paper. Pay particular attention to the underlined words.

Benny <u>preceded</u> down a deserted path that ran along <u>a</u> embankment behind his house. The night was clear and cold, so <u>different than</u> the climate of his last stopover. Benny stuck his hands in his jacket pockets and walked quickly <u>passed</u> a deserted farmhouse. He began an <u>all together</u> silent whistle to accompany his lonely footsteps. Suddenly, he tripped on something <u>among</u> his feet. Knowing he was dangerously close to the precipice, Benny knelt to find the object: a single sneaker <u>laying</u> at just the point where the land ended and the cliff dropped away. Benny slipped his hand inside and felt the worn lining.

It was still warm.

20.1 Capitalization of Sentences and the Pronoun *I*

■ Capitalize the first word of every sentence, including the first word of a direct quotation that is a complete sentence.

> **D**id you know that Beethoven, who was born in Bonn, Germany, in 1770, was completely deaf by the time he composed his Ninth Symphony?
>
> **T**he poet Edna St. Vincent Millay responded to a Beethoven symphony by writing, "**S**weet sounds, oh beautiful music, do not cease!"

■ Capitalize the first word of a sentence in parentheses that stands by itself. Do not capitalize a sentence within parentheses that is contained within another sentence.

> Scott Joplin composed ragtime piano music. (**R**agtime music was originally called rag music.)
>
> Fiddles and banjos (**t**he piano was used later) were the original instruments in a ragtime band.

Do not capitalize the first word of a quotation unless the entire quotation can stand as a complete sentence or is capitalized in the original text.

> The writer Thomas Carlyle said that music is "**t**he speech of angels."
>
> The American composer Aaron Copland said, "**M**elody is what the piece is about."

Do not capitalize the first word of an indirect quotation. An **indirect quotation,** often introduced by the word *that,* does not repeat a person's exact words.

> Beethoven said that **m**usic should bring tears to the eyes of the listeners.

■ Always capitalize the pronoun *I* no matter where it appears in the sentence.

> Since **I** already know how to play the drums, **I** do not need to take lessons before **I** join the band.
>
> You'd think **I** would be surprised, but **I** am never surprised by anything my uncle does.

Capitalization

Exercise 1   Identifying Errors in Capitalization

On a separate sheet of paper, write the words that are incorrectly capitalized and correct them.

in a darkened room in Overland Park, a twenty-five-inch television set sits unlit and alone. just because the Fitzpatricks have jilted their television doesn't mean they have thrown aside their love of action-packed color video. they just get it from a new source—a multimedia computer.

Before the PC, the Fitzpatricks lay sprawled on the floor for up to five hours a day, watching sports, cartoons, and sitcoms. now watching TV has given way to their current favorite activity—aiming the icon at the computer screen. As Shaun Fitzpatrick said, "i don't watch TV anymore."

"nearly fifty years after the commercial launch of broadcast television, the PC is emerging as the first serious challenger to television's hold on the free time of the American family," claims media analyst Dr. Murray Cantor.

Exercise 2   Capitalizing Sentences and the Pronoun *I*

Rewrite each sentence, correcting any errors in capitalization. If a sentence has no errors write the word *correct*.

What They Said

1. The first line of Margaret Walker's poem "Lineage" is "my grandmothers were strong."
2. The Irish novelist Margaret Wolfe Hungerford's 1878 novel *Molly Bawn* contains the famous line "Beauty is in the eye of the beholder."
3. Less than a week after Britain and France had declared war on Nazi Germany on September 3, 1939 (On September 1, Germany had invaded Poland), the French diplomat Paul Reynaud assured radio listeners, "we shall win because we are the stronger."
4. In *Blue Highways,* William Least Heat-Moon writes of how he traveled America's back roads "in search of places where change did not mean ruin and where time and men and deeds connected."
5. In her essay "No Name Woman," Maxine Hong Kingston describes how immigrants in decades past "Who could not reassert brute survival died young and far from home."
6. An insightful piece of advice was given by First Lady Eleanor Roosevelt when she wrote, "no one can make you feel inferior without your consent." (she wrote this in her book *This Is My Story,* published in 1937.)
7. In an interview about her writing techniques, the novelist Toni Morrison declared, "i always know the ending; that's where i start."
8. When asked why the color yellow appeared so frequently in his fiction, Jorge Luis Borges said that Perhaps it was because yellow was the last color he was able to see as he gradually lost his vision.
9. In a letter the author F. Scott Fitzgerald commented, "all good writing is swimming under water and holding your breath."
10. A week after John F. Kennedy's assassination, President Lyndon Johnson addressed the United States Congress and stated that He regretted having to stand where Kennedy ought to have stood.

Capitalizing Sentences and the Pronoun *I*

Rewrite each sentence, correcting any errors in capitalization. If the sentence has no errors, write the word *correct.*

SAMPLE   every afternoon before rehearsals, the actress recited, "i can achieve greatness."

ANSWER   Every afternoon before rehearsals, the actress recited, "I can achieve greatness."

1. Albert Einstein, the brilliant physicist who was awarded the Nobel Prize for Physics in 1921, described science as "Nothing more than a refinement of everyday thinking."
2. Toni Morrison said that her writing has Holes and spaces so that the reader can create his or her own understanding of the story.
3. When Sylvia Plath was seventeen years old, she wrote, "i am afraid of growing older."
4. She continued, "i want to be free. spare me from cooking three meals a day—spare me the relentless cage of routine and rote."
5. Calvin Coolidge broke the police strike in Boston and declared, "there is no right to strike against the public safety by anybody, anywhere, anytime."
6. She said, "the guests have arrived, so please let them in."
7. "The tables and chairs are all set up," she said, "Although we still have to put out all the food and cutlery."
8. The magazine article stated that children spend too much money on video games.
9. "i came, i saw, i conquered."—Julius Caesar
10. Ralph Waldo Emerson said, "every hero becomes a bore at last."
11. The painting (is it an original?) depicts a knight jousting in a tournament.
12. According to this article, "when a wife becomes a second wage earner, husband-wife families spend more on work-related and time-saving expenses such as child care and carry-out food."
13. Juan told his friends that The bands performed better than he had expected.
14. The video was extremely popular. (it made over $50 million.)
15. The first line of Gwendolyn Brooks's poem "The Bean Eaters" is "they eat beans mostly, this old pair."
16. When a network shows a pilot television show (a sample episode from a new series), it monitors the audience's response.
17. The philosopher Seneca advised, "if you wish another person to keep your secret, first keep it yourself."
18. South African writer Doris Lessing believes that a twentieth-century writer must be especially creative during this age, which she claims is "One of the great turning points of history."
19. Her short story "To Room Nineteen" begins, "this is a story, i suppose, about a failure of intelligence; the Rawlingses' marriage was grounded in intelligence."
20. that the Rawlingses had waited so long (But not too long) for the real thing proved their good sense; a good many of their friends had married young and now (They felt) regretted lost opportunities.

Capitalization of Proper Nouns

■ Capitalize a proper noun.

Capitalize a common noun only when it is the first word of a sentence. Capitalize only the important words in proper nouns composed of several words. Do not capitalize articles (*a, an, the*), coordinating conjunctions (*and, but, for, or, nor, yet*), or prepositions of fewer than five letters.

1. Names of individuals

Michael Chang	Jackie Joyner-Kersee
Maria Martinez	Catherine the Great

2. Titles of individuals

■ Capitalize titles used before a proper name and titles used in direct address.

President Carter	Mr. Louis Armstrong
Sir Arthur Conan Doyle	Surgeon General C. Everett Koop
Queen Victoria	Rear Admiral Mary F. Hall
Dr. Paul Dudley White	Yes, Senator. [direct address]

■ In general, do not capitalize titles that follow a proper name or are used alone. Most writers, however, capitalize *president* when referring to the current president of the United States.

> In the Oval Office, the President met with Corazón Aquino, the former president of the Philippines.
> Can you tell me who the third president of the United States was?

■ In general, capitalize a title that describes a family relationship when it is used with or in place of a proper name. Do not capitalize it when it is used with a possessive pronoun such as *my, our, your, their, his,* or *her.*

I wrote to Aunt Olga.	*but*	My aunt Olga lives abroad.
We spoke to Father.		Our father is a lawyer.
Did you visit Grandpa Roberts?		Our grandpa was out.
What did you say, Grandmother?		What did my grandmother say?
Yesterday Grandmother spoke at her garden club.		

3. Names of ethnic groups, national groups, and languages

Maori	Aborigine	Iroquois
Swedish	Kenyan	French
Latin	Spanish	English

4. **Names of organizations, institutions, political parties and their members, and firms**

Girl Scouts of America	Republican Party
Salvation Army	a Democrat
University of Miami	American Express Company
House of Representatives	Wang Laboratories, Inc.

Do not capitalize common nouns such as *museum* or *university* unless they are part of a proper noun.

Jesse visited the art museum on his lunch hour.
He visited the Dallas Museum of Fine Arts.

5. **Names of monuments, bridges, buildings, and other structures**

Grant's Tomb	Hoover Dam
Graybar Building	Greater New Orleans Bridge

6. **Trade names**

Toyota	Tide detergent
Bayer aspirin	Ivory soap

7. **Names of documents, awards, and laws**

Magna Carta	Congressional Medal of Honor
Treaty of Paris	Heisman Trophy
Emmy Award	Sixteenth Amendment

8. **Geographical terms**

■ Capitalize the names of continents, countries, states, counties, and cities, as well as the names of specific bodies of water, topographical features, regions, and streets.

North America	Mackinac Island
Greece	Pocono Mountains
Illinois	Red River Valley
West Virginia	Painted Desert
Chester County	Tropic of Capricorn
Richmond	Central America
Indian Ocean	Michigan Avenue

9. **Names of planets and other celestial bodies**

Mercury	Pleiades	the Sun
Uranus	Little Dipper	the Moon
Andromeda galaxy	the constellation Orion	

Capitalize *earth* only when it refers to the planet. In that case, do not use the definite article *the.*

They dug deep into the earth to find water.
The planets **M**ars and **E**arth are similar in many respects.

10. Compass points

■ Capitalize the words *north, east, south,* and *west* when they refer to a specific area of the country or the world or when they are part of a proper name. Do not capitalize them when they merely indicate direction.

the Far **E**ast	*but*	the **e**ast coast of Australia
South Carolina		Travel **s**outh on Route 9.
the **S**outhwest		a **s**outhwest wind

11. Names of ships, planes, trains, and spacecraft

U.S.S. *Intrepid*	*City of New Orleans*
Concorde	*Apollo 12*

12. Names of most historical events, eras, and calendar items

World **W**ar **I**	**P**leistocene
Great **D**epression	**M**emorial **D**ay
Age of **R**eason	**D**ecember

You should not capitalize a historical period that refers to a general span of time.

the **f**ifth century	the **t**hirties

■ Capitalize the days of the week and the months of the year, but do not capitalize the names of the seasons (*spring, summer, autumn, fall, winter*).

13. Religious terms

■ Capitalize names of deities, religions and their denominations and adherents, words referring to a supreme deity, and religious books and events.

Allah	**C**hurch of **E**ngland
God	the **A**lmighty
Catholicism	the **B**ible
Islam	the **G**ospels
Shintoism	**G**ood **F**riday
Lutherans	**P**assover

14. Names of school courses

■ Capitalize only those school courses that are the name of a language or the title of a specific course. Do not capitalize the name of a subject.

French	*but*	foreign language
World History I		a course in world history
Calculus 303		I am studying calculus.

15. Titles of works

A Connecticut Yankee in King Arthur's Court [book]

"To a Child Running with Outstretched Arms in Canyon de Chelly" [poem]

the *Philadelphia Inquirer* [newspaper]

"Home on the Range" [song]

■ Always capitalize the first and last word of a title or subtitle. Capitalize all other words except articles, coordinating conjunctions, and prepositions of fewer than five letters.

■ Capitalize articles (*a*, *an*, and *the*) at the beginning of a title only when they are part of the title itself. It is common practice not to capitalize (or italicize) articles preceding the title of a newspaper or a periodical. Do not capitalize (or italicize) the word *magazine* unless it is part of the title of a periodical.

The Invisible Man	*but*	a *Life* magazine photograph
The Red Pony		the *Chicago Tribune*

Exercise 4 **Capitalizing Proper Nouns**

On your paper, rewrite the following sentences, correcting the capital letters as necessary.

The Underground Railroad

1. In your History class, you may have discussed the Underground railroad—a secret network that helped Enslaved people escape to freedom in the period before the civil war.
2. In the Decades before the Civil War, the antislavery movement began to flourish in the United States, especially in the north.
3. Pitted against this Movement were those who supported the fugitive slave act—a 1793 law that gave legal support to owners seeking their runaway enslaved servants.
4. The term *underground* in Underground Railroad refers to the secrecy necessary to transport the enslaved people, most of whom traveled North either at night or in disguise.
5. The operation was called a Railroad because railway terms were used to discuss the travellers' progress from the south to safe locations: routes were called lines; those who helped along the way were conductors; and their charges were known as freight or packages.
6. A wide array of people throughout the country—men and women of all ages, african americans, whites, quakers, presbyterians, congregationalists—worked for the Underground Railroad.

(continued)

Capitalization

7. Among the most Prominent were two United States representatives, Joshua Giddings and gerrit smith, as well as the reputed leader of the entire operation, Levi Coffin of cincinnati.

8. Using the railroad, many enslaved people crossed the ohio river to find freedom, and some managed to travel all the way to canada.

9. Harriet Tubman of maryland escaped from slavery in 1849 and became a conductor of hundreds of other enslaved people along the railroad.

10. The Underground Railroad continues to fascinate people, as we can see by the success of the novel *The house of dies drear* by Author Virginia Hamilton.

| Exercise 5 | Capitalizing Proper Nouns |

Rewrite each sentence. Correct any errors in capitalization. If a sentence has no errors, write the word *correct*.

Santha Rama Rau

1. Born in madras, india, Writer Santha Rama Rau traveled around the world with her father, a high-ranking Civil Servant in india's british Colonial Administration.

2. By the time she was eighteen years old, Rau had lived in england and south america as well as in india.

3. She traveled to America for her college education, studying english and Writing at wellesley college in Massachusetts.

4. Rau's first book, *Home to india* (1945), was an autobiography that drew upon her unusual childhood experiences around the world.

5. Rau was comfortable writing in a number of literary forms: in 1960, for example, she dramatized novelist E. M. forster's famous Novel *A Passage To India* for performance in a theater in london.

6. One of her most famous stories is "by any other name," an excerpt from her acclaimed autobiographical novel *Gifts Of Passage.*

7. In the story, Santha puts away her religious books with their stories of the lord krishna (one of the most important gods of hinduism, the major Religion of India) to study at a school run by the british.

8. Santha has to go to this school because her Mother is ill and her Father is away on a business trip.

9. The teacher refuses to learn how to pronounce the names of indians, so Santha's name is changed to "cynthia."

10. Her sister premila becomes "pamela," and the girls feel like outsiders because they follow indian, rather than british, traditions.

| Exercise 6 | Writing Sentences |

Prepare to write a report on a well-known writer. Select a writer and then research facts to include in the report, such as the writer's date of birth, place of birth, education, important writings, travels, languages spoken, and notable awards. Be sure to use capital letters correctly in your notes.

Exercise 7 Capitalizing Proper Nouns

Write the letter of the sentence from each pair that has proper nouns correctly capitalized.

Gabriel García Márquez

1. **a.** The colombian writer gabriel garcía márquez is one of the most innovative writers of today.
   b. The Colombian writer Gabriel García Márquez is one of the most innovative writers of today.

2. **a.** Márquez was born in 1928 in aracataca, a town in Colombia's caribbean zone near the Northern coast.
   b. Márquez was born in 1928 in Aracataca, a town in Colombia's Caribbean zone near the northern coast.

3. **a.** He identifies with the mixed African and Native American heritage of the region and feels little sympathy with the Spanish colonial legacy of his nation's capital, Bogota.
   b. He identifies with the mixed african and native American heritage of the region and feels little sympathy with the spanish colonial legacy of his Nation's capital, bogota.

4. **a.** Although he was born into a large family, Márquez spent the first years of his life with his grandmother, from whom he heard traditional folktales.
   b. Although he was born into a large family, Márquez spent the first years of his life with his Grandmother, from whom he heard traditional Folktales.

5. **a.** He was especially close to his Grandfather, a famous man who had fought in the war of a thousand days (1899–1902).
   b. He was especially close to his grandfather, a famous man who had fought in the War of a Thousand Days (1899–1902).

6. **a.** The influence of william faulkner and ernest hemingway is evident in márquez's early novels *leaf storm* (1955) and *No one writes to the Colonel* (1962).
   b. The influence of William Faulkner and Ernest Hemingway is evident in Márquez's early novels *Leaf Storm* (1955) and *No One Writes to the Colonel* (1962).

7. **a.** Márquez's unique blend of keen observation and outrageous fantasy reached its height in 1967 with his masterpiece *One Hundred Years of Solitude.*
   b. Márquez's unique blend of keen observation and outrageous fantasy reached its height in 1967 with his masterpiece *one hundred years of solitude.*

8. **a.** Speaking of Márquez's work, professor Minta said, "He knows all about the power of nostalgia and never loses sight of the need to resist it."
   b. Speaking of Márquez's work, Professor Minta said, "He knows all about the power of nostalgia and never loses sight of the need to resist it."

9. **a.** In his 1982 nobel address, Márquez discussed the "disorderly reality" of latin America and his hopes for the future of this region and the world.
   b. In his 1982 Nobel address, Márquez discussed the "disorderly reality" of Latin America and his hopes for the future of this region and the world.

10. **a.** During his remarks to the audience, he quoted from Pablo Neruda of Chile and William Faulkner of the United States.
    b. During his remarks to the audience, he quoted from pablo neruda of chile and william faulkner of the united states.

Capitalization

20.3 Capitalization of Proper Adjectives

■ Capitalize proper adjectives (adjectives formed from proper nouns).

Below are some of the categories into which most proper adjectives fit:

1. **Adjectives formed from names of people**

   Georgian architecture
   Mosaic teachings [the teachings of Moses]
   Copernican system
   Jeffersonian agrarianism
   Freudian psychology
   Elizabethan era
   Shakespearean drama

2. **Adjectives formed from place names and names of national, ethnic, and religious groups**

Athenian democracy	**I**rish folk music
Virginian soil	**H**ispanic cooking
African pottery	**J**ewish holidays
German chocolate	**B**uddhist temple

   When used as adjectives, many proper nouns do not change form.

Vermont maple syrup	**U**nited **S**tates foreign policy
Inuit artifacts	**B**eethoven symphonies
Beatles songs	**I**ndia ink

Exercise 8   **Capitalizing Proper Adjectives and Proper Nouns**

Rewrite the following sentences correctly on your paper. As you write each sentence, add or drop capital letters as necessary.

Columbus's Voyage of Discovery

1. On october 12, 1492, a sailor on the spanish ship *pinta* sighted an island in what are now believed to be the bahamas.
2. The italian captain of the expedition, Christopher Columbus, went ashore with the flag of spain and named the place san salvador.
3. Although Columbus's voyage opened up the americas to the people of europe, this achievement had not been his original goal.
4. Columbus's original goal had been to prove that the important commercial and trading centers of asia—china, japan, and the east indies—could be reached by sailing westward from europe.
5. European demand for chinese, japanese, and indian products was great.

6. Such asian spices as pepper, cinnamon, ginger, and cloves were important products to europeans, who also prized such Asian food as rice, figs, and oranges.
7. On his return to spain, Columbus persuaded queen isabella, who had sponsored his voyage, to give him political control over the lands he had reached.
8. Columbus and his brothers subsequently abused their political power by exploiting and enslaving the People of these Lands in the new world.
9. Although he had sailed to a Continent previously unknown to europeans, Columbus still believed that he had reached the east indies.
10. Columbus called the new world inhabitants indians.

Exercise 9 **Capitalizing Proper Nouns and Adjectives**

Write the sentences, correcting any errors in capitalization. If a sentence has no errors, write *correct*.

SAMPLE Oakland university in rochester, michigan, sponsored a debate between reporters from the *Detroit news* and the *Washington post*.

ANSWER Oakland University in Rochester, Michigan, sponsored a debate between reporters from the *Detroit News* and the *Washington Post*.

Saint Petersburg

1. Saint Petersburg, considered one of the most beautiful cities in Europe, is in the northwestern part of Russia.
2. It has long played an important part in russian history.
3. Built by Peter the Great, it was the capital of the Russian Empire during the Eighteenth and Nineteenth Centuries.
4. Students of Modern History learn of its memorable siege.
5. During world war ii, it was the target of a grueling nine-hundred-day siege by the German and Finnish armies.
6. Saint Petersburg's location produces long, cold nights in the Winter and long, warm days in the Summer.
7. The city is filled with famous Museums, such as the hermitage, and Historic Buildings, such as the marble palace.
8. The City has been known by several names, including Saint petersburg (1703–1914), petrograd (1914–1924), and leningrad (1924–1991).
9. In 1991 the russians restored the name Saint Petersburg.
10. That year the Communists lost power, and former heroes such as Lenin were no longer revered.

Exercise 10 **Sentence Writing for a Speech**

Imagine that you are going to give a speech about a notable historical event. To prepare for your speech, make notes to help you organize your information. Write down several sentences in which you describe important aspects of the event, such as where and when the activity took place, who was involved in the action, and what impact it had on history.

Write the letter of the sentence that is correctly capitalized in each of the following pairs.

1. **a.** After reading the novel *1984,* i shuddered to think of living in an orwellian society.
   b. After reading the novel *1984,* I shuddered to think of living in an Orwellian society.

2. **a.** The author of a recent article published in *Real Archaeology* magazine stated that the deluxe version of the Illuminate Company's flashlight was the best on the market.
   b. The author of a recent article published in *Real archaeology* magazine stated that the deluxe version of the illuminate company's flashlight was the best on the market.

3. **a.** The National Association for the Advancement of Colored People was established in 1910 to effect racial equality between African Americans and whites throughout the United States.
   b. The national association for the advancement of colored people was established in 1910 to effect racial equality between african americans and whites throughout the United States.

4. **a.** Over a thousand lives were lost when a torpedo from a German submarine struck and sank the British Liner *lusitania* in 1915.
   b. Over a thousand lives were lost when a torpedo from a German submarine struck and sank the British liner *Lusitania* in 1915.

5. **a.** Accepting the Nobel peace prize, Martin Luther King Jr. said that the road from Montgomery, Alabama, to Oslo, norway, would one day "Be widened into a super-highway of justice."
   b. Accepting the Nobel Peace Prize, Martin Luther King Jr. said that the road from Montgomery, Alabama, to Oslo, Norway, would one day "be widened into a super-highway of justice."

6. **a.** Can you ask the librarian to help me find out whether Spanish is widely spoken in Oregon and other parts of the Northwest?
   b. Can you ask the librarian to help me find out whether Spanish is widely spoken in Oregon and other parts of the northwest?

7. **a.** Before boarding *air force one* for his trip to the Middle East, the president said that he was hopeful about the Peace Talks.
   b. Before boarding *Air Force One* for his trip to the Middle East, the President said that he was hopeful about the peace talks.

8. **a.** My cousin Anita met mom and dad at the neighborhood Shopping Mall, and then they all drove in my parents' car to visit Uncle Carlos.
   b. My cousin Anita met Mom and Dad at the neighborhood shopping mall, and then they all drove in my parents' car to visit Uncle Carlos.

9. **a.** Is anyone in history 102 writing a report on life in the urban centers or the rural areas of America in the Nineteenth Century?
   b. Is anyone in History 102 writing a report on life in the urban centers or the rural areas of America in the nineteenth century?

10. **a.** Among the most complex figures in American history is Chief Crazy Horse of the Sioux nation.
    b. Among the most complex figures in American History is chief Crazy Horse of the Sioux nation.

Review: Capitalizing in Sentences

The following sentences are about the opera *Porgy and Bess*. Rewrite each sentence, correcting any errors in capitalization. If a sentence has no errors, write *correct*.

SAMPLE   Auditions for the spring musical *Porgy and Bess* were held in the madison high school auditorium.

ANSWER   Auditions for the spring musical *Porgy and Bess* were held in the Madison High School auditorium.

1. According to the *Oxford Companion to American Theatre*, the play *Porgy* (Written by Dorothy and Dubose Heyward) "Remains one of the greatest of all American folk dramas."
2. The musical *Porgy and Bess* (1935), considered "A folk opera," was based on that play.
3. Dubose Heyward and Ira Gershwin wrote the musical's lyrics. (The music was composed by Ira's brother, George.)
4. Experts have said that The distinctly American musical owes much to George Gershwin and his use of jazz rhythms.
5. One review of *Porgy and Bess* asserted, "this opera is one of the great achievements of the American musical theater."

Review: Capitalizing in Sentences

In each sentence, write the words that are incorrectly capitalized. Some sentences may have more than one error; some sentences may not have any errors at all. If a sentence does not have any errors, write *correct*.

SAMPLE   Ms. Martin's class is studying *the age of reason*.

ANSWER   *The Age of Reason*

The Father of the Chocolate Bar

1. According to *the great american candy bar book*, Milton S. Hershey is the father of the Chocolate bar business in America.
2. Hershey was an unsuccessful caramel maker when he saw a demonstration of the art of german chocolate making at the chicago world's fair in 1893.
3. Hershey decided to give up making Caramels and start manufacturing Chocolate.
4. He built a factory in his home state, Pennsylvania, and planned an entire city around it.
5. To find a name for his "candytown," hershey decided to hold a contest.
6. The $100 prize for the best name was awarded to "hersheykoko."
7. Soon the town's name was shortened to the less imaginative but easier "hershey," and hershey, pennsylvania, became the center of america's chocolate business.
8. Hershey's chocolate factories were astonishingly productive during world war II when the main Hershey plant produced 500,000 chocolate bars per hour for American soldiers stationed at home and overseas.
9. Hershey chocolate became america's favorite, and Hershey refused to advertise his product on radio or television until 1970.
10. His Policy was "give them quality. that's the best advertising."

Rewrite each sentence, correcting any errors in capitalization. If a sentence has no errors, write *correct.*

Consumer Advocate Ralph Nader

1. The most famous consumer advocate in america, ralph nader, became well known in the 1960s for his book *unsafe at any speed,* documenting the dangers of driving the corvair, a car made by the Chevrolet Division of General motors.
2. Because of nader's victory in this case, the ford motor company felt compelled to warn consumers about a suspension system problem in some of its automobiles.
3. Even more significantly, the case provided the primary impetus for the national traffic and motor vehicle safety act of 1966.
4. Not content to rest on his successes, nader has since then been involved in a number of cases, including another famous one in which he blocked the house of representatives from overruling the immigration and naturalization service.
5. Nader also started a program to monitor the teamster union's pension fund, which the teamsters considered a punitive measure but which nader did not see as cruel at all.
6. Nader's consumer activism has also included drug effectiveness and aviation safety.
7. Despite the high profile of these cases, Nader believes that his most important accomplishment was the creation of the citizen's utility board in wisconsin, which he sees as a cornerstone in the fight for Consumers' Rights.
8. Other issues of corporate ethics and human safety to which he has drawn attention include Environmental Pollution; the danger of Atomic Energy Plants; health hazards in food, medicine, and occupations; Fraud; and the secrecy and immunities of large corporations.
9. Nader organized investigative teams of young lawyers, consumer specialists, and students, popularly called "nader's raiders," to conduct surveys of companies, federal agencies, and the U.S. congress.
10. Nader is not without his critics; his investigations have at times been criticized as being superficial and biased against big business and government.

Rewrite each sentence, correcting any errors in capitalization.

1. The recipe for german noodles in the original *new york times cookbook,* which was written by craig claiborne, calls for butter, noodles, bread crumbs, parsley, and mushrooms.
2. This dish goes well with mexican meatballs, which are also relatively easy to prepare.
3. The deepest gorge in the united states is not the grand canyon, as most of us would expect; actually, the deepest gorge is hells canyon, located between idaho and oregon on the snake river.
4. According to a study conducted at the mayo clinic in rochester, minnesota, more heart attacks among men occur on saturdays and sundays than on other days of the week.
5. The mayo clinic study came up with very different results from those of an earlier canadian study of royal canadian air force pilots, which found that monday was the leading day for heart attacks.

Summary of Capitalization Rules

Capitalize	Do Not Capitalize
Before making repairs, the mechanic ordered parts for our car. (**O**ur car is a foreign model.)	The mechanic ordered parts for our car (**o**ur car is a foreign model) before making repairs.
Anne Frank said, "**I**n spite of everything, I still believe that people are really good at heart."	Anne Frank said that **i**n spite of all that was happening around her, she believed people are fundamentally good.
Mayor Richard Daley	the **m**ayor
Aunt Carmen	my **a**unt Carmen
Vanderbilt **U**niversity	the **u**niversity
San **D**iego **Z**oo	the **z**oo
a **T**oyota	a **c**ompact **c**ar
the **V**olstead **A**ct	an **a**ct passed by Congress
Mississippi **R**iver	the **r**iver
Ventnor **A**venue	the **a**venue
Mercury; **P**luto; **E**arth; **S**un	a **p**lanet; the **e**arth
World **W**ar **II**	Another **w**orld **w**ar began.
the **B**ible; **B**uddhism	a **h**oly **b**ook; a **r**eligion
Geography 101; **C**reative **W**riting	**g**eography; a **c**reative **w**riting class
Pulitzer **P**rize	the **p**rize
"**T**he **S**tar-**S**pangled **B**anner"	the **n**ational anthem

Grammar Review

Capitalization

CAPITALIZATION

The Muses Are Heard is Truman Capote's memoir of a trip he made to the Soviet Union in 1955 with a troupe of African American actors who had come to perform George Gershwin's opera *Porgy and Bess*. In this passage, the Americans are met by their interpreters, a woman named Miss Lydia and three young men, and the delegate from Moscow's Ministry of Culture, Nikolai Savchenko. This excerpt has been annotated to show some of the rules of capitalization covered in this unit.

Place name (city)

Name of a firm

Proper adjective formed from a place name

Title used directly before a person's name

Name of an institution

Name of a national group

Name of a person

Name of a language

First word of a complete sentence within quotation marks

Literature Model

from **The Muses Are Heard**
by Truman Capote

We reached Brest Litovsk in a luminous twilight. Statues of political heroes, painted cheap-silver like those souvenir figures sold at Woolworth's, saluted us along the last mile of track leading to the station. The station was on high ground that afforded a partial view of the city, dim and blue and dominated, far-off, by an Orthodox cathedral, whose onion-domes and mosaic towers still projected, despite the failing light, their Oriental colors.

It seemed natural that Miss Lydia and the young men should react awkwardly to this, their first encounter with Westerners; understandable that they should hesitate to test their English, so tediously learned at Moscow's Institute of Foreign Languages but never before practiced on bona fide foreigners; forgivable that they should, instead, stare as though the Americans represented pawns in a chess problem. But Savchenko also gave an impression of being ill at ease, of preferring, in fact, a stretch in Lubyanka [a prison] to his present chores. . . . He delivered a small speech of welcome in gruff Russian, then had it translated by Miss Lydia. "We hope each and all have had a pleasant journey. Too bad you see us in the winter. It is not the good time of year. But we have the saying, Better now than never. Your visit is a step forward in the march toward peace. When the cannons are heard, the muses are silent; when the cannons are silent, the muses are heard."

The muse-cannon metaphor, which was to prove a Savchenko favorite, the starring sentence of all future speeches, was an instant hit with his listeners. ("A beautiful thing." "Just great, Mr. Savchenko." "That's cool cookin', man.")

> First word of a sentence that stands by itself in parentheses

We crossed a hundred yards of track, walked down a dirt lane between warehouses, and arrived at what appeared to be a combination of a parking lot and market place. Brightly lighted kiosks circled it like candles burning on a cake. It was puzzling to discover that each of the kiosks sold the same products: cans of Red Star salmon, Red Star sardines, dusty bottles of Kremlin perfume, dusty boxes of Kremlin candy.

> Trade name

Mixed Review

Rewrite the following sentences about Truman Capote [kə pō´ tē]. Correct all the errors in capitalization. If a sentence has no errors, write *correct*.

Truman Capote

1. truman capote was born truman streckfus persons in 1924.
2. His Mother's second marriage was to Joe Capote.
3. By 1928 Capote had moved to monroeville, alabama.
4. Harper Lee (She later became the Award-winning author of *to Kill A Mockingbird*) was one of his best friends there.
5. at seventeen he was working at the *new yorker* magazine.
6. In 1948 his first novel, *Other voices, other rooms,* became a success. (he was just twenty-four at the time.)
7. Capote trained his powers of recall by memorizing ever-longer sections of the Sears, Roebuck catalog.
8. writing about his russian experience helped inspire Capote to pioneer the "nonfiction novel," which uses Novelistic Techniques to report facts.
9. Capote said that He gave his life to the nonfiction novel *In cold blood,* in which he used "Journalism as an art form."
10. Capote won many Prizes, including the edgar award of the Mystery writers of America and an emmy award.

Capitalization

Review: Exercise 1

Proofreading

This passage describes Marc Chagall, whose painting appears on this page. Correct the errors in spelling, capitalization, grammar, and usage. Add any missing punctuation. There are ten errors.

Marc Chagall

¹Marc Chagall was born in 1887 in Vitebsk, a town in Russia near the polish border. ²Although he spends most of his adult life in france, Chagall never forgot the village of his youth; indeed, his dreamlike paintings are filled with images from the past: village dances, weddings, harvest festivals, and funerals.

³When chagall was twenty-three years old, he moved to Paris. ⁴Although his work was influenced by the surrealists, he always remained true to his own stile. ⁵He returned to Russia in October 1917 after the revolution and served as Commissar of fine arts in Vitebsk. ⁶His irreverent style met with disapproval (A banner he designed to commemorate the revolution showed green cows floating upside down), and he returned to Europe. ⁷Chagall pays tribute to the Town where he was born in *The Market Place, Vitebsk*. ⁸Chagall's village is dominated by an Eastern Orthodox Cathedral (as is Brest-Litovsk the town Truman Capote describes).

Marc Chagall, *The Market Place, Vitebsk*, 1917

Writing Application

TIME

For more about the writing process, see **TIME Facing the Blank Page,** pp. 111–121.

Capitalization in Writing

You have learned that the first word in a sentence and the pronoun *I* are always capitalized. Read the following passage from the novel *An American Tragedy* by Theodore Dreiser. Focus especially on the italicized words.

"Well, now, *Clyde,* as you have seen, it has been charged here that you took *Miss* Alden to and out on that lake with the sole and premeditated intent of killing her—murdering her—and finding some unobserved and quiet spot and then first striking her with your camera, or an oar, or club, or stone maybe, and then drowning her. Now, what have you to say to that? Is that true, or isn't it?"

"No, sir! It's not true!" returned Clyde, clearly and emphatically. *"I* never went there of my own accord in the first place, and I only went there because she didn't like *Grass Lake."* And here, because he had been sinking down in his chair, he pulled himself up and looked at the jury and the audience with what measure of strength and conviction he could summon—as previously he had been told to do.

Techniques with Capitalization

When you proofread your writing, make sure that you follow these capitalization guidelines.

❶ Always capitalize the first word of a sentence.

❷ Capitalize all proper names: Clyde Griffiths, Roberta Alden.

❸ Capitalize the titles before proper names: Miss Alden, Mr. Griffiths.

❹ Capitalize the pronoun *I.*

❺ Capitalize place names: Grass Lake; Lycurgus House; Terre Haute, Indiana.

❻ Capitalize languages, nationalities, and religions: German, Cherokee, Judaism.

❼ Capitalize historical events, eras in history, and documents: Civil War, Middle Ages, Declaration of Independence.

Practice Practice these techniques by revising the following passage from "The Third Level" by Jack Finney. Rewrite it on your paper. Pay particular attention to words that need to be capitalized.

I turned into grand central from Vanderbilt avenue, and went down the steps to the first level, where you take trains like the Twentieth century. then I walked down another flight to the second level, where the suburban trains leave from, ducked into an arched doorway heading for the subway—and got lost. That's easy to do. I've been in and out of grand central hundreds of times, but i'm always bumping into new doorways and stairs and corridors. Once I got into a tunnel about a mile long and came out in the lobby of the roosevelt hotel. another time I came up in an office building on forty-sixth street, three blocks away.

Punctuation, Abbreviations, and Numbers

21.1 The Period

■ Use a period at the end of a declarative sentence and at the end of a polite command.

DECLARATIVE SENTENCE	The banjo is an American folk instrument. Playing the banjo is an American tradition.
POLITE COMMAND	Think of some other folk instruments besides the banjo. Consider the banjo, a symbol of American culture.

Exercise 1 Using the Period

None of the sentences below show end punctuation. On your paper, write *No* if the sentence should not end with a period, and explain why. Write *Yes* if it should end with a period, and write *declarative* or *polite command* to show what type of sentence it is.

SAMPLE	What other instruments are symbols of American culture
ANSWER	No/The sentence is a question.
SAMPLE	Remember the importance of the banjo to folk music
ANSWER	Yes/polite command

The Banjo

1. You may have wondered about the relationship between a banjo and a guitar
2. The banjo is the same general type of instrument as the guitar
3. The body of a banjo is made of parchment stretched over a metal hoop, and the body of the guitar is made out of wood or metal
4. When you listen to a banjo, does it sound as if the music is being made from the same number of strings as a guitar
5. Think about the quality of sound from both of these magnificent instruments
6. When it is played, the banjo sounds as if it has a higher pitch than most guitars
7. Do you think the banjo originated in the United States or in another part of the world
8. The first people in the United States to use the banjo were enslaved people from Africa
9. Consider the banjo, then, as possibly having African origins
10. The banjo may originally have been an African instrument, and that is why it was used by some African American musicians
11. Can you make a connection between the geographical origins of the banjo and its use in early jazz bands
12. Classify the small-sized zither banjo and the higher-pitched tenor banjo as stringed instruments
13. The tenor banjo and the zither banjo have very different sounds from the traditional banjo
14. You can marvel at the inventiveness of the musician who first figured out how to tune the banjo to get the odd, high-pitched sound of the tenor banjo
15. What do you think encouraged this musician, whoever he or she was, to try this musical experiment

21.2 The Exclamation Point

■ Use an exclamation point to show strong feeling and indicate a forceful command.

EXCLAMATORY SENTENCE	What a great movie that was**!**
	How lovely you look**!**
	That's the spirit**!**
FORCEFUL COMMAND	Don't you dare go without me**!**
	Look out**!**
	Write that letter**!**

Exercise 2 **Using the Exclamation Point**

On your paper, write *No* if the sentence should *not* end in an exclamation point and *Yes* if it should.

The Titanic

1. The *Titanic* sank in the North Atlantic Ocean
2. It happened on April 15, 1912
3. What a terrible tragedy that was
4. The ship was a British ocean liner
5. It was hailed as fast and unsinkable
6. Imagine the passengers' shock when the ship hit the iceberg
7. How awful a night that was
8. There weren't enough lifeboats on board to save everyone
9. After the accident, people probably yelled, "Abandon ship"
10. Books have been written about the sinking of the *Titanic*

Exercise 3 **Writing with Exclamation Points**

Write an original sentence based on each sentence below. Your new sentence should end with an exclamation point. Remember that an exclamation point ends a sentence that shows strong feeling or indicates a forceful command.

SAMPLE	There was an iceberg in front of the *Titanic* that night.
ANSWER	There's an iceberg!

1. The loss of life on the *Titanic* was considered great by everyone who heard about the tragedy.
2. One of the ironies of the event was that the ship's first voyage was also its last.
3. Warnings about the iceberg were signaled to the ship, but they were either ignored or not received.
4. The *Titanic* traveled at full speed after the warnings were sent to its crew.
5. Other ships were nearby, but they could not get to the *Titanic* in time.

Punctuation, Abbreviations, and Numbers

21.3 The Question Mark

■ Use a question mark to indicate a direct question.

> Was Aaron Copland an American composer**?**
>
> Did Copland write *Appalachian Spring***?**

A question mark should not follow a declarative sentence that contains an indirect question.

> My friend asked whether Aaron Copland wrote *Appalachian Spring***.**
>
> She wondered what folk tune is the central melody in *Appalachian Spring***.**

Exercise 4   Using Question Marks

On your paper, write *No* if the sentence should not end in a question mark and *Yes* if it should.

Aaron Copland

1. Who was the first American composer to be accepted by the European music world
2. Aaron Copland, son of Russian immigrants, grew up to be a uniquely American composer
3. When he studied in Europe, he learned from great teachers about the traditions of classical music
4. How was he able to use inventive techniques to transform his music into a new, exciting sound
5. When Copland began writing film scores, he altered previous Hollywood practices by employing a variety of styles to "evoke a specific landscape"
6. How did his teacher from Paris, Mademoiselle Boulanger, feel about playing this piece in her American debut
7. What American music characteristics did Copland use to rid his compositions of their European influence
8. By adding elements of jazz, he was able to inject an American sound into his classical compositions
9. Have you heard his most popular compositions—*Billy the Kid* (1938), *Rodeo* (1942), and *Appalachian Spring* (1944)—in live performance
10. Copland wrote *Appalachian Spring* as a ballet, but it is also well loved as a musical composition on its own

Exercise 5   Writing Sentences with Question Marks

On your paper, write a paragraph that describes music you know about or appreciate. Your paragraph should include four sentences that end with question marks.

Read the following sentences, and correct them by adding periods, exclamation points, and question marks.

Zora Neale Hurston, Author

1. My friend asked me how I enjoyed Zora Neale Hurston's novel *Their Eyes Were Watching God*
2. Wow What a great book that was
3. I wonder why it took me so long to discover this wonderful writer
4. Did you know that Hurston writes tales of African American folk culture
5. In her autobiography, *Dust Tracks on a Road,* Hurston recounts her early years in Eatonville, Florida
6. As a teenager, she traveled with a theatrical troupe
7. She also attended Columbia University, where she studied anthropology
8. Hurston studied at Columbia with the famous ethnographer of Native American cultures, Franz Boas
9. What a thrill it must have been to study with the great Franz Boas
10. Are you aware that Hurston traveled widely—to such places as Louisiana, Alabama, Haiti, Jamaica, and the Bahamas
11. She traveled to these places as a scholar and student of African American folkways and culture
12. Don't you dare walk away with my only copy of *Mules and Men*
13. After I read *Mules and Men,* I had to ask myself what could be more fascinating than collecting and studying the folktales, prayers, jokes, and games of an unfamiliar culture
14. When you finish reading it, please tell me your reactions to *Mule Bone: A Comedy of Negro Life in Three Acts*
15. Zora Neale Hurston wrote *Mule Bone* with Langston Hughes
16. Zora Neale Hurston was born in 1901 and grew up in Eatonville, Florida
17. If you have finished reading the works that I've already mentioned, "Book of Harlem" should be next on your list
18. If you enjoy this story, you may also want to read "The Bone of Contention," which I can lend you
19. She is so talented
20. She was a writer for Paramount Studios
21. Would you have guessed that a novelist, short story writer, and cultural anthropologist also worked in Hollywood
22. She was also a professor in the drama department at North Carolina College for Negroes (now North Carolina Central University)
23. The other day, a friend of mine remarked that Zora Neale Hurston was his favorite author
24. "Read every page carefully because she writes with such detail" was the last thing this friend told me before I borrowed a book of Hurston's stories
25. As I took the book, I asked, "What else should I know"

The Colon

Colons to Introduce

1. Lists

■ Use a colon to introduce a list, especially after a statement that uses such words as *these, the following,* or *as follows.*

> The elements of a good detective story are **these:** a crime, interesting characters, and an arrest.
>
> Of classical composers, I have most enjoyed **these:** Beethoven, Brahms, and Mozart.
>
> Listen to a recording of one of **the following** concert vocalists: Justino Diaz, Martina Arroyo, or Jessye Norman.
>
> A teacher often gives **the following** instructions: (1) find books on your topic, (2) take notes, (3) write an outline, and (4) write a first draft.

A colon is not used to introduce a list that immediately follows a verb or a preposition.

> Three important American composers **are** Aaron Copland, Scott Joplin, and Philip Glass.
>
> The woman **ordered** a blue jacket, a brown belt, and black shoes.
>
> What kind of music is most popular **in** South America, Africa, and Asia?

2. Illustrations or restatements

■ Use a colon to introduce material that illustrates, explains, or restates the preceding material.

> Many African instruments are made of natural materials**:** Pottery, shells, gourds, and beads are often used to make African percussion instruments.
>
> The cause of the fire was obvious**:** Children were playing with matches.
>
> The joyous news was told to the patiently waiting crowd**:** The concert would take place on Saturday.

A complete sentence following a colon is capitalized, as in the preceding examples.

Colons Before Quotations

■ Use a colon to introduce a long or formal quotation. A formal quotation is often preceded by such words as *this, these, the following,* or *as follows.*

> Patrick Henry's memorably eloquent speech before the Virginia Convention closed resoundingly with **the following** patriotic exclamation: "I know not what course others may take; but as for me, give me liberty, or give me death!"

Quotations of more than one line of poetry or more than four or five lines of prose are generally written below the introductory statement and are indented on the page.

> Walt Whitman celebrated freedom in the following lines:
>
>> The earth expanding right hand and left hand,
>> The picture alive, every part in its best light,
>> The music falling in where it is wanted, and stopping where
>>   it is not wanted,
>> The cheerful voice of the public road, the gay fresh sentiment
>>   of the road.

> As a comment upon the way to read her place in the world, Emily Dickinson wrote **these** lines of poetry:
>
>> I read my sentence—steadily—
>> Reviewed it with my eyes,
>> To see that I made no mistake
>> In its extremest clause—

Other Uses of Colons

■ Use a colon between the hour and the minute of the precise time, between the chapter and the verse in biblical references, and after the salutation of a business letter.

6:40 A.M.	Matthew 2:5
9:20 P.M.	Dear Sir or Madam:
Exodus 3:4	Dear Ford Motor Company:
Greetings:	To Whom It May Concern:
Dear Volunteers:	Dear Chairperson:

Exercise 7   Using the Colon

Rewrite the following sentences correctly, adding colons where they are needed. For the sentence that does not need a colon, write *correct*. Remember that colons are not needed when a list immediately follows a verb or a preposition.

Memory Skills

1. The information that we need to remember can be classified into the following three categories things we hear, things we see, and things we read.
2. In developing memory skills, you might therefore focus on these three kinds of memory aural memory, visual memory, and memory for written material.
3. Social situations often require you to use aural memory skills at a party, for example, you will want to remember the names of people you meet.
4. Your visual memory will be important if you witness a crime or an accident a police officer may ask you to recall details about a person's appearance or a car's color, make, and license-plate number.
5. Your memory for written material will help you in such subjects as history, social studies, science, spelling, and foreign languages.
6. The following steps will help you to remember information (1) concentrate on the information, (2) repeat the information to yourself, (3) write and rewrite the information, and (4) make up a mnemonic device.
7. A mnemonic device for remembering the colors of the spectrum is the name Roy G. Biv, which stands for the following colors red, orange, yellow, green, blue, indigo, and violet.
8. By using a series of mnemonic devices, Angela memorized portions of the Bible, including Genesis 1 1–31 and Psalms 23 1–6.
9. To remember the locker combination 53-7-15, you could use this mnemonic device "We often have dinner from 5 30 to 7 15."
10. Rhymes and repetition make it easy to memorize the following lines from "The Raven," a poem by Edgar Allan Poe

> While I nodded, nearly napping, suddenly there came a tapping,
> As of someone gently rapping, rapping at my chamber door—

Exercise 8   Using Colons in Your Writing

Number your paper from 1 to 4. Write four sentences, using colons. Use the directions given in the following list.

1. This sentence should introduce a list.
2. This sentence should contain an illustration of a point.
3. This sentence should include a quotation.
4. This sentence should include a time of day.

21.5 The Semicolon

Semicolons to Separate Main Clauses

■ Use a semicolon to separate main clauses that are not joined by a coordinating conjunction (*and, but, or, nor, yet,* or *for*).

> I enjoy reading; mysteries are my favorite books.
> Wilkie Collins wrote mysteries; his books are suspenseful.

■ Use a semicolon to separate main clauses joined by a conjunctive adverb (such as *however, therefore, nevertheless, moreover, furthermore,* or *consequently*) or by an expression such as *for example* or *that is*.

> George Gershwin wrote popular music as well as traditional music; moreover, he combined the two forms in pieces such as *Rhapsody in Blue.*

A comma usually follows a conjunctive adverb or an expression such as *in fact*.

> Much jazz is improvised; however, all the instruments are played in the same key.

Semicolons and Commas

■ Use a semicolon to separate the items in a series when one or more of these items contain commas.

> Three important jazz musicians of the twentieth century were Louis Armstrong, a trumpet player; Duke Ellington, a composer; and Sarah Vaughan, a singer.

■ Use a semicolon to separate two main clauses joined by a coordinating conjunction when one or both of the clauses contain several commas.

> Arthur Ashe, one of the world's most famous tennis players, was the first African American to win the U.S. Open and Wimbledon; but he is also remembered for his work after his retirement from tennis, which included the formation of the National Junior Tennis League.

Exercise 9 — Using the Semicolon

Rewrite the following sentences correctly, adding semicolons where they are needed.

Film Successes

1. "The subjective actress thinks of clothes only as they apply to her the objective actress thinks of them only as they affect others, as a tool for the job." —Edith Head
2. Film buffs might know that Edith Head, the famous costume designer, won eight Academy Awards for costuming such films as *All About Eve, Sabrina,* and *The Sting* but few probably remember that she actually appeared in a movie, *The Oscar,* in which she played herself.
3. The Beatles starred in three movies: *A Hard Day's Night,* made in 1964 *Help!,* made in 1965 and *Let It Be,* made in 1970.
4. "I've never sought success in order to get fame and money it's the talent and the passion that count in success." —Ingrid Bergman
5. Ingrid Bergman was graced with both talent and passion consequently, she made a success of her career.
6. The classic film *Casablanca* was a perfect vehicle for Bergman's talents the film also starred Humphrey Bogart, Peter Lorre, Claude Rains, Sidney Greenstreet, and Dooley Wilson.
7. The story, which unfolds in wartime Morocco, depicts Rick Blaine, the cynical American café owner Ilse Lund, a former love of his and Captain Louis Renault, the head of the French police in Morocco.
8. Casablanca has become a refuge for an assortment of characters who have fled the Nazi occupation of France the characters are caught up in the intrigues of the city as they await visas to America.
9. Bogart plays Rick, whose hard-boiled cynicism is overcome by memories of his love for Ilse (Bergman) in prewar Paris Rick helps Ilse escape with her husband.
10. "As Time Goes By" is the most famous song from *Casablanca* like the film itself, it has become a favorite among film buffs.

Exercise 10 — Using the Semicolon

For each sentence that is written correctly, write *correct*. Insert semicolons in those sentences that are written incorrectly.

Alfred Hitchcock

1. Alfred Hitchcock, a British-born American film producer and director, appeared in his own films, his roles, however, were minor.
2. You might think that *The 39 Steps* from 1935 is an old film, yet, it is still studied with enthusiasm at film schools.
3. By using carefully selected screen images, Hitchcock, a brilliant technician, created suspense for a movie audience.
4. He repeated images in his films for example, *North by Northwest* and *Vertigo* involve great heights, while *Psycho* and *The Birds* show a world where people or things go out of control.
5. His popular television show opened each week with macabre music and an image of his portly silhouette he then delivered a dark but humorous introduction to the nightly episode.

The Comma

Commas and Compound Sentences

■ Use commas between the main clauses in a compound sentence.

You should use a comma before a coordinating conjunction (*and, but, or, nor, yet,* or *for*) that joins two main clauses.

> Beethoven was a musical genius, **for** he continued to compose major works after he had become completely deaf.
>
> Mozart and Schubert were both classical musicians, **but** each had his own unique style.

The comma may be omitted when two very short main clauses are connected by a coordinating conjunction, unless the comma is needed to avoid confusion.

> Min prepared the meal and Ralph washed the dishes. [clear]
>
> Min prepared the meal and the dishes needed washing. [confusing]
>
> Min prepared the meal, and the dishes needed washing. [clear]

Commas in a Series

■ Use commas to separate three or more words, phrases, or clauses in a series.

> The television show *I Love Lucy* was clever, entertaining, and very funny.
>
> Charles Chaplin wrote, directed, and starred in many film comedies.
>
> Some movies make audiences laugh, others make them cry, and still others amaze them with dazzling special effects.

Commas are unnecessary when the items in a series are joined by conjunctions.

> Langston Hughes's poetry is insightful and expressive and powerful.

Nouns used in pairs (*spaghetti and meatballs, bacon and eggs, pen and ink*) are considered single units and should not be divided by commas.

I like salt and pepper, oil and vinegar, and croutons on my salad.

Swimming and diving pools, football and baseball fields, and tennis courts are located in the park.

Commas and Coordinate Adjectives

■ Place a comma between coordinate adjectives that precede a noun.

Coordinate adjectives modify the same noun to an equal degree. One way to tell whether adjectives in a sentence are coordinate is to reverse their order or put the word *and* between them. The adjectives are coordinate if the sentence still sounds natural.

Julia is a beautiful, happy, intelligent child.

A comma should not be used between adjectives preceding a noun if they sound unnatural with their order reversed or with *and* between them. Adjectives that describe size, age, shape, color, and material usually do not need a comma between them.

Julia wore a long blue wool scarf.

Exercise 11   Using the Comma (Part 1)

Rewrite the following sentences correctly, adding commas where they are needed. For the one sentence that needs no commas, write *correct*.

The Tomb of Shih Huang-ti

1. Shih Huang-ti was emperor of the Ch'in Dynasty from 221 to 210 B.C. and his accomplishments had long-lasting effects on the history of China.
2. Shih Huang-ti unified the Chinese Empire oversaw construction of the Great Wall and built himself a truly magnificent tomb.
3. His very extensive well-equipped funeral compound may be the greatest of his many extraordinary accomplishments.
4. The twenty-square-mile tomb was built two thousand years ago yet it was discovered only in 1974.
5. The compound consists of underground chambers filled with ceramic statues of soldiers bronze chariots and such weapons as spears and swords.
6. The life-size statues number more than six thousand but no two are alike.
7. The ancient ceramic soldiers face east and are poised for battle.
8. The military formation is manned with infantrymen archers and mounted cavalry.
9. Bronze jade and gold artifacts complete the rich treasure buried with Emperor Shih Huang-ti.
10. Shih Huang-ti of Ch'in was the first emperor of the unified nation and his rule gave China its name.

Commas and Nonessential Elements

1. Participles, infinitives, and their phrases

■ Use commas to set off participles, infinitives, and their phrases if they are not essential to the meaning of the sentence.

> The children, excited, ripped open their presents.
>
> Mari made her way along the beach, jogging happily.
>
> I have no idea, to tell you the truth, what this really means.

You should not set off participles, infinitives, and their phrases if they are essential to the meaning of the sentence.

> The most famous documentary film directed by Robert J. Flaherty is *Nanook of the North.* [The participial phrase limits *most famous documentary* to the most famous one that Flaherty directed.]
>
> Flaherty made the film to show the realities of Eskimo life. [The infinitive phrase tells *why* Flaherty made the film.]
>
> To film *Nanook of the North* was a difficult undertaking. [The infinitive phrase is used as the subject of the sentence.]

2. Adjective clauses

■ Use commas to set off a nonessential adjective clause.

A nonessential (nonrestrictive) clause gives additional information about a noun. Because it does not change, but adds to, the meaning of a sentence, it is set off with commas.

> My cousin Ken, who lives in California, works as a film editor. [*Who lives in California* is a nonessential clause.]

Avoid using commas in an essential adjective clause. An essential (restrictive) clause provides information about a noun that is needed to convey the precise meaning of the sentence.

> The person who actually films a movie is called the camera operator. [*Who actually films a movie* is an essential clause. It tells which person.]

3. Appositives and appositive phrases

■ Use commas to set off an appositive or an appositive phrase if it is not essential to the meaning of a sentence.

A nonessential (nonrestrictive) appositive or appositive phrase can be considered *extra* information and therefore needs commas.

> Sherlock Holmes**, the famous fictional detective,** was the invention of Sir Arthur Conan Doyle.

> Holmes is often accompanied by Dr. Watson**, the narrator of many of Conan Doyle's stories.**

A nonessential appositive or appositive phrase is sometimes positioned before the word to which it refers.

> **The narrator of many of Conan Doyle's stories,** Dr. Watson often accompanies Holmes on his investigations.

An essential (restrictive) appositive or appositive phrase provides necessary information about a noun and is therefore not set off with commas.

> Conan Doyle's novel *A Study in Scarlet* was the first to include the famous detective. [If a comma were placed before the essential appositive, *A Study in Scarlet,* the sentence would imply that this was Conan Doyle's only novel.]

Commas with Interjections, Parenthetical Expressions, and Conjunctive Adverbs

■ Use commas to set off interjections (such as *oh* and *well*), parenthetical expressions (such as *on the contrary, on the other hand, in fact, by the way, for example,* and *after all*), and conjunctive adverbs (such as *however, moreover,* and *consequently*).

> **Alas,** I have not read all of Conan Doyle's novels.

> I have not read *Valley of Fear,* **for example.**

> Holmes is a memorable character; **consequently,** he is known around the world. [conjunctive adverb]

Rewrite the following sentences correctly, adding commas where they are needed. For the one sentence that needs no commas, write *correct*.

Citizen Kane, a Movie Classic

1. Orson Welles's film *Citizen Kane* won only one Academy Award; nevertheless it is now considered one of the finest movies ever made.
2. In fact few American films have been as influential as *Citizen Kane.*
3. *Citizen Kane* directed by and starring Orson Welles has a newsreel quality that makes it seem very realistic.
4. The movie which traces the life of a rich and powerful man has had a stormy history to say the least.
5. Some of those criticizing the film thought that Welles had insulted the powerful newspaper publisher William Randolph Hearst.
6. The character Kane played by Orson Welles had many things in common with Hearst.
7. For instance Kane built a great mansion Xanadu just as Hearst built a great mansion San Simeon.
8. Indeed Orson Welles was severely criticized by those people who felt that he had exposed their private lives in order to make his film.
9. On the other hand in 1970 Welles was publicly celebrated as one of the greatest American directors in the history of motion pictures.
10. He also received a special Oscar which was given to him for his outstanding achievements in the film industry.

Commas and Introductory Phrases

1. Prepositional phrases

■ Use a comma after a short introductory prepositional phrase only if the sentence would be misread without the comma.

> During the winter, snowstorms are common in New England.
> [The comma is needed to prevent misreading.]

■ Use a comma after a long prepositional phrase or after the final phrase in a succession of phrases.

> On the rug by the fireplace, a large dog slept.

A comma is not used if the phrase is immediately followed by a verb.

> On the rug by the fireplace slept a large dog.

2. Participles and participial phrases

■ Use commas to set off introductory participles and participial phrases.

Laughing, I watched my three-year-old brother try to hide the bag of cookies.

Covered in chocolate, my brother's smiling face revealed his secret.

Commas and Adverb Clauses

■ Use commas after all introductory adverb clauses.

Lately, I have been somewhat forgetful.

■ Use commas to set off internal adverb clauses that interrupt the flow of a sentence.

Before he became a locksmith, Mr. Beam used to work as a fire-fighter.

In general, set off an adverb clause at the end of a sentence only if the clause is parenthetical or the sentence would be misread without the comma.

Mr. Beam used to work as a firefighter **before he became a locksmith.** [no comma needed]

I attended the bake sale, **although I don't like sweets.**

Commas and Antithetical Phrases

■ Use commas to set off an antithetical phrase.

An **antithetical phrase** uses a word such as *not* or *unlike* to qualify what precedes it.

Augusta, not Bangor, is the capital of Maine.

Unlike Kansas, Colorado is very mountainous.

Exercise 13 **Using the Comma (Part 3)**

Read the five sentences below. Then rewrite the sentences correctly, adding commas where they are needed. If a sentence is correct, write *correct*.

Alberta Hunter

1. Unlike most singers Alberta Hunter enjoyed a successful career in music late in life.
2. Retiring from the nursing profession at the age of eighty-two Hunter decided that she would return to her previous career—as a singer.
3. Because she sang the blues so well many audiences requested blues numbers.
4. In each song lyrics and tone blended for a powerful rendition.
5. Because Hunter had a talent for learning languages she was able to perform successfully in several European countries.

Commas with Titles, Addresses, and Numbers

1. Titles of people

■ Use commas to set off a title when it follows a person's name.

   Henry VIII, king of England, was a songwriter and musician.

2. Addresses, geographical terms, and dates

■ Use commas to separate the various parts of an address, a geographical term, or a date.

   The company is located at 840 Pierce Street, Friendswood, Texas 77546, and it has another office in Lansing, Michigan.

   Paris, France, is the setting of some of Hemingway's works.

   On Friday, October 12, 1492, Christopher Columbus landed on the New World island now called San Salvador.

A comma is not used when only the month and the day or the month and the year are given.

   In July 1776 the Declaration of Independence was signed.

   The signing of the Declaration of Independence on July 4 is celebrated every year.

3. References

■ Use commas to set off the parts of a reference that direct the reader to the exact source.

   The theme is expressed in *The Scarlet Letter*, pages 3–4.

   We performed act 1, scene 1, of William Shakespeare's *Julius Caesar.*

Commas and Direct Address

■ Use commas to set off words or names used in direct address.

   Mona, can you meet me this afternoon?

   You, my dear, are leaving at once.

   Thank you for the book, Mrs. Gomez.

Commas and Tag Questions

■ Use commas to set off a tag question.

By using a tag question such as *have you?* or *shouldn't I?* you emphasize an implied answer to the statement that precedes it.

You have seen Paul's new car, **haven't you?**

He bought a red sports car, **didn't he?**

Commas in Letter Writing

■ Place a comma after the salutation of an informal letter and after the closing of all letters.

Dear Mario,
Dear Cousin Agnes,

Yours truly,
Best wishes,

Use the following style for the heading of a letter:

23 Silver Lake Road
Sharon, Connecticut 06069
February 15, 1992

Misuse of Commas

Do not use a comma before a conjunction that connects a compound predicate or a compound subject.

INCORRECT	Our school never wins the championship, but has a spectacular losers' party every year.
CORRECT	Our school never wins the championship but has a spectacular losers' party every year.

Do not use a comma alone to join two main clauses that are not part of a series. Such a sentence punctuated with a comma alone is called a *run-on sentence* (or a *comma splice* or a *comma fault*). To join two clauses correctly, use a coordinating conjunction with the comma, or use a semicolon.

INCORRECT	The navigator Juan Rodríguez Cabrillo sighted land in 1542, the history of modern California began.
CORRECT	The navigator Juan Rodríguez Cabrillo sighted land in 1542, **and** the history of modern California began.
CORRECT	The navigator Juan Rodríguez Cabrillo sighted land in 1542; the history of modern California began.

Never use a comma between a subject and its verb or between a verb and its complement.

INCORRECT	What she considered an easy ballet step to master, was quite difficult for me.
CORRECT	What she considered an easy ballet step to master was quite difficult for me.
INCORRECT	Popular tourist attractions in Florida include, Disney World, Palm Beach, and the Everglades.
CORRECT	Popular tourist attractions in Florida include Disney World, Palm Beach, and the Everglades.
INCORRECT	Their motto was, "All for one."
CORRECT	Their motto was "All for one."

Exercise 14   Using the Comma (Part 4)

Rewrite the following letter, adding commas where they are needed or removing them where necessary. (Twenty-five corrections are needed altogether.)

> 4615 Oak Street
> Kansas City Missouri, 64101
> January 2 2000

Dear Kim

Happy New Year Kim! We haven't spoken on the phone for some time have we? I am enclosing an article about American colleges that appeared in the Sunday December 30 1999 issue of the *Kansas City Star*. You still haven't decided on a college have you?

I've been looking through the college catalogs at the local library. Mrs. Hom the head librarian was a big help. Colleges I'm thinking of applying to include, Hood College in Frederick Maryland; Kansas State University; and the University of Texas.

The enclosed article contains recent information, and so should prove useful to you. Wouldn't it be nice if we could go to the same college Kim? It's been three years since you moved to Winchester Virginia and left Kansas City. I hope to hear from you soon Kim.

> Your friend
> *Maureen*

P.S. I forgot to tell you about the vacation my family took, last month. Kim you may be surprised to hear that I actually climbed a path up a huge waterfall in Hawaii, and developed a serious interest in studying botany. Although I had planned to major in science, I did not have a focus until this trip. Studying plant life, will set me up for a fascinating, not boring career.

21.7 The Dash

In typed material a dash is indicated by two hyphens (--). A comma, semi-colon, colon, or period should not be placed before or after a dash.

Dashes to Signal Change

■ Use a dash to indicate an abrupt break or change in thought within a sentence.

> "I think the answer is—I've forgotten what I was going to say."
> All of us—I mean most of us—look forward to vacations.

Dashes to Emphasize

■ Use a dash to set off and emphasize supplemental, or extra, information or parenthetical comments.

> Yellowstone Park's geyser Old Faithful has erupted faithfully—every hour on the hour—for over eighty years.

Exercise 15   **Using the Dash**

Some of the sentences of dialogue below need dashes. Rewrite those that need dashes, inserting the dashes correctly. For the two sentences that do not need dashes, write *correct*.

Yellowstone National Park

1. Alex said, "Someone I think Sharisse told me that Yellowstone National Park covers over two million acres."
2. Maime remarked, "No, Alex, it wasn't Sharisse. It was oh, I forgot!"
3. "Never mind," Alex answered. "There are so many sights to see especially Old Faithful before we leave."
4. "Mammoth Hot Spring now that's my kind of tourist attraction. It consists of a series of five terraces with reflecting pools," Maime said.
5. Alex countered, "Just let me see one bison, moose, or elk just one before I take my leave of this magnificent wonder of nature."
6. Maime replied, "Well, even if we don't see a single animal, the trip will still be great."
7. Alex said, "Whatever we see and there's plenty to see here let's not forget the fine art of photography, Maime."
8. "I could take pictures at least one a minute our entire stay here. The landscape is so overwhelming," Maime remarked.
9. "A roll or two of the park's attractions will suffice," Alex said.
10. "We'll put together a vacation album of the adventures of Maime and Alex or should I say Alexander? at Yellowstone National Park."

21.8 Parentheses

■ Use parentheses to set off supplemental material.

Supplemental material may also be set off by commas and dashes. The difference between the three marks is one of degree. Use commas to set off material that is closely related to the rest of the sentence. Use parentheses to set off material that is not intended to be part of the main statement. Use dashes for emphasis or for material that abruptly interrupts the sentence.

> The city is about 6.4 kilometers (4 miles) from here.
>
> At the national convention, representative Marta Ramirez (Texas) took first place in the tall tales competition.

Do not capitalize or add end punctuation to a complete sentence within parentheses if the parenthetical material is contained within another sentence. If a sentence in parentheses stands by itself, both a capital letter and end punctuation are necessary.

> Martha Jane Cannary (she was known as Calamity Jane) knew Wild Bill Hickok.
>
> Paul Bunyan is a famous figure in American folklore. (You can learn all about him if you visit the Paul Bunyan Center in Minnesota.)

Exercise 16   Using Parentheses

If the sentence uses parentheses correctly, write *correct* on your paper. If parentheses are not used correctly, write the sentence and make any needed corrections.

Paul Bunyan

1. Where Paul Bunyan comes from (Minnesota), everyone knows at least one tale about him.
2. Without question, his most prized possession was Babe (an ox), a friendly creature with a peculiar blue hue.
3. This massive blue ox had a span between its two horns that far surpassed that of any real ox on earth (it measured forty-two ax handles and a plug of tobacco).
4. With his enormous size and strength, Paul Bunyan ruled a gargantuan lumber camp for part of each year. (From the winter of blue snow to the spring that came up from China.)
5. If you travel to lumber camps in southern regions of the United States, you may learn about another legendary lumberjack. (Tony Beaver.)

Parentheses with Other Marks of Punctuation

1. With a comma, a semicolon, or a colon

■ Always place a comma, semicolon, or colon *after* the closing parenthesis.

> The writer Bret Harte is associated with the West (his stories include "The Outcasts of Poker Flat" and "The Luck of Roaring Camp"**)**, but this celebrated American author was actually born in Albany, New York.

2. With a period, a question mark, or an exclamation point

■ Place a period, a question mark, or an exclamation point *inside* the parentheses if it is part of the parenthetical expression.

> The most famous guide of the Lewis and Clark expedition was Sacajawea. (A novel based on her life was published**.)**

> Owatonna is the name of a Native American princess (a member of the Santee nation**?)** who lived hundreds of years ago.

■ Place a period, a question mark, or an exclamation point *outside* the parentheses if it is part of the entire sentence.

> The code of laws that governed Iroquois society was the Great Binding Law (known as the Iroquois Constitution**).**

> How surprised I was to learn that the British still call corn *maize* (which comes from the West Indian word for "corn"**)!**

Exercise 17　　　**Using the Dash and Parentheses**

Rewrite the following sentences correctly, adding dashes and parentheses where they are needed. Use the marks of punctuation indicated in parentheses at the end of each sentence.

American Writers

1. Because the novelist Louise Erdrich had supportive parents they encouraged her reading and writing endeavors, she knew at an early age that she wanted to be a writer. (parentheses)
2. The gifted writer F. Scott Fitzgerald 1896–1940 wrote the screenplays for several Hollywood films. Did you know that he never liked to publicize this fact? (two sets of parentheses)
3. Stephen Crane the author of *The Red Badge of Courage* was once shipwrecked while traveling from the United States to Cuba. What an adventurous life he led! (dashes and parentheses)
4. The Chilean poet Gabriela Mistral her real name was Lucila Godoy Alcayaga won the Nobel Prize for literature in 1945. (parentheses)
5. I consider the *Narrative of the Life of Frederick Douglass* and I gave this evaluation much thought to be the most compelling autobiography I have ever read. (dashes)

Brackets and Ellipsis Points

Brackets

■ Use brackets to enclose information that you insert into a quotation for clarity.

He [Dr. Martin Luther King, Jr.] gave us back our heritage.
—Alice Walker

■ Use brackets to enclose a parenthetical phrase that already appears within parentheses.

The word *tycoon* comes from the Japanese word *taikun,* meaning "mighty lord" (which in turn comes from two Chinese words [*ta,* "great" and *kiun,* "prince"]).

Ellipsis Points

■ Use a series of three spaced points, called **ellipsis points,** to indicate the omission of material from a quotation.

Use three spaced points if the omission occurs at the beginning of a sentence. If the omission occurs in the middle or at the end of a sentence, use any necessary punctuation (for example, a comma, a semicolon, or a period) plus the three spaced points. When it is necessary to use a period, do not leave any space between the last word before the omission and the first point, which is the period.

"Listen, my children, and you shall hear. . ."
—Henry Wadsworth Longfellow

| Exercise 18 | Using Brackets and Ellipsis Points |

On your paper, write each sentence below correctly, using brackets where they are needed. For two sentences, omit part of a quote by using ellipsis points correctly.

Fictitious Captions from Photographs in the Calhoun County Gazette

1. "When you see them officers of the law, greet them like the most respected members of your own family," the mayor was quoted to have said.
2. "Today," the mayor began his address to the council, "you can pass it a city bill on recycling and conserve the environment for generations to come."
3. County fair blue ribbon holder Brenda Holt said, "After I put him a Brahman bull in the pen, the crowds gathered around just to stare at his strength and beauty."
4. Sheriff Grand's nickname comes from the French term *les yeux* (which means "eyes" related to his keen insights into how to abide by the law).
5. This is a photograph from the mayor's trip to Maine where he camped out on Isle au Haut. (The island's name comes from the French word for "high" referring to the two mountains at the island's center.)

21.10 | Quotation Marks

Quotation Marks for Direct Quotations

■ Use quotation marks to enclose a direct quotation.

Place quotation marks around the quoted material *only*, not around introductory or explanatory remarks. Such remarks are generally separated from the actual quotation with a comma.

> Samuel Johnson, the British author, said, "What is written without effort is in general read without pleasure."
>
> Franklin Delano Roosevelt proclaimed, "There is nothing to fear but fear itself."
>
> The national anthem begins with the words, "Oh say can you see," and ends with "and the home of the brave."

■ When a quotation is interrupted by explanatory words such as *he said* or *she wrote*, use separate sets of quotation marks.

Two marks of punctuation, such as two commas or a comma and a period, should be used to separate each part of the quotation from the interrupting phrase. If the second part of the quotation is a complete sentence, it should begin with a capital letter.

> "Genius," said the great inventor Thomas A. Edison, "is one percent inspiration and ninety-nine percent perspiration."
>
> "Free verse," Robert Frost begins a famous poetry definition, "is like playing tennis without a net."
>
> "The Lord prefers common-looking people," Abraham Lincoln once said. "That is the reason He made so many of them."

You should not use quotation marks in an indirect quotation (a quotation that does not repeat a person's exact words).

> **ORIGINAL QUOTATION**   Toni Morrison said, "I wrote my first novel because I wanted to read it."
>
> **INDIRECT QUOTATION**   Toni Morrison said that she wrote her first novel because she wanted to read it.

■ Use single quotation marks around a quotation within a quotation.

> In speaking to her students, the teacher said, "Benjamin Franklin once wrote 'Lose no time; be always employed in something useful.'"

- In writing dialogue, begin a new paragraph and use a new set of quotation marks every time the speaker changes.

> "Are you going to pass this collection of abalone shells on to your children?" I said.
>
> "No," he said. "I want my children to collect for themselves. I wouldn't give it to them."
>
> "Why?" I said. "When you die?"
>
> Mr. Abe shook his head. "No. Not even when I die," he said. "I couldn't give the children what I see in these shells. The children must go out for themselves and find their own shells."
>
> —Toshio Mori

Quotation Marks with Titles of Short Works

- Use quotation marks to enclose titles of short works, such as short stories, short poems, essays, newspaper and magazine articles, book chapters, songs, and single episodes of a television series.

> "Araby" [short story]
> "When I Was One-and-Twenty" [poem]
> "A Modest Proposal" [essay]
> "The Third Side" [newspaper article]
> "Ahab" [chapter]
> "The Star-Spangled Banner" [song]

Quotation Marks with Unusual Expressions

- Use quotation marks to enclose unfamiliar slang and other unusual or original expressions.

> A once-popular expression was "zounds."
> "Groovy" was a popular expression that meant "terrific."

Quotation Marks with Definitions

- Use quotation marks to enclose a definition that is stated directly.

> *Ukelele* comes from the Hawaiian word for "flea."
> *Isle au Haut* comes from the French word *haut,* which means "high."

Quotation Marks with Other Marks of Punctuation

1. With a comma or a period

■ Always place a comma or a period *inside* closing quotation marks.

Robert Browning once said, "Oppression makes the wise man mad."

"Not to oversee workmen," Benjamin Franklin cautioned, "is to leave them your purse open."

2. With a semicolon or a colon

■ Always place a semicolon or a colon *outside* closing quotation marks.

Chuck Berry wrote "Johnny B. Goode"; the song was one of the first examples of rock-and-roll music.

There is only one main character in Ernest Hemingway's short story "Big Two-Hearted River": Nick Adams.

3. With a question mark or an exclamation point

■ Place the question mark or exclamation point *inside* the closing quotation marks when it is part of the quotation or title.

We read Leonard Bernstein's essay "What Makes Music American?"

Walt Whitman's poem "Beat! Beat! Drums!" is about the Civil War.

■ Place the question mark or exclamation point *outside* the closing quotation marks when it is part of the entire sentence.

Have you read Gwendolyn Brooks's poem "We Real Cool"?

How I adore old Cole Porter songs such as "Anything Goes"!

When the sentence, as well as the quotation at the end of the sentence, needs a question mark (or an exclamation point), use only one question mark (or exclamation point), and place it *inside* the closing quotation marks.

What was the name of the French poet who asked, "Where are the snows of yesteryear?"

| **Exercise 19** | **Using Quotation Marks** |

Rewrite the following sentences correctly, adding quotation marks where they are needed. For the sentences that need no changes, write *correct*.

General Colin Powell

1. I have been reading about General Colin Powell in preparation for a newspaper article I am writing entitled What Makes a Great Military Mind?
2. My sources tell me that General Powell was born in New York City and graduated from the City College of New York in 1958.
3. My parents, Powell reportedly stated, expected their children to do something with their lives.
4. Powell has said that he enrolled in the Reserve Officers' Training Corps while he was in college because he felt comfortable with military discipline and had learned to take advantage of any promising opportunities that came his way.
5. One of Powell's classmates recalled, He displayed rare leadership ability on campus; another said, He motivated many other students to succeed.
6. Over the years, Powell completed various tours abroad, won numerous medals for his service in Vietnam, and served as a senior military assistant in Washington, D.C., where one of his associates said of him: He is more of an expediter than a global thinker.
7. Many years later, General Powell relinquished command of the Fifth Corps, a seventy-two-thousand-troop force stationed in West Germany, to serve in the White House. Mr. President, I'm a soldier, he said, and if I can help, I'll come.
8. As chairman of the National Security Council's policy review group, he was responsible for turning down what he termed pet rocks, those wild plans that had little chance of approval at higher levels.
9. In 1989, before becoming the first African American chairman of the Joint Chiefs of Staff, Powell reportedly said, I remember those who suffered and sacrificed to create the conditions and set the stage for me.
10. The word *ideology* means the set of doctrines or opinions of a person or group. A close friend of Powell's once said, He has almost no ideology, unless belief in country and public service qualify as ideology.

| **Exercise 20** | **Writing with Quotation Marks** |

Imagine that you were named "Student of the Year" and your school newspaper published an article about you. Write sentences from the newspaper article, based on the instructions below. Each sentence should include quotation marks.

1. Write a sentence that contains a comment by a teacher or peer about your award.
2. Write a sentence that mentions the title of a song or short story you wrote.
3. Write a sentence that mentions and defines an unusual nickname of yours.
4. Write a sentence with a quotation from the principal in the form of a question.
5. Write a sentence with a direct quote from you; the quote should be followed by a semicolon and the rest of the sentence.

21.11 Italics (Underlining)

Italic type is a special type that slants upward and to the right. *(This sentence is printed in italics.)* When typing or writing by hand, indicate italics by under-lining. (<u>This sentence is underlined.</u>) When you are using a computer, learn the special keystrokes for italics by referring to your software manual.

Italics for Titles and Foreign Words

■ Italicize (underline) titles of books, long poems, plays, films and television series, paintings and sculptures, long musical compositions, and court cases. (A "long poem" or "long musical composition" is any poem or musical composition published under its own title as a separate work.) Also italicize the names of newspapers and magazines, ships, trains, airplanes, and spacecraft.

The Invisible Man [novel]	*Billy the Kid* [ballet]
Leaves of Grass [long poem]	*St. Louis Post-Dispatch* [newspaper]
A Raisin in the Sun [play]	*Psychology Today* [magazine]
Casablanca [film]	U.S.S. *Intrepid* [ship]
Nature [television series]	*City of New Orleans* [train]
Christina's World [painting]	*Spruce Goose* [airplane]
David [sculpture]	*Apollo 9* [spacecraft]
Brown v. Board of Education of Topeka Kansas [court case]	

■ Italicize (underline) and capitalize articles (*a, an, the*) written at the beginning of a title only when they are part of the title itself. It is common practice not to italicize (underline) the article preceding the title of a newspaper or a magazine. Do not italicize the word *magazine* unless it is part of the title of a periodical.

The Color Purple	*but*	the *Arabian Nights*
A Night at the Opera		a *Business Week* reporter
The Scarlet Letter		the *New Yorker* magazine

Do not italicize the apostrophe and -*s* in the possessive of italicized titles.

Time's editorial	*Macbeth*'s plot

■ Italicize (underline) foreign words and expressions that are not used frequently in English.

Such words are not italicized if they are commonly used in English.

James always puts ***hasta la vista*** at the end of his letters to me.
The health spa offers courses in **judo** and **karate**.

Italics with Words and Other Items Used to Represent Themselves

■ Italicize (underline) words, letters, and numerals used to represent themselves—that is, words used as words, letters used as letters, and numerals used as numerals.

> To make your essays read more smoothly, connect ideas with conjunctive adverbs such as **_therefore_** and **_however._**
>
> Did you say **_F_** or **_S_**?
>
> There is no **_9_** in my phone number.
>
> Should I use the dollar sign (**_$_**) or spell out the word?

Exercise 21 **Using Italics**

Rewrite the following sentences correctly, underlining the words, letters, and numerals that should be italicized.

Award-Winning Achievers

1. According to books such as The World Almanac and magazines such as Time and U.S. News & World Report, high achievers in many fields are often recognized by well-known awards.
2. The American composer Samuel Barber twice won Pulitzer Prizes—in 1958 for the opera Vanessa and in 1963 for his piano concerto.
3. In 1984 Haing S. Ngor won an Academy Award for best supporting actor for his role in the film The Killing Fields.
4. A person might use the word impressive to describe Michael Jackson's achievement at the 1983 Grammys, where he won awards for both best record and best album of the year.
5. The actress Ruth Brown won Broadway's Tony Award for best actress for her part in the 1989 hit musical play Black and Blue.
6. Soon after the spacecraft Apollo 11 returned from the moon in 1969, Neil Armstrong, Edwin "Buzz" Aldrin, and Michael Collins were awarded the Presidential Medal of Freedom by President Richard M. Nixon.
7. After several of her books were published to great acclaim, Toni Morrison's Beloved won a Pulitzer Prize for fiction in 1988.
8. The award-winning chef Julia Child uses the expression Mangez bien during her television broadcasts.
9. The poet Juan Ramón Jiménez, winner of the Nobel Prize for Literature in 1956, published his most famous volume of prose poems, Platero and I, in 1914.
10. In 1984 Love Medicine, the first novel by Louise Erdrich, won the National Book Critics Circle Award for fiction.

21.12 The Apostrophe

Apostrophes with Possessives

1. Pronouns

■ Use an apostrophe and *-s* for the possessive of a singular indefinite pronoun. Do not use an apostrophe with any other possessive pronouns.

no one**'s** business	*but*	**its** engine
each other**'s** books		the car is **hers**

2. Singular Nouns

■ Use an apostrophe and *-s* to form the possessive of a singular noun, even one that ends in *-s*.

the child**'s** toy
the bus**'s** muffler
the duchess**'s** problem
the lynx**'s** habitat
Peru**'s** mountains
Ray Charles**'s** music
Wallace Stevens**'s** poetry
Mr. Lax**'s** accounts

This rule does have some exceptions, however. For example, to form the possessive of ancient proper nouns that end in *-es* or *-is*, add an apostrophe only.

Ulysses**'** journey
Paris**'** apple
Xerxes**'** army
Socrates**'** pupils

3. Plural nouns ending in *-s*

■ Use an apostrophe alone to form the possessive of a plural noun that ends in *-s*.

the Girl Scouts**'** badges
the Hugheses**'** vacation
the teachers**'** cafeteria
the tennis rackets**'** strings

4. Plural nouns not ending in *-s*

■ Use an apostrophe and *-s* to form the possessive of a plural noun that does not end in *-s*.

> the children**'s** surprise
> the women**'s** decision
> his feet**'s** arches
> her teeth**'s** crowns

5. Compound nouns

■ Put only the last word of a compound noun in the possessive form.

> my great-grandfather**'s** watch
> her brother-in-law**'s** family
> the foster child**'s** happiness
> my fellow employees**'** offices
> my pen pal**'s** family members

6. Joint possession versus individual possession

■ If two or more persons (or partners in a company) possess something jointly, use the possessive form for the last person named.

> my father and mother**'s** house
> Lerner and Loewe**'s** musicals
> Bill and Julia**'s** e-mail address
> Greene, Jones, and Smith**'s** firm

■ If two or more persons (or companies) possess an item (or items) individually, put each one's name in the possessive form.

> Julio**'s** and Betty**'s** test scores
> the Murphys**'** and the Ramirezes**'** houses
> the winner**'s** and loser**'s** times

7. Expressions of time and money

■ Use a possessive form to express amounts of money or time that modify a noun.

> two hours**'** drive
> eighty cents**'** worth
> five miles**'** walk

You can also express the modifier as a hyphenated adjective. In that case the possessive form is not used.

> a two-hour drive
> an eighty-cent loaf
> a five-mile walk

Apostrophes in Contractions

■ Use an apostrophe in place of letters omitted in contractions.

I'd	*formed from*	I had, I would
can't		cannot

■ Use an apostrophe in place of the omitted numerals of a particular year.

the '96 election results
the summer of '82

Apostrophes with Special Plurals

■ Use an apostrophe and -*s* to form the plural of letters, numerals, symbols, and words used to represent themselves.

Do not italicize the apostrophe or the -*s*. Only the letter, numeral, symbol, or word should be italicized (underlined).

Cross your *t*'s and dot your *i*'s.
Please be sure to write *and*'s instead of *&*'s.
I typed *5*'s instead of *6*'s.

Do not use an apostrophe (or italics) in the plural of dates.

F. Scott Fitzgerald set many of his novels in the 1920s.

Exercise 22   **Using the Apostrophe**

Rewrite the following sentences correctly, adding apostrophes where they are needed. For the one sentence that needs no changes, write *correct*.

Ishi and the Yanas

1. I looked under the *I*s in the encyclopedia to find out about Ishi, the last Stone Age man known to have lived in North America.
2. Ishi was introduced to civilizations wonders by Professor Waterman.
3. Waterman first learned of the mans existence from one of San Franciscos newspapers.
4. The story attracted Waterman because of its human drama.
5. Ishi was a member of the Yanas, a group of Native Americans who had lived in California and practiced their ancestors way of life.
6. The Yanas tragedy began in the 1840s, when the white settlers desire for gold overshadowed all else.
7. With Californias gold rush, many people moved into the Yanas territory.
8. Theres no need to exaggerate the impact this migration had on the Yanas and other tribes existence.
9. The foreigners desire to take over the land drove away the Yanas.
10. The Yanas culture was practically destroyed in one years time.

Hyphens with Prefixes

Hyphens are not ordinarily used to join a prefix to a word. Some exceptions are described below. If you are in doubt about using a hyphen, consult a dictionary.

■ Use a hyphen after any prefix joined to a proper noun or a proper adjective. Use a hyphen after the prefixes *all-*, *ex-* (meaning "former"), and *self-* joined to any noun or adjective.

> pre-Raphaelite
> all-purpose
> ex-senator
> self-sealing

■ Use a hyphen after the prefix *anti-* when it joins a word beginning with *i-*. Also use a hyphen after the prefix *vice-*, except in *vice president.*

> anti-inflammatory
> vice-consul

■ Use a hyphen to avoid confusion between words beginning with *re-* that look alike but are different in meaning and pronunciation.

> re-cover the sofa   *but*   recover a lost watch

Hyphens in Compound Adjectives

■ Use a hyphen in a compound adjective that precedes a noun.

A compound adjective that follows a noun is generally not hyphenated.

> a plum-colored shirt   *but*   The shirt was plum colored.

Compound adjectives beginning with *well, ill,* or *little* are usually not hyphenated when they are modified by an adverb.

> an ill-tempered man   *but*   a rather ill tempered man

Do not hyphenate an expression when it is made up of an adverb ending in -*ly* and an adjective.

> a badly torn blanket
> a superbly modeled sculpture

Hyphens in Numbers

1. Compound numbers

■ Hyphenate any spelled-out cardinal or ordinal compound number up to *ninety-nine or ninety-ninth*

twenty-seven	twenty-ninth
fifty-eight	thirty-second

2. Fractions used as adjectives

■ Hyphenate a fraction that is expressed in words.

a one-eighth portion	one-half of the pie
a two-thirds majority	two-thirds of the population

We walked three and one-half miles.
BUT We walked three and a half miles.

3. Connected numerals

■ Hyphenate two numerals to indicate a span.

1899–1968   pages 151–218

When you use the word *from* before a span, use *to* rather than a hyphen.
When you use *between* before a span, use *and*.

from 1899 **to** 1968   **between** 2:45 **and** 3:15 P.M.

Hyphens to Divide Words at the End of a Line

If a word must be divided at the end of a line, divide it between syllables or pronounceable parts. When you are unsure of where to divide a word, check a dictionary.

■ In general, if a word contains two consonants occurring between two vowels or if it contains a double consonant, divide the word between the two consonants.

con-sonant	pul-ley
per-tinent	scis-sors

■ If a suffix has been added to a complete word that ends in two consonants, divide the word after the two consonants.

dull-est	steward-ship
reck-less	fill-ing

Exercise 23 — Using the Hyphen

Rewrite the following sentences, adding hyphens wherever they are needed. If a sentence is correct, write *correct.* Then make a list of all the italicized words, not including the book title, and show where each would be divided if it had to be broken at the end of a line.

Ancient African Civilizations

1. Motivated by antiEgyptian feeling, the people of Kush conquered Egypt around 800 B.C. and emerged as a newly *powerful* African empire.
2. During its seven *century* reign as a great power, the Kushite Empire based its wealth on ironworking.
3. Around A.D. 1000, in the interior sections of Africa, where few nonAfricans dared travel, there existed rising empires, large towns, and *intricate* trading systems.
4. Axum, another ancient African kingdom, was Christianized by fourth century missionaries, resulting in the origin of the Coptic *Christian* Church.
5. Axum's farmers *practiced* terracing and irrigation, and its very well trained artisans carved great churches out of stone mountains.
6. *According* to an eleventh century Arabic scholar, the kings of the empire of Ghana defended their self interests with a huge army.
7. Well trained ironworkers, the Ghanaians *controlled* vast areas of West Africa for almost ten centuries.
8. Mansa Musa, who headed the *kingdom* of Mali for twenty five years, could never be accused of anti intellectualism—he established universities.
9. Fabulously wealthy, this much discussed king *embarked* on a pilgrimage to Mecca in 1324 with sixty thousand followers and more than eighty camels loaded with gold dust.
10. These little known facts, and others about the African empire of Songhay, can be found on pages 75 96 of *Understanding Africa* by E. Jefferson Murphy.

Exercise 24 — Writing with Hyphens

Write the letter corresponding to the correctly written word or phrase for each item below.

1. (a) self-esteem (b) self esteem (c) selfesteem
2. (a) a well received-idea (b) a well-received idea (c) a well received idea
3. (a) a poorly understood notion (b) a poorly-understood notion (c) a poorly understood-notion
4. (a) one third-reports (b) one-third of the reports (c) one third of the reports
5. (a) from noon to midnight (b) from noon-to-midnight (c) from noon and midnight

21.14 Abbreviations

Use **abbreviations,** or shortened forms of words, to save space and time and to avoid wordiness. A period follows many abbreviations. Check your dictionary for guidance on how to write a particular abbreviation.

■ Use only one period if an abbreviation occurs at the end of a sentence that would ordinarily take a period of its own.

■ If an abbreviation occurs at the end of a sentence that ends with a question mark or an exclamation point, use the period *and* the second mark of punctuation.

He awoke at 5:00 **A.M.**   Did he awake at 5:00 **A.M.?**

Capitalization of Abbreviations

■ Capitalize abbreviations of proper nouns.

Thurs.   **U.S.A.**   **U.S.** Army

Many abbreviations of organizations and government agencies are formed by using the initial letters of the complete name. Pronounced letter by letter or as words, these abbreviations do not take periods.

UN   NASA   ABC   RCA   IRS   WNBA

When abbreviating a person's first and middle names, leave a space after each initial.

Robert **E.** Lee   **W. H.** Auden   **J. S.** Bach

The following abbreviations related to historical dates and times should be capitalized:

A.D. (*anno Domini,* "in the year of the Lord" [since the birth of Christ]); place before the date: **A.D.** 67

B.C. (before Christ); place after the date: 500 **B.C.**

B.C.E. (before the common era; equivalent to *B.C.*); place after the date: 1000 **B.C.E.**

C.E. (common era; equivalent to *A.D.*); place after the date: 60 **C.E.**

A.M. (*ante meridiem,* "before noon"); place after exact times: 9:30 **A.M.**

P.M. (*post meridiem,* "after noon"); place after exact times: 5:15 **P.M.**

Abbreviations of Titles of People

■ Use abbreviations for some personal titles.

Among the titles that are generally abbreviated are *Mrs., Mr., Ms., Sr.,* and *Jr.* Professional and academic titles, including *Dr., M.D.,* and *Ph.D.,* are almost always abbreviated.

Mr. Julian Escobedo	Madeleine Albright, **Ph.D.**
Mrs. William Buckley	**Dr.** Jonas Salk
Victoria Proudfoot, **M.D.**	Martin Luther King **Jr.**
María García, **M.F.A.**	Paul Chin, **D.V.M.**

Abbreviations of Units of Measure

■ Abbreviate units of measure used with numerals in technical or scientific writing but not in ordinary prose.

The abbreviations below stand for plural as well as singular units.

ENGLISH SYSTEM		METRIC SYSTEM	
ft.	foot	**cg**	centigram
gal.	gallon	**cl**	centiliter
in.	inch	**cm**	centimeter
lb.	pound	**g**	gram
mi.	mile	**kg**	kilogram
oz.	ounce	**km**	kilometer
pt.	pint	**l**	liter
qt.	quart	**m**	meter
tbsp.	tablespoon	**mg**	milligram
tsp.	teaspoon	**ml**	milliliter
yd.	yard	**mm**	millimeter

Exercise 25   Using Abbreviations

Write the abbreviations for the italicized words or phrases in the following sentences. Write *correct* if no abbreviation should be used.

1. Does the Amtrak train to New York leave Cleveland at 2:00 *ante meridiem?*
2. Bernice's car took fifteen *gallons* of gasoline.
3. Christopher Columbus landed in the New World in *anno Domini* 1492.
4. The *Federal Bureau of Investigation* is part of the *United States* Department of Justice.
5. Yuki ran ten *kilometers* in record time.

Numbers and Numerals

In nontechnical writing, some numbers are spelled out and others are expressed in figures. Numbers expressed in figures are called *numerals*.

Numbers Spelled Out

■ In general, spell out cardinal (such as *twenty*) and ordinal numbers (such as *twentieth*) that can be written in one or two words. Also, spell out any number that occurs at the beginning of a sentence.

> **Two hundred twenty** singers performed.
>
> She was the **fifteenth** person in line.

Numerals

■ In general, use numerals to express numbers that would be written in more than two words.

> There were **220** singers in the chorus.

Write large numbers as numerals followed by *million* or *billion*.

> The area of Australia is roughly **2.95 million** square miles.

■ If some numbers in a sentence should be written out while other related numbers should appear as numerals, use all numerals.

> This year the number of women marathon runners increased from **55** to **429**.

1. Money, decimals, and percentages

■ Use numerals to express amounts of money, decimals, and percentages.

> She owed me **$2.75**.
>
> The bottle holds **1.5** quarts of liquid.
>
> The bank paid **8** percent interest.

Spell out amounts of money that can be expressed in a word or two.

> **forty-four** cents   **twenty-two thousand** dollars

2. Dates and time

■ Use numerals to express the year and day in a date and to express the precise time with the abbreviations A.M. and P.M.

> My sister will celebrate her twentieth birthday on April **23, 2010**.
>
> The movie was scheduled to begin at **7:05 P.M.**

- Spell out expressions of time that do not use the abbreviation A.M. or P.M.

  The film starts at **seven** o'clock.

- To express a century when the word *century* is used, spell out the number. Likewise, to express a decade when the century is clear from the context, spell out the number.

  The **twentieth century** saw the beginnings of rock-and-roll music in the **fifties.**

- When a century and a decade are expressed as a single unit, use numerals followed by an *-s.*

  The baby boom reached its peak in the **1950s.**

3. **Addresses**

- Use numerals for streets and avenues numbered above ninety-nine and for all house, apartment, and room numbers. Spell out numbered streets and avenues with numbers of ninety-nine and below.

  The office is near **Fifth** Avenue, at **4** West **34th** Street, Room **9**.

| Exercise 26 | **Using Numbers and Numerals** |

Write out the paragraph below, correcting the use of numbers and numerals.

American Women Champions

[1]Since the advent of television, America's female athletes have been followed regularly by audiences of as many as fifty million viewers. [2]You can find some interesting statistics on female athletes in *For the Record: Women in Sports,* published in nineteen eighty-five by World Almanac Publications, two hundred Park Avenue, New York, New York. [3]You will learn, for example, that the ancient Olympics began in Athens, Greece, in the 8th century B.C., whereas the modern Olympics began in Athens in the 1890s; American women began competing only in nineteen twelve. [4]The United States record holder in the international figure-skating competition, Carol Heiss, collected 5 world championships and a gold medal; she was runner-up or United States champion for 8 successive years. [5]The 1st African American gymnast to win a national championship was Dianne Durham of Gary, Indiana (population one hundred forty-three thousand), who accomplished the feat in nineteen eighty-three. [6]Mary Lou Retton, the popular American gymnast, not only achieved 2 perfect scores on 2 successive vaults at the 1984 Olympics in Los Angeles but also won the gold medal for all-around performance. [7].06 of a second behind teammate Evelyn Ashford, sprinter Chandra Cheeseborough finished 6th in the 100-meter dash in the nineteen seventy-six Montreal Olympics. [8]At the Los Angeles games, Cheeseborough broke her own previous national record for running 400 meters, coming in at forty-nine and five one hundredths seconds; yet she was still beaten by her teammate Valerie Brisco-Hooks. [9]At the 1988 Calgary Olympics, speed skater Bonnie Blair set a new world's record of thirty-nine and one-tenth seconds for the 500-meter race.

Grammar Review

PUNCTUATION

Best known for her novels, Mary McCarthy was also a fine travel writer, as shown in the following excerpt from *The Stones of Florence*. In this passage from the book, which has been annotated to show the kinds of punctuation covered in this unit, McCarthy gives us a deft sketch of one of Italy's most celebrated cities.

Literature Model

from The Stones of Florence
by Mary McCarthy

"How can you stand it?" This is the first thing the transient visitor to Florence, in summer, wants to know, and the last thing too. . . . He means the noise, the traffic, and the heat, and something else besides, something he hesitates to mention, in view of former raptures: the fact that Florence seems to him dull, drab, provincial. Those who know Florence a little often compare it to Boston. It is full of banks, loan agencies, and insurance companies, of shops selling place mats and doilies and tooled-leather desk sets. The Raphaels and Botticellis in the museums have been copied a thousand times; the architecture and sculpture are associated with the schoolroom. For the contemporary taste, there is too much Renaissance in Florence: too much "David" (copies of Michelangelo's gigantic white nude stand on the Piazza della Signoria and the Piazzale Michelangelo; the original is in the Academy), too much rusticated stone, too much glazed terracotta, too many Madonnas with Bambinos. In the lackluster cafés of the dreary main piazza (which has a parking lot in the middle), stout women in sensible clothing sit drinking tea, and old gentlemen with canes are reading newspapers. Sensible, stout, countrified flowers like zinnias and dahlias are being sold in the Mercato Nuovo, along with straw carryalls, pocketbooks, and marketing baskets. Along the Arno, near Ponte Vecchio, ugly new buildings fill the cavities where the German mines exploded. . . .

(continued)

Quotation marks to enclose a direct quotation

Question mark to indicate a direct question

Ellipses to indicate the omission of material from a quotation

Colon to introduce an explanation of the preceding material

Period at the end of a declarative sentence

Semicolon to separate two main clauses

Parentheses to set off supplemental material

Commas to separate coordinate adjectives

Commas to separate items in a series

Punctuation, Abbreviations, and Numbers

Grammar Review

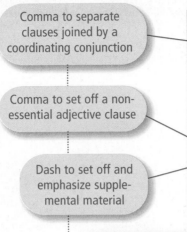

Comma to separate clauses joined by a coordinating conjunction

Comma to set off a non-essential adjective clause

Dash to set off and emphasize supplemental material

> Florence is a manly town, and the cities of art that appeal to the current sensibility are feminine, like Venice and Siena. What irritates the modern tourist about Florence is that it makes no concession to the pleasure principle. It stands four-square and direct, with no air of mystery, no blandishments, no furbelows—almost no Gothic lace or baroque swirls. . . . The general severity is even echoed by the Florentine bird, which is black and white—the swallow, a bachelor, as the Florentines say, wearing a tail coat.

Review: Exercise 1   Using the Comma

These sentences describe Florence. Rewrite each one, adding or deleting commas as needed.

SAMPLE The Uffizi Museum houses art by some of the great Renaissance painters such as, Raphael Michelangelo and da Vinci.

ANSWER The Uffizi Museum houses art by some of the great Renaissance painters such as Raphael, Michelangelo, and da Vinci.

1. Florence which is known as *Firenze* in Italian lies 145 miles northwest of Rome the capital of Italy.
2. Often called the Athens of Italy Florence remains a major, world, art center.
3. The magnificent buildings proud bridges and famous statues make the city itself a work of art a treasure to be enjoyed and protected.
4. This great city which is situated on the banks of the River Arno probably dates back to Caesar's Rome.
5. At various times during the Middle Ages walls were built around Florence and parts of a medieval wall still stand.
6. In fact inside the walled section the city takes on a distinctly, medieval flavor that enchants visitors.
7. Making Florence a tourist mecca its churches palaces and artwork attract visitors to the older section of the city.
8. Florence unlike Rome was never sacked but over the years it has suffered from many, damaging floods.
9. On November 4 1966 flood waters rose steeply, and destroyed many glorious irreplaceable works of art.
10. Although the occasional floods can be disastrous, the weather for most of the year is really quite pleasant.

Proofreading

The following passage describes the artist Thomas Cole, whose painting appears on this page. Rewrite the passage, correcting the errors in spelling, grammar, and usage. Add any missing punctuation. There are ten errors.

Thomas Cole

¹Born in a busy industrial town in Lancashire County in England, Thomas Cole (1801–1848) was one of Americas' great nineteenth-century landscape painters. **²**Before he and his family moved to Ohio in 1818 he worked for an engraver and a fabric designer. **³**When he was twenty two, his family moved to Philadelphia. **⁴**There Cole studied the paintings in the Pennsylvania Academy of the Fine Arts and he began to be attracted to landscape painting.

⁵By the time he was twenty four, Cole had moved to New York and had begun to make a name for himself as a landscape painter. **⁶**His scenes of the rugged New England countryside has an epic granduer. **⁷**The painting shown here inspired by Coles' travels through Italy in the early 1830s, include some large impressive monuments that are built in a severe style.

Thomas Cole, *View of Florence from San Miniato,* 1837

Grammar Review

Mixed Review

The following sentences describe Mary McCarthy's life and writings. Rewrite each sentence, correcting all errors in punctuation.

Mary McCarthy

1. Mary McCarthy was born in Seattle Washington and she grew up in Minneapolis Minnesota.
2. McCarthy did not plan to be a writer: in fact her first ambition was to pursue a career in the theater.
3. Her only brother Kevin McCarthy did pursue that career, and became a noted actor. (He starred in the original version of the film "Invasion of the Body Snatchers".
4. Like the women in her novel "The Group" McCarthy attended Vassar College, and graduated in 1933.
5. Early in her career, McCarthy wrote mostly nonfiction which included literary criticism, and articles, and essays.
6. Although she wrote for the magazines, "the Nation," and "the New Republic" McCarthy is most closely linked to the "Partisan Review."
7. McCarthys' second husband Edmund Wilson—also a famed writer and critic encouraged her to write fiction.
8. McCarthy was thirty years old, when she published her first book of fiction "The Company She Keeps."
9. The book presents a bright, young woman named Margaret Sargent who like McCarthy has a passion for truth.
10. By 1960, McCarthys novels included the following: *The Oasis,* published in 1949, *The Groves of Academe,* published in 1952, and *A Charmed Life,* published in 1955.
11. Need you ask what these novel's popularity did for McCarthy's writing career!
12. Critics of her novels' wondered, why they contained so much autobiographical material?
13. McCarthy answered as follows, What I really do she said is take real plums and put them in an imaginary cake.
14. Some of her books are memoirs, including the following; "Memories of a Catholic Girlhood," and "How I Grew".
15. Her travel writing as you have seen is elegant and she wrote many pieces about Venice as well as Florence.
16. After the publication of her novel, "The Group" in 1962—its my favorite, McCarthy's popularity soared.
17. This book which received mixed reviews tells of eight womens' lives, loves and careers.
18. The book was a best seller, moreover it was turned into a movie starring Candice Bergen who went on to star in the television series, "Murphy Brown."
19. Did you read McCarthy's sixth novel "Birds of America."
20. Often called Americas First Lady of Letters, McCarthy is noted for her analytic witty prose style.

Writing Application

TIME

For more about the writing process, see **TIME Facing the Blank Page,** pp. 111–121.

Punctuation in Writing

V. S. Naipaul uses punctuation in this passage as a tool for creating varied sentences at the beginning of his novel *The Enigma of Arrival.* Examine the passage, focusing especially on the use of commas, semicolons, question marks, and hyphens.

> The narrow public road ran beside the dark, yew-screened grounds of the manor. Just beyond the road and wire fence and the roadside scrub the down sloped sharply upwards. Stonehenge and the walk lay in that direction. There would have been a lane or path leading off the public road. To find that lane or path, was I to turn left or right? There was no problem, really. You came to a lane if you turned left; you came to another lane if you turned right. Those two lanes met at Jack's cottage, or the old farmyard where Jack's cottage was, in the valley over the hill.
>
> Two ways to the cottage. Different ways: one was very old, and one was new. The old way was longer, flatter; it followed an old, wide, winding riverbed; it would have been used by carts in the old days. The new way—meant for machines—was steeper, up the hill and then directly down again.

Techniques with Punctuation

Try to apply some of V. S. Naipaul's writing techniques when you write and revise your own work.

❶ Use commas between adjectives that modify the same noun if they are not separated by a conjunction. If the adjective is a compound, use a hyphen.

NAIPAUL'S PUNCTUATION the dark, yew-screened grounds

ANOTHER VERSION the dark and yew-screened grounds

❷ Use a question mark to end interrogative sentences in which a question is communicated.

NAIPAUL'S INTERROGATIVE SENTENCE To find that lane or path, was I to turn left or right?

A DECLARATIVE VERSION I could turn left or right to find that lane or path.

❸ Use semicolons to separate two independent clauses in a sentence that are not joined by a coordinating conjunction.

NAIPAUL'S SENTENCE You came to a lane if you turned left; you came to another lane if you turned right.

ANOTHER VERSION You came to a lane if you turned left, and you came to another lane if you turned right.

Practice Practice these techniques by revising the following passage. In your revision, either add needed punctuation or omit punctuation used incorrectly.

How do tourists find the well known beach on this tropical island. First, they must navigate the many paths, each lined with tall-graceful trees. With one path they may find brightly colored flowers with another they may discover ripening fruit on plants or small trees. Which path should they take. There's no easy answer each path unfolds its own mystery. I must admit; though, that I am satisfied with whatever path I take on this island? One path presents a fascinating variety of wild-bird life another presents dense tropical plants with fragrances sweet, bitter, and exotic.

"*The woods are lovely, dark and deep./But I have promises to keep,/And miles to go before I sleep,/And miles to go before I sleep.*"

—Robert Frost, "Stopping by Woods on a Snowy Evening"

William Fraser Garden,
The Wood at Dusk

History and Development of English

22.1 A Multicultural Linguistic Heritage

When the first English settlers arrived in North America, they spoke a language that had been influenced by centuries of contact with many cultures. This influence was most evident in the settlers' vocabulary.

Words from Many Lands

Throughout the history of English, the language has readily borrowed words from other languages. The chart below gives a small sampling of some of these loan words, the languages from which they were borrowed, and the approximate dates they first appeared in English.

Persian illustration, 1554

Early Loan Words in English			
LANGUAGE	**ORIGINAL WORD**	**ENGLISH WORD**	**APPEARED IN ENGLISH**
LATIN	crystallum librarius	cristal (crystal) library	13th century 14th century
GREEK	kōmōidia oligarchia	comedy oligarchy	14th century about 1500
SCANDINAVIAN LANGUAGES	vindauga skule	windowe (window) skoulen (scowl)	13th century 14th century
FRENCH	atourne magique	attourney (attorney) magik (magic)	14th century 14th century
SPANISH	sombra	sombrero	about 1600
ITALIAN	madrigale maccheroni	madrigal macaroni	late 16th century about 1600
ARABIC	qutuh nāranj	coton (cotton) orange	14th century 14th century
PERSIAN	kaarwaan bāzār	caravan bazaar	late 16th century early 17th century

American English

As the English settlers established communities on the eastern coast of North America, their language and customs were influenced by the many cultures they encountered. As contact with these cultures increased, words

History and Development of English

22.1 A Multicultural Linguistic Heritage   **759**

from Native American languages soon became part of the settlers' vocabulary. Many of these loan words were place names and names of plants and animals that did not exist in England.

As the settlers pushed westward, they encountered other Native Americans, some of whom spoke languages heavily influenced by the Spanish of the conquistadores. The English settlers also encountered Spanish-speaking settlers. Thus many Spanish words entered the developing vocabulary of American English.

Early Loan Words In American English		
ORIGINAL WORD	**ENGLISH WORD**	**APPEARED IN ENGLISH**
NATIVE AMERICAN LANGUAGES		
chocolatl (Nahuatl)	chocolate	about 1600
äräkun (Algonquian)	raccoon	early 17th century
mokasin (Algonquian)	moccasin	early 17th century
askoot-asquash (Narraganset)	squash	mid-17th century
pawcohiccora (Algonquian)	hickory	mid-17th century
chitmunk (Ojibwa)	chipmunk	early 19th century
SPANISH		
mestengo	mustang	early 19th century
patio	patio	early 19th century
estampida	stampede	early 19th century
cañón	canyon	mid-19th century
bonanza	bonanza	mid-19th century
vigilante	vigilante	mid-19th century
AFRICAN LANGUAGES		
banäna (Wolof)	banana	about 1600
mbanza (Kimbundu)	banjo	mid-18th century
gombo (Bantu)	gumbo	early 19th century
vodu (Ewe)	voodoo	mid-19th century

Exercise 1

Use a dictionary to discover the language from which each of the following English words originated. If your dictionary provides dates, find out when each word first entered English.

1. circle
2. skirt
3. lieutenant
4. roast
5. trombone
6. hoosegow

Think of at least three more words that originated in another language and find out when each of them entered the English language.

History and Development of English

Wordworks

BLENDS AND COMPOUNDS

The Blend-o-rama

Lewis Carroll, the author of *Alice's Adventures in Wonderland*, loved to experiment with language. When writing stories and poems, Carroll invented many new words, such as *chortle, galumph,* and *snark.* What do these words mean, and how did Carroll come to create them?

Chortle, galumph, and *snark* are examples of blends—new words made by combining two existing English words. *Chortle* is a blend of **chuck**le and s**nort**; *galumph* could be a blend of **gall**op and tri**umph**; *snark* is probably a blend of **sn**ake and s**hark.**

As people use English to conduct their daily lives, words that no longer effectively communicate ideas pass gradually out of use, while new, more effective words are born. Thus, *dumbfound* was created, a blend of **dumb** and con**found.** And, similarly, **fl**utter and **hurry** may have been blended to make *flurry.*

Another way new words are created is by compounding, or joining, two words. Some compounds are closed (one word), such as *greenhouse* and *shipwreck.* Others are open (two words), such as *post office* and *ice cream.* Still others are hyphenated: *fire-eater* and *go-between.* Whether a compound is closed, open, or hyphenated is often a seemingly arbitrary matter established by tradition rather than by the application of a set of rules for compounding.

Like blends, compounds have a long history. In Old English, for example, *full* and *fyllan* were joined to create *fullfyllan* (to fulfill). Despite the long history of compounding, some compounds are short-lived. *Splashdown* was created in the earliest days of the United States space program to describe the return of space capsules that left orbit by parachuting into the ocean. Today's space shuttles glide onto airport runways, relegating *splashdown* to linguistic history.

> #### ⟨ACTIVITY⟩
>
> #### Blend-o-rama
> Try your hand at creating your own blends and compounds. Write three of each and then use your newly created words in a story, a dialogue, or a poem.

22.2 | An African-English Creole

The enslaved Africans in the American colonies spoke a variety of West African languages. To make communication possible between the colonists and the enslaved people (who sometimes knew little of each other's languages), a pidgin, or hybrid language, slowly evolved.

Pidgin Speech

A pidgin is a hybrid language that combines elements of two or more languages. Pidgins arise out of contact between different cultures through trade, war, colonization, or, in this case, slavery. Pidgins develop to enable people from different cultures to communicate on a rudimentary level.

The pidgin that enabled enslaved people and their owners to communicate was part English and part native Caribbean and African languages. The mixture, which melded different vocabularies, grammars, and pronunciations, flourished in the United States during the eighteenth century and the first half of the nineteenth century. With the end of slavery and the plantation system, this pidgin English slowly died out except in one area of the United States where a form of it is still spoken today.

A Creole Called Gullah

Many descendants of former enslaved people still live on the Sea Islands, off the coasts of South Carolina and Georgia, and on the nearby mainland, where profitable cotton plantations once thrived. These people speak Gullah, sometimes called Geechee, the pidgin English that their ancestors spoke.

Gullah, however, is no longer considered a pidgin by linguists, since from birth its speakers learn it as their primary language. When a pidgin becomes the primary language learned from birth, it is called a creole.

An English speaker who did not understand Gullah would undoubtedly recognize some of the words. Most words, however, would be completely unfamiliar. Read the following Gullah sentence. Say the sentence aloud. Which words do you recognize? Can you decipher the meaning of the sentence?

Uma-chil' nyamnyam fufu and t'ree roll roun, but 'e ain't been satify.

Now read the English translation and compare it with the Gullah original.

The girl ate mush and three biscuits, but she wasn't satisfied.

What is the Gullah verb for *ate?* How is the noun *biscuits* expressed in Gullah? Can you suggest a reason why *uma-chil'* means 'girl'?

Gullah exhibits some grammatical patterns derived from English. Notice the auxiliary verbs in the following sentences.

> I be shell 'em. (I am shelling them.)
> I ben shell 'em. (I shelled them.)
> I bina shell 'em. (I have been shelling them.)
> I ben don shell 'em. (I shelled them some time ago.)

Gullah, like any language that started as a pidgin, shows evidence of linguistic inventiveness. *Dawn* in Gullah is an open compound: *day clean. Flatter* is a closed compound: *sweetmouth.* Even an intensifier like *very* is expressed inventively. In Gullah, *very ugly* becomes *ugly too much.*

Exercise 2

Research and report on the Gullah language and the culture of the people who speak it. Use the library and/or the Internet to do your research. Answer questions like the following: Where did the Gullah-speaking people come from? How do you think they came to live on the Sea Islands? Why do you suppose Gullah has thrived on these islands when throughout the rest of the South this language died out with slavery? What is taking place on the Sea Islands today? Do you think the culture of the people will survive?

Wordworks

ILLOGICAL JUXTAPOSITION

Include Me Out

> Wagner's music's better than it sounds.

Samuel Goldwyn was a legendary Hollywood studio tycoon, the head of MGM during its golden years. Goldwyn is remembered, however, not just for his movie-making prowess but also for his creativity with the English language. Sam Goldwyn once said of an MGM contract actor, "We're overpaying him, but he's worth it." Another time Goldwyn defended his studio's films by asserting, "Our comedies are not to be laughed at!"

And what was a Goldwyn associate to make of the following remark: "I never liked you, and I always will"?

Goldwyn's remarks are illogical juxtapositions. An illogical juxtaposition is a humorous statement that results when two contradictory ideas get tangled up in the same sentence. "Include me out," for example, is an illogical juxtaposition because to *include* means to bring *in,* not to leave *out.* Although illogical juxtapositions are usually unintentional, sometimes they are deliberate, such as Mark Twain's satirical critique, "Wagner's music is better than it sounds."

In addition to Goldwyn and Twain, another well-known practitioner of illogical juxtapositions was New York Yankee catcher Yogi Berra. After Berra turned to managing, reporters wondered whether he would succeed in the dugout after so many years on the field. His answer? "Sometimes you can observe a lot by watching." Berra is also reported to have said of the national pastime, "Ninety-nine percent of this game is half mental."

Illogical juxtapositions remind us that we are, after all, human, and that what we say is not always what we mean. Unless, that is, you subscribe to Samuel Goldwyn's oft-quoted philosophy: "I may not always be right, but I'm never wrong!"

ACTIVITY

Figure It Out

With a partner, try translating the following illogical juxtapositions. What did the speaker mean to say?

1. A girl who is seventeen is much more of a woman than a boy who is seventeen.
2. Don't pay any attention to him; don't even ignore him.
3. Her death leaves a void in the community that will be hard to replace.
4. No wonder nobody comes here—it's too crowded.
5. Let's have some new clichés.
6. This book has too much plot and not enough story.

22.3 Immigration and American English

How many languages do you speak? One? Two? You may not realize it, but if you speak English, you are acquainted with quite a few other languages as well: Greek, Latin, Algonquian, Hopi, German, French, Spanish, and Thai, to name just a few. You may not be fluent in any of these languages, but every day you use words from their vocabularies.

In fact, whenever two or more different cultures establish and maintain contact over an extended period of time, the vocabulary of each culture's language reflects word borrowing from each of the other cultures' languages. Throughout the long history of English, the language has borrowed words liberally from other languages to enrich its vocabulary.

In the United States, much of this word borrowing has resulted from immigration. The United States has been peopled largely by immigrants, from its birth to the present day.

A Cultural Bonanza

One great wave of immigration to the United States took place from about 1820 to 1850. Millions of people fled poverty and famine in their countries of origin in the hope of improving the quality of their lives in the United States. From western Europe came millions of immigrants—Irish, Germans, Scandinavians. In addition, hundreds of thousands of Chinese arrived from Asia. Each of these groups brought with it a unique culture. The foods, music, literature, history, religious and social traditions, and language of each culture eventually would be woven into the cultural fabric of the developing nation.

Beginning about 1880 and continuing into the 1920s, another wave of immigration enhanced the cultural vitality of the United States. The new immigrants included Italians, Greeks, Poles, Hungarians, Russians; and smaller numbers of people from other cultures throughout the world. Each of these cultures has expanded the vocabulary of American English.

New Arrivals

Immigration to the United States continues to this day. Over the past several decades, people have immigrated to the United States from Vietnam, Cambodia, Laos, Thailand, Haiti, Central America and South America, Korea, Mexico, Ireland, the Middle East, and the Philippines. Immigrants continue to arrive from Europe, Asia, and Africa. The chart on the next page shows just a few of the words from other languages that have reshaped American English during the past two centuries.

Borrowed Words in American English

LANGUAGE	WORD	WHEN BORROWED
FRENCH	levee	mid-18th century
	cent	late 18th century
	depot	late 18th century
	jambalaya	late 19th century
SPANISH	plaza	mid-19th century
	adobe	mid-19th century
	corral	mid-19th century
	serape	late 19th century
GERMAN	pretzel	late 19th century
	kindergarten	mid-19th century
	hamburger	late 19th century
DUTCH	cookie	early 18th century
	boss	early 19th century
	bakery	early 19th century
	snoop	early 19th century
ITALIAN	spaghetti	late 19th century
	minestrone	late 19th century
HAWAIIAN	ukulele	late 19th century
IRISH	phony	about 1900
CHINESE	chop suey	late 19th century
	chow mein	about 1900
	wok	mid-20th century
JAPANESE	hara-kiri	mid-19th century
	hibachi	mid-19th century

Exercise 3

Use your dictionary to identify the language from which each boldfaced word below was borrowed.

Alberto's mom asked him to go to the **delicatessen** for some **coleslaw.** Alberto replied that he would also pick up some **bagels** while he was there. His sister Marcella reminded him to get some **Parmesan** cheese for the next night's **lasagna,** and their little brother asked Alberto to buy some **tacos.**

Wordworks

CONTRONYMS

Is the Moon Out?
Are the Lights Out?

It's a hot, humid Saturday in July, and your neighbor tells you, "I think it's about time to trim that tree!" What is your neighbor going to do?

It's a cold, snowy Saturday in December, and your neighbor tells you, "I think it's about time to trim that tree!" Now what is your neighbor going to do?

It's clear from this example that the word trim has two nearly opposite meanings. *Trim* can mean "take away from," as in "**trim** (cut off) some branches," or it can mean "add to," as in "**trim** (hang some ornaments, tinsel, and strings of popcorn on) the tree." *Trim* is a contronym, a word that has two opposite meanings that depend on the context in which the word is used.

English has a number of contronyms. *Left* can mean "departed," as in "Rick and Maria **left** two hours ago." Left can also mean "remaining," as in "Only Rick and Maria were **left.**"

Wear is another contronym. "That leather **wears** well" means the leather endures. "Rain will **wear** that suede" means the suede will decay.

When you **dust** a table, you remove something. When you **dust** a pan of brownies with powdered sugar, you add something.

How about *cleave?* You can **cleave** to someone (become one together, as in marriage or close friendship), or you can **cleave** a log (split it in two).

It's possible that on some dark night you may find yourself saying, "It's a good thing the moon is **out,** because the lights are **out!**"

ACTIVITY

Controquizonyms

Test your contronym knowledge. Each of the contronyms below is used to convey a certain meaning in the sentence provided. Think of the opposite meaning for each word and then write a sentence using that meaning.

1. Clip (to join): I will clip the coupon to the letter.
2. Handicap (advantage): The golfer's handicap allowed competition.
3. Temper (to soften): Temper your anger or it will get you in trouble.
4. Swear (to pledge): The soldier will swear loyalty to her country.
5. Commencement (beginning): At the commencement of the war, the outcome was uncertain.

History and Development of English

Regional American English

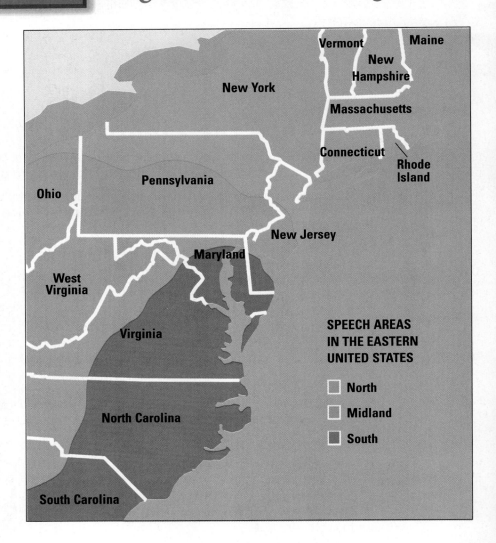

SPEECH AREAS
IN THE EASTERN
UNITED STATES

☐ North

☐ Midland

■ South

When you go to the grocery store, are your purchases put in a **bag** or a **sack?** Does the water in your kitchen sink flow from a **tap,** a **faucet,** or a **spigot?** Do you enjoy **cottage cheese, Dutch cheese, smearcase,** or **clabber cheese?** And when you sit down to a summer supper, do you bite into **corn on the cob** or **roasting ears?**

The United States is a land of diversity, and people in different parts of the country speak slightly different forms, or dialects, of English. A dialect is a regional variety of a language that differs from other regional varieties in vocabulary, grammar, and pronunciation. The map above shows parts of the three major dialect regions of the eastern United States: North, Midland, and South. Each dialect can be divided further into many subgroups, some of them distinguished by region and some by socioeconomic factors.

History and Development of English

British Influence

Where did these dialects come from? They didn't just spring up in America; their roots go back across the Atlantic to England, where people also speak regional dialects.

When English immigrants began settling in North America, they tended to settle in groups; that is, people who lived in the same area in England often settled together in America. One group settled in the southern colonies, while another group settled in the middle colonies. These groups of settlers typically had little contact with each other. Thus, the regional dialects they brought with them from England were preserved in America. Although mass communication has diminished some speech differences, traces of them can still be heard.

One Language, Many Variations

American English dialects differ in vocabulary, grammar, and pronunciation. You have already been introduced to some vocabulary differences. Here's another example: What do you call a sandwich made from cold meats, cheeses, and condiments served on a long slice of French bread? If you're from New York, you probably call it a **hero.** In Philadelphia it's a **hoagie,** and in Iowa, a **Dagwood.** The people of Illinois call it a **sub,** or **submarine,** while in Rhode Island, it's a **grinder.** And in New Orleans? Why, it's a **poor boy,** of course!

Grammatical differences in dialects occur as well. A Northerner might say "you might be able to," whereas a Southerner might say "y'all might could." The Northern personal pronouns *ours, yours,* and *his* might become *ourn, yourn,* and *hisn* in the Midland dialect region.

Different dialects also exhibit variations in pronunciation. In some Northern and Southern dialects, the *r* in the following words is barely pronounced, if at all: *father, card, far, fort.* In Northern and Midland speech, the *s* in *grease* and *greasy* is pronounced like the *ss* in *hiss.* In Southern dialect, the same *s* has a *z* sound.

Whenever you hear a dialect that is different from yours, remember that "different" English is not incorrect or uneducated English. The Northern, Midland, and Southern dialects, as well as the many socioeconomic dialects, are simply different ways to express the same ideas.

Exercise 4

Investigate regional differences in language within your own community. Seek out students and teachers who have moved from other areas of the country. Listen closely to the ways they speak and to the words and expressions they use. Which words and expressions that you use are unfamiliar to them? Do they use any expressions that are unfamiliar to you? Report on your findings to the class.

Wordworks

PUSH-BUTTON WORDS

Button, Button

Suppose you want to borrow your sister's car next Saturday. At first she says no, so you have some major persuading to do. Do you remind your sister how inconsiderate and selfish she can be sometimes, how her bad attitude and unfriendly manner turn people off, and how lending you her car might make her appear less self-centered? Or do you tell her how much you have always admired her openness and generosity and that you appreciate the trust she places in you when she lets you use her car?

Assuming you are sincere, the second approach is clearly the better one. Using language that makes people feel good (or bad) is known as "pushing their buttons," because many people react automatically to certain words.

Politicians long ago figured out that certain words evoke either a strong positive or negative response in most people. The power of a push-button word is in its connotations—all the ideas and emotions associated with the word. For example, how many times have you heard *America, freedom,* and *democracy* strung together by politicians? These words are meant to give you a warm emotional glow, stirring up your feelings of pride and patriotism. The politician hopes that these good feelings about your country will inspire good feelings—and votes—for him or her.

Advertisers employ plenty of push-button words as well. Think about the phrase "warm, golden rolls, made just like Grandma baked at home, from all-natural ingredients." Can you identify the push-button words in this pitch? Most people associate pleasant feelings with *warm, golden, Grandma, home,* and *natural.* The advertiser hopes you will feel those same emotions about its dinner rolls, even when the closest anybody's grandma comes to them is in picking up a package at the grocery store!

> Think Globally
> Act Locally

> I thought
> I was wrong
> once, but I was
> mistaken

> SAY NO
> TO
> DRUGS

> ### ACTIVITY
> #### Whose Button Is It?
> Try this "push-button" activity. For each word in the following list, do some free association. Write down whatever words come to you as you think about each word. Try to come up with five to eight words that you associate with each listed word. Then, looking over your responses, note how each word and its associations make you feel. Where might you encounter such words? Compare your words and feelings with those of your classmates. Do you all have the same "buttons"?
>
> - used
> - dictator
> - antique
> - nutritious
> - artificial
> - wholesome
> - improved
> - responsibility

22.5 Impact of the Mass Media

During the 1980s, teenagers of the San Fernando Valley, in Los Angeles, developed a unique manner of speech. It included such colorful expressions as *tubular, to the max, I'm totally sure, gag me with a spoon, grody,* and *narly.* In an earlier era, this way of speaking would have remained localized to southern California and, because it was based largely on slang, eventually would have died out. But something very different happened.

What happened was the intervention of the mass media. Television news shows broadcast stories on the language and culture of "Valley girls" (and boys). Hollywood joined the bandwagon with a popular movie, *Fast Times at Ridgemont High.* Newspapers and magazines ran stories about how young people in the Valley seemed to spend all of their free time at shopping malls. Moon Unit Zappa, daughter of sixties rocker Frank Zappa, had a hit record, *Valley Girl,* that satirized the speech of the Valley teens. Soon teenagers all across America and overseas were affecting the language, mannerisms, and even the dress of "the Valley."

Media Presence and Speed

The "Valley" phenomenon is just one example of how the mass media can affect the language we speak. Two critical characteristics enable the media to dominate our culture: presence and speed.

First of all, media presence is everywhere. The Internet, television, radio, newspapers, magazines, billboards, advertising, movies, records—all spread, influence, and promote popular culture. In the early 1990s, a German automobile manufacturer launched an advertising campaign that used a German word, *fahrvergnügen,* to describe the driving experience its cars offered. The word was plastered across billboards, sung about in television and radio commercials, and featured in magazine ads. Before long, the word was even being joked about on late-night television talk shows. *Fahrvergnügen* will likely never assume a permanent place in the English language, but thanks to the mass media, it has certainly made an impact on American consciousness.

The second important characteristic of the media is speed. Throughout history, change has come slowly to the English language. Until recently a word from a foreign language might take decades, if not centuries, to become fully integrated into the English language. Today, however, this process has been accelerated. We live in an age in which communication is instantaneous over television, radio, and the Internet. For example, we can watch wars fought "live" on network television, receive instantaneous e-mail from friends across the world, and become aware of language we might otherwise never know.

Advances in media even add new words to the English language. In just the recent past, new terms have become part of our everyday language—for example, *the Internet, e-mail, the Web, modem, search engine, URL,* and *CD-ROM.*

Future Talk

In the future, how will the mass media's ability to create, import, and export language nearly instantaneously influence American English and other languages? Will the constant presence of the mass media in the daily lives of people throughout the world lead one day to a global language that everyone will understand? If it does, will that language resemble any that people now speak?

Already the world shows signs of moving toward a global language, and many indications suggest that English could become that language. English is standard in international civil aviation, allowing professionals in that field to communicate effectively despite differences in their native languages. In addition, partly because of European colonial expansion during the eighteenth and nineteenth centuries, English is now widely used—and is sometimes even an official language—in countries as varied as India, Jamaica, and Nigeria.

Whether a global language will evolve and what form it will take are questions yet to be answered. But whatever the future holds, one fact about the present has become quite apparent: every day the mass media affect the way we understand and talk about our world.

Exercise 5

Examples of how the mass media affect American English are all around you. Spend some time reading, watching, and listening to advertisements. How many newly invented words or foreign words can you find? Make a list of these words. Which words do you think are likely to endure? Why?

Wordworks

A R G O T

On the Lam

If you're a fan of the old gangster movies of the 1930s and 1940s, you've probably already figured out the language used in those stories. But if phrases like *on the lam* sound completely foreign to you, welcome to the world of argot!

Argot is a special kind of language, the more or less secret lingo of a particular group. Argot is often associated with a shady, underworld culture. Criminals use argot, also called cant, to conceal their plans and to foster a sense of group identity. Some sociologists have suggested that since organized crime is, after all, a profession, it has developed its jargon in the same way other professions develop their jargon.

Argot is probably as old as professional crime itself. Argot was described as the special language of crime as early as the sixteenth century. Much later, in 1690, an author identified only as B. E. compiled a dictionary of terms used by what the author called "the canting crew."

Although most argot remains a mystery to the general public, argot has never-theless enriched American slang with terms such as *hot* (for stolen merchandise), *to take for a ride, to hijack,* and *to muscle in.* And like all living languages, argot continues to evolve and change.

ACTIVITY

Awright, Wise Guys

Look at the list of argot terms and definitions below. Many terms date from the 1920s, an era famous for its bank robbers and outlaws. Use this list, plus any other argot you may know or can locate in the library, to write a brief scene for a gangster movie. Try to use as many terms as you can and make the dialogue as realistic as possible. Share your scene with classmates.

- **C-note** (a $100 bill)
- **canary** (one who confesses, or "sings," to the police)
- **cannon** (a pickpocket)
- **cut** (an individual's share of the loot)
- **finger** (to turn in to the law)
- **G-man** (a federal agent)
- **grifter** (a con artist)
- **heater** (a gun)
- **loot** (stolen goods)
- **mark** (a victim)
- **moll** (popularly, a gangster's girlfriend; also, a gun moll, or female pickpocket)
- **on the lam** (running from the law)
- **paperhanger** (one who passes forged checks)
- **rap** (the blame for a crime)
- **slammer** (prison)
- **up the river** (in or into prison)

Library Resources

23.1 How to Locate Books and Other Library Materials

Think about all the services your library offers. You can take out a book to read for pleasure, do research for a term paper, borrow a video or a CD, use the Internet, or find out about events in your community.

Today, in addition to books and magazines, modern public libraries provide free access via the Internet and other databases to a world of multimedia information. Most libraries even offer their own Web sites. Library Web sites provide connections to the library catalog, and sometimes to magazine indexes, allowing you to begin your research at home or at school.

Most Important Parts of a Library

- **Fiction Books** are works of the imagination, such as novels and collections of short stories.
- **Nonfiction Books** are fact-based and are about subjects such as history, science, and the arts.
- **Reference Works** include encyclopedias, dictionaries, almanacs, and atlases.
- **Periodicals** include magazines, journals, and newspapers. Periodicals are usually published on a daily, weekly, monthly, or quarterly schedule.
- **Audio-Visual Materials** include films, slides, videos, records, audio cassettes, and compact discs.
- **Catalogs,** either in card form or on a computer, index each book in the library.
- **Computers.** Modern libraries offer computer access to electronic databases and indexes, as well as to the Internet.

When doing research your first task is to locate the materials you need. For most topics, your search starts with the resources of a public library. Some topics, however, might lead you to specialized libraries, which have more books on particular subject areas such as medical science, business, art, or law. In either type of library, your search will probably begin with the catalog.

Using the Catalog

Traditionally, libraries offered a card catalog to help users locate books. Information was filed alphabetically, by title and by author, on paper cards in long drawers. Today computer catalogs help you locate library materials. These catalogs allow searches by **subject, author, title,** or **keyword.** Become familiar with the online screens, including the help screens that provide tips for more effective searching.

A Typical On-Screen Book Search

SCREEN 1 The first screen allows you to select a search category—*Keyword, Author, Title,* or *Subject.* If a *Subject* search returns no results, try the same word as a *Keyword* search. If you desire only recent titles, you can also limit your search by date.

SCREEN 2 Then, on the screen 2, you can type as much or as little of the subject as you want. For example you might type *hurricanes, Texas.*

SCREEN 3 Examine the initial results. If they reflect what you are searching for, hit enter.

SCREEN 4 Note the classification, or "call" number, so you can locate the book on the shelf.

```
You searched for the
Subject: Hurricanes
Texas

1 Hurricanes Texas
Galveston History
20th Century  1
```

```
You searched for the Subject:
Hurricanes Texas
Author    Larson, Erik
Title     Isaac's Storm: a
          man, a time, and the
          deadliest hurricane in
          history
Imprint   New York: Crown
          Publishers, 1999
Location  976.413 La
```

Classification Sytems

To organize books, libraries use either the Dewey decimal system or the Library of Congress classification (LC). The Dewey system divides nonfiction books into ten numerical categories, based on topic. Books are shelved by call number and then alphabetically. Fiction books are shelved alphabetically by author's last name and then by title. The Library of Congress classification uses letters to divide books into twenty categories. Most academic libraries and large specialized libraries use this system.

Dewey Decimal System

CATEGORY NUMBERS	MAJOR CATEGORY
000–099	General works
100–199	Philosophy
200–299	Religion
300–399	Social sciences
400–499	Language
500–599	Sciences
600–699	Technology
700–799	Arts
800–899	Literature
900–999	History and geography

Library of Congress System

LETTERS AND CATEGORIES		LETTERS AND CATEGORIES	
A	General works	N	Fine arts
B	Philosophy and religion	P	Language and literature
C–F	History	Q	Science
G	Geography and anthropology	R	Medicine
H	Social sciences	S	Agriculture
J	Political science	T	Technology
K	Law	U	Military science
L	Education	V	Naval science
M	Music	Z	Bibliography and library science

When searching for books in the online catalog, be careful to note when materials appear in special collections. Local history, science fiction, reference books, career titles, and other books may be shelved in a separate section of the library. These locations will be noted in the online catalog.

How to Locate Periodicals and Current Materials

Print periodicals, such as newspapers, magazines, and journals, are still excellent sources for current information; however, the Internet may be the most up-to-date source. Many online indexes and databases provide the full text of articles, speeches, and media transcripts. Sometimes these databases give only a summary of the article, and you have to search the library's periodical stacks or microfilms for the full article. For materials more than ten years old, you may need to search the library's periodicals stacks.

Although databases differ, they share common features. At the first screen, or query screen, you are asked to type in your search words. Display screens will then list the titles of the articles found. The list will give a brief summary and the source and date of the article. If the full text of a particular article is available, a symbol for full text will be displayed. These periodical displays may be arranged by date, or by *relevancy*—how well they relate to the terms you entered. Many databases will give you an opportunity to refine your search further with additional keywords.

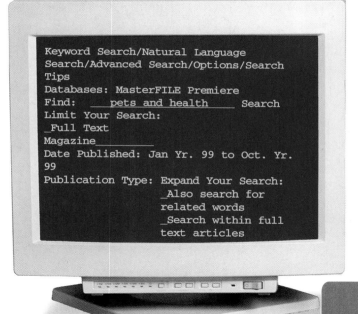

An Online Periodical Search

Remember that each database is different, so the search screens will be different, but the principles are basically the same. The search shown here is from an *EBSCO Host* database, *MasterFILE Premier*. *Masterfile Premier* provides full text for over 1,800 periodicals covering nearly all subjects. The *EBSCO Animal* database provides information on topics relating to animals.

When you enter the database, you see a menu screen. Each of these databases has a box that you can select. Once you have chosen your database, you will see a screen like the following.

First Search Screen In the query box (the line after "find"), type your search terms. To search more than one term, separate them by *and, or,* or *not*. For example, if you want to search viruses but not computer viruses, type *virus not computer*.

Notice that this search is limited by certain dates; you don't want all articles on this subject, only within that time frame. If you wanted to search only *Newsweek,* you could type that title in the space next to *Magazine*.

Library Resources

If you come up with no hits, or results, try expanding your search by selecting one of the options listed on the screen under *Expand Your Search.*

Second Screen, Search Results The titles with *X*'s next to them include the whole article. Two articles have full-page images listed—which is important to know if you need a graphic for your report. The Mark category means you can choose that article to look at later. You can mark all the articles that look interesting and then view them or e-mail them to your home computer or print the list of them in the library.

```
Searched: MasterFILE Premier for pets and health
(1 to 10) of 66   Refine Search   Print/Email/Save
Mark   Full Text   Select Result for More Detail
X      When Pets Pop Pills.; By: Meyer, Michael., Newsweek,
       10/11/99, Vol. 134 Issue 15, p60, 2p, 1 graph, 2c
       Pudgy Pups and Chubby Cats.;p By: McCullough, Susan., Family
       Circle, 10/05/99, Vol. 112 Issue 14, p167, 1p, 2c
       Pet life,: By: King, Linda K.., McCall's, Oct99, Vol. 127 Issue
       1, p128, 2/3p, 1 cartoon, 1c
       Fido's More Than a Friend.; By: C. M.., Weight Watchers, Oct99,
       Vol. 32 Issue 8, p16, 2p, 1c
       Pesticide Spray Is Said to Pose Almost No Risk To Humans.; By:
       Sullivan, John., New York Times, 09/07/99, Vol. 148 Issue 51638,
       pB5, 0p
X      Studies Show Anti-Oxidants Have Benefits For Aging Pets.,
                            Full Page Image
X      10 Hints for a Healthy Dog., Dog World, Sep99, Vol 84 Issue 9,
       p10, 1/4p, 1 chart
                            Full Page Image
X      Insurance coverage that goes to the dogs.; By: Sutton, Judy.,
       Crain's Chicago Business, 08/02/99, Vol. 22 Issue 31, p4, 1/3p
X      Poison on the Farm.; By: Geller, Jon., Mother Earth
       News, Aug/Sep99, Issue 175, p66, 3p, 1c
                            Full Page Image
(1 to 10) of 66          Refine Search Print/E-mail/Save
```

Types of Computerized Indexes

For many years, the most popular paper index for periodicals has been the *Readers' Guide to Periodical Literature.* The *Readers' Guide* alphabetically indexes articles, both by author and subject, covering a wide range of subjects in more than 260 magazines and newspapers. Today you can access the *Readers' Guide* online at your library. Other online periodical indexes include *The Electric Library* and *Magazine Article Summaries.* Like the *Readers' Guide,* these indexes search current general interest magazines and newspapers.

Other specialized databases allow you to search for materials on specific subjects, such as biography, sociology, art, science, and literature. For example, *Biography Resource Center* is a database that contains biographies about people from all over the world.

You do not need the Web site address to access these databases at your public library. Your library, either individually or as part of a group of libraries, subscribes to these or similar databases. To access a database, just use the computers in your library that offer these databases.

Exercise 1

1. Use your library's computer to look up your library Web site on the Internet. Does the site provide links to other library catalogs? Which ones? What are your library hours? What other pieces of information does your library Web site provide?
2. Ask your librarian about the different databases your library provides. Take notes on the answer. If you were researching a report on nuclear accidents, which of these databases would make a good resource and why? If you were searching for information about Virginia Woolf, which database would you select? If you needed to do a report on Alzheimer's Disease, which database would you select?
3. Imagine that you had a term paper assignment to write a ten-page paper on a topic currently important in the news. Choose three library resources that would provide information on that topic. Which resource provides the most up-to-date information? Which is easiest to search and why?

23.2 Reference Sources

General reference works will satisfy many of your research needs, so investigate general reference works first. They do not take much time to survey, and they provide excellent background information. If you do not locate what you need, you may then move on to more specialized reference sources.

General Reference Works

General reference works include sources such as encyclopedias, dictionaries, atlases, and yearbooks. Online versions of these sources are available and may provide video, film, and audio clips in addition to traditional text and photos. Since these sources are frequently updated, they often provide more current information than print versions.

Internet reference sites also can answer many reference questions. One advantage of these sites is that they are available twenty-four hours a day. You can connect from home if you have access to a computer and a modem. One disadvantage of these sites is that there are no librarians available to help you find the information you need quickly. Examples of online reference sites include *The Internet Public Library,* sponsored by the School of Information at the University of Michigan, and *Thor: The Virtual Reference Desk +*, the online resource site of Purdue University Library.

The chart on the next page gives examples of some of the most commonly used reference resources.

General Reference Works

TYPE OF REFERENCE	EXAMPLES OF SOURCES
Dictionaries arrange words alphabetically and include definitions and pronunciations.	**Dictionaries**—*Merriam Webster's Collegiate Dictionary*, tenth edition; *Random House Webster's Collegiate Dictionary; Dictionary of Slang* **Online examples**—*WWWebster Dictionary*, which is based on *Merriam Webster's Collegiate Dictionary*, tenth edition
Encyclopedias are multi-volume works containing alphabetically arranged articles covering all branches of knowledge.	**Encyclopedias:** *World Book, Encyclopedia Americana, New Book of Knowledge* **Online examples:** *Britannica Online, Encarta, Grolier, Encyclopedia Americana, New Book of Knowledge*
Biographical Works contain brief life histories of notable individuals. Search by name or by profession or art.	**Biographical Works:** *Contemporary Authors, Current Biography, The International Who's Who, Cyclopedia of World Authors* **Online example:** *Biography Index*
Yearbooks and Almanacs contain information and statistics for the past year.	**Yearbooks and Almanacs:** *Time/Information Please Almanac, World Almanac, ESPN Information Please Sports Almanac, Statistical Abstracts of the United States*
Atlases contain maps, charts, plates, or tables illustrating any subject.	**Atlases:** *Times Atlas of the World: Comprehensive Edition, Cambridge Atlas of Astronomy, History Atlas of North America* **Online examples:** *Information Please Almanac, Texas Almanac*
Gazetteers are geographical dictionaries.	**Gazetteers:** *Merriam-Webster's Geographical Dictionary, Columbia Gazetteer of the World* **Online examples:** *The U.S. Gazetteer*

Specialized Reference Sources

Some reference resources target specific areas of knowledge. *The McGraw-Hill Encyclopedia of Science and Technology,* for example, available in both print and online, is a source for scientific information. For help on the format of a term paper you might consult *The Chicago Manual of Style* or the style guides published by the Modern Language Association or the American Psychological Association. For information on careers, you might investigate *The Encyclopedia of Careers and Vocational Guidance.* Sources like these provide quick answers to reference questions in specific subject areas.

Using Literature Reference Works to Answer Questions

QUESTIONS	SOURCES FOR AN ANSWER
1. Who are the main characters in Thomas Hardy's novel *Far from the Madding Crowd?* Where is this novel set?	*Oxford Companion to English Literature, A Literary Gazetteer of England, A Mapbook of English Literature*
2. Who were the most prominent authors in colonial America?	*Oxford Companion to American Literature, American Authors and Books, Cambridge History of American Literature*
3. For which form of poetry is Matsuo Bashō best known?	*Cassell's Encyclopedia of World Literature*
4. What are the titles of the epic poems about the Greek hero Odysseus?	*Oxford Companion to Classical Literature; Penguin Companion to Classical, Oriental, and African Literature*
5. Who wrote *Le Misanthrope?* What is it about?	*The New York Public Library Desk Reference, Penguin Companion to European Literature, Oxford Companion to French Literature*

Answer the questions in the chart on page 780, using references other than those listed. For each question, write the answer, cite the source or sources you used, and tell how you located those sources. Share your answers with the class.

23.3   The Internet

Your public library will also provide access to the Internet, a valuable source of information. The Internet, also known as *the Net, Cyberspace,* or *the Information Highway,* provides information on any subject and gives access to e-mail—still the most popular feature of the Net. The Internet is divided into various domains, or neighborhoods: .com, .edu, .gov, .mil, .net, or .org. The period at the beginning is referred to as <dot>. So <dot>com is usually, but not always, a commercial organization; <dot>edu is always an educational entity such as *harvard.edu* or *berkeley.edu;* <dot>gov is a governmental organization such as *whitehouse.gov;* and <dot>mil denotes military sites.

When doing research on the Internet, choose sites sponsored by organizations, the government, or educational institutions. These sites usually offer the most reliable information, and they tend to be more accurate than business sites or those of private individuals. However, always check any Web site for accuracy and timeliness. Check to see when it was last updated. Check for errors and omissions. Check to see what agency sponsors the site. Is it reputable? See Unit 7, "Research Paper Writing," page 322, for guidance on evaluating sources and detecting bias. Many libraries now provide a list of recommended Web sites—for instance, for government, news, and reference.

Because there are so many Internet sites, the best way to find worthwhile information on the Net is by using a *search engine.* Search engines work by sending out software agents, called spiders, which search every link they can find.

If you do not find any worthwhile hits with one search engine, try several others. Each search engine searches the Internet differently, and no single search engine will search comprehensively.

Online Search Terms	
ABSTRACT	A summary of an article or information source.
DATABASE	A collection of information resources that can be searched electronically. Some databases, such as *Biography Index,* only search a specific subject; others such as *Nexus/Lexus* or the *Electric Library* search all subjects.
DISCUSSION GROUPS	A virtual place where you can ask questions or discuss problems and current events. Discussion groups on the Internet exist on almost every topic, including the environment, pets, music, and sports.
HIT	The term for a successful result after you have searched online.
FULL TEXT	This means that the entire article is present online. However, sometimes full-text articles do not include charts and graphics.
INTERNET	A computer network that is composed of many smaller computer networks. The Internet is the largest computer network in the world.
RELEVANCY	When used in computer searching, relevancy describes how closely your search results answer your search query. Many databases and search engines display results in a hierarchy from the most relevant to the least. These relevancy relationships are usually given in percentages.
SEARCH ENGINE	Computer software that browses the Internet for places where your words appear. Examples are Yahoo, Goober, Lycos, and Ask Jeeves.
URL	Stands for Universal Resource Locator. This is an address for a Web site. It contains the computer name, directory name, and Web page name.
WORLD WIDE WEB	The part of the Internet that provides information in various formats, including print, sound, photos, graphics, and video. Links allow you to move from place to place.

Exercise 3

1. Log onto www.yahoo.com and search for a topic related to one of your classes. Now log onto www.dogpile.com and search for this same subject. What are the differences? Which search engine would you rather use when you don't really know what specific topic you are looking for? Why? Which search engine would you rather use when you know exactly what you are looking for? Why?
2. Go to www.deja.com and search again for the same topic. What is the difference between the information found on Yahoo, Dogpile, and Deja? For what type of research would you choose to search Deja first? Report on your findings to the class.

Using Dictionaries

24.1 Varieties of Dictionaries

One of the most famous dictionaries in the English language is the *Oxford English Dictionary,* or *OED*. This multivolume dictionary contains more than 15,000 pages and lists over 80 meanings just for the word *get*.

General Dictionaries

Although people often use the phrase "the dictionary," there are many different kinds of dictionaries, some general and some specialized. General dictionaries are all-purpose dictionaries that contain a broad range of words in common usage.

Types of General Dictionaries Your first dictionary was probably a school dictionary, featuring the relatively few common words that you would be most likely to encounter in your school years.

Later, most people acquire college dictionaries, which have more than 150,000 entries with detailed definitions sufficient for most college students as well as general users. College dictionaries separately list abbreviations, biographical and geographical names, foreign words and phrases, and tables of measures. *Random House Webster's College Dictionary* and *American Heritage Dictionary* are popular college dictionaries.

For the scholar or researcher, unabridged dictionaries provide as many as 500,000 entries that have detailed definitions and extensive word histories. You will find these dictionaries, spanning several volumes, primarily in libraries. Examples of these dictionaries include the *Oxford English Dictionary* and the *Random House Dictionary of the English Language.*

Main Entries A dictionary entry consists of many elements, such as preferred spellings, plural and capitalized forms, synonyms, and antonyms. Also, the entry may provide American regional expressions (such as "batter-cake" for "pancake"), cross-references, idioms, and other elements. The example on the next page shows many of these elements in a dictionary entry for the word *battle.*

Notice the entry for **battle²**, which indicates it is a homograph, a word that is spelled the same as another word but has a different word history. The label *Archaic* means that particular usage is no longer common. You may encounter archaic terms when you read Shakespeare or other classic literature. The label **See** BATTLEMENT is a cross-reference to the entry for the word *battlement.*

Using Dictionaries

bat•tle¹ (bat'l), *n., v.,* ***-tled, -tling.*** *—n.* **1.** a hostile encounter between opposing military forces. **2.** participation in such an encounter or encounters; wounds received in battle. **3.** any fight, conflict, or struggle, as between two persons or teams. **4.** *Archaic.* a battalion. *—v.i.* **5.** to engage in battle. **6.** to struggle; strive. *—v.t.* **7.** to fight (a person, army, cause, etc.). **8.** to force or accomplish by fighting, struggling, etc. ***—Idiom.*** **9. give** or **do battle,** to engage in conflict; fight. [1250–1300; ME *bataile* < OF < VL *BATTĀLIA, for LL *battuālla* gladiatorial exercises = *battu(ere)* to strike (see **BATE²**) + *-ālia,* neut. pl. of *-ālis* -AL¹] **—bat'tler.** *n.*

bat•tle² (bat'l), *v.t.* ***-tled, -tling.*** *Archaic.* to furnish with battlements; crenelate [1300–50; ME *batailen* < MF *bataillier.* SEE BATTLEMENT]

> Homographs, marked by small raised numbers, are words that are spelled the same but are given separate entries because they have different word histories, called etymologies.

> Main entries begin with the syllabicated spelling of the word, its pronunciation, and its part-of-speech label.

> Etymologies appear in brackets within entries. The first use of "battle¹" occurred during A.D. 1250 to A.D. 1300.

Accessing Dictionaries Online

You can obtain CD-ROM versions of many major dictionaries. You can also access numerous dictionaries, including *WWWebster's Dictionary,* on the Internet. Online dictionaries allow you to enter a search word to see a definition and sometimes even an illustration. If you are not sure how to spell the word, just type it in. If the spelling is incorrect, the dictionary will give you a list of words that might include the one you wanted. Online dictionaries also offer features such as word games, language tips, and amusing facts about words. Some online dictionary services allow you to access numerous general and specialized dictionaries in one search.

Using Specialized Dictionaries

Specialized dictionaries provide in-depth information about words in a particular field. For example, a dictionary called *DARE* (*Dictionary of American Regional English*) provides regional definitions of words. Other examples of specialized dictionaries follow.

Specialized Dictionaries	
QUESTIONS	**SOURCES FOR AN ANSWER**
1. What does a "head gaffer" do on a movie set?	1. *NTC's Mass Media Dictionary*
2. Who is a Middle East mufti?	2. *Political Dictionary of the Arab World*
3. What was W. C. Handy's full name?	3. *Dictionary of American Negro Biography*
4. When was *Common Sense* first published?	4. *Dictionary of Historic Documents*
5. What does the Biblical name *Canaan* mean?	5. *Dictionary of Bible Place Names*
6. Where was ancient Cahokia, and why is it significant?	6. *The Facts on File Dictionary of Archaeology*
7. Who was nicknamed "Edward Longshanks"?	7. *The Dictionary of Historic Nicknames*
8. What was the Gang of Four?	8. *The Facts on File Dictionary of 20th-Century History*
9. Who helped the enslaved Dred Scott in his lawsuit for freedom?	9. *The Civil War Dictionary, Dictionary of American History*
10. Who said, "Learning without thought is Labor Lost"?	10. *Similes Dictionary*

Decide which of the specialized dictionaries listed in the previous chart might be useful for providing answers to the following questions.

1. What is archaeologist Heinrich Schliemann's greatest find?
2. Where could you learn the identity of the person whom Chief Sitting Bull nicknamed "Little Sure Shot"?
3. Where could you read a summary of the Vietnam War?
4. Where could you find out whether Mount Sinai is the same as Mount Horeb?
5. Where could you learn whether Abner Doubleday, who may have been the founder of baseball, played a role in the Civil War?
6. Where could you learn the political history and significance of the Negev, a desert area in Israel?
7. Where could you find out who said: "Grief sat on his chest like a dragon"?

24.2 Kinds of Thesauruses

Thesauruses list synonyms and are the most commonly used specialized dictionary. Words are arranged by category in a traditional-style thesaurus and alphabetically in a dictionary-style thesaurus.

You can also access thesauruses electronically—on CD-ROMs, on the Internet, and even on some word processing software.

Traditional Style

The best-known thesaurus is *Roget's Thesaurus,* named for Peter Mark Roget, a British doctor who first developed large categories of words related to a basic concept. Using a traditional *Roget's* involves two steps. First, look up a word in the index, and choose its subentry that is closest to the meaning you have in mind. The subentry is followed by a number. Next, look up that number in the body of the thesaurus to find synonyms for the subentry. Look at the example for *think* that follows. Words similar in meaning are grouped together and set off with semicolons.

If you want a synonym for the verb "think," the index gives you four categories from which to choose. If the meaning that you want is closest to "cogitate," the index directs you to look up entry 478.8, shown here.

478.8 VERBS **think, cogitate,** cerebrate, intellectualize, ideate, conceive, conceptualize, form ideas, entertain ideas; **reason** 482.15; **use one's head,** use or exercise the mind, set the brain or wits to work, bethink oneself, put on one's thinking or considering cap [informal].

Dictionary Style

Thesauruses in dictionary form present words in alphabetical order. Each word is followed by several synonyms and cross-references to any related major category. A major category includes nouns, verbs, and adjectives related to one main idea. See the entry for ELEVATION below.

ELEVATION

Nouns—**1,** elevation; raising, lifting, erection; sublimation, exaltation; prominence, eminence; advancement, promotion, preferment; uplift, IMPROVEMENT; HEIGHT, hill, mount, mountain.

2, lever, crane, derrick, windlass, capstan, winch, crowbar, jimmy, pulley, crank, jack, dredge, elevator, lift, dumbwaiter, hoist, escalator, moving stairway.

Verbs—**1,** heighten, elevate, raise, lift, erect, set up, stick up, heave, buoy, weigh.

2, exalt, sublimate, place on a pedestal, promote, advance, improve.

3, take up, fish up; dredge.

4, stand up, spring to one's feet; hold one's head up, rise up, get up, jump up.

Adjectives—**1,** elevated, raised, lifted up; erect; eminent, lofty; stilted.

2, ennobled, exalted, uplifted.

Antonym, **see** DEPRESSION.

> Major categories appear in capital letters. ELEVATION is the major category in this example. IMPROVEMENT and HEIGHT are other major categories in which you could find additional synonyms.

> Synonyms are listed by part of speech.

> For antonyms for "elevation," a cross-reference (see DEPRESSION) tells you to look under that entry. Not all thesauruses refer you to antonyms.

Exercise 2

Use a thesaurus to find two synonyms for each word below. Then write an original sentence to illustrate the meaning of each synonym. Check the exact meaning of each word in a dictionary before you use it in a sentence.

1. shortness
2. order
3. insanity
4. disclosure
5. converge
6. convex
7. to chance
8. to love
9. to travel
10. authority
11. to broaden
12. to clothe
13. cloudy
14. present (as an adjective)
15. to prepare
16. slowness
17. to prosper
18. test

25.1 Expanding Your Vocabulary

The best way to add new words and phrases to your vocabulary is through reading widely, listening carefully, and participating actively in conversations. Using English effectively requires continuous effort because the language is always changing. For example, English acquires new vocabulary through contact with other languages; *rodeo, potato,* and *pizza* were once words used only in foreign languages, but today they are commonly used by English speakers.

You can often determine the meaning of an unfamiliar word or phrase by paying attention to the words and sentences that surround it. Sometimes this context provides obvious clues to meaning, but at other times you may need to verify a word's meaning by looking it up in a dictionary. A dictionary also provides pronunciation guidelines, multiple meanings of words, and even meanings of figurative expressions.

Specific Context Clues

If you learn to watch and listen for the clues in language, you can often determine the meanings of new words, phrases, and expressions. Context can also point you to the meaning of a familiar word used in a new way. In the following paragraph, unfamiliar words are in italic type, and clue words are underscored. Can you guess the meanings of the unfamiliar words?

> The death of Sam Houston's beloved mother served as a *fulcrum,* or a hinge, on which his life turned. Whereas previous personal failures had led him to sink into despair and inactivity, this tragedy *galvanized* Houston's political career. Like his valiant friend, President Andrew Jackson, Houston plunged into public service and became a *stalwart* defender of Jackson's political beliefs.

In the first sentence, the clue word *or* allows you to figure out that a *fulcrum* functions like a hinge. *Or* signals that a restatement or a more familiar explanation follows. Other clue words introducing restatements include *in other words, also known as,* and *also called.*

Contrasts show unfamiliar words as opposites of familiar words. The clue word *Whereas* contrasts "sink into despair and inactivity," and "galvanized Houston's political career"; thus, you know that *galvanized* must mean "stimulated." Other clue words indicating contrasts are *but, although, on the contrary, however, on the other hand,* and *in contrast to.*

Comparisons liken unfamiliar words to familiar ones. The clue word *like* compares the two men, one valiant and the other *stalwart.* You know that stalwart must mean "brave" or "strong of mind." Other clue words introducing comparisons are *also, likewise, similarly, in the same way, similar to, resembling,* and *as.* Use the clue words in the paragraph that follows to figure out the mean-

Vocabulary

ings of the words in italic type. Before you read the explanation, jot down on scratch paper what you think the words mean.

> When we visit our cousins in Arizona, we love to dine on their *patio, which is* the little paved courtyard right next to the house. The patio overlooks several Southwestern landforms, *such as* valley-like canyons and table-*like mesas,* which are always beautiful to gaze upon. I remember how amazed I was the first time I saw an *arroyo* brimming with flood water after a heavy rain, *since* we had ridden along its dusty bottom only the previous afternoon.

The clue words *which is* in the first sentence signal that a definition for *patio* follows. Other clue words introducing definitions include *which means* and *that is.* Examples illustrate unfamiliar words. You probably deduced that a *mesa* is a landform. Other clue words introducing examples include *for example, for instance, other, these, including,* and *especially.*

Sometimes an unfamiliar word in a cause and effect sentence is explained by the cause or the effect. The content indicates that an *arroyo* may be a stream bed in a dry region. Clue words introducing causes and effects include *because, as a result, therefore, when,* and *consequently.*

In addition to clue words, punctuation marks can also supply context clues. For example, many restatements and definitions are set off by commas, dashes, or even semicolons.

General Context Clues

If there are no specific clue words, use general context clues. Begin by determining an unfamiliar word's part of speech. For instance, if you read that "the defendant leaned toward his lawyer, and the two had a brief interlocution," you know that *interlocution* is a noun. You might guess that an interlocution is a kind of conversation. In the following paragraph, examine the general context of the unfamiliar words in italic type.

> Although Ramone had left for the play in a *jocund* mood, laughing and telling amusing stories to his buddies, he returned home amazingly changed. He described to his parents the *poignant* scene of the play in which Macduff learns that his wife and children have been murdered.

Even if you do not know the meaning of *jocund,* you do know that it is an adjective describing *mood.* From supporting details ("laughing and telling amusing stories"), you may correctly guess that *jocund* means "merry or cheerful." Using the same process with *poignant,* you might deduce that the scene was sad and touching.

In addition to general context clues, the tone, setting, and situation may provide clues to the meaning of a word, as in the sample paragraph on the next page.

> I don't know how she does it, but my older sister always manages to *cajole* Dad into increasing her allowance. First, she warms him up with excessive flattery. After she flatters him, she reminds him of every little good deed she's done. Then she offers to prepare one of his favorite desserts, and before I know it, she has an allowance that's three times larger than mine. You'd think Dad would recognize a *sycophant* when he sees one.

You know that *cajole* is a verb. It has to do with warming up Dad and flattering him. In fact, *cajole* means "to persuade by pleasant words" or "to wheedle." The word *sycophant* is a noun and indicates a type of person. You can tell that the writer has a low opinion of her sister's actions, so you may guess that to be called a *sycophant* is not complimentary. In fact, a sycophant is a self-serving flatterer.

Exercise 1

Each of the following sentences contains a word in italic type that may be unfamiliar to you. Try to determine each word's meaning from its context; then write the word and your definition of it on your paper. Check your accuracy with a dictionary.

1. Gold is a very *ductile* metal; it can be hammered quite thin.
2. I would feel like an *ingrate* if I failed to express my gratitude to all those who have so generously assisted me.
3. Schubert's "Ave Maria" is known for how smoothly the notes flow into each other; in contrast, his "Marche Militaire" is known for its dramatic *staccato* notes.
4. We enjoyed the *legerdemain* of the magician and wondered just how she managed to move her hands so quickly.
5. Though usually so graceful, Marcia felt absolutely *maladroit* when she dropped the tray containing tea cups.
6. Some people who have trouble falling asleep have found that drinking a glass of warm milk before going to bed has a *somniferous* effect.
7. The pile of rotting garbage was as *odoriferous* as any skunk.
8. Unlike the *feral* cats in the woods, the domesticated barn cats were friendly and purred as they rubbed against us.
9. Professional mountain climbers almost never suffer from *acrophobia*; on the contrary, the higher the mountain, the happier they are.
10. No one can top Carlos as a *gastronome*; he buys only the finest cheese and the choicest meats, drives to the pier to handpick the freshest of fish, and uses only fresh herbs.

Although the English language borrows words from many languages, many English words have their origins in Latin, Greek, or Anglo-Saxon words and word parts. Knowing some of these word parts from other languages will help you analyze an unfamiliar word and determine its meaning.

The main part of a word is its **root.** A root may be a complete word, such as *gram,* or it may be a part of a word. Roots such as *jur* and *cand* are unable to stand alone as words and must be combined with other elements in order to form words.

Roots are often combined with a **prefix** (a word part attached to the beginning of a word), a **suffix** (a word part attached to the ending of a word), or another root. Many students learn lists of word parts to prepare for the vocabulary portion of college entrance examinations. Look at how you might analyze the word encryption.

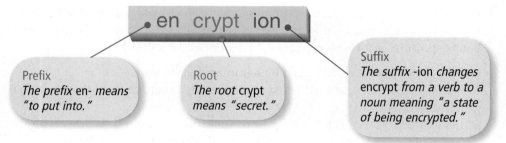

en crypt ion

Prefix
The prefix en- means "to put into."

Root
The root crypt means "secret."

Suffix
The suffix -ion changes encrypt from a verb to a noun meaning "a state of being encrypted."

The word *encryption* means something that has been put into a secret code or message. Although this word's parts add up to its meaning, sometimes an analysis of a word's parts do not yield its meaning. Use a dictionary to verify what a word means.

Word Roots

While prefixes and suffixes can give you hints about a word's meaning, the word's root provides the real clue. In the word *encryption,* the prefix *en-* and the suffix *-ion* have been attached to the root *crypt.* Other words formed from the same root include *cryptic,* meaning mysterious in meaning; *cryptograph,* meaning a message in secret code; and *cryptographer,* meaning a person who specializes in studying the techniques of secret codes. The root *crypt* is also an English word; it is a noun meaning a subterranean chamber that is used as a burial place or as a location for secret meetings.

Look at the list of word roots that follows on the next page. Some roots have more than one form. If you have studied a foreign language, you might notice that some word roots mean the same thing in another language.

	Word Roots	
ROOTS	**MEANINGS**	**EXAMPLES**
aqua, aqui	water	aquatic, aquifer
astr, astro	star	astral, astronomical
aut, auto	self-acting	autism, autobiography
biblio	book	bibliography, bibliophile
bio	life	biology, biosphere
cand	shine, glow	candle, candescent
chron	time	chronicle, chronological
circ	circle	circular, circus
clin	bend, lean	recline, incline
cogn	know	cognition, incognito
crypt	hidden, secret	cryptic, cryptogram
culp	fault, blame	culprit, exculpate
fac, fec	do, make	factual, infect
fin	end, limit	define, finite
fix	fasten	fixate, fixative
gen	birth, kind	engender, genealogy
geo	earth	geocentric, geode
graph, gram	write, writing	autograph, telegram
hydr, hydra	water	hydroelectric, dehydration
jac, ject	throw, cast, hurl	trajectory, injection
jud	judge	adjudication, prejudge
junct	join	conjunction, juncture
jur, jus	law	jury, justice
log, logy	word, thought, speech	monologue, theology
luc	light	lucid, translucent
meter, metr	measure	thermometer, metric
nym	name	antonym, pseudonym
op, oper	work	operate, operator
omni	all	omnipresent, omnivorous
path, patho	suffering	pathetic, pathology
ped	foot, child	pedicure, pediatrics
port	carry, bear	exportation, portfolio
psych	soul, mind	psychotherapy, psychology
phys	body, nature	physical, physiology
reg, rig	rule, straight	regular, rigid
scop	examine, instrument	periscope, telescope
spect	sight	perspective, spectator
tele	far, distant	telepathy, telephone
terr	earth	terrace, territory
therm	heat	thermal, thermometer
verb	word	verbal, verbose
vid, vis	see	videogame, visual

Vocabulary

Word Prefixes

Prefixes are word parts attached to the beginnings of words to change their meanings. Prefixes may show quantity, size, time, direction, or position. Some prefixes reverse the meaning of a word root. Notice that some of the following prefixes have more than one meaning.

	PREFIXES	MEANINGS	EXAMPLES
Word Prefixes			
PREFIXES SHOWING DIRECTION OR POSITION	circum-	around	circumlocution, circumspect
	col-, com-, con-	together	collect, compact, concentrate
	de-	lower	depress, devalue
	en-	in, put into	encapsulate, enlargement
	ex-, exo-	out of	export, exclaim, exotic
	in-, im-	into	insight, immigrant
	inter-	between, among	international, interdependent
	mid-	middle of	midnight, midriff
	peri-	around, about, enclosing	periscope, periphery, peripatetic
	sub-	below, outside of	submarine, subterranean, sublet, subsist
	super-	above, over	supervise, supersede
	trans-	across, over	transmit, transcend
PREFIXES SHOWING QUANTITY OR SIZE	semi-, hemi-	half	semiannual, hemisphere
	uni-, mon-	one	unicycle, monarchy
	bi-, di-	two	bimonthly, dilemma
	tri-	three	tripod, triangle
	oct-, octa-	eight	octopus, octave
	deca-	ten	decade, decathlon
	cent-	hundred	century, centigrade
	milli-	thousand	milliliter, million
PREFIXES SHOWING NEGATION	a-, an-	not, without	amoral, aseptic, anemia
	ant-, anti-	against	antacid, antifreeze
	counter-	opposite to	counterclockwise, counterspy
	de-, dis-	do the opposite	defrost, decaffeinate, disarm
	il-, im-, in-, ir-	without, not	illegal, immodest, incomplete, irreligious
	non-, un-	not	nonconformist, unmoved
	mis-	wrongly, bad	misdeed, misjudge
PREFIXES SHOWING TIME	post-	after	postgame, postwar
	pre-, pro-	before	precede, prologue
	re-	again	revisit, rewrite
	syn-	together	synchronized, syncopated

Word Suffixes

Each **suffix** has its own meaning and is added to the end of a word root to create a new word with a new meaning. Besides having a specific meaning, a suffix may also make a word a different part of speech.

Word Suffixes				
	SUFFIXES	**MEANINGS**	**ORIGINAL WORD**	**NEW WORD**
SUFFIXES THAT FORM NOUNS	-ee	receiver of action	train	trainee
	-ance, -ence	state, quality	relevant	relevance
			persist	persistence
	-ant, -eer	agent, doer	contest	contestant
			puppet	puppeteer
	-ist	quality, state	theory	theorist
	-ness	action, state	bright	brightness
	-tion, -ion	the act of	prosecute	prosecution
SUFFIXES THAT FORM ADJECTIVES	-able	capable of	read	readable
	-al	characterized by	person	personal
	-ful	full of, having	wonder	wonderful
	-ial	relating to	manor	manorial
	-ic	characteristic of	Byron	Byronic
	-ical	related to	geology	geological
	-less	lacking, without	care	careless
	-ly	akin to	queen	queenly
	-ous	full of	joy	joyous
SUFFIXES THAT FORM VERBS	-ate	become, form	valid	validate
	-en	make, cause to be	length	lengthen
	-ify	cause, make	terror	terrify
	-ize	make, cause to be	eulogy	eulogize

Adding New Words to Your Vocabulary

You can add new words to your spoken and written vocabulary in a variety of ways. For example, you might keep a list of new words as you encounter them. Be sure to include familiar words used in new ways. Then you can quiz yourself on your list at regular intervals. If you have a computer, you might want to create a personal dictionary. Your dictionary may contain the pronunciation, definitions, figurative uses, synonyms, and antonyms for new words or phrases. You may even want to create a program to quiz yourself on the vocabulary in your dictionary.

The best way to increase your vocabulary is to read a wide variety of material, both fiction and nonfiction. The more frequently you encounter a word as it appears across content areas, the deeper your understanding of that word will be. No matter how you expand your word knowledge, try to use your new vocabulary as you speak and write every day.

Analyze the following words for their roots, prefixes, and suffixes. (Not every word has all three parts.) Write what you think each word means—but be careful: not every word's meaning will add up to the sum of its parts. Check your accuracy with a dictionary.

antipathy	incandescent
aquaplane	inclination
bicentennial	inoperable
bioengineering	interjection
biped	intermediary
circumscribe	interject
circumspection	millipede
combustible	misdeed
commingle	pedicab
conjunction	preseason
contravene	rehydrate
culpable	seer
deport	spectral
ejection	superstructure
geothermal	trilogy

Use the roots, prefixes, and suffixes that follow, plus words and word parts that you already know, to create a list of fifteen words. Your list might include words you know as well as combinations that you think might be words. Use at least one word part in each word. Check your spelling in a dictionary.

Roots	Prefixes	Suffixes
aqua	*anti-*	*-able*
auto	*en-*	*-ance*
clin	*ex-*	*-ee*
fix	*fe-*	*-eer*
geo	*in-*	*-en*
gram	*ir-*	*-er*
log	*mid-*	*-ful*
meter	*mis-*	*-ify*
op	*non-*	*-ion*
reg	*sub-*	*-ist*
spect	*trans-*	*-ize*

UNIT
26 | Spelling

Mastering the Basics

English spelling is complex. If spelling frustrates you at times, you're in good company. Playwright George Bernard Shaw, a frustrated speller, even bequeathed part of his fortune to establish a new system of spelling! One of the best ways to become a good speller is to be an avid reader. Another way is to notice and remember common spelling patterns.

Basic Spelling Rules

Besides noticing the common letter patterns in English words, learning basic spelling rules will help you improve your spelling.

Forming Plurals Some basic rules can help you form most plurals, but you need to memorize the spellings of plurals that are exceptions to rules. Study the following list to review some of the rules.

Rules for Regular Plurals	Examples
To form the plural of most nouns, including proper nouns, add -s. If the noun ends in -ch, -s, -sh, -x, or -z, add -es.	bell + -s = bells bunch + -es = bunches bus + -es = buses
To form the plural of common nouns ending in a consonant + -y, change the y to i and add -es.	ally (change the y to i) + -es = allies dairy (change the y to i) + -es = dairies jury (change the y to i) + -es = juries
To form the plural of most nouns ending in -f, including all nouns ending in -ff, add -s. For some nouns ending in -f, especially those ending in -lf, change the f to v and add -es.	belief + -s = beliefs puff + -s = puffs loaf (change the f to v) + -es = loaves elf (change the f to v) + -es = elves

Rules for Irregular Plurals	Examples
Some nouns become plural by adding -en, -ren, or by substituting letters.	child + -ren = children woman—women
Some nouns are the same in the singular and the plural.	swine—swine sheep—sheep

Spelling

Adding Prefixes You are probably already familiar with some common prefixes, such as *anti-*, *hyper-*, and others mentioned in Unit 25. Look at the rules for spelling words containing prefixes.

Adding Prefixes
When adding a prefix to a word, retain the spelling of the original word.
anti- + gravity = antigravity   *co-* + authors = coauthors
When adding a prefix to a lowercase word, do not use a hyphen in most cases. When adding a prefix to a capitalized word, use a hyphen. Always use a hyphen with the prefix *ex-* meaning "previous" or "former."
co- + worker = coworker   *mid-* + ship = midship   *un-* + American = un-American   *ex-* + coach = ex-coach

Many different suffixes can be added to words. Most words that contain suffixes are spelled in a straightforward manner.

Adding Suffix *-ly* When adding *-ly* to a word that ends in a single *l*, keep the *l*. When the word ends in a double *l*, drop one *l*. When the word ends in a consonant + *le*, drop the *le*:

   equal + *-ly* = equally   dull + *-ly* = dully
   comfortable + *-ly* = comfortably

Adding Suffix *-ness* When adding *-ness* to a word that ends in *n*, keep the *n*.

   common + *-ness* = commonness   mean + *-ness* = meanness
   plain + *-ness* = plainness   brazen + *-ness* = brazenness

Adding Suffixes to Words Ending in a Silent e When you are adding a suffix to a word ending in a consonant + silent *e*, pay attention to the first letter of the suffix.

Rules	Examples	Exceptions
Drop the final silent *e* before a suffix that begins with a vowel.	fine + *-est* = finest value + *-able* = valuable	Drop the final *e* after the letters *u* or *w*: *due, duly; awe, awful.*
Keep the final silent *e* before a suffix that begins with a consonant.	definite + *-ly* = definitely white + *-ness* = whiteness	

Keep the final *e* in words ending in *-ee* and *-oe*: see, seeing; woe, woeful. Keep the final silent *e* before the suffix *-ing* to avoid ambiguity: singe, singeing; toe, toeing. Keep the final silent *e* in words ending with *-ce* or *-ge* that have suffixes beginning with *a* or *o*: service, serviceable.

Adding Suffixes to Words Ending in a Consonant The following chart contains rules and examples concerning the doubling of a final consonant when adding a suffix to a word.

If	Then
If the original word is a one-syllable word . . .	Double the final consonant: *hop, hopping*
If the original word has its accent on the last syllable and the accent remains there after the suffix is added . . .	Double the final consonant: *begin, beginning*
If the original word is a prefixed word based on a one-syllable word . . .	Double the final consonant: *reset, resetting*

Do not double the final consonant . . .
if the accent is not on the last syllable or if the accent shifts when the suffix is added. *travel, traveling*   *refer, reference*
if the final consonants are *x* or *w*.   *wax, waxing*   *saw, sawing*
when adding a suffix that begins with a consonant to a word that ends in a consonant. *annul, annulment*

Forming Compound Words When joining a word that ends in a consonant to a word that begins with a consonant, keep both consonants:

air + man = airman   book + keeper = bookkeeper
back + ground = background   row + boat = rowboat

There are many exceptions to this rule. Many compounds are hyphenated: for example, *know-how*. Some compounds remain separate words, such as *cross section*, while related words, such as *crosswalk*, are joined. Use a dictionary to check the spelling of compounds.

ie* and *ei Learning this rhyme can save you many misspellings: "Write *i* before *e* except after *c*, or when sounded like *a* as in *neighbor* and *weigh*." There are notable exceptions to the rule, and they include *seize, seizure, leisure, weird, height, either, neither,* and *forfeit*.

-cede, -ceed,* and *-sede Because of the relatively few words with sēd sounds, these words are worth memorizing.

These words use *-cede:* accede, precede, secede.
One word uses *-sede:* supersede.
Three words use *-ceed:* exceed, proceed, succeed.

Using a Computer Spelling Checker

Although spelling checkers have certain advantages, they are not foolproof. Use the following tips to learn what spelling checkers can and cannot do for you.

Tips for Using a Spelling Checker

1. When the spelling checker highlights a misspelled word and suggests a replacement, do not rely on the spelling checker's judgment. It searches for words that look similar to the misspelled word, but it does not know the particular word that you need. For example, if you type *mett,* the spelling checker will give you a choice of *met, net, mitt, nit,* and so on.

2. After using the spelling checker, proofread for sense. If you typed *wing* for *ring,* for example, the spelling checker will not pick up the error because both *wing* and *ring* are correctly spelled words. Even grammar checkers that check for grammatical agreement are not very accurate, so don't rely on them. A computer has yet to be invented that has the reasoning ability of a human being.

3. Use the spelling checker to target spelling problems. Keep a list of words that the spelling checker highlights and quiz yourself on the words until you master them.

Exercise 1

Each of the following sentences contains one, several, or no misspelled words. Write each misspelled word correctly and state whether a rule applies to each case. Check your answers in a dictionary.

1. The ranches hireing cowboys are owned by the Joneses and the Diazes.
2. Midship-men at the Naval Academy are participating in antigravity experiments.
3. I like the plainess of white walls for displaying Southwestern art.
4. My arguement for replacing that aweful wallpaper was finally begining to win her over.
5. Fifteen attorneys representing forty companys are trying to sue the bakery for allowing its chimneys to pollute the air of three valleys.
6. Since the warehouse was empty at mid-day, the railroad delivery service decided to make the delivery at that time.
7. If you precede me on the highway I will probably not excede the speed limit, so let us procede on our journey.
8. You should sieze this opportunity to do a little travelling.

Spelling Challenges

Not everyone misspells the same words. Each person has an individual set of "problem" words. One strategy for learning these words is to develop a list of words that you frequently misspell. Order the words by subject area and keep the list in a notebook, where you can refer to it. Review words until you have mastered their spellings.

Commonly Misspelled Words

Some words fool most spellers at least some of the time, because the words contain unusual combinations of letters, do not follow spelling rules, or are not spelled as they sound. A list of such words follows. Try quizzing yourself to see how many of the words you can spell correctly.

> Some words have more than one correct spelling; for example, "adviser" is also correctly spelled "advisor."

Commonly Misspelled Words			
abundant	consciousness	inoculate	personnel
accelerator	controlling	intellectual	persuade
accidentally	cruelty	judgment	picnicking
accomplishment	deceitful	larynx	possessed
acknowledge	desirable	license	precede
adequately	devastation	livelihood	prestige
admittance	dilemma	magistrate	prevalent
advantageous	disastrous	maintenance	procedure
adviser	discrimination	manageable	propagate
alliance	dissatisfied	marriageable	questionnaire
apologetically	embarrass	mediocre	rebellion
apparent	emphasize	melodious	recommendation
arrangement	enormous	miniature	referred
ballet	environment	mosquito	remittance
beginning	exhilaration	necessity	reveal
benefited	exuberant	negligence	rhythmical
biscuit	February	negotiable	ridiculous
buffet	feminine	newsstand	salable
burial	fission	nuisance	separation
capitalism	gaiety	occurrence	souvenir
caricature	gauge	omission	sponsor
cataclysm	guidance	opportunity	strategic
calendar	hereditary	outrageous	unscrupulous
changeable	horizontal	pamphlet	vacuum
colleague	ideally	parliament	vaudeville
coming	incidentally	peasant	vengeance
competition	influential	permanent	Wednesday

Easily Confused Words

Some words are frequently confused with other words that have similar pronunciations or spellings. Study the following list of easily confused words. Other words that are frequently confused are in Unit 19.

Easily Confused Words		
carat	diamond weight	She wore a two-carat diamond.
caret	proofreader's mark	Use a caret to insert a word.
carrot	vegetable	We like peas and carrots.
complement	to go well with	Tartar sauce complements fish.
compliment	to express admiration	I complimented her on her dress.
precedence	priority	What takes precedence over safety?
precedents	previous events	Are there legal precedents?
rap	to knock	Rap on the door.
wrap	to cover	I will wrap the presents.
root	part of a plant	The plant's roots are dry.
rout	to defeat	We will rout our rivals.
route	a traveler's way	Which route should I take?
en route	along the way	We expect trouble en route.
shear	to cut	He should shear the sheep.
sheer	utter, steep	The cliff is a sheer drop.
weather	atmosphere	The weather is sunny and dry.
whether	if	Whether you go is your choice.

Exercise 2

Rewrite the following sentences to correct misspellings.

1. The disasterous buffet included enormus old carots, stale minature biskets, and some rather mediocer fish.
2. When one considers the devestation caused by his unscrupulus enemies, it is no wonder that General Lee exuberantly lead the charge to route them.
3. The wheather analyst's accomplishements were acknoledged by many complements from her colleages.
4. The maintainance personnel sponsered a campaigne for enviromental awareness.
5. Does the calendar show Febuary forth as being a Wensday or a Thursday?

27.1 Boost Your Study Skills

Think of accomplished musicians, athletes, and scholars you know. As they develop and maintain their skills, they focus precisely on activities that will increase their abilities for a specific task, and they change those activities to fit new challenges. When you study efficiently, your focus should be on monitoring how well you understand specific information. Using good study habits means applying whatever strategies you need to fully understand important information.

Taking Meaningful Notes

Good notes do two things: they condense main ideas and important details, and they show relationships between ideas and details. When you take notes, paraphrase ideas. Double-space your notes, using a question mark to indicate missing information. Later, add any information you discover in your reading or discussions. The following notes are from a biology class.

Taking Notes in Modified Outline Form

Cell Division — 2 Forms

I. Mitosis: cell divides, forms 2 ident. cells—4 stages in animals
   (1) prophase—chromosomes condense and appear
   (2) metaphase—   "   line up midcell
   (3) anaphase—   "   move apart
   (4) ? —   "   elongate, become invisible
II. Meiosis

> Identify main ideas by giving them prominence in your notes and list details underneath the main ideas to indicate relationships.

> Use abbreviations such as *2* for "two" and *ident.* for "identical" whenever possible to save time.

Making Study Time Count

Think about developing and using good study habits, not just about spending time studying. If you work in front of a blaring television set while stretched out on a sofa, you probably won't gain much from your effort. Trying to cram a week's studying into a panicky two hours is actually time poorly spent.

Think about when, where, and how you learn best. What works for another may not work for you, so experiment to discover which study habits suit you. Consider the suggestions on the next page.

Study Skills

Study Tips

1. **Find a quiet place to study.** Distractions will break your concentration and waste time.
2. **Choose a regular time to study.** If studying becomes a routine, it will seem less like a chore.
3. **Set achievable study goals.** Divide long-term assignments into stages and complete them over a period of time. For nightly homework, prioritize assignments. Do the dreaded assignments first, when you have the most energy.
4. **Before beginning to read or study, skim the material to get a sense of what is before you.** If you preview the material, it will make more sense to you when you read it in depth because you can anticipate how main ideas are connected and will develop.
5. **Study with a pen and paper ready.** Jot down key words and ideas to reinforce them in your mind and to provide yourself with material for review at another study session.
6. **After reviewing the material on your own, ask someone to quiz you to see whether you have mastered the material.** Although you understand the material, you may not know it well enough to rephrase it for a test.
7. **Refresh your attention by taking occasional breaks.**
8. **Don't cram for tests.** Research shows that you will learn more in several short review sessions than in one long session.
9. **If you know the time will be well spent, form a study group.** Quiz each other to prepare for tests.

Reading to Remember

To understand and remember what you read, first spend some time previewing the material. Skim chapter headings, key terms, photo captions, and chapter summaries to gain a general sense of the material and an overview of main ideas. The study or review questions at the end of sections or chapters indicate what information the author considers most important.

Next, read in depth. Try having a mental conversation with yourself as you read, stopping when something does not make sense. Reread or adjust your pace while working through difficult material. You may want to take two-column notes. Divide a piece of paper in half vertically. Take notes from your reading on the left side; on the right side record your questions, summaries, clarifications and comments for later review. Your writing will "reflect" the ideas in your mind and help reinforce what you've learned.

During other study sessions, review important material. Scan your textbook again for main ideas and supporting details. Reread your notes and supply answers you have found to questions. When studying your notes and class handouts, you might use a highlighting marker to emphasize important points. Highlight judiciously: if an entire page is colored in, you will see no differentiation between important ideas and minor details.

Evaluating What You Read

When you read textbooks and other library sources, first read for understanding; then read critically. You may evaluate a passage, making a judgment or forming an opinion about an idea or an author. You may analyze the completeness of information or consider the logic of certain conclusions. Sometimes word choices in a selection can help you judge an author's bias. At other times, you may need to rely on your own knowledge or outside sources to help you evaluate a selection. Look at the following paragraph about pesticides and try to answer the questions that follow.

Many pesticides that are banned in wealthy nations are shipped to Central America, often with disastrous results. Pesticide containers have safety instructions written in a language farmers can't read. Some pesticides are so toxic that anyone applying them should wear a tightly sealed rubber suit and a respirator. Unfortunately, most farmers are too poor to afford any protection; those who can afford the gear don't buy it because rubber suits are impractical in the tropics.

- What are the facts?
- What additional information might you need to understand the situation fully?
- What words might be clues to the writer's bias? Is the writer's viewpoint well supported?

Writers show bias when they demonstrate strong, personal, and sometimes unreasonable opinions. Writers use persuasive techniques when they try to get readers to believe something or to act in a particular way. Writers may have strong personal bias and still compose persuasive essays that are logical and well supported. On the other hand, writers can be vague or less than accurate in order to be persuasive. How would you evaluate the paragraph above?

Some word choices are clues to bias: *wealthy* countries, *disastrous* results, and *unfortunately*. What other information would you want to know before evaluating this writer's thoughts?

Exercise 1

Find a news article and an editorial on the same subject. Analyze the news article for fact, opinion, exaggeration, and bias; then do the same for the editorial.

As an alternative, choose a magazine article that you feel contains unsupported opinions or bias and write a one-page essay stating and defending your views.

Understanding Graphics

The graphics in your textbooks and in other reading materials can clarify complex relationships, untangle complicated descriptions, and summarize key information. Accurately interpreting these visual aids will help you get the most from your reading. Most graphics are easy to read once you recognize their basic form, usually that of a diagram, table, chart, or graph. Be sure you understand the labels on any graphic.

Analyzing Diagrams

Diagrams, such as organizational trees and maps, illustrate the steps in a process or the breakdown of abstract concepts into concrete terms. The diagram that follows illustrates how a concept can be more easily understood when it is rendered as a diagram.

> Arrows within the diagram provide important information. Why is Stage 1 presented at the bottom of the diagram instead of at the top?

> Notice that the overall design of the diagram not only lists the stages of Maslow's theory but also shows that one stage cannot be reached without the previous stage being completed.

Abraham Maslow's Psychological Theory of the Hierarchy of Needs

STAGES	EXAMPLES	PERIOD OF GROWTH
Stage 5 Self-actualization	Self-acceptance Self-confidence	Adult
Stage 4 Esteem needs	Respect and acceptance from others	Adolescent
Stage 3 Love needs	Attention from friends and family	Child
Stage 2 Safety needs	Secure environment	Infant
Stage 1 Physiological needs	Air, sustenance, warmth	Developing fetus

Reading Tables, Charts, and Graphs

Suppose you are doing some research about video viewing in your community during the last half of the 1980s, before DVD (digital video disc) players became popular. How might you use visual aids? After collecting data from your local video stores, you could present your findings about both video sales and rentals in a table, graph, or chart.

Tables These graphics work well when you are presenting several categories of detailed, statistical data. The following hypothetical table presents the number of dollars spent on video sales and rentals in one town during a five-year time span in the first half of the 1990s.

Video Sales and Rentals in Heatherfield, 1991–1995 (in dollars)		
YEAR	VIDEO RENTALS	VIDEO SALES
1991	$164,250	$ 7,215
1992	$243,790	$10,150
1993	$392,640	$18,973
1994	$529,106	$19,005
1995	$599,838	$19,621

The table can be read across or down.

Both rentals and sales increased from 1991 to 1995, but rentals exceeded sales by a much greater percentage.

While the table illustrates that a trend took place in one town during that particular five-year period, you cannot assume that the same statistics applied to video sales and rentals in other towns or even in Heatherfield during the next decade. Other variables may have affected video statistics from 1996 to the year 2000. For example, did DVD player purchases increase the number of videos purchased in the later 1990s?

Read tables carefully—numbers are sometimes written in a kind of short-hand in which zeroes are dropped. Always check the labels.

Line Graphs These graphs dramatically show trends, movements, and cycles. Line graphs are often used to show amounts, or quantitative information, such as sales figures, temperatures, or rainfall over a period of time.

The vertical axis, or scale, usually appears on the left side and is used to show the dependent variable, such as dollars or temperature. The horizontal axis usually appears below the graph and shows the independent variable, such as time.

As in the preceding table, you cannot infer facts beyond those illustrated in the graph. For example, this sample graph does not give any information about video sales in Heatherfield or about video rentals in any other town.

The information on both axes is presented in equal increments. How would your visual perception of the trend alter if the vertical axis used larger units? Smaller units?

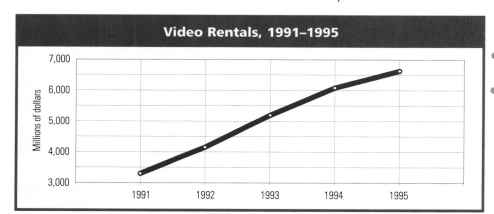

Video Rentals, 1991–1995

The vertical axis measures thousands of dollars; the line within the graph shows approximate rental dollars per year. Note that figures in the table are more exact than those indicated by the line graph.

Study Skills

Bar Graphs Bar graphs compare amounts of items. The bars can be horizontal or vertical. This bar graph uses the same data as the line graph.

How does your perception of the data change when you see this bar graph versus the same information in the line graph and in the table?

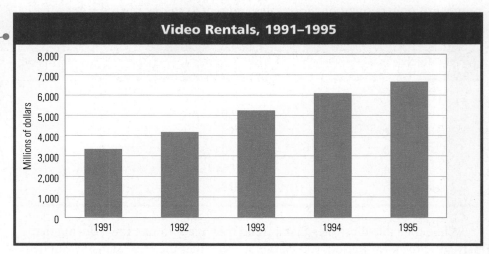

Pie Charts These graphics show a circle representing 100 percent of a whole. Divisions within the circle, or "slices" of the pie, represent proportions of the whole and must visually reflect the percentages they represent. To evaluate the accuracy of a pie chart, compare pie slices to divisions on a clock face. In fifteen minutes, the minute hand travels around 25 percent of the pie; thirty minutes equals 50 percent. The shapes of the slices in a pie chart compare to percentages of the whole.

Compare the size of the slice labeled 41.3% on each chart. On the "incorrect" chart, it occupies 50% of the circle.

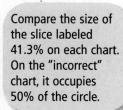

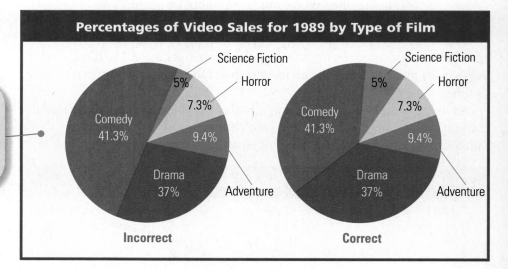

Exercise 2

Find a table, chart, graph, or diagram. Make a copy of it; then, in writing, tell what information the visual aid illustrates.

Study Skills

UNIT 28

Taking Tests

28.1 Taking Essay Tests

Essay tests require you to use your knowledge of a given topic to produce a well-written essay in a limited amount of time. Prepare thoroughly so your thoughts about test information are organized in your head before you walk into class. Then, when you take the test, allocate enough time for each stage of the writing process.

Planning the Essay

As you study, begin planning possible answers to essay questions that are likely to appear on the test. If you know beforehand how many essay questions you will be required to complete, you can estimate how much time you'll have for each question.

An essay test may consist of one in-depth question or several less-complex ones. When you receive the test, first read it through. Determine how much time to spend on each question. Then reread each question for signal words that indicate the thinking processes you'll need to use in your answer: *compare, contrast, analyze, explain, trace, define, summarize,* or *prove.* Look at the following example questions.

Analyzing an Essay Test Question

History Question: Trace the expansion of railroads in the American West.

Analysis: To *trace* is to describe, one stage at a time, how something changes or develops.

What to consider:

- What caused the change to begin?
- What were the stages of change? How long did each last?
- What were the particular elements of each stage? (Consider major political events, people, and obstacles.)
- In each stage, what remained the same? Changed? Why? (Consider how and why economic, social, and natural forces compelled changes to occur.)
- When and why did the development end?

Similarly, if you are asked to *define* something, begin with an actual definition; then develop and expand the definition. Use examples or illustrations and comparisons and contrasts.

Analyzing an Essay Test Question

Literature Question: <u>Contrast</u> the poems of Anne Sexton with those of Emily Dickinson.

Analysis: To *contrast* is to describe how items are different.

What to consider:

- Which items (poems) will you contrast?
- Which elements of those items make effective contrasts? (Consider subject matter, tone, images, rhythm, and rhyme.)
- Which details provide the best support? (Consider summarizing poems and paraphrasing lines from poems.)
- How are the poets' lives reflected in their poems?

Writing the Essay

If you must write more than one essay, apportion enough time for each. Begin your answer to a question by brainstorming and prewriting on scratch paper for several minutes. Read the test question again to make sure that you are answering what has been asked. Create a rough outline to organize main ideas and key details. Next, jot down your thesis statement. Then begin drafting your answer.

State your thesis in the first paragraph of your draft so you can refer to it to keep your ideas on track. Use transition words to help move smoothly from one idea to the next. Provide complete information, including examples and illustrations, where necessary. Be specific; your teacher will not be impressed if you pad your answer with unnecessary details about the subject.

You won't have time to revise your answer. Instead, spend the remaining minutes that you have proofreading your answer and making corrections neatly.

Exercise 1

Prepare an outline and a thesis statement for each of the following sample essay questions. Spend no more than ten minutes on any one question. Discuss your work in groups.

1. Trace the development of civil rights in the United States.
2. Define "point of view" as it applies to literature and give examples of the kinds of point of view.
3. Defend or disprove the following statement: "Education is the great emancipator."
4. Contrast the benefits of aerobic exercise and weight lifting.

28.2 Preparing for Standardized Tests

Standardized tests are a part of almost every student's high school experience. Perhaps at no time, though, is the strain of taking standardized tests more acute than when you are preparing to apply to colleges that you may want to attend. Being prepared for these standardized tests is the best way to lessen the strain.

The Purpose of Standardized Tests

Standardized tests are given to many people under similar circumstances and are objectively graded to determine an average, or "standard," score. Three of the most widely known standardized tests, all part of the college application process, are the PSAT (Preliminary SAT), the ACT, and the SAT. The ACT measures achievement in English, math, social studies, and natural sciences. The SAT measures verbal and mathematical abilities and is the most frequently administered standardized test. The PSAT, typically the first test that students take, is designed to predict results on the SAT. For most students, the PSAT is simply a practice test. Those who do exceptionally well on the PSAT will qualify for the National Merit Scholarship competition.

There are actually two SAT tests—the three hour SAT-I: Reasoning Test and a variety of one-hour SAT-II: Subject Tests. The SAT-I tests general verbal and math skills. Each SAT-II subject test evaluates mastery in a particular subject area.

Colleges use standardized test scores as one element in determining students' admission status and probable success in college courses. Many students take both the SAT and the ACT in order to apply to a variety of colleges. Most high school students take the PSAT and SAT in their junior year and have the option of repeating the SAT in their senior year. If you are not satisfied with your first SAT performance, then repeat the test. In fact, some guidance counselors recommend taking the SAT for the first time just to demystify the experience.

Preparing to Take Standardized Tests

Because standardized tests of ability measure overall scholastic aptitude, you can't study for the tests in the same way you would study for classroom tests. You can, however, almost always improve your results by preparing for standardized tests, using the methods described in the box that follows.

Before You Take a Standardized Test

- Gather information about the test. Your school counselor's office is a good place to begin your search for information.
- Get a schedule of test dates, and mail in the appropriate forms and any required fees well before the deadline date.
- Take practice exams, such as the PSAT (Preliminary SAT). Practice exams give you an idea of the kinds of questions you can expect and help you to learn how to pace yourself. You can also buy practice books or borrow them from a library.
- Review general principles, but don't cram for the test. Rely on practice exams, books, and study guides. Also ask your counselor about tutors and study groups.

On the morning of the test, be sure that you are well rested and have eaten a sustaining breakfast. Arrive at the testing center early and have necessary items with you, such as your entrance card, identification, #2 pencils, an eraser, and a watch. The box below provides tips for taking standardized tests.

Tips for Taking Standardized Tests

- If you don't already know, find out whether the test is designed to be completed; some are not. Also find out whether there is a penalty for incorrect answers. If there is a penalty, it is to your advantage not to guess if you don't know an answer. If there is no penalty, do not hesitate to guess.
- Before you begin any section of the test, read the directions carefully. Directions may change from section to section.
- Before beginning each section, check to see how many questions there are so you can pace yourself accordingly.
- If you can't answer a question, don't waste precious minutes dwelling on it. Go on to the next question. If there is time, you can return to the questions you skipped.
- You will probably use a #2 pencil and fill in circles on a computer-readable form. Be sure that your marks are heavy and remain within the answer circle.
- If you skip a question in the test booklet, make sure you skip the corresponding answer circle. Periodically check that the number of the test question matches that of your answer.

Exercise 2

Use a bulletin board in your classroom to create an information center for standardized tests. Your class and other English classes can work together on the project. Use the following suggestions for assigning duties.

1. Visit the counseling center to interview counselors and to gather information, such as sample forms.
2. Make a chart listing application deadlines.
3. See what test-taking resources and practice exams are available in libraries and at bookstores. Prepare a summary of your findings.
4. Write reviews of study guides and practice books. Include prices, quality, and availability.
5. Contact colleges that you and others may want to attend. Find out which exams each college requires and post your findings.

28.3 | Standardized Test Items

Standardized tests such as the SAT measure your understanding of word meanings; your level of reading comprehension in various subject areas; and your knowledge of grammar, usage, and mechanics.

Multiple-Choice Vocabulary Test Items

Vocabulary test items are followed by five possible answers. First, examine the given word or words and try to determine an answer before you read the choices. You will be less likely to be confused by a misleading or ambiguous answer choice. Next, choose the best answer from those listed.

Antonym Test Items These items require you to look at a capitalized word and then choose, from a list of words, one that is most nearly opposite in meaning. Look at the capitalized word below and choose its antonym.

PRELUDE: (A) postpone (B) preamble (C) fugue (D) epilogue (E) symphony

A *prelude* is "an introductory performance"; in context, it often refers to a piece of music. You should look for a word that describes the closing of something, such as *epilogue,* choice (D), which is the correct answer even though it refers to the afterword in a novel rather than to a piece of music. You may be distracted by choice (A), *postpone,* which means "to put off," but it's neither a good match nor the same part of speech as *prelude.*

Analogy Test Items These items test your ability to identify the relationship of a word pair. The item, then, requires that you find a parallel relationship in another word pair from a list of word pairs. Always begin by determining the relationship of the first word pair. Some possible relationships are presented in the chart below.

Analogy Relationships	
WORD PAIR	**RELATIONSHIP**
TREPIDATION : PERTURBATION	synonyms
PROCESSIONAL : RECESSIONAL	sequence in time
OEDIPUS REX : DRAMA	an item in a classification
DROUGHT : STARVATION	cause and effect
ASTROLABE : ASTRONOMER	tool and user

To determine an analogy relationship, formulate a simple sentence that contains and describes the relationship. For astrolabe : astronomer, you might think, "An astrolabe was used by early astronomers." Determine the relationship of the following capitalized word pair.

PENICILLIN : MEDICINE :: (A) sickness : invalid   (B) aggravation : rash
(C) Ibsen : playwright   (D) insurance : liability   (E) punctuation : language

You may decide that penicillin is a kind of medicine. The relationship of the given pair is *an item in a class*. Now consider the choices, putting each answer choice in your relationship sentence. Thus, "Sickness is *not* a kind of invalid"; "aggravation is *not* a kind of rash." (Watch out for answers that would be correct if their order were reversed: a rash *is* a kind of aggravation.) "Ibsen is *not* a kind of playwright," but he is one author in that class. Neither of the last two choices suits the relationship of object to class. While *punctuation* is related to *language*, "punctuation is *not* a kind of language," nor is it a class of language. Even if your relationship sentence is "penicillin is an example of medicine" or "penicillin is used in the practice of medicine," choice (E) still does not work. Choice (C) is correct.

Sentence-Completion Test Items

These test items present sentences in which critical words are missing. You must recognize the relationships among the parts of the sentence in order to choose the word or words that make the sentence correct, both grammatically and logically. Decide which answer choice makes the following sentence correct.

Taking a stand in favor of animal rights, the researcher _____ an end to vivisection and _____ using monkeys in experiments.
(A) applauded . . . extolled   (B) denied . . . continued   (C) condemned . . . supported
(D) cheered . . . threatened   (E) advocated . . . denounced

Before you begin to answer the question, read the entire sentence to understand the ideas expressed; then try out each answer choice. Thus, someone in favor of animal rights would certainly applaud the end of vivisection but would hardly extol the use of monkeys in experiments. To be sure that both words fit the logic and grammar of the sentence, try all the choices in the blanks until you find the best answer. Only answer (E) makes sense in the sentence above.

Reading-Comprehension Test Items

This section of the test presents passages of varying length and difficulty from writing in different fields of study. The questions about the passages are designed to test your understanding of what you read. Try the sample questions on the next page. Read the questions first to determine what to look for as you read the passage.

Taking Tests

One of the most important archaeological finds in history is the discovery of the tomb of Chinese Emperor Qin Shihuangdi. Qin came to power when he was only thirteen years old. As soon as he ascended the throne, he ordered laborers to begin work on his tomb, a project believed to have taken thirty-six years to complete. An army of life-size terra-cotta figures holding authentic weapons is buried in standing formation with the emperor. Each statue was apparently modeled after a specific soldier—an astounding feat considering the vast number of statues: approximately six thousand archers, officers, and charioteers with their horses.

1. The best title for this passage would be:
   (A) Burial Practices in Ancient China
   (B) Emperor Qin Shihuangdi
   (C) Qin's Army in the Tomb
   (D) Archaeology in China
   (E) A Forgotten Emperor

2. Which of the following conclusions could be made after reading the passage?
   (A) The greatest archaeological finds are in China.
   (B) Qin's society held its emperors in great esteem.
   (C) Qin's soldiers respected him.
   (D) Qin greatly feared his enemies.
   (E) Profiteers are attracted to archaeological sites.

Most questions deal with finding the main idea, drawing inferences, identifying facts, and recognizing tone. The first question above asks for a title, the main idea of the passage. The answer is (C): (A) and (D) are too broad; (B) and (E) focus on the emperor, not the tomb.

The second question asks you to draw an inference. In the passage, none of the choices is directly stated. But only answer (D) can be concluded, based on the information provided. When answering a question that asks for facts from a passage, find the choice that answers that specific question. In evaluating an author's tone, look for words that indicate attitude.

English-Composition Test Items

These items test your ability to identify and correct errors in grammar, sentence structure, word usage, and correctness of expression according to standard written American English.

Usage Test Items These test items require you to recognize sentence parts that are grammatically incorrect or unclear. Each test item is a sentence that contains several underlined parts labeled (A) through (D), followed by choice (E), "no error." As you read, determine in which part an error exists or, if there is no error, choose (E). Remember that an error can occur only in an underlined section. Try the following question.

At the Jacobean drama festival honoring Shakespeare's birthday, minstrels, dressed in
            (A)
bright colors, playing old ballads and love songs, walked among the crowds; everywhere
            (B)   (C)
was music and laughter. no error
        (D)   (E)

Be sure to read the entire sentence, or you may overlook an error. In the example above, the singular verb "was" in (D) does not agree with the plural subject "music and laughter." Because the structure reverses the order of these elements, the problem is hard to spot.

Sentence-Correction Test Items These test items require you not only to find the error in an underlined sentence part, but also to decide on the best revision to correct the error. Your answer, selected from choices that follow the sentence, should reflect the most effective expression and should be free of awkward, illogical, or faulty sentence structure. Typically, choice (A) contains the exact wording of the underlined section and means "no error." As with usage test items, an error can occur only in an underlined portion.

Try to determine the error before reading the answer choices. Read the following sentence and its possible corrections.

The company president should either resign, or he should learn about responding to employee complaints in a serious way.
(A) he should learn about responding to employee complaints in a serious way.
(B) he should learn serious responses to employee complaints.
(C) learn to respond seriously to employee complaints.
(D) should take the employee complaints with greater seriousness.
(E) could respond in a serious manner to employee complaints.

Choice (C) contains the most clear and concise wording and corrects the faulty parallelism in the original sentence.

Exercise 3   Vocabulary

Antonym Test Items Find the best antonym for each of the words below.

1. recidivism: (A) advancement (B) deterioration (C) disavow (D) rubbish (E) elitism
2. jocular: (A) irksome (B) angular (C) laughable (D) morose (E) happy

Analogy Test Items For each question, find the pair of words that represents the same relationship expressed in the first word pair.

3. computer : microchip : : (A) program : people (B) injection : rash
   (C) universe : constellation (D) irrigation : flood (E) reporter : news
4. benevolent : forgives : : (A) beneficial : receives (B) radiant : obscures
   (C) proficient : bungles (D) musical : develops (E) haughty : boasts

(continued)

Exercise 3

Sentence-Completion Test Items Find the words that best complete each sentence below.

5. When one thinks of _____, Lorraine comes to mind: she always puts the needs of others before her own comfort and convenience.
   (A) goodness (B) affectation (C) altruism (D) prestige (E) ennui

6. The dissident writer continued to _____ the current political system in her lectures, even though the government had _____ her books.
   (A) attack . . . banned (B) praise . . . sold (C) admonish . . . praised
   (D) uphold . . . criticized (E) laud . . . destroyed

Exercise 4

Reading-Comprehension Test Items Read the passage and answer the questions that follow it.

Bedouin are Arabic-speaking nomadic peoples of the Middle Eastern deserts. They inhabit or utilize a large part of the land area, though they are only a small part of the total population in the Middle East. Most Bedouin migrate between the desert, where they live during the rainy winter season, and the cultivated land, where they live in the dry summer months.

Family is the most important feature of Bedouin social structure. The extended family provides viability and functions as one entity in economic, political, and military ventures. Each family is headed by a sheikh, who is assisted by an informal tribal council of male elders.

Bedouin are most often animal herders and have been traditionally classified according to the animal species that are the basis for their livelihood. Camel nomads from large tribes in the Sahara, Syrian, and Arabian deserts have the most prestige. Beneath them in rank are sheep and goat nomads and cattle herders.

7. Which of the following statements is not true?
   (A) Weather conditions play an important role in the nomadic patterns of Bedouin.
   (B) A sheikh does not have dictatorial rule over his tribe.
   (C) The proportion of Bedouin to other Middle Eastern peoples is small.
   (D) Bedouin live in villages in the desert.
   (E) Bedouin elders advise the sheikh.

8. The Bedouin extended family is important because
   (A) it appoints a sheikh as leader.
   (B) it helps ensure economic, political, and military survival.
   (C) it helps ensure the availability of camels.
   (D) the sheikh is advised by a council of elders.
   (E) of a system of dowries.

English-Composition

Usage Test Item Read the sentence below and decide whether any part of it contains an error. Choose (E) if the sentence is grammatically correct.

9. The <u>effect of chlorofluorocarbons</u> on the protective <u>ozone layer, which surrounds</u>
   (A)   (B)

   the <u>earth, will have</u> disastrous consequences for plant and animal life unless the
       (C)

   <u>use of these chemicals is abandoned.</u> <u>no error</u>
                (D)   (E)

Sentence-Correction Test Item Choose the answer that produces the clearest, most effective sentence.

10. As I see it, students who want to pursue a liberal arts education should take classes in history, economics, literature, and philosophy, <u>and they should also take classes in math and science, as well.</u>
   (A) and they should also take classes in math and science, as well.
   (B) as well as in math and science.
   (C) and in math and science, as well.
   (D) and they should, as well, take classes in math and science.
   (E) including classes in math and science.

28.4 Standardized Test Practice

The following exercises are designed to familiarize you with two standardized tests—the SAT II Writing and the ACT English exams—that you may take during the school year. These exercises are similar to those in the actual tests in how they look and what they ask you to do. Completing these exercises will provide you with practice and make you aware of areas you might need to work on.

The **SAT II Writing Test** contains four types of questions separated into two parts: Part A and Part B. In Part A, you will be asked to compose a clear and effective essay on a specific assignment. This section of the SAT II Writing Test is not addressed in the following exercises.

Part B is all multiple-choice questions. The first section is called **Error ID.** In this section, you will be asked to find an error in one of four underlined portions of a sentence. If there is no error in the sentence, you will choose answer choice E.

The second section is called **Improving Sentences.** In this section, you will be given a sentence that has parts underlined or that is completely underlined. You will be asked to choose from among five ways of phrasing the underlined portion. Choice A always repeats what is in the original question; the other four answer choices are different.

The third section is called **Improving Paragraphs.** In this section, you will be given a short series of paragraphs to read. The paragraphs are followed by questions that require you to make decisions about sentence structure, word choice, and usage within the passage. You may also be asked questions concerning the organization, development, and coherence of a particular part of this series of paragraphs.

On the **ACT English Exam,** you will be given five passages with questions corresponding to each passage. The passages differ in their style, voice, and content. Some are informal first-person narratives, while others are more formal informational essays written in the third person. The questions for each passage test a variety of subject matter—grammar, sentence structure, usage, style, logic, coherence, organization, and consistency. While some questions focus on an underlined portion of the passage, other questions involve an entire paragraph, or even the entire passage. You must consider all features of standard written English in order to answer each question effectively.

Taking Tests

Preparing for the Tests

The exercises listed in the chart below should help to improve your writing and make you more comfortable with the format and types of questions you will see on the SAT II Writing and the ACT English exams.

SAT II WRITING EXERCISES	
Exercise	**Pages**
• Error ID Exercises	824–825
	826–827
	832–833
	834–835
• Improving Sentences Exercises	828–829
• Improving Paragraphs Exercises	830–831

ACT ENGLISH EXERCISES	
Passage	**Pages**
• Passage 1	836–837
• Passage 2	838–839
• Passage 3	840–841
• Passage 4	842–843
• Passage 5	844–845
• Passage 6	846–847

Directions: The following sentences test your knowledge of grammar, usage, diction (choice of words), and idiom.

   Some sentences are correct.
   No sentence contains more than one error.

You will find that the error, if there is one, is underlined and lettered. Elements of the sentence that are not underlined will not be changed. In choosing answers, follow the requirements of standard written English.

If there is an error, select the <u>one underlined part</u> that must be changed to make the sentence correct.

If there is no error, choose answer choice E.

EXAMPLE: SAMPLE ANSWER

   <u>The other</u> delegates and <u>him</u> <u>immediately</u>   Ⓐ ● Ⓒ Ⓓ Ⓔ
         A   **B**   **C**
   accepted the resolution <u>drafted</u> by the
                                  D
   neutral states. <u>No error</u>
                        E

---

1. After Gary tripped and broke <u>his</u> ankle, he
                                    A
    <u>has been</u> <u>very careful</u> when <u>walking</u> down
      B   **C**   **D**
    the stairs. <u>No error</u>
                    E

2. The teacher was happy <u>to see</u> that her
                             A
    students <u>had started</u> <u>to comprehend</u> the
               B   **C**
    difference <u>between</u> a proximal cause and a
                 D
    final cause. <u>No error</u>
                     E

3. The snakes <u>attracted</u> a crowd on the
                  A
    playground, <u>for</u> <u>it was</u> unlike anything the
                  B   **C**
    children <u>had ever seen</u> before. <u>No error</u>
               D   **E**

4. <u>Some of</u> the most interesting cities on
      A
    earth <u>are</u> in <u>dry</u> areas where there are
            B   **C**
    <u>hardly no</u> nearby lakes or rivers. <u>No error</u>
      D   **E**

5. The director of a local charity <u>claims that</u> a
                                       A
    <u>curiously low</u> percentage of <u>their</u>
      B   **C**
    donations comes <u>from</u> people with a lot of
                       D
    money. <u>No error</u>
               E

6. Slight differences in air temperature may
    seem <u>unimportant</u> to you and <u>I</u>, but they
           A   **B**
    <u>can have</u> <u>serious</u> effects on the pilots of
      C   **D**
    light aircraft. <u>No error</u>
                        E

GO ON TO THE NEXT PAGE

7. In many small towns, jobs in factories <u>are</u>
   A
   plentiful, but <u>it</u> <u>do not require</u> a <u>lot of</u> skill.
   B   C   D
   <u>No error</u>
   E

8. <u>Showing</u> the deplorable conditions <u>under</u>
   A   B
   <u>which</u> poor immigrants <u>lived</u>, Jacob Riis
   C
   used photography in order <u>for protesting</u>
   D
   unsafe housing. <u>No error</u>
   E

9. Neither Larry's mother <u>nor</u> his father <u>were</u>
   A   B
   able <u>to attend</u> the opening of the school
   C
   play <u>on</u> Saturday. <u>No error</u>
   D   E

10. I was eager <u>to see</u> Jason's new ten-speed
    A
    bicycle, <u>which</u> was very different <u>to any</u>
    B   C
    other bike I had <u>ever seen</u>. <u>No error</u>
    D   E

11. Kathleen, <u>the newest of</u> the two employees
    A
    <u>who</u> have recently <u>been hired</u>, <u>has</u> an
    B   C   D
    excellent education and is a conscientious
    worker. <u>No error</u>
    E

12. <u>The more</u> you <u>look at</u> the early paintings of
    A   B
    Jackson Pollock, the more <u>they</u> begin <u>to</u>
    C   D
    provoke an emotional reaction. <u>No error</u>
    E

13. Robert <u>was asked</u> <u>to read</u> just one chapter
    A   B
    of the book, and so <u>having</u> only a vague
    C
    idea <u>of</u> the main idea. <u>No error</u>
    D   E

14. <u>Since</u> 1970, <u>less than</u> three Americans have
    A   B
    <u>won</u> the <u>highly prestigious</u> Nobel Prize in
    C   D
    literature. <u>No error</u>
    E

STOP

Directions: The following sentences test your knowledge of grammar, usage, diction (choice of words), and idiom.

Some sentences are correct.
No sentence contains more than one error.

You will find that the error, if there is one, is underlined and lettered. Elements of the sentence that are not underlined will not be changed. In choosing answers, follow the requirements of standard written English.

If there is an error, select the <u>one underlined part</u> that must be changed to make the sentence correct.

If there is no error, choose answer choice E.

EXAMPLE:

<u>The other</u> delegates and <u>him</u> <u>immediately</u>
   A   **B**   **C**
accepted the resolution <u>drafted by</u> the
                D
neutral states. <u>No error</u>
         E

SAMPLE ANSWER

Ⓐ ● Ⓒ Ⓓ Ⓔ

---

1. <u>Even though</u> her injury was mild, the
  A
gymnast <u>was told</u> that she would not be
      B
able to practice <u>for</u> an <u>indecisive</u> period of
         C   **D**
time. <u>No error</u>
    E

2. The extremely low-fat foods <u>eaten by</u>
           A
people who are trying to lose weight may

be <u>hazardous to</u> <u>their</u> health. <u>No error</u>
B **C**   **D**   **E**

3. <u>Roger's</u> strong moral convictions <u>led</u> <u>him</u>
  A   **B** **C**
to <u>protest over</u> his school's unfair
   D
admissions practices. <u>No error</u>
           E

4. Of the many ideas <u>recommended by</u> my
               A
staff for <u>this year's</u> fund-raising <u>event</u>, the
       B   **C**
one I like <u>better</u> is Olivia's. <u>No error</u>
      D   **E**

5. <u>Vital</u> to any analysis <u>of</u> the causes of World
  A   **B**
War I <u>are</u> an understanding of the many
     C
alliances between European <u>countries in</u>
                D
the early 1900s. <u>No error</u>
         E

6. Placing baking soda <u>in</u> a glass filled with
           A
vinegar <u>normally</u> <u>result</u> in an <u>interesting</u>
      B   **C**   **D**
chemical reaction. <u>No error</u>
         E

GO ON TO THE NEXT PAGE ⟩

7. Though thousands of college basketball
    _A_
    players dream of becoming a professional
                   _B_   _C_
    athlete, few will ever reach that goal.
    _____   _D_
    No error
    _E_

8. According to the survey, neither banana
    _A_
    nor coconut are likely to become a popular
    _B_   _C_   _D_
    flavor of ice cream. No error
                         _E_

9. Many of the lecturers were professors who,
    _A_
    in light of their years of excellent teaching,
    _B_
    had received the Marshall Scholarship.
        _C_
    No error
    _D_

10. Since the removal of his tonsils last week,
          _A_
    Jason is feeling far better than he did
          _B_   _C_
    before the operation. No error
    _D_   _E_

11. The religion of the ancient Babylonians

    was very similar to the Egyptians, as they
    _A_   _B_
    both worshipped the same sun god.
    _C_   _D_
    No error
    _E_

12. In the early 1930s, England did not want to
    _A_   _B_
    declare war on Germany because they were
                                    _C_
    afraid of another bloody world war.
             _D_
    No error
    _E_

13. To investigate the history of a word and
                      _A_
    learning to use it properly are very
    _B_   _C_   _D_
    different tasks. No error
                     _E_

14. The doctor was thrilled to see that the
                         _A_
    cancer had started to recede after the
          _B_   _C_
    patient's fifth treatment. No error
    _D_   _E_

Directions: The following sentences test correctness and effectiveness of expression. In choosing answers, follow the requirements of standard written English; that is, pay attention to grammar, choice of words, sentence construction, and punctuation.

In each of the following sentences, part of the sentence or the entire sentence is underlined. Beneath each sentence, you will find five ways of phrasing the underlined part. Choice A repeats the original; the other four are different.

Choose the answer that best expresses the meaning of the original sentence. If you think the original is better than any of the alternatives, choose it; otherwise choose one of the others. Your choice should produce the most effective sentence—clear and precise, without awkwardness or ambiguity.

EXAMPLE:

Laura Ingalls Wilder published her first book

and she was sixty-five years old then.

   (A)   and she was sixty-five years old then

   (B)   when she was sixty-five

   (C)   being age sixty-five years old

   (D)   upon the reaching of sixty-five years

   (E)   at the time when she was sixty-five

SAMPLE ANSWER

Ⓐ ● Ⓒ Ⓓ Ⓔ

1. A large predatory insect, <u>the elongated body of a dragonfly</u> can reach five inches in length.

   (A) the elongated body of a dragonfly
   (B) a dragonfly whose elongated body
   (C) a dragonfly's elongated body
   (D) the dragonfly has an elongated body that
   (E) as well as having an elongated body, the dragonfly

2. Herodotus wrote a collection of <u>histories and they give</u> us a good idea of what life was like in Greece around 400 B.C.

   (A) histories and they give
   (B) histories, being the giving to

   (C) histories, they give
   (D) histories that give
   (E) histories, and giving

3. The final grade was better than Dave could possibly have <u>expected, having received</u> a B– when he counted on a C+.

   (A) expected, having received
   (B) expected; and so he received
   (C) expected; he received
   (D) expected: including he reception of
   (E) expected, he was receiving

GO ON TO THE NEXT PAGE ▷

4. Steel production in our factory could be greatly increased by installing new ovens <u>and increasing the number</u> of furnace operators.

   (A) and increasing the number
   (B) and if they increase the number
   (C) also by increasing the number
   (D) and the number being increased
   (E) and if there was a larger amount

5. Bathing your cat too often is as unhealthy <u>than if you do not bathe it</u> often enough.

   (A) than if you do not bathe it
   (B) as not bathing it
   (C) as if one were not to bathe it
   (D) than not bathing
   (E) as for not bathing it

6. <u>It was the sinking of American ships, along with a telegram threatening the United States as well, that encouraged the president to enter the war.</u>

   (A) It was the sinking of American ships, along with a telegram threatening the United States as well, that encouraged the president to enter the war.
   (B) It was the sinking of American ships, along with a telegram threatening the United States, encouraging the president to enter the war.
   (C) American ships were sunk and a telegram threatening the United States was published, and these helped encourage the president to enter the war.
   (D) The sinking of American ships, along with a telegram threatening the United States as well, were encouraging the president to enter the war.
   (E) The sinking of American ships, along with a telegram threatening the United States, encouraged the president to enter the war.

7. <u>The lack of credible eyewitnesses to the crime posing</u> a serious problem for police detectives who are trying to solve the case.

   (A) The lack of credible eyewitnesses to the crime posing
   (B) The crime with its lack of credible eyewitnesses having posed
   (C) The lack of credible eyewitnesses to the crime has been posing
   (D) It is the lack of credible eyewitnesses to the crime posing
   (E) The lack of credible eyewitnesses to the crime poses

8. The oxygen tank in the cockpit allowed the pilots to breathe at altitudes where the air was thin <u>and they could fly</u> much higher than ever before.

   (A) and they could fly
   (B) as well as flying
   (C) so they could be flying
   (D) and to fly
   (E) and the flying

9. The teacher received advice from the office on how many tests to give <u>and getting money</u> to purchase new school supplies.

   (A) and getting money
   (B) as well as given money
   (C) as well as money
   (D) and also getting money
   (E) and also being given money

Directions: The following passage is an early draft of a student essay. Some parts of the passage need to be rewritten.

Read the passage and answer the questions that follow. Some questions are about particular sentences or parts of sentences and ask you to make decisions about sentence structure, word choice, and usage. Other questions refer to the entire essay or parts of the essay and ask you to consider organization, development, and appropriateness of language. Choose the answer that most effectively expresses the meaning and follows the requirements of standard written English.

Questions 1–6 are based on the following passage.

(1) Many of my friends and I used to think that learning algebra was a waste of time. (2) It was something you needed for school. (3) It was meaningless in real life.

(4) One day after school, my friends and I went to play soccer. (5) My friends were changing into their soccer clothes. (6) I ran into Mr. Davies, the local baker, who looked worried. (7) He was trying to figure out how many assistants he needed to hire to help him prepare for the bake sale. (8) He needed to bake fifty cakes for the sale, and he only had five cakes in his store. (9) Each assistant could bake nine cakes per day. (10) I make a quick calculation and had the solution in no time.

(11) I casually told Mr. Davies that he will need five assistants to finish the job. (12) He was so impressed that he promised me a free cake. (13) He asked if I wanted to work in his store. (14) That's how I learned that mathematics can be very useful.

1. Which of these is the best way to combine sentences 2 and 3 (reproduced below)?

   It was something you needed for school. It was meaningless in real life.

   (A) It was something you needed for school, as well as meaningless in real life.
   (B) It was something you needed for school, but it was meaningless in real life.
   (C) It was something you needed for school, but being meaningless in real life.
   (D) It was something you needed for school, meaningless in real life.
   (E) It was something you needed for school, while in real life meaningless.

2. Which of the following sentences should be added after sentence 3 in order to connect the first paragraph to the second paragraph?

   (A) I have believed this since I was a young child in grade school.
   (B) I was never very good at mathematics anyway.
   (C) I don't know why our parents make us learn mathematics.
   (D) My teachers tell me that it will be very important in college.
   (E) A recent experience, however, made me change my mind.

GO ON TO THE NEXT PAGE

3. Which is the best way to combine sentences 5 and 6 (reproduced below)?

My friends were changing into their soccer clothes. I ran into Mr. Davies, the local baker, who looked worried.

(A) My friends were changing into their soccer clothes, I ran into Mr. Davies, the local baker, who looked worried.

(B) I ran into Mr. Davies, the local baker, who looked worried, in contrast to my friends who were changing into their soccer clothes.

(C) While my friends were changing into their soccer clothes, I ran into Mr. Davies, the local baker, who looked worried.

(D) I ran into the local baker, whose name was Mr. Davies, at the same time as my friends were changing into their soccer clothes.

(E) After my friends were changing into their soccer clothes, I ran into Mr. Davies, the local baker, who looked worried.

4. Which of these is the best way to rewrite the underlined portion of sentence 10 (reproduced below)?

I make a quick calculation and had the solution in no time.

(A) (As it is now)
(B) I make a quick calculation and has
(C) I make a quick calculation and will have
(D) I made a quick calculation and had
(E) I have made a quick calculation and had

5. Which of these is the best way to rewrite sentence 11 (reproduced below)?

I casually told Mr. Davies that he will need five assistants to finish the job.

(A) (As it is now)
(B) I told Mr. Davies that he will casually need five assistants to finish the job.
(C) I told Mr. Davies that he would casually need five assistants to finish the job.
(D) I casually told Mr. Davies that he would need five assistants to finish the job.
(E) Casually I tell Mr. Davies that he will need five assistants to finish the job.

6. Which of these is the best way to combine sentences 12 and 13 (reproduced below)?

He was so impressed that he promised me a free cake. He asked if I wanted to work in his store.

(A) He was so impressed that he promised me a free cake and asked if I wanted to work in his store.

(B) He was so impressed that he promised me a free cake, but asked if I wanted to work in his store.

(C) He was so impressed that he promised me a free cake, asking if I wanted to work in his store.

(D) So impressed he was that he promised me a free cake, asked if I wanted to work in his store.

(E) He asked if I wanted to work in his store because he was so impressed that he promised me a free cake.

Directions: The following sentences test your knowledge of grammar, usage, diction (choice of words), and idiom.

Some sentences are correct.
No sentence contains more than one error.

You will find that the error, if there is one, is underlined and lettered. Elements of the sentence that are not underlined will not be changed. In choosing answers, follow the requirements of standard written English.

If there is an error, select the <u>one underlined part</u> that must be changed to make the sentence correct.

If there is no error, choose answer choice E.

EXAMPLE:

<u>The other</u> delegates and <u>him</u> <u>immediately</u>
   A   **B**   **C**
accepted the resolution <u>drafted by</u> the
                   D
neutral states. <u>No error</u>
           E

SAMPLE ANSWER

Ⓐ ● Ⓒ Ⓓ Ⓔ

---

1. Clever film producers <u>expect</u> that people
                  A
will pay <u>more</u> to see an <u>action</u> film <u>than</u>
       B   **C**
<u>they will seeing</u> a documentary. <u>No error</u>
   D   **E**

2. <u>Even though</u> the opening of Karen's store is
   A
<u>set for</u> January 1, she believes that it <u>would</u>
  B   **C**
<u>be</u> delayed <u>because of</u> her son's illness.
          D
<u>No error</u>
  E

3. The employees looked <u>skeptical</u> at their
               A
manager <u>as he told</u> <u>them</u> that the
      B   **C**
conditions at the plant <u>would improve</u> in
                 D
the near future. <u>No error</u>
           E

4. Students who want to be <u>a lawyer</u> should
               A
<u>know</u> that law school is expensive <u>and that</u>
 B   **C**
many lawyers are <u>unhappy with</u> their jobs.
           D
<u>No error</u>
  E

5. Most European <u>countries</u> <u>are committed</u> to
           A   **B**
principles of international law, <u>which</u> in
                  C
some cases take precedence <u>over</u> national
                 D
laws. <u>No error</u>
     E

6. Although <u>they</u> are <u>widely</u> used, standard-
       A   **B**
ized test scores <u>are</u> not <u>reliant</u> indicators of
         C   **D**
a student's academic potential. <u>No error</u>
                    E

GO ON TO THE NEXT PAGE

7. His <u>quick</u> wit and his superior command
  A
of English <u>makes</u> Shakespeare a joy <u>to read</u>,
  B   C
even for students <u>unfamiliar with</u> other
        D
British writers. <u>No error</u>
       E

8. <u>According to</u> my economics professor, a
  A
high sales tax <u>does</u> <u>not always discourage</u>
       B   C
people <u>to buy</u> goods and services. <u>No error</u>
    D   E

9. Though he was asked by many <u>to run</u> for
           A
class president, Michael <u>did not think</u> of
         B
himself <u>as</u> a good <u>candidate</u>. <u>No error</u>
    C   D   E

10. Now that Sally <u>completed</u> her math
       A
homework, she will start <u>to think</u> <u>about</u>
         B C
<u>beginning</u> her report on the <u>history of</u> the
          D
Declaration of Independence. <u>No error</u>
         E

11. The apples that Martin <u>bought</u> for
         A
<u>his sister</u> at the supermarket were not <u>as</u>
  B   C
ripe as <u>the local fruit stand</u>. <u>No error</u>
    D   E

12. <u>Regardless</u> of how <u>careful</u> planes are flown,
  A   B
they <u>need</u> expert pilots <u>to ensure</u> that they
   C   D
reach their destinations safely. <u>No error</u>
         E

13. People who <u>have studied</u> electrical engi-
      A
neering <u>are</u> likely <u>to receive</u> job offers in
     B   C
<u>such fields as</u> computer architecture and
  D
software design. <u>No error</u>
      E

14. A committee of <u>recently</u> <u>elected</u> public
       A B
officials <u>have discussed</u> the mayor's
     C
<u>proposal for</u> the new highway. <u>No error</u>
  D   E

STOP

Directions: The following sentences test your knowledge of grammar, usage, diction (choice of words), and idiom.

> Some sentences are correct.
> No sentence contains more than one error.

You will find that the error, if there is one, is underlined and lettered. Elements of the sentence that are not underlined will not be changed. In choosing answers, follow the requirements of standard written English.

If there is an error, select the <u>one underlined part</u> that must be changed to make the sentence correct.

If there is no error, choose answer choice E.

EXAMPLE:

<u>The other</u> delegates and <u>him</u> <u>immediately</u>
   A   B   C
accepted the resolution <u>drafted by</u> the
                       D
neutral states. <u>No error</u>
             E

SAMPLE ANSWER

Ⓐ ● Ⓒ Ⓓ Ⓔ

1. <u>According to</u> the article, <u>excessively</u> high
     A   B
airline fares may prevent some people

  <u>to see</u> <u>their</u> families during the holidays.
    C   D
<u>No error</u>
  E

2. There has never been a great deal <u>of</u>
                         A

  <u>contact</u> between <u>Richard and I</u>, even
    A   B
though there <u>are</u> several clubs <u>to which</u> we
          C   D
both belong. <u>No error</u>
          E

3. The giant pandas recently arrived from

  China <u>lured</u> a crowd to the zoo, <u>for</u> <u>it was</u>
        A   B   C
unlike anything the public <u>had ever seen</u>
                   D
before. <u>No error</u>
     E

4. Petra <u>has</u> not yet <u>began to</u> work <u>on</u> her
      A   B   C
science project, even though it is due

tomorrow <u>before</u> noon. <u>No error</u>
        D   E

5. Mr. Smith is more a teacher <u>than like</u> a
                      A
principal; he never <u>scolds</u> students <u>but</u>
             B   C
rather <u>helps them become</u> better learners.
          D
<u>No error</u>
  E

6. If one <u>considers</u> all of the <u>possible</u>
        A   B
consequences <u>before</u> taking any action,
         C
<u>you will probably</u> make the right decision.
         D
<u>No error</u>
  E

GO ON TO THE NEXT PAGE

7. Even though I <u>have not known</u> Jason <u>for</u>
                          A   **B**
<u>very long</u>, I consider <u>him</u> <u>my best friend</u>.
B   **C**   **D**
<u>No error</u>
  E

8. My sister looked <u>cautious</u> around the
                       A
entryway, <u>as if</u> <u>she</u> believed she <u>would find</u>
        B **C**   **D**
a stranger in the house. <u>No error</u>
                      E

9. Our school conductor <u>believes</u> that <u>more</u>
                         A   **B**
people will come to hear one of

Beethoven's symphonies <u>than</u> <u>seeing</u> a rock
                      C   **D**
and roll concert. <u>No error</u>
               E

10. Children who want to be <u>a jockey</u> should
                      A
<u>begin</u> taking riding lessons <u>at</u> a young age
B   **C**
and should <u>always wear</u> helmets. <u>No error</u>
         D   **E**

11. Walter's bouquet <u>contained</u> flowers that
                A
<u>were</u> very different <u>to the ones</u> in <u>Alice's</u>
B   **C**   **D**
bouquet. <u>No error</u>
         E

12. My grandfather has <u>noticed that</u> the pain
                A
in his joints is <u>noticeably</u> reduced
            B
<u>whenever</u> it <u>rained</u> before noon. <u>No error</u>
  C   **D**   **E**

13. Even though <u>there were</u> <u>barely</u> no visible
                A   **B**
marks, it was obvious that the tree <u>had</u>
                         C
<u>been struck</u> <u>violently</u>, probably by an axe.
  C   **D**
<u>No error</u>
  E

STOP

DIRECTIONS: In the passage that follows, certain words and phrases are underlined and numbered. In the right-hand column, you will find alternatives for each underlined part. You are to choose the one that best expresses the idea, makes the statement appropriate for standard written English, or is worded most consistently with the style and tone of the passage as a whole. If you think the original version is best, choose "NO CHANGE."

You will also find questions about a section of the passage or about the passage as a whole.

These questions do not refer to an underlined portion of the passage but rather are identified by a number or numbers in a box.

For each question, choose the alternative you consider best. Read each passage through once before you begin to answer the questions that accompany it. You cannot determine most answers without reading several sentences beyond the question. Be sure that you have read far enough ahead each time you choose an alternative.

Memory

[1]

One of our most remarkable human characteristics is our capacity for <u>memory. The</u>
₁
human brain is capable of storing and retrieving reams of information, but how do our brains <u>decide, which</u> memories to keep and which
₂
memories to discard? In order to <u>make the most</u>
₃
of memories retained with the amount of space available for new memories, our <u>brains, you see,</u>
₄
classify each piece of new information as either "trivial" or "important."

[2]

For the most part, "important" information receives top priority, because it is the <u>base or</u>
₅
<u>foundation</u> for all our other memories. Each of these "important" memories <u>are vital</u> to the
₆

1. **A.** NO CHANGE
   B. memory, the
   C. memory; the
   D. memory and

2. **F.** NO CHANGE
   G. decide which
   H. decide that
   J. decide of which

3. **A.** NO CHANGE
   B. measure the quantity
   C. balance the number
   D. weigh the amount

4. **F.** NO CHANGE
   G. brains, for sure,
   H. brains, as a result,
   J. brains

5. **A.** NO CHANGE
   B. base, or foundation;
   C. base, or foundation,
   D. base or, foundation

6. **F.** NO CHANGE
   G. is vital
   H. are being vital
   J. are in use

GO ON TO THE NEXT PAGE →

preservation of our species. [7] The simplest of such memories involve the answers to questions such as "What can I eat?" "Where can I find it?" and "Which animals are dangerous?" These types of memories aid and help basic survival skills. Without them, an individual would be unable long enough to survive to reproduce consequently, his genes would die with him.
       8   9

[3]

    Then, the other category of information is "trivial." Ideas and information we would normally consider worthwhile are still, for the purpose of
                            10
memory, considered "trivial." For example, we can
                         11
look at cultural behaviors by starting with reading,
                         12
writing, and learning to play a musical instrument. While these are all meaningful activities, they are not strictly necessary to our survival. A sizable portion of our memories, is filled by so-called
                         13
"trivial" information that is given a different order of significance.

7. At this point, the author is deciding whether or not to add the following sentence:

Memory, in all its forms, is an area of interest to many brain surgeons.

    Would this sentence be a logical and relevant addition to the essay?
    A. Yes, because it serves to establish a background for the essay.
    B. Yes, because it helps to legitimize the study of memory by mentioning its interest to brain surgeons.
    C. No, because the concerns of brain surgeons are unimportant.
    D. No, because it sheds no new light on the issue of "important" memories.

8. F. NO CHANGE
    G. (Place after *survive*)
    H. (Place after *reproduce*)
    J. (Place after *individual*)

9. A. NO CHANGE
    B. reproduce, and
    C. reproduce and
    D. reproduce so

10. F. NO CHANGE
    G. still for,
    H. still, for,
    J. still

11. A. NO CHANGE
    B. Furthermore,
    C. (Begin new paragraph) For example,
    D. (Begin new paragraph) Furthermore,

12. F. NO CHANGE
    G. which for instance would be
    H. such as
    J. like the ones of

13. A. NO CHANGE
    B. memories is
    C. memories, was
    D. memories, would be

THE PRINCETON REVIEW

The Futurists

[1]

Where can we look for the <u>beginning</u> origin of
                              1
modern art? We might start with <u>the</u> impulse to
                                 2
overthrow tradition and shock the middle class.

The <u>originators</u> of a controversial movement who
        3
wanted to do just that were known as Futurists.

These artists formulated theories about art, and its

role in society, during the <u>first half</u> of the
                            4
twentieth century.

[2]

[1] The Futurist movement began with Filippo

Tommasso Marinetti. [2] He advocated <u>that which</u>
                                       5
<u>was then</u> a revolutionary approach to both the

making of art and its reception by society. [3]

Instead of clinging to the values of an earlier time,

1. **A.** NO CHANGE
   B. starting
   C. start,
   D. OMIT the underlined portion

2. **F.** NO CHANGE
   G. their
   H. it's
   J. your

3. **A.** NO CHANGE
   B. originator's
   C. originator's,
   D. originators'

4. At this point, the author wants to provide specific chronological information about the formulation of Futurist theories. Which alternative does that best?
   F. NO CHANGE
   G. beginning
   H. start of the theory
   J. first three decades

5. **A.** NO CHANGE
   B. what was then
   C. which was then, but not now
   D. that was then, but not now

GO ON TO THE NEXT PAGE

Marinetti's agenda <u>it was</u> emphasized the values
                        6
of originality, change, and innovation. [4] He called
for a sweeping rejection of all the traditional
political, cultural, and social values of the time.
[5] He was an Italian poet and editor who, in
<u>1909 and</u> published a manifesto in the Parisian
  7
newspaper *Le Figaro*. ☐8☐

[3]

Yet, surprisingly, Marinetti and his fellow
Futurists adopted the manner and dress of the
very society they argued against. <u>They being</u> such
                                       9
middle-class items as fancy ties, tailored coats, and
pocket-handkerchiefs, in keeping with the latest
styles. They did so in order to also destroy the
middle-class notion of the bohemian artist, a
label they <u>were seeking</u> to avoid. They wanted
                10
<u>to live free from all conventions</u>.
              11
    The Futurists saw themselves as members of a
future society, in which all the traditions and
cultural habits of the past no longer existed.

6. **F.** NO CHANGE
   G. it is
   H. they found it
   J. OMIT the underlined portion

7. **A.** NO CHANGE
   B. 1909;
   C. 1909,
   D. 1909, and

8. For the sake of logic and coherence,
   Sentence 5 should be placed
   F. where it is now.
   G. before Sentence 1.
   H. before Sentence 2.
   J. before Sentence 4.

9. **A.** NO CHANGE
   B. They, wearing
   C. They wore
   D. They , which wore

10. **F.** NO CHANGE
    G. were sought
    H. was seeking
    J. been seeking

11. At this point, the writer wants to provide
    readers with a general description of the
    Futurists' vision of a life free from all
    conventions. Assuming all are true, which
    alternative does that best?
    A. NO CHANGE
    B. to be free to earn as much money from
       their art as they could.
    C. to invent a new society, in which each
       member created a value system of his
       own.
    D. to discover new techniques in painting,
       sculpture, and poetry.

DIRECTIONS: In the passage that follows, certain words and phrases are underlined and numbered. In the right-hand column, you will find alternatives for each underlined part. You are to choose the one that best expresses the idea, makes the statement appropriate for standard written English, or is worded most consistently with the style and tone of the passage as a whole. If you think the original version is best, choose "NO CHANGE."

You will also find questions about a section of the passage or about the passage as a whole.

These questions do not refer to an underlined portion of the passage but rather are identified by a number or numbers in a box.

For each question, choose the alternative you consider best. Read each passage through once before you begin to answer the questions that accompany it. You cannot determine most answers without reading several sentences beyond the question. Be sure that you have read far enough ahead each time you choose an alternative.

Bathing in Japan

[1]

When I was a young man, I lived in Tokyo for two years. In my time there, I experienced many aspects of Japanese culture, <u>which</u> were all
1
pleasurable in their own way. But if <u>there were</u>
2
<u>anyone who</u> asked me to name my favorite experience, my answer might sound a bit strange—I loved taking baths.

[2]

You see, I lived in an old residential neighborhood. Because the buildings were so old, they did not have the <u>conveniences</u> of a modern
3
shower, let alone a modern bathtub. So every night, I would follow the <u>neighborhood crowd</u> to
4
the local *sento*, or public bath. There, for a small fee, I was able to bathe like a king.

1. **A.** NO CHANGE
   B. in which
   C. that
   D. OMIT the underlined portion.

2. **F.** NO CHANGE
   G. of the people there, there was someone who
   H. anyone
   J. there was a person and this person

3. **A.** NO CHANGE
   B. convenience, like
   C. convenience, that
   D. convenience

4. **F.** NO CHANGE
   G. neighborhoods crowds
   H. neighborhood's crowd
   J. neighborhoods' crowd

GO ON TO THE NEXT PAGE

840 Unit 28 Taking Tests

[3]

The bathing area was enormous. Large faucets were placed along the walls, just below a shelf for your grooming <u>supplies. Soap,</u> shampoo,
5
toothpaste, etc. To wash, I would invert the plastic bucket <u>(which were available in many colors)</u> I
6
brought my supplies in and sit on it in front of one set of faucets. A drain along the wall instantly washed away all the water I used.

[4]

In the center of the cavernous room were two large hot tubs for soaking and relaxing. After bathing, I would walk out onto a lovely outdoor terrace and dry myself off while watching fish swim in a pond the owner <u>were building</u>. Of
7
course, tall shrubs surrounded the terrace, and no one could look within. ☐8☐

[5]

The room had a counterpart <u>right next door.</u>
<u>For female bathers,</u> I knew this because the main
9
entrance had two doors, one for each gender. ☐10☐

5. **A.** NO CHANGE
   B. supplies—soap,
   C. supplies; soap,
   D. supplies soap,

6. **F.** NO CHANGE
   G. (the colors of which were varied)
   H. (bucket choice was up to the individual)
   J. OMIT the underlined portion.

7. **A.** NO CHANGE
   B. having built
   C. was building
   D. being built

8. The writer wants to add another relevant detail to paragraph 4. Which alternative does that best?
   F. Sometimes, even after drying off, I could not resist taking another bath right away.
   G. Cleanliness is considered a virtue in Japan.
   H. However, my favorite experience had to be my time spent on the local trains.
   J. In my family, you had to clean the bathtub very thoroughly after using it.

9. **A.** NO CHANGE
   B. right next door. For female bathers I
   C. right next door for female bathers. I
   D. right next door, for female bathers, I

10. The writer wants to add the following sentence to the essay:

Each of the doors had a banner displaying the Japanese character for the appropriate sex, which I committed to memory on my first visit.

This sentence would fit most logically into Paragraph
   F. 2, before the first sentence.
   G. 3, after the last sentence
   H. 4, before the first sentence.
   J. 5, after the last sentence.

DIRECTIONS: In the passage that follows, certain words and phrases are underlined and numbered. In the right-hand column, you will find alternatives for each underlined part. You are to choose the one that best expresses the idea, makes the statement appropriate for standard written English, or is worded most consistently with the style and tone of the passage as a whole. If you think the original version is best, choose "NO CHANGE."

You will also find questions about a section of the passage or about the passage as a whole.

These questions do not refer to an underlined portion of the passage but rather are identified by a number or numbers in a box.

For each question, choose the alternative you consider best. Read each passage through once before you begin to answer the questions that accompany it. You cannot determine most answers without reading several sentences beyond the question. Be sure that you have read far enough ahead each time you choose an alternative.

Horse Games

[1]

Even though the people of Kyrgyzstan, a nation in Central Asia, <u>which being achieved</u> their independence from the former Soviet Union a decade ago, <u>we</u> are steeped in centuries of their own national identity. The cornerstone of their national consciousness is a relationship with horses that is displayed at all festivals and celebrations.

[2]

Many different races, <u>testing</u> both riding speed and agility, have been passed down <u>like</u> generation to generation. In one game, two riders try to wrestle each other out of the saddle.

[3]

<u>Consequently</u> another horse game is similar to the ball games played in Western <u>countries,</u> Kyrgyz players use quite a different type of ball. In it, two teams of horseback riders try to carry, or

1. **A.** NO CHANGE
   B. achieved
   C. at one time being achieved
   D. OMIT the underlined portion

2. **F.** NO CHANGE
   G. they
   H. it
   J. them

3. **A.** NO CHANGE
   B. testing and proving
   C. with the intention of testing and proving
   D. tested

4. **F.** NO CHANGE
   G. into
   H. from
   J. on

5. **A.** NO CHANGE
   B. Despite
   C. In addition,
   D. Although

6. **F.** NO CHANGE
   G. countries
   H. like countries.
   J. countries and

GO ON TO THE NEXT PAGE ⇒

throw, a weighted goat carcass across their opponent's goal. This game is also far rougher than any of its Western equivalents, in that <u>Western players might enjoy the game as well</u>.
7

[4]

Perhaps the most outrageous of all these traditional horse games is *kesh kumay*, or "kiss the girl." In this game, men are pitted <u>over</u> women,
8
and while the prize is love, the price of failure is scorn. One male and one female rider are set loose on a wide-open meadow, where the male rider tries to catch the female rider and plant a kiss on her lips. The female rider does everything she can to avoid being kissed, and if she is able to do so, she gets to strike her unsuccessful pursuer as a demonstration of her scorn. If, <u>while</u>, the
9
male is successful, the woman is considered unable to resist falling in love with him, as he has proved himself a master of horsemanship, which for the Kyrgyz, <u>is similar to marrying a stranger</u>.
10

11 All of these games aptly demonstrate the proud heritage of the Kyrgyz. These timeless <u>traditions along with</u> their practitioners, will be at
12
the center of national culture for years to come.

7. Which of the following alternatives provides the most relevant and appropriate contrast?
   A. NO CHANGE
   B. Western games are enjoyed around the world.
   C. Central Asian games are usually free from violence.
   D. it has no rules or regulations whatsoever.

8. F. NO CHANGE
   G. to
   H. against
   J. for

9. A. NO CHANGE
   B. as,
   C. however,
   D. OMIT the underlined portion

10. Which of the following alternative clauses would best support the assertion made in the sentence that a woman is considered unable to resist falling in love with a master of horsemanship?
   A. NO CHANGE
   B. is a quality to be shunned at all costs.
   C. is the fastest way to earn a living.
   D. is the most attractive of all achievements.

11. Which of the following provides the best transition from the topic of the previous paragraph to the new topic of this paragraph?
   A. The ancient traditions embodied in such horse games are part of the character of the people of Kyrgyztan.
   B. Many people in Kyrgyztan believe in ghosts.
   C. As can be seen, there are many different horse games in Kyrgyztan.
   D. Very few Western women would consider marrying a stranger.

12. F. NO CHANGE
   G. traditions along with,
   H. traditions, along with,
   J. traditions, along with

DIRECTIONS: In the passage that follows, certain words and phrases are underlined and numbered. In the right-hand column, you will find alternatives for each underlined part. You are to choose the one that best expresses the idea, makes the statement appropriate for standard written English, or is worded most consistently with the style and tone of the passage as a whole. If you think the original version is best, choose "NO CHANGE."

You will also find questions about a section of the passage or about the passage as a whole.

These questions do not refer to an underlined portion of the passage but rather are identified by a number or numbers in a box.

For each question, choose the alternative you consider best. Read each passage through once before you begin to answer the questions that accompany it. You cannot determine most answers without reading several sentences beyond the question. Be sure that you have read far enough ahead each time you choose an alternative.

Jan Cunningham, Preservationist

[1]

Jan Cunningham works for some interesting clients. She works for houses, factories, hotels,
<u>1</u>
and many other types of buildings. She is a historic preservation consultant. <u>It were her job to</u>
<u>2</u>
get these old <u>buildings listed</u> on the National
<u>3</u>
Register of Historic Places. She leads the way in the preservation of New York City's historic land-marks. Jan has been doing this job for <u>much</u> than
<u>4</u>
twenty years.

[2]

<u>Jan tries to ensure that these buildings are</u>
<u>5</u>
<u>recognized for their historical significance</u>. This

1. **A.** NO CHANGE
   B. clients, she
   C. clients. She,
   D. clients, specializing

2. **F.** NO CHANGE
   G. Her job is to
   H. Being her job, it is to
   J. Her job, it being to

3. **A.** NO CHANGE
   B. buildings list's
   C. building's listed
   D. building's lists

4. **F.** NO CHANGE
   G. further
   H. many
   J. more

5. Which of the following alternatives best provides new and specific details about how Jan gets recognition for these buildings?
   A. NO CHANGE
   B. As part of her work, Jan researches the names and family histories of each of the former tenants of the building.
   C. Jan makes the case she can for why these buildings are of historic value.
   D. Jan knows a lot about the buildings.

GO ON TO THE NEXT PAGE ⇒

secures them a special <u>place</u> in American history.
6
The Register is a list of buildings that have played

an important role in the economic, cultural, or

architectural history of this country.

[3]

[1] Owners of commercial buildings receive a

tax break if their building makes it on to the

<u>Register, it was this</u> can save them a lot of money.
7
[2] However, owners of residential buildings that

make it on to the Register do not get a tax break.

[3] What they get is the right to put a plaque on

their building. [4] Many <u>proud, homeowners</u>
8
<u>display this plaque</u> right next to their front

entrance. [9]

[4]

[1] The owner hired Jan because he wants to

preserve the sense of history surrounding the

house. [2] Jan is currently working for the owner

of a 250-year-old farmhouse. [3] It can take up to

a year for Jan to argue successfully on behalf of a

client. [4] However, for a building over two

centuries old, one year does not seem like a long

time at all. [10]

Jan's <u>clients are successfully remarkable</u>. In over
11
twenty years of work, she has never failed to gain

<u>a client</u> a place on the Register.
12

6. F. NO CHANGE
G. place, that of recognition
H. place, which is especially recognized
J. place, these old buildings

7. A. NO CHANGE
B. Register, so that this
C. Register. This
D. Register, this

8. F. NO CHANGE
G. proud homeowners, display this plaque
H. proud homeowners display this plaque
J. proud homeowners, display this plaque,

9. The writer wants to add the following explanation to Paragraph 3:

The plaque lists the year in which the building was built and the year it was added to the Register.

This sentence would most logically be placed:
A. before Sentence 1.
B. after Sentence 3.
C. before Sentence 3.
D. after Sentence 4.

10. Which of the following sequences of sentences will make Paragraph 4 most logical?
F. 1, 2, 4, 3
G. 1, 4, 3, 2
H. 2, 1, 3, 4
J. 2, 4, 3, 1

11. A. NO CHANGE
B. clients' are remarkably successful
C. client's are successfully remarkable
D. clients are remarkably successful

12. The writer wishes to link the essay's opening and closing sentences. Which of these alternatives best achieves this effect?
F. NO CHANGE
G. a client or two
H. a client of hers
J. any of her unusual clients

DIRECTIONS: In the passage that follows, certain words and phrases are underlined and numbered. In the right-hand column, you will find alternatives for each underlined part. You are to choose the one that best expresses the idea, makes the statement appropriate for standard written English, or is worded most consistently with the style and tone of the passage as a whole. If you think the original version is best, choose "NO CHANGE."

You will also find questions about a section of the passage or about the passage as a whole.

These questions do not refer to an underlined portion of the passage but rather are identified by a number or numbers in a box.

For each question, choose the alternative you consider best. Read each passage through once before you begin to answer the questions that accompany it. You cannot determine most answers without reading several sentences beyond the question. Be sure that you have read far enough ahead each time you choose an alternative.

Night of Fire

Imagine it is the year 1833. It is a cold November night and you lie sleeping in bed, <u>where its</u> immersed in the comfort of a dream.
₁
Suddenly, you are awoken by the sound of voices outside your window. You open your eyes to a bedroom awash with flashes of light. <u>It paints</u> the
₂
walls in streaks that pulse with intensity. You <u>crept</u>
out of bed to the window. The voices grow louder₃
as you approach. Outside, everyone from your neighborhood seems to fill the streets, their heads arched toward the heavens, each face illuminated by the night sky. You guess a great storm is passing overhead, but there is no sign of rain. The <u>people's faces</u> are dry. You are compelled to
go out₄ into the street and join the crowd.

Once on the <u>street. You</u> also look up and
₅
cannot believe what you see: the sky above is

1. **A.** NO CHANGE
   B. and you are
   C. you are
   D. OMIT the underlined portion.

2. **F.** NO CHANGE
   G. Its paint
   H. They paint
   J. They paints

3. **A.** NO CHANGE
   B. creep
   C. had crept
   D. were creeping

4. **A.** NO CHANGE
   B. peoples faces
   C. people's face's
   D. peoples eyes

5. **F.** NO CHANGE
   G. street: you
   H. street, you
   J. street—you

GO ON TO THE NEXT PAGE

streaked with light and smoke. [1] It seems the heavens are ablaze with fire. [2] Thousands of brilliant rays of light appear across the sky, disappearing only briefly before being replaced again by a thousand more. [3] You are not sure whether to join them or to remain silent and admire the brilliant scene. [4] Some neighbors gasp, as if they believe the world were coming to an end. 6

The sky continues to emit the strange, glowing flares and one does not move for even a moment,
⁷
paralyzed by the unmatched beauty of the pretty
⁸
night sky. Then, finally, the flashes grow more
intermittent. Slowly, the earth's shimmering ceiling turns black once again. The crowd begins to disband. You remain still as each of them leave
⁹
amazed and return to their homes.

Much later, you will learn that the world was
¹⁰
not in fact ending. You will read about the Leonid meteor shower of 1833, the largest in history. But for now, it is you remaining on the street, simply
¹¹
awestruck and mesmerized by the beauty and trepidation of a cold November, night when the
¹²
world caught on fire.

6. Which of the following sequences of sentences makes this paragraph most logical?
   A. NO CHANGE
   B. 1, 4, 2, 3
   C. 4, 1, 3, 2
   D. 1, 2, 4, 3

7. Which of the choices is most consistent with the style established in the essay?
   F. NO CHANGE
   G. one cannot
   H. you do not
   J. they refuse to

8. Which of the choices best emphasizes how the state of the sky affects the writer?
   A. NO CHANGE
   B. nice
   C. radiant
   D. attractive

9. F. NO CHANGE
   G. they leave amazed and returns to their homes.
   H. they each leave amazed and return to their homes
   J. they each leaves and returns to their homes.

10. A. NO CHANGE
    B. was not, in fact ending
    C. was not, in fact, ending
    D. was not in fact, ending

11. F. NO CHANGE
    G. you remain
    H. remaining there, is you
    J. what is remaining is you

12. A NO CHANGE
    B. trepidation, of a cold, November night
    C. trepidation of, a cold November night,
    D. trepidation of a cold, November night

STOP

Listening and Speaking

29.1 Listening Effectively and Critically

Your ability to listen has important effects on your success in school, sports, jobs, and personal relationships. In this lesson, you'll gain some essential advice on how to improve your listening comprehension.

Listening Actively

When you listen, you need to do more than just hear the words that the person says. Only by listening carefully and actively will you be able to understand, interpret, and respond effectively.

The chart below shows some important types of active listening. Keep in mind, however, that these types of listening cannot really be neatly separated. For any particular situation, you will probably need to use a combination of these types of listening.

Types of Listening

TYPE	EXAMPLE
Empathic listening: understanding and responding to another's feelings	Participating in an informal conversation with an old friend
Critical listening: separating facts from opinions and evaluating the speaker's message	Listening to a persuasive message such as a political speech or a commercial
Reflective listening: identifying main ideas and thinking about their implications	Listening to an informational message, such as a science lecture
Appreciative listening: enjoying and interpreting a performance	Listening to a performance of a play

Particular listening situations differ greatly, yet you can still benefit from understanding general strategies for active listening. The chart that follows presents such strategies.

Strategies for Active Listening

PREPARE TO LISTEN

- Eliminate physical distractions.
- Clear your mind of other thoughts.
- Adopt a positive attitude and an open mind about what you are going to hear.
- Identify the situation and the type of listening called for.

(continued)

Listening and Speaking

Strategies for Active Listening (continued)

LISTEN TO THE MESSAGE
- Focus your attention on what the speaker is saying.
- Maintain concentration by finding something of interest in the message.
- Take notes if the situation calls for it.

INTERPRET THE MESSAGE
- Summarize the message. Identify the purpose of the message and the main ideas or themes.
- Reflect on what you hear. Ask yourself: Does this information sound reasonable? Does it conflict with anything else I know? Is the speaker knowledgeable and reliable?

RESPOND TO THE MESSAGE
- Ask questions.
- Discuss the message.
- Assess the message. What significance or consequences does the message have for you or for others?

Evaluating What You Hear

You can use the Strategies for Active Listening to absorb, understand, and interpret the messages you hear. In certain situations, you'll want to do even more with the information you hear. Some situations—such as persuasive messages and performances of poems, short stories, plays, and other literary works—require you to critically analyze and evaluate what you hear.

Analyzing Persuasive Messages Each day, you are confronted by numerous persuasive messages—from friends, teachers, parents, the media, and other sources. How do you decide when a persuasive message is worthwhile? Use the following criteria to analyze and evaluate persuasive messages.

Criteria for Evaluating Persuasive Messages

- **Purpose.** What is the speaker trying to sell or get people to do?
- **Audience.** To what audience is the message targeted?
- **Facts/opinions.** What are the facts and what are the opinions in the message? Do the facts support the opinions or claims? What facts or opinions are missing?
- **Errors in reasoning.** Does the message contain errors in reasoning, such as overgeneralizations and either/or arguments?
- **Persuasive techniques.** What kinds of persuasive techniques—such as bandwagon appeal, loaded language, celebrity testimonial, and exaggeration—are used in the message? How does the message appeal to people's emotions?
- **Values and biases.** What values or biases does the message reflect? Do these values coincide with yours?
- **Your opinion.** After analyzing the message, what is your opinion of it? Do you agree, disagree, or need more information to make a decision?

Evaluating Literary Performances Some literary works, such as poems and plays, are intended to be read aloud or performed. Many short stories and essays also come alive more fully in a performance. You can use the following Criteria for Evaluating Literary Performances both to evaluate literary performances and to improve your own performance of literary works.

Criteria for Evaluating Literary Performances

- **Voice qualities.** Does the performer effectively use such voice qualities as volume, stress, tone, and articulation to present the work?
- **Body language.** Does the performer use body language—including posture, eye contact, facial expressions, gestures, and movements—to engage the audience and bring the work to life?
- **Literary elements.** What element of the literary work—such as character development, plot, imagery, rhyme, or figurative language—does the performance emphasize? What is the effect of this element?
- **Your rating.** How would you rate the performer's interpretation of the literary work? Why?

Exercise 1

Listen to an oral presentation by a teacher, student, or visitor in your school and apply the Strategies for Active Listening. Then answer the following questions:

1. What kind of listening did the situation call for?
2. Did you take notes? Why or why not?
3. What was the purpose of the message? What were the main ideas?
4. What questions do you have about the message?
5. What is the significance of the message to you or to others?

Exercise 2

Listen closely to a commercial or public service message on the radio. Use the Criteria for Evaluating Persuasive Messages to write an analysis and evaluation of the message. Then present your analysis and evaluation orally to the class.

Exercise 3

Working in a small group, take turns to present and listen to literary performances of a poem, short story, or scene from a play. As you listen, apply the appropriate Strategies for Active Listening. Then use the Criteria for Evaluating Literary Performances to write critiques of the performances. Discuss your critiques in your group and use the feedback you receive—both positive and negative—to improve your performances for a second round of presentations.

29.2 Speaking Effectively

How well you speak can influence your social relationships as well as your success in school and in the workplace. In this lesson, you'll learn how to speak effectively in both informal and formal situations.

Speaking Informally

You speak informally all the time. Whether telling your friends about a movie you saw, explaining the life cycle of a particular plant when called on in class, or giving directions to the mall, you are speaking informally. In such informal speaking, you do not usually plan what you will say, and others might do as much talking as you. The chart below describes some typical informal speech situations.

Tips for Informal Speaking		
TYPE	**DESCRIPTION**	**HINT**
In-person and phone conversations	Conversations are the most common and least formal speaking situations. Subjects are usually spontaneous and varied, and each party both listens and speaks. A phone conversation, however, usually has a more defined purpose.	Letting others speak without interruption helps encourage participation of all those engaged in the conversation. A phone conversation will be more effective if you explain your reason for calling. Be sure to call at a time that is convenient for the person you are phoning and keep the call to a reasonable length.
Announcements	Announcements provide brief, important information about events, meetings, projects, and other such occurrences. Announcements should be clear and give all necessary details.	Encouraging questions after the announcement helps to ensure that you have clearly communicated the necessary information.
Giving directions or instructions	Providing directions or instructions usually involves an explanation of a procedure or process.	Present your points as a series of logical steps. Speak slowly and be sure the listener understands. Encourage the listener to ask questions. You might even ask questions yourself to help your listener understand.

Making Formal Speeches

Formal speeches are prepared, rehearsed, and then delivered at a pre-arranged place and time. Preparing a formal speech is similar to writing a research paper or a persuasive essay; you follow many of the same steps.

Purpose and Audience Once you have a topic, focus on your purpose for making the speech. Do you want to inform your audience, persuade them, or entertain them? You may end up doing all three—an audience that is entertained is more likely to listen attentively, and an audience that hears solid evidence is more likely to be persuaded. But as you start out, write a clear statement of your main purpose, such as "I want to persuade my audience to lower their standard of living to conserve natural resources."

After clearly defining your purpose, identify your audience. Are they suburban teenagers? Are they urban adult professionals? Evaluate what your audience already knows about your topic, even interviewing some of them if possible. What concerns or biases do they have? What misconceptions do you need to dispel? Then think about the level of language that fits your audience. For a formal speech, you'll use standard English, but you may need to tailor your vocabulary to your audience and explain any technical terms you use.

Research Gather facts, examples, and experts' opinions on your topic by conducting library and Internet research, polls, and interviews. After studying the information you gather, formulate a clear, concise thesis statement. Then select accurate, relevant evidence from reliable sources to support your thesis.

Outline Choose a pattern of organization that fits your information. (To review possible methods of organizing an informational speech, see pages 76–77. For a persuasive speech, see pages 270–273.) Outline your information using your thesis as the controlling idea. At this point, consider whether visual aids might be useful in presenting your topic.

Drafts and Revisions Use your outline as a guide to draft your speech, following the standard structure of an introduction, a body, and a conclusion. An old saying about the format for speeches is, "Tell 'em what you're gonna tell 'em—tell 'em—then tell 'em what you told 'em." If you are preparing a persuasive speech, review the appropriate appeals and rhetorical strategies for persuasive writing on pages 270–305.

In your introduction, think of a way to grab your audience's attention. You might consider using humor, telling an interesting story, asking an intriguing question, using a memorable quote, or stating a notable fact.

For your conclusion, you might refer to the method you used in your introduction and provide a twist that sums up your speech. For example, if you began with a question, you might state the question again and give the answer. Whatever method you use, strive for a strong finish that drives home your message. Your last words are the ones your audience will be most likely to remember.

Revise your speech, just as you would any other work of informative or persuasive writing. Then read your speech aloud and make further changes so that it flows smoothly. You have to be able to say what you write. If your sentences are too long, shorten them. If you stumble over a group of words, change them.

Preparation Unless you choose to memorize your speech, you'll need to prepare materials to use during your delivery. Some speakers read from manuscript pages; others speak from an outline or note cards. If you are not required to use a particular method, choose the method that works best for you and your situation. If you read your speech, prepare a double- or triple-spaced manuscript with wide margins. If you choose to speak from an outline or note cards, use your written speech to prepare these materials. Underline topic sentences, number supporting points, and transfer the ideas to an outline or note cards. Be sure to number your manuscript pages, outline pages, or note cards at the top.

Practice Practice your speech a few times in front of a mirror. Then ask a friend or relative to listen to your speech or to videotape it. As you rehearse, pay attention to the points listed in the following chart. Even if you read your speech, be sure to look up often and make eye contact with your audience, especially at the beginning and end of sentences.

Techniques for Delivering a Speech

VERBAL TECHNIQUES
- **Volume.** Speak loudly enough so that everyone in the audience can hear you.
- **Pronunciation.** Speak clearly, pronouncing all the words.
- **Pace.** Speak at a moderate speed, but vary the rate and use pauses to convey your meaning.
- **Tone.** Speak in an animated tone.
- **Emphasis.** Stress important words and ideas.

NONVERBAL TECHNIQUES
- **Posture.** Stand up tall with your head straight.
- **Eye contact.** Make eye contact with people throughout your audience.
- **Facial expressions and gestures.** Vary your facial expressions to reflect what you are saying and use natural gestures to reinforce your ideas.
- **Visual aids.** If appropriate for your topic, use charts, diagrams, graphs, or video clips to enhance your speech and convey important information.

Audience Questions and Comments At the end of your speech, encourage your audience to respond. Answer questions honestly and respectfully. Use the question-and-answer period to clarify misunderstandings, to reiterate points that listeners may have missed, to treat objections, and to learn what may have been unclear in your speech.

Exercise 4

Choose a topic that interests you and prepare, organize, and present an informative or persuasive speech, following the steps described in this section. As you listen to the speeches of your classmates, apply the Strategies for Active Listening presented on pages 849–850.

29.3 Group Participation

You participate in many groups—families, classes, study groups, teams, clubs or organizations, and work groups. To be an active group participant, you need listening and speaking skills as well as an understanding of how to function in a group. In this lesson, you'll learn how to participate effectively in a variety of group situations.

Participating in a Study Group

In a typical study group or discussion group, members have roles, such as leader (or facilitator), recorder, and participants. The leader guides the discussion and keeps the group focused on the topic or task. The recorder takes notes on ideas and records final decisions. The participants contribute ideas, respond to the ideas of others, and vote on decisions. A study group operates most effectively if all members follow the guidelines listed in the chart below.

Guidelines for Participating in a Study Group

- **Be prepared.** Complete any assigned reading or research before the group meets.
- **Focus on the issue.** Don't stray from the main idea by bringing up irrelevant topics.
- **Listen actively.** Make an effort to understand each person's viewpoint.
- **Show respect.** Recognize that each person has something worthwhile to contribute. An effective group draws upon the diversity of its members.
- **State your ideas clearly and concisely.** Don't talk on and on so that others have little chance to speak.
- **Respond constructively to the ideas of others.** Explain why you agree or disagree with someone's idea, providing reasons or evidence. Provide praise and other positive support when appropriate.
- **Encourage everyone to participate.** If someone has not spoken, ask for his or her opinion.

Participating in a Formal Meeting

Most formal meetings follow a modified version of a set of rules known as *parliamentary procedure,* which developed from the procedures of the British Parliament. The book *Robert's Rules of Order* is a standard guide to parliamentary procedure. The United States Congress, state and local governments, and many community organizations base the conduct of their meetings on parliamentary procedure.

Parliamentary procedure promotes orderly, democratic meetings by providing an established order of business and procedures for proposing, discussing, and voting on issues. The order of a formal meeting follows this format.

A Formal Meeting

1. The presiding officer calls the meeting to order.
2. The secretary reads the minutes of the previous meeting.
3. Officers, boards, and/or committees give reports.
4. Members discuss unfinished business from previous meetings.
5. Members discuss new business.
6. Members make announcements that do not require formal action.
7. The presiding officer adjourns the meeting.

According to parliamentary procedure, only one topic is discussed at a time. To introduce a topic for discussion, a member makes a motion, or a proposal for action, and another member seconds the motion.

In general, most of the guidelines for participating in a study group also apply to a formal meeting. In addition, you should become familiar with the standard procedures of the group and adhere to those procedures.

Exercise 5

In a group of five or six students, choose a poem to discuss. Ask a volunteer from the group to read the poem aloud. Following the Guidelines for Participating in a Study Group, share your reactions to the poem and analyze such literary elements as imagery, rhyme, rhythm, and figurative language. Then discuss the oral presentation of the poem, using the Criteria for Evaluating Literary Performances on page 851.

Exercise 6

Attend a formal meeting in which a version of parliamentary procedure is followed, such as a student council meeting or a town council meeting. Take notes on the procedures that the group follows. Use your notes to give a brief oral report to the class.

29.4 Taking Part in an Interview

You are quite likely to take part in a job or college interview soon. Both job and college interviews are two-way exchanges of information that challenge your listening and speaking skills. Prospective colleges and employers are looking for the same thing—likeable, energetic people who have the necessary skills, are eager to learn and willing to work hard, will fit into the environment, and won't drop out or leave soon. The following guidelines will help you in both college and job interviews.

Guidelines for Being Interviewed

Be prepared. Find out all you can about the college or business before you go to the interview. Make a list of questions that can't be answered by your research. Be prepared to answer questions about your skills, interests, assets, school or work experience, goals, and what you're looking for in a school or job.

Make a good initial impression. Arrive on time. Be well groomed but wear comfortable clothes. Shake hands with the interviewer.

Listen actively. Maintain eye contact with the interviewer and listen attentively to what he or she says. If you don't understand a question or a point, ask for clarification.

Answer questions honestly, thoughtfully, and positively. If you need to, take time to think about a question before responding. Be sure to answer just the question asked; avoid straying from the topic.

Present a positive attitude and self-image. Show your interest and enthusiasm.

Use positive body language. Sit up straight and lean slightly toward the interviewer to convey your interest. Don't fidget or stare at the floor.

Thank the interviewer. At the end of the session, thank the interviewer for his or her time. Then send a thank-you letter. If you are genuinely interested in the school or job, use the letter to express your interest.

Exercise 7

Work with a partner and take turns interviewing each other for a specific job of your choice and for admission to a college of your choice. As the interviewer, prepare clear questions and provide feedback on the performance of the interviewee based on the Guidelines for Being Interviewed. As the interviewee, focus on listening attentively and on speaking clearly and effectively as you respond to the interviewer's questions.

Viewing and Representing

By the age of eighteen, the average student has spent more time watching television than learning in a classroom. Television and the other mass media have an immense influence on your life. Whether you are aware of it or not, they help shape your attitudes, values, and behavior. The media not only *reflect* your culture, but they also help *create* it. By developing *media literacy*—the ability to interpret, analyze, and evaluate media messages as well as create your own—you can exert some control over the way media messages shape your thinking and your life.

Except for radio, all the mass media include visual messages, which have their own language just as verbal messages do. Understanding the language of visual messages will help you read and interpret such messages.

Understanding Visual Design

To understand the design of a photograph or illustration, you examine its *composition,* or arrangement of elements. The following chart lists some basic elements in the composition of a photograph or illustration and describes effects that can be achieved by manipulating these elements. The actual effect of an element depends on the overall context of the picture, however.

Elements of Visual Design	
ELEMENT	**SOME POSSIBLE EFFECTS**
Line	Lines can be real or implied. An example of a real line is the edge of a building; a person's gaze can create an implied line. Lines can be used to direct a viewer's attention or to suggest a mood or theme.
Straight lines	Point in a direction or lead the eye to something
Curved lines	Suggest motion, warmth
Vertical lines	Suggest dignity, status, power
Horizontal lines	Suggest peace, stillness
Diagonal lines	Suggest tension, action, energy
Shape	
Circle	Suggests wholeness, lovableness, softness
Square	Suggests firmness, stability
Triangle	Suggests unity and balance or tension
Positioning of subjects	
Center of frame	Conveys stability
Top of frame	Conveys importance, power
Bottom of frame	Conveys subordinance, weakness, vulnerability
Color or tone	
Cool colors (blue, green, gray)	Convey calm, emotional distance

(continued)

Viewing and Representing

Elements of Visual Design (continued)

ELEMENT	SOME POSSIBLE EFFECTS
Warm colors (red, yellow, orange)	Convey energy, vibrance, warmth
Bright colors	Convey joy, action, excitement
Subdued or pastel colors	Suggest innocence, softness, vulnerability
Light tones	Create a happy, playful mood
Dark tones	Convey sadness, mystery, dullness
Light	
Bright light	Draws the eye to a specific area; creates a cheerful mood
Dim light or shadows	Creates a sense of mystery or doom
Texture	
Smooth, flat	Might suggest emptiness or something modern and streamlined
Rough, woven	Might convey wholesomeness, naturalness, a sense of home
Silky, shiny	Might convey a sense of luxury
Space	
Large space around subject	Draws attention to subject; isolates details; can create a sense of openness, vastness, emptiness, loneliness
Little space around subject	Subject seems dominating, overwhelming

To understand how elements of visual design work together in a photograph, study this picture of a high school history classroom, which appeared in a major newsmagazine. Horizontal lines—those created by the desktops in the middle and foreground and the bookcase in the back-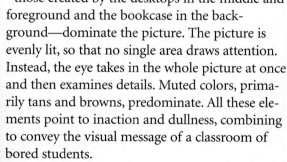ground—dominate the picture. The picture is evenly lit, so that no single area draws attention. Instead, the eye takes in the whole picture at once and then examines details. Muted colors, primarily tans and browns, predominate. All these elements point to inaction and dullness, combining to convey the visual message of a classroom of bored students.

A viewer may look at this photograph and think that the photographer simply captured the reality of the situation. But the photographer made a conscious decision about what to include and what to exclude from the picture. What if the photographer had chosen instead to shoot a close-up of one particular student? Or a shot focusing on the teacher and showing the backs of a few students in the front desks? In the resulting photographs, the impression given of the "reality" of the situation might be different. Every photograph presents one view of reality from a particular perspective.

Look through books and magazines to find a dramatic picture that illustrates something about people and their culture. Use the Elements of Visual Design chart to describe the effects of lines, shapes, positioning of subjects, color, light, and space in the photograph. Summarize what the photograph conveys in general and about people and culture in particular.

Understanding Film Techniques

The basic elements of visual design apply to the media of motion pictures and videos as well as to photographs and illustrations. Motion picture and television directors use a wide variety of film techniques to tell stories and to convey messages. The following chart describes some of these techniques and the effects they can have.

Film Techniques	
TECHNIQUE	**POSSIBLE EFFECTS**
Camera angle	
High (looking down)	Minimizes importance or status of subject
Low (looking up)	Emphasizes importance or power of subject
Straight-on (eye level)	Puts viewer on equal level with subject; promotes identification with subject
Camera shots	
Close-up (magnified view)	Promotes identification with subject
Long shot (wide view)	Establishes relationship between characters and a setting
Reaction shot	Shows effect of one character on another or of an event on a character
Lighting	
High-key (bright, even)	Creates cheerful, optimistic tone
Low-key (producing shadows)	Creates gloomy, eerie tone
Lit from above	Subject seems to glow with significance
Lit from below	May raise audience apprehension
Movement	
Slow motion	Emphasizes movement and heightens drama
Blurred motion	Suggests speed, confusion, or dreamlike state
Editing	
Selection and arrangement of scenes	Sequence of short shots builds tension, creates a rushed mood; sequence of long shots may convey a feeling of stability
Special effects	
Artwork and miniature models	Can be filmed to appear real
Computer enhancement	Can create composite images or distort qualities of a character or scene
Background music	Evokes audience's emotional response; sets mood; reinforces theme

Examine the elements of visual design and the film techniques used in this still from the movie *Titanic* (1997). The dark blue and steely gray of the ocean create a feeling of doom. The low camera angle causes the viewer to look up at the propellers, just as the people in the lifeboat do. The propellers fill the frame behind the people and appear overpowering and dominating, like a huge monster. The light reflecting off the lifeboat draws attention to the boatful of people. The colors, camera angle, positioning of subjects, and lighting all reinforce the theme of the people's helplessness in the face of a monstrous technological disaster. This scene was created through special effects. The picture is a digital composite—the people in the lifeboat were filmed in a tank, and then that film was combined with a shot of a model of the *Titanic*.

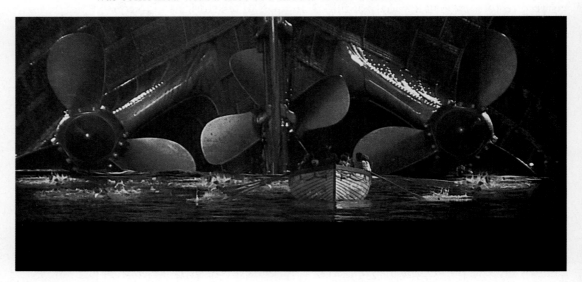

Exercise 2

Select and view a videotape of a movie that was made from a book or story you have read in literature class. Choose two scenes from the movie to analyze. Refer to the Film Techniques chart and take notes on at least two aspects of each scene, such as camera angle and lighting. Use your notes to give a brief oral report to the class, describing the scenes, the techniques used, and their effects.

30.2 Analyzing Media Messages

Photographs, movies, and television programs often seem to capture scenes from life just as they are. But all media messages are constructed for a purpose (typically to inform, entertain, or persuade) and show only a particular view of life from one perspective. Even in a documentary that you might consider strictly factual, a director has made many decisions about how to shoot scenes, what information to include and exclude, and what effects to strive for. The purpose or goal may or may not be worthwhile—that's for you to decide. To make an informed decision, you need to be able to analyze media messages.

Recognizing Forms of Media

Media messages reach you in a wide variety of forms. These forms can be grouped into four main types: print, broadcast, film, and Internet. *Print media* include newspapers, magazines, billboards, books, and other products that convey messages through printed words and images. *Broadcast media* consists of radio and television, in which either just sounds or both sounds and moving images are transmitted to a wide public audience. *Film media* include movies and videotapes, which also consist of sounds and moving images. The *Internet* contains a wide variety of Web sites that consist of some combination of printed words, still and moving images, and sounds.

The form of a media message affects its meaning, or how you interpret it. Watching a baseball game on television and then reading the coverage of the same game on the sports page of a newspaper may give you a different impression of the same game. The Kennedy-Nixon presidential debates of 1960 are a famous example of the influence that a form of media can have on the way a message is interpreted. The majority of radio listeners thought that Richard Nixon won the debate, while most of the television audience believed John F. Kennedy had won. The visual impression that Nixon made differed radically from the verbal impression he gave—enough to change people's opinions.

Exercise 3

Follow the media coverage of a news event of your choice on television, in a newspaper, in a newsmagazine, and on the Internet. Write a brief report comparing and contrasting the coverage in the different media. Consider each of the following aspects in your comparison:

- what information you gain from each form of media
- the perspective from which each medium approaches the subject
- the impression of the event each medium leaves you with
- the unique properties of each medium, and how those properties affect news coverage

Deconstructing Media Messages

Before you form an opinion about a media message—whether it's a TV commercial, an informational Web site, or a popular movie—you need to think about how and why it was created, or constructed. The following chart describes how to **deconstruct** a media message, that is, how to take it apart and analyze how its parts contribute to the overall message.

How to Analyze a Media Message		
IDENTIFY	**BY ASKING YOURSELF**	**EXAMPLE**
• source	Who made this? How does the source affect the message?	A lobbying group for coal companies sponsors an Internet ad that presents global warming as a theory, not a fact. The group has a pro-environment-sounding name.
• purpose	Why was it made? Is it meant to inform, entertain, or persuade?	A documentary on the Alaskan wilderness is informative and entertaining, but its primary purpose is to persuade the audience to support wilderness preservation.
• target audience	Who is the message intended for? How has the content been shaped to appeal to the intended audience?	A TV sitcom is targeted to teenagers. The main characters live in an upper-middle-class suburban home and dress in the latest fashions.
• main idea	What is the intended message?	In a feature article on public high schools, a newspaper article identifies low academic standards as the main problem.
• design elements and/or film techniques	How are design elements or film techniques used to communicate a message or manipulate a viewer's response?	Computer enhancement is used in a cover photo for a woman's magazine to make the model look thinner than she actually is. The thin model sets a beauty standard for women.
• cultural elements	What cultural values and assumptions, stated or unstated, are built into the message?	A U.S. movie portrays a hero who becomes rich and, as a result, gains happiness, reinforcing a cultural emphasis on material success.
• persuasive techniques	What persuasive techniques does the message use, such as glittering generalities, emotional appeals, logical fallacies, loaded language, and celebrity testimonials? Are the arguments persuasive, or do they contain logical fallacies?	Professional athletes endorse a brand of athletic shoes and suggest that their own performance improved after buying these shoes. (false cause-and-effect) Announcer states that everyone using a new shampoo will feel happier and healthier. (glittering generality)
• missing content or viewpoint	What relevant information has been left out? Whose viewpoint has not been heard?	A TV news program reports on declining standardized test scores among U.S. students. The viewpoints of educators who question the relevance and validity of such tests are not discussed.

Use the How to Analyze a Media Message chart to examine a newspaper or news-magazine ad, a TV commercial, or an Internet ad. Create a chart of your own, in which you fill in the third column by answering the questions in the second column.

Form a small discussion group with classmates and consider the following questions. Share the results of your discussion with the entire class.

1. How do the television shows and movies you view affect your perception of reality? For example, how have they shaped your perception of the following:
   - the standard of living that most people in our nation enjoy
   - the most important values that most people in our nation share
   - how a person's success in life should be measured
   - what makes a person happy
2. In general, what values do you think the mass media promote? For example, do they promote any of the values listed below? Support your opinions with facts.
   - an emphasis on self-gratification rather than the good of a larger group
   - instant gratification of personal needs and wants
   - simple solutions to complex problems
   - romantic ideals of truth, justice, and love
   - consumerism
3. How have media messages influenced your values, behavior, and perception of reality? Discuss specific examples.

30.3 Producing Media Messages

Another way to increase your understanding of media messages and the decisions that go into their creation is to produce your own. Creating your own media messages also gives you a way to interact with your culture, not just absorb it.

Making a Video

The creation of a video requires many skills and the cooperation of a group of people. Each group member takes on one or more of the following roles, based on his or her skills and interests.
- **Director:** coordinates the group members and supervises filming
- **Researcher:** finds background information on the topic and the interviewees
- **Scriptwriter:** writes and revises the script
- **Storyboard designer:** prepares a series of simple sketches of each video scene to go along with the dialogue or narration

- **Interviewer:** prepares questions and conducts the interviews
- **Narrator:** provides the spoken commentary by reading the script aloud
- **Camera operator:** films the interviews and other shots

Depending on the size of the group, some members may take on two or more roles. For example, the scriptwriter might also function as the researcher and narrator. Making a video provides an opportunity to try out different roles and learn new skills.

As you plan and produce your video, consider the elements of visual design and the film techniques described in the first section of this unit. Make sure you have a clear focus that can be summarized in a paragraph.

TIPS ON PRODUCING AND PRESENTING A VIDEO

1 BEGIN BY BRAINSTORMING. In your group, consider these questions: Who are the intended viewers? What do they already know or think about the subject? What is the purpose and focus of the video? What information do we need to find out? Who will we interview? What scenes will we shoot?

2 PLAN YOUR VIDEO BY CREATING A STORYBOARD. A storyboard provides a blueprint for shooting your video. It consists of simple sketches of the sequence of scenes you will shoot, with the dialogue or narration. You want your video to tell a story—so create a beginning, middle, and end. Include scenes that set the stage, show the location, or provide details that enrich the story.

3 WHEN YOU SHOOT, VARY YOUR SCENES. Mix long shots that show a location with closer shots that focus on a single subject. Shoot from different angles and heights to achieve different effects. Vary the length of the shots you take as well.

4 PAY ATTENTION TO LIGHTING. Shoot in strong light—outside during daylight or inside near windows and with all the lights on. Set up your own lights if necessary.

5 SHOOT TO EDIT. To make it easier to edit scenes later, leave a little room before and after each scene by letting the camera run. Reshoot scenes that don't turn out well.

6 EDIT TO CREATE A POLISHED FINAL PRODUCT. At the editing stage, you can eliminate bad footage, add music and sound effects, and insert titles. You also can mix short cuts and long cuts to achieve the pacing you want.

7 ASK FOR VIEWER FEEDBACK. After you present your video, ask the audience to fill out a questionnaire or participate in a discussion to give you feedback. Ask viewers to state the main idea of your video and to comment on how effectively it was conveyed. In addition, elicit their comments on the pacing, the camera techniques, and the audio and visual quality.

Working in a small group, choose one of the following video projects to undertake:

- a ten-minute documentary
- an advertisement for a product, service, or political candidate
- an adaptation of a short story

Decide on a topic and agree on roles for each group member. Then work together to plan, write, shoot, edit, and present your video to the class. Elicit feedback by holding viewer discussion groups and by preparing a questionnaire for the audience to complete after viewing your video.

Designing a Web Site

Using a software program or hypertext mark-up language (HTML), you can create a Web site that incorporates striking photographs, graphics, text, and even sound. A good Web site is attractive, informative, and easy to use. For additional background on Web sites, see Unit 31, Electronic Resources, pages 869–889. The following guidelines will help you design an effective Web site.

GUIDELINES FOR DESIGNING A WEB SITE

1 **BEGIN WITH A CLEAR PURPOSE.** Identify your audience and make sure you have something useful to share. Your home page, or main page, should convey what the site is about in a way that gets viewers' attention.

2 **PLAN YOUR SITE BEFORE YOU BUILD IT.** View related sites and brainstorm ideas about what to include and how to present it. Design a layout for each page that is logical and easy to follow, and create a flowchart showing how the pages of your site will be connected.

3 **KEEP THE DESIGN SIMPLE AND CONSISTENT.** Pick just a few colors and fonts for your site. Unify the pages by using the same background color and by repeating a logo (your own "trademark") or icon (symbol) that identifies your site. Talk to friends to evaluate the appeal of your logo or icon. Avoid a busy background that detracts attention from your message. Keep key design features, such as the method of moving around the site, consistent on all the pages.

4 **BE SURE THE SITE IS QUICK TO DOWNLOAD.** Viewers will give up if your home page takes too long to download. Keep the images small enough and few enough so that the page downloads quickly.

5 **MAKE THE SITE EASY TO MOVE AROUND ON.** Use a clear, simple navigation scheme on all your pages. Make all your pages accessible from your home page within four or fewer clicks.

(continued)

Viewing and Representing

6 KEEP THE TEXT SHORT AND EASY TO READ. If you have a lot of information, break it up into short and medium-length sections and put the sections on linked pages. Use a font that is easy to read and a background color that provides enough contrast for reading ease. Carefully proofread and correct all text.

7 TEST YOUR SITE AND REVISE IT. Ask your friends or classmates to visit your site and test how well it works. Make a user-response form based on these guidelines and ask them to complete it.

Exercise 7

Working in a small group, plan and create a Web site for your school. Use the Web site shown above as a model, or design a site all your own. Decide what you want visitors to the site to know about your school, such as where it is, what classes are offered, and what different groups and cultures are represented. Ask friends to visit your Web site and complete a form critiquing the site. Analyze the responses you receive, reflect on changes you might make to improve the site, and revise your site as necessary.

Viewing and Representing

UNIT 31
Electronic Resources

31.1 Word Processing

Word processing is not just for writing papers. As you become familiar with more uses of the computer, you will realize that word processing is used in many ways in computer technology. An e-mail message is word processed and then sent. When you add text to a graph, you need to know how to word process. Presentation software also includes a word processor, as do database programs and spreadsheets. Fortunately, many of the familiar word processing commands and techniques carry over to other software programs. The more expert you are at word processing, the better you will be able to navigate in the world of computer technology.

Word Processing Across Applications

Word processing is more than simply typing words on the computer. Most programs include similar drafting, editing, and publishing features. Compare the following menu bars and toolbars from three different types of programs.

From a Word Processing Program

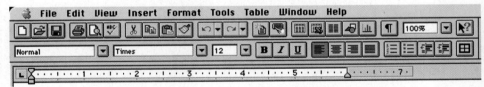

From a Spreadsheet Program

From a Presentation Program

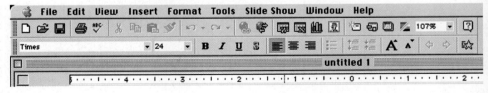

Although each program has its own unique tools, you can see many similarities. All offer users the ability to use similar typefaces, such as Times Roman and Arial, and styles, such as **bold,** *italic,* and ***bold italic.*** In each program, you can use similar tools to change the size of the type, adjust spacing, set different types of margins, and much more. There is a consistency to the word processing tools no matter what the application.

Keyboard Shortcuts In addition to the similarities in the toolbars, there are also similarities in the keyboard shortcuts that you can use. While you can become fairly speedy with the mouse, it is helpful to understand that the notations on the right side of the pull-down menus indicate the keystrokes, or shortcuts, that will perform the same actions as a menu item. For example, there is more than one way to cut and paste.

From a
Word Processing Program

Edit	View	Insert	For
Undo Typing			⌘Z
Repeat Typing			⌘Y
Cut			⌘X
Copy			⌘C
Paste			⌘V
Paste Special...			
Clear			Clear
Select All			⌘A
Find...			⌘F
Replace...			⌘H
Go To...			⌘G
AutoText...			
Bookmark...			⌘⇧F5
Links...			
Object			
Publishing			▶

From a
Spreadsheet Program

Edit	View	Insert	Format
Undo Typing "44" in A1			⌘Z
Can't Repeat			⌘Y
Cut			⌘X
Copy			⌘C
Paste			⌘V
Paste Special...			
Paste as Hyperlink			
Fill			▶
Clear			▶
Delete...			⌘K
Delete Sheet			
Move or Copy Sheet...			
Find...			⌘F
Replace...			⌘H
Go To...			
Publishing			▶
Links...			
Object			

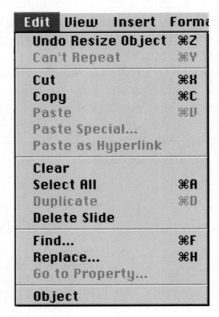

**From a
Presentation Program**

Method 1—using the menu:
- Use the mouse to highlight the text you want to move.
- Pull down the **Edit** menu and click on **Cut.**
- Move the cursor to the place where you want to input the text.
- Pull down the **Edit** menu and click on **Paste.**

Method 2—using keyboard shortcuts:
- Use the mouse to highlight the text you want to move.
- Macintosh: press the **Command** key and the *x* key at the same time to cut. Windows: press the **Ctrl** [control] key and the *x* key at the same time to cut.
- Move the cursor to the place where you want to input the text.
- Press **Command** (or **Ctrl**) and the *v* key at the same time to paste.

There are still more ways of doing the same thing. With most software, you can select the text you want to move and, while holding down the mouse button, drag the text to a new position and release the mouse button. This procedure is called click and drag. In addition, your function toolbar probably has cut, copy, and paste icons you can click on to perform the operation, and the function (F) keys across the top of your keyboard, provide cut and paste capabilities. One of the great things about word processing is that there are often several ways to perform an action, and you can choose the way that best suits you.

Electronic Resources

Memorizing keyboard shortcuts for frequently used word processing functions will help you save time and become more efficient in your writing. They will also give your mouse hand a rest from repetitive wrist and hand movements that can lead to serious aches. These keyboard shortcuts are included in many programs you are likely to use. Learning to use them is similar to learning to touch-type. Although touch-typing is not a requirement, the better typist you are, the better able you will be to concentrate on your writing rather than on the act of typing.

Exchanges Across Applications Make your software programs work together by transferring information from one application to another. If you are most comfortable creating text with your word processing program, you may want to continue to do all your text creation that way. But you often need to use another program, perhaps a desktop publishing program to create a brochure. No problem! You can cut and paste copy from the word processing document to the desktop publishing program. Similarly, graphics such as artwork and graphs can be copied from the software that created them (or from Internet downloads) and pasted into a word processing document. There's no end to the possibilities of cross-application exchanges because these options are built into most software.

Exercise 1

To learn more keyboard shortcuts, find a list of them through an Internet search. As keywords on your browser, try "Mac" or "Windows" (depending on which operating system you use), followed by "keyboard shortcuts." Explain a few of the shortcuts you find for the class. The class may wish to compile a list of those they find most useful.

Revising and Editing Your Writing

You know that good writing is largely a matter of revising and editing. Your word processing program probably has tools, such as spell checkers and grammar checkers, that will help you in the revising and editing stages. In addition, many word processing programs offer a Track Changes tool that can be found under **Tools** on your toolbar. If you choose **Track Changes/Highlight Changes,** you will see onscreen all changes, deletions, or additions you make in a document. You can also choose **Compare Documents** under the **Tools** menu and compare what you are currently working on with a previous version. The illustration below shows what a paragraph might look like if the changes had been tracked.

TIME
For more about the writing process, see **TIME Facing the Blank Page,** pp. 111–121.

Rules at the side indicate lines with changes

Strikethrough indicates deletion

Word processing is ~~much~~ more than ~~just~~ simply typing <u>words on the computer.</u> Most programs include similar drafting, editing, and publishing features. Compare the <u>following</u> menu bars and toolbars from <u>three</u> different types of programs.

Underline indicates addition

Electronic Resources

Publishing

After hours, or even days or weeks, of research, writing, and editing, your writing project is done. Yet it looks somewhat plain. Word processing programs offer you many options for making your work look better. Experiment with different type styles—for example, you can make the title bold and your name italic, or you can use bold and italic to emphasize a particularly important point. Change the size of the type, add bulleted items, or put lists into columns. These are only a few of the things you can do to change your work's appearance. Most programs also allow you to add illustrations (such as photos, artwork, graphs, and maps) to your work.

Many word processing programs also include some of the features of more complex desktop publishing programs. These features allow you to design professional looking newsletters and brochures. The program may include style templates with attractive layouts you can use or adapt to meet your needs. Working with classmates, you can collaborate on an attractive booklet of class writings, including full-color illustrations if you have access to a color printer.

Choosing Typefaces

There are literally thousands of different typefaces. They break down into two broad categories: those with serifs (the little lines at the edges of letters) and those without serifs. The serifs are more traditional and thought by some to be easier to read. San serifs are more modern and clean looking, which makes them good choices for bold headings. Here are a few examples of each type.

Serif Faces	San Serif Faces
Times Roman	Frutiger
Garamond	Helvetica
Palatino	Univers

Find out how many typefaces you have access to on your computer and try them out.

Create a Template The illustration on page 875 shows a **template** for a page. A template is a grid used as the basic layout guide in the design of a page. This one is for the first page of a newsletter. The later pages would have their own templates, possibly only a single one for all inside pages. This template was created using only the functions available on a word processing program.

The broken-line boxes you see on the example would not appear in the printed page. They are there only to indicate the various blocks of type or graphics that will go onto the page. The text in the template serves only to show what a complete page will look like and to help the user know what goes into each field. (A **field** is a shape, usually a box, on a template that defines an area into which text or art can be inserted.)

Electronic Resources

KENNEDY HIGH SENIORS'

CLASS NEWSLETTER

Month 2000   Vol. 0, No. 0

Place Headline for Lead Story Here.

Text for lead story begins in column one and continues through this column and the next column. Text is justified—flush left and right.

Text for lead story begins in column one and continues through this column and the next column. Text is justified—flush left and right.

Text for lead story begins in column one and continues through this column and the next column. Text is justified—flush left and right.

Text for lead story begins in column one and continues through this column and the next column.

Heading (if necessary)

Text for lead story begins in column one and continues through this column and the next column. Text for lead story begins in column one

PHOTO
OR
ART
Depth can vary.

Caption for photo or artwork if needed. Two-line maximum. Text is 10 pt. Arial, ragged right.

and continues through this column and the next column.

Text for lead story begins in column one and continues through this column and the next column. Text for lead story begins in column one and continues through this column and the next column. Lead story continues to page three if necessary.

Second Story Heading Here

Byline

Number two story begins here and continues on page two. Text is justified—flush left and right. Number two story begins here and continues on page two. Text is justified—flush left and right. Number two story begins here and continues on page two.

Text is justified—flush left and right. Number two story begins here and continues on page two. Text is justified—flush left and right.

Continued on page 2

Inside . . .

- Teaser with bullets for one or two stories inside. Text is set flush left and ragged right.

- Teaser with bullets for one or two stories inside. Text is set flush left and ragged right.

Electronic Resources

Your word processing software may include ready-made templates for different types of writing, such as a newsletter, a business letter, a report, and a résumé. To create a template yourself, start with some sketches that include all the things you want to see on a page. In the case of a newsletter, include the masthead (which shows the newsletter's title and information about the volume, number, and date), each column of text, and places for photos or art. When you are satisfied with your design, use your word processing program to build your template. The program should include a pop-up art menu that allows you to create text fields and art fields. You can go to the Help menu to get further help in creating such a template.

Once your template is complete, you can use it to create new issues of your newsletter (or whatever other publication you design it for). Just give the template a name ("Newsletter Template," for example) and store it on your hard drive. When you want to create an issue, open the template document, rename it ("Newsletter April 2002," for example), and replace all the type currently on the document with your copy for the new issue. After you rename it (using the Save as function), the original template document will remain unchanged, ready to be used again.

Exercise 2

Work together to create a collection of class writings. Include works of fiction, poetry, news reports, opinion pieces, reviews, and other writings. Have someone act as editor in chief; a few other students can be copy editors. Another group can take responsibility for designing and publication, making templates, and laying out the text and graphics. Also try to include advertisements (even if they are fictional) and illustrations. Print copies on a printer and distribute them to class members.

31.2 Finding Information

We live in the information age, when technology makes it possible to find, retrieve, and send data almost instantaneously. Therefore, a premium is placed on what you know, how adept you are at getting information, and how well you can express yourself. The Internet and the World Wide Web are increasingly important vehicles for gaining this knowledge and communicating.

The Internet

The Internet mirrors society: There are government sites, educational sites, business sites, communities of like-minded people, and even military sites. Although the World Wide Web, the most-used part of the Internet, is enormous, it is highly organized. Every Web site has a domain name. Typed into your browser's address or "go to" window (located under the toolbar), the domain name will take you to a specific site. Following is a typical Web address, or URL (Uniform Resource Locator), that will take you to a particular page of a domain.

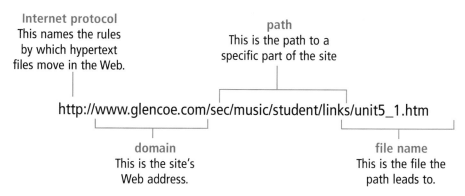

Internet protocol
This names the rules by which hypertext files move in the Web.

path
This is the path to a specific part of the site

http://www.glencoe.com/sec/music/student/links/unit5_1.htm

domain
This is the site's Web address.

file name
This is the file the path leads to.

Domain names end with a suffix that identifies the category the site belongs to. For instance, the Glencoe site has the suffix *.com*, which indicates that it is a commercial, or business, site. As you conduct your Internet search, be aware of the site suffixes. At the very least, these suffixes will give you a clue as to the identities of the people who own the sites.

Site Categories	Suffix
Commercial	.com
Education	.edu
Government	.gov
Organizations	.org
Military	.mil
Network Organizations or Internet Service Provider (ISP)	.net

The key to finding what you want on the Internet is the use of search tools. You don't need any extra software for these tools; they are on Internet sites of their own waiting to be used. To get to one, just copy its URL into the address window of your browser and hit your Return (or Enter if you use Windows) key.

Search Engines Search engines allow you to use keywords to locate sites with the information you want. For example, suppose you want to find information about colonial missions in Texas. You could go to the main page of a search engine and type "colonial missions" in the keyword window. The quotation marks tell the engine to look for the two words as a phrase. Otherwise, you would get hits for sites that used only the word "colonial" and other sites that used only "missions", neither of which might meet your needs. To avoid getting information about colonial missions in states other than Texas, you could add "Texas" as another keyword and put a + before it. The plus sign tells the search engine that you want only sites that include both "colonial missions" and Texas.

There are more tricks to doing an intelligent keyword search. However, since each search engine may differ slightly from the others, go to the search engine site and look for notes on searching in its Help menu.

Subject Directories Subject directories can also be used to conduct keyword searches, but their real strength lies in their hierarchies of subject listings. A subject guide works like this:

- On its home page is a list of about a dozen broad areas, such as computers, education, government, and science.
- Clicking on one of these subjects brings up a more detailed list within that subject area and possibly some specific sites as well. For example, click on Computers and you'll get a new screen with a list of subtopics, such as Internet, Programming, Software, and Technology News. A list of some specific sites may follow that.
- Click on a subtopic, and the next screen will have a list of subtopics of the subtopic you clicked on plus another group of sites. For example, click on Software and the new list might include software topics such as Business, Education and Reference, and Graphics. Clicking on Graphics, in turn, might lead you to such topics as Animation, Clip Art, and Exhibits.

A subject directory is particularly useful when you are searching for a topic to write about. It allows you to explore a subject by continuously narrowing the focus and, at the same time, suggesting some specific sites.

Remember that using the Internet is a process. Keep your eyes open as you conduct your search. You may unexpectedly find valuable information while searching for something different. Follow the links and trails as you explore. The list on page 879 provides the names and URLs of some leading search engines and subject directories.

Electronic Resources

Search Engines	URL (all begin with http://)	Features
Alta Vista	www.altavista.com	One of the most comprehensive search engines
Excite	www.excite.com	Includes "search for more documents like this one" option; can search for ideas or concepts
HotBot	www.hotbot.com	Includes choices to search the news, companies, or newsgroups
Infoseek	www.infoseek.com	Offers guides to subjects of popular interest
Lycos	www.lycos.com	Offers subject directory options to narrow your search
MetaCrawler	www.metacrawler.com	A meta-search engine; searches through several other search engines

Subject Directories	URL (all begin with http://)	Features
About.com	www.about.com	Offers more than five hundred guides, each of whom takes responsibility for sites on a specific subject
The Argus Clearinghouse	www.clearinghouse.net	Lists sites by topic; offers ratings of each site
Yahoo!	www.yahoo.com	Contains topics that are well geared toward student research

Bookmarks Bookmarks (one of the two most-used browsers calls them "favorites") can be a shortcut that will make researching via the Internet infinitely easier. Bookmarks provide a way of mapping your research and keeping track of your sources. As you conduct your search, create a bookmark for every site that is particularly interesting or that might not be useful now but could be in the future. Just pull down the bookmark menu to save a bookmark. Saving puts a file of the site's URL on your hard drive so that you can return to the site quickly by clicking on its name in the bookmarks menu.

Exercise 3

Visit the sites of at least three of the search engines and subject directories listed above. Try a few searches on each one. Then use either "search engine" or "subject directory" as keywords in one of the search engines to find a search engine or subject directory not included on the list. Visit that new site and evaluate it. Compare your findings with those of your classmates.

Electronic Resources

E-mail

E-mail is one of the most-used features of the Internet. It's a great way to collaborate with someone else on a project. You can exchange messages with anyone in the world who has an e-mail account. The great advantage of e-mail is that whether you are collaborating with a student across town or a student in Australia, your messages will get there sooner than by regular mail. They travel to their destination in a matter of seconds. You can also attach documents, pictures, video clips, and audio clips to an e-mail message.

Remember, since e-mail messages are word processed documents, you can compose them in your word processing software and then copy and paste them into the e-mail message when you are online. You will cut down on telephone costs and compose the best messages possible. You can even do a spelling check before sending a message.

Exercise 4

Find a photograph that you like and write a short piece about it. (A good source for downloadable photos is the Library of Congress: http://www.loc.gov/) Using e-mail, send the document and a copy of the photo to a friend or classmate. Have your correspondent comment on your writing and e-mail the comments back to you. If you are not sure how to send a picture file via e-mail, use the help function of your e-mail software to find directions for adding attachments to a message.

Chat Rooms and Newsgroups

Chat rooms and newsgroups are another possible source of information available on the Internet. Chat rooms are sites on which people with a similar interest can gather and hold a conversation by writing and responding to messages that all online members can see. Since a chat room functions in real time and there are several people conversing via computer simultaneously, be succinct and clear in your comments.

You must also be aware that the information available in chat rooms is likely to be mostly opinion. Take everything you read with a grain of salt. Unless you know the person you are chatting with is an authority, it's not a good idea to use that person's information in a report (or anywhere else) without getting confirmation from another source.

A newsgroup is rather like a chat room in which ideas and information are exchanged not in real time but by way of e-mail. Once you know what you are interested in, try looking for a newsgroup devoted to that topic. There are thousands of newsgroups, and chances are good that you can find at least one devoted to a topic that interests you.

If you are new to chat rooms and newsgroups, take time to learn something about them before you plunge in with comments or questions. A site will almost always have a hyperlink to a FAQ (Frequently Asked Questions) page. Click on it. It will help keep you from appearing to be a "newbie," a newcomer who bothers the old timers with questions that have been asked and answered previously. Read the FAQs—and the site's list of rules and regulations if it has one—and observe for a while before you get active.

CD-ROMs & DVDs

Some of the information you need may not be available on the Internet. However, information can also be gathered from specific software packages on CD-ROMs (compact disc–read-only memory). CD-ROMs can contain video clips, animation, and sound as well as text and are placed directly into a drive on your computer. Entire encyclopedias, both general and topical, are contained on CD-ROMs, as are databases and, of course, computer games. Check your school or local library to see whether they have a list of CD-ROM references you can use for your research.

DVDs (digital videodiscs) represent a more advanced technology. In fact, the video and audio capabilities of DVD software are so great that with a DVD you can view an entire full-length movie on your computer. It's likely that DVD drives, which can also play CD-ROMs, will eventually replace CD-ROM drives on computers.

Exercise 5

Pick a hobby or an extracurricular activity and research it on the Internet. List the appropriate sites you have found. Create an evaluation form and evaluate the sites. If you can, include chat rooms or newsgroups among your sites. Exchange this information via e-mail with a friend or fellow student.

Electronic Resources

31.3 Communicating Visually

Before computers, people in charge of design and layout for books and other printed matter had to painstakingly sketch out their design specifications. Type then consisted of pieces of lead that were individual letters and spaces set by hand or single lines of text cast in one piece by a keyboard-operated machine. Changes were costly and not encouraged. However, now we have computers with powerful software programs that offer a myriad of layout possibilities. Making changes is relatively simple, and you can easily add and delete design elements. Keep in mind that designers want to create a look and feel, while writers and editors want to keep text readable and ideas clear. When you, or a group of you and others, work on a project, try to balance readability and an attractive design.

Design Elements

Graphic designers follow some of the following simple rules that you can apply to your work.

- Keep it simple, especially if you are new to design work. You can do almost anything with your computer, but don't get carried away. Just because you *can* do it doesn't mean that you *should* do it.

- Do not use multiple fonts in a sentence or paragraph. Choose an attractive typeface in a readable size for your basic text and stick with it.

- Do not use too many different typefaces. In addition to the typeface for your basic text, you might choose a second one for headings and a third if you have something like boxed sidebars in your work. There's seldom any reason to go beyond that limit.

- Use lists to make ideas easy to understand and access. Word processing software allows you to make numbered or bulleted lists easily, sometimes with the click of a button.

- Balance your text with headings and graphics to make it more readable.

Many of the rules are common sense, and you do not need sophisticated publishing software in order to follow them. Your word processing program should allow you to use all of these ideas. Adding them to your writing is as easy as the press of a mouse button.

Design Elements

Using four simple design elements, you can give your published work a polished look that will appeal to your readers.

Contrast Nothing looks duller than a page on which everything looks the same—a mass of black type on white paper. Contrast breaks up the gray look of a dull page. Boldface headings contrast with normal type. Larger display type contrasts with smaller text type. Color contrasts with black and white, and, of course, different colors contrast with one another. Wisely used, and not overdone, contrast can make your pages look interesting, even dynamic.

Repetition When elements are repeated on a page or a two-page spread, they give the page or spread a uniform appearance. Headings that break the text into parts that are of equal importance, for example, should be similar in size and style. Graphics—graphs or tables, for example—should be done in a similar style throughout a report or an article. Icons or other ornaments can be repeated regularly throughout a work. Color schemes should also be similar.

Alignment All the elements on a page should align in a sensible way. This does not mean that everything must align at the left or right margin, but indentations should be used systematically and for a purpose. Don't just fling elements around without thinking about how they affect the appearance of the whole page or, in the case of a booklet, two facing pages.

Grouping Related elements should be placed near one another. Proximity makes your material easier to read and helps the reader understand the organization of your content.

Graphics and Writing

The greeting card industry is enormous: each year people buy millions of congratulations cards, birthday cards, thank you cards, cards to just say hi, and many others. Part of the reason is the power of the images on the cards. They enhance and emphasize the written statements on the inside. Visual images—photographs, drawings, cartoons, graphs, and tables—enrich your writing. Images also help with difficult explanations.

Suppose you were writing about the growth of newborn babies. When you describe the growth increments in writing they seem exceedingly small. You can write about how a baby gained nine pounds in three months, but a graph such as the one on the next page shows more dramatically the rapid increase in weight as the baby matures. It also allows for an easy comparison of two children's growth.

Two Children's Growth: First 3 Months

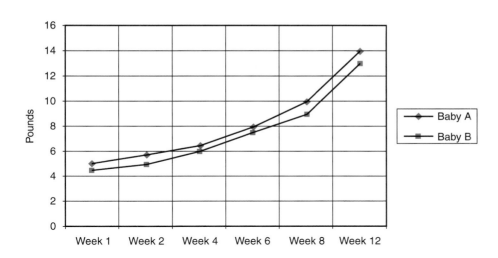

The use of a computer in writing allows you to include such graphic elements. You simply create, copy, and paste in the same way that you copy and paste text. The various creative software programs all have additional tools, such as paintbrushes for color, circle and square makers, and an ability to add text. Following is a picture of a sample graphics program toolbar.

Most graphics programs are relatively easy to use, but it may take practice to feel comfortable with some of the drawing tools. As with your writing, you can save different versions and cut and paste until you get what you want. These programs come with manuals, guidelines, templates, and a Help function that provides answers to frequently asked questions.

Graphic Explanations

Sometimes when simple description fails you, a graphic will help. It may be difficult to describe the organization of a company. It's much easier to see the relationship between departments and individuals in an organizational chart. A sample is shown on page 886. Note how the relationships are shown. You can tell at a glance to whom each person reports. Note, too, how color is used to show different departments and different levels within a department.

Multimedia Experts, Inc.

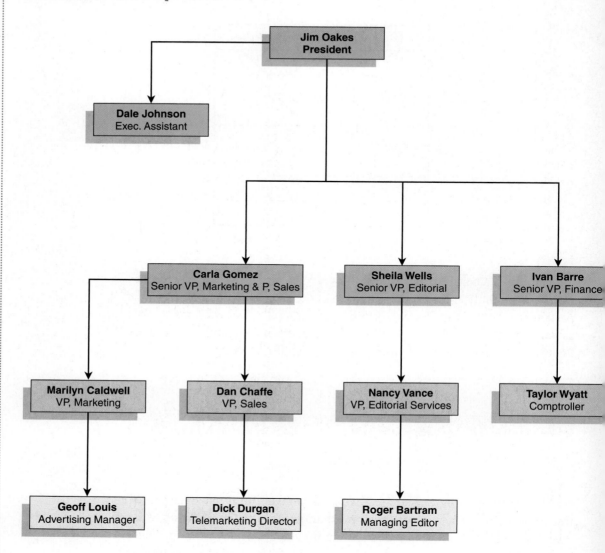

Jim Oakes
President

Dale Johnson
Exec. Assistant

Carla Gomez
Senior VP, Marketing & P, Sales

Sheila Wells
Senior VP, Editorial

Ivan Barre
Senior VP, Finance

Marilyn Caldwell
VP, Marketing

Dan Chaffe
VP, Sales

Nancy Vance
VP, Editorial Services

Taylor Wyatt
Comptroller

Geoff Louis
Advertising Manager

Dick Durgan
Telemarketing Director

Roger Bartram
Managing Editor

The best way to gain a better understanding of the power of graphics is to experiment. Try creating different graphs with the same information to help you see the differences and understand how different concepts can be illustrated.

Exercise 6

Working with a group, think of a company that you could start. Then create all the items you would need to run a business—a name, a logo, business cards, letterhead, a half-page advertisement, and a two-page company profile. Have a class competition, with a panel of student judges. See which designs are deemed the best.

31.4 Producing in Multimedia

Writing reports used to be relatively dull work. You wrote a piece and put it in a nice binder with a cover page. Businesses depended on slides and overhead projectors for presentations. It was difficult to include graphics or images, and both slides and transparencies were produced off-site. Making changes was difficult and time consuming.

Personal computer technology has made these difficulties a thing of the past. Presentation software allows you to create slide shows that can be viewed on a computer monitor. Transparencies can be made with computer software and printed on transparency paper with a laser printer. You can scan in pictures, create graphs, and include images on every page. You can even make changes up to the last moment.

Types of Multimedia Productions

Multimedia is the merging of text with sound (speech, music, sound effects) and images (photos, graphics, video clips) for a presentation. Productions can be as relatively low-tech as a slide show with a tape recorder or as high-tech as your own Web page with QuickTime video and audio clips. Currently there are several different software packages that create slides or cards that can be linked together for a multimedia production.

Here are three relatively easy ways to create a multimedia production.

Hardware & Software	How to Use
Camera, slide or overhead projector, screen, and tape recorder.	Use 35-mm slides or overhead transparencies for the visuals (text and images). Use a tape recorder for narration, music, or other sounds.
Computer with presentation software (PowerPoint or Persuasion) and a microphone.	Use presentation software to create a computer-based slide show combining text, graphics, images, and sound.
Computer with hypertext software (HyperStudio, HyperCard) and a microphone.	Use a hypertext program to combine text, graphics, images, and sound to create a series of cards that can be viewed in sequence.

You can also include scanners, digital cameras, video cameras, and other drawing and graphic programs to the hardware and software list. The more sophisticated the equipment, the more sophisticated the production.

Multimedia Techniques

There are two kinds of multimedia productions. One is an author-controlled piece in which the user/viewer follows the path that the author has predetermined. The other is a more open-ended production with links that allow the user/viewer to navigate a compendium of material. Either kind is a good choice. Which kind is selected depends on the subject matter and how and what the author wishes to create.

For example, if you were hired to do a multimedia production for a political candidate, you would want to control the subject matter. You would want to focus on the candidate's background, the issues, the candidate's previous experience in office, and perhaps his or her voting record. You would want to include family pictures, sound bites from speeches, and perhaps a photograph of the candidate with the president or another important political figure. It would be important to present a certain image, and you would not want people to deviate from what you had created. This would be an author-controlled production.

However, if you were hired to author a production on a certain piece of legislation, you might want the viewers to explore and learn on their own. You would include the text of the bill, possibly with hyperlinks to explanations of the bill's parts. You would also include information about both sides of the issue, sound bites from rallies and debates over the bill, and photographs of supporters. You might even offer links to a history of the piece of legislation or information about similar bills and their successes or failures. The users would navigate this production, deciding for themselves which links to follow and in what order.

Creating a Project

Beginning a multimedia project is the same as beginning a piece of writing. Start by creating an outline and then expand your outline into a storyboard. Think about the look and feel of your project. Decide whether the goal is to entertain, to inform, or to persuade. Then add details to your script. You can do it all with word processing software.

Once the script is completed, cutting and pasting it into your presentation software is easy. Think of each slide as a chance to present a single thought or idea. Do not overload the slide with too much information. If there are tangential items you want to add, think about making them links that the viewer can choose to read and explore. When the images are particularly powerful, you may not need any text. You may use a narrator for some segments rather than use written text. Create a title slide to begin your presentation and include a segment at the end to credit your sources.

Evaluating a Project

For a larger or complex presentation, you may wish to collaborate with several others, dividing the work among the group. Even when you are working alone, you may wish to collaborate with a friend to make sure you have accomplished your goal. What an author thinks is obvious is often not so to the viewer. You may have left out information or provided too much information. Once you have gone through your presentation, set up a dress rehearsal with a friend. First, create an evaluation sheet your friend can use. You might want to include some of the following questions.

✔ Does the project flow?
✔ Are the ideas easy to understand?
✔ Are there enough images and sound bites?
✔ Are you able to navigate through all the links?
✔ Are there too many fancy cuts and fades that are distracting?

Once your critic has gone through the production alone, go through it together. Talk about what your viewer liked or disliked and why. Listen to the comments and try not to take them personally. Remember, any criticism is meant to help you improve your work. Also view other people's work and note what you like or dislike; adapt the positive elements into your project.

Like many other skills, being a good multimedia producer takes practice.

Exercise 7

Choose a poem you like and, together with another student, turn it into a multimedia production. Include the text of the poem, with each stanza on a separate sheet or slide if the poem is long. Illustrate the events that are happening and provide necessary historical background and background on the poet. If you're using presentation software, create hyperlinks so viewers can determine how they will navigate through your presentation.

WRITING AND LANGUAGE
GLOSSARY

This glossary will help you quickly locate grammatical and other terms useful for writers.

A

Abstract noun. *See* Noun.

Action verb. *See* Verb.

Active voice. The form of a verb used when the subject of the sentence performs the action.

Adjective. A word that modifies a noun or pronoun by limiting its meaning. An adjective may tell *what kind, which one, how many,* or *how much.* Adjectives appear in various positions in a sentence.
  The **positive degree** is the simple form of the adjective. (*tall, difficult, bad*)
  The **comparative degree** compares two persons, places, things, or ideas. (*taller, more difficult, worse*)
  The **superlative degree** compares more than two persons, places, things, or ideas. (*tallest, most difficult, worst*)

Adjective clause. A dependent clause that modifies a noun or pronoun. *See also* Clause.

Adverb. A word that modifies a verb, an adjective, or another adverb by making its meaning more specific. Adverbs answer the questions *How? When? Where?* and *To what degree?* Certain adverbs of time, place, and degree have a negative meaning. (She *never* saw the car.) Some adverbs have different forms to indicate degree of comparison.
  The **comparative degree** of an adverb compares two actions. (*more promptly, better*)
  The **superlative degree** compares three or more actions. (*most promptly, best*)

Adverb clause. A dependent clause that modifies a verb, an adjective, or an adverb. *See also* Clause.

Allusion. A reference to a well-known person, place, event, or creative work.

Analogy. A comparison based on a similarity between things that are otherwise dissimilar.

Analysis. The process of taking apart, examining, and explaining a topic, a piece of literature, or a media presentation.

Anecdote. A short written or oral account of an event.

Antecedent. *See* Pronoun.

Appositive. A noun or a pronoun placed next to another noun or pronoun that further identifies or gives additional information about it. (My friend *Kathy* has freckles.) An **essential,** or **restrictive, appositive** is a word or phrase that is needed to make the meaning of a sentence clear. If the appositive is not needed for clarity, it is **nonessential** or **nonrestrictive.**

Argument. A statement, reason, or fact for or against a point; a type of persuasive writing in which logic or reason is used to try to influence a reader.

Article. The adjectives *a, an,* and *the.* **Indefinite articles** *a* and *an* refer to one of a general group of persons, places, or things. The **definite article** *the* indicates that the noun is a specific person, place, or thing.

Atmosphere. The general mood, or emotional quality, of a literary work. Authors create atmosphere primarily through details of setting, such as time, place, and weather.

Audience. The reader, listener, or viewer for whom writing and other forms of communication are intended.

Author's purpose. An author's intent in writing a literary work. Typical purposes are to persuade, to instruct, to inform or explain, to entertain, to describe, or to tell a story.

Autobiography. A person's account of his or her own life.

Auxiliary verb. *See* Verb.

B

Bias. An inclination to present a settled and often prejudiced or narrow outlook on a subject.

Bibliography. A list of writings or other sources used as reference for a work.

Biography. A nonfiction account of a person's life written by someone other than the subject.

Body. The main part of a piece of writing; the section in which ideas are developed.

Bookmarks/Favorites. The feature on many Web browsers that allows the user to save addresses of Internet sites so that the sites can be accessed quickly.

Brainstorming. Surfacing ideas by listing all that come to mind without evaluating them.

C

Case. The form of a noun or pronoun that is determined by its use in a sentence. A noun or pronoun is in the **nominative case** when it is used as a subject or after a linking verb, in the **objective case** when it is used as an object, and in the **possessive case** when it is used to show possession.

Cause and effect. An organizational technique that presents events and conditions as reason and result, motive and reaction, or stimulus and response.

Characterization. The methods used by a writer to reveal the personality of a character.

Chronological order. An organizational technique that presents events in time sequence.

Clarity. The quality of a piece of writing that makes it easy to understand.

Classification. Any method of grouping according to a common principle or characteristic.

Clause. A group of words that has a subject and a predicate and that is used as part of a sentence.

A **main,** or **independent, clause** has a subject and a predicate and can stand alone as a sentence. A **subordinate,** or **dependent, clause** has a subject and a predicate, but it cannot stand alone as a sentence. A subordinate clause may be an **adjective, adverb,** or **noun** clause. An **elliptical clause** is an adverb clause in which words have been omitted but are clearly implied. (An elephant can run faster than you [*can run*].) An **essential,** or **restrictive, clause** is a clause that is needed to make the meaning of a sentence clear. If the clause is not needed for clarity, it is **nonessential** or **nonrestrictive**.

Cliché. An expression that has lost its impact through overuse.

Climax. The point of greatest emotional intensity, interest, or suspense in the plot of a narrative. *See also* Plot.

Clustering. A technique for generating writing ideas, which involves writing a word, circling it, and surrounding it with other words and phrases.

Coherence. The quality of a paragraph or composition in which sentences are clearly and logically connected; also called cohesiveness.

Cohesive writing. A type of writing in which sentences and paragraphs are logically connected to one another.

Collaboration. Working with others on a common project.

Collective noun. *See* Noun.

Colloquial language. Informal, conversational speech.

Common noun. *See* Noun.

Comparative degree. *See* Adjective; Adverb.

Comparison and contrast. The technique that measures items against one another and shows similarities and differences.

Complement. A word or phrase that completes the meaning of the verb in a sentence. The four basic kinds of complements are **direct objects, indirect objects, object complements,** and **subject complements**.

Complex sentence. *See* Sentence.

Compound sentence. *See* Sentence.

Compound-complex sentence. *See* Sentence.

Conceptual map. A graphic device that develops a central concept by surrounding it with examples or related ideas in a weblike arrangement.

Conclusion. A restatement or summing up of the ideas in a composition that brings it to a definite close; also a judgment or decision.

Conflict. A struggle between opposing forces. An **external conflict** pits a character against an outside force, such as another person, nature, a physical obstacle, or a cultural expectation. An **internal conflict** occurs within a character and may involve a decision to be made or a challenge to be faced and overcome.

Conjunction. A word that joins single words or groups of words.

A **coordinating conjunction** joins words or groups of words that are equal in grammatical importance.

Correlative conjunctions, such as *both . . . and, just . . . so, not only . . . but also, either . . . or, neither . . . nor, whether . . . or,* work in pairs to join words and groups of words of equal importance.

A **subordinating conjunction** joins a dependent idea or clause to a main clause.

Conjunctive adverb. An adverb used to clarify the relationship between clauses of a compound sentence. (*however, consequently*) Conjunctive adverbs have several uses: to replace *and,* to replace *but,* to state a result, to state equality.

Connotation. The thoughts and feelings associated with a word apart from the dictionary definition of the word.

Constructive criticism. Comments on another person's writing made with the intention of helping the writer improve a particular draft.

Context. The setting or situation in which an action takes place; also, in reading, the words and sentences that come before and after a specific word and help to explain its meaning.

Convention. An established or traditional technique or way of doing things.

Coordinating conjunction. *See* Conjunction.

Correlative conjunction. *See* Conjunction.

Credibility. The quality of a speaker or writer that makes that person's words believable.

Criticism. An analysis or evaluation of something, based on clear reasons and/or examples.

Culture. The attitudes, beliefs, and customs of any group, usually developed over a period of time.

D

Deductive reasoning. A way of thinking or explaining that begins with a general statement or principle and applies that principle to specific instances.

Definite article. *See* Article.

Demonstrative pronoun. *See* Pronoun.

Denotation. The dictionary definition of a word.

Dénouement. *See* Plot.

Dependent clause. *See* Clause.

Descriptive writing. Writing that uses sensory details to convey a dominant impression of, for example, a setting, a person, an animal, and so on.

Desktop publishing. The preparation of a text by formatting it on a computer and printing it out for presentation. Additional computer generated information may be included, such as graphs, photographs, and diagrams to enhance the written text.

Dialect. A way of speaking that is characteristic of a particular region or group of people.

Dialogue. Conversation between characters.

Diction. A writer's choice of words to convey meaning. Writers choose their words carefully to express meaning precisely.

Direct object. *See* Complement.

Documentation. Identification of the sources used in writing research or other informative papers, usually in the form of endnotes or footnotes, or using parenthetical documentation.

Drafting. One of the steps in the writing process; the organization and wording of a piece of writing. A writer may make many drafts before producing a final product.

Drama. A story intended to be performed by actors for an audience.

E

Editing. A step in the writing process that prepares material for presentation. The revised draft is checked for standard usage, varied sentence structure, and appropriate word choice.

Editorial. A newspaper or magazine article that expresses the personal ideas and opinions of the writer.

Effective listening. Listening that includes careful evaluation and critique of an oral presentation.

Elaboration. The use of facts, details, anecdote, quotations, or examples to develop an idea or support a statement.

Ellipses. Punctuation used to indicate the omission of words within a text. A series of evenly-spaced periods (. . .) is the common punctuation used.

E-mail. Short for electronic mail; messages, usually text, sent from one person to another by way of computer.

Empathy. An individual's close identification with a person, place, or thing, as when audience members experience the same emotions as a character in a play.

Emphatic form. *See* Verb tense.

Essay. A short piece of nonfiction writing in which the author presents his or her view on a particular topic.

Essential clause. A subordinate clause that cannot be omitted without changing the intended meaning of a sentence.

Evaluation. Making a judgment about the strengths and weaknesses of a draft in content, organization, and style.

Exposition. *See* Plot.

Expository writing. Writing that informs an audience by presenting information and explaining concepts and ideas; also called informative or explanatory writing.

External conflict. *See* Conflict.

Falling action. *See* Plot.

Feedback. The response a listener or reader gives a speaker or writer about his or her work.

Fiction. A narrative in which situations and characters are invented by the writer.

Figurative language. Forms of language used for descriptive effect and not meant to be interpreted literally—often to imply ideas indirectly.

Figure of speech. A specific device or kind of figurative language such as **metaphor, personification, simile,** or **symbol.**

First-person point of view. *See* Point of view.

Foreshadowing. The author's use of hints or clues to prepare readers for events that will happen later in a narrative.

Formal language. Language that uses correct grammar and omits slang expressions and contractions. It is especially common in nonfiction writing that is not personal.

Freewriting. A way of identifying ideas or topics by writing for a specific length of time without stopping or limiting the flow of ideas.

Gender-neutral language. Language that avoids sexism by using inclusive terms.

Generalization. A statement that presents a conclusion about a subject without going into details or specifics. *See* Overgeneralization.

Genre. A division or type of literature. Fiction, nonfiction, poetry, and drama are examples of genres. Each of these is further divided into subgenres.

Gerund. A verb form that ends in *-ing* and is used as a noun.

Glittering generality. An attractive claim based on insufficient evidence.

Graphic organizer. A visual way of organizing information; types of graphic organizers include graphs, outlines, charts, tables, webs or clusters, and diagrams.

Home page. The location on a Web site by which a user normally enters the site. A typical home page may explain the site, summarize the content, and provide links to other sites.

Hyperlink. A highlighted or underlined phrase or word on a Web page that, when clicked, moves the user to another part of the page or to another Web page.

Hypertext. Links in some text that can be clicked with a mouse to take the user to another document or to a different section in the same document.

Idiom. A word or phrase that has a special meaning different from its standard or dictionary meaning. (*In the same boat* is an idiom that means "having the same problem.")

Imagery. The word pictures that writers create to evoke an emotional response in readers. In creating effective images, writers use **sensory details** to help readers see, hear, feel, smell, and taste the scenes described in the work.

Imperative mood. *See* Mood of a verb.

Independent clause. *See* Clause.

Indicative mood. *See* Mood of a verb.

Indirect object. *See* Complement.

Inductive reasoning. A way of thinking or explaining that uses specific facts to draw a general conclusion.

Infinitive. A verb form that begins with the word *to* and functions as a noun, an adjective, or an adverb in a sentence.

Intensifier. An adverb that emphasizes an adjective or another adverb. (*very* important, *quite* easily)

Intensive pronoun. *See* Pronoun.

Interjection. A word or phrase that expresses emotion or exclamation. An interjection has no grammatical connection to other words.

Internal conflict. *See* Conflict.

Internet. A worldwide computer network that allows users to link to any computer on the network electronically for social, commercial, research, and other uses.

Interpretation. An explanation of the meaning of something.

Interrogative pronoun. *See* Pronoun.

Intransitive verb. *See* Verb.

Introduction. Part of a written or oral work that identifies the subject, gives a general idea of what the body of the composition will contain, sets the tone, and may provide other information necessary for the audience.

Inverted order. A sentence in which the predicate comes before the subject. Questions, or interrogative sentences, are generally written in inverted order.

J–L

Jargon. Terminology peculiar to a specific profession, trade, or other group of people.

Journal. A daily record of events kept by a participant in those events or a witness to them; also a personal notebook for freewriting, collecting ideas, and recording thoughts and experiences.

Learning log. A type of journal used for recording, questioning, and evaluating information.

Lexicon. A wordbook or dictionary.

Listening strategies. Techniques that include analysis, evaluation, and identification of oral material.

Literary criticism. A type of writing in which the writer analyzes and evaluates a work or works of literature.

Logic. The process of clear and organized thinking that leads to a reasonable conclusion. *See also* Logical fallacy.

Logical fallacy. An argument that seems to be plausible but which uses an invalid inference.

M

Main clause. *See* Clause.

Manual of style. Any one of several texts published to inform writers of the conventions of style.

Mechanics. In writing, the use of punctuation and capitalization.

Media. A plural term used to refer to the methods of communication such as newspapers, magazines, television, and radio. The singular form, *medium,* may be defined as "a means by which something is conveyed."

Memoir. A type of narrative nonfiction that presents the story of a period in the writer's life and is usually written from the first-person point of view. A memoir may emphasize the impact of significant historical events on the writer's life.

Memorandum. A short written reminder commonly referred to as a **memo**.

Metaphor. A figure of speech that makes a comparison between two seemingly unlike things. A metaphor does not use words such as *like* or *as*.

Mood of a verb. The **indicative mood** makes a statement or asks a question. The **imperative mood** expresses a command or makes a request. The **subjunctive mood** expresses a formal demand, suggestion, or statement of necessity. The subjunctive mood may also state a condition or wish that is contrary to fact.

Multimedia presentation. The presentation of a piece of writing accompanied by other media, such as video, music, and visual art.

N

Narrative writing. A type of writing that tells about events or actions as they change over a period of time and often includes story elements such as character, setting, and plot.

Nominative pronoun. *See* Pronoun case.

Nonessential clause. A clause that adds information but is not absolutely needed to express the meaning of the sentence.

Nonfiction. Literature that deals with real people, events, and experiences. Among the categories of nonfiction are **biographies, autobiographies,** and **essays.**

Nonverbal strategies. Techniques of a speaker to get across ideas in ways other than by the use of words. Gestures, body language, and facial expression are common strategies used by speakers.

Noun. A word that names a person, place, thing, quality, characteristic, or idea.
An **abstract noun** names an idea, a quality, or a characteristic.
A **collective noun** names a group of people or things.
A **common noun** names a general type of person, place, thing, idea, characteristic, or quality.
A **proper noun** names a particular person, place, thing, or idea.

Noun clause. A dependent clause that functions as a noun. *See also* Clause.

Number. The form of a noun, pronoun, or verb that indicates whether it refers to one (**singular**) or to more than one (**plural**).

O

Objective pronoun. *See* Pronoun case.

Omniscient point of view. *See* Point of view.

Oral tradition. Literature that passes by word of mouth from one generation to the next and perpetuates history and values of a culture.

Order of importance. A way of organizing details in a paragraph or composition from least to most or most to least important.

Organization. A system of ordering ideas into a coherent composition.

Outline. A condensed arrangement of main topics and supporting ideas, usually including numbered words or phrases in a logical sequence.

Overgeneralization. Drawing a broad conclusion that is not supported by facts. *See also* generalization and deductive reasoning.

Paragraph. A unit of writing that consists of related sentences.

Parallelism. The use of a series of words, phrases, or sentences that have similar grammatical form.

Paraphrase. A restatement of a passage in different words that retains the meaning, tone, and general length of the original.

Parenthetical documentation. A specific reference to the source of a piece of information; it is placed in parentheses directly after the information appears in a piece of writing.

Participle. A verb form that can function as an adjective. **Present participles** always end in *-ing*. **Past participles** often end in *-ed*, but can take other forms as well.

Passive voice. The form of a verb used when the subject of the sentence receives the action of the verb.

Peer response. The suggestions and comments provided by peers, or classmates, about a piece of writing or another type of presentation.

Personal pronoun. *See* Pronoun.

Personal writing. Writing that expresses the writer's thoughts, feelings, and ideas.

Persuasive writing. Writing, usually nonfiction, that seeks to move the reader to the author's viewpoint by one or more means, such as logic, emotion, entreaty, or salesmanship.

Phrase. A group of words that functions as a unit in a sentence. A **prepositional phrase** consists of a preposition, its object, and any modifiers of the object and can function as an adjective or adverb. A **verb phrase** consists of one or more auxiliary verbs followed by a main verb.

Plagiarism. The presentation of another's words or ideas as one's own; the use of material without crediting the source or without the permission of the original creator or owner of the work.

Plot. The sequence of events in a narrative work. The plot begins with the **exposition,** or the introduction of the characters, the setting, and the conflict. The **rising action** adds complications to the conflict, leading to the **climax,** or emotional high point. The climax gives way rapidly to its logical result in the **falling action,** and finally to the **resolution,** or **dénouement,** in which the final outcome is revealed.

Point of view. The relationship of the narrator to the story. Most writing is written from the **first-person, third-person limited,** or **third-person omniscient** point of view.

Portfolio. A set of creative works representing the achievements of a writer or artist.

Positive degree. *See* Adjective.

Précis. A brief summary of main ideas.

Predicate. The part of a sentence that expresses the essential thought about the subject of the sentence; includes the **simple predicate** (the key verb or verb phrase) and all the words that modify it.

Preposition. A word that shows the relationship of a noun or pronoun to some other word in the sentence.

Prepositional phrase. *See* Phrase.

Presenting/Publishing. The final step in the writing process; the presentation of the finished work. Any method of sharing a completed piece of writing is a form of presenting.

Prewriting. Gathering information, checking facts, and organizing and discussing the substance of a planned work are among the steps used by writers in the prewriting phase.

Primary Source. Original documents such as letters, newspaper or magazine articles, interviews, or historical documents from a specific time period.

Problem solving. The use of skills to identify a problem, list possible solutions, and determine an action.

Progressive form. *See* Verb tense.

Pronoun. A word that takes the place of a noun, a group of words acting as a noun, or another pronoun. The word or group of words that a pronoun refers to is called its **antecedent.**

A **demonstrative pronoun** points out specific persons, places, things, or ideas.

An **indefinite pronoun** refers to persons, places, or things in a more general way than a noun does.

An **intensive pronoun** has the same form as a reflexive pronoun. An intensive pronoun adds emphasis to another noun or pronoun.

An **interrogative pronoun** is used to form questions.

A **personal pronoun** refers to a specific person or thing.

A **reflexive pronoun** reflects back to a noun or pronoun used earlier in the sentence, indicating that the same person or thing is involved. (I will admire *myself* in the mirror.)

A **relative pronoun** is used to begin a subordinate clause.

Pronoun case. The form of a pronoun that is determined by its use in a sentence. Personal pronouns may be in the **nominative, objective,** or **possessive** case, depending upon their function in a sentence. *See also* Case.

Proofreading. The last part of the editing process that involves checking work to discover typographical and spelling errors.

Propaganda. The spreading of information for the purpose of influencing thoughts and actions to help or harm a group, idea, or person.

Proper noun. *See* Noun.

Prose. Writing distinguished from poetry by its similarity to the diction and rhythms of ordinary speech.

Publishing. The presentation to an audience of a creative work in its final form.

Purpose. The aim of writing, which may be to express, discover, record, develop, reflect on ideas, problem solve, entertain, influence, inform, or describe.

R

Reflection. The careful consideration of an idea or creative work.

Relative pronoun. *See* Pronoun.

Representation. A way in which information or ideas are presented to an audience; a dramatic or artistic presentation.

Research. The action of locating information on a topic from a variety of reputable sources.

Resolution. *See* Plot.

Résumé. A written summary of one's education and work experience.

Revising. The stage of the writing process in which a writer goes over a draft, evaluating the writing for clarity, purpose, and suitability to the audience, and making changes in content, organization, and style in order to improve it. Revision techniques include adding, elaborating, deleting, combining, and rearranging text.

Rhetoric. The art of using language to present facts and ideas in order to persuade.

Rising action. *See* Plot.

Root. The part of a word that carries the main meaning.

S

Script. The written text to be used in a performance.

Secondary source. Writings about a specific event or time period, written after the time described. Historical essays, biographies, and critics' reviews are examples of secondary sources.

Sensory detail. *See* Imagery.

Sentence. A group of words expressing a complete thought. Sentences can be classified by structure:
> **simple sentences** with a main clause,
> **compound sentences** with two or more main clauses,
> **complex sentences** made up of a main clause and one or more subordinate clauses, and
> **compound-complex sentences** with two or more main clauses and at least one subordinate clause.

Sentence variety. The use of different types of sentences to add interest to writing.

Setting goals. Determining the end for which an activity is taking place.

Sexist language. Word choice that promotes prejudice or discrimination based on gender.

Short story. A brief fictional narrative in prose. A short story will usually concentrate on a single event with only a few characters.

Simile. A figure of speech that compares two unlike things, using the word *like* or *as.*

Source. The point of origin of any piece of information. A **primary source** is the original source of the information. A **secondary source** is a report based on a primary source.

Spatial order. The arrangement of the details of a setting according to their location—for example, from left to right or from top to bottom.

Speech. An oral communication; a public address.

Standard English. The most widely used and accepted form of the English language.

Stereotype. A generalization about a group of people that is made without regard for individual differences.

Structure. The framework or general plan of a literary work. Structure refers to the relationship of the parts of a work to each other and to the whole piece.

Style. The expressive qualities that distinguish an author's work, including **diction, sentence structure,** and **figures of speech.**

Subject. The part of a sentence that tells what the sentence is about; includes the **simple subject** (the key noun or pronoun) and all the words that modify it.

Subjunctive mood. *See* Mood of a verb.

Subordinate clause. *See* Clause.

Subordinating conjunction. *See* Conjunction.

Summary. A brief statement of the main idea of a written work or of a proceeding.

Superlative degree. *See* Adjective; Adverb.

Support. In nonfiction writing, details that verify or add credence to a main idea.

Symbol. Any person, animal, place, object, or event that exists on a literal level within a work but also represents something on a figurative level.

Technology. A way of accomplishing a task using technical processes or knowledge.

Tense. *See* Verb tense.

Theme. The main idea or message of a story, poem, novel, or play, sometimes expressed as a general statement about life.

Thesis. A position or proposition advanced by a speaker or writer.

Tone. A reflection of the writer's attitude toward a subject as conveyed through such elements as word choice, punctuation, sentence structure, and figures of speech.

Topic sentence. A sentence that expresses the main idea of a paragraph.

Transition. A connecting word that clarifies the relationship of words or ideas.

Transitive verb. *See* Verb.

U–V

Unity. The quality of a composition in which all the sentences and paragraphs support one main idea.

URL. The standard form of an Internet address; stands for Uniform Resource Locator.

Venn diagram. A visual representation consisting of two or more overlapping circles used to show similarities and differences in two entities.

Verb. A word that expresses action or a state of being and is necessary to make a statement.
An **action verb** tells what someone or something does.
A **transitive verb** is an action verb that is followed by a word or words that answer the question *What?* or *Whom?*
An **intransitive verb** is an action verb that is not followed by a word that answers the question *What?* or *Whom?*
A **linking verb** links, or joins, the subject of a sentence with a word or expression that identifies or describes the subject.

Auxiliary verbs, or helping verbs, are words that accompany the main verb.

Verb tense. The tense of a verb indicates when the action or state of being occurs.
In addition to **present**, **past**, and **future** tenses, there are three perfect tenses: the **present perfect, past perfect,** and **future perfect.**
The **progressive form** of a verb expresses a continuing action with any of the six tenses. To make the progressive forms, use the appropriate tense of the verb *be* with the present participle of the main verb.
The **emphatic form** adds special force, or emphasis, to the present or past tense of a verb. For the emphatic form, use *do, does,* or *did* with the base form.

Verbal. A verb form can function as a noun, an adjective, or an adverb. The three kinds of verbals are **gerunds**, **infinitives**, and **participles**. *See* Gerund; Infinitive; Participle.

Voice. The distinctive use of language that conveys the writer's or narrator's personality to the reader. Sentence structure, word choice, and tone are elements that communicate voice.

W

Web site. A site on the World Wide Web that can be reached through links or by accessing a Web address or URL. *See* URL.

Word processing. The use of a computer for the writing and editing of written text.

World Wide Web. A global system that uses the Internet and allows users to create, link, and access fields of information. *See* Internet.

Writing process. The series of stages or steps that a writer goes through to develop ideas and to communicate them.

GLOSARIO
DE ESCRITURA Y LENGUAJE

Este glosario permite encontrar fácilmente definiciones de gramática inglesa y términos que usan los escritores.

Abstract noun/Nombre abstracto. *Ver Noun.*

Action verb/Verbo de acción. *Ver Verb.*

Active voice/Voz activa. Forma verbal usada cuando el sujeto de la oración realiza la acción.

Adjective/Adjetivo. Palabra que modifica, o describe, un nombre (*noun*) o pronombre (*pronoun*), limitando su significado. Un adjetivo indica *qué tipo, cuál, cuántos* o *cuánto*. Los adjetivos aparecen en varias posiciones en la oración.

> **Positive degree/Grado positivo.** Forma simple del adjetivo (*tall, difficult, bad*; en español: *alto, difícil, malo*).
> **Comparative degree/Grado comparativo.** Adjetivo que compara a dos personas, lugares, cosas o ideas (*worse, sadder*; en español: *peor, más triste*).
> **Superlative degree/Grado superlativo.** Adjetivo que compara más de dos personas, lugares, cosas o ideas (*worst, saddest*; en español: *el peor, la más triste*).

Adjective clause/Proposición adjetiva. Proposición dependiente que modifica un nombre o pronombre. *Ver también Clause.*

Adverb/Adverbio. Palabra que modifica a un verbo, adjetivo u otro adverbio, haciendo que su significado sea más específico. Los adverbios responden a las preguntas *cómo, cuándo, dónde, de qué manera* y *qué tan seguido* sucede algo. Determinados adverbios de tiempo, lugar y grado tienen un significado negativo. (Ella *nunca* vio el auto.)

Algunos adverbios tienen diferentes formas para indicar el grado de comparación.

> **Comparative degree/Grado comparativo.** Compara dos acciones (*more, promptly, better*; en español: *más, de inmediato, mejor*).
> **Superlative degree/Grado superlativo.** Compara tres o más acciones (*most promptly, best*; en español: *lo más pronto, lo mejor*).

Adverb clause/Proposición adverbial. Proposición dependiente que modifica un verbo, un adjetivo o un adverbio. *Ver Clause.*

Allusion/Alusión. Referencia en un texto escrito a un personaje, lugar o situación muy conocidos de una obra literaria, musical, artística o histórica.

Analogy/Analogía. Comparación basada en la similitud de cosas que son diferentes.

Analysis/Análisis. Proceso de separar, examinar y explicar un tema, una obra de literatura o una presentación de los medios.

Anecdote/Anécdota. Narración oral o escrita de un suceso.

Antecedent/Antecedente. *Ver Pronoun.*

Appositive/Apositivo. Nombre colocado junto a otro para identificarlo o agregar información sobre él. (Mi amiga, *Kathy*, tiene pecas.) La aposición **esencial** (*essential*) o **no restrictiva** (*non restrictive*) es una palabra o frase necesaria para aclarar el sentido de una oración. Si la aposición no es necesaria para dar claridad, se llama **no esencial** (*non essential*) o **no restrictiva** (*non restrictive*).

Argument/Argumento. Afirmación, razón o hecho en favor o en contra de algún comentario; texto escrito persuasivo en el que se aplican la lógica o la razón para influir en el lector.

Article/Artículo. Nombre dado a las palabras *a, an* y *the* (en español: *un, uno/a, el, la*). *A* y *an* son artículos **indefinidos** (*indefinite articles*), que se refieren a cualquier cosa de un grupo. *The* es un artículo **definido** (*definite article*); indica que el nombre al que precede es una persona, lugar o cosa específicos.

Atmosphere/Atmósfera. Ambiente general o cualidad emocional de una obra literaria. Los autores crean la atmósfera a partir de detalles, como el tiempo, el lugar y el clima.

Audience/Público. Lector, escucha u observador a los cuales se dirige una comunicación, ya sea escrita o de cualquier otra forma.

Author's purpose/Finalidad del autor. Intención del autor al escribir una obra literaria. En general busca persuadir, enseñar, informar o explicar, entretener, describir o contar una historia.

Autobiography/Autobiografía. Relato que hace una persona sobre su propia vida.

Auxiliary verb/Verbo auxiliar. *Ver Verb.*

Bias/Tendencia. Inclinación a presentar una perspectiva establecida y con frecuencia prejuiciada o miope sobre un tema.

Bibliography/Bibliografía. Lista de los libros, artículos y otras fuentes que se utilizan como referencia en una investigación.

Biography/Biografía. Narración de no ficción de la vida de una persona, escrita por alguien más.

Body/Cuerpo. Parte central de una obra escrita; sección donde se desarrollan las ideas.

Bookmarks/favorites/Marcadores/favoritos. Característica de muchos buscadores de red que permiten guardar direcciones de Internet para entrar a ellas rápidamente.

Brainstorming/Lluvia de ideas. Actividad por medio de la cual se generan ideas al hacer una lista de todo lo que se nos ocurre sin evaluarlo.

Case/Caso. Forma de un nombre o pronombre que se determina por su uso en la oración. El nombre o pronombre está en caso **nominativo** (*nominative case*) cuando se utiliza como sujeto o después de un verbo copulativo; en caso **acusativo** y **dativo** (*objective case*) cuando recibe la acción del verbo; y en caso **posesivo*** (*possessive case*) cuando se utiliza para indicar posesión o propiedad.

Cause and effect/Causa y efecto. Técnica de organización que presenta los sucesos y condiciones como causa y resultado, motivo y reacción, o estímulo y respuesta.

Characterization/Caracterización. Métodos que utiliza un escritor para crear sus personajes.

Chronological order/Orden cronológico. Técnica de organización que presenta los sucesos en secuencia de acuerdo con el tiempo en que sucedieron.

Clarity/Claridad. Cualidad de un escrito que lo hace fácil de entender.

Classification/Clasificación. Cualquier método de agrupar según un principio o característica en común.

Clause/Proposición. Grupo de palabras que consta de sujeto y predicado y que se usa como parte de una oración.

Independent clause/Proposición independiente. También llamada **proposición principal** (*main clause*); tiene sujeto y predicado y hace sentido por sí misma.

Dependent clause/Proposición dependiente. También llamada **proposición subordinada** (*subordinate clause*); tiene sujeto y predicado pero depende de la proposición principal. Puede ser una proposición adjetiva, adverbial o nominal.

Elliptical clause/Proposición elíptica. Proposición adverbial donde las palabras han sido omitidas pero están claramente implícitas. (Un elefante corre más rápido que tú [*puedes correr*]).

Essential clause/Proposición esencial. También llamada proposición restrictiva *(restrictive clause);* es necesaria para el significado de la oración, a diferencia de las proposiciones **no esenciales** o **no restrictivas** (*nonessential* o *nonrestrictive*).

Cliché/Cliché. Expresión que perdió su efecto por usarla demasiado.

Climax/Clímax. Momento donde ocurre la mayor intensidad emocional, interés o suspenso en la trama de una narración. *Ver también Plot.*

Clustering/Agrupamiento. Técnica para generar ideas que consiste en escribir una palabra, ponerla dentro de un círculo y rodearla con otras palabras y frases.

Coherence/Coherencia. Cualidad de un párrafo o composición en que las oraciones tienen una relación clara y lógica; también se llama cohesión.

Cohesive writing/Escritura coherente. Tipo de escritura en que las oraciones y párrafos están lógicamente relacionados entre sí.

Collaboration/Colaboración. Proceso de trabajar en equipo para escribir un texto o realizar un proyecto.

Collective noun/Nombre colectivo. *Ver Noun.*

Colloquial language/Lenguaje coloquial. Lenguaje informal de conversación.

Common noun/Nombre común. *Ver Noun.*

Comparative degree/Grado comparativo. *Ver Adjective; Adverb.*

Comparison-and-contrast/Comparación y contraste. Técnica de organizar ideas, señalando sus similitudes y diferencias.

Complement/Complemento. Palabra o frase que completa el significado de un verbo en una oración. En inglés hay cuatro clases de complementos: **directo** (*direct object*), **indirecto** (*indirect object*), **de objeto** (*object complement*) y **predicativo** (**atributo**) (*subject complement*).

Complex sentence/Oración compleja. *Ver Sentence.*

Compound sentence/Oración compuesta. *Ver Sentence.*

Compound-complex sentence/Oración compuesta-compleja. *Ver Sentence.*

Conceptual map/Mapa conceptual. Recurso gráfico que desarrolla un concepto central rodeándolo con ejemplos o ideas relacionadas a manera de red.

Conclusion/Conclusión. Afirmación que resume las ideas de una composición, antes de ponerle punto final.

Conflict/Conflicto. Lucha entre dos fuerzas opuestas. Un **conflicto externo** enfrenta un personaje a una fuerza externa, como otra persona, la naturaleza, un obstáculo físico o una expectativa cultural. Un **conflicto interno** ocurre dentro del personaje y puede implicar que se tenga que tomar una decisión o enfrentar un reto y solucionarlo.

Conjunction/Conjunción. Palabra que une dos palabras o grupos de palabras.

Coordinating conjunction/Conjunción coordinante. Las palabras *and, but, or, nor, for, yet* (*y, pero, o, no, para, aun*) unen palabras o grupos de palabras que tienen igual importancia gramatical.

Correlative conjunction/Conjunción correlativa*. Las palabras *both . . . and, just as . . . so, not only . . . but also, either . . . or, neither . . . nor* (*tanto . . . como, así como, no sólo . . . sino, . . . o*) son palabras en pares que vinculan palabras o frases de igual importancia.

Subordinate conjunction/Conjunción subordinante. Une una idea u proposición subordinada con la proposición principal.

Conjunctive adverb/Adverbio de coordinación. Adverbio para aclarar la relación entre las proposiciones de una oración compuesta (*however, consequently*; en español: *sin embargo, en consecuencia*). Tiene varios usos: sustituir *and (y)*, sustituir *but (pero)*, afirmar un resultado o afirmar igualdad.

Connotation/Connotación. Pensamientos y sentimientos relacionados con una palabra, más que con su definición de diccionario.

Constructive criticism/Crítica constructiva. Comentario sobre lo que escribe otra persona, con la intención de ayudar a que mejore el borrador.

Context/Contexto. Escenario o situación en la que tiene lugar la acción. También en la lectura, las palabras y oraciones que están antes y después de una palabra determinada y que sirven para explicar su significado.

Convention/Convención. Técnica o forma tradicional o establecida de trabajar en un campo.

Coordinating conjunction/Conjunción coordinante. *Ver Conjunction.*

Correlative conjunction/Conjunción correlativa*. *Ver Conjunction.*

Credibility/Credibilidad. Cualidad de un hablante o escritor que hace creer sus palabras.

Criticism/Crítica. Análisis o evaluación con razones o ejemplos claros.

Culture/Cultura. Actitudes, creencias y costumbres de un grupo determinado, que se crean a través del tiempo.

Deductive reasoning/Razonamiento deductivo. Pensamiento o explicación que parte de una afirmación o principio generales y los aplica a casos específicos.

Definite article/Artículo definido. *Ver Article.*

Demonstrative pronoun/Pronombre demostrativo. *Ver Pronoun.*

Denotation/Denotación. Definición de una palabra que da el diccionario.

Dénouement/Esclarecimiento. *Ver Plot.*

Dependent clause/Proposición dependiente. *Ver Clause.*

Descriptive writing/Escritura descriptiva. Tipo de escritura que da detalles sensoriales para comunicar una impresión predominante de un escenario, persona, animal, etcétera.

Desktop publishing/Edición por computadora. Uso de programas de computadora para formar un documento con texto escrito, gráficas y/o imágenes.

Dialect/Dialecto. Forma de lenguaje hablado característico de una región o grupo particular.

Dialogue/Diálogo. Conversación entre personajes en un escrito.

Diction/Dicción. Palabras que escoge un escritor para comunicar un significado. Los escritores seleccionan las palabras cuidadosamente para expresar su significado con toda precisión.

Direct object/Complemento directo. *Ver Complement.*

Documentation/Documentación. Identificación de las fuentes que se emplean para escribir un documento u otros textos informativos; generalmente se ponen como notas al pie, al final del texto o entre paréntesis.

Drafting/Borrador. Paso del proceso de escritura; organización y formulación de un texto escrito. Antes de llegar a un producto final, el escritor suele tener varios borradores.

Drama/Obra dramática. Narración actuada por los actores ante un público.

E

Editing/Edición. Paso del proceso de escritura en que se revisa que el borrador corregido tenga un lenguaje estándar, una estructura sintáctica variada y la elección adecuada de palabras.

Editorial/Editorial. Artículo en un periódico u otro medio que expresa las ideas personales y la opinión del escritor.

Effective listening/Atención eficaz. Forma de escuchar que implica evaluación cuidadosa y crítica de una presentación oral.

Elaboration/Elaboración. Uso de hechos, detalles, anécdotas, citas o ejemplos para desarrollar una idea o sustentar una afirmación.

Ellipsis/Puntos suspensivos. Signo de puntuación que consiste en dejar tres puntos con espacios iguales para indicar que se están suprimiendo una o varias palabras.

E-mail/Correo electrónico. Abreviatura de correo electrónico; mensajes, generalmente textos, que se envían por computadora.

Empathy/Empatía. Identificación cercana de una persona con otra persona, un lugar o cosa, como cuando el público experimenta las mismas emociones que el personaje de una obra.

Emphatic form/Forma enfática. *Ver Verb tense.*

Essay/Ensayo. Pieza breve de no ficción en la que el autor presenta su punto de vista sobre un tema determinado.

Essential clause/Proposición esencial. Proposición subordinada que no puede omitirse sin cambiar el significado de una oración.

Evaluation/Evaluación. Juicio sobre las fallas y los aciertos de un texto en borrador en cuanto a contenido, organización y estilo.

Exposition/Exposición. *Ver Plot.*

Expository writing/Texto descriptivo. Tipo de escritura que informa al público presentando información y explicando conceptos e ideas; también llamada escritura informativa o explicativa.

External conflict/Conflicto externo. *Ver Conflict.*

F

Falling action/Acción descendente. *Ver Plot.*

Feedback/Retroalimentación. Respuesta del escucha o lector al mensaje de un hablante o escritor.

Fiction/Ficción. Narrativa donde las situaciones y los personajes son inventados por el escritor.

Figurative language/Lenguaje figurado. Formas lingüísticas usadas con un efecto descriptivo y que no deben ser interpretadas literalmente; con frecuencia implican ideas de manera indirecta.

Figure of speech/Tropo. Recurso específico o tipo de lenguaje figurado como la **metáfora** (*metaphor*), la **personificación** (*personification*), el **símil** (*simile*) o el **símbolo** (*symbol*).

First person point of view/Punto de vista de primera persona. *Ver Point of view.*

Foreshadowing/Presagio. Pistas o claves que utiliza un autor para advertir a los lectores de los acontecimientos que ocurrirán más adelante en la narración.

Formal language/Lenguaje formal. Lenguaje que utiliza una gramática correcta y omite contracciones y expresiones coloquiales. Es adecuado para textos de no ficción, que no son de carácter personal.

Freewriting/Escritura libre. Búsqueda de ideas escribiendo durante un tiempo determinado, sin detenerse ni limitar el flujo de ideas.

Gender-neutral language/Lenguaje de género neutro. Lenguaje que evita el sexismo al usar términos inclusivos.

Generalization/Generalización. Afirmación que presenta una conclusión acerca de un tema sin entrar en detalles específicos. *Ver* Sobregeneralización.

Genre/Género. Clasificación o tipo de literatura. La ficción, la no ficción, la poesía y el teatro son ejemplos de géneros. Cada uno se divide en subgéneros.

Gerund/Gerundio. Verboide que termina en *–ing* y se usa como nombre (en inglés).

Glittering generality/Generalización deslumbrante. Afirmación atractiva sin pruebas suficientes.

Graphic organizer/Organizador gráfico. Manera visual de organizar la información, como las tablas, las gráficas, las redes y los árboles de ideas.

Home page/Página principal. Página por medio de la cual un usuario entra normalmente a un sitio de Web. Por lo general, explica el sitio, resume el contenido y proporciona vínculos con otros sitios.

Hyperlink/Hipervínculo. Oraciones o palabras sombreadas o subrayadas en una página en red que al activarse con un clic conectan al usuario con otra parte de la página o con otra página de la red.

Hypertext/Hipertexto. Vínculos en algunos textos que con el clic del ratón el usuario llega a otro documento o a una sección distinta del mismo documento.

Idiom/Modismo. Palabra o frase cuyo significado es diferente del significado estándar o de diccionario. (*Hacer la vista gorda* es un modismo que significa "pasar por alto".)

Imagery/Imaginería. Imágenes que crean los escritores con palabras para evocar una respuesta emocional en los lectores. Al crear imágenes eficaces, los escritores usan **detalles sensoriales** (*sensory details*) para que los lectores puedan ver, oír, sentir, oler y gustar las escenas descritas.

Imperative mood/Modo imperativo. *Ver Mood of a verb.*

Independent clause/Proposición independiente. *Ver Clause.*

Indicative mood/Modo indicativo. *Ver Mood of a verb.*

Indirect object/Objeto indirecto. *Ver Complement.*

Inductive reasoning/Razonamiento inductivo. Pensamiento o explicación que parte de varios ejemplos para llegar a una afirmación general.

Infinitive/Infinitivo Verboide que consta de la palabra *to* y la base del verbo (en español terminan en *–ar, -er* o *-ir*). En inglés se usa como sustantivo, adjetivo o adverbio en la oración.

Intensifier/Intensificador. Adverbio que refuerza un adjetivo u otro adverbio (*very* important, *quite* easily; en español: *muy* importante, *bastante* fácil).

Intensive pronoun/Pronombre intensivo*. *Ver Pronoun.*

Interjection/Interjección. Palabra o frase que expresa emoción o exclamación. No tiene relación gramatical con las demás palabras.

Internal conflict/Conflicto interno. *Ver Conflict.*

Internet/Internet. Red mundial computarizada que permite comunicarse electrónicamente con cualquier computadora de la red para buscar información social, comercial, de investigación y de otro tipo.

Interpretation/Interpretación. Explicación del significado de algo.

Interrogative pronoun/Pronombre interrogativo. *Ver Pronoun.*

Intransitive verb/Verbo intransitivo. *Ver Verb.*

Introduction/Introducción. Parte de una obra escrita u oral que identifica el tema, da la idea general de lo que contendrá el cuerpo de la composición y determina el tono; puede proporcionar información adicional necesaria para el público.

Inverted order/Orden invertido. Oración en la que el predicado se encuentra antes del sujeto. Las preguntas, u oraciones interrogativas, por lo general se escriben en orden invertido.

J-L

Jargon/Jerga. Terminología peculiar de una profesión, comercio u otro grupo de personas.

Journal/Diario. Registro diario de sucesos de la persona que participa en ellos o que los presencia; también una libreta personal para escribir libremente, reunir ideas y registrar pensamientos y experiencias.

Learning log/Registro de aprendizaje. Diario para registrar, cuestionar y evaluar información.

Lexicon/Léxico. Diccionario.

Listening strategies/Estrategias para escuchar. Técnicas que incluyen el análisis, la evaluación y la identificación de material oral.

Literary criticism/Crítica literaria. Tipo de escritura en la que el escritor analiza y evalúa una o varias obras literarias.

Logic/Lógica. Proceso de pensamiento claro y organizado que conduce a una conclusión razonable. *Ver también Logical fallacy.*

Logical fallacy/Falacia lógica. Argumento que parece creíble pero que usa una inferencia inválida.

M

Main clause/Proposición principal. *Ver Clause.*

Manual of style/Manual de estilo. Texto publicado para informar a los escritores acerca de las convenciones de estilo.

Mechanics/Reglas ortográficas. En escritura, uso correcto de puntuación y mayúsculas.

Media/Medios. Término en plural para referirse a los métodos de comunicación como periódicos, revistas, televisión y radio. El singular, *medio* (*medium*), puede definirse como "forma por la cual se comunica algo".

Memoir/Memoria. Tipo de narrativa de no ficción, por lo general escrito en primera persona, que presenta el relato de un período de la vida del escritor. Una memoria puede resaltar el efecto que ciertos sucesos históricos importantes tuvieron en su vida.

Memorandum/Memorando. Recordatorio breve conocido comúnmente como **memo**.

Metaphor/Metáfora. Tropo que compara dos cosas aparentemente distintas sin usar las palabras *like* o *as (como).*

Mood of a verb/ Modo verbal. Indicative mood/Modo indicativo. Hace una afirmación o pregunta. **Imperative mood/Modo imperativo**. Expresa una orden o hace una petición. **Subjunctive mood/Modo subjuntivo.** Expresa una orden formal, una sugerencia o afirmación de una necesidad. También puede señalar una condición o deseo que es contrario al hecho.

Multimedia presentation/Presentación multimedia. Uso de una variedad de medios como el video, el sonido, un texto escrito y artes visuales para presentar ideas e información.

N

Narrative writing/Narrativa. Tipo de escritura que narra sucesos o acciones que cambian con el paso del tiempo; por lo general tiene personajes, escenario y trama.

Nominative pronoun/Pronombre nominativo. *Ver Pronoun case.*

Nonessential clause/Proposición no esencial. Proposición que agrega información pero que no es absolutamente necesaria para expresar el significado de la oración.

Nonfiction/No ficción. Literatura que trata sobre personas, sucesos y experiencias reales. Entre las categorías de la no ficción están:

la **biografía** (*biography*), la **autobiografía** (*autobiography*) y el **ensayo** (*essay*).

Nonverbal strategies/Estrategias no verbales. Técnicas de un hablante para exponer ideas sin usar las palabras. Los gestos, el lenguaje corporal y la expresión facial son estrategias comunes usadas por los hablantes.

Noun/Nombre (o sustantivo). Palabra que nombra a una persona, lugar, cosa, o a una idea, cualidad o característica.

    Abstract noun/Nombre abstracto. Nombra una idea, una cualidad o una característica.
    Collective noun/Nombre colectivo. Nombra un grupo de personas o cosas.
    Common noun/Nombre común. Nombra a cualquier persona, lugar, cosa o idea.
    Proper noun/Nombre propio. Nombra a una persona, lugar, cosa o idea específica.

Noun clause/Proposición nominal Proposición dependiente que se usa como nombre. *Ver también Clause.*

Number/Número. Forma del nombre, pronombre o verbo que indica si se refiere a uno (**singular**) o a más de uno (**plural**).

O

Objective pronoun/Pronombre personal de complemento directo o indirecto. *Ver Pronoun case.*

Omniscient point of view/Punto de vista omnisciente. *Ver Point of view.*

Oral tradition/Tradición oral. Literatura que se transmite de boca en boca de una generación a otra y que perpetúa la historia y los valores de una cultura.

Order of importance/Orden de importancia. Forma de organizar los detalles en un párrafo o composición según su importancia.

Organization/Organización. Sistema para ordenar las ideas de modo que resulte una composición coherente.

Outline/Esquema. Distribución condensada de ideas principales y secundarias; casi siempre tiene palabras o frases numeradas en una secuencia lógica.

Overgeneralization/Sobregeneralización. Conclusión general que no está sustentada por hechos. *Ver también Generalization; Deductive reasoning.*

Paragraph/Párrafo. Una unidad de texto que consta de oraciones relacionadas.

Parallelism/Paralelismo. Uso de una serie de palabras, frases y oraciones que tienen una forma gramatical similar.

Paraphrase/Parafrasear. Reformulación de un pasaje en palabras diferentes que conservan el significado, el tono y la longitud general del original.

Parenthetical documentation/Documentación parentética. Referencia específica a la fuente de la información que se pone entre paréntesis directamente después de ésta.

Participle/Participio. Verboide que se usa como adjetivo.
>   **Present participle/Participio presente.** Siempre termina en *–ing.*
>   **Past participle/Pasado participio.** Por lo general termina en *–ed*, pero también tiene otras formas.

Passive voice/Voz pasiva. Forma verbal usada cuando el sujeto de una oración recibe la acción del verbo.

Peer response/Respuesta de compañeros. Sugerencias y comentarios que dan los compañeros de clase sobre un texto escrito u otro tipo de presentación.

Personal pronoun/Pronombre personal. *Ver Pronoun.*

Personal writing/Escritura personal. Texto que expresa los pensamientos y sentimientos del autor.

Persuasive writing/Texto persuasivo. Tipo de escritura, generalmente de no ficción, encaminado a llevar al lector a aceptar el punto de vista del escritor mediante la lógica, la emoción, la súplica o la sugestión.

Phrase/Frase. Grupo de palabras que funcionan como unidad en una oración.
>   **Prepositional phrase/Frase preposicional.** Consta de una preposición, su objeto y cualquier modificador del objeto; puede funcionar como adjetivo o adverbio.
>   **Verb phrase/Frase verbal.** Consta de uno o más **verbos auxiliares** (*auxiliary verbs*) seguidos del verbo principal (*main verb*).

Plagiarism/Plagio. Presentación de palabras o ideas ajenas como si fueran propias; uso de material sin acreditar la fuente o sin el permiso del creador original o propietario del trabajo.

Plot/Trama. Secuencia de sucesos en una obra narrativa. La trama comienza con la **exposición** (*exposition*), o introducción de los personajes, el escenario y el conflicto. La **acción ascendente** (*rising action*) agrega complicaciones al conflicto y conduce al **clímax** (*climax*) o momento emotivo más intenso. El clímax conduce rápidamente al resultado lógico en la **acción descendente** (*falling action*) y, por último, al **desenlace** (*resolution*) o **esclarecimiento** (*dénouement*), en el cual se revela el desenlace.

Point of view/Punto de vista. Relación del narrador con la historia. La mayoría de las obras están escritas en **primera persona, tercera persona, o tercera persona omnisciente.**

Portfolio/Portafolio. Colección de obras creativas que representan el logro de un artista o escritor.

Positive degree/Grado positivo. *Ver Adjective.*

Précis/Sumario. Resumen breve de ideas principales.

Predicate/Predicado. Parte de la oración que expresa el pensamiento esencial acerca del sujeto de la oración; incluye el **predicado simple** (*simple predicate*) (el verbo o frase verbal clave) y todas las palabras que lo modifican.

Preposition/Preposición. Palabra que muestra la relación de un nombre o pronombre con otra palabra en la oración.

Prepositional phrase/Frase preposicional. *Ver Phrase.*

Presenting/Publishing/Presentación/Publicación. Último paso del proceso de escritura; presentación de un trabajo terminado. Cualquier método de compartir una obra escrita completa es una forma de presentación.

Prewriting/Preescritura. Recopilación de información, revisión de datos, organización y discusión del tema de una obra en planeación.

Primary source/Fuente primaria. Documentos originales como cartas, artículos de periódicos o revistas, entrevistas o documentos históricos de un periodo específico.

Problem solving/Resolución de problemas. Proceso de identificar un problema, enumerar posibles soluciones y determinar un curso de acción.

Progressive form/Durativo. *Ver Verb tense.*

Pronoun/Pronombre. Palabra que va en lugar del nombre; grupo de palabras que funcionan como un nombre u otro pronombre. La palabra o grupo de palabras a que se refiere un pronombre se llama **antecedente** (*antecedent*).

Demonstrative pronoun/Pronombre demostrativo. Señala personas, lugares, cosas o ideas específicas.

Indefinite pronoun/Pronombre indefinido. Se refiere a personas, lugares o cosas de manera más general que el nombre.

Intensive pronoun/Pronombre intensivo*. Tiene la misma forma que un pronombre reflexivo. Agrega énfasis a otro nombre o pronombre.

Interrogative pronoun/Pronombre interrogativo. Se usa para formular preguntas.

Personal pronoun/Pronombre personal. Se refiere a una persona o cosa específica.

Reflexive pronoun/Pronombre reflexivo. Se refiere a un nombre o pronombre usado con anterioridad en la oración e indica que se trata de la misma persona o cosa. (*I will admire* myself *in the mirror*; Me admiraré *a mí mismo* en el espejo.)

Relative pronoun/Pronombre relativo. Se usa para iniciar una proposición subordinada.

Pronoun case/Caso del pronombre. Forma del pronombre que se determina por su uso en la oración. El pronombre está en caso **nominativo** (*nominative case*), en caso **acusativo** y **dativo** (*objective case*) y en caso **posesivo*** (*possessive case*), dependiendo de su función en la oración. *Ver también Case.*

Proofreading/Corrección de pruebas. Último paso del proceso editorial en que se revisa el texto en busca de errores tipográficos y de otra naturaleza.

Propaganda/Propaganda. Información difundida con el fin de influenciar los pensamientos y las acciones para ayudar o perjudicar a un grupo, idea o persona.

Proper noun/Nombre propio. *Ver Noun.*

Prose/Prosa. Escritura que se diferencia de la poesía por su similitud con la dicción y los ritmos del lenguaje común.

Publishing/Publicación. Presentación de una obra creativa en su forma final.

Purpose/Finalidad. Objetivo de la escritura: expresar, descubrir, registrar, desarrollar o reflexionar sobre ideas, resolver problemas, entretener, influir, informar o describir.

R

Reflection/Reflexión. Consideración cuidadosa de una idea o una obra creativa.

Relative pronoun/Pronombre relativo. *Ver Pronoun.*

Representation/Representación. Forma en que se presenta información o ideas al público; presentación teatral o artística.

Research/Investigación. Proceso de localizar información sobre un tema en diversas fuentes confiables.

Resolution/Resolución. *Ver Plot.*

Résumé/Currículo. Resumen escrito de los antecedentes educativos y laborales de una persona.

Revising/Revisión. Paso del proceso de escritura en que el autor repasa el borrador; evalúa la claridad, propósito y adecuación al público; y cambia el contenido, la organización y el estilo para mejorar el texto. Las técnicas de revisión son agregar, elaborar, eliminar, combinar y reacomodar el texto.

Rethoric/Retórica. Arte de usar el lenguaje para presentar hechos e ideas con el fin de persuadir.

Rising action/Acción ascendente. *Ver Plot.*

Root/Raíz. Parte de una palabra que contiene el significado principal.

S

Script/Guión. Texto escrito para una representación teatral o de cine.

Secondary source/Fuente secundaria. Textos acerca de un suceso o período específico, escritos después del tiempo que se describe. Los ensayos históricos, las biografías y las reseñas críticas son ejemplos de fuentes secundarias.

Sensory details/Detalles sensoriales. *Ver Imagery.*

Sentence/Oración. Grupo de palabras que expresa un pensamiento completo. Las oraciones se clasifican según su estructura:
> **Simple sentence/Oración simple.** Consta de una sola proposición principal.
> **Compound sentence/Oración compuesta.** Tiene dos o más proposiciones principales.
> **Complex sentence/Oración compleja.** Formada por una proposición principal y una o más proposiciones subordinadas.
> **Compound-complex sentence/Oración compuesta-compleja.** Consta de dos o más proposiciones principales y por lo menos una proposición subordinada.

Sentence variety/Variedad de oraciones. Uso de diferentes tipos de oraciones para agregar interés al texto.

Setting goals/Determinación de objetivos. Definir el propósito con que se realiza una actividad.

Sexist language/Lenguaje sexista. Elección de palabras que promueven el prejuicio o la discriminación de género.

Short story/Cuento. Narrativa breve de ficción en prosa. Por lo general se concentra en un solo suceso con unos cuantos personajes.

Simile/Símil. Tropo que compara dos cosas esencialmente distintas, usando las palabras *like* o *as* (*como*).

Source/Fuente. Punto de origen de cualquier información. Una **fuente primaria** (*primary source*) es la fuente original de la información. Una **fuente secundaria** (*secondary source*) es un informe basado en una fuente primaria.

Spatial order/Orden espacial. Forma de presentar los detalles de un escenario según su ubicación: de izquierda a derecha o de arriba hacia abajo.

Speech/Discurso. Comunicación oral; charla pública.

Standard English/Inglés estándar. La forma más ampliamente usada y aceptada del idioma inglés.

Stereotype/Estereotipo. Generalización acerca de un grupo de personas sin tomar en cuenta las diferencias individuales.

Structure/Estructura. Marco o plan general de una obra literaria. Relación de las partes de una obra entre sí y con la obra como un todo.

Style/Estilo. Cualidades expresivas que distinguen la obra de un autor, como la **dicción** (*diction*), la **estructura sintáctica** (*sentence structure*) y los tropos (*figures of speech*).

Subject/Sujeto. Parte de la oración que informa sobre qué trata ésta; incluye al **sujeto simple** (*simple subject*) (el nombre o pronombre clave) y las palabras que lo modifican.

Subjunctive mood/Modo subjuntivo. *Ver Mood of a verb.*

Subordinate clause/Proposición subordinada. *Ver Clause.*

Subordinating conjunction/Conjunción subordinante. *Ver Conjunction.*

Summary/Resumen. Breve explicación de la idea principal de una obra o de un suceso.

Superlative degree/Grado superlativo. *Ver Adjective; Adverb.*

Support/Sustento. En escritos de no ficción, detalles que verifican o confirman una idea principal.

Symbol/Símbolo. Persona, animal, lugar, objeto o suceso que existe en el nivel literal en una obra pero que también representa algo más en el nivel figurado.

Technology/Tecnología. Conjunto de procesos o conocimientos técnicos para realizar una tarea.

Tense/Tiempo. *Ver Verb tense.*

Theme/Tema. Idea o conclusión principal de un cuento, poema, novela u obra, algunas veces expresada como afirmación general sobre la vida.

Thesis/Tesis. Posición o propuesta de un hablante o escritor.

Tone/Tono. Reflejo de la actitud del escritor hacia un tema, que se comunica mediante elementos como la elección de las palabras, la puntuación, la estructura sintáctica y los tropos.

Topic sentence/Oración temática. Oración que expresa la idea principal de un párrafo.

Transition/Transición. Palabra conectora que aclara las relaciones entre de palabras e ideas.

Transitive verb/Verbo transitivo. *Ver Verb.*

Unity/Unidad. Integridad de un párrafo o composición; coherencia entre todas las oraciones o párrafos para expresar o sustentar una idea principal.

URL/URL. Forma estándar de una dirección de Internet. (Son iniciales de *Uniform Resource Locator*.)

Venn diagram/Diagrama de Venn. Representación visual que consta de dos círculos que se traslapan, usado para comparar dos cosas con características comunes y diferentes.

Verb/Verbo. Palabra que expresa acción o estado y que es necesaria para hacer una afirmación.

  Action verb/Verbo de acción. Indica qué hace alguien o algo.

  Transitive verb/Verbo transitivo. Verbo de acción que va seguido de una palabra o palabras que responden a la pregunta *what*? (¿qué?) o *whom*? (¿a quién?)

  Intransitive verb/Verbo intransitivo. Verbo de acción que no va seguido de una palabra que responde a la pregunta *what*? (¿qué?) o *whom*? (¿a quién?)

  Linking verb/Verbo copulativo. Une al sujeto de una oración con una palabra o expresión que identifica o describe al sujeto.

  Auxiliary verb/Verbo auxiliar. Verbo que acompaña al verbo principal.

Verb tense/Tiempo verbal. El tiempo de un verbo indica cuándo ocurre la acción o estado. Además de los tiempos **present tense/ presente, past/pasado** y **future/futuro**, hay tres tiempos perfectos: **present perfect/ presente perfecto, past perfect/pretérito perfecto** y **future perfect/futuro perfecto.**

  Progressive form/Durativo. Expresa acción continua con cualquiera de los seis tiempos. Se forma con el tiempo correspondiente del verbo *be (estar)* y el presente participio del verbo principal.

  Emphatic form/Forma enfática. Agrega fuerza especial, o énfasis, al tiempo presente o pasado de un verbo. Para la forma enfática se usa *do, does,* o *did* con el infinitivo.

Verbal/Verboide. Forma del verbo que funciona como nombre, adjetivo o adverbio en la oración. Las tres clases de verboides son **gerund/gerundio, infinitive/infinitive** y **participle/participio.** *Ver Gerund; Infinitive; Participle.*

Voice/Voz. Uso del lenguaje que transmite al lector la personalidad del escritor o narrador. La estructura de la oración, la elección de las palabras y el tono son elementos que comunican la voz.

Web site/Sitio Web. Sitio de World Wide Web que puede ser alcanzado mediante vínculos o una dirección Web o URL. *Ver también URL; World Wide Web.*

Word processing/Procesador de palabras. Programa de computadora para escribir y editar un texto.

World Wide Web/World Wide Web. Sistema global que usa Internet y permite a los usuarios crear, vincularse y entrar a campos de información. *Ver también Internet.*

Writing process/Proceso de escritura. Serie de pasos y etapas por los que atraviesa un escritor para desarrollar sus ideas y comunicarlas.

*Este término o explicación solamente se aplica a la gramática inglesa.

INDEX

software for creating, 422, 423, 424, 426
tables, 809
time lines, 183, 185, 237, 239
tree diagrams, 57–59, 332
Venn diagrams, 228, 231
Group participations, 855–856
Gullah, 762–763

H

Heavenly bodies, capitalizing names of, 697–698
Helping verbs, 453
Historical events, capitalizing names of, 698
Historical writing
narrative, use of, 168–176
present tense in, 579
Home page, 894
How-to writing. *See* Process explanation
Humanities Index, 779
Hung, hanged, 678
Hyperbole, 290–291
Hyperlink, 894
Hypertext, 894
Hyphens
in compound adjectives, 744
in compound words, 744
to divide words at end of lines, 745
in numbers, 745
with prefixes, 744
Hypothesis building, 215, 240–243
in prewriting, 241

I

I, capitalization of, 693–695
Idiom, 894
Illogical juxtaposition, 764
Illusion, allusion, 675
Imagery, 246, 250, 894
Imperative mood, 591, 896
Imperative sentences, 550
Importance, order of, 76, 129, 130, 135, 271, 330
Impression, order of, 129, 130, 135, 163, 261, 330
In, into, in to, 678
Incomplete comparisons, 656
Indefinite articles, 459, 673, 890
Indefinite pronouns, 447, 898
as antecedents, 394

and pronoun-antecedent agreement, 637
and subject-verb agreement, 392, 611, 612
Independent clauses, 891. *See also* Main clauses
Index, of a book, 782
Indicative mood, 591, 896
Indirect objects, 497, 498, 503, 508, 892
diagraming, 566
Indirect questions, 715
Indirect quotations, 736
Inductive reasoning, 282–283
pitfalls in, 284, 895
Infinitive clauses, 521
Infinitives and infinitive phrases, 521, 895
commas with, 405, 724
diagraming, 569
Informal speaking, 852
Informal English, 761–765, 768, 769, 773
Information sources, 325–327
documenting, for research paper, 338–339
electronic, 781
evaluating, for research paper, 343
formatting citations for, 339–342
Informative writing. *See* Expository writing
Institutions, capitalizing names of, 697
Intensifier, 895
Intensive pronouns, 444, 629, 898
Interjections, 479, 895
commas with, 406
Internal conflict, 892
Internet, 877–881, 895
bookmarks/favorites, 879, 891
chat rooms, 880
e-mail, 419, 880, 893
hyperlink, 894
hypertext, 894
keyword, 775, 878
newsgroups, 880
search engine, 878–879
subject directories, 878
types of Web sites, 877
URL, 877, 900
World Wide Web, 900
Interpretation, 895
Interrogative pronouns, 446, 898
Interrogative sentences, 550

who/whom in, 630
Intervening expressions, and subject-verb agreement, 388, 390, 609
Interviews, 52, 856–857
Intransitive verbs, 450, 483, 900
Introduction, 782, 895
drafting effective, 336
in technical writing, 430
Invention. *See* Prewriting
Inverted order, 895
subject-verb agreement, 507, 604–605
Irregardless, regardless, 679
Irregular comparisons, 651–653
Irregular verbs, 399, 576–578
Italics
with foreign words, 739
with titles of trains, ships, aircraft, spacecraft, 739
for titles of works, 699, 739
with words as words, 740
It's, its, 404, 624

J

Jargon, 895
Journal, 12–15, 16, 21, 895
Journal writing, 9, 13, 15, 17, 21, 25, 29, 33, 39, 53, 57, 61, 65, 69, 73, 77, 79, 83, 87, 91, 93, 97, 103, 129, 133, 137, 141, 145, 149, 152, 173, 175, 179, 183, 187, 191, 197, 215, 219, 223, 227, 229, 233, 237, 241, 245, 249, 255, 271, 275, 279, 283, 285, 289, 291, 295, 299, 303, 309
contents of, 14
form of, 14
reader-response, 29
writer's, 12–15
See also Learning Log

K

Keyword, 776, 878, 879

L

Languages
capitalizing names of, 696
See also English language
Laws, capitalizing names of, 697
Lay, lie, 680
Learn, teach, 680

identifying theme in, 186–189
literature models in, 166, 168, 172, 174, 178, 180, 182, 184, 198–205
presenting, 197
prewriting, 169, 194–195
revising, 196–197
sentence combining in, 366–369
structuring, 182–185
National groups, capitalizing names of, 696
Negatives
 as adverbs, 465
 double, 658
Newsletters, 4–6
Newspapers, 147, 341, 699, 739, 777–778
Nominative, predicate, 500, 508
Nominative absolutes, 523–525
Nominative case, 623–624, 891, 893
Nonessential clause, 891, 896
Nonessential elements, 405–406, 693–696, 724–725, 890, 891
Nonfiction, 896
 responding to, 28–31
 writing about, 28–30
Nonfiction books, 775
Nonfiction narratives, 172–177
Nonverbal communication, 854, 864. *See also* Body language
Nonverbal strategies, 896
Note cards, 327–329, 852–854
Note numbers, 342
Note taking, 805
 on computer, 239
 in prewriting, 133
 for research paper, 327–329
 as study skill, 805
Noun clauses, 547–548, 891, 896
 diagraming, 572–573
 using in sentences, 549
Noun identification, 440
Nouns
 abstract, 435, 896
 of amount, 606
 capitalization in titles, 696
 collective, 439, 606, 633, 634, 896
 common, 438, 440, 896
 compound, 742
 concrete, 435
 definition of, 435, 896
 of direct address, commas to set off, 728
 as direct objects, 497

gerunds as, 519
infinitive used as, 521
as objective complements, 497
possessive form of, 435, 742–743
as predicate nominatives, 700
proper, 438, 440, 696–701, 896
singular/plural, 435–437
special, 606
as subject complements, 500
using specific, 441
Nouns of amount, and subject-verb agreement, 606
Numbers, 896
 hyphens in, 749
 for notes, 342
 pronoun-antecedent agreement in, 632
 spelled out, 749
Numerals, 749–750

Object complements, 497, 499
 diagraming, 566, 892
Objective case, 891, 893. *See also* Direct objects; Indirect object; Prepositions
 for pronouns, 623–624
Objects of prepositions, 513
 observing, 68–71, 789–791
 noun clauses as, 547
Opinions, distinguishing between facts and, 274–277
Oral tradition, 896
Order of importance, 896
 descriptive writing, 144–146
 essay writing, 76–80
 explaining a process, 218–220
 narrative writing, 182–184
Order of impression, in descriptive writing, 130
Organization, 896
 cause and effect, 222–225, 891
 charts, 422
 chronological, 76–77, 330–332, 891
 compare and contrast, 76–77, 226–231, 330, 892
 order of importance, 76–77, 129, 135, 271, 330, 896
 order of impression, 129–130, 135, 330
 pro and con, 76
 process explanation, 215, 330
 spatial, 76, 129, 130, 135, 330

transitions for, 216
Organizations, 697, 745
 charts, 422
Outline, 896
 alternative forms of, 332
 on computer, 151, 332
 drafting from, 334–335
 for formal speech, 853
 formal outline, 330–331
 in personal writing, 11
 for research paper, 330–331
Overgeneralization, 896
Oversimplification, 290–291

Paragraphs, 897
 coherence, 82–85
 transitions, 216
 See also Transitions
 expository, 214–217
 supporting sentences, 78–79, 82
 thesis, 97
 topic, 78–79
 unity, 72–74
Parallelism, 82, 83, 363, 896
Paraphrasing, 29, 897
 in note taking, 327–328
Parentheses, 693, 732–733
Parenthetical documentation, 339–340, 897
Parenthetical expressions, commas with, 393, 406, 733
Participials and participial phrases, 517–518, 520, 529–530, 897
 as adjectives, 517
 commas with, 405, 517, 724, 726–727
 diagraming, 568
 past, 518, 897
 present, 517, 897
Parts of speech, 435, 479
Passed, past, 680
Passive voice, 589–590, 897
Past participles, 518, 897
 correcting improper use of, 400
 of irregular verbs, 576–577
 of regular verbs, 576
Past, passed, 680
Past perfect tense, 583, 900
Past tense, 580, 900
Peer editing, 91
Peer review, 10, 11, 86–89, 91, 345, 897
 checklist for, 87

Q

R

imperative, 550
interrogative, 550
inverted, 507
run-on, 386–387, 553
simple, 538, 539, 899
simple subject and predicate
    in, 489
subjects of, 489, 490, 494, 496
word order in, 495–496
varying, 345, 563
Sequence of events, 236–239
Series
    commas in, 407
    semicolons in, 720
Set, sit, 682
Setting
    in descriptive writing, 129
    in determining theme, 187
Setting goals, 899
Sexist language, 899
Ships, capitalizing names of, 698
Short story, 62, 156–163, 899
    capitalization of, 699
    quotation marks with, 736
*Should of, would of, could of, might
    of, must of,* 677
Similarities, analysis of, in
    expository writing, 245
Simile, 899
Simple predicates, 489, 897
Simple sentences, 538–539, 899
    diagraming, 565
Simple subjects, 489, 899
Single quotation marks, 735
Sit, set, 682
Source cards, 327–328
Sources, 328–329, 899. *See also*
    Reference works; Research
    paper
Spacecraft, capitalizing names of,
    698
Spatial order, 76, 129–130, 135,
    330, 899
Speaking, 852–854
    in writing conference, 38, 102,
    154, 196, 254, 308
Special nouns, subject-verb agree-
    ment with, 606
Specific context clues, 789–790
Speech, 852–854, 899
Spelling
    basic rules in, 798–800
    checking, on computer, 247,
    297, 801
    commonly misspelled words,
    802

easily confused words, 803
ie and *ei,* 800
plurals, 798
prefixes, adding, 799
suffixes, adding, 799–800
Sports history, 166–170
Spreadsheet programs
    for creating graphic organizers,
    424, 426
    in technical writing, 429
Standard English, 899
Standardized tests
    English-composition questions,
    818–819
    multiple-choice vocabulary
    questions, 816–817
    preparing to take, 814–815
    purpose of, 814
    reading-comprehension
    questions, 817–818
    sentence-completion questions,
    817
Stereotype, 899
Structure, 899
Student models, 13, 16, 20, 24, 34,
    56, 72, 79, 83, 98, 146, 150,
    175, 176, 188, 218, 226, 227,
    234, 296, 350–356
Study groups, 855
Study skills
    analyzing graphics, 808–810
    analyzing problems, 232–235
    evaluating what you read, 807
    for exam, 19
    making study time count,
    805–806
    note taking in, 805
    reading to remember, 806
    See also Tests
Style, 899
Style manuals, 341, 427, 895
Subject, 899
    adding to sentence fragment,
    384–385
    complete, 490–491, 502, 505
    compound, 390–391, 492, 502,
    506, 608
    diagraming, 565
    identifying, 493
    in inverted sentences, 496
    noun clause as, 547–549
    position in sentence, 495, 496,
    502
    simple, 489, 493, 502, 506, 899
Subject approach, in

compare-and-contrast essay,
    229
Subject complements, 497, 892
    diagraming, 566
    predicate adjectives, 501
    predicate nominatives, 388, 500
Subject-verb agreement
    in adjective clauses, 613–615
    with collective nouns, 389, 606
    with compound subjects, 390,
    608
    correcting problems in,
    388–392
    with indefinite pronouns as
    subjects, 391, 611–612
    with intervening expressions,
    391, 609–610
    with intervening prepositional
    phrases, 388, 601–602
    in inverted sentences, 604–605
    with linking verbs, 603
    with nouns of amount, 389,
    606, 749
    with special nouns, 606–607
    with titles, 607
    with verbal phrases, 517–522
Subjunctive mood, 591–592, 896
Subordinate clauses, 446, 536,
    542–543, 545, 547, 891
    correcting as sentence
    fragments, 385
    who, whom in, 446, 630
Subordinating conjunctions, 474,
    477, 536–537, 542, 545, 892
Suffixes, 795, 800
Summarizing, in note taking,
    327–328
Summary, 899
Superlative degree
    of adjectives, 458, 649–651, 890
    of adverbs, 464, 649–651, 890
Support, 899
Syllabication, 713
Symbol, 899
Symbols, apostrophe to form
    plural of, 743
Synonyms. *See* Thesauruses

Table of contents, 782
Tables, 429, 809–810
Tag questions, commas to set off,
    728
Take, bring, 677
Teach, learn, 680

ACKNOWLEDGMENTS

Text

UNIT ONE From *Cruising the Caribees* by Cléo Boudreau, reprinted by permission of the author.

"On Remembering the Beara Landscape" by Christopher Nolan from *Dam-Burst of Dreams* by Christopher Nolan. Copyright © 1981 by Christopher Nolan. Published by the Ohio University Press.

From *Black Ice* by Lorene Cary. Copyright © 1991 by Lorene Cary. Reprinted by permission of Alfred A. Knopf, Inc., a division of Random House, Inc.

UNIT TWO "Knoxville, Tennessee" from *Black Feeling, Black Talk, Black Judgment* by Nikki Giovanni. Copyright © 1968, 1970 by Nikki Giovanni. Reprinted by permission of HarperCollins Publishers, Inc.

From "Who's on First?" by Bud Abbott and Lou Costello reprinted by permission of TCA Television Corp., The Estate of Bud Abbott Jr. and Hi Neighbor.

From *An American Childhood* by Annie Dillard. Copyright © 1987 by Annie Dillard. Reprinted by permission of HarperCollins Publishers, Inc.

UNIT THREE From "Late Pleistocene Human Friction Skin Prints From Pandejo Cave, New Mexico" by Donald Chrisman, Richard S. MacNeish, Jamshed Mavalwala, and Howard Savage, from *American Antiquity*, 61(2), 1996, pp. 357–376. Copyright © by the Society for American Archaeology. Reprinted by permission. All rights reserved.

From "The Signature" by Elizabeth Enright. Reprinted by permission of Russell & Volkening as agents for the estate of Elizabeth Enright. Copyright © 1951 by Elizabeth Enright, renewed in 1979 by Elizabeth Enright.

UNIT FOUR From *Viva Baseball! Latin Major Leaguers and Their Special Hunger,* by Samuel O. Regalado. Copyright © 1988 by the Board of Trustees of the University of Illinois. Used with permission of the University of Illinois Press.

"The Case of Harry Houdini," from *Star of Wonder* by Daniel Mark Epstein. Copyright © 1986 by Daniel Mark Epstein. Reprinted by permission of the Overlook Press, Woodstock, NY 12498.

UNIT FIVE From "R.M.S. *Titanic*" by Shelley Lauzon, Reprinted by permission of the author.

"To My Dear and Loving Husband" by Anne Bradstreet. Copyright © 1967 by the President and Fellows of Harvard College. Published by Harvard University Press.

"In Retrospect" by Maya Angelou from *And Still I Rise* by Maya Angelou. Copyright © 1978 by Maya Angelou. Reprinted by permission of Random House, Inc.

From *The Soul Of A New Machine* by Tracy Kidder. Copyright © 1979 by John Tracy Kidder. Reprinted by permission of Little, Brown and Company.

UNIT SIX From "Native American Burials: Legal and Legislative Aspects" by Walter R. Echo-Hawk, reprinted by permission of the author.

From "Of Accidental Judgments and Casual Slaughter" by Kai Erikson from *The Best American Essays 1986*. Copyright © 1985 by Kai Erikson. First published by The Nation.

UNIT SEVEN From *The Concord Review*, Spring 1990, Volume Two, Number Three. Copyright © 1990 by The Concord Review, P. O. Box 661, Concord, MA 01742. Reprinted with permission.

UNIT THIRTEEN Reprinted with permission of Scribner, a Division of Simon & Schuster, from *The Great Gatsby* (Authorized Text) by F. Scott Fitzgerald. Copyright 1925 by Charles Scribner's Sons. Copyright renewed 1953 by Frances Scott Fitzgerald Lanahan. Copyright © 1991, 1992 by Eleanor Lanahan, Matthew J. Bruccoli and Samuel J. Lanahan as Trustees under Agreement dated July 3, 1975 created by Frances Scott Fitzgerald Smith.

UNIT SEVENTEEN Excerpt from *I Wonder As I Wander* by Langston Hughes. Copyright © 1956 by Langston Hughes. Reprinted by permission of Hill and Wang, a division of Farrar, Straus & Giroux.

UNIT EIGHTEEN Reprinted with permission of Scribner, a Division of Simon & Schuster, from *A Moveable Feast* by Ernest Hemingway. Copyright © 1964 by Mary Hemingway. Copyright renewed © 1992 by John H. Hemingway, Patrick Hemingway, and Gregory Hemingway.

UNIT TWENTY Excerpts from *The Muses Are Heard* by Truman Capote. Copyright © 1956 by Truman Capote. Reprinted by permission of Random House, Inc.

UNIT TWENTY-ONE Excerpt from *The Stones of Florence* by Mary McCarthy. Copyright by Mary McCarthy. Reprinted by permission of Harcourt, Inc.

Photo

Cover KS Studio; **vi** National Museum of American Art, Washington, D.C./Art Resource, NY; **vii** ©1945 Universal Pictures, Inc./SuperStock; **ix** (t)Schlowsky Photography, (b) Art Resource, NY; **x** Muskegon Museum of Art; **xi** ©Warner Brothers, Inc; **xii** Grant V. Faint/The Image Bank; **xiii** *Edward Hopper* by Lloyd Goodrich ©1978, *Edward Hopper Light Years* by Harry N. Abrams ©1988, Photo by Schlowsky Photography; **xiv** Collection Haags Gemeentemusem-The Hague; **xv** (t)Brown Brothers, (b)Phil Cantor/SuperStock; **xvi** Robert Houser/COMSTOCK; **xvii** Courtesy Journal Communications; **xviii** Ant Farm ©1974; **xix** Art Resource, NY; **xx** Jen and Des Bartlett/Bruce Coleman, Inc; **xxi** ©PhotoDisc, Inc; **xxii** (t)Drawing by David Levine, ©1966 Reprinted with permission for The New York Review of Books, (b)Schlowsky Photography; **xxiv** Schlowsky Photography. **xxxi-1** The Bowers Museum of Cultural Art/CORBIS; **2-3** Adam Woolfitt/CORBIS; **5** Don Hebert; **6** Schlowsky Photography; **7** Schlowsky Photography; **8** National Museum of American Art, Washington, DC/Art Resource, NY; **10** (t)Jeffry W. Myers/FPG, (b)Mike and Carol Werner/COMSTOCK; **12** Joan Bennett; **13 16** Schlowsky Photography; **18** John Elk III/Bruce Coleman, Inc; **20** Schlowsky Photography; **22** (t)Culver Pictures, (b)UPI/CORBIS-Bettmann; **24** Michael Quackenbush/The Image Bank; **26** ©1987 Universal Press Syndicate. Reprinted with permission. All rights reserved; **28** Judith Aronson/Ligature, Inc; **32** Bernard Kappelmeyer/FPG;

35 Musees Royaux Des Beaux-Arts De Belgique, Brussels/ Bridgeman Art Library, London/New York; 41 Collection of the artist; 43 Art Resource, NY; 45 Adam Woolfitt/CORBIS; 46-47 Layne Kennedy/ CORBIS; 48 (l)Chris Denney, (tr, br)Barbara Brandon/Schlowsky Photography; 49 (t)Barbara Brandon/ Schlowsky Photography, (b)Chris Denney; 55 Collection Haags Gemeentemusem-The Hague; 58 COMSTOCK; 60 ©1945 Universal Pictures, Inc./SuperStock, Kobal Collection; 64 The Far Side ©1985 Universal Press Syndicate. Reprinted with permission; 67 *Carafe, Jug, and Fruit Bowl,* 1909 (Summer). Pablo Picasso. Solomon R. Guggenheim Museum, NY. Gift, Solomon R. Guggenheim, 1937. Photograph by David Heald. Photograph © Solomon R. Guggenheim Foundation; 68 (detail)National Gallery of Art, Washington DC. Collection of Mr. And Mrs. Paul Mellon; 69 Robert Houser/COMSTOCK; 72 Michael Rothwell/FPG; 76 Tate Gallery, London/Art Resource, NY; 81 Private collection/Art Resource, NY; 82 Culver Pictures; 85 Giraudon/Art Resource, NY; 90 Ken Sherman/Bruce Coleman, Inc; 107 Collection of Douglas and Beverly Feurring, Courtesy of Tibor de Nagy Gallery, NY; 110 Layne Kennedy/CORBIS; 122-123 Roine Magnusson/Tony Stone Images; 125 126 Eric Roth; 128 Charles Cambell/CORBIS/ Westlight; 130 Roger Farrington/The Wang Center, Boston; 132 Schlowsky Photography; 135 The Metropolitan Museum of Art, George A. Hearn Fund, 1943 (43.159.1); 136 Harold Lambert/ SuperStock; 140 Drawing by David Levine. ©1966 Reprinted with permission from The New York Review of Books; 141 Scott Darrow/SuperStock; 142 Schlowsky Photography; 144 David Henderson/Eric Roth Studio; 148 ©1972 by Edward Gorey from "The Listing Attic" in Amphigorey. Published by G.P. Putnam & Sons; 157 Art Resource, NY; 161 Milano, Coll. Jesi/Art Resource, NY; 162 Christie's Images/ SuperStock; 165 Roine Magnusson/Tony Stone Images; 166-167 CORBIS; 168 (t)Mark Tuschman, (b)Schlowsky Photography; 170 (tl, tr)Mark Tuschman, (b)Meckler Publishing Corporation/ Schlowsky Photography; 171 Schlowsky Photography; 172 UPI/ CORBIS-Bettmann; 178 (l)Nicholas Hilliard by courtesy of the Board of Trustees of the Victoria and Albert Museum/Bridgeman Art Library, London/New York, (r)Methuen Collection, Corsham Court, England; 183 Sophia Smith Collection, Smith College; 189 The Metropolitan Museum of Art, Purchase Alfred N. Punnett Endowment Fund and George D. Pratt Gift, 1934; 190 Russ Kinney/COMSTOCK; 192 Smithsonian Institution; 198 PhotoDisc, Inc.; 200 Brown Brothers; 201 Posters Please, Inc; 203 AKG, Berlin/SuperStock; 207 CORBIS; 208 William A. Bake/CORBIS; 210 (t) Frank Siteman, (b) Titanic Historical Society; 212 Woods Hole Oceanographic Institute; 214 Jen and Des Bartlett/Bruce Coleman, Inc; 218 Jack Elness/COMSTOCK; 222 ©Warner Brothers, Inc; 225 Culver Pictures; 226 Drawing by Jonik ©1991 The New Yorker Magazine, Inc; 231 Alan Berner; 240 Schlowsky Photography; 248 Abby Aldrich Rockefeller Folk Art Center; 256 PhotoDisc, Inc.; 257 Bavaria/Viesti Associates; 258 David Em "Transjovian Pipeline" ©1979 David Em/Represented by Speickerman Associates, SF; 263 William A. Bake/CORBIS; 264-265 Raymond Gehman/CORBIS; 266 DeSciose Productions; 268 (t)Linda J. Echo-Hawk, (b)DeSciose Productions; 269 Schlowsky Photography; 274 Smithsonian Institution; 276 Phil Cantor/ SuperStock; 278 Cadge Productions/ The Image Bank; 284 Grant V. Faint/The Image Bank; 289 Ralph Morse/Life Magazine ©1958 Time, Inc; 294 The John F. Kennedy Library (KN-C29248); 301 Ant Farm ©1974; 302 Curtis Publishing Company; 303 Uniphoto Picture Agency/Consolidated Press; 310 PhotoDisc, Inc.; 314 Courtesy of the artist, Francine Seders Gallery, Seattle. Photo by Chris Eden; 317 USAF; 321 Raymond Gehman/CORBIS; 322-323 CORBIS; 324 W. King/FPG; 330 Collection of the Whitney Museum of American Art, NY. Josephine N. Hopper Bequest. 70.183a; 334 Schlowsky Photography; 338 (t)Schlowsky Photography, (b)Group III/Bruce Coleman, Inc; 344 Friends of American Art Collection, 1930.934. The Art Institute of Chicago. All rights reserved; 348 The Joslyn Art Museum, Omaha NE; 357 CORBIS; 358-359 382 Dave Bartruff/CORBIS; 383 CORBIS; 410 421 PhotoDisc, Inc.; 432-433 Burstein Collection/CORBIS; 485 Patricia Gonzalez; 509 Courtesy Journal Communications; 531 The Metropolitan Museum of Art, Gift of Mrs. Frank B. Porter, 1992 (22.207); 562 The Metropolitan Museum of Art, Gift of Chester Dale, 1963; 598 University Museum, University of Pennsylvania,T4-9c2; 620 National Museum of American Art/Art Resource, NY; 645 Courtesy Mary-Anne Martin/Fine Art; 669 The Metropolitan Museum of Art, Robert Lehman Collection (1975.1.227); 690 Collection of The Whitney Museum of American Art. Gift of an anonymous donor. 54.58; 710 The Metropolitan Museum of Art, Bequest of Scofield Thayer, 1982 (1984.443.6); 753 The Cleveland Museum of Art, Mr. And Mrs. William H. Marlatt Fund, 61.39; 756-757 Christie's Images/ SuperStock; 759 Giraudon/ Art Resource, NY; 761 through 773 (gears)VCG/FPG; 763 Southern Historical Collection, Wilson Library, University of North Carolina at Chapel Hill; 764 Drawing by David Levine. ©1966 Reprinted with permission for The New York Review of Books; 771 823 Mark Burnett; 856 Ken Chernus/ FPG; 860 Bob Sacha; 862 Photofest; 868 NASA; 870 871 872 file photo; 882 Mark Burnett; 883 file photo.